MARKETING MANAGEMENT

MARKETING MANAGEMENT

Macmillan Publishing Company
New York

Collier Macmillan Publishers
London

Donald S. Tull
University of Oregon

Lynn R. Kahle
University of Oregon

Macmillan Publishing Company
866 Third Avenue, New York, New York 10022

Collier Macmillan Canada, Inc.

Library of Congress Cataloging in Publication Data

Tull, Donald S.
  Marketing management / Donald S. Tull, Lynn R. Kahle.
      p.   cm.
  Includes indexes.
    1. Marketing—Management.   I. Kahle, Lynn.   II. Title.
HF5415.13.T85 1990
658.8—dc20   89–32662
                                                    CIP
  ISBN 0–02–421700–X (Hardcover Edition)
  ISBN 0–02–946278–9 (International Edition)

IE Printing: 1 2 3 4 5   Year: 0 1 2 3 4

ISBN 0-02-946278-9

TO
Marge
Susan
David
Brooks
Debra
and
Kevin

THE MACMILLAN SERIES IN MARKETING

PREFACE

The underlying reason for the discipline of marketing is the understanding and improvement of marketing management. It is the ultimate reason for broadly based courses in marketing, such as consumer behavior and marketing research, as well as for the more specialized courses, such as retailing, wholesaling, communication, pricing, and distribution and logistics.

The primary characteristic of marketing management and the principal concern of this book is the making of marketing decisions. Toward this end the book has sections on:

- Marketing management and marketing strategy to provide the context for marketing decision making (Section I)
- The marketing environment to assist in understanding the origin of marketing problems, to help identify them, and to describe ethical concerns that arise in solving them (Section II)
- Decision making, market measurement, and marketing planning and forecasting to describe how decisions are made and how one obtains information to help make them (Section III)
- Marketing programs: managing the marketing mix to describe the areas where decisions have to be made and the bases for making them (Section IV)
- Marketing organization, marketing controls, controls and audits, and international marketing to discuss how marketing departments are organized to facilitate decision making and implementation, how controls can be used and audits conducted to evaluate and to improve them, and to describe an increasingly important arena for decision making—international marketing (Section V)

We have attempted to deal with these topics as clearly and as directly as possible. A continuing concern has been the illustration of concepts and techniques discussed by the use of actual examples. (One measure of how well we have done this is the fact that references were made to a total of 494 American and foreign companies.) There are extensive sets of discussion questions and problems at the end of each chapter, and a total of 49 short cases at the end of each section, all involving actual marketing situations. An accompanying book of computer-based analytic exercises has also been provided to cover that important area.

Regardless of how well our objectives have been achieved, we are in the debt both of our students, who have used earlier versions of the book, and of our colleagues who have read and made many helpful suggestions for improving the manuscript. The reviewers of the manuscript made many insightful and useful comments, and so deserve individual recognition. They were:

Mark Alpert
University of Texas–Austin

Shirley Anderson
California State University–Northridge

Madan Batra
Indiana University of Pennsylvania

Barry Bayus
Cornell University

Sharon Beatty
University of Alabama

William Browne
Oregon State University

Gregory Carpenter
Columbia University

Clarke Caywood
University of Wisconsin–Madison

John Crawford
University of North Texas

Rohit Deshpande
Dartmouth College

O. C. Ferrel
Memphis State University

Ed Grubb
Portland State University

Ashok K. Gupta
Ohio University

Robert R. Johnson
College of William and Mary

G. E. Kiser
University of Arkansas

Raymond LaForge
Oklahoma State University

Max Lupal
California State University–Northridge

Stuart Mandell
University of Lowell

Steven Miller
Oklahoma State University

Wayne Norvell
Kansas State University

Terry Neustrom
Westmar College

Edward T. Popper
Northeastern University

William Pride
Texas A&M University

George Prough
University of Akron

C. P. Rao
University of Arkansas

Peter B. Shaffer
Western Illinois University

Bruce Smakey
Lehigh University

Daniel Toy
Penn State University

Gerald Waddle
Clemson University

John Walton
Miami University

Ken Williamson
James Madison University

We would also be remiss if we did not recognize the contributions of our editors, Ron Stefanski, David Shafer, and Bill Oldsey of Macmillan.

Russell Till of Till & Till, Inc. provided invaluable support during the production process.

We are indebted to all, but we alone must be held accountable for any errors of omission or commission that remain.

D.S.T.
L.R.K.

BRIEF CONTENTS

Section V MARKETING ORGANIZATION, CONTROLS AND AUDITS, AND INTERNATIONAL MARKETING

CONTENTS

Chapter 12   Product Line Management, Brand Management, and the Product Life Cycle   385

Chapter 13   Pricing Decisions   424

Chapter 14   Marketing Communication Planning   461

MARKETING MANAGEMENT AND STRATEGY

I

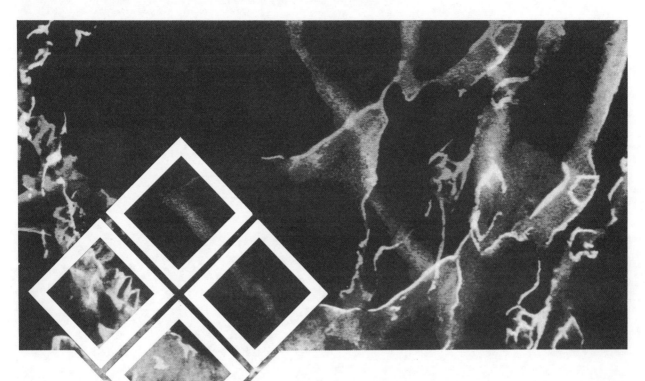

"Marketing" was the answer of a majority of more than 100 top-level American executives when asked (in 1986), "What is the most important management area in the company?" Marketing is important because it forms the link between the company and the markets it serves. The making of mutually satisfactory exchanges of goods and services with users in those markets is the reason for the company's existence and the principal concern of marketing management.

Marketing strategy is the focal point of corporate strategy. A coherent overall strategy must be grounded in the products to be offered, the markets to be entered, and the marketing programs used to serve them.

The role of marketing management in the company, in the economy, and to consumers, is described in Chapter 1. The translation of company objectives to market strategies and the development of marketing program strategies to implement the market strategies are discussed in Chapter 2.

MARKETING AND MARKETING MANAGEMENT

Marketing is that complex of activities of the company or organization that link it with those who have need for its products or services. The primary concerns of marketing are markets and the making of mutually satisfactory exchanges with those who comprise those markets. Adding the tasks that result in satisfactory exchanges being made leads to the following definition:

> **Marketing** is the process of planning and executing the conception, pricing, promotion, and distribution of ideas, goods, and services to create exchanges that satisfy individual and organizational objectives.[1]

Marketing management has the responsibility for managing the process that leads to the exchanges being made. That is,

> **Marketing management** consists of the making and implementing of the decisions necessary for the marketing of specific ideas, goods, and services.

Management of marketing, like management in any other functional area, is mainly concerned with the making and implementing of decisions.

The principal concerns of this chapter are to examine the roles of marketing management to the *consumer*, in the *firm*, and in the *economy*.

The Exchange Process

Companies exist to serve markets through exchanges. By its nature, the exchange process requires an ***offering*** and an ***acceptance***. The offering consists of a product or service, to be sure, but it is far more than that. There is an associated bundle of benefits—some physical, some psychological, some social—that collectively comprise the offering. It is not incidental that the largest-selling cigarette is promoted with the symbols of virility and rugged independence, or that a university increased its enrollment by 20 percent and cut its dropout rate in half by developing a program to help meet students' psychological and social needs as well as providing a more appealing set of courses for freshmen (Exhibit 1–1). The importance of the benefits associated with buying a car beyond just acquiring a means of transportation is illustrated in the statement that follows:

> An automobile is not simply a tangible machine for movement, visibly or measurably differentiated by design, size, color, options, horsepower, or miles per gallon. It is also a complex symbol denoting status, taste, rank, achievement, aspiration, and, these days, being "smart"—that is, buying economy rather than display.[2]

As this statement implies and Figure 1–1 shows, the offering in an exchange consists of a *generic* product (or service), the *tangible* product, and the *augmented* product. These terms are defined as follows:

Generic product. *the utilitarian benefits provided by the product.* An automobile provides transportation; a television set provides entertainment, news, and information.

Tangible product. *the physical features of the product that have precise specifications.* An automobile has a specific set of features (model, size, horsepower rating, and so forth), design, and brand; a television set has a set of specified features (size of cathode ray tube, color or black and white, and capacity to handle a given number of channels), design of cabinet, and brand.

Augmented product. *the ancillary products and services that accompany the tangible product and the image associated with its use.* The buyer of a new car receives a warranty, postpurchase service, and an owner's manual as well as an image of luxury and status if the car is, say, a Jaguar or Cadillac, an image of sportiness if it is a Porsche or Corvette, or one of economy if it is a Volkswagen or Honda CVCC; a buyer of a new television set receives a warranty, postpurchase service, and a set of operating instructions along with being accorded more status if it is a Sony than if it is an off-brand.

EXHIBIT **1-1**

Three Successful Marketing Campaigns

MARLBORO CIGARETTES

Marlboro is the leading brand of cigarettes in terms of sales, both in the United States and worldwide.

It was not always an industry leader. It was introduced in the 1950s as a low-tar filtertip that did not obtain the market share expected of it. After learning through marketing research that it had acquired a "feminine" image, the company decided to reposition the brand. For several reasons, it decided that it should be marketed as a masculine product: The proportion of women who smoke is lower than that for men, per capita consumption among women who do smoke is substantially lower than that for men who smoke, women smokers stop smoking more often then men because of pregnancies, women tend to continue to use "masculine" products whereas men typically do not use "feminine" products, and there was then no other cigarette on the market positioned as a women's cigarette (as Virginia Slims was later).[3]

What should be done to create a masculine image for the product? Television viewers and print media readers the world over now know how this was done. The "Marlboro Country" theme was created using the virile Marlboro cowboy image. The campaign was backed with a sizable budget. Young men started smoking the brand because of the rugged masculine role model, and women Marlboro smokers did not switch away from it.

Thirty years later, annual sales of Marlboro cigarettes exceed $4 billion, making the brand alone big enough to be one of the top 100 corporations in the United States, or about the same size as the Campbell Soup Company.[4]

Institutions (including universities) also can market services successfully, as the following case history illustrates.

THE UNIVERSITY OF OREGON

In 1983, student enrollment at the university was down to 15,500, and was projected to drop substantially over the next 10 years. Based on federal census data and school attendance records, the number of high school graduates in Oregon was on a long-term trend downward and was expected to reach the lowest levels in 40 years by the early 1990s.

The university administration was convinced it had a first-rate product to sell, and set out to devise a program of attracting and retaining students. A television advertising campaign was developed and aired. A direct-mail program, involving as many as 40,000 pieces per mailing, was developed using computerized sorting of census data and information collected by the SAT and ACT testing services to provide addresses of potential students across the country. And a retention program was developed to help keep previously enrolled students at the university.

Nationally, one-eighth of all students drop out of universities during their freshman year, and the U. of O.'s drop-out rate was then 11.3 percent (slightly below the national average). A program based on identifying high student stress periods and then supplying the information to help them get involved with the appropriate student and faculty groups and services was devised. Freshmen seminars, small classes of 15 to 25 students, were developed and offered by faculty on a voluntary, overload basis.

By 1988 the drop-out rate had declined to 9.5 percent. And university enrollment was up more than 2,800 students from its level five years earlier.[5]

Competently planned and conducted marketing programs also work in international marketing, as the following case history demonstrates.

THE TOYOTA MOTOR CORPORATION

Toyota entered the U.S. market in 1958 and sold 288 cars. Twenty years later it was selling cars in the United States at the rate of 500,000 per year.

The success did not come immediately, however. The car it introduced in 1958 was the Toyopet, a boxy, noisy, uncomfortable car that sold for $700 more than the VW Beetle. Some improvements were made in the Toyota Crown that came out the next year, but the sales results remained about the same.

After this initial failure, Toyota management took a careful look at the U.S. market and at the other car makers, both U.S. and foreign, that were selling cars here. A series of marketing research projects disclosed that an increasing proportion of the U.S. market was ready for a smaller car, and that a significant part of Volkswagen's success had been due to the superior service organization it established. The research also profiled the demographic and psychographic market segments that should be targeted. After this was done, the Toyota engineers designed the car to be sold to those segments—the Toyota Corona. It was twice as powerful as the VW Beetle, as well as being more comfortable and handling better.

The U.S. car makers remained supremely confident that large and expensive automobiles were what the public really wanted. GM and Ford had brought out compact models, but only as a result of government prodding rather than because of any conviction that this was the way the market was heading.

Toyota established West Coast dealerships in four urban areas—Los Angeles, San Francisco, Portland, and Seattle. It priced the Corona aggressively and advertised heavily. When sales grew, it rolled its marketing territory eastward.

It has not had to look back.[6]

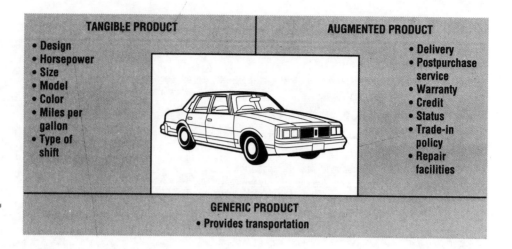

FIGURE 1-1
The offering: a new automobile.

An exchange requires an offering and an acceptance. The process of exchange is shown in Figure 1–2.

In a commercial exchange situation, there are the four possible outcomes shown in Figure 1–3.[7] Buyers are naturally concerned that the outcome of a purchase is either the one in cell (3) or in cell (4) in the figure, and are probably largely indifferent as to which of the two it is. One might speculate that sellers exhibit a similar indifference to the outcome as long as it is either cell (1) or (4).

Such speculation would be wrong, however. It might make little difference to the financial health of the company if every buyer made only one (lifetime) purchase within the product line and did not discuss his or her reaction to the product or its purchase price with anyone else. Neither of these conditions is typical, however. Buyers purchase products in most product lines with some degree of regularity, and offer opinions on them when asked. (Repeat purchases of frequently purchased products, such as toothpaste or salad dressing, constitute an average of over 85 percent of the sales of mature brands.) Repeat purchases of products are highly dependent on prior purchase satisfaction, and even initial trial is somewhat dependent on word-of-mouth evaluation. (Word-of-mouth evaluation greatly affects the attendance of new movies, for example.)

FIGURE 1-2
The exchange process.

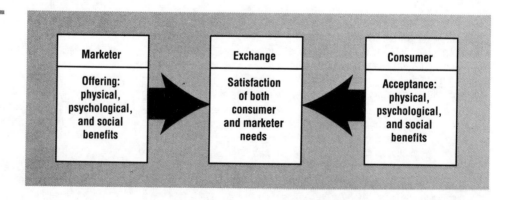

	Buyer gains	Buyer loses
Seller gains	Mutually beneficial exchange (4)	Conflicting outcomes exchange (1)
Seller loses	Conflicting outcomes exchange (3)	Mutually injurious exchange (2)

FIGURE 1-3
Gain/loss outcomes of exchanges involving a seller and a buyer.

One might expect, therefore, that, within limits, companies that provide greater value to their customers themselves tend to receive the benefits of larger market shares and higher profits. There is persuasive evidence that this is the case. A study of the operations of some 2,000 business units indicates that the higher the relative value (product quality and service in relation to price) provided the customer, the higher the market share and gross margin for the product line.[8]

A common belief is that commercial exchanges are "zero-sum" transactions resulting (usually) from the seller's gaining and the buyer's losing by equal amounts. Not so. If the marketing effort that brought about the exchange was carried out competently, it was a "positive-sum" transaction in which both the buyer and the seller gained.

The Marketing Concept

The ***marketing concept*** bears on the issue of benefits to buyer and seller. The earliest version of it (although not by that name) is by Adam Smith and was written more than 200 years ago: "Consumption is the sole end and purpose of all production; and the interest of the producer ought to be attended to only as far as it is necessary for promoting that of the consumer."[9] McCarthy and Perrault state it as follows: "The marketing concept means that an organization aims all of its efforts at satisfying its customers—at a profit."[10] They hint, but stop short of saying, that the marketer as well as the customer will benefit from any sale or purchase carried out in accord with the concept.

We have already seen that companies that provide high relative value (high product quality and service in relation to price) to customers tend to have high market shares and gross margins for their product lines. This indicates that the marketing concept has implications beyond being a desirable ethical precept—it is a principle that, when followed, leads to operationally sound practices as well.

ROLE OF MARKETING MANAGEMENT IN THE FIRM

Marketing Management—If It's Competent, It Works

Perhaps the most important question that one can ask about any applied field from the standpoint of the firm is, "If it's done right, does it work?" Competency of management in any applied field never guarantees success, but inevitably and significantly raises the odds that the project or program being managed will succeed. It is in this sense that we can say that soundly planned and competently executed marketing programs "work."

Three examples of marketing programs that were highly successful are given in Exhibit 1–1.

The assertion that competent marketing makes a sizable contribution to the success of the firm is supported by the results of a study conducted in 1985 by Coopers & Lybrand, one of the "Big Eight" accounting firms. Consultants from that firm, along with researchers from Yankelovich, Skelley, and White, interviewed 140 chief executive officers and other top executives of companies and found that about two-thirds of them (64 percent) believe that marketing is "the most important management area" for a company.[11]

It is obvious that we (the authors) believe that sound marketing is a valuable asset to any concern. We do not want to imply that it is a panacea, however. It will only work when the quality and availability of the product supports its price and the promotional claims made for it, and an appropriate distribution system has been developed. Since engineering and manufacturing bear responsibility for product quality, and finance often plays a substantial role in setting price, a coordinated program with those departments is required to assure the ultimate success of the marketing program.

The Responsibilities of Marketing Management

The Generic Responsibility of Management— Decision Making

It will be recalled that marketing management was defined as consisting of "the making and implementing of the decisions necessary for the marketing of specific ideas, goods, and services." **Decision making**— identifying the problem, getting the necessary information about it, developing viable alternative solutions, choosing an alternative, and implementing it—underlies and permeates the managing of any activity, and marketing is no exception.

Marketing management decisions are (or should be) based on assessments of how the markets served by the company will react to each of the alternative actions being considered, and the ethical, political, and legal contexts in which the decision is to be made. Market reactions are in turn affected and conditioned by consumer and organizational buying behavior, competitors' actions, and the state of the economy. Figure 1–4 illustrates the complex of forces and interactions that bear on marketing decisions.

The four functions that comprise the marketing effort of the firm are:

Product planning

Pricing

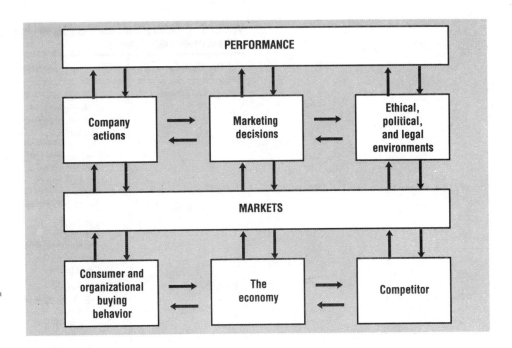

FIGURE 1-4
Forces and their interactions that affect marketing decisions.

Promotion

Distribution

These are known as the **marketing mix** elements. If the marketing department is a fully integrated one, it is these functions for which the marketing manager is responsible, and for which decisions have to be made.

Table 1–1 provides a partial list of decisions that have to be made for each of these mix elements for a single product or service. Multiply this list by the number of products or services the company has, and, recognizing that some of these decisions have to be made several times a year, one begins to gain an understanding of how decision-making-intensive the marketing manager's job is.

The Marketing Management Process

A marketing program involving the four mix elements just listed needs to be developed for each offering. Managing the program involves six steps:

1. *setting marketing strategy*
2. *planning the nature and level of the mix elements* required for its accomplishment
3. *organizing* for operations
4. *coordinating* (and coordinating it with other departments)
5. *implementing* the plans
6. *controlling* to ensure that objectives are met to the extent possible

Table 1-1 A Partial List of Decisions Required for Each of the Marketing Mix Elements

Mix Variable	Decision

Product or service	Product assortment
	   New products
	     Product deletions
	Quality
	Features or attributes
	Performance characteristics
	Product design
	Package design
	Repair and service
	Guarantees and warrantees

Price	Unit price Allowances Quantity discounts Cash discounts Credit terms

Promotion	Advertising
	   Budgets by product
	   Themes
	   Campaigns
	   Media
	   Frequency
	   Cooperative
	     Amounts
	     Who receives
	   Evaluation
	Personal selling
	   Budgets by area
	   Number of reps
	   Remuneration
	   Quotas
	   Hiring
	   Training
	   Evaluation
	Sales promotion
	   Budgets by product
	   Type
	   Frequency
	   Evaluation

Distribution	Channels
	Logistics
	   Budgets
	   Storage facilities
	     Locations
	     Size
	   Inventories
	   Transportation

We discuss each of these responsibilities in turn below.

1. Setting Marketing Strategy: Marketing strategy involves deciding on the fundamental means of achieving the company's objectives through the markets entered and the marketing programs used to serve them.

Setting marketing strategy is such an important step in the management of a company that it is seldom delegated completely to the marketing department. Rather, the responsibility of the marketing manager typically is to recommend strategy to top management and, if there are any changes to be made, to participate in making them. (Setting marketing strategy is the subject of the next chapter.)

2. Planning the Nature and Level of the Marketing Mix Elements: Decisions have to be made about the marketing objectives to be realized, the kinds of products and services to be offered, the pricing policies to be established, the advertising and promotional campaigns to be used, and the distribution system to be employed.

Setting prices and allocating the marketing budget by mix element by product is a critical step in the planning process. This requires that the sales response function for the appropriate range of each mix element be estimated.

> The ***sales response function*** for a particular marketing mix element for a given product (or service) is the relationship between the level of that element and the sales of the product for a specified period, during which time the level of the other marketing mix elements are held constant.

For example, the demand curve described in basic microeconomics classes is a sales response function for price. It and sales response functions of the forms commonly assumed for product quality and advertising are shown in the graphs below.

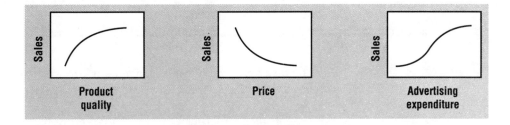

It is only when the sales response functions for these and the other marketing mix elements for each product are estimated accurately (over the relevant range) that sound allocations of resources can be made.

The marketing departments in most progressive companies have a standard set of procedures that they use for planning, implementing, controlling, and revising the marketing program for each of their products and product lines. The procedure used by one successful processed food company for planning, developing, testing, and introducing new products, for example, is as shown in Exhibit 1–2.

The existence of a set of procedures is evidence of at least two things. First, it signifies that the needs of the marketing program have been analyzed, and the way in which it is to be conducted has been planned, so that its management does not consist solely of a series of ad hoc decisions made when crises arrive. Second, it suggests that the marketing department is likely to be well accepted by top management, and its activities integrated where necessary with those of engineering, manufacturing, and finance. A procedural blueprint for operating a major department does not get published and used unless it has at

EXHIBIT **1-2**

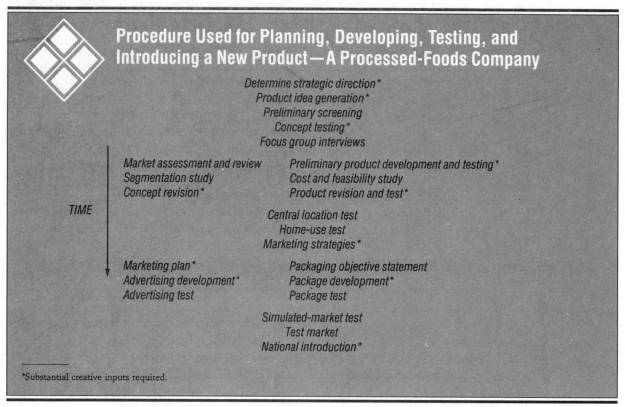

Procedure Used for Planning, Developing, Testing, and Introducing a New Product—A Processed-Foods Company

Determine strategic direction*
Product idea generation*
Preliminary screening
Concept testing*
Focus group interviews

Market assessment and review	Preliminary product development and testing*
Segmentation study	Cost and feasibility study
Concept revision*	Product revision and test*

TIME

Central location test
Home-use test
Marketing strategies*

Marketing plan*	Packaging objective statement
Advertising development*	Package development*
Advertising test	Package test

Simulated-market test
Test market
National introduction*

*Substantial creative inputs required.

least the tacit approval of top management, and such approval isn't given unless it meshes with the operations of other major departments.

3. Organizing: A crucial aspect of marketing management in the firm is to what extent the planning and day-to-day operating decisions concerning the elements of the marketing mix are the responsibility of one office. The organizational assignments for the responsibilities for the product, price, promotion, and distribution elements are central both to how marketing is being managed and *who* is doing it.

Ideally, the responsibility for all of the marketing-related activities is vested in a single office within the company. The only form of organization that meets this requirement completely is the *fully integrated marketing department* that has as its head a *marketing manager* or *marketing vice-president*. An example of one form of such an organizational arrangement, called a **functional organization**, is given in Figure 1–5.

Alternative ways of organizing that result in integrated marketing that tend to be found in larger companies are **product management, market management,** and **matrix** organizations. These are discussed in the chapter on marketing organization (Chapter 19).

Most companies today have marketing departments, but the responsibility for one or more of the mix elements is not always assigned to them. An

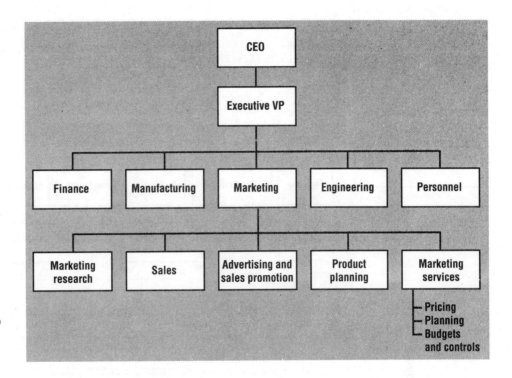

FIGURE 1-5
Functional marketing organization
(fully integrated).

example of a badly fragmented organization insofar as marketing is concerned is given in Figure 1–6.

It is apparent that this is a very inefficient organizational arrangement for managing the marketing effort. Even though the person in charge of the Marketing Department may have the title "Marketing Manager," the actual marketing manager is the Executive Vice-President. The persons controlling the marketing mix elements report to that office, and it is there, and only there, that any real coordination of them can take place. Unfortunately, the work load of that position rarely allows the time for assuming the marketing manager's role in addition to its regularly assigned responsibilities.

Marketing departments are the most frequently reorganized—and the marketing executives in charge most frequently replaced (whether from choice or necessity is not clear)—among the sample companies' marketing, production, engineering, finance/accounting, and purchasing departments.[12]

4. Coordinating: Once the product markets and market segments have been selected, the firm must carry out a series of functions to develop its offerings. These functions, and the departments to which they typically are assigned, are shown in Figure 1–7.

Unless there is a "new product" department responsible for development of products to the point of introduction, marketing is customarily "on the point" with coordinating the efforts of the various departments involved. It is also usually marketing's responsibility to coordinate special orders, rush deliveries, and individual financing arrangements for current products.

It is apparent that there is a substantial amount of coordination within the firm in which marketing is involved.

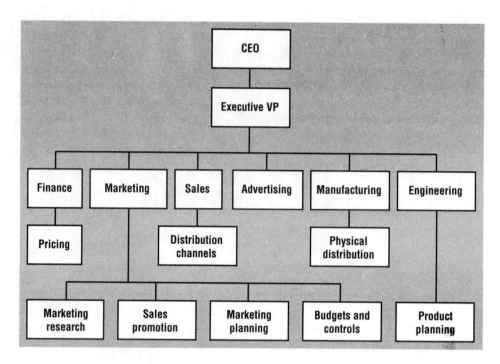

FIGURE 1-6
Badly fragmented marketing
organization.

5. Implementing: Implementation is the "tactics" half of the "strategy and tactics" combination. The two are interdependent to the point that

- both have to be done well if the program is to be a success; if either is done poorly, trouble or failure results;
- good implementation moderates the effects of bad strategy, and provides more time for diagnosis and change of strategy before failure; and

FIGURE 1-7
Functions required for developing
the offering for selected product
markets and market segments,
and departmental responsibilities
for them.

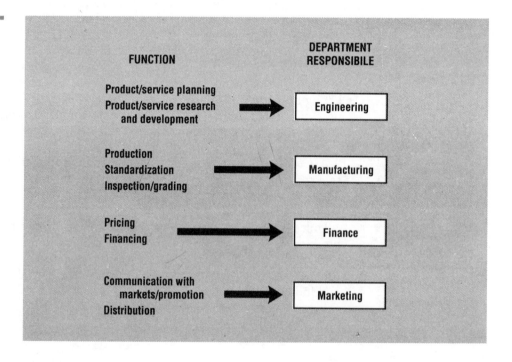

- poor implementation camouflages good strategy, and makes it difficult to diagnose the cause of the problem.

Whereas top management typically reserves the prerogative of setting marketing strategy, implementation is by definition the responsibility of the marketing department (if the department is fully integrated). This arrangement is somewhat ironic because, in the usual case, it is probably faster, and may be easier, for competitors to emulate a good strategy than a good implementation. (Exceptions obviously exist to this statement, for example, having a strategy of marketing products for which there is good patent protection, and having strategies that require extensive finances.)

Good implementation can be a powerful stimulant for success. Some companies have enjoyed continued outstanding success by executing one part of their marketing program unusually well. Three cases in point are Frito-Lay and its distribution system, BiC and its advertising program, and Midwest Typewriter (a company in Kansas City which won the IBM award as its best dealer in the United States in 1987) and its excellent service program.

6. Controlling: Controlling involves setting up performance standards (sales, market share, profit, and so forth), measuring actual performance, designing feedback systems, and taking action when marketing objectives are not being met.

If one were looking for the weakest link in the management of marketing programs, in many companies controlling would be a prime candidate. One of the reasons is that market-share measurements require knowing what industry sales are by the sales territory or segment, and for the time period, desired. It is often difficult to obtain industry sales data by sales territories, and especially difficult to obtain them by market segment. Another reason is that measurement and feedback for many of the performance standards is the province of another department—accounting. Accounting departments are typically busy, and setting up internal variable costing systems that allow the determination of such things as contribution to profit and fixed costs by product, or even by product line, is typically expensive and time consuming.

Management Style for Marketing Managers

Earlier, we described the central role decision making plays in marketing management. In understanding what it is that marketing management does and how it goes about doing it, it is instructive to look at the management style appropriate for marketing managers:

> ***Management style*** refers to a recurring set of characteristics that are associated with the decisional processes of the manager.[13]

There are at least five style elements that are of interest as they apply to marketing managers. They are

1. Planning versus improvisation—a determinant of the time period covered by the decision.

2. Innovation versus imitation—the source(s) of alternative courses of action considered in the decision.

3. Empiricism versus rationalism—influences the manner in which information is acquired to be used for choosing among alternatives.

4. Risk acceptance versus risk aversion—affects the alternative chosen.

5. Individual versus group decision making—defines with whom responsibility rests and how it is shared.

A brief assessment of the appropriate stance for the marketing manager on each of these style elements follows.

Planning versus Improvisation: There is little room for back-of-the-envelope, hip-pocket management in marketing. The good marketing manager is one who plans extensively.

Innovation versus Imitation: Innovation is needed to generate alternative solutions for problems that have not been considered before. A new product cannot be introduced, a new advertising campaign cannot be developed, or a new distribution channel cannot be adopted with a good probability of success without substantial innovative effort being involved. For example, as indicated by the asterisks in Exhibit 1–2, about one-half of all the steps involved in developing and introducing a new product require major creative inputs if they are to be carried out competently.

Empiricism versus Rationalism: Empiricists tend to make decisions based on analogous situations and on intuitive generalizations. When confronted with a decision to be made, they rely on "experience" and "judgment" as guides. Rationalists, on the other hand, tend to analyze problems and the data they have about them to try to find rules and relationships they can apply in making the decision. They too use experience and judgment in making decisions, but they are applied to the results of the analysis.

The advent of management science and the growing use of digital computers in the past three decades have resulted in marketing managers' moving toward (haltingly, perhaps, but toward) the rationalist end of the continuum. Major reasons for greater rationalism in marketing decisions have been the development of electronic data bases appropriate for use in marketing, the development of software (spreadsheets, for example) permitting "what-if" simulations of outcomes, and the development of formal marketing models to help solve marketing problems.

Risk Acceptance versus Risk Aversion: Marketing is arguably the riskiest area of the business. More money may well be risked on marketing activities whose outcomes can be predicted less accurately than for any other function of the firm. Does this mean that marketing managers should be more risk assuming than the managers of other functional areas? No, it does not. Observation of companies suggests that most have an implicit, but generally well-understood, stance toward risk assumption. As employees of the company, marketing management should abide by this implicit policy on risk in the same way it abides by other company policies.

Individual versus Group Decision Making: The degree of coordination required by marketing managers means that many of the decisions made by them have to be based on group consensus. It may therefore be that marketing managers are involved in more group decisions than the managers of other, more isolated departments of the company.

THE ROLE OF MARKETING MANAGEMENT IN THE ECONOMY

Marketing was defined earlier as the process of planning and executing the conception, pricing, promotion, and distribution of ideas, goods, and services to create exchanges that satisfy individual and organizational objectives. From this definition it is evident that such diverse exchange situations as

- the exchange of ideas in political campaigns,
- the barter or purchase of goods, and
- the purchase of services from nonprofit institutions (such as universities or health-care organizations)

all clearly fall within the domain of marketing.

Marketing also is a necessary function in every economy, regardless of the way it is organized. Any economy has five basic functions:

1. Decide what is to be produced.
2. Decide who is to produce it.
3. Allocate resources for it to be produced.
4. Decide who is to receive what share.
5. Distribute it physically.

The principal way of characterizing the organization of economies with respect to these functions is by where they fall on the continuum shown below.

At one end is the completely managed, or "command," economy, of which the closest approximation (at least until the late 1980s[14]) is that of Soviet Russia. The USSR does not have solely a managed economy, however; it allows each peasant family a small plot of land on which it can cultivate products for sale for its own profit, for example, rather than restricting agricultural production only to collectivized farms. At the other end is the economy of the United States, which is perhaps the closest example of an economy organized solely by market forces. Market constraints exist in the U.S. economy, however;

subsidies paid to farmers producing selected agricultural products are an example.

"Mixed" economies fall at various points along the continuum between the USSR and the United States. China, Yugoslavia, the Western European countries, Japan, and Canada are examples.

In command economies, state planning organizations carry out the functions done by marketing in free-enterprise economies. The central planning organization therefore becomes the primary "marketer" for the state. The five basic functions of the economy are handled as follows in the two types of economies:

1. *DECIDING WHAT IS TO BE PRODUCED.*
   Command economy—Central planning does the product planning.
   Free-enterprise economy—Marketing management coordinates the product planning, often using marketing research information.

2. *DECIDING WHO PRODUCES IT.*
   Command economy—Central and regional planning organizations determine the relative efficiency of producers and assign production responsibilities to state-owned companies.
   Free-enterprise economy—Done by price system. Marketing management recommends prices to top management.

3. *ALLOCATING RESOURCES FOR IT TO BE PRODUCED.*
   Command economy—Central and regional planning organizations make allocation decisions.
   Free-enterprise economy—Done by price system. Marketing management recommends prices to top management.

4. *DECIDING WHO RECEIVES WHAT SHARE.*
   Command economy—Effective demand working through centrally set prices and wages or salaries.
   Free-enterprise economy—Effective demand working through prices and wages or salaries set by individual firms. Marketing management affects demand through promotion, recommends prices to top management.

5. *DISTRIBUTING IT PHYSICALLY.*
   Command economy—Centrally planned and controlled distribution system.
   Free-enterprise economy—Planned and controlled by marketing departments of individual firms.

This list of functions and how they are performed demonstrates that marketing management collectively plays a key role in the operation of free-enterprise economies. If one wishes to characterize the command economy planners as being pseudo "marketers" when they are making product and pricing decisions, then the same comment applies to command economies as well.

SUMMARY OF IMPORTANT POINTS

1. *Marketing* is the process of planning and executing the conception, pricing, promotion, and distribution of ideas, goods, and services to create exchanges that satisfy individual and organizational objectives.

   Marketing management consists of the making and implementing of the decisions necessary for the marketing of specific ideas, goods, and services.

2. An *offering* in an exchange consists of a *generic* product (or service), the *tangible* product, and the *augmented* product.

3. The terms *generic product*, *tangible product*, and *augmented product* are defined as follows:

   generic product the utilitarian benefits provided by the product.
   tangible product the physical features of the product that have precise specifications.
   augmented product the ancillary products and services that accompany the tangible product and the image associated with its use.

4. In a commercial exchange situation, the possible outcomes are

	Buyer gains	Buyer loses
Seller gains	Mutually beneficial exchange (4)	Conflicting outcomes exchange (1)
Seller loses	Conflicting outcomes exchange (3)	Mutually injurious exchange (2)

5. Companies that provide greater value to their customers themselves tend to receive the benefits of larger market shares and higher profits. For the sake of both the customer and the company, therefore, marketing management should attempt to ensure that the (positive-sum) outcome (4), the "win-win" outcome in the above matrix, occurs as often as possible.

6. The *marketing concept* means that an organization aims all of its efforts at satisfying its customers—at a profit.

7. Managing marketing programs involve six steps:
   a. setting marketing strategy
   b. planning the nature and level of the mix elements required for its accomplishment
   c. organizing for operations
   d. coordinating with other departments
   e. implementing the plans
   f. controlling to ensure that objectives are met to the extent possible

8. *Management style* refers to a recurring set of characteristics that are associated with the decisional processes of the manager.

9. There are at least five style elements that are of interest as they apply to marketing managers:
   a. *planning versus improvisation*   a determinant of the time period covered by the decision
   b. *innovation versus imitation*   the source(s) of alternative courses of action considered in the decision
   c. *empiricism versus rationalism*   influences the manner in which information is acquired to be used for choosing among alternatives
   d. *risk acceptance versus risk aversion*   affects the alternative chosen
   e. *individual versus group decision making*   defines with whom responsibility rests and how it is shared.

10. Marketing management helps to carry out each of the five basic functions of an economy:
   a. **Deciding what is to be produced.**
   Command economy. Central planning does the product planning.
   Free-enterprise economy. Marketing management coordinates the product planning, often using marketing research information.
   b. **Deciding who produces it.**
   Command economy. Central and regional planning organizations determine the relative efficiency of producers and assign production responsibilities to state-owned companies.
   Free-enterprise economy. Done by price system. Marketing management recommends prices to top management.
   c. **Allocating resources for it to be produced.**
   Command economy. Central and regional planning organizations make allocation decisions.
   Free-enterprise economy. Done by price system. Marketing management recommends prices to top management.
   d. **Deciding who receives what share.**
   Command economy. Effective demand working through centrally set prices and wages or salaries.
   Free-enterprise economy. Effective demand working through prices and wages/salaries set by individual firms. Marketing management affects demand through promotion, recommends prices to top management.
   e. **Distributing it physically.**
   Command economy. Centrally planned and controlled distribution system.
   Free-enterprise economy. Planned and controlled by marketing departments of individual firms.

REVIEW QUESTIONS

1.1.   What is *marketing*?

1.2.   What is *marketing management*?

1.3. What is an *offering?*

1.4. What is a
   a. *fragmented* marketing department?
   b. *fully integrated* marketing department?

1.5. What are the steps involved in managing a marketing program?

1.6. On what basis can we make the assertion that "marketing management works"?

1.7. What are the five basic functions of any economy?

1.8. In a free-enterprise economy, what is marketing management's role in carrying out the functions given in answer to question 1.6?

1.9. In a command economy, how are the functions given in answer to question 1.6 carried out?

1.10. In a commercial exchange situation, what are the possible outcomes?

1.11. Which of the outcomes given in answer to question 1.10 should the marketing manager try to bring about as often as possible? Why?

1.12. In your own words, what is the *marketing concept?*

DISCUSSION QUESTIONS AND PROBLEMS

1.13. At the beginning of the chapter, marketing management was defined as "the making and implementing of the decisions necessary for the marketing of specific ideas, goods, and services." This definition implies that marketing managers are only involved in making and implementing decisions—they have no other responsibilities. Is this implication true? Explain.

1.14. A definition of marketing management that is an alternative to the one used in this chapter (see the preceding question) is "setting marketing strategy, planning for its accomplishment, organizing for marketing operations, implementing plans, and controlling to ensure that company objectives are met to the extent possible." Is this definition preferable to the one used in the chapter? Why or why not?

1.15. "It is not possible for a marketing program for an in-business-for-profit company to be designed for the benefit of the buyer as well as for the firm. After all, doesn't making a profit require that the company takes in more than it gives out? And doesn't that mean that the buyer *cannot* be a beneficiary of the exchange?" Comment.

1.16. Does the marketing concept imply that the marketer should try to satisfy only those needs and desires that consumers say they have? Explain.

1.17. How does the marketing concept relate to the buyer loses–seller gains, buyer gains–seller loses, buyer loses–seller loses, buyer gains–seller gains possible outcomes of an exchange?

1.18. The following ad appeared in London newspapers in 1900:

> **Men Wanted For Hazardous Journey.** Small wages, bitter cold, long months of complete darkness, constant danger, safe return doubtful. Honor and recognition in case of success.
> —ERNEST SHACKLETON.

There was an immediate response of unprecedented proportions.
a. What was the *offering?*
b. Why do you think it was so successful?

1.19. In the survey of 140 executives (described in the chapter), about two-thirds of them when asked "Which is the most important management area in the firm?" replied "marketing." The remaining one-third gave some other management area. Side with the minority and make a case for
a. finance
b. manufacturing
being the most important management area.

1.20. Can it reasonably be asserted that planners in command economies make *marketing* decisions? Why or why not?

1.21. a. Can advertising contribute to a "win" outcome for the consumer in an exchange? Explain.
b. Can a higher price (for the same product) contribute to a "win" outcome for the consumer in an exchange? Explain.

1.22. "Buick is counting on a new ad campaign featuring upbeat music, scenic roads and portraits of its 1988 model cars to replace its stodgy image with a more upscale one" (*Advertising Age*, August 31, 1987, p. 52).
a. Does this new campaign change the Buick "offering"? Explain.
b. Can this new campaign create added value to consumers? Explain.

1.23. The Lorillard Company has a new cigarette named "Harley-Davidson." In product information prepared for its sales force, the company states that "the Harley-Davidson name was chosen because of its all-American quality image.... The objective is to capitalize on Harley-Davidson's pre-existing image to generate interest and appeal to the male segment of the cigarette market."

Suppose that the names "Harley-Davidson" (which was licensed from the motorcycle company) and "Pure Pleasure" were the finalists in the selection of the new cigarette's name. Would the selection of "Pure Pleasure" have provided a different level of perceived value to the male smoker? Explain.

Endnotes

[1] The definition adopted by the Board of the American Marketing Association in 1985.

[2] T. Leavitt, *The Marketing Imagination*, Free Press, 1983, 74.

[3] As reported in J. N. Sheth, *Winning Back Your Market*, John Wiley & Sons, 1985, 76–77.

[4] *Advertising Age*, August 25, 1986, 28.

[5] As described in M. Hoy, "Winning the Numbers Game," *Old Oregon*, Summer 1986, 22–26. Later data supplied by the director of admissions and records have been added.

[6] See P. Kotler, L. Fahey, and S. Jatusripitak, *The New Competition*, Prentice-Hall, 1985, Chap. 3, for a more complete description of Toyota's entry and growth in the U.S. market.

[7] Adapted from K. E. Boulding, "The Economics of Human Conflict," in *Nature of Human Conflict*, E. B. McNeil (ed.), Prentice-Hall, 1965.

[8] D. F. Duhan, "The Marketing Influence of the Benign Shift of Transaction Relationships and Firm Value Added Productivity," Ph.D. diss., University of Oregon, 1984, Chaps. 4 and 5.

[9] A. Smith, *The Wealth of Nations*, Random House, 1937, 336.

[10] E. J. McCarthy and W. J. Perrault, Jr., *Basic Marketing*, 8th ed., Richard D. Irwin, 1984, 35.

[11] "Strategic Marketing Top Priority of Chief Execs," *Marketing News*, January 31, 1986, 1.

[12] According to a study conducted by the authors in 1987. A random sample of 350 companies was taken from Standard & Poor's Register of Executives. Twenty-five letters were returned because the addressee was no longer there. Sixty-three companies responded.

[13] Adapted from D. S. Tull, "Solutions for Marketing Cases: Implicit Model and Management Styles," paper presented at the Forty-first National Meeting of the Operations Research Society of America, 1971.

[14] With the advent of *perestroika*, the program of restructuring of the Soviet economy introduced by Mikhail Gorbachev, some of the economies of the Soviet bloc countries (East Germany, for example) may be closer to being prototype command economies than is the USSR.

MARKETING STRATEGIES

By the end of the usual day in the typical company, several marketing decisions will have been made. They will have involved such concerns as increasing the inventory in a regional warehouse, making a price adjustment to reflect an increase in materials prices, settling on a theme for an advertising campaign, hiring a new sales representative, or any of a large number of other marketing-related, day-by-day matters.

These are examples of ***operating marketing decisions***. They are made on an everyday, continuing basis at varying levels of the marketing organization depending on the subject area and their importance. Over time, hundreds of them are made. Collectively they are vital to the well-being, and ultimately the survival, of the company.

In the well-managed company, however, these operating decisions are made within the context of a much smaller set of decisions. These are the ***strategic management and marketing decisions*** of the firm.

Consider the following examples of strategic marketing decisions:

> The Hewlett-Packard Company has been successful in the highly competitive hand-held calculator market by offering high-priced, quality products for selected segments of the market. Hewlett-Packard has been a major innovator in special features for calculators and has been able to command higher-than-average prices as a result.
>
> Lukens Steel Co. has differentiated its offerings from those of its competitors by becoming "specialists in steel plate." The company makes only steel plate, and more grades and sizes of it than any other steel company.
>
> The Stroh Brewery Company, a regional brewery located in Detroit, moved to reposition its regular beer as a premium rather than as a popularly priced beer. Prices have been raised, promotional budgets increased, and advertising themes adapted in keeping with a premium image.
>
> Compaq Computer Corp., a manufacturer of microcomputers, was founded in 1982 and became one of the 500 largest companies in the United States in 1985. It sells only to the business market, staying out of the home and educational markets. It distributes only through dealers.
>
> White Castle Co., a fast-food restaurant chain with outlets located in nine cities in the midwestern part of the United States, sells hamburgers only—no chicken, no salad, no breakfast food. It has the lowest prices for hamburgers—30 cents—with the highest average sales per outlet in the industry. Its hamburgers are cooked with steam, which leaves them with a high moisture content. This makes them compatible with both freezing and microwave reheating. The company sells more than 20 million frozen hamburgers per year through grocery stores.

These examples share at least two common characteristics. First, they are each part of a "grand design" of the operations of the company involved. As such, the decisions they represent had to involve the top management, as well as the marketing management, of the firm. Second, in each case they emphasize marketing considerations. They are planned means of achieving the company's objectives through the markets to be served or the marketing programs to be used.

We can employ the characteristics of the marketing strategies just described in arriving at the following generic meaning of the term:

> *Marketing strategy* is the fundamental means planned for achieving the company's objectives by developing a sustainable competitive advantage through the markets entered and the marketing programs used to serve them.

This definition is a useful one for a number of reasons. First, by referring to the "fundamental" means of achieving objectives, it differentiates *strategies* from tactics. Tactics are means employed to carry out strategies. (The decision to have differing market programs in different parts of the market is a segmentation **strategy**; deciding how the programs are to differ is a segmentation **tactic**.)

Second, it emphasizes that strategies have to be planned, a topic that is discussed in a later chapter of this book.

Finally, it states that company objectives are achieved by developing a *sustainable competitive advantage* through two primary means—the choice of *markets* to enter and the *marketing programs* to employ in serving them.

Table 2–1 Principal Marketing Strategies

   I. Translation of Company Strategic Objectives to Market Strategies
    A. Market share now, profit later
    B. Profit now

  II. Market Strategies
    A. Choice of product markets
       1. Market penetration
       2. Market development
       3. Product development
       4. Diversification
       5. Segmentation
       6. Portfolio management

 III. Marketing Program Strategies
    A. Product
       1. Quality level
          a. low
          b. competitive
          c. high
       2. Variety
          a. limited
          b. extensive
    B. Pricing
       1. Level
          a. penetration
          b. matching
          c. skimming
       2. Price leadership
          a. lead
          b. follow
    C. Communication
       1. Level
          a. low
          b. parity
          c. high
       2. Target audiences
          a. distributors (push)
          b. consumers (pull)
       3. Degree of comparison
          a. own-product-oriented
          b. comparison-oriented
    D. Distribution
       1. Level
          a. mass
          b. selective
          c. exclusive
       2. Degree of directness
          a. direct
          b. middlemen
       3. Degree of integration
          a. integrated
          b. nonintegrated

An Overview of Marketing Strategies

An overview of marketing strategies is given in Table 2–1. As shown in the table, there are three major sets of strategic marketing decisions that need to be made:

1. Translation of company objectives to market objectives—choosing between a ***market share now, profit later*** and a ***profit now*** strategy. A choice has to be made for each market as to whether some potential short-term profits will be deferred in the interest of building market share, or profits will be taken as the opportunity allows.
2. Strategic ***choice of markets***—choosing the product markets to be served through strategies of market penetration, market development, product development, and diversification, and through management of the resulting portfolio of product markets.
3. ***Developing marketing program strategies***—devising appropriate strategies for the marketing program for each product market.

These strategies are necessarily sequential in nature. That is, a decision about whether "market share now, profit later" or "profit now" (strategic decision 1) is to be the principal objective to be made before the choice of markets (decision 2) is made, and markets obviously have to be chosen before developing marketing program strategies (decisions). A discussion of the principal strategic decisions in each of these areas is the primary concern of this chapter.

TRANSLATION OF COMPANY STRATEGIC OBJECTIVES TO MARKET STRATEGIES

The Decision Concerning Adopting a "Market Share Now, Profit Later" or a "Profit Now" Strategy

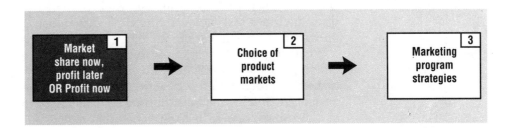

The choice between a "market share now, profit later" and a "profit now" strategy is tied closely to company strategies. Company strategic objectives determine market strategies.

Table 2–2   Strategic Objectives of Eighty Two Large Corporations

Category	Number	Percent*
Profitability	73	89
Growth	67	82
Market share	54	66
Social responsibility	53	65
Employee welfare	51	62

*Adds to more than 100 percent because most companies have multiple objectives.
Source: Adapted from Y. K. Shetty, "New Look at Corporate Goals," *California Management Review*, Winter 1979, p. 73.

What are the objectives of companies? A list of the stated strategic objectives of 82 large corporations is shown in Table 2–2. The strategic objectives of a majority of these companies can be summarized as follows:

To be profitable (89 percent) and to grow (82 percent) and/or to increase market share (66 percent) using means that are socially responsible (65 percent) and that contribute to employee welfare (62 percent).

The means of achieving these strategic objectives include conducting ongoing programs of research and development, diversifying, providing quality products and services, and pricing, promoting and distributing them in a manner that benefits the customer as well as the company.

Whereas profitability and growth/market share are generally compatible objectives for a product line over the long term, they are usually *incompatible* in the short term. Building market share normally requires lower prices and higher promotional budgets than would maximize profits during the building period.[1] When the desired level of market share is reached, however, prices can be raised and promotional budgets reduced to levels that will maintain share and, not incidentally, increase profits. A strategy of building market share that is successful over the long term will result in higher profits overall (and higher discounted net cash flows at the time it is initiated) than will a strategy of attempting to maximize profits with each price and advertising budget set.[2]

Whether a company chooses to build market share or to maximize present period profits dominates both the choice of product markets to enter and the marketing programs used to serve them. The number and kinds of products developed, in what markets they are sold, and how they are priced, promoted, and distributed are each likely to be different under a market-share strategy than they are under a profit-now strategy. As we shall see shortly, the choice between these two strategies also has far-reaching consequences with respect to how the manufacturing and financing functions within the company are conducted.

Considerations
Involved in
Choosing
between the
"Market Share
Now, Profit
Later" and "Profit
Now" Strategic
Alternatives

The decision to build market share and thus to delay taking (some) potential profits as the opportunity permits is not any easy one. It depends on considerations of the industry, market, product, and competitors, and of company capabilities and willingness to assume risk.

These considerations may even lead two different companies in the same industry to adopt different strategies simultaneously. An example is the two largest domestic producers of hand-held electronic calculators, Texas Instruments and Hewlett-Packard. Since the early days of the calculator market, "Texas Instruments has used the strategy of driving down prices to gain market share. . . . The calculator . . . market is a prime example."[3] Hewlett-Packard has used the reverse strategy of high quality and high price with no concern about market share.

A consideration of the general factors involved in the market-share-now versus take-profits-now issue will help explain the bases on which the general strategic decision should be made. The key considerations leading to adopting a market-share strategy are as follows:

1. The company should be in an industry in which sustainable competitive advantages can be developed and in which higher market share can be expected to lead to higher long-term profits.
2. The product(s) should be in an early stage of the product life cycle.
3. The potential market should be large enough and sufficiently price-elastic (relative to product quality) to permit sizable economies of scale in manufacturing or marketing to result in substantial potential profits.
4. The product(s) should be of good quality relative to those of competitors.
5. After considering the relative qualities of the products, the company should have either an actual or a potential cost advantage relative to competitors.
6. The company must be willing to devote substantial resources to both product and manufacturing R&D and to plant and equipment improvement and expansion.
7. The company must have, or be willing to acquire, a marketing capability that is at least the equal of its nearest competitor.
8. The number of competitors, their capabilities, and their strategies should be such as to provide for a reasonable chance of success for a market-share strategy.
9. The company needs to be well financed.
10. The management must be willing to undergo a higher level of risk.

We do not suggest that all of these factors need to be met in order to choose the market-share-now option. However, the potential effects of the absence of one or more of them should be considered carefully before going ahead with the market-share strategy.

A brief discussion of each of the factors follows.

1. *The company should be in an industry in which one or more sizable and sustainable competitive advantages can be developed and in which higher market share can be*

expected to lead to higher long-term profits. The attractiveness of a market share now–profit later strategy varies with industries both in terms of the opportunities for developing sustainable competitive advantages and the amount of expected profit resulting from increasing market share.

The Boston Consulting Group has developed a matrix of "competitive environments" that groups industries by the number of ways competitive advantages can be attained, and the potential size of the advantage gained.[4] This matrix is shown in Figure 2–1.

Of the industries in the four quadrants in the figure, only two of them—the specialization (quadrant 1) and volume industries (quadrant 4)—are promising prospects for a market-share-now strategy.

Specialization industries contain companies that have found a market niche and that serve it well. They typically provide quality products and services at a premium price. Examples of such industries are specialized magazines, high-priced cosmetics, specialty metals, fashion clothes, chain-saw chain, special-

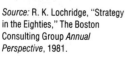

FIGURE 2-1
Matrix of competitive environments.

Source: R. K. Lochridge, "Strategy in the Eighties," The Boston Consulting Group *Annual Perspective*, 1981.

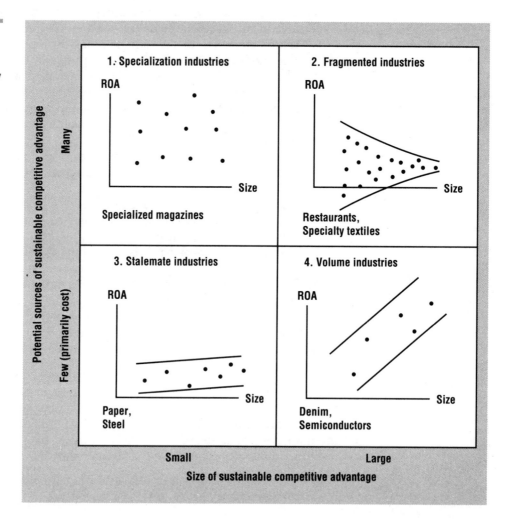

purpose computers, and luxury cars. There are many sources of competitive advantage in these industries—quality products that can be customized if desired, prestige, service, and advanced technology are examples.

Increasing market share may or may not result in added profits (ROA = return on assets in the figure) in specialization industries, however. Mercedes-Benz, for example, is a highly profitable company with a limited overall market share, whereas Harley-Davidson, the holder of the major market share of the market for high-performance (and high-priced) motorcycles, is only marginally profitable. Both are in a specialization industry. If a management were inclined to pursue a market-share strategy in a specialization industry, therefore, it would be well advised to look not only to whether it could sustain one or more competitive advantages, but also whether the long-term added profitability would be such as to make such a strategy worthwhile.

No such profitability concerns need be raised in the "volume" industries, however. Here sustainable competitive advantage rests largely on cost, and a high market share brings lower costs through economies of scale. Examples of volume industries include semiconductors, most household appliances, minicomputers, commercial airliners, and low- and medium-priced automobiles.

Texas Instruments forecast in the early 1970s that the hand-held calculator market was destined to become a volume industry. Given this forecast, it was appropriate for the company to consider using a market-share-now strategy for its calculators.

Companies in the industries in the two other quadrants in Figure 2–1, the fragmented (quadrant 1) and stalemate (quadrant 3) industries, are typically not good candidates for the market-share-now strategy. Fragmented industries include restaurants, specialty textiles, general-purpose automobile repair, custom home construction, and hospitals and dental clinics. For these industries there may even be a negative association of return on assets with market share.[5] The stalemate industries are the "smokestack" industries that include steel, paper, forest products, fertilizer, and basic industrial chemicals. For these industries the added return from higher market share is so limited as to make a market-share-now strategy unattractive.

2. *The products should be in an early stage of the product life cycle.* The product life cycle is typically portrayed as shown in Figure 2–2. That is, it is an S-shaped sales curve that is commonly divided into the stages of ***product development, rapid sales growth, competitive turbulence, mature market, declining market,*** and ***death.*** (The product life cycle is discussed in detail in Chapter 12.)

There is a corresponding product life cycle measured with respect to profits. The profits cycle is also shown in Figure 2–2.

If a market-share strategy is adopted, it obviously needs to be implemented early in the product life cycle, during the introduction or early in the growth stage. The underlying strategy is to build market share during the introduction and growth stages and to "harvest" profits during the maturity stage.

3. *The potential market should be large enough and sufficiently price-elastic (relative to product quality) to permit sizable economies of scale in manufacturing or marketing to result in substantial prospective profits.* Strategically, it makes little sense to invest heavily in attempting to capture a large share of a small market. The market must potentially be large and, in order for a market-share strategy to succeed,

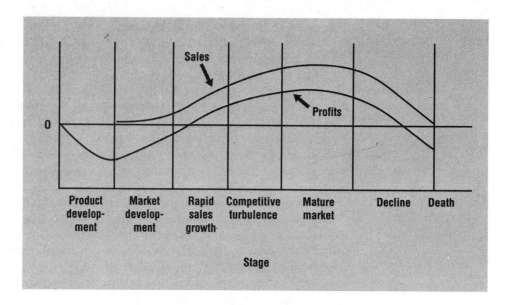

FIGURE 2-2
Product life cycles—sales and profits.

must also be one in which buying decisions are influenced substantially by lower prices or higher promotional budgets.

By the mid 1980s, more than 50 million hand-held calculators were being sold each year.

4. *The product(s) should be of good quality relative to those of competitors.* PIMS (*Profit Impact of Marketing Strategies*) is a database of the operating characteristics and results of nearly 3,000 business units of over 200 companies. (The PIMS database is discussed in more detail in a later section of this chapter.) One of the findings from this database is:

> Whether connected with new product introductions or not quality improvement is a powerful means of building market share. . . . In all three groups of businesses—consumer products, raw materials, and industrial products—competitors that increased relative quality enjoyed much greater gains in share than those whose quality ratings remained constant or diminished.[6]

There is further evidence from one study using the PIMS database that high relative product quality is not incompatible with achieving a low relative cost position in an industry.[7] This may have resulted from the

**high relative quality → high market share →
high cumulative output → low unit cost**

causal chain described in the discussion of factor 4.

5. *After considering the relative qualities of the products, the company should have either an actual or a potential sustainable cost advantage relative to competitors.* One of the key competitive strategies is cost leadership.[8] And, as long as there is an opportunity to reduce unit costs substantially by increasing the volume produced, a powerful argument follows for building market share, even at the cost of delaying some potential profits. The increased market share contributes to cost reductions, which in turn allow prices to be reduced. Lower prices can lead to further increases in market share, and so, in "volume" industries, the process has the potential to ratchet itself to successively lower costs, lower prices, higher market shares, and higher profits.

There is evidence for some products that the reduction in costs takes the form of an experience curve. This cost reduction curve is defined as follows:

> The *experience curve* is a cost curve such that each time the accumulated output of a product doubles, the total cost per unit goes down by a fixed percentage.

Two aspects of this definition should be noted. First, it is the *accumulated* output that must double before costs fall by a fixed percentage. That is, if 100,000 units of a product have been produced since the first one came off the line, 100,000 more units will have to be produced before costs fall by the fixed percentage that applies. Second, the cost referred to is the *total* cost, and not just the manufacturing cost. Total costs include marketing, engineering, and overhead costs as well as manufacturing costs.

An example is the cost history of videotape recorders. Each time the *accumulated output* of one of the manufacturers doubled, *total costs* per unit declined an average of about 20 percent.[9] Assuming that the first unit cost of that manufacturer was about $25,000 and that this same industry average of a 20 percent reduction in unit costs was experienced each time cumulative output was doubled, the costs of successive units would be as shown in Table 2–3.[10] These are dramatic reductions and, assuming that other producers have had similar cost reductions, illustrate the sizable cost advantages that the major videotape recorder producers (Sony and RCA, for example) have had.

By convention, the experience curve is referred to as the complement of the percentage of cost reduction that results from a doubling of cumulative output. The curve for videotape recorders would therefore be called an 80 percent experience curve (100 percent minus 20 percent).

Table 2-3 Reductions in Unit Costs of Producing Videotape Recorders as Cumulative Output Increases — 80 Percent Experience Curve

Cumulative No. of Units Produced		Total Unit Cost (in $)
1		$25,000
2	(1.0–2.0) $25,000 =	20,000
4	(1.0–2.0) $20,000 =	16,000
100		5,675
1,000		2,704
10,000		1,288
100,000		614
1,000,000		292

There is evidence to indicate that although the percentage of cost reduction varies, the same general relationship between cost reduction and cumulative output holds for a variety of products and services. Some examples:

Long-distance telephone calls	72 percent
Integrated electronic circuits	74 percent
Electric shavers	77 percent
Broiler chickens	79 percent
Japanese beer	84 percent
Model "T" Ford	85 percent
Primary magnesium	93 percent

Sources: With the exception of the Model "T" Ford, the data are from the Boston Consulting Group as reported either in *Perspectives on Experience* (no publisher shown, 1972) or in D. F. Abell and J. S. Hammond, *Strategic Market Planning*, Prentice-Hall, 1979. The Model "T" figure is given in N. J. Abernathy and K. Wayne, "Limits to the Learning Curve," *Harvard Business Review*, September–October 1974, 111.

The experience curve is discussed in detail in Appendix A.

6. *The company must be willing to devote substantial resources to both product and manufacturing R&D and to plant and equipment improvement and expansion.* The company needs to defend itself against new technological developments by competitors that would make its product(s) less desirable before it reaches the high-profit stage. It also needs to develop lower-cost manufacturing methods to help it obtain a substantial lowering of unit costs.

Design of the product for ease of manufacturing is an important determinant of the slope of the experience curve. Toward this end, companies should strive to simplify the product over time in terms of either design or number of parts or both. For example, between 1974 and 1978, the number of parts of one Texas Instrument calculator was reduced from 119 to 17.[11]

7. *The company must have, or be willing to acquire, a marketing capability that is at least the equal of its nearest competitor.* There is an obvious need for high capabilities, and either excess capacity or the willingness to build additional capacity, in both of these areas to allow a market-share strategy to be pursued successfully.

8. *The number of competitors, their capabilities, and their strategies should be such as to provide for a reasonable chance of success for a market-share strategy.* It is desirable for the company to have a relatively high market share initially when the management elects a market-share strategy for an existing product. The PIMS data disclose that "for most markets a good approximation of the natural (market share) structure is one in which the market leader has a 40 percent share, and numbers 2, 3, and 4 have shares of 25 percent, 15 percent, and 10 percent, respectively."[12] Starting in even the number 2 position in an existing product line gives the company seeking a cost advantage a sizable handicap unless it has developed manufacturing technology or product characteristics that compensate for not being first.

It is also desirable that none of the other competitors are going for, or are likely to go for, a market-share strategy. Two companies pursuing the same strategy can lead to a costly victory at best, and an expensive loss or stalemate at worst.

Texas Instruments' management knew in 1974 (when it entered the calculator market) that there were several Japanese companies that were attempting to get a foothold in the American calculator market. This could have been interpreted as an indication of later problems. (In recent years, the Japanese and other Asian electronics companies exporting to this country have followed a market-share strategy almost without exception.)

9. *The company needs to be well financed.* The market-share strategy requires substantial investment in the earlier periods.

10. *The management must be willing to undergo a higher level of risk.* There can be no question but that foregoing potential present profits to build market share is a riskier strategy than taking profits as the situation allows. By following a market-share strategy, risks are being taken that the sizable market projected will not materialize, that new technological developments will make current products obsolete, that competitors will capture the major share of the market, and even that the Antitrust Division of the Department of Justice will break the company up if the strategy is too successful.

The high risk involved makes it undesirable for a multi-product-line company to elect market-share strategies for more than, say, 25 percent of its lines. For single-product-line companies using such a strategy, it also makes it desirable to diversify.[13]

Conclusions with Respect to Market Share Now, Profit Later versus Profit Now Strategic Decisions	Given the differences in markets, in products and their stage of the life cycle, and in competitor strengths and strategies, the same overall market share and other company objectives cannot reasonably be applied indiscriminately across products and markets. A preferable strategy is to adapt the overall objectives to the needs and opportunities of each of the products and the markets in which they are sold.

Without being privileged to the deliberations that both the Hewlett-Packard (HP) and Texas Instruments (TI) managements had concerning this issue, one cannot say with certainty what led to the opposing strategic decisions. However, it appears that market conditions, initial product designs, and company financial strengths would have permitted either company to move in either direction. A greater engineering orientation, along with lesser manufacturing and marketing capabilities, a strong presupposition that TI and foreign competitors would elect the market-share strategy, and a more conservative management may have been the major reasons that HP adopted the strategy it did. The reverse of these considerations may account for the contrary decision by TI.

For whatever reason(s), given the later erosion of TI's share and substantial drop in calculator profits, and the continuing stable and profitable market enjoyed by HP for its calculators, one has to conclude that the HP strategy was the better one.

Choice of Product Markets

The choice of products and the markets in which they are sold is of obvious importance to the success or failure of the marketing program. These choices are the sole determinants of market potential, have substantial effects on the degree of competition and the cost of marketing, and ultimately are important determinants of the profitability of the firm.

Market Strategies

After a market-share or a profit-now strategy is chosen, one has to select appropriate *market* and *marketing program* strategies. Market strategies are discussed in this section; marketing program strategies are discussed in the section that follows.

A market can only be defined with reference to the product (or products) that is to be sold to it. Note that this is the case in the following definition:

> A **market** is a geographic area or a group of actual or potential users of a product or product class.

Since the term *market* is necessarily tied to the product offered in it, when one refers to *market strategies*, one is referring to *product market strategies* as well. The two terms are used here interchangeably.

One way of viewing the strategic alternatives for product market choice for an existing company is shown in Figure 2–3. That is, a company can attempt to increase market share in existing markets with existing products. Such a strategy is one of **market penetration**. Or the company can try entering new markets with existing products; this is a strategy of **market development**. Another strategic alternative is to develop new products for existing markets, a strategy of **product development** or **product differentiation**; or the company might choose to develop both new products *and* new markets. This is a strategy of **diversification**. Finally, any one of these strategies might involve dividing the product market into two or more segments, and using different marketing programs for each of the segments. This is a strategy of **market segmentation**. We discuss these strategic possibilities in terms of the following example:

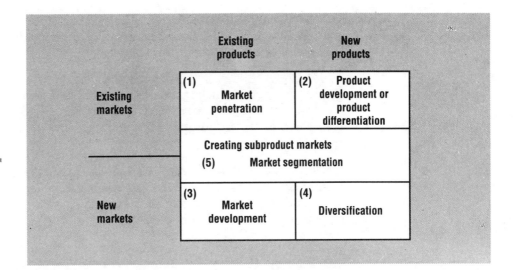

FIGURE 2-3
Product market strategic
alternatives matrix.

Source: Adapted from H. I. Ansoff,
"Strategies for Diversification,"
Harvard Business Review,
September–October 1957,
113–124.

In the early 1980s, Sears-Roebuck management took stock of the recent poor performance of the company. Sales increases each year had been less than that accounted for by inflation since 1978 and profits per share had declined by about one-third since 1977.

Management believed there were several reasons for this poor performance record. By the mid 1970s the company had passed through the post–World War II rapid-growth phase of not only its retail and mail-order business, but its insurance (Allstate) and financing (Sears-Roebuck Acceptance Corp.) businesses as well. It had reached virtual saturation of good locations for its more than 850 retail stores. A "trading-up" strategy in the late 1970s had moved it away from its core lower-to-middle-income market segments. Both K-Mart and J. C. Penney had made substantial gains during this period, because of both aggressive expansionary programs of their own and the failure of Sears to remain as competitive as it had been.

Sears' management was looking for ways to improve the company's performance.

Product Market Strategy One: Market Penetration

A market-penetration strategy is one involving existing products and existing markets. It can be defined as follows:

> A ***market-penetration strategy*** is one in which an attempt is made to increase the market share for existing products in existing markets.

How can market share be increased? Reflection suggests there are four possible ways.

Attract Competitors' Customers: The objectives of the usual marketing program include winning customers away from competitors while maintaining the loyalty of one's own customers.

> A general price reduction by Sears or increased advertising and sales promotion would have been moves calculated to divert customers from K-Mart, Penney's, and other competitors to shopping at Sears.

Convert Nonusers into Users: Every market contains a certain proportion of persons who are nonusers. In the case of mail and telephone sales, for example, only about 12 percent of general merchandise is sold to a somewhat greater proportion of people who buy by this means.

> As a means of converting nontelephone buyers to ordering via telephone, as well as to increase purchases from present users, Sears has considered establishing a cable TV catalog network to display merchandise on home-television receivers.

Increase the Frequency of Purchase: If purchase frequency is increased, as long as average purchase amounts do not decrease proportionately as much, market share will increase.

> The use of a cable TV catalog network would almost certainly increase ordering frequency by Sears' customers.

Increase the Average Amount per Purchase: An increase in the average sale will also increase market share, other things remaining the same.

> In order to increase the size of the average purchase, some mail order and telephone order companies have returned coupons good for a certain amount on the next purchase as long as the amount of the purchase exceeds a certain level. Sears might consider such a promotional device.

Product Market Strategy Two: Product Development or Product Differentiation

A ***product-development*** or ***product-differentiation strategy*** is one in which new products are offered in existing markets.

New products can be either ***innovative***, ***emulative***, or ***adaptive***.

Innovative New Products: An innovative new product is a new-to-the-economy product; neither the company nor its competitors have had such a product before. An example is the digital computer, penicillin, and video tape recorders, at the time each was developed originally and introduced.

As a retailer, Sears has not supported the research and development of innovative new products in the past. It could do so in the future, of course, if the management chose to do so.

Emulative New Products: An emulative new product is a new-to-the-company but not a new-to-the-economy product. An example is the more than 50 brands of electric toothbrushes that are emulations of the original Sunbeam electric toothbrush.

Sears has traditionally been very active in the development and retailing of housebrand items (Diehard batteries, Craftsman tools, Kenmore appliances, etc.) which are often emulative in origin.

Adaptive New Products: An adaptive new product is an adaptation of an existing product. The adaptive new product either can be a *replacement* for an existing product (the new model of the Compaq DeskPro microcomputer replaces the previous one) or can be an *addition* to the existing product line (a portable version of the Compaq computer is added). Adding a new adaptive product is known as **product differentiation**. (Product differentiation is described more fully in the section on market segmentation.)

Sears has also been active in adapting the products it offers.

Product Market Strategy Three: Market Development

A market-development strategy involves developing new markets for existing products. It can be defined formally as:

A **market-development strategy** is one in which new markets are sought for existing products.

New markets can be from new geographic areas, new market segments, or both.

New Geographic Areas: Aggressive, growth-oriented companies have traditionally sought new market areas. The expansion of U.S. firms into the Canadian, Western European, Japanese and other markets in the 1960s and the movement of firms from those countries into the U.S. market in the 1970s and 1980s illustrate the use of a market-development strategy.

Although Sears has virtually saturated the bigger metropolitan areas in the United States with its larger stores, only a limited number of smaller stores (less than 400) have been built in less densely populated areas. These areas could be developed if it were judged profitable to do so.

New Market Segments: We discuss later in this section the dividing of product markets into more homogeneous submarkets, or market segments, as a separate product market strategy.

Product Market Strategy Four: Diversification

A ***diversification strategy*** is one in which new products are offered in new markets.

Companies diversify to reduce risks, to even out demand over time, to increase profits, and for other reasons. An example of a diversifying move is:

> Sears has contemplated entry into the market for automobiles with an electric car. It would be sold and serviced by Sears, and financing, insurance, and tires, batteries, and accessories would be provided through its retail stores.

Collectively, the products offered by a firm and the market in which they are sold comprise a ***portfolio*** of product markets. The portfolio of product market holdings as of a point in time are analogous to a portfolio of securities held by an investor.

The literature on the management of investment portfolios stresses that a potential new security to be bought should be analyzed in terms of its future effects on the overall holdings. That is, the value of an individual security is determined within the context of the portfolio of holdings rather than independently. This is necessary because the levels of risk and of yield of the portfolio are likely to change with the addition of each security. Investment portfolios with individual holdings that have differing life cycles and payout periods are stronger than those that are more homogeneous in these respects, again because they result in more favorable prospects for risk and yield.

A diversified portfolio of product markets, like a diversified portfolio of securities, potentially has less risk than a single holding. The risk that can potentially be eliminated by diversification is called ***specific risk***. This is the risk that is attached to each product market specifically and stems from uncertainties in consumer patronage, competitor actions, and other non-economy-wide perils.

But you can't avoid all risk however much you diversify. There is some risk that results from economic and market fluctuations that affect all product markets in the industry. Recessions and depressions, increases in interest rates, wars, and changes in government regulations are examples. Collectively, these risks are known as ***systematic risk***.[14]

The relationship of risk to number of product markets in a reasonably well diversified portfolio is shown in Figure 2–4.

Diversification as a means of reducing *specific risks* is a common strategy. Virtually every aerospace company in the United States has, at one time or another, attempted to enter industrial product markets to reduce its dependence on governmental budgets and spending. Conversely, almost all machinery and heavy equipment manufacturers have attempted to market products to governmental agencies, in part to reduce the effects of potential decline in the industrial markets they serve. Textbook publishers have added trade departments, and publishers of trade books have added textbook departments; accounting firms have begun to offer management consulting services, and consulting firms to offer accounting services; and manufacturers in the United States have begun marketing their products abroad, and foreign manufacturers have entered the U.S. market, all in part to hedge against potential decline in their initial product markets.

Product Market Strategy Five: Market Segmentation

A strategic choice has to be made as to whether the markets chosen will be undifferentiated with respect to marketing programs or, alternatively, whether some or all of them are to be treated as different **market segments**.

Until the 1950s, most marketers of both consumer and industrial products had followed a policy of differentiating *products*, but not of differentiating *markets*. That is, most manufacturers had recognized that a number of sizes, styles, and models of a product would increase total sales beyond that of a single, standard model. However, they had not yet reached the stage of identifying separate segments of the market that could be served better by one configuration of product than another, or of differing prices, kinds and levels of promotion, or distribution, and of acting on that knowledge.

The need to do so was first described in 1956 in a now classic article by Wendell Smith.[15] He referred to the need for differential treatment of portions of the market as **market segmentation**.

We can define market segmentation as follows:

> **Market segmentation** is the strategy of offering a different product configuration, charging a different price, or using a different kind or level of promotion or distribution in one part of the market than in one or more other portions of the market.

FIGURE 2-4
Relationship of number of product markets to risk.

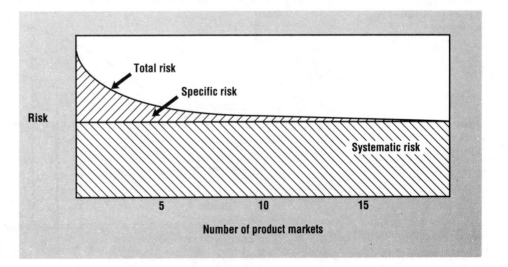

Rationale of Market Segmentation: Whether or not market segmentation is a *possible* strategy in a given situation is dependent on the **response functions** of each potential market segment to each mix variable. For example, Figure 2–5 shows the sales response of each of three hypothetical market segments to differing levels of advertising expenditures. Since the segments have differing optimum levels of advertising (if short-term profit maximization is the objective), segmentation on the basis of advertising expenditures is possible. If the response functions for other marketing mix variables also vary among segments, segmentation on the basis of one or more of the other variables might also be possible.

Whether or not segmentation is a *viable* strategy, however, is dependent on the following conditions:

1. *Identifiability.* The portion of the market with one or more differing response functions that is to form the segment must be identifiable as such.
2. *Economic attractiveness.* A portion of the market may have one or more different response functions, but it is either so small or the cost of treating it as a separate segment is so great as to make it uneconomical to do so.
3. *Accessibility.* The potential segment must be accessible to differential treatment. That is, the marketer must be able to offer different products, charge different prices, or use different kinds or levels of promotion and distribution to a segment for it to be a potentially viable one.

Sears (and its competitors such as Ward's, K-Mart, and Penney's) has recently separated its stores into a series of specialty shops. There are, for example, young women's, matrons', and men's apparel; sporting goods, white goods; furniture; and housewares shops each separately identified

FIGURE 2-5
Hypothetical sales response functions to advertising for three market segments.

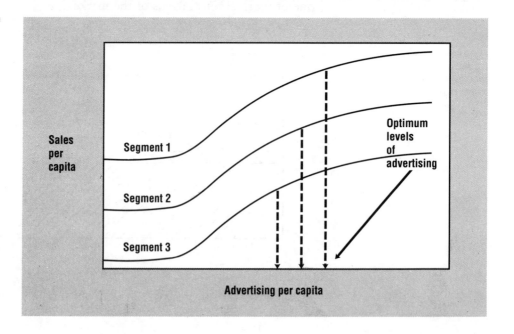

and housed within the same Sears "store." This is a recognition that the different segments of shoppers need a more-specialized shopping environment than the previous configuration of Sears stores had provided, and that it was economically viable to do so.[16]

Bases for Market Segmentation: Any characteristic that results in a differing response function is a potential basis for segmentation. The many possible bases for segmenting markets include (1) geographic location, (2) demographic characteristics, (3) socioeconomic characteristics, (4) psychological characteristics, and (5) product-related characteristics. The marketing research methods for identifying potential segments based on these characteristics range from the use of cross-tabulations to more sophisticated multivariate methods such as cluster analysis.[17]

Some examples of using each of these bases for market segmentation are as follows:

Campbell Soup: "Instead of developing a single set of products and marketing programs to win over American consumers, Campbell . . . is tailoring its products, advertising, promotion, and sales efforts to fit different regions of the country. . . ."[18] (*geographic location*)

Oshkosh B'Gosh: "Sales of Oshkosh's adult clothing line, a familiar sight on farms, railroads, and in factories, have suffered from unemployment in those occupations. As a result the company in the 1970s moved into children's clothing. . . . Its children's wear, which now comes in fashion colors and a variety of styles, now accounts for 80% of the company's sales. . . ."[19] (*demographic characteristics*)

America West: "America West (has) carefully positioned itself as an airline for business travelers—that small percentage of the population that does the lion's share of flying."[20] (*socioeconomic characteristics*)

Designer jeans manufacturers: "Although TV channels are ablaze with such brand names as Jordache, Gloria Vanderbilt, and Calvin Klein, . . . none of them really talk about the product itself, or how it is made, or the material that goes into the product. Rather, each is attempting to mold consumer's perception by associating its products with such issues as life styles and/or sex appeal."[21] (*psychological characteristics*)

Procter & Gamble: "At Procter & Gamble several detergent products coexist, each having a different positioning: Cheer is for washing in all temperatures, Oxydol is to get your whites whiter. Dash is for low-suds concentrated cleaning power, Bold has fabric softener."[22] (*product-related characteristics*)

Product Differentiation and Positioning: If market segmentation is the *strategy* of treating different segments of the market differently, product differentiation and positioning are the methods of *implementing* it. These two concepts overlap in usage to the point that they are sometimes difficult to distinguish. **Product differentiation** has been defined as occurring when

> a product offering is perceived by the consumer to differ from its competition on any physical or nonphysical product characteristic, including price.[23]

Positioning has been defined as

> the act of designing the company's image and value offer so that the segment's customers understand and appreciate what the company stands for in relation to its competitors.[24]

These definitions overlap insofar as each includes the differentiating of nonphysical product characteristics (including price). In addition, there is the suggestion that positioning may also include differentiating physical product characteristics ("designing the . . . value offer").

It may help to separate the two conceptually to think of product differentiation as being mainly concerned with changing *physical* attributes of the product, and positioning chiefly concerned with changing the consumer's conception of the product on one or more *psychological* dimensions.

Product positioning is illustrated in Figure 2–6. Perceptual maps of this kind can be generated by a statistical technique known as **multidimensional scaling**.[25]

Either physical changes in products or changes in the consumers' perception of the product, or both, can be used for target-market segments. Virginia Slims cigarettes is an example of both being used on a product targeted at women. The product and its package were changed from the traditional forms to have a more feminine appearance, and both the media and the advertising copy used were planned to reach and to appeal to women rather than to men. Coors beer is an example of another product in which women were added as a new target segment through an advertising campaign designed for them.[26]

Product Market Strategy Six: Portfolio Management

To assist management in adding or deleting products and markets and allocating resources among the current product markets, many companies have turned to the use of one or more portfolio models. A **portfolio model** is

> a means of classifying product markets on two or more dimensions such as market share, market growth, company's competitive capabilities, industry attractiveness, and stage in the product life cycle.

There are several standardized portfolio models that use differing dimensions and means of classification. They include the models of the Boston Consulting Group (BCG), Shell International, General Electric, McKinsey, and A. D. Little. In addition, many companies have developed models of their own.[27]

Although the models each result in a two-dimensional matrix, they vary considerably in the number of factors that go into the dimensions. For example, the General Electric model at one time used 40 factors (which have since been

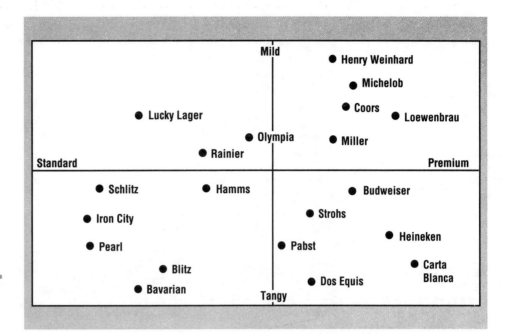

FIGURE 2-6
Positioning map for two characteristics of 20 brands of beer.

reduced to 15), whereas the BCG model uses only 2. Both for reasons of its popularity and for simplicity, we confine our discussion here to the BCG model.

The BCG model is a **market growth, market share matrix** in which the entrants are classified on the basis of the *real growth rate of the market* they are in and the *relative market share* they have attained. (Relative market share is defined as the share of the company divided by that of its largest competitor.) The two-by-two matrix that results from "high" and "low" categories on both the growth rate and market share dimensions is shown graphically in Figure 2–7.

The quadrants of the matrix have differing strategic implications as far as marketing and investment are concerned. Product market entries that fall in the upper-left quadrant—the "stars" quadrant—are the high-growth, high-share entries that are the leaders of the industry. They are in the growth stage of the product life cycle, and the company has been successful in building a large market share for them. A common strategy employed with them is to attempt to maintain or to increase this share, even at the expense of forgoing present profits that could be generated by increasing prices, lowering quality, or decreasing promotional expenditures. Substantial investments may even be required to support such a strategy. If it is successful, however, the returns at the time the product matures will more than offset the deferred profits and current investments.

The entries in the lower-left quadrant—the "cash cows"—are those that are in the mature stage of the life cycle and for which a high relative market share is enjoyed. They are products for which the usual strategy is to "harvest" or to cash in the market share prior to the beginning of the decline stage. Such a strategy results in large positive cash flows, which can be used to invest in the "star" or the "question mark" entries as needed.

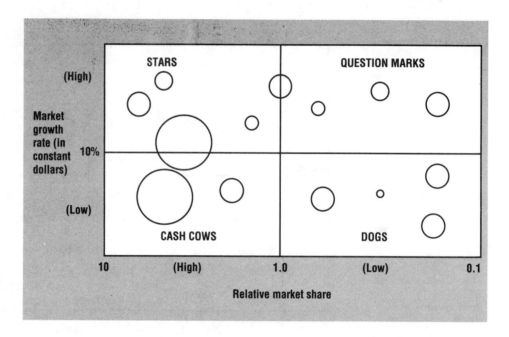

FIGURE 2-7
Market growth, relative market share matrix.

Those in the upper-right quadrant—the "question marks"—are the subject of the most difficult strategic decisions. They are in high-growth markets, but to date have not fared well in terms of relative market share. To try and build market share is always risky and, based on past results for these products, almost always costly. To remain and to lose, or even to maintain, share may not be profitable. The strategic decision makers in these cases are involved in high-risk and potentially costly choices.

The final quadrant, the lower-right corner of Figure 2–7, contains the candidates for liquidation. They are products in the mature or declining stage of the life cycle for which the company has not been successful in building or maintaining relative market share. They are generally low-return products with bleak prospects. Unless there are other reasons for retaining them, an early internment is an appropriate strategy for many of them.

The product market portfolio can be used for examining the entries of competitors and judging what their strategic moves are likely to be. In Figure 2–8, for example, the positions are shown of the entries of General Motors and American Motors in the domestic market in the mid-1980s. From this diagram, the relatively weak position of American Motors in all but the van and four-wheel-drive markets (and its much stronger position in those two markets) suggests that AMC may move to concentrate in that area.

The product market portfolio has also been used as a basis for selecting managers.[28] Cautious, conservative managers may be appropriate for low-share, low-growth businesses, but they are hardly the proper choice for low-share, high-growth businesses.

There are at least three problems with using portfolio models. First, they are designed primarily for developing strategies for dealing with existing product markets rather than reaching an optimum portfolio.[29] Second, the classifications of product markets are very sensitive to how the dimensions are defined. (One can define *market growth* in unit or dollar terms, for example, and if growth in dollars is used, it can be measured in deflated dollars, current dollars, or deflated dollars forecast for the short or long term.) Wind and Mahajan used 4 of the standardized models for a comparison of 15 business units using differing definitions of dimensions and found that the cell in which a product market was classified was often dependent on the definitions of the dimensions used.[30] And third, the classifications of product markets are sensitive to some extent on the standardized model that is used.[31]

Given these problems, Wind and Mahajan have concluded that

... the risk is high when employing a single portfolio model as a basis of portfolio analysis and strategy. It further suggests the need to test the sensitivity of the portfolio classification of businesses to various definitions, cut-off rules, weights, and models. Carefully examine the pattern of classification of businesses into the various categories and consider the use of multiple models, rather than on a single portfolio model.[32]

Strategic Considerations in the Choice of Product Markets

In the early 1980s Boeing Aircraft, which had built about 60 percent of the roughly 7,000 jet airliners then in service, was being forced to take an increasing number of trade-ins of used jetliners in order to sell its new models. To Boeing management this was an undesirable development— the management looked on the aircraft business of Boeing as consisting solely of the manufacturing and marketing of new airplanes, not the acquisition and sale of used ones. If it were necessary to take trade-ins to close new orders, Boeing would do so, but only as a service to its prospective new-plane customers. Whenever possible, Boeing acted only as a broker, finding a buyer for the used airplane(s) and bringing buyer and seller together.[33]

FIGURE 2-8
Market growth, relative market share matrix for General Motors (GM) and the American Motors Corporation (A) in subcompact (SC), compact (C), intermediate (I), full-size (F), luxury (L), and vans and four-wheel drive Vehicles (V-FW) markets, mid 1980s.

Source: Wards Automotive Yearbook, Wards Communications, Inc., 1985.

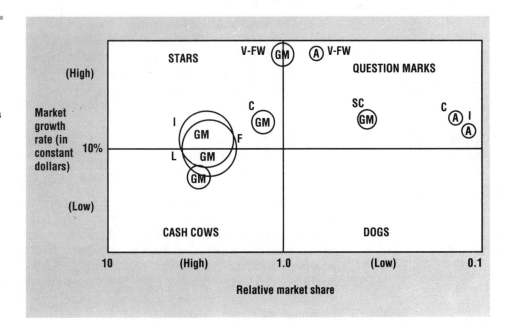

Suppose Boeing management had raised the question (which it in fact later did) of whether the company should stop viewing the used commercial aircraft business as only a necessary means to the end of selling new aircraft and begin aggressively to acquire and to sell used commercial airplanes as a major business in its own right? What strategic considerations might Boeing management have weighed in reaching a decision on entering the used-aircraft product market on this basis?

There are a number of strategic considerations that might have been involved in the decision by Boeing or, more generally, that might be involved in the decision by any company concerning whether or not to enter a particular product market. They include the following:

Market-Related Strategies

1. Offset seasonal or cyclical sales lulls
2. Round out a product line
3. Realize marketing efficiencies
4. Combat competitive entry
5. Exploration
6. Defend market-share position
7. Increase market share

Engineering or Production-Related Strategies

8. Utilize technical capability
9. Use production expertise and/or excess capacity
10. Use by-products of existing products

Risk-Related Strategies

11. Diversification to reduce risk

Management Preference

12. Owner/manager preference

Financial Strategies

13. Tax and other financing considerations
14. Size and potential profitability

Market-Related Strategies

1. *Offset seasonal or cyclical sales lulls.* The turn-of-the-century coal and ice dealer is a classic example of a company whose product lines were chosen, at least in part, because the sales patterns compensated each other. In this case, the sales patterns of the two products were determined by the season, but compensating patterns can result from economic fluctuations as well. As an example, in periods of high housing prices, the number of new housing units sold falls, and so the sales of new-home builders tend to decline. The amount of remodeling of existing homes has a tendency to increase during such periods, however, as some homeowners who can't afford to buy a newer or larger house remodel their current one. The new-home builder who also does remodeling therefore can take advantage of the compensating changes in these two markets.

2. *Round out a product line.* A complete product line always contains two types of products: (a) the full range of models and sizes of the basic product that are likely to be demanded by customers and (b) products that are complementary to it. For some types of primary products, another type of product is also needed to complete the line; these are called adjunct products.

Complementary products are those products that tend to be used together, such as computer hardware and software, cameras and film, or bacon and eggs. Where such complementarity exists, wholesalers and retailers typically carry (but manufacturers do not necessarily manufacture) the associated lines.

Adjunct products include used units of the primary product, spare parts, and repair (and other) services for it. The requirement for Boeing to enter the used-aircraft market to support sales of its new models is an example, and it is a reason for product market selection that is well known to automobile dealers, industrial equipment suppliers, and to most computer and major appliance retailers.

3. *Realize marketing efficiencies.* Companies sometimes enter a product market because they believe they have a differential advantage arising from their marketing capabilities. For example, the movement in the late 1970s and early 1980s by many financial brokerage firms into adding banking services, and the reciprocal movement of banks into supplying brokerage services, were both prompted by ready marketing access to a client base that was financially oriented.

When the Boeing management seriously began to examine the possibility of entering the used commercial aircraft market as a separate business (as well as an adjunct to the sale of new airplanes), it did not escape their attention that the company would have a marketing advantage in that product market. Its sales staff already routinely called on most of the potential buyers for such aircraft in an attempt to sell them new airplanes. If the sale of a new jetliner did not work out, the sale of a used one might.

4. *Combat competitive entry.* Preemption (taking something in order to prevent someone else from getting it) is the central element in this strategy. It is a common practice to preempt brand names, for example, by registering names that are not used. The registration of these names is solely to prevent competitors from using them. Some companies practice preemptive patenting as well by building a "fence" of patents of similar products around their basic product to prevent competitors from entering that market. Oil-exploration firms routinely extend their leaseholds beyond the boundaries of the areas in which they are interested in drilling because they don't want competitors bidding up lease prices if the exploration is successful.

Aerospace companies often bid on governmental research contracts on new technical developments or systems, not because they themselves want the contract, but because they don't want a competitor to get it and develop a capability or a new system that may benefit them in bids for later contracts. Although it is not commonly publicized, industrial companies no doubt introduce products or enter markets on occasion also to preempt competitors from doing so. During the 1960s, when IBM had an approximate 80 percent share of the computer market, its competitors believed that it stockpiled new computer designs. It did not want to compete with itself by introducing new computers, and thus making the ones it was already leasing obsolete, but neither did it want to lose to competitors its technical superiority of the computers it had on the market. Stockpiling advanced computer designs, and introducing a new computer only when there was reason to believe that a competitor might be about to introduce a new design of its own, was a strategy that served both objectives.

5. *Exploration.* Entering a product market on an exploratory basis is an informal means of test marketing that is not uncommon. If it is not costly to "try out" a product market, this can be a sound strategy.

Corning Glass has used this approach successfully for putting a number of products on the market. It has formed a department that does exploratory marketing of products that do not appear to have the potential to warrant the full, formal product development and evaluation process. It has had some notable successes: Heat-resistant glass for doors for fireplaces and wood-burning stoves is an example.

6. *Defend market-share position.* When a competitor brings out a new product that has added or different features and is successful, the usual reaction is for other companies in the industry to develop and introduce a "me too" version of it. The spate of minivans that followed the introduction of the first one by Chrysler in the mid 1980s is an example.

7. *Increase market share.* Within reasonable limits and other factors being equal, the more products one has, the greater the market share for the product line is going to be. This is the primary reason for "line extensions" in packaged goods in which multiple brands of essentially the same product are offered. Proctor & Gamble has followed this practice by having several brands of shortening and detergents, for example. Although introducing line extension products may be successful in increasing market share, it is clear that the number must be held to reasonable levels or the costs will exceed the returns from the added share.

Engineering or Production-Related Strategies

8. *Utilize technical capability.* Many decisions on entry into product markets are based on a technical capability that the makers believe gives their company a differential advantage. By definition the entry of companies into "high-tech" businesses requires a substantial technical capability and often is the result of a technical breakthrough. Apple's entry into the personal computer field was based largely on its early lead in the development of microcomputers, for example.

9. *Use production expertise or excess capacity.* The Ford Motor Company entered (but later abandoned) the aircraft field in the 1920s in part because of Henry Ford's conviction that if the company's production expertise and the excess plant capacity it then had were applied to airplanes, costs would be lowered significantly.

Excess plant capacity is the usual reason for companies to produce "house" brands for large retailers. The washer-dryers made by Whirlpool and the television sets made by RCA for Sears to be sold under the Sears name are cases in point.

10. *Use by-products of existing products.* It is sometimes profitable for a company to utilize the by-products that result from the production of a primary product to produce and sell other products. For example, USX (formerly United States Steel Corporation) has a sizable chemical business in products that it extracts from the gases produced by the coking of coal.

Risk-Related Strategies

11. *Diversification to reduce risk.* This was discussed earlier as one of the product market strategies.

Management Preference

12. *Owner/manager preference.* Just as personal preference is an important consideration in our choice of occupation, it often is an important factor in the decision by the management of companies concerning which product markets to enter. In a study of entrepreneurs, N. R. Smith showed that some, whom he calls "craftsman" entrepreneurs, seem never to want their firm to expand beyond the point that they can directly manage day-to-day operations, whereas others, the "opportunistic" entrepreneurs, want the firm to grow by moving into new markets and products so that they can assume a general-manager role.[34]

In a general sense, when the top management defines the business(es) the company is to be in, it is expressing management preferences, at least in part. When the Boeing management initially viewed the company as being in the *new*, and not the *used*, aircraft business, there must have been some element of personal preference, as well as economic considerations, involved.

Financial Strategies

13. *Taxes and other financing considerations.* In some cases, companies acquire others for financial reasons that have little or nothing to do with the product markets of the company taken over. As a result of the complexities of tax laws, for example, tax savings from acquiring companies with substantial tax credits can be the determining reason for an acquisition that adds a sizable number of new product markets to the portfolio of the acquirer. Similarly, a "leveraged buyout" is an opportunity for the buyers to acquire a company profitably with little of their own capital, and the product markets entered as a result may be largely incidental to the transaction.

14. *Size and potential profitability.* The **potential profitability** of a product market is a kind of encompassing criterion for the selection of product markets since, with the exception of owner/manager preference, all of the criteria for selecting product markets considered thus far also affect potential profitability. The **size** of a prospective product market obviously has a close relationship to its potential profitability too.

The size and potential profitability are such important considerations in the choice of product markets that we devote an entire chapter (Chapter 8) to how they can be determined.

Marketing Program Strategies

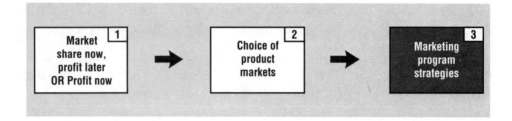

After market choices have been made, strategic decisions have to be made concerning the marketing programs that are to be used to serve them. That is, strategic decisions have to be made concerning the **products** to be offered (quality level, variety), **price** (level, whether to lead or follow), **communication** (level, target audiences, degree of comparison), and **distribution** (level, degree of directness, degree of integration).

The strategic decisions for each of the mix variables are discussed in the chapters on product management, pricing, communication, and distribution. However, there are some generalizations that are beginning to emerge about overall marketing program strategies that can be reported here. These generalizations are from the Profit Impact of Market Strategies (PIMS) project conducted by the Strategic Planning Institute.

The PIMS Project

One of the advantages of multi-product-line companies is the opportunity to apply the operating lessons learned in one product area to other product areas. In 1960, General Electric set up an internal project to study the factors that accounted for variations in operating performance. After extensive research and testing, a computer-based model was developed in which return on investment (ROI) in GE business units was related to a number of factors in each unit. This model "explained" a large proportion of the variation in ROI among the business units.

This method distilled the operating experience of GE business units so that the major strategic factors accounting for good (and poor) operating performance across its business units could be identified. It was recognized, however, that the findings would necessarily be affected by the organizational and management styles used by GE; better information would be obtained if the operating experiences of other companies were also incorporated. This was done in 1972 when the PIMS program was initiated. "Since that time, more than 450 companies have contributed information to [PIMS] documenting the strategies and financial results of nearly 3,000 strategic business units (SBUs) for periods that range from 2 to 12 years."[35] Later a nonprofit corporation, the Strategic Planning Institute, was set up by the member companies to manage the project.

The findings from the PIMS project with respect to marketing strategies are as follows:

1. *In general, the strategies of market development and product development are superior to that of diversification.* A company that concentrates on a set of products and markets that are sufficiently related to permit selling to the same customers or sharing the same marketing programs can expect better performance (higher ROI) at the business unit level.

   The evidence is that this is especially true for consumer goods companies; the relationship is not as strong for industrial goods companies.

2. *Businesses tend to be most successful in using a premium price strategy when the product line is distinctive and expenditures on advertising and promotion are heavy.* Highly advertised products probably carry a distinctive brand image which successfully supports a premium price. Discount prices may cause customers to suspect the quality claims in the advertising and that customers unfamiliar with a new and unique product may tend to link premium prices with premium quality.

3. *Product quality is an important determinant of business profitability; high quality and high return on investment usually go together.* The evidence is that quality is positively and significantly related to ROI for almost all kinds of products and market situation.

4. *Providing "value"—a low relative price for a product of comparable quality—generally results in higher returns on investment. The most profitable "value" offering is a premium-quality product at a relatively lower price.* For lower-quality products, the higher profits that result from lower prices are the result of increases in market share. For higher-quality products, the producer generally realizes higher ROIs because "(1) the market values quality so highly that it is willing to pay more for it than the incremental cost of producing quality, and (2) the market is so happy about not having to pay a premium price for 'value' that it is willing to reward the seller by granting a disproportionately increased share of the market."[36]

The pooling of experience represented in the PIMS database and the analysis to determine relationships between strategies and outcomes is an obviously useful approach to evaluating marketing strategies. Since the project is still relatively new and more companies and the operating experiences of a larger number of business units over a longer period of time are being analyzed, we can expect a more substantial set of findings for marketing program strategies to emerge over time.

Some inherent problems with the PIMS approach exist, however. First, the findings are *associative* but not necessarily *causal* in nature. Higher ROIs in business units are *associated* with higher-quality products, and this suggests they *may* also be *caused* by the quality increment. It does not *prove* that this is the cause, however. It may be, for example, that more competent managements are the causes of higher ROIs, and that they also tend to prefer higher-quality products. Judgment rather than statistical linkage must then be used to conclude that higher-quality products result in higher ROIs.

Second, the findings are inextricably tied to the sample of business units represented in the database. This is a nonrandom sample of larger companies—primarily manufacturing companies from the Fortune 500 list—so the generality of the findings is limited to the population of business units from which the sample came. Other factors being equal, larger companies are better managed than smaller companies. The findings may not apply to smaller companies, for this or other reasons.

Finally, the data are self-reported. Perceptual biases concerning the relative quality of the reporting company's products versus those of competitors and other items reported are possible.

SUMMARY OF IMPORTANT POINTS

1. *Marketing strategy* is the fundamental means planned for achieving the company's objectives by developing a sustainable competitive advantage through the markets entered and the marketing programs used to serve them.
2. Three major sets of strategic marketing decisions have to be made:
   a. choosing between a *market share now, profit later* and a *profit now* strategy
   b. *selecting markets* to enter
   c. *developing marketing program strategies* to serve them.
3. The decision either to build market share or to maximize present-period profits dominates both the choice of product markets to enter and the marketing programs used to serve them.
4. The key considerations leading to adopting a market-share strategy are as follows:
   a. The company should be in an industry in which sustainable competitive advantages can be developed and in which higher market share can be expected to lead to higher long-term profits.
   b. The product(s) should be in an early stage of the product life cycle.
   c. The potential market should be large enough and sufficiently price-elastic (relative to product quality) to permit sizable economies of scale in manufacturing or marketing to result in substantial potential profits.
   d. The product(s) should be of good quality relative to those of competitors.
   e. After considering the relative qualities of the products, the company should have either an actual or a potential cost advantage relative to competitors.
   f. The company must be willing to devote substantial resources to both product and manufacturing R&D and to plant and equipment improvement and expansion.
   g. The company must have, or be willing to acquire, a marketing capability that is at least the equal of its nearest competitor.
   h. The number of competitors, their capabilities, and their strategies should be such as to provide for a reasonable chance of success for a market-share strategy.
   i. The company needs to be well financed.
   j. The management must be willing to undergo a higher level of risk.

5. The Boston Consulting Group has developed a *matrix of competitive environments* that classifies industries by the number of ways that sustainable competitive advantages can be attained, and the potential size of the advantage gained.

6. There are four groups of industries that result from the competitive environment matrix: (a) specialization, (b) volume, (c) stalemate, and (d) fragmented.

7. Only products in *specialization* and *volume* industries are generally viable candidates for a market share now, profit later strategy.

8. An *experience curve* is a cost curve such that each time the accumulated output of a product doubles, the total cost per unit goes down by a fixed percentage.

9. By convention, the experience curve applicable to a product is identified by the complement of the percentage of the cost reduction that results from a doubling of cumulative output. (Example: If the fixed per-unit cost reduction is 15 percent each time the accumulated output doubles, the experience curve is known as an 85 percent curve.)

10. A *market* is a geographic area or a group of actual or potential users of a product or product class.

11. Because the term *market* is necessarily tied to the product offered in it, the terms *product market* and *market* are interchangeable.

12. The strategies that can be used for choosing product markets are market penetration, product development or product differentiation, market development, diversification, and market segmentation. These strategic alternatives are shown in the figure below.

	Existing products	**New products**
Existing markets	(1) Market penetration	(2) Product development or product differentiation
	Creating subproduct markets (5) Market segmentation	
New markets	(3) Market development	(4) Diversification

13. A *market-penetration strategy* is one in which an attempt is made to increase the market share for existing products in existing markets.

14. There are four ways of increasing market share using a market-penetration strategy:
   a. Attract competitors' customers.
   b. Convert nonusers into users.
   c. Increase the frequency of purchase.
   d. Increase the average amount per purchase.

15. A *product-development or product differentiation strategy* is one in which an attempt is made to increase market share through developing and marketing new products.

16. A *market-development strategy* is one in which new markets are sought for existing products.

17. There are three kinds of new products:
   a. innovative
   b. emulative
   c. adaptive.

18. *Product differentiation* has been defined as occurring when a product offering is perceived by the consumer to differ from its competition on any physical or nonphysical product characteristic, including price.

19. *Positioning* has been defined as the act of designing the company's image and value offer so that the segment's customers understand and appreciate what the company stands for in relation to its competitors.

20. A *diversification strategy* is one in which new products are offered in new markets.

21. A diversified portfolio of products usually has less risk than a single holding.

22. The risk that is potentially reduced by diversification is known as *specific risk*. The risk that cannot be eliminated by diversification is called *systematic risk*.

23. A *portfolio model* is a means of classifying product markets on two or more dimensions such as market share, market growth, company's competitive capabilities, industry attractiveness, and stage in the product life cycle.

24. There are at least three problems with using portfolio models:
   a. They are designed primarily for developing strategies for dealing with the company's current product markets rather than selecting an optimum portfolio.
   b. The classifications of product markets are very sensitive to how the dimensions are defined.
   c. The classification of product markets is sensitive to some extent to the standardized portfolio model that is used.

25. *Market segmentation* is the offering of a different product configuration, charging a different price, or using a different kind or level of promotion or distribution in one part of the market than in one or more other portions of the market.

26. Market segmentation is a *possible* strategy when there is a different response function for one or more of the mix variables in one part of the market than for the other parts.

27. Market segmentation is a *viable* strategy when the segment(s) with the differing response function(s) is
   a. identifiable
   b. economical, attractive
   c. accessible.

28. Any characteristic that results in a differing response function is a potential basis for segmentation. The many possible bases for segmenting markets include

a. geographic location

b. demographic characteristics

c. socioeconomic characteristics

d. psychological characteristics

e. product-related characteristics.

29. The decisions of companies concerning whether or not to enter a particular product market turn on one or more of the following strategic considerations:

   a. Market-related strategies

      (i) offset seasonal or cyclical sales lulls

      (ii) round out a product line

      (iii) realize marketing efficiencies

      (iv) combat competitive entry

      (v) exploration

      (vi) defend market-share position

      (vii) increase market share

   b. Engineering or production-related strategies

     (viii) utilize technical capability

      (ix) use production expertise or excess capacity

      (x) use by-products of existing products

   c. Risk-related strategies

      (xi) diversification to reduce risk

   d. Management preference

      (xii) owner/manager preference

   e. Financial strategies

     (xiii) tax and other financing considerations

     (xiv) size and potential profitability

30. The reported findings on marketing strategies from more than 200 companies operating in excess of 2,000 business units (the reported data comprise the *Profit Impact of Marketing Strategy* [PIMS] database) include the following:

   a. In general, the strategies of market development and product development are superior to that of diversification.

   b. Businesses tend to be most successful in using a premium-price strategy when the product line is distinctive and expenditures on advertising and promotion are heavy.

   c. Product quality is an important determinant of business profitability; high quality and high return on investment usually go together.

   d. Providing "value"—a low relative price for a product of comparable quality—generally results in higher returns on investment. The most profitable "value" offering is a premium-quality product at a relatively lower price.

31. Three cautionary considerations need to be kept in mind regarding the PIMS findings:

   a. The findings are associative but not necessarily causal in nature.

   b. The data are from a nonrandom sample of larger companies. The findings may not apply to smaller companies, for this or other reasons.

   c. Perceptual biases may exist in the data since they are self-reported.

REVIEW QUESTIONS

2.1. What is a *marketing strategy*?

2.2. What are the three major sets of strategic marketing decisions that have to be made?

2.3. What are the key considerations leading to adopting a market-share strategy?

2.4. a. Which types of industries have products that are generally viable candidates for a market share now, profit later strategy?
     b. Which types of industries have products that are generally *not* viable candidates for a market share now, profit later strategy?

2.5. What is an *experience curve*?

2.6. Why are the terms *product market* and *market* interchangeable?

2.7. What are the strategies that can be used for choosing product markets?

2.8. What are the possible ways of increasing market share using a market-penetration strategy?

2.9. a. What is the type of risk that can be reduced by diversification?
     b. What is the type of risk that cannot be reduced by diversification?

2.10. What is a *portfolio model*?

2.11. What are the potential problems with using portfolio models?

2.12. What is *market segmentation*?

2.13. a. When is marketing segmentation a *possible* strategy?
      b. When is it a *viable* strategy?

2.14. What are the bases that can be used for market segmentation?

2.15. On what considerations do the decisions of companies concerning entering a particular product market turn?

2.16. What are the findings with respect to marketing strategies from the PIMS database?

2.17. What cautionary considerations need to be kept in mind with respect to the PIMS findings?

DISCUSSION QUESTIONS AND PROBLEMS

2.18. List 10 competitive advantages that a company might have. Assign each a rank in terms of how sustainable you believe it is compared to the others. (Let "1" be most sustainable, "10" least sustainable.)

2.19. Do you believe that a company that updates plans each year for the next 10 years is more likely to be strategically oriented than one that plans only for the coming year? Why or why not?

2.20. One of the problems in strategic management is how to motivate middle-level executives to work toward the company's long-term well-being at the expense of short-term goals. In particular, it is difficult to determine how much to reward managers now for performance on programs whose outcomes may not be known for several years. What steps might be taken to solve this problem? Explain.

2.21. Macmillan Publishing Company is a major publisher and marketer of college textbooks. Should it be using a market share now, profit later strategy in pricing, promoting, and distributing its books to colleges and universities? Why or why not?

2.22. The Honda Spree has the highest market share (approximately 25 percent) of the motor scooters now on the market in the United States. Should Honda be using a market share now, profit later strategy in pricing, promoting, and distributing the Spree? Why or why not?

2.23. According to findings from the PIMS database, the strategies of market development and product development are superior to that of diversification. Why do you think that is the case?

2.24. Recently the makers of Dr Pepper, a soft drink, decided to drop their market development strategy and pursue a market-penetration strategy instead. Traditionally the strongest market area for Dr Pepper has always been in the South.
   a. What are the principal ways in which this new strategy could have been implemented?
   b. What price changes, if any, might have resulted?
   c. What changes in marketing communication themes might have resulted from this change in strategy?
   d. What changes in marketing promotions might have resulted?
   e. What problems might this change have caused in the distribution channel (franchised bottlers) for the product?

2.25. For a number of years, the Mars Company used an advertising campaign for its Snickers candy bar that showed it being used by blue-collar workers as an on-the-job between-meals snack.
   a. Is this an example of the use of a market-segmentation strategy? Why or why not?
   b. Is this an example of the use of a product-differentiation strategy? Why or why not?
   c. Is this an example of the use of a market-penetration strategy? Why or why not?
   d. Is this an example of positioning?

2.26. In the mid 1980s the Colgate-Palmolive Company entered the detergent market with Surf, a product that contains deodorizing chemicals and is advertised as being effective in removing odors from clothes. In the first two years after it was introduced, it gained an 8 percent share of the detergent market, second only to Procter & Gamble's Tide (with 17 percent).
   a. Is this an example of the use of a market-segmentation strategy? Why or why not?
   b. Is this an example of the use of a product-differentiation strategy? Why or why not?
   c. Is this an example of the use of a market-penetration strategy? Why or why not?

2.27. Choose a recent example (from *The Wall Street Journal, Advertising Age, Business Week*, or some other source) of a company that entered a new product market. Decide which of the strategic considerations listed in the text (p. 48) might apply in this case.

2.28. The management of American General, an insurance company, stated in a recent company annual report that it intended to increase the company's sales (and profits) through five separate means: market growth, market penetration, new products, new markets, and mergers and acquisitions.
   How do these means compare with the strategies shown in Figure 2–4 (p. 41)?

2.29. A General Motors executive has stated that the company is targeting 19 different segments for its automobiles. He did not indicate what those segments are. What is your best guess as to what they are? Why?

2.30. As stated in the text (p. 43), America West Airline adopted a strategy of positioning itself as an airline for business travelers. What steps could the company have taken toward accomplishing that result?
   Solving problems 2.31 and 2.32 may require that you consult Appendix A.

2.31. Suppose that Company A and Company B each started manufacturing video tape recorders at the same time. Further suppose that the total cost to each company for the first unit produced was $25,000 and that each was operating with an 80 percent experience curve.

a. Prepare a graph of the 80 percent curve using log-log graph paper. Plot the experience curve line by using the first unit cost of $25,000 and a fourth unit cost of $16,000 (cost of unit 2 = $25,000 × 0.8 = $20,000; cost of unit 4 = $20,000 × 0.8 = $16,000) and drawing a straight line through the two points.

b. Suppose that by the end of the first year Company A had produced 100,000 recorders and Company B had produced 50,000. What would have been the per-unit cost advantage (in terms of dollars, not percent) of Company A over Company B at the end of the year?

c. Suppose A and B are both pricing with a 50 percent mark-up on cost (i.e., if cost is $1.00, price is $1.50). How much of a price advantage would A have?

d. Calculate the percent unit cost advantage A has over B using the formula $[(P_B - P_A)/P_B] \times 100$.

e. Suppose that instead of operating on 80 percent experience curves, both companies were on 70 percent curves. What would A's percent unit cost advantage be?

2.32. Suppose that Company A is in the hand-held calculator business and has just produced its one hundred thousandth unit. Assume further that the cost of the first unit it produced was $1,000, and it has been operating on a 70 percent experience curve.

Assume that Company B has just entered the field and produced its first calculator at a cost of $750. Assume further that it will be operating on an 80 percent experience curve.

a. Using 3 × 5 cycle log-log graph paper, prepare a graph of the experience curves for the two companies. Plot both curves on the same graph. Denominate the unit cost axis cycles as $10, $100, and $1,000 and the cumulative quantity axis cycles as 10, 100, 1,000, 10,000, and 100,000. (Plot the experience curve line for Company A by using the first unit cost of $1,000 and a fourth unit cost of [cost of unit 2 = $1,000 × 0.7 = $700; cost of unit 4 = $700 × 0.7 = $490] and drawing a straight line through the two points. Use a similar procedure for plotting the line for Company B.)

b. At what number of units produced, and at what unit cost, will B's cost per unit be equal to A's?

c. At what number of units produced will A have a $50 per-unit cost advantage over B?

2.33. Prepare a market growth, market-share matrix for the portfolio of products held by a company of your choice.

2.34. What other product markets, if any, might be useful additions to the portfolio of the company in question 2.33 for purposes of

a. risk reduction?

b. increasing net present value of cash flow?

Endnotes

[1] R. D. Buzzell and F. D. Wiersema, "Successful Share Building Strategies," *Harvard Business Review*, January–February 1981, 135–145.

[2] V. J. Cook, Jr., "The Net Present Value of Market Share," *Journal of Marketing*, Summer 1985, 49–63.

[3] "Texas Instruments Shows U.S. Business How to Survive in the 1980's," *Business Week*, September 18, 1978, 67.

[4] R. K. Lochridge, "Strategy in the Eighties," The Boston Consulting Group Annual Perspective, 1981.

[5] C. Y. Woo and A. C. Cooper, "The Surprising Case for Low Market Share," *Harvard Business Review*, November–December 1982, 106–113; C. Y. Woo, "Market Share Leadership—Not Always So Good," *Harvard Business Review*, January–February 1984, 50–54.

[6] Buzzell and Wiersema, "Successful Share Building Strategies," 140.

[7] L. W. Phillips, D. R. Chang, and R. D. Buzzell, "Product Quality, Cost Position, and Business Performance: A Test of Some Key Hypotheses," *Journal of Marketing*, Spring 1983, 26–43.

[8] M. E. Porter, *Competitive Advantage: Creating and Sustaining Competitive Advantage*, Free Press, 1985, Chap. 3, 12–14.

[9] This figure was provided privately by one of the firms in the industry.

[10] The formula for calculating unit cost at a specified level of cumulative output, given the first unit cost and the level of the experience curve, is given in Appendix A.

[11] *Business Week*, September 18, 1978, 89.

[12] Buzzell and Wiersema, "Successful Share Building Strategies," 139.

[13] P. N. Bloom and P. Kotler, "Strategies for High Market Share Companies," *Harvard Business Review*, November–December 1975, 67.

[14] R. Brealey and S. Meyers, *Principles of Corporate Finance*, 2nd ed., McGraw-Hill, 1984, 125.

[15] W. R. Smith, "Product Differentiation and Market Segmentation as Alternative Marketing Strategies," *Journal of Marketing*, July 1956, 3–8.

[16] "Can Sears Get Sexier But Keep the Common Touch?" *Business Week*, July 6, 1987, 93–95.

[17] For a discussion of segmenting methods, see P. E. Green, D. S. Tull, and G. S. Albaum, *Research for Marketing Decisions*, 5th ed., Prentice-Hall, 1987, Chap. 17.

[18] "Marketing's New Look," *Business Week*, January 26, 1987, 1.

[19] "Oshkosh Out to Cover Adult Market," *Advertising Age*, April 28, 1986, 69.

[20] "Air West Is One of Deregulation's Big Winners," *Marketing News*, December 4, 1987, 26.

[21] "Positioning Revisited," *Advertising Age*, March 15, 1982, M-43.

[22] "Positioning Reigns for Consumer or Industrial Products," *Marketing News*, May 9, 1986, 44.

[23] P. R. Dickson and J. L. Ginter, "Market Segmentation, Product Differentiation, and Marketing Strategy," *Journal of Marketing*, April 1987, 4.

[24] P. Kotler, *Marketing Management: Analysis, Planning, Implementation and Control*, 6th ed., Prentice-Hall, 1988, 308.

[25] This technique is described in D. S. Tull and D. I. Hawkins, *Marketing Research: Measurement and Method*, 4th ed., Macmillan, 1987, 298–301.

[26] "New Print Ads for Coors Beer Target Women," *The Wall Street Journal*, June 2, 1987, 29.

[27] For a description of standardized portfolio models, see Y. Wind, V. Mahajan, and D. J Swire, "An Empirical Comparison of Standardized Portfolio Models," *Journal of Marketing*, Spring 1983, 89–99. For advice on how to construct portfolio models, see Y. Wind and V. Mahajan, "Designing Product and Business Portfolios," *Harvard Business Review*, January–February 1981, 155–165.

[28] "Mead's Technique to Sort Out the Losers," *Business Week*, March 11, 1972, 124–126.

[29] For a discussion of the product market portfolio and some of its shortcomings, see S. Day, "Diagnosing the Product Portfolio," *Journal of Marketing*, April 1977, 29–38.

[30] Wind and Mahajan, "Designing Product and Business Portfolios," 92–94.

[31] Ibid., 95–98.

[32] Ibid., 98.

[33] Based in part on "Used Market a Fertile Ground for Cultivating New Buyers," *International Herald Tribune*, September 16, 1985, 1–2.

[34] N. R. Smith, *The Entrepreneur and His Firm: The Relationship between Type of Man and Type of Company*, Bureau of Business Research, Michigan State University, 1967, Chap. 4.

[35] R. D. Buzzell and B. T. Gale, *The PIMS Principles: Linking Strategy to Performance*, Free Press, 1987, 1.

[36] M. Chussil and S. Schoeffler, "Pricing High Quality Products," The PIMSLETTER on Business Strategy, No. 5, 1978.

MINICASES

MINICASE **I-1**

Fast Foods versus Supermarkets: What Strategies Should the Supermarkets Use?

About 40 cents of each food dollar spent in the United States is for food eaten outside the home. This represents a doubling of the 20 cents per dollar spent in commercial food-serving establishments 20 years ago. And of the $100 billion or so spent in restaurants each year, more than $20 billion is in fast-food operations.

The growth in eating out is the product of changes in the lifestyles of Americans, and especially of American women. More women are postponing marriage and, when married, are deciding to have fewer children or none at all. More married women are working outside the home. Even with those with children, more than 50 percent have outside jobs. There is less time in the two-job household to prepare meals, and more money to buy them already prepared by stopping by a fast-food restaurant.

What strategies can the food manufacturers and supermarkets use to counteract the effects of the fast-food trend on their sales? Explain.

Kitch'n Cook'd Maui Potato Chips Company*

Dewey Kobayaski is part owner and manager of the Kitch'n Cook'd Maui Potato Chips Company in Hawaii. The chips produced by his company are big, thick, slow-cooked, and hand-packaged, and have a reputation of being the world's best.

His company packages only 1,000 pounds of chips (2,287 seven-ounce bags) each day. With the exception of 144 packages he sends to a friend who runs a grocery store in Honolulu, the chips are sold only on Maui. The seven-ounce bags sell for as much as $2 per package. The day's production is sold out within an hour after delivery to the hotels, stores, and gift shops that handle them.

He does not want his company to get any larger because, he says:

It would increase overhead, increase problems. I could triple production and still not fill the demand on Maui.

I could open franchises on the mainland, become one of the major potato chip producers, but I really like it the way it is. My dad and I come here every day and work 12 hours. We both believe in doing an honest day's work to keep our minds functioning.

If we got into mass production, our chips would not be as good as they are today. I would lose my reputation. I have pride in what I am doing. I wouldn't want to sacrifice that just to become a millionaire.

1. What are Dewey Kobayaski's objectives?
2. Would you have the same objectives if you were he? Why or why not?

---

*This case is taken from a story filed by Charles Hillinger of the LA Times–Washington Post Service, and reported in *The Oregonian*, April 24, 1977, p. F2.

Speedi-Lube

In the past decade, several hundred drive-in oil and lube service establishments have come into being in the United States and Canada. Some are independently owned, others are parts of franchised chains or chains owned by major companies. All are designed to give a fast 10-minute-or-so oil change and lubrication service for an automobile while the driver remains with the car.

This service was traditionally provided for a customer's car at full-service gasoline stations. Service station owners have become increasingly less interested in doing so, however, as many have converted to "mini-serve" or self-serve operations to decrease labor costs, and others have turned to doing tune-ups and minor repairs that give a higher return for the use of the two or three service bays the typical gasoline station has.

Speedi-Lube is a company with multiple locations in the Seattle area that provides a drive-in oil change and lubrication service. It has an ad budget of approximately $100,000 and uses an umbrella campaign with the slogan "We're good and we're fast."

Should Speedi Lube attempt to segment its market? If so, to what segments and by what means? If not, why not?

PPG Industries

Approximately one-third of the revenues of PPG Industries (formerly the Pittsburgh Plate Glass Company) are derived from the production and sale of glass products. The management of PPG has recognized for some time that the trends in the two largest markets for glass products, the transportation and construction industries, are not favorable. Both the automobile and the housing markets are depressed and, over the long term, both are changing in ways that decrease the requirements for glass.

Since 1973 the reduction in size of automobiles has decreased the use of glass per car by more than 10 percent. There are indications that the drive to increase gasoline mileage may result in even further decreases in the use of glass; glass is heavy and contributes to higher inside temperatures in summer, leading to greater use of automobile air conditioners. In the design of houses, the use of ordinary plate glass, of which PPG is the leading producer, is a major contributor to energy loss.

1. What strategies are available to PPG to counter the adverse trends in the automobile and construction markets?
2. What strategies do you believe PPG should seriously consider adopting?

United States Navy: Pilot Shortage

The U.S. Navy has been plagued with a persistent shortage of airplane pilots. The shortage was up to 2,600 pilots in the mid 1980s. Since it requires about three years to recruit and train a pilot competent to fly today's aircraft in combat, the Navy's air arm was, and would continue to be for some time, at less than combat readiness.

The Secretary of the Navy asked that a plan be prepared and submitted to his office for eliminating the shortage within four years. The officer in charge of preparing the plan started holding exit interviews of flying officers leaving the service to obtain their suggestions. Two suggestions were obtained for correcting the problem: (1) raising flight-duty pay and (2) a new bonus solely for pilots eligible to leave the Navy who reenlisted.

1. What other alternatives might be considered?
2. Prepare a plan to correct the problem within the four years allowed.

The Owens-Illinois Company Social Objectives

The following statement appeared in a recent annual report of the Owens-Illinois Company:

Our credo for corporate social responsibility has long been to operate facilities which are assets to the communities in which they are located, whether in the United States or abroad.

Owens-Illinois is strongly committed to a continuing policy of equal opportunity for employment and advancement. As a result of our Affirmative Action programs, there are more qualified minorities and women in the Company's work force than ever before. Our programs also provide for employment and training of substantial numbers of persons classified as hard-core unemployed.

In the area of environmental concern, Owens-Illinois has an enviable record, particularly in air and water quality control.

In addition to philanthropic contributions to charitable organizations, both nationally and in communities where we have facilities, the Company encourages employees to actively participate in governmental, social, and civic activities.

Once again, in responding to social demands, it is important that we not lose sight of the fact that the corporation was created and exists to produce, at a profit, goods and services which people want and need. While we must be sensitive to social pressures, business alone cannot solve all the complex social problems of the world. Earning a reasonable profit may not be the sole function of a corporation, but for any enterprise not earning an adequate return, all other considerations are academic.

Provide an evaluation of this statement indicating (1) areas of agreement or disagreement and (2) any considerations you feel are not covered.

Industrial Fan and Blower Manufacturer

The management of an industrial fan and blower manufacturer has developed and stated the following policies with regard to the company's marketing program:

In general, our marketing principles or rules can be outlined as follows, but at the same time they must be interpreted in terms of the specific markets:

1. The company should establish prices based on what the market will bear and still purchase the product in sufficient quantities to utilize near-full manufacturing capacity, to obtain maximum profit. Prices should not be based on cost plus a fixed margin.

2. The company should strive for individuality in product design, or innovation, to achieve a position of market leadership.

3. Marketing intelligence is to be aware of market trends and requirements, competitors' activities, and competitors' prices. . .

4. Customers will pay more for products when the value received is actually or apparently recognized as greater, and the company should establish prices accordingly.

5. Marketing which attempts to sell the customer on the company approach rather than attempting to copy competitors' products is most likely to prove more profitable.

1. How does this statement relate to
   a. a "market share now, profit later" strategy?
   b. the PIMS findings on marketing strategies?
2. What potential general marketing strategies are not referred to in the statement? Explain.

THE MARKETING ENVIRONMENT

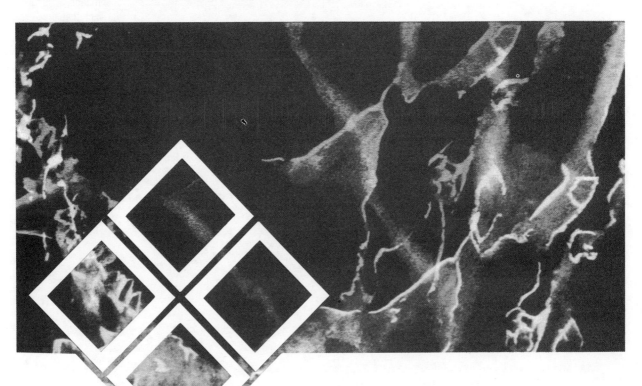

Before marketing strategies can be designed and marketing plans can be formulated intelligently, the strategist and the planner have to understand the overall environment in which the marketing program is to be conducted. Seven specific environments can be identified that shape and affect the marketing program. They are the environments of

- the firm itself
- the industry of which it is a part
- the state of technology that affects its products and services
- the economy
- the consumer market
- the commercial/industrial market
- the ethical codes, political climate, and legal system relating to the economy.

These environments are described in this section. The firm, the industry, technology, and the economy are discussed in Chapter 3. The consumer market environment is considered in Chapter 4, and the organizational (commercial/industrial) market in Chapter 5. The ethical, political, and legal environments are described in Chapter 6.

THE MARKETING ENVIRONMENT: THE FIRM, THE INDUSTRY, THE STATE OF TECHNOLOGY, AND THE ECONOMY

This chapter is a wide-ranging one. In it, we consider four of the marketing environments as they relate to and affect the firm's marketing program: the internal environment of the **firm** (of which the "corporate culture" is an essential part), the nature of the **industry** and its trade practices, the level of **technology** that relates to the company's products and services, and the state of the **economy**. The remaining environments of marketing (the **organizational** [industrial/commercial] market, the **consumer** market, and the **ethical, political, and legal** environments) are described in the subsequent chapters of this section.

It is evident that these environments all continuously interact, so a change in one can have marked effects on the others. As examples of these interactions, consider the case of Xerox Corporation:

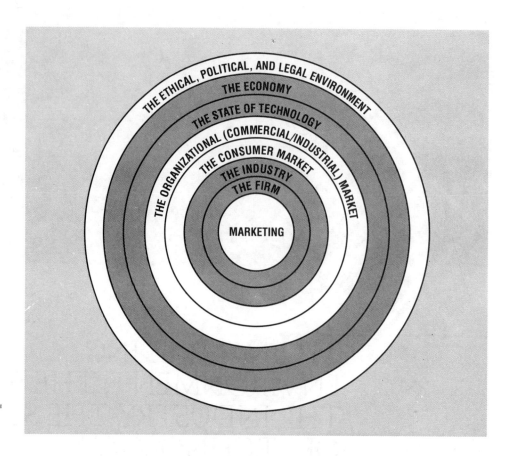

FIGURE 3-1
The environments of marketing.

Xerox was a firm formed to commercialize the technological development (xerographic copying) that made inexpensive reproduction of documents possible.

Almost single-handedly, the Xerox machine began to change the industry of which it was a part (information processing and storage).

The development of word-processing programs and equipment have in turn brought about further sweeping changes in how information is processed and stored. This has affected the use of copiers and so, in turn, has had pronounced effects on Xerox.

Xerography and word processing have had substantial effects on the economy, both in terms of efficiency and as direct contributors to gross national product. In 1987, sales of xerographic copying alone amounted to about $14 billion.

The "corporate culture" as a determinant of the actions, and even the level of success, of the firm has received considerable attention in recent years. We begin with it as the central element of the environment within the firm, and proceed to the external environments of industry, technology, and economy as the chapter progresses.

THE ENVIRONMENT WITHIN THE FIRM: THE CORPORATE CULTURE

Culture has been defined as

> the implicit beliefs, norms, values, and customs that underlie and govern conduct in a society.[1]

If we exchange the word *corporation* for *society*, we have a suitable definition of the term *corporate culture*.

This term has been popularized by a best-selling book in the early 1980s titled *In Search of Excellence*.[2] In an attempt to distill the principles of successful management from the shared experiences of companies, the authors (T. J. Peters and R. H. Waterman, Jr.) interviewed managers at 43 successful American companies. They were struck by the fact that all of these companies have a distinct set of beliefs, norms, values, and customs that are usually implicit—they are often not written down anywhere—but are nonetheless well understood. They report their observations in part as follows:

> Without exception, the dominance and coherence of culture proved to be an essential quality of the excellent companies. Moreover, the stronger the culture and the more it was directed toward the marketplace, the less need was there for policy manuals, organization charts, or detailed procedures and rules. In these companies, people way down the line know what they are supposed to do in most situations because the handful of guiding values is crystal clear.[3]

The companies about which this statement was made were all among the 500 largest in the United States. If a similar study had been done using a sample of smaller companies, the authors would no doubt have found an even greater "dominance and coherence" of company culture. Fewer people, a smaller number of levels, and lesser departmentation all permit more direct transmission and quicker assimilation of cultural norms and values.

The culture of the company permeates all of its operations, including its marketing program. The basic functions of a company that manufactures and markets one or more products are those of **research and development** (R&D), **engineering, manufacturing, finance**, and **marketing**. A well-managed company achieves a balance among these functions such that none dominates the other; rather, all receive and give the kind of support needed to complement the others so that the final results will be a well-coordinated and smoothly functioning whole.

Department managers in R&D, engineering, manufacturing, and finance who are attempting to operate their respective departments as efficiently as possible will inevitably have conflicts with each other and with the marketing manager (who is also trying to run his or her department efficiently). These conflicts arise because of attempts to optimize departmental goals that are sometimes not fully congruent with company goals. For example, R&D has a natural leaning toward the design of technically sophisticated products. Engineering tends to design the appearance of products more from a functional than from an aesthetic viewpoint. Manufacturing prefers a few models with long, stable runs. Finance would like limited inventories and stringent credit terms. Each of these preferences may be at odds with marketing's interest in serving the customer to the best of its ability.[4] The nature of these conflicts is shown in Table 3–1.

The culture of the company usually emphasizes one of these functions more than it does the others. For example, some companies are known as being engineering-oriented, some as being chiefly concerned with manufacturing, others as being preoccupied with "by the numbers" financial considerations, and still others as emphasizing marketing.

It is not unusual for companies to emphasize different functions at different stages of their development. The Pillsbury Company, formed in 1869, is an example. It was first production-oriented. Later Pillsbury centered its efforts on selling, and more recently it became genuinely marketing-oriented.[5]

Companies that are marginal survivors, or that fail, often have not achieved a proper balance among these constituent functions. Consider in this respect a little-known manufacturer of a cosmetic/home remedy:

Since its founding in 1866, the E. E. Dickinson Company of Essex, Connecticut, until recently was identified with a single product—witch hazel. Witch hazel is an astringent (a product that shrinks swollen areas and reduces wrinkles) that the company has claimed variously to be efficacious as a beauty aid, an application for bumps and bruises, an aftershave, a skin freshener, and a shrinking agent for hemorrhoids. It has been advertised modestly since 1979, but was not advertised at all for the 15 years preceding that.

A consumer study in the early 1980s showed favorable responses to new witch hazel product forms including a skin cream, a first-aid remedy, and a towelette with witch hazel in it. The towelette was subsequently introduced.[6]

This is an example of a company that for most of its existence had a high degree of imbalance in the emphasis placed on its basic functions. Although it survived, and even enjoyed a modest degree of prosperity for more than a hundred years, there was no research and development, and marketing seemingly received scant attention over most of its lifetime. When compared with other, more-successful companies in the cosmetics field (say, Gillette or Alberto-Culver) that have continued aggressively to develop and to market new products, the difference in orientation is dramatic.

The best-managed companies avoid this tendency toward imbalance. The emphasis on product quality of Procter & Gamble, Johnson and Johnson, or Hewlett-Packard has resulted in substantial R&D budgets, to be sure, but careful attention and adequate financial support have also been given to the other functional areas of the business. The management of IBM, whose corporate culture centers in marketing, similarly has not permitted that emphasis to act to the detriment of R&D, engineering, manufacturing, or finance. Apple Computer, where management earlier gave preferential attention to engineering, has more recently devoted greater efforts to marketing.[7]

Table 3–1 Conflicting Emphases among the Research and Development, Engineering, Manufacturing, Finance, and Marketing Departments

Department	Its Emphasis	Marketing's Emphasis
Research and development	Basic research Intrinsic quality Technically sophisticated	Applied research Perceived quality Level of technical sophisticated market demands
Engineering	Long design lead time Standard components Functional appearance	Short design lead time Many models Custom components Aesthetic appearance
Manufacturing	Long production lead time Long runs with few models No model changes Standard orders	Short production lead time Short runs with many models Many model changes Custom orders
Finance	Small inventories Tight budgetary controls Pricing to cover costs Stringent credit terms Demanding collection procedures	Large inventories Flexible budgetary controls Pricing to develop market Easy credit terms Easy collection procedures

Source: Adapted from P. Kotler, *Marketing Management: Analysis, Planning, and Control*, Prentice-Hall, 6th ed., 1988, 717.

What can the marketing manager do if the company is unbalanced in terms of an undue emphasis being given to, say, manufacturing or engineering at the expense of marketing? In such cases an internal "marketing of marketing" program is called for. If comparative data on competitor organizational structures, numbers of personnel, and expenditures by function can be obtained, and if they show that competitors' marketing departments receive relatively more support, this can be a useful approach to convincing management to bolster the company's marketing efforts.

THE INDUSTRY ENVIRONMENT

The nature of the industry does much to shape and to mold the marketing efforts in it. Consider the following market characteristics:

Type of business. The type of products (or services) and the markets to which they are sold.

Life cycle stage of the product. Whether the product is in the introductory, growth, maturity, or decline stage.

Number and concentration of customers. Whether the customers for the product(s) or services are fragmented (many small buyers) or concentrated (few large buyers).

Number and size of competitors. Whether the industry tends toward being a competitive market (many small suppliers) or an oligopoly (a few large suppliers).

Each of these industry characteristics can play an important role in determining the marketing programs of the companies in it. For example, two companies in different industries with the characteristics described in Table 3–2 will each tend to have the kinds of marketing programs indicated for them.

The topics of type of business, life cycle stage, and number and concentration of customers are discussed in later chapters.[8] However, the important topic of the competitive environment is not treated elsewhere, and so needs to be dealt with here.

The Competitive Environment

As Porter has stated, "The fundamental basis of above-average performance in the long run is *sustainable competitive advantage*."[9] Although a knowledge of competitor actions may not be an absolute necessity for developing and maintaining a competitive advantage, it is obviously important to learn as much as one can about them and what they are doing—and are planning to do—in planning the course of action of one's own firm.

Competitor
Intelligence

Learning about competitors and their actions requires obtaining competitor intelligence information. **Competitor intelligence** has been defined as

highly specific and timely information about a corporation.[10]

Table 3–2 Industry Characteristics and Their Effects on Marketing Programs

Company ABC	Company XYZ
Industry characteristics The industry markets frequently purchased, nondurable products in the growth stage of the product life cycle to consumers, and has a large number of small firms.	**Industry characteristics** The industry markets infrequently purchased, capital equipment items in the mature stage of the product life cycle to industrial buyers, and has a large number of has a small number of large firms.
Marketing program The company will be concerned with developing adaptations (line extensions) of the basic product, pricing to maintain or increase market share, advertising heavily, selling to wholesalers who in turn sell to retail stores, all the while maintaining an aggressive overall marketing stance.	**Marketing program** The company will be concerned with developing different products that will carry out the same functions more efficiently, pricing to increase profits, primarily relying on sales representatives rather than advertising, and selling directly to end users, being very conscious of competitors and the possibility of retaliation to marketing moves.

The name has been adapted from the term ***military intelligence*** because of the obvious similarities in purposes and uses.

The following is an example of competitor intelligence:

1. You may come across a competitor's help-wanted ad that says the company is hiring a host of programmers to produce a new software product.
2. In addition, through your sales force you discover that this same competitor is opening a sales office in a different region.
3. You have also heard through the grapevine that certain prospective clients whom you have been wooing for months have suddenly been approached by the competitor for possible test marketing of a new product.
4. A credit report states that the same competitor has just submitted new Uniform Commercial Code (UCC) filings for major pieces of equipment. (UCC filings occur when a commercial loan is taken out to purchase equipment.)

You think about this information and draw the following inferences:

1. The competitor is planning to hire or has already hired a considerable number of new programmers for a soon-to-be-released product.
2. The product may be further along than the help-wanted ad suggests, since the company is already opening new sales offices. You decide you should track these new offices to find out where they are located, since they may form a pattern that will tell you in which states or regions the competitor is planning to concentrate sales.
3. The clients the competitor approached may become valuable sources of information about the new product.
4. The UCC filings usually make clear what the equipment was that the competitor purchased. You should find out how the equipment is being used; it very likely could be for the marketing or production of the new product.[11]

Uses of Information on Competitors

Competitor intelligence can be used for answering questions concerning your competitors'

Competitive position. Strengths, weaknesses, positioning of products, vulnerability to strategies we are considering, and our vulnerability to their potential strategies.

Marketing strategy. Goals and objectives, product features, impending product announcements, prices, advertising budgets, trade channels, trade discounts, and sales force deployment.

R&D projects. Types of products being developed and forecast completion dates.

Production capabilities. Plant capacity, production levels, production costs, and sources of supply.

Financial status. Current sales and changes from preceding year's sales, current profits and changes from preceding year's profits, amount of liquid assets, levels of cash flow, loans outstanding, loan repayment schedules, and stock issuance plans.

There are many applications of such information. For example, if the competitor's financial information in the above listing discloses that large firms in the industry are significantly more profitable than small ones, the smaller firms are likely to experience serious profit pressures in the next recession from price reductions by the larger firms. This possibility should be anticipated and countering actions planned for when needed by the smaller firm.[12]

Sources of Competitor Information

How can the information for these purposes be obtained? The following are some of the applicable sources:

Buyers' guides
City directories
Classified ads
Credit services
Current industrial reports
Databases
Dealers
Environmental impact statements
Financial periodicals
Government documents
Industry directories
Investment manuals
Patent disclosures

Sales representatives
SEC filings
Special magazine issues
State corporate filings
State industry directories
Statistical sources
Syndicated data services
Trade associations
Trade press
Trade shows
UCC filings
Visual sightings
Yellow pages

Some companies have formalized the collection of competitor information by appointing a "Director of Competitive Analysis" whose job involves the continuing collection and analysis of data from these and other sources.[13] However, more modest monitoring programs, especially suited for smaller companies or cost-conscious larger ones, can be used successfully.[14]

The Ethics of Acquiring Information on Competitors

Many ethical questions arise as to which sources to employ and how to use them. Although it is clear such practices as computer "crashing" (eavesdropping) and the hiring of industrial spies should not be used—both are not only ethically shabby, but are also illegal—what about the following practices?

- Buying competitors' products and dissecting them
- Taking plant tours anonymously
- Counting tractor trailers leaving competitors' plant loading bays
- Analyzing labor contracts
- Buying competitors' garbage
- Studying aerial photographs
- Asking customers and buyers about the sales of competitors' products

- Asking suppliers about sales to competitors to determine production levels
- Debriefing competitors' former employees
- Sending employees to technical conferences to question competitors' technical people.[15]

Patterns of Doing Business

All industries have accepted patterns and norms by which business is conducted by its members. These are implicit working "rules" that relate to such things as credit terms, services that are provided, return policies on products, "chiseling" on price, gifts and gratuities to buyers, and so forth. These patterns of expected behavior collectively constitute a kind of culture for the industry.

In many industries, the more important of these implied rules get made explicit by the Federal Trade Commission (FTC). This has been done through the preparation of FTC-approved "Commercial Practices." Under Section 5 of the Federal Trade Commission Act, the FTC is empowered to declare illegal all "unfair methods of competition" (see pp. 168–170). What constitutes an "unfair" method of competition is left to the Commission to decide. The Commission does this by convening panels of industry executives and jointly working out with them a set of approved "Commercial Practices" rules. These rules are mainly concerned with marketing practices. (An example of the rule that governs how the size of television receiving set screens may be advertised is given in Exhibit 6–6, p. 169.) These rules, which have the force of law but stem from the industry itself, clearly affect the marketing programs of companies within the industry.

The Technological Environment

Technology affects marketing programs in three important ways. The first and most direct effect is through the *research and development (R&D) that is done on new products*, both by the firm and by its competitors. It is from this source that the patented new products the firm markets, and the new products with which they will compete, originate.

The second effect is the result of the *R&D that is done on improving the designing and manufacturing processes*. It is through this means that better-quality and lower-cost products are produced—a continuing vital requirement for successful marketing programs.

The third way in which technology affects marketing programs is through the *development of new means of performing the marketing functions themselves*. "Telemarketing" replacing sales calls at the customer's office and computerized checkout scanning in supermarkets are two examples.

Each of the ways in which technology affects marketing programs is discussed in more detail below.

Research and Development for New Products

Research to generate potential new products and processes and the development of them to bring them to a usable state is a primary driving force in our economy. A number of studies indicate that between 80 and 90 percent of the long-term per capita economic growth that has occurred over the past century in the United States can be attributed to improved technology resulting from research and development expenditures.[16]

Industrial R&D expenditures in the United States in 1985 were $80 billion.[17] Although there has been concern about reduced R&D expenditures in recent years, *this amounted to more than twice the combined expenditures on R&D of Japan, West Germany, and Great Britain.*

An aspect of industrial R&D that is of special interest to marketers is the way in which its output is adopted.

Patterns of Adoption of R&D Innovations

There are four patterns (or tendencies) of adoption of R&D innovations within an industry that are of significance to marketing. The first is that often the company that becomes the leader in manufacturing and marketing an innovative new product is either a newly formed company or an existing company in a different industry. The following are only a few of the many examples that could be cited:

Studebaker was the only manufacturer of wagons and buggies that entered the automobile business; the early leading automobile companies—including Ford, Chrysler, Dodge, Overland, Chevrolet, and Olds—were companies that were either formed to enter the business or else were involved in other businesses.

The leading manufacturer of diesel-electric locomotives, General Motors, came from the automotive rather than the steam locomotive industry. The company with the largest market share of the steam locomotive industry, Baldwin Locomotive, didn't come on the market with a diesel-electric locomotive until 12 years after General Motors introduced its diesel-electric engine.

The independent inventor of the electric typewriter was unsuccessful in his attempts to sell that development to manual typewriter companies. He later sold it to IBM, which became the leading producer of nonportable electrics. From 1960 to 1980, IBM sold over 9 million electric typewriters. Manual typewriters are no longer produced in the United States.

None of the existing electromechanical calculator manufacturers entered the electronic calculator business (and only one, NCR, became a computer manufacturer). The early leaders in electronic calculators were Texas Instruments and Hewlett-Packard, both associated with the instrument (as well as other) industry.

We should not use hindsight to judge the managements of these companies too harshly. It is very difficult to forecast the future sales of a potential product with even a modest degree of accuracy. This is compounded by the fact that sales of the traditional product often continue to grow for a period of time after the product that will replace it eventually is introduced. For example, sales of steam locomotives continued to increase through the mid 1940s even though the diesel-electric locomotive was introduced in 1931.[18]

A second, and related, pattern is that many companies rely on the technical innovations of others which they buy or license (or they even buy an innovating company itself) rather than develop innovations internally. For example, General Motors got into the diesel-electric locomotive field by acquiring two small firms in that industry. Reynolds Pen, the company that introduced the ballpoint pen, was neither the developer nor even in the writing instrument business until it acquired the rights to and marketed the ballpoint pen. IBM did not initially develop the computer and, in fact, reportedly has made only limited contributions to the advancement of computer technology in the 30 or so years it has been the leading producer of computers.

A third pattern is the frequent use of a hedging strategic response to the new technology. Companies with substantial market shares for the traditional product often divide resources "so as to participate in a major way in both the old and the new technologies."[19] For example, American Locomotive developed both an advanced turbine-powered steam locomotive and a diesel-electric locomotive in the 1930s.[20] CBS and Raytheon, both producers of vacuum tubes, responded to the new semiconductor technology by developing new lines of vacuum tubes while also committing themselves heavily for R&D and production facilities for transistors.[21] For the companies in one study of five different industries, this hedging strategy was "unsuccessful more often than successful."[22]

A fourth pattern appears to be the inability of companies with a low market share in the traditional product to adopt the new technology successfully. This may well be the result of some of the same reasons that caused the low market share in the traditional product—lack of marketing abilities, inadequate financing, or poor overall management, for example.

It is of obvious importance to the long-term economic well-being of the company to be conversant with the technical state of the art of the industry. Marketing can assist in this process by keeping abreast of current developments (through marketing research and technological forecasting—see pages 235–250 and 314–325) and participating in the formulation of the strategic response to each development as it arises.

Research and Development on Designing and Manufacturing Processes

One does not need to be an economist, or a marketing manager, to appreciate the critical role that quality products produced at low cost play in the success of a company. In recent years the computer has played an increasingly important role in achieving high-quality, low-cost production.

CAD (computer-assisted design) and CAM (computer-assisted manufacturing) systems, although developed earlier, began to be adopted on a sizable scale in the United States around 1980. Their use grew so rapidly that by the mid 1980s they accounted for about 20 percent of all U.S. plant and equipment expenditures.[23]

Computerized design and manufacturing do not only improve quality and reduce costs. They are more flexible—can be retooled much faster—and so make it easier, cheaper, and faster to launch new products. This will very likely mean shorter product life cycles and more frequent model updates.

Technological Developments Used in Marketing

In addition to bringing about dramatic alterations in the products marketed, changing technology has resulted in sweeping changes in the marketing process itself. Improved packaging made self-service, and the supermarket, possible. First radio and then television permitted advertising to move out of print and into the electronic media, and automobiles, trains, and airplanes enabled sales representatives to make more frequent calls and deliveries to be made much faster. More recently, the use of **computerized scanning using product codes** in supermarkets and department stores has provided management with more and more timely information on which to base pricing, advertising, and ordering decisions.

We can confidently expect that technologically based changes in the ways in which marketing is conducted will continue to be made. For example, the use of the television set as a communication medium for electronic catalogs, or the home computer used for the same purpose plus transfer of funds for payment (videotex)—while still in their infancy—may well have substantial effects on how consumers buy durable and specialty products and services in the future.

THE ECONOMY

Changing Patterns of Consumer Expenditures, Incomes, and Savings

Effective aggregate demand is the result of expenditures of buyers. For consumers, the relationship between personal consumption expenditures, nonconsumption expenditures, income, and changes in level of personal savings is:

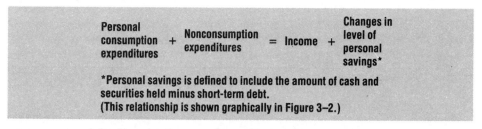

This is a basic equation that states, in effect, that total expenditures can be no more, or less, than the amount available to be spent.

This equation can be rewritten to show personal consumption expenditures directly as

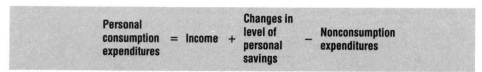

The levels and trends in each of these variables are described below. Personal income is discussed first because it is the major determinant of the others.

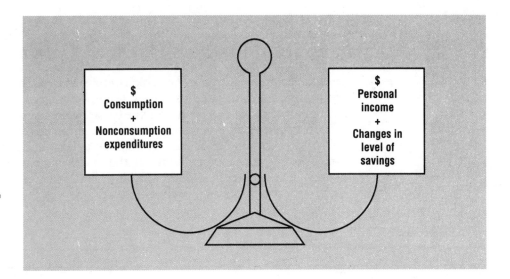

FIGURE 3-2
Relationship of personal consumption and nonconsumption expenditures to personal income and changes in level of net savings.

Level of Personal Income

The predominant trend in personal income since 1970 in the United States has been one of growth. Money income per capita in 1970 was $9,640; in 1986 it was $11,670 (both in 1986 dollars). This is an increase of more than 21 percent for that period. The increase in per capita income after adjustment for inflation means that the average living standard in the United States has increased. One might expect that when living standards rise, shifts in consumer expenditure patterns would occur. Some recognizable shifts have in fact taken place in the United States as a result of the rise in real income.

Patterns of Personal Consumption Expenditures

In 1857, Ernst Engel, after studying the budgets of German blue-collar families, published his "Laws" of consumer expenditures. He found that as incomes increased, expenditures tended to increase as well, but with changes in the relative demand for different classes of products and services. He observed that, as personal income increased, the percentage spent on food declined, the percentage spent on housing remained about constant, and the sum of that spent on other products and services (transportation, clothing, medical care, education, and entertainment) and that saved increased.

Engel did the research for his "Laws" during a period of stable prices. As tendencies, they have generally been descriptive of changes in consumer expenditure patterns in the United States until the 1970s when inflation rates rose substantially. Since 1970, the predictive record of the "Laws" has not been a very good one, however. The percentage spent on food has in fact declined (as Engel would have predicted), but housing expenditures as a percentage have increased (rather than staying constant, per Engel), and the combined percentage amounts of transportation, clothing, medical care, education, and entertainment expenditures have stabilized (rather than increasing, as the "Laws" suggest they should have).[24]

The findings of budget studies are always to be interpreted as averages. There may be substantial variation around the average for any one income class. Marketers are well advised to look carefully at both the expenditure variations *within* income classes and the expenditure variations *between* income classes for the product categories with which they are concerned. For example, transportation expenses as a percentage of total consumption expenditures may stay relatively constant across income classes—at least one budget study shows that they do[25]—but the expenditures at the lower income levels may be predominantly for public transportation and maintenance of older automobiles, whereas that of the higher income levels may be for relatively frequent purchase of new cars.

Nonconsumption Expenditures

Disposable personal income is

personal income minus tax and nondiscretionary transfer payments.

The major items deducted from personal income to reach disposable income are federal, state, and local taxes and social security contributions.

Taxes and social security contributions are obviously nonconsumption expenditures. Lesser nonconsuming expenditures include life insurance and such incidentals as passport fees and fines and penalties.

Changes in Levels of Personal Savings

Personal savings was defined earlier as the amount of cash and securities held minus short-term debt. For example,

If a family has $10,000 in savings but owes $3,000 on an automobile, its personal savings would be $7,000.

Changes in level of personal savings during a given time period (a year, for example) is the difference between the beginning and ending level of savings.

The trend in savings since 1975 has been downward. In that year it was about 8.6 percent of disposable income; in recent years it has fallen to as low as 3.2 percent (1987). Personal savings as a percentage of disposable personal income in the United States is substantially lower than that of many other industrialized countries (including Japan [about 16 percent] and West Germany [about 13 percent]). Since savings are used to finance part of the investment in capital goods, this does not bode well for the ability of the United States to remain fully competitive in world markets.

Expenditure category	Engel's Laws	United States	
	When income rises, the percentage spent on	Until 1970, Engel's Laws were reasonably good predictors of the direction of percentage changes in expenditures by category. As income rose, the percentage spent on	Since 1970, Engel's Laws have not been good predictors of the direction of percentage change in expenditures by category. As income has risen, the percentage spent on
Food	Declines	Declined	Has declined
Housing	Remains constant	Remained constant	Has increased
Sum of clothing, education, entertainment, medical care, and transportation	Increases	Increased	Has increased substantially
Savings	Increases	Increased	Has declined substantially

FIGURE 3-3
The direction of percentage changes in expenditures by category as predicted by Engel's Laws, and actual changes in the United States.

Sources: The National Income and Product Accounts of the United States, 1929–1974, U. S. Bureau of Economic Analysis; *Three Budgets for an Urban Family of Four Persons, 1981*, U. S. Bureau of Labor Statistics; and *Consumer Expenditure Survey: Interview Survey, 1985*, U. S. Bureau of Labor Statistics.

Inflation

The recent history of the changes in the general price level in the United States has been one of persistent inflation. The greatest increase in prices in recent years took place during the mid 1970s. The Consumer Price Index (CPI), compiled by the U.S. Bureau of Labor Statistics, showed an average increase of almost 10 percent per year from 1972 to 1977. Prices continued to rise after 1977, and were at double-digit levels in 1979 to 1981. Since then, the level has dropped, but inflation persists at a rate of 3 to 6 percent.

It seems likely that inflation over the near future will continue. Deficit financing by federal and state governments induces inflation unless savings increase to offset it. Neither the recent history of deficit financing nor that of savings rates suggests that these forces are likely to be brought into balance soon.

Buyers and markets alike have reacted and adjusted to inflation. In this section, we examine changes that consumers and marketing managements have taken to deal with the problem.

Consumer Adaptation

Consumers began to adjust their shopping habits and patterns as inflation rose in the early 1970s. Studies conducted of consumers indicate at that time that they began

doing more comparison shopping

using coupons more heavily

preparing shopping lists more frequently

postponing appliance purchases

repairing the family car rather than buying a new car

choosing automobiles and appliances with fewer "extras" when purchases have to be made

remodeling their present home rather than buying a new one

doing home canning

cooking more from scratch rather than using prepared foods and mixes

stocking up on bargains or advertised specials

buying a reduced variety of food products

making fewer shopping trips[26]

These changes have been characterized as reflecting a "conservation ethic" and a trend toward "voluntary simplicity." Although they may in fact reflect a change in consumer attitudes and values, they appear to have been the result of inflation-induced tighter budgets. One would have to suspect that if real personal incomes were to rise, the economizing shopping behaviors described above—"Keeping down with the Joneses," as one writer has described them—might largely disappear.

Marketing Management Adaptation

Inflation results in increases in both production and marketing costs. These cost increases have resulted in changes in the marketing mix primarily in three areas: pricing, products offered, and promotion.

Price Changes

As costs increase, the maintenance of margins (mark-ups) requires that commensurate increases in prices be made. Most companies have made price increases on their products to pass increased costs along, and consumers, although not always continuing to buy as much at the higher prices, have become resigned to the necessity of companies' raising prices.

Products Offered	***Generic products*** are an adaptation to increased prices brought about by inflation. Generics were begun in France in the early 1970s by the Carrefour chain of hypermarkets as a direct response to the relatively high inflation rates being experienced there. (A ***hypermarket*** is a giant supermarket that carries a much wider range of product lines than supermarkets in the United States.) Generics generally are of a lower quality than branded products and no advertising is done for them. Both of the resulting cost savings can be passed on to the consumer via lower prices. In some lines of food products and drug sundries, generics have captured as much as a 20 percent share of the market.
Sales Promotion	A way of adjusting to resistance on the part of consumers to increased prices is to increase the use of sales promotions. A ***sales promotion*** to consumers

is a short-term price, prize, or product incentive designed to induce purchase.

Coupons, rebates, contests, games, premiums, trading stamps, and free product samples are examples of consumer promotions. During the period of (mostly) double-digit inflation from 1976 through 1980 sales promotion budgets rose substantially. The estimated number of coupons distributed in the United States, for example, increased from about 48 billion in 1976 to 900 billion in 1980 (from an average of about 700 to more than 1,100 per U. S. household).[27] Not only did the number of coupons distributed rise dramatically during that period, but the average value per coupon also increased.

Other types of promotions to consumers (rebates, games, and free samples of products, in particular) also were used to an increasingly greater extent over that same period. The result was that for products such as packaged foods and drug sundries, sales promotions budgets as a percentage of sales increased markedly during that period, and advertising budgets as a percentage of sales actually decreased.

Reactions to rising marketing costs have also brought about some changes in promotion by the firm. Rapid increases in travel costs combined with a concerted advertising campaign by American Telephone and Telegraph, for example, have resulted in telephone sales calls—"telemarketing"—being used increasingly at the expense of personal sales calls.

One other apparent adjustment to inflation should not pass unnoticed. According to the Secret Service, counterfeiters have reduced their output of 10 and 20 dollar bills. They have begun printing 50 and 100 dollar bills instead.

Prosperity and Recession

Although a free-enterprise economy has much to recommend it over a command economy, it has the disadvantage of being subject to larger fluctuations in level. The so-called business cycle is a characteristic of economic life in the

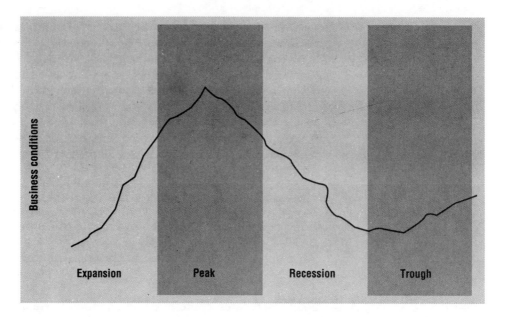

FIGURE 3-4
The four phases of the business cycle.

western industrialized countries that plagues all companies, and all the functional areas of each of them.

Not only does the overall level of free-enterprise economies fluctuates, but the level of local and regional economies within them can vary substantially as well. The year 1986 was a prosperous one overall in the United States, and yet one study indicated that the economies of 31 of the 50 states were in a recession.[28]

A major problem in dealing with business cycles is the difficulty of predicting them accurately. In this respect, the use of the term *cycle* to describe them is somewhat misleading, as it has the connotation of regular, predictable, periodic, metronome-like movements. This is anything but the case. As Samuelson states,

> No exact formula, such as might apply to the motions of the moon or of a simple pendulum, can be used to predict the timing of future (or past) business cycles. Rather, in their rough appearance and irregularities, business cycles more closely resemble the fluctuations of disease epidemics, the weather, or a sick child's temperature.[29]

Still, as for the spread of an epidemic, the weather, or a sick child's temperature, attempts to forecast must be made. The critical element to forecast is the **turning points** represented by the peak and the trough in Figure 3–4. If the peak of a cycle can be forecast accurately, for example, production schedules can be trimmed, inventories can be reduced, financial arrangements can be made, and counter-recession marketing plans can be laid. Similar accommodations can be made as a result of an accurate prediction of the turning point at the trough, although the actions taken obviously will differ.

The cost of not predicting a turning point accurately or, alternatively, of predicting one that doesn't occur, can be high. The example of a forecasting error made by the chairman of the board of Montgomery Ward more than 35 years ago whose effects are still being felt by the company today is instructive in this respect:

Just after the end of World War II, Sewell Avery, chairman of the board of Montgomery Ward, was being urged by his senior management to begin a major expansion of Ward's retail department stores. It was known that Sears-Roebuck was then launching an expansion program that would modernize, upgrade, and substantially increase the number of its retail stores. Avery remembered the short but sharp recession that had occurred after World War I, however, and was confident that there would be another one following World War II. He decided to wait and not to begin acquiring sites and adding stores until after the downturn, when land and building costs would be lower.

He was still waiting for the recession when he retired 10 years later. In the interim, Sears had gained a lead in both the number and quality of retail outlets that it still has not relinquished.

Forecasting turning points is discussed in Chapter 9.

High versus Low Interest Rates

The level of interest rates, and especially that of "real" interest rates (the difference between the rate of interest paid and the rate of inflation) affects marketing in a number of ways. The effects of *high* interest rates include the following:

1. *Delay in purchase of items that traditionally are paid for in installments or with borrowed funds.* In the consumer goods field, purchases of such items as houses, automobiles, and appliances are delayed. Investment in plant and equipment in the industrial goods field slows.
   Secondary effects: The remodeling, used, and repair markets prosper.
2. *Increasing saving.* Both the inducement of higher interest payments to save and the cost of paying higher interest rates to buy results in more saving.
   Secondary effects: The supply of funds available for lending increases relative to demand; interest rates fall.
3. *The seller assumes a greater share of the financing of purchases.* "Creative" financing takes place in which the seller finances at least a part of the purchase price.
   Secondary effects: The net prices realized from the sale falls, profits fall, the seller experiences cash flow problems.
4. *Delay in accounts receivable payment.* Buyers attempt to get free financing by delaying payment. Average time to payment (which is near 30 days in periods of low interest rates) climbs to 50–60 days when rates are high.
   Secondary effects: Collection efforts on the part of the seller increase tensions between the sales representative and the buyer; some accounts are lost or dropped.

5. *Attempts are made to reduce inventories by both seller and trade channel members.*
   Secondary effects: Deliveries are slowed, tensions increase between sellers and channel members, marginal brands are discontinued by wholesalers and retailers, retailers become less willing to stock new products even of well-known brands. The selection of models and sizes available at retailers becomes less.
6. *Costs increase.* Production costs rise because of lack of investment in new plant and equipment, higher financing costs.
   Secondary effects: Prices are raised to reflect the cost increases.
7. *Promotional efforts increase in an attempt to offset the effects of higher prices.* Advertising, rebates, coupons, and other sales promotion methods are used to a greater extent.
   Secondary effect: Marketing costs rise.

Rising interest rates call for an increasing degree of cooperation between the marketing and the finance departments of the firm. Both should set aside the desire to further their own immediate interests and work out changes in credit terms, collection policies, buyer financing arrangements, and other matters that affect both areas in a manner that is best for the company.

Changes in such important economic variables as personal income, savings rates, the level of inflation, and interest rates translate almost immediately into effects on company sales and output; manufacturing, marketing, and financing costs; and cash flows and profits. Companies whose sales are especially income-, inflation-rate-, or interest-rate-sensitive need good forecasts of these variables in order to take advantage of favorable upcoming economic developments, and to prepare adequately for the unfavorable ones.

SUMMARY OF IMPORTANT POINTS

1. *Corporate culture* can be defined as the implicit beliefs, norms, values, and customs that underlie and govern conduct in a corporation.
2. The culture of a company usually tends to emphasize one of the following functions: research and development, engineering, manufacturing, finance, and marketing. The well-managed company is one in which the functions that are not emphasized in the culture nonetheless receive adequate attention and support.
3. The industry characteristics of type of business, life cycle stage of the product(s) sold, number and concentration of customers, and number and size of competitors are important determinants of the marketing programs of the companies in the industry.
4. All industries have accepted patterns and norms of doing business that constitute an industry "culture." The more important of these patterns and norms for many industries are codified by the Federal Trade Commission into Trade Practice Rules. These Rules are mainly concerned with marketing practices and have the force of law.

5. *Competitor intelligence* has been defined as highly specific and timely information about a corporation.

6. Some of the applicable sources for competitive intelligence gathering purposes are

Buyers' guides	Sales representatives
City directories	SEC filings
Classified ads	Special magazine issues
Credit services	State corporate filings
Current industrial reports	State industry directories
Databases	Statistical sources
Dealers	Syndicated data services
Environmental impact statements	Trade associations
Financial periodicals	Trade press
Government documents	Trade shows
Industry directories	UCC filings
Investment manuals	Visual sightings
Patent disclosures	Yellow pages

7. Technology affects marketing programs in two ways: (a) by periodically altering the nature of the products(s) sold by the company or its competitors; (b) by altering the way in which marketing itself is conducted.

8. Researchers at the Strategic Planning Institute have found that, for the companies providing data to the PIMS database, $1 of R&D expenditure over the preceding eight years contributed an average profit of $3 in 1978. The average internal rate of return for R&D expenditures was 33 percent.

9. There are four common patterns of companies with respect to adoptions of R&D innovations. They are:

a. Often the company that becomes the leader in manufacturing and marketing an innovative new product is either a newly formed company or an existing company in a different industry.

b. Many companies rely on the technical innovations of others, which they acquire (or acquire the rights to use) rather than innovate themselves.

c. A hedging strategic response—committing substantial resources to develop the new technology while committing resources to improve the traditional product(s)—is frequently used by companies. Limited evidence suggests that such a strategy is unsuccessful more often than not.

d. Companies with a low market share in the traditional product usually do not adopt the new technology successfully.

10. A recent technological advance that has affected the way retail marketing is conducted is the adoption of the product code and the reading of it with electronic scanners.

11. The amount of personal consumption expenditures is determined as:

Personal consumption expenditures	=	Income	+	Changes in level of personal saving	−	Nonconsumption expenditures

12. The rate of growth in personal income, after adjustment for inflation, has slowed markedly in recent years.
13. Engel's "Law" is that as personal income increases, the percentage spent on food declines, the percentage spent on housing remains about constant, and the sum of that spent on other products and services and that saved increases.
14. Engel did his research during a period of stable prices. In periods of inflation, it appears that as income increases, the percentage spent on food does in fact decline, but the percentage spent on housing *increases*, and the sum of the percentages spent on other products and services and saved declines.
15. The major nonconsumption expenditures in the United States are social security contributions and taxes.
16. Personal savings as a percentage of income in the United States has declined over the past decade. Since savings are used to finance part of the investment in capital goods, this reduction means there has been a shift in relative demand from industrial to consumer goods.
17. Consumers tend to adapt to inflation by postponing purchases, shopping more carefully, repairing or remodeling the old rather than buying new products, and tending to "do it themselves" rather than paying to have it done for them.
18. Marketing management tends to adapt to inflation by raising prices; marketing generic products; increasing the use of sales promotions and other promotions such as rebates, games, and the distribution of free samples; and increasing the use of "telemarketing."
19. The effects of high interest rates include
    a. delay in purchase of items that traditionally are paid for in installments or with borrowed funds
    b. increased saving
    c. increased use of seller financing
    d. delays in receipt of accounts receivable
    e. reduced inventories
    f. increased production and financing costs
    g. increased promotional efforts

REVIEW QUESTIONS

3.1. How would you define the term *corporate culture*?

3.2. What are the differences in emphasis in product design between the
    a. Marketing and Research & Development departments?
    b. Marketing and Engineering departments?

3.3. What are differences in emphasis in the manufacturing of products between the Marketing and Manufacturing departments?

3.4. What are the differences in emphasis in financial arrangements between the Marketing and Finance departments?

3.5. What are the major market characteristics for an industry that shape the marketing programs of the firms that comprise that industry?

3.6. In what ways does technology affect marketing programs?

3.7. What proportion of the long-term economic growth in the United States can be attributed to improved technology?

3.8. What would you say is the average rate of return from R&D expenditures for companies that contribute to the PIMS databank?

3.9. What patterns that are of significance to marketing can be discerned with respect to adoption of research and development innovations?

3.10. What is the formula that relates personal consumption, expenditures, nonconsumption expenditures, income, and changes in level of savings?

3.11. What are Engel's "Laws" of consumer expenditures?

3.12. a. How have consumer expenditures in the United States differed from Engel's "Laws" in recent years?
b. What caused these differences?

3.13. What portion of the typical family budget is made up of taxes and social security contributions?

3.14. What adjustments in their developing habits and patterns have consumers made to adapt to inflation?

3.15. What adjustments have marketing managers made in their marketing programs to adapt to inflation?

3.16. What are the effects on marketing of high interest rates?

DISCUSSION QUESTIONS AND PROBLEMS

3.17. When one goes to a foreign country for the first time, one normally experiences what is known as "culture shock." What would you say are
a. Its symptoms?
b. Its causes?

3.18. Do you believe most students experience a form of culture shock when they first enter a college or university?
   a. If your answer is "yes,"
      (i) What are its symptoms?
      (ii) What are its causes?
   b. If your answer is "no," why don't they experience it?

3.19. Do you believe most college graduates experience culture shock when they first begin work after graduation? Why or why not?

3.20. Casual observation suggests that executives who have been highly successful in a company over a number of years often are not nearly as successful for the first few months when they move to a different company. Assuming (for the moment) that this is generally the case, how might it be explained?

3.21. It has been suggested that firms located in smaller cities (e.g., Amana, Iowa [Amana] or Midland, Michigan [Dow Chemical] often have stronger corporate cultures than firms located in New York or Los Angeles. Do you believe that is likely to be the case? Why or why not?

3.22. It has been observed by a partner in an executive search firm that consumer packaged-goods companies typically have one of three "marketing cultures": marketing preculture, analysis-driven, or advertising-driven. What would you expect to be the differences among these culture types?

3.23. What differences would you expect to exist between the marketing programs for the:
   a. General Electric Company strategic business unit (SBU) that manufactures and sells jet engines for aircraft and the SBU that manufactures and sells light bulbs?
   b. IBM SBU that manufactures and sells mainframe computers and the SBU that manufactures and sells personal computers?
   c. Omark Industries SBU that sells chain-saw chain to manufacturers of chain saws and the SBU that sells the same chain-saw chain to the replacement market?

3.24. In your opinion, which of the following practices, if any, are unethical as a means of competitor intelligence?
   a. Buying competitors' products and dissecting them
   b. Taking plant tours anonymously
   c. Counting tractor trailers leaving competitors' plant loading bays
   d. Analyzing labor contracts
   e. Buying competitors' garbage
   f. Studying aerial photographs
   g. Asking customers and buyers about the sale of competitors' products
   h. Asking suppliers about sales to competitors to determine production levels

    i.   Debriefing competitors' former employees

    j.   Sending employees to technical conferences to question competitors' technical people

3.25.   Assume that research and development expenditures for the years 1980 through 1986 and that the profits for the year 1987 for the products in which they resulted are as shown below:

R&D expenditures ($000)		Profits for products resulting from R&D ($000)	
1980	$ 100	1987	$10,000
1981	200		
1982	400		
1984	800		
1985	1,600		
1986	3,200		

What is the internal rate of return for R&D?

3.26.   The fact that companies that are leaders in marketing traditional products either don't adopt innovative new technology or else adopt it late is attributed in the text to the difficulty of forecasting. Are there other reasons that might explain this phenomenon?

3.27.   In Japan, a part of the Universal Product Code (UPC) is reserved for the price* of the product. That is not the case for the UPC in the United States.

    a.   What are the advantages of the Japanese practice relative to that in the United States?

    b.   What are the disadvantages of the Japanese practice relative to that in the United States?

    c.   Which do you believe is better?

3.28.   Suppose your company forecaster predicts rising rates of inflation during each of the next four years. How would you expect this to affect sales if your company manufactures and markets:

    a.   Murphy beds (beds that fold into a closet when not in use)?

    b.   New automobiles?

    c.   Replacement parts for automobiles?

    d.   Home canning equipment?

    e.   Home electric appliances?

    f.   Camping equipment?

    g.   Downhill skis?

    h.   Cross-country skis?

*"Price" here means the price at which the product is sold to the first buyer in the trade channel.

3.29. Suppose your company manufactures and sells dentifrices, shaving creams, and shampoos. Suppose further that the person responsible for forecasting for your company predicts a sharp increase in inflation over the next 12 months.
   a. What changes in the marketing programs of your company's competitors might you expect?
   b. What changes in your own company's marketing program might you consider?

Endnotes

[1] As given in H. Assael, *Consumer Behavior and Marketing Action*, 3rd ed., Kent, 1987, 668.

[2] T. J. Peters and R. H. Waterman, Jr., *In Search of Excellence: Lessons from America's Best-Run Companies*, Harper & Row, 1982.

[3] Ibid., 75–76.

[4] See R. W. Reukert and O. C. Walker, Jr., "Marketing's Interaction with Other Functional Units: A Conceptual Framework and Empirical Evidence," *Journal of Marketing*, January 1987, 1–19, for a discussion of the nature of interfunctional interactions within the firm.

[5] As described in R. J. Keith, "The Marketing Revolution," *Journal of Marketing*, January 1960.

[6] "One-Product Dickinson Sees Change Ahead," *Advertising Age*, May 31, 1982, 4.

[7] "Apple Computer: The Worm Turns," *The Economist*, April 5, 1986, 76–78.

[8] See relevant sections of Chapter 4, "Consumer Buying Behavior," Chapter 9, "Financial Evaluation of Product Markets," Chapter 10, "Marketing Planning and Forecasting," Chapter 11, "Product Management," Chapter 12, "Brand Management, Product Line Management, and the Product Life Cycle," and Chapter 16, "Personal Selling and Sales Management" for detailed discussions of these topics.

[9] M. E. Porter, *Competitive Advantage: Creating and Sustaining Superior Performance*, Free Press, 1985, 10.

[10] L. M. Fuld, *Competitor Intelligence*, John Wiley & Sons, 1985, 9.

[11] Ibid., 11.

[12] See M. E. Porter and V. E. Millar, "How Information Gives You Competitive Advantage," *Harvard Business Review*, July–August 1985, 149–160; J. J. Brock, "Competitor Analysis: Some Practical Approaches," *Industrial Marketing Management*, October 1984, 225–231; S. Ghosbal and S. K. Kim, "Building Effective Intelligence Systems for Competitive Advantage," *Sloan Management Review*, Fall 1986, 49–58; and T. Gilad and B. Gilad, "Business Intelligence—The Quiet Revolution," *Sloan Management Review*, Summer 1986, 53–61, for an elaboration of uses.

[13] R. MacAvoy, "Corporate Strategy and the Power of Competitor Analysis," *Management Review*, July 1983, 9.

[14] R. Hershey, "Commercial Intelligence on a Shoestring," *Harvard Business Review*, September–October 1980, 22–30.

[15] S. Flax, "How to Snoop on Your Competitors," *Fortune*, May 14, 1984, 29–33.

[16] See, for example, M. Abramovitz, "Resource and Output Trends in the U.S. Since 1870," *American Economic Review, Papers and Proceedings*, Vol. 46, 1956, 5–23; and R. Solon, "Technical Change and the Aggregate Production Function," *Review of Economics and Statistics*, Vol. 39, 1957, 312–320.

[17] *Statistical Abstract of the United States, 1988*, Bureau of the Census, Table 954, 560.

[18] A. Cooper, E. Demuzzio, K. Halten, E. Hicks, and D. Tock, "Strategic Responses to Technical Threat," Krannert Graduate School of Industrial Administration, Purdue University, Paper no. 431, November 1973, 7.

[19] Ibid., 11.

[20] Ibid.

[21] Ibid.

[22] Ibid. The industries and the new technological innovations were (1) the steam locomotive industry and the diesel-electric locomotive, (2) the vacuum tube industry and the transistor, (3) the fountain pen industry and the ballpoint pen, (4) the producers of boilers for fossil fuel plants and nuclear power plants, and (5) the safety razor and the electric razor.

[23] "The Retooling of America," *The Economist*, August 23, 1986, 24–25.

[24] As reported in, U.S. Bureau of Economic Analysis, *The National Income and Product Accounts of the United States, 1929–1974*; U.S. Bureau of Labor Statistics, *Three Budgets for an Urban Family of Four Persons, 1981*; and U.S. Bureau of Labor Statistics, *Consumer Expenditure Survey: Interview Survey, 1985*. The data given in this report do not take into account the appreciation of housing unit prices. For those persons who owned their own homes in 1970, there may well have been a *negative* cost of housing during the next decade when one takes into account the substantial rise in its value.

[25] Ibid.

[26] As described in Z. E. Shipchandler, "Inflation and Life-styles: The Marketing Impact," *Business Horizons*, February 1976, 134–138; "Inflation Affects Couples' Behavior in Marketplace," *Marketing News*, May 19, 1978, 2; "Inflation Changes Supermart Buying Habits," *Marketing News*, August 10, 1979, 1.

[27] *Advertising Age*, December 15, 1980, 41.

[28] "Economic Conditions in States Vary Dramatically as a Study Shows 31 Are Experiencing Recession," *The Wall Street Journal*, August 26, 1986, 50.

[29] P. A. Samuelson, *Economics*, 11th ed., McGraw-Hill, 1980, 237.

CONSUMER
BUYING BEHAVIOR

Ultimately, marketing efforts converge on consumers and attempt to gain their interest and purchases. Even industrial marketing most often leads, with a few additional levels of transactions, to the consumer because industrial demand is derived from consumer demand. Industrial products that fail to contribute to eventual consumer satisfaction have a future as precarious as consumer products that do not meet consumer needs and desires. Consumers who attain satisfaction often repeat their purchases and help a company gain a long-term successful franchise with the buying public, but frustrated or angry consumers can undermine marketplace progress for a firm that is the focus of their agitation through hostile word-of-mouth campaigns and by purchasing substitute products from competitors.

Marketing managers therefore need to understand how and why consumers purchase a product and how they assess products already owned. The better a company understands its consumers, the more likely it is to succeed in the marketplace. John Smale, chairman and CEO of Procter & Gamble, believes, "Our business is based on understanding the consumer and providing the kind of products that the consumer wants. We place enormous emphasis on our product development area and our marketing area, and on our people knowing the consumer."[1]

A knowledge of consumer behavior is useful for helping both to set and to implement marketing strategies. For setting strategies, it helps in:

- selecting and segmenting markets.
- planning marketing strategies.
- evaluating strategies.
- assessing consumer trends that will affect strategies in the future.

For implementing strategies, an understanding of consumer behavior is necessary to assist in:

- understanding fully the sources of any market-response problems.
- gauging response to prospective product, price, promotion, and distribution changes.
- planning the marketing program.
- evaluating the marketing program.

We begin this chapter with the presentation and discussion of a simplified model of consumer buying behavior. We then discuss the major elements of the model in sections on the social, situational, and informational influences that affect buying behavior. (The applications of consumer behavior to the managing of the product, price, promotion, and distribution elements of the marketing program are discussed in the chapters dealing with those topics.)

The influences on consumers are varied and complex. Three major sources of influence are (1) social, (2) situational, and (3) informational. **Social influences** have to do with the people associated with a consumer. In what country and region does the consumer live? Who are his or her friends and family? How have these influences shaped the consumer into a unique human being? Social influences determine what wants and needs will guide the consumer when making purchases. **Situational influences** have to do with the context in which a product will be used. Different contexts demand different approaches to product use. Where will the product or service be used? How? **Informational influences** have to do with the facts and beliefs a person has about a product or service. Does such a product even exist? Why would someone want to have it? What brands have what attributes? We consider each of these types of influences separately, starting with social influences.

Although every consumer decision may not involve every single type of influence, the shrewd marketing manager will at least contemplate how each type of influence may relate to decisions about his or her products because of improved understanding and because each of these variables, alone or in combination, has potential as a criterion for market segmentation. Figure 4–1 describes how each of these factors relates to consumer buying behavior. A person who has experienced particular social influences develops particular needs and desires. These needs and desires depend on the situation in which the person finds himself or herself. Needs and desires motivate a person to seek, to attend to, and to process information about products and purchases. Once information has been gathered, a purchase decision is made. Although we do not consider consumer decision making in this book, it is quite similar to manager decision making, as described in the next chapter. Finally, once a product has been purchased and used, that experience will influence subsequent purchase decisions because the use information will be processed before the next buying decision is made.

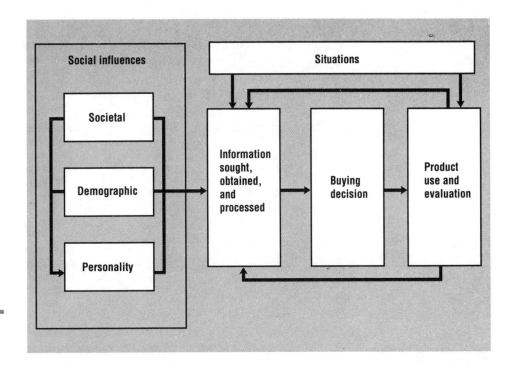

FIGURE 4-1
A simplified model of consumer
buying behavior.

SOCIAL INFLUENCES ON CONSUMERS

Hundreds of social influences impinge on consumers at any given moment, and only certain combinations will allow a company to gain purchase behavior. Some causes are more distant and may influence decisions only in extreme cases. Influences from geography, government, history, and culture can be dramatic and intense, but often they are in the background and overlooked. For example, the nuclear power disaster at Chernobyl in the USSR unquestionably altered the shopping behavior of local consumers, yet few consumers there would have considered the lack of a nuclear power accident as a major influence on their purchase behavior the day before the tragedy. Similarly, a far greater percentage of people in the United States than in Norway own microwave ovens, in spite of similar levels of development and income in the two countries. Yet few Americans would state that a major cause of their purchase of a microwave oven had to do with not being Norwegian.

Figure 4–2 describes the major social influences on consumers: societal, demographic, and personality. Each in turn has a number of subcategories, several of which are listed. Influences are listed from more abstract to more specific. We consider each influence as it relates to consumer behavior in the following section.

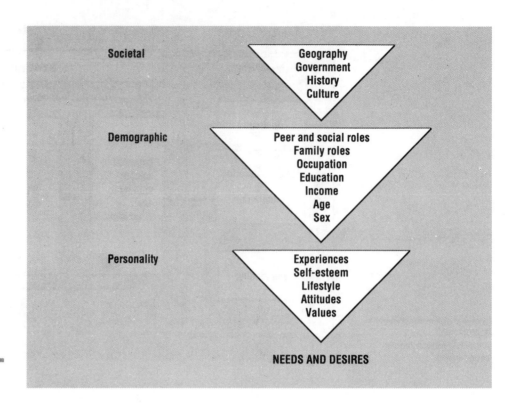

Societal Influences on Consumer Behavior

As shown in Figure 4–2, societal influences include the dimensions of **geography**, **government**, **history**, and **culture**.

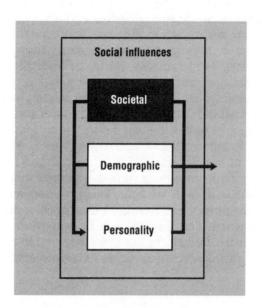

Geography: Different places have different resources, climates, values, and traditions.[2] These factors and others help determine what products people find attractive at different points in time. Just consider the differences between the marketing opportunities during Mardi Gras in New Orleans versus during ski season in Aspen versus during the Macy's Thanksgiving Day parade in New York City. Or consider the January clothing market in Honolulu versus that in Oslo, Norway. The customs, climates, and values of the regions influence what will be purchased and by whom.

Few tasks of marketing are carried out as effectively when geographic areas are ignored as when they are carefully considered. Companies that sell coffee soon discover that people in the West like their coffee somewhat stronger than in other regions of the United States. People in the South tend to like a hint of chicory. Hot coffee has more appeal in Minneapolis during January than in Miami during July. And in Utah, religious beliefs influence coffee consumption. If you have traveled through Europe, you know that tastes in coffee vary from country to country, with some countries selling coffee that many Americans find extremely strong and others selling brews hard to distinguish from what is served back home in the United States.

The Campbell's Soup Company recently changed its marketing policies to emphasize greater responsiveness to regionalism.[3] For example, Campbell's nacho cheese soup now is spicier in Texas and California, where spiciness is prized, than in other regions of the country. In New York City, local radio ads tied Swanson frozen dinners to the New York Giants football team, which is distinctly more popular in New York City than in, say, Denver.

Computer technology and universal product codes have recently enabled companies to use geographic segmentation efficiently where previously mass marketing efficiency dictated less-sensitive marketing plans. The combination of the two allows stores to keep efficient records of what sells where. Computerized inventory control allows quick shifting of specialized products to where they are selling.

A key to successful regional marketing is defining the relevant region. What regions have different needs and desires for your product? If you sell pencils, and your marketing research shows that folks everywhere pretty much want the same things in pencils, then a regional marketing strategy may make no sense. If Bureau of the Census regions capture the divisions of your market, they may be what you should use. Table 4–1 describes both the four-region and the nine-region system used by the Bureau of the Census. Some marketers

Table 4–1 Bureau of the Census Geographic Regions in the United States

Nine Regions	Four Regions	States
New England	Northeast	ME, NH, VT, MA, RI, CT
Middle Atlantic	Northeast	NY, PA, NJ, DE
South Atlantic	South	WV, MD, DC, VA, NC, SC, GA, FL
East South Central	South	KY, TN, MS, AL
West South Central	South	TX, OK, AR, LA
East North Central	Midwest	WI, IL, MI, IN, OH
West North Central	Midwest	ND, SD, MN, NE, KS, IA, MO
Mountain	West	NV, ID, MT, WY, UT, AZ, CO, MN
Pacific	West	CA, OR, WA, AK, HI

are even using postal zip codes as geographic segmentation units because consumers in different parts of the same city often differ substantially.

Within the United States, regional shifts in population density are occurring. In particular, people are moving to the South and to the West. The air conditioner has made warmer climates more attractive, as people flee the "Snow Belt" and the "Rust Belt" for the "Sun Belt." The decline in the manufacturing and industrial sector, long dominant in the Northeast, has contributed to this movement.

Government: The chapter on the legal and political environment tells how government can influence consumers and marketing efforts. When Congress required all passenger cars to have seatbelts, the sale of seatbelts increased. When the U.S. government allows tariffs to rise or fall, the relative attractiveness for consumers and marketers of some imports and exports can change.

Some of the most significant changes in consumer behavior have resulted from legislation initiated by the consumer movement and consummated by Congress. Quack druggists have virtually been forced out of business, and diseased meat rarely is sold these days in U.S. supermarkets. Likewise, political actions can restructure relationships. In the short period of time from when the powerful Shah of Iran courted the United States until the Ayatollah overthrew him and allowed employees of the American Embassy in Iran to be taken hostage, every kind of commercial exchange between Iran and the United States, from travel plans and educational exchanges to Persian rugs and oil, declined.

History: When people share a history, they may also share consumer behaviors related to that history. Common perceptions about products emerge. People who visit a particular vacation spot may want to buy a t-shirt announcing that they've been there. People who watch their college basketball team win the national championship may want to buy commemorative items. On a more global level, marketers from the United States have an easier time selling products in Canada than in Vietnam because the history of the relationship of the United States with Canada has been much friendlier than with Vietnam. Managers need to know historic contexts when evaluating marketing opportunities.

Culture: In international marketing, understanding cultural subtleties often determines the difference between success and failure. Anecdotes about differences between national cultures abound. For example, "Body by Fisher" translates into Japanese to "Corpse by Fisher," a distinctly less appealing marketing slogan. Marketers must take care to recognize the distinctive aspects of any cultural group.

The same principle applies to domestic marketing. Campbell's, for example, advertises V8 juice in northern California on Spanish-speaking radio, in order to appeal especially to the Hispanic market.[4] Hispanic people often have encountered political, social, and economic circumstances quite different from what other Americans have encountered, and non-Hispanics often will not appreciate or grasp the richness of these experiences, especially as that richness relates to consumer responses. The same could be said for appreciating Asian

Americans, blacks, or other culturally unique groups. Of course, within each of these cultural groups significant subgroups also exist.[5]

Within the United States, differences between blacks and whites have received the most research attention. Black consumers are indeed different from whites in many respects. For example, black consumers respond more favorably to advertisements that feature blacks than to ads that use only whites.[6] Within the limits that blacks' lower income allows, blacks tend to innovate in clothing more than whites.[7] And blacks listen to AM radio more than whites.[8] With blacks making up over 10 percent of the population of the United States—and a much higher percentage in most major cities—marketers usually cannot afford to ignore black cultural traditions.

Most people understand their own cultural and subcultural groups better than any other group. As long as they want to deal only with "their own kind," intuitive subcultural and cultural understanding may be sufficient to allow adequate marketing. But as the people in the target market become more culturally diverse, the probability of misunderstanding increases tremendously. Many of these issues are covered in the chapter on international marketing.

Conclusions about Societal Influences

Often, marketers forget that marketing always occurs in a societal context. If a marketing program occurs only in one society and nothing disruptive occurs within that society, the consequences of this omission may not be too great. But as a global economy becomes more important and as the diversity of people continues to increase, the relevance of societal considerations will loom larger.

Demographic Influences on Consumer Behavior

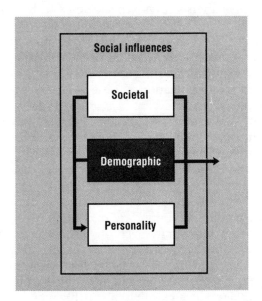

Demographic influences include *peer and social roles*, *family roles*, *occupation*, *education*, *income*, *age*, and *sex*.

Peer and Social Roles: Friends and social roles greatly influence how people behave as consumers. A **role** is:

the pattern of behavior performed by a person who occupies a particular position in the social system.

Consider your role as a student in a college class. Many purchases you make are directly related only to that role. Although the authors hate to admit it, you probably would not have purchased this book had it not been required for your class and your role as a student. The clothes you wear, the way you wear your hair, the container for your books, the activities you pursue on Friday nights, even your choice of beverage at a party all probably will reflect the roles you occupy and who your friends are in those roles. If you are the mayor, the coach, the boss, the leading scorer, the clown, the new kid, or the membership chairperson, your role will help you decide on certain purchases.

The critical concept here is the **role-related product cluster**. Consumers generally consider an entire set of otherwise-unrelated products necessary to fulfill the requirements of a certain role.[10] For example, in 1950 Mason Haire showed that a woman who purchased instant coffee was viewed as a lazy housewife who failed to fulfill her role obligations.[11] (This study also illustrates how role obligations can change over time, since it is doubtful that use of instant coffee would signify laziness today.)

New members generally are socialized about norms when they arrive in a new context. A **norm** is

a standard of behavior prescribed and enforced by a group through the use of rewards and sanctions.[12]

The boss explains that all employees must dress "as if they worked for IBM." The new member then knows what clothes to buy for the role. The union shop steward explains that coffee breaks come at 10:15 A.M. and 2:30 P.M. but that no one actually drinks coffee. The worker now knows what beverage not to buy and when not to buy it. Fellow students tease you about wearing a suit to class until you justify violating the norm ("I have a job interview today") or you suffer sufficient humiliation to observe the blue-jeans norm tomorrow.

Family Roles: Whether you are the daughter, the dad, or the great-aunt, your family role will influence your purchase decisions. Mothers buy chicken soup for sick kids. Sons buy their mothers greeting cards for Mother's Day. Parents clothe and feed their small children. And when the whole family decides to vacation at Disney World and the Epcot Center, your individual dream to surf in Hawaii evaporates in the interest of domestic tranquility.

In some ways families simply are one additional group with roles, norms, and socialization. Some family decisions are hard to aggregate, and some consumer decisions are not family decisions at all. Yet families deserve special attention in consumer analysis because, first of all, many decisions are made for all family members ("Tonight for dinner we'll all have chicken cacciatore."). And many families are economic units. A big pay raise for mom means more money for a child's tennis shoes and tennis lessons. Expensive tuition bills for one member may mean no money for a new car for another member. Shifting from one employed parent to two parents with jobs may change the family discretionary income or housing budget substantially. Divorce means maintaining two households instead of one, with constant or even diminished income. And families are important also because they tend to mediate the influences of other role and reference groups in that families dominate time and training for most members.[13]

Families are closely related to life cycle stage,[14] in some ways more closely than age. What you buy and how you buy it depends heavily on whether you are single, cohabiting, married, divorced, or widowed. How many children you have, their ages, and whether they live at home helps to determine what kinds of clothes, foods, toys, entertainment, and transportation you buy. Parents with only teenagers do not generally buy rattles for their children, as an obvious example.

Some family decision making requires role specialization or cooperation.[15] The person who normally cooks the evening meal will decide what food to purchase. The person who does the gardening may exert more influence when selecting gardening tools. But purchases may require several different roles, each of which is important for understanding marketing:[16] (1) The information gatherers obtain knowledge, expertise, and facts from friends, users, consumer magazines, or salespeople. (2) Influencers lobby other family members to make individual desires known. (3) Decision makers reach the conclusion about a purchase. (4) Purchasers carry out the decision. (5) Consumers are the actual users.

Consider a family planning to purchase a second car primarily for the mother to drive to work, but also for the teenagers to use on weekends. The father may have the most knowledge of automotive mechanics and thus may dominate the information-gathering stage. The teenagers as influencers may argue intensely for particular style considerations, such as a sporty exterior. Preteen children may also try to influence color choice. The mother may make the final decision because her income provides the funding and the need for the car. But if she is busy at a time when the father is free and the dealer eager to sell, he may conclude the actual negotiation as purchaser at the automobile dealership. The consumers then will be the mother and the teenagers. Who, then, bought the car? It was truly a family acquisition.

Occupation: Clearly, vocation dictates certain consumer expenditures. As with family, occupation is another role, but again it is a role of such import in our society that it warrants special attention. Uniforms or suits for certain occupations may influence purchase decisions. What books you read, what clubs you join, and how you relax may all stem from your job. Truck drivers buy coffee at economical roadside restaurants. Salespeople for expensive industrial equipment manufacturers entertain clients at posh restaurants and on golf courses. Some professors plan summer vacations around professional conferences. Some people travel extensively as a part of their occupation, and many people purchase occupational supplies, services, and equipment. Thus, occupation directly dictates a good deal of consumer activity.

Education: Education can influence consumers in two ways. First, it alters how people shop. Educated consumers tend to make more informed decisions about purchases. They tend to read periodicals such as *Consumer Reports* more often. And they tend to understand price, warranty, and product attribute information more precisely. Second, education alters what people want and appreciate. Although symphony tickets may cost about the same as professional wrestling tickets, people who purchase the former on average have a higher educational level. Clearly, people with different educational levels behave differently as consumers.[17]

Income: Perhaps the importance of income for consumers is most obvious of all demographic variables. All consumers must purchase products and services with money, and a lack of income (unless wealth comes from elsewhere) limits options. People with a higher income will be more likely to shop at Sak's Fifth Avenue than at K-Mart. People with a higher income will be more likely to vacation in European hotels than to camp in the Ozarks. The decision to buy a first-class plane ticket and the choice of alcoholic beverage once in that first-class seat will both correlate with income. What major appliances a person purchases will also depend on income.[18]

Some scholars have advocated combining income and other demographic variables into a composite called **socioeconomic status**. The Bureau of the Census, for example, combines income, occupation, and education into its measure of socioeconomic status. Although some of these methods are quite sophisticated,[19] the trend has been away from such combination.[20] Most often the worth of the uncombined measures of income, education, and occupation is greater than the measures combined. As O. D. Duncan (one of the earliest proponents of the composites who now prefers the separate measures) reportedly asked, "Why would anyone want hash [combined measures] when they could have steak [separate, untransformed measures]?"

Age: Many products appeal more to people in one age group than another—Poligrip, skateboards, Geritol, acne cream, music by the Beatles. People in different age groups have different needs and wants, as well as different opportunities to buy. The astute marketer must recognize how age groups respond to each product in his or her control and how the critical age groups might change.

The teenage market has been shrinking in size, but it is still large. It consists of over 25 million people, and it will return to that level again around 1997 after some decline. Teens spend over $40 billion per year in the United States,[21] hardly a trivial amount. Many teenagers have part-time jobs that generate income that is almost exclusively discretionary. Thus, although they may earn only a limited amount, much of it will be spent on luxuries. Furthermore, teens spend a lot of money that is not their own. One survey found that 49 percent of teenage girls had shopped for the family groceries in the previous week, a side effect of working mothers. Nevertheless, teens tend to be quite skeptical about advertisements.[22]

People in their twenties face independence, initiation into new roles, and establishment of a household. They are a prime market for appliances and furniture. Although their incomes tend to lag behind those of older groups, their needs generally are stronger than in many groups for first-purchase durable products. This age group is relatively small right now, which is a disadvantage for marketers but an advantage in the career paths of these people because of less competition. These people respond best to marketing pitches that are straightforward, respectful, and personal.[23]

People in their thirties have often been called "Yuppies," short for "young, urban professionals." True Yuppies are, of course, a subset of people in their thirties, but this age cohort is especially important because of its sheer size. During World War II (1939–1945), their future parents were too busy fighting and supporting the war effort to have babies, but when the future parents returned and settled into postwar life, starting in the late 1940s and continuing to the early 1960s, they made up for lost time fertility-wise, leading to a "baby boom." Like the proverbial pig in a python, this cohort has appeared in demographic charts as an abnormally large group, and it has created marketing opportunities at each age. To make the picture even rosier for marketers, many families in this group have two incomes.

Who are these people called the Yuppies? They have many unique characteristics. They were raised in a permissive environment by parents who read Dr. Spock and who were relatively affluent. Their permissiveness was accentuated by widespread availability of the pill and no fear of AIDS. (We consider how the family has changed in the next section on sex differences.) They are the first generation raised with television, including the first televised war—Vietnam. They prefer quality of life and self-fulfillment to wealth and self-sacrifice. They enjoy leisure but also want to succeed in a business world where competition with one another may limit opportunities for advancement. They want quality even if it costs a bit more.[24] Marketers who have understood this group and anticipate its coming needs have been richly rewarded.

During their forties many college-educated men reconsider their life goals and accomplishments.[25] They may experience a midlife crisis and may decide to make significant career, family, or lifestyle changes as they approach the middle of their lives. They may approach the marketplace differently, trading in a station wagon for a sports car. They may want to discover new and exciting characteristics they have previously left uncovered. Usually the crisis ends and these men return to their former selves, but the reconsidered lifestyle may linger. Much has been made about women and menopause during this age period, but it seems that most of the associated psychological changes are at best modest.[26] Probably the most significant events for women in this age cohort have to do with changing relationships with their children as those children grow up.

After the forties but before retirement often is a quite happy time. Careers are established, and people can cash in on what has gone before. As children leave home and the house becomes an "empty nest," people can enjoy the fruits of their labors. Financial concerns shift from child rearing to retirement security. The concept of luxury plays a more dominant role in the thoughts of many consumers here. Gardening, golf, and needlework may increase in interest here.[27] Travel opportunities increase as more discretionary income is available due to decreased child-rearing expenses.

Because life expectancy has increased so much in recent years, the retired market segment is also growing rapidly. Although retirement frequently implies a drop in income, this group actually has considerable discretionary income because mortgages often are paid off and children usually are no longer dependent. Health, travel, and recreation are important to retired people. They tend to be price-sensitive and conscientious shoppers. Especially after loss of a spouse, loneliness can be a major issue.[28] For some of the older members of this category, diminished information-processing capacity (diminished hearing, diminished vision) may impede shopping if retailers are not sensitive to these changes.[29] Advertisers also must be aware of this concern. For example, time-compressed advertisements do not work as effectively with elderly consumers as with college students.[30] However, it is not true that elderly people resist all technological progress. If information is conveyed to retired people effectively and if the product meets their needs, change will be accepted and even embraced.[31]

Sex: Perhaps the most lasting changes in our society over the past two decades have been in the role of women within our society. For the first time in the history of the United States, most women work for pay outside the home, abandoning the role of exclusive housewife both for economic and for philosophic reasons.[32] As women continue to march toward equality with men (there are still rank and salary disparities), their purchasing power and economic clout will continue to increase.[33] At the same time, new needs will emerge to cover functions previously covered by the exclusive housewife, such as child care, cleaning, and cooking. Availability of day care for children has mush-roomed over the past decade, but in many locations supply lags far behind demand. Quality convenience foods have grown in popularity. Other time-saving products will continue to appear. Work tools for women have increased as more women need cars to drive to work and need wardrobes appropriate for their positions. And when working women are married to a working spouse, families with two incomes usually have much greater purchasing power than single-income families.

Families have also changed in structure over the past several decades. Fewer people are married; more are single and divorced. More people cohabitate with-out marrying, or at least before marrying. And family size has declined. Each of these trends implies that a new market may be growing for down-sized, down-priced products associated with households, such as refrigerators, tele-phones, and laundry hampers.

Conclusions about Demographic Influences

This partial list of demographic influences illustrates a number of ways of describing consumers and tracking their changing characteristics. Knowing about demographic patterns and trends can help the marketing manager iden-tify new opportunities or changing circumstances. New products and new segments often are discovered from careful examination of demographic in-formation. But demographics rarely demonstrate the underlying reasons for changes. Managers need to understand *why* changes are taking place, not merely that they are happening. For that understanding it is often necessary to turn to personality analysis.

Personality Influences on Consumer Behavior

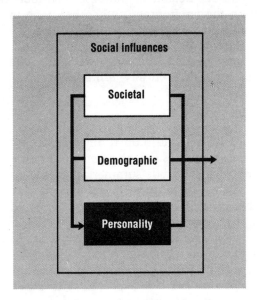

Personality as an influence on consumer behavior has the dimensions of *experiences*, *self-esteem*, *lifestyle*, *attitudes*, and *values*.

Experiences: No matter what categories you use to describe a person or how that person fits into social categories, each person has to some degree unique experiences and therefore unique responses to marketing efforts. Many of the societal and demographic factors we have just considered simply represent shorthand summaries of probable experiences a person has had similar to others in that category. But any given person may deviate from that pattern, giving rise to individual differences that characterize what animates behavior in a particular context.

Self-Esteem: People develop self-esteem (or a self-concept) that reflects their prior experiences in various situations and that guides their encounter with new situations.[34] *Self-concept* is

> an attitude about one's self, defining what one is and what one does.

This attitude is quite complex. Self-evaluation leads to the way and the ability to relate to other people, and it leads to social information gathering.[35] People constantly behave in ways that manifest their self-concept. For example, people who consider themselves to be generous buy and give more gifts.

Many purchase decisions may directly express the self-concept. Often the purchase of a product implements that self-image in one form or another. The product symbolizes what type of person the consumer is.[36] For example, imagine two recent college graduates who have just obtained their first career-path jobs. Each plans to splurge on improved transportation with the new-found wealth of a lucrative job. If one has found that she adapts to situations most effectively when behaving as a "solid American," she may prefer to purchase a Plymouth Reliant. If the other considers herself most effective in interaction with the environment when behaving in a "sporty and worldly" manner, she may prefer to buy a Nissan Pulsar or a Volkswagen Jetta.[37]

Attitudes: Simply stated, attitudes summarize what a person likes and does not like. Stated more theoretically, **attitudes** are

> schemas,[38] stored as preferences, that provide abstract accounts of adaptation.

Each experience with an attitudinal object, such as a product, will influence the attitude. For example, suppose a person has an attitude, "I like Smucker's strawberry jam." This attitude summarizes previous experiences with Smucker's strawberry jam. It is a much more efficient method of information summarization than to recall every single experience with strawberry jam. (E.g., "On June 7 of last year I ate Smucker's strawberry jam, and it tasted good. On July 23 of last year I ate it, and it tasted good. On July 24 of last year I ate it, and it tasted good. On . . .")

Presumably such an attitude schema would develop from a history of positive experiences with the jam. For a person with hundreds of experiences with Smucker's strawberry jam, this attitude would be a well-honed abstraction and therefore resistant to change if all of the evidence had fit the attitude schema well. High-involvement products probably are conducive to more elaborate attitude schemas than low-involvement products. People probably also spend a greater amount of time seeking and processing information relevant to high involvement products.[39]

Attitudes change when the equilibrium described in the attitudinal schema demonstrably fails.[40] When one state of equilibrium proves to be inadequate, an improvement in the attitude is necessary. For example, if the local grocery store suddenly raises the price on a jar of Smucker's strawberry jam to $5, the attitude may change from "I like to buy Smucker's strawberry jam" to "Smucker's strawberry jam tastes good but costs too much."

Many of the most significant changes in attitudes result from shifting social equilibrium, as when a person moves to a new job or a new social context. For example, if you take a new job at double the salary working for an otherwise wonderful boss who hates Fords, your long-standing love of Fords may be suppressed or revised as a part of adapting to the new environment.

The question of attitude-behavior consistency is, of course, quite important to marketing strategy. Most marketing research measures attitudes based on the assumption that attitudes are closely related to behaviors. Advertising usually seeks to alter behavior *indirectly* through changing attitudes, whereas couponing and sampling are techniques aimed *directly* at behaviors. One theory of the relationship between attitudes and behaviors is described in Exhibit 4–1— not a simple and direct one.[41] Rather, marketing managers who want to predict sales from attitudes will need to chart other factors as well.

The answer to the question of the relative importance of attitudes and behaviors influencing each other has direct bearing on the marketing manager's decision about resource allocation for advertising versus couponing and sampling.[44] It has also stirred up a great deal of controversy among consumer behavior researchers.[45]

EXHIBIT **4-1**

Multi-attribute View of Attitudes and Behaviors

Advertisers frequently state that the goals of advertising are to inform, to persuade, and to change intention to buy. The roots of this concept can be found in the multi-attribute model, also known as the "Theory of Reasoned Action," and the Fishbein model, in honor of its creator.[42] The model assumes that attitudes (A) toward purchase are the attitudes of interest. These attitudes come from the combination of all beliefs (B) about a product multiplied times the evaluation (E) of those beliefs:

$$A = B(E)$$

The beliefs are viewed by the person as facts, and the evaluations are measured like attitudes. For example, Henry may believe that Hawaiian shirts are colorful and like that fact, and he may believe that they are comfortable and also like that fact. The combination of these two beliefs plus any others, each multiplied by its evaluation, will lead to the attitude toward purchasing.

A parallel concept to attitude is subjective norm (S). It results from multiplying normative beliefs (N) times motives to comply (M):

$$S = N(M)$$

A normative belief is what other important people think, such as Henry's friends and family. A motive to comply is whether other important people matter in this context. For example, if Henry's friends all hate Hawaiian shirts but Henry does not care, what Henry's friends think will not matter in this case. But if Henry's parents like Hawaiian shirts and he cares what his parents think, that will influence his subjective norm.

Purchase intentions (I) result from the weighted combination of attitudes toward purchase and subjective norms. The weight (w) is based on how important each element is in a particular decision:

$$I = (w)A + (w)S$$

Behavior results from purchase intention, but many other factors can interfere with the actual purchase of a product. Henry may plan to buy a Hawaiian shirt but fail to do it because of intervening factors if the shirt is too expensive, if it is not stocked in any store he visits, if Henry does not have time to go to Hawaii, or if the Hawaiian shirt makers are all on strike, to give a few examples.

From this model we can see that attitude and behavior are related, with attitude generally leading to behavior; however, subjective norms, the importance of attitudes and subjective norms, purchase intention, and intervening factors all have an influence on purchase behavior, too. Thus, the relationship between attitudes and behaviors includes several factors and is somewhat complex.

The debate over this model, its measurement, and its elements has been one of the hottest in consumer research for more than a decade. Many important articles have been written about this model, and many issues have not yet been resolved.[43] The model does, however, provide a useful starting point for marketers to understand how to inform, to persuade, and to change intention to buy.

The concept of abstraction is pivotal to understanding how attitudes and behaviors are related. Abstraction in a sense provides an attitudinal prototype from which behaviors are manufactured. Attitudes are abstractions about the adaptive consequences of various behaviors. The attitude "I like Burpee seeds" probably summarizes the results of previous purchases and product usage, and it provides a guide for future purchases as well. The strategy implied by the attitudinal abstraction ("I like Burpee seeds") will be applied in appropriate circumstances (by purchasing Burpee seeds).

Habit is a concept that has also been invoked in this context.[46] As an attitude is applied more and more, habit develops.

This general-abstraction principle will break down during several situations.[47] When a situation has either no apparent adaptive significance or ambiguous significance, abstractions will not necessarily guide behavior because they will not be seen as relevant. Neither will this principle apply when new abstractions are forming or transforming. When people believe that the rules they've used to purchase products (e.g., solid hand soap) have been revised (e.g., the introduction of soft, liquid hand soap), they will be more likely to experiment with alternatives.

Lifestyle: **Lifestyles** can be defined as

> clustered patterns of attitudes, interests, and behaviors.

Attitudes do not exist in isolation; rather, many attitudes often are interrelated with one another. Consider the person who buys large amounts of shotgun ammunition:

> We know from demographic analyses that he tends to be a young craftsman or blue-collar worker from the South or Mountain states with a relatively low income. And we could guess that he likes to hunt. But he has a whole list of other interests and attitudes that fit into a lifestyle quite different from others.[48] His preferences include fishing, camping, out-of-doors activities, smoking, playing poker, danger, war stories, and auto repair. He would not mind being a policeman or a professional football player, but he also does not mind occasionally pushing the law to its limits, and he does not watch sporting events on television more than other people. Many of his lifestyle characteristics defy common sense and have major implications for marketing: He does not shop at discount stores any more than others, he does not read the newspapers as much as others, nor does he have an abnormal love for spectator sports. If we relied exclusively on demographic data and ignored lifestyle data, we could well advertise in the wrong places, develop ads that do not appeal to our consumer, and even use inappropriate channels of distribution. Hunter safety ads, for example, typically warn against the dangers of firearms, yet danger is a special joy to ammunition consumers.

Values: The study of values examines the most fundamental aspect of personality. A **value** can be defined as

> an enduring belief that a specific mode of conduct or end-state of existence is personally or socially preferable to an opposite or converse mode of conduct or end-state of existence.[49]

Values are more abstract than attitudes. People have attitudes *about something*, but values do not have such objects. They play an equally important role in consumer behavior.[50] Values also summarize adaptive strategies, which have been acquired through experience, into adaptive value schemas. Several recent studies have demonstrated that a large range of values relate directly to consumer behavior.[51] For example, people who value fun and enjoyment in life are especially likely to consume a lot of alcoholic beverages and to read *Playboy*;

people who value self-fulfillment avoid television, because self-advancement is rare while watching television; and people who value a sense of accomplishment have unusually high incomes that result from many accomplishments.

One way to state the principle of the marketing orientation would be to assert that effective marketing helps people fulfill their values. Products and product usage become elements of value schemas. Products tied to values will be experienced more favorably than products that deliver more-mundane benefits. This tie between value and product can be literal, as when an effective children's toothpaste is purchased to promote motherhood, or it can be purely psychological, as when an urbanite purchases a cigarette to apply a value schema about cowboy-like rugged independence.

The principle of abstraction is at least as important in this context as it is in the context of attitude-behavior consistency.[52] Often attitudes and behaviors change when aspects of them are linked to more abstract principles or values. For example, opponents of gun-control legislation have complained that gun-registration laws threaten freedom; thus, they seek to tie one specific but controversial attitude to an abstract but widely held value. Their goal is to foster assimilation of opposition to gun-control legislation into the abstract value schema about freedom.

Table 4–2 summarizes key characteristics of people who endorse different values, based on research using the List of Values (LOV). People who identify each different value as most important differ in numerous ways, sometimes quite profoundly. Companies that understand what their consumers value will be better equipped to help those consumers find value fulfillment in the context of certain products and services. The table reports what percentage of Americans endorsed each value both in 1976 and in 1986.

Table 4–2 Brief Description of Value Segments[53]

1. *Self-respect* is the "all-American" value, selected by the largest number of Americans and having the least distinctive endorsers. People from all age and income groups selected this value as most important. About 21.1 percent of Americans selected it in 1976; 23.0 percent in 1986.
2. *Security* is a deficit value, endorsed by people who lack economic and psychological security. Blacks, southerners, and retired people also select this value frequently. It was selected by 20.6 percent of Americans in 1976, 16.5 percent in 1986.
3. *Warm relationships with others* is an excess value, endorsed by people—especially women—who have a lot of friends and who are friendly. The percentage here has risen from 16.2 to 19.9.
4. Likewise, people who endorse *sense of accomplishment* have accomplished a lot. These people tend to be successful middle-aged men. About 11.4 percent endorsed it earlier, but more recently it grew to 15.9 percent. The percentage is higher in the Northeast.
5. People—mostly Yuppies—who endorse *self-fulfillment* are relatively well fulfilled economically, educationally, and emotionally. They resent excessive demands from their families. Overall, 9.6 percent of Americans subscribed to this value in 1976, falling more recently to 6.5 percent.
6. *Being well-respected* is selected by the Rodney Dangerfields of the world. It's interesting to contrast self-respect, which one can achieve alone, with being well-respected, which requires the cooperation of others. People who value self-respect are much better adjusted, according to our measures. Endorsers have low educational and income attainment, and they tend to be older (8.8 percent in 1976; 5.9 percent in 1986).
7. *Sense of belonging* also requires the help of others. As with warm relationships with others, it is a social value selected by women. But sense of belonging is less reciprocal and seems to result in greater dependency. Procter & Gamble must love this value group—it's a home-and-family-oriented value particularly popular in the Mountain states. The endorsement rate was 7.9 percent and has fallen to 5.1 percent.
8. You might think that *fun and enjoyment in life* would isolate the hedonists in America, but the cliché that describes these people is, "Stop and smell the roses." Young people who appreciate life especially like this value. About 4.5 percent of Americans endorsed it in 1976, and the percentage has risen to 7.2 percent. The rise has been especially dramatic among young males.

Conclusions about Personality Influences

Personality research, sometimes called *psychographic* research in marketing, has made many contributions to understanding consumer behavior, although some of the contributions have been modest or equivocal.[54] Too often, marketing research has been atheoretical, with no rationale for why any personality variable ought to relate to particular consumer behaviors. Personality variables have no magical powers, and researchers who assume that they do are often disappointed. But careful and thoughtful examination of how experiences in situations, self-esteem, attitudes, lifestyles, and values might relate to a particular product or service will often lead to a better understanding of the nature of sales and of how to service the consumer.

Conclusions about Social Influences

Without a doubt, social forces dictate most of what we do as consumers. College students in the United States differ from Australian Aborigines and Zulu warriors primarily due to social influences. The reason we want a personal computer rather than a boomerang or a nose ring can be tied quickly to social forces. Indeed, the social context in which we find ourselves will define our desires and needs. Marketing succeeds or fails to the extent that it effectively addresses those wants and needs.

SITUATIONAL INFLUENCES ON CONSUMERS

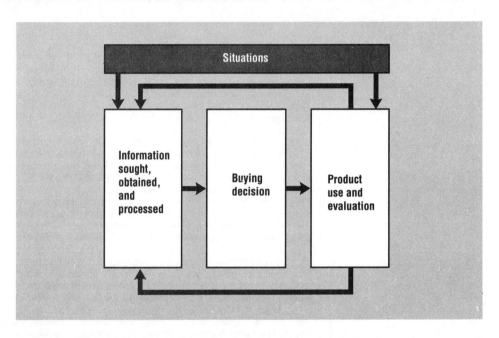

Each person has faced many individual situations and developed patterns of dealing with those situations. One goal of a marketer is to develop products that will please unique consumers in unique usage situations.[53]

EXHIBIT **4-2**

Procter & Gamble's 800 Number

Sometimes consumers want to use a product but are having a difficult time figuring out how to do it in a particular use situation. If that product is a household product, you might ask your mother. But what if you are at Princeton and your mother is in Peoria? If you are curious about how to use a Procter & Gamble product, you could telephone the manufacturer's toll-free (800) number. Some people call with complaints or compliments, but most of the 800,000 callers each year want to know how to use a product. Every December the company receives a rush of calls for baking recipes using Crisco. In April, spring cleaners want advice from Mr. Clean. Each June, mothers baking wedding cakes for their daughters with Duncan Hines mixes want coaching on this activity.

Although P&G does not view the toll-free number as its primary source of data about use situations, several product modifications have resulted from situational information generated from these calls. P&G learned, for example, that Downy had a tendency to freeze easily during cold spells and that the company should provide high-altitude instructions for baking Duncan Hines brownies.[57]

The marketing manager must try to understand what each consumer experiences in each situation. Wants and desires for products will vary from one situation to another, and the marketer must understand that.

Task definition or usage plan is perhaps the most important aspect of the situation to impinge on consumers.[54] Consumers buy products because they plan to use the products for a particular purpose in a specific situation. Consider Arm & Hammer baking soda. Although it occupied a dominant position in the market for baking soda as a cooking ingredient, the company was able to increase sales considerably by marketing its baking soda as a refrigerator deodorant, thus defining a new usage situation. Orange growers experienced a similar success by convincing consumers, in the words of their ad, that "Orange juice isn't just for breakfast anymore." Exhibit 4–2 provides an example of a source of information about how to use a product in a particular situation.

INFORMATIONAL INFLUENCES ON CONSUMERS

The other major class of influences on consumer behavior besides social and situational is informational. Consumers process information from advertisements, from friends, from experiences—all to form beliefs about products that will ultimately influence decisions about what to buy. A number of books have been written about how consumers process information,[58] and thousands of articles have discussed the topic of human information processing. Approaches to how people use information are almost as numerous as authors who write about it. The approach we take here elaborates on Piaget's cognitive theory of

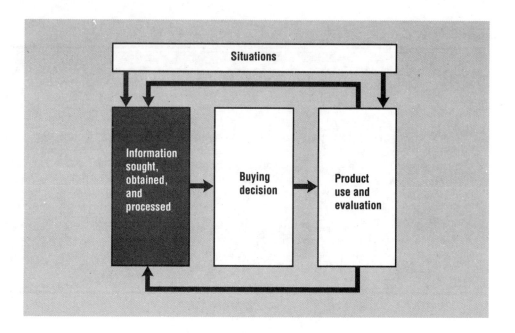

information processing.[59] This approach is the most frequently cited information-processing approach in social science.

External and Internal Information Search

Information is not something that inadvertently arrives in people's heads via some obscure path. Humans are active information seekers and active information processors. When we want to know about a particular product or service, we have ways of finding out. Some of the ways are dominated by marketers. We may read an advertisement in the newspaper to find out who is having a sale, we may look through the Yellow Pages for the address of the nearest place to buy what we want, we may study a point-of-purchase display or a package, or we may talk to retailers. We may also seek advice from sources independent of marketers. We may talk to friends and relatives, or we may read the most recent article from *Consumer Reports* about our planned purchase.[60] All of these activities are known as external search, because we are looking beyond ourselves. Generally consumers do not spend enormous amounts of time searching for products, but if a particular decision has important consequences, they will.

Internal search involves memory scanning and self-analysis. It is much more difficult for marketers to study,[62] but we can learn something about it.[63] People have a vast store of memories of similar circumstances and experiences, and this store will usually be used in any attempt to assemble the relevant information for a particular decision. Although it is difficult to study, it probably constitutes the single largest source of influence on any consumer decision.

Schemas and New Information

Everyone has a large number of schemas about how the world works. Specific self-concepts, attitudes, lifestyles, and values all are examples of schemas. So are bodies of individual knowledge about specific products. Figure 4–3 describes what happens to schemas when new information is encountered, when internal and external searches are wedded. First, we judge whether the information is even relevant. If the information is not judged to be relevant, low-involvement information processing results.[64] (This topic is discussed more fully later in this chapter.) When someone encounters relevant new information, high-involvement information processing occurs. High-involvement information can be assimilated into existing mental schemas without altering them, or it can lead to accommodation (revision) of the schemas. *Assimilation* is the fusion of a new object to an already-established schema. *Accommodation* is the most direct sense in which the environment acts on the individual's cognitive structure.

In many cases, assimilation and accommodation occur simultaneously. Their joint action is known as *adaptation*. Adaptation is the fundamental goal of information processing, as well as of many other human and biological activities. People seek to establish equilibrium with the environment through adaptation.

> When a person transforms the environment or is transformed by the environment to promote more effective interchanges between the person and the environment,

this is known as *equilibration through adaptation*.

To provide an example of how these functions work, consider the following example:

John believes that Fords are good cars. As new information is encountered, he will assimilate it, if it fits or is made to fit, into the attitude schema about Fords. As long as that attitude schema fosters effective interchanges between John and his environment (e.g., a family Ford provides adequate transportation), positive new information will be primarily assimilated,

FIGURE 4-3
How people process new information

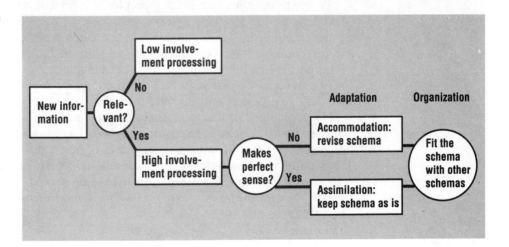

even if at times that information does not fit into the schema neatly. For example, if Bill claims that Fords have bad transmissions, that information may be interpreted as a personality flaw of Bill (negativism) rather than as a mechanical flaw of Fords.

Some accommodation will also take place as the attitude schema becomes more complex. The view may develop that Fords are good cars in spite of (or except for) fuel-system problems. As long as a state of equilibrium exists between the external environment and that schema, it will be resistant to major change. If that system should inhibit adaptation and effective interchanges with the environment (e.g., the Ford has a mechanical problem that ruins the family vacation), then the schema would be ripe for a phase of extensive accommodation, or reequilibration, and for change.

A complementary function to adaptation is **organization**. It is

> the tendency to systematize processes into coordinated, coherent systems.

It is the mechanism through which internal representations of the external environment are related·to one another. What we know about Ford relates to what we know about General Motors, about large industrial companies in the United States, about the labor union movement, about life in Detroit, Michigan, and about transmissions, to name only a few of the relevant schemas.

An advertising stimulus or other marketing information will have a unique impact on an individual, depending on that person's previous experience and knowledge about the world. But at the same time, that impact is not entirely random or arbitrary. Even if the external world is only interpreted through current schemas unique to the individual, schemas reflecting the environment poorly will change more readily than schemas that closely approximate the environment or something correlated with the environment because of their inhibition of adaptation. That is, people will interact inappropriately with the world when they have poor schemas, and the inappropriate interaction will provide feedback that change is needed.

To continue with our Ford example, if John knows from experience that Fords have good electrical systems and good air conditioning systems, organization may push him to believe that the cooling system on Fords is superior to the cooling system on other cars, in spite of the lack of direct experience with particularly impressive success stories about Ford cooling systems. John may also conclude that large American companies can manufacture fine, high-technology products and that the future of Detroit, Michigan, is promising.

Do people see products as they "really" are? We know that people often miscomprehend television commercials.[65] Certainly people often construe many other things in ways that may deviate from "reality," but external reality does influence the construing. It depends, however, on the person who does the observing and the information that is presented. The metaphor of food ingestion is apt in this context. The unique characteristics of a person influence how food or information is ingested. Potatoes provide energy to the athlete and extra weight to the sedentary person.

Or to use a climate-related example, the Eskimo will likely perceive snow in a more complex manner than the Californian, and the Californian will likely perceive surfboards in a more complex manner than the Eskimo. But just as the sedentary person and the athlete will both respond differently to meat than to potatoes, the Californian and the Eskimo also will both distinguish between snow and surfboards (or else risk constructing some unusual igloos). If a sporting goods store created a pile of snow and tried to sell it as surfboards, no one would be tricked. But the ability to note subtle differences in surfboards may depend on prior knowledge of the product category.

Because people understand only aspects of a product, it is important for marketers to make certain that consumers actually perceive the attributes that have been built into products. Neither the product nor the person is static. They are dynamic, active, changing entities. Some theories view schemas as stable, like statues, but in fact they are dynamic, like movies. For example, when we buy a product and interact with it, that interaction alters exactly what we think of the product, sometimes on a daily basis. This changing nature of schemas is one reason research can sometimes mislead marketers: If the people change from the time of the research until the time of implementing the marketing program, the program may fail even if the research accurately predicted success.

One study showed how these processes can account for information processing in an advertising context.[66] It examined how people respond to print advertising by manipulating the physical attractiveness and likelihood of celebrity sources and participant product involvement in a simulated print advertisement for "Edge" disposable razors:

> Celebrities with extreme ratings on physical attractiveness and likableness were selected for inclusion in the simulated advertisements. The authors expected that for products such as disposable razors, for which consumer interest is relatively low, people would not examine information from an advertisement very long. Any information conveyed in the advertisement would probably be observed within the first second or two of observing the advertisement. Thus, the effect of the celebrity's image would be crucial in determining the effectiveness of the advertisement. More specifically, they predicted that, because razors are used more to enhance physical attractiveness than to increase likableness, the endorsement of physically attractive celebrities would facilitate attitude change and advertisement effectiveness more than the endorsement of likable celebrities. The results were consistent with this prediction. Advertisements that included attractive celebrities were associated with higher levels of favorable attitudes toward the product and with optimal levels of favorable intentions to purchase the product than ads that included only likable celebrities.

Emotion and Information Processing

In recent years, scholars have recognized that emotion plays a significant role in how people respond to information.[67] When people experience emotional arousal, they tend to process information more quickly. The emotion functions like a catalyst, stimulating the processing. Advertisements that arouse people emotionally probably are processed more quickly. Products that arouse people probably generate more attention. Although historically consumer researchers have viewed consumers as rational, computer-like information-processing machines, in recent years the trend has been to realize that emotions also influence consumption.

Involvement and Information Processing

Involvement has also generated a good deal of interest in recent years.[68] At one time, for the most part only high-involvement models were considered, such as we have done thus far in this chapter. But more recently, scholars have recognized that many consumer decisions are unimportant from the point of view of the consumer.[69] Executives at Procter & Gamble care deeply about the fate of their Crest toothpaste, but most consumers would probably not be willing to fight and die over the issue of selecting the correct brand of toothpaste. When consumers watch an advertisement for Crest, few would feel a deep obligation to master every detail of the ad, as if their future well-being depended entirely on it. More likely, consumers may try to tune out the ad or to pursue some other activity. Consumers generally are just not that involved in the decision for certain products. When involvement is low, information processing is turned off more quickly. Superficial aspects of marketing communication, such as music and attractiveness of a celebrity endorser, may play a greater role in consumer influence and consumer decision making than product facts.[70] The most difficult task for the advertiser may not be conveying cogent product information; rather, it may be capturing the attention of the consumer in the first place.

The entire way of marketing a product will vary as a function of the involvement level.[71] Table 4–3 compares the two approaches. The ideal strategy for marketing a product very much depends on whether it is generally a low- or high-involvement product. Low-involvement products are generally purchased based on price and convenience. Initial purchases usually are not based on very much information, and repeat purchases will usually only use information based on prior personal experience.

Table 4–3 High- versus Low-Involvement Product Marketing

Marketing Variable	High Involvement	Low Involvement
Advertising goals	Convey information	Repetition
Positioning	Deliver benefits	Solve problems
Price	Depends on quality	Low
Sales promotions	Less important	More important
Distribution	Depends on quality	Widespread

Satisfaction and Postpurchase Information Processing

Satisfaction with product use constitutes a special category of information processing because it includes the consumer's direct experiential evidence about the product. Expectation and expectancy disconfirmation lead to level of satisfaction, and these in turn lead to attitudes toward the product and future purchase intention.[72] People generally trust their own experiences with a product as much as any other source of information; hence, positive experiences will fuel satisfaction, repeat purchase, and brand loyalty, whereas negative experiences will lead to dissatisfaction, brand switching, and negative word-of-mouth communication.[73]

Complaints provide one source of information about dissatisfaction. Retailers and manufacturers ought to deal with legitimate consumer complaints promptly and courteously because negative word-of-mouth communication, if allowed to spread, can have devastating consequences on future sales and future relationships between consumers and a company. Consumers who complain, if treated politely, can provide a company with valuable evidence to consider in current product appraisal and in future product design. Consumers who complain and obtain adequate redress often like a company and its products more than consumers who have not complained. Although dealing with complaining customers can be unpleasant, it can also be a valuable source of marketing research on how consumers process information about a particular product or service.

Postpurchase information sources ought to include more than just complaints. Firms should constantly seek to learn how consumers are using and responding to their products and services. All of the types of research that can help identify new product opportunities, such as the types of methods discussed in the chapter on information for marketing decisions, apply to postpurchase evaluation.

Conclusion on Information Influence

Many of the information-processing strategies we discuss in the chapter on manager decision making also apply to consumer decision making. Indeed, the two sets of decisions—managerial and consumer—often represent identical processes, especially when high-involvement products are under consideration. Both need to develop theory about what will work and then implement that theory. Both types of decisions are often difficult, and errors are made in both. Yet the very process of making highly complex decisions after processing complex, perplexing information is what distinguishes the *homo sapiens* from other primates. And the history of success at such endeavors is what distinguishes twentieth-century civilization from the hunter-gatherer species of our genetic endowment.

CONSUMER BEHAVIOR AND MARKET SEGMENTATION

One major reason marketing managers need to understand consumer behavior is for market segmentation. Companies often can increase profits by serving subgroups or segments of the entire market well. Different consumers constitute different segments, and marketers need to deal with each different segment appropriately. Marketers must decide how to allocate resources and how to plan strategy based on the nature of the relevant segments.

Initially defining segments is often a difficult task. Given the wealth of information covered in this chapter, what is useful for defining segments and what is irrelevant? The answer is that in principle all of the information about consumer behavior[74] is relevant and that what is irrelevant depends upon the product and the situation. It will, of course, often be impossible to measure every single construct in a segmentation study. Managers must decide what variables to use in a segmentation study based on specific needs and the current state of knowledge about a particular product. Usually managers will have some idea about what does and does not relate to consumption of a certain product. Managers typically will know something about what benefits are relevant, what needs and desires the relevant potential segments might have, and what types of questions need to be answered in this context. That is, managers have theories about what should be used for segmentation before any research is conducted.

Consider a segmentation study conducted by the Canadian Office of Tourism.[75] The government wanted to promote tourism to Canada from the United States, and it wanted to develop an understanding of the relevant segments. Because a wide variety of types of vacations are available in Canada and because people in the United States vacation in many different forms and for many different reasons, the researchers knew that a segmentation approach would likely be more effective than a mass-marketing approach. Once potentially interested segments could be matched with vacation opportunities in Canada, the Office of Tourism could decide which segments to pursue most aggressively.

Before conducting the segmentation study, the researchers needed to decide (1) whom they would interview, (2) the frame of reference for segmentation, and (3) alternative potential methods for segmentation.

1. Deciding whom they would interview was not easy. To interview only U.S. citizens who have traveled to Canada would restrict the sample to 5 percent of the population of the United States and would, perhaps, bury untapped opportunities in unsampled respondents. The goal was to expand market share, not simply to preserve it; therefore, it was necessary to interview people who had never been to Canada. On the other hand, for many people a trip to Canada is unlikely because they never vacation far away from home. Because research has shown that how far people have traveled on previous vacations is predictive of how far they will travel on future vacations, it was decided to restrict the sample to people who had traveled at least three-fourths of the distance from their home to Canada at least once. Furthermore, the sample was restricted to people who at least once had previously taken a vacation of at least a week's duration during the past three years. Thus, the sample consisted of people who, based on prior experiences, could at least potentially be expected to consider a Canadian vacation.

2. The frame of reference for product evaluation is sometimes an important issue. In this case the use of a "dream vacation" as the standard of comparison would perhaps generate unrealistic comparisons. Many people have fantasies about vacations they are quite unlikely to purchase. Likewise, using "vacations in general" as the standard would be difficult because many people have taken multiple vacations, some with quite different purposes. In this study, the researchers decided to anchor all comparisons to the respondent's most recent vacation.

3. To control the amount of data collected, the researchers used their knowledge of vacationing to focus on a benefit-based segmentation system. They could have considered favorableness toward Canada as a segmentation criterion, but this system fails to recognize that Canada is not a single entity, vacation-wise, nor is it one toward which attitudes are highly polarized. Or they could have emphasized geographic area in the United States as a criterion for segmentation. The difficulty with this standard is that desires for types of vacations do not vary as much by region in the United States as they do by other factors. Thus, segmentation by desires sought seemed the most promising.

The researchers started gathering data with a pilot sample of 200, in order to test whether the three above-mentioned decisions were viable. When the approach was supported by the pilot data, the researchers conducted 1,750 interviews. The data were reduced using a Q-mode factor analysis with principal components extraction of the eigenvalues and a varimax rotation. Based on this analysis, they identified six segments.

Segment I. *Friends and relatives—nonactive visitor* (29 percent). These people want to visit family and friends in familiar surroundings. They rarely participate in activities.

Segment II. *Friends and relatives—active city visitor* (12 percent). These people differ from Segment I in that they like to practice sightseeing, to shop, and to attend entertainment events.

Segment III. *Family sightseers* (6 percent). These people want a different, new vacation spot children would enjoy and find enriching.

Segment IV. *Outdoor vacationers* (19 percent). Clean air and peaceful, beautiful scenery attract this group. Camps, recreational facilities, and accommodations for children matter for these people.

Segment V. *Resort vacationers* (19 percent). Good weather, good water sports, and good urban atmosphere attract Segment V people.

Segment VI. *Foreign vacationers* (26 percent). These people want a foreign atmosphere and beautiful scenery. They like to vacation in places they have never been before. Good accommodations and service are more important to them than cost. They want an exciting and enriching experience.

The results of this study were put to use immediately. Segments I and II were eliminated from further consideration because they do not provide a good profit opportunity. The other segments were then profiled in terms of behavior, psychographics, travel incentives, and image of a vacation in Canada. Results were disseminated to all interested parties. Advertising content, media choices, and promotional materials were geared toward the appropriate segments. This information was used for planning for future hotels, accommodations, and tourist facilities by both the Canadian government and private groups.

Note how consumer-behavior information was utilized in this research. Societal factors were considered but essentially rejected as a basis for segmentation. In general, demographic factors played a minor role relative to what had been anticipated, although family roles proved highly relevant. Personality turned out to provide the major insight into knowing what Canadian vacations are likely to attract people from the United States. Although information-processing strategy did not help define segments in this study, in some instances it could. For example, consider the schema complexity of people who buy a bicycle from a mass merchandiser (e.g., Sears), where decisions are usually based on little product information, versus the schema complexity of people who buy a bicycle from a local bicycle shop, where owners are often also the sales staff, repair staff, and neighborhood expert. Likewise, involvement has been used as a segmentation strategy basis.

SUMMARY OF IMPORTANT POINTS

1. Consumer behavior is useful for setting strategies. It helps in selecting and segmenting markets, planning marketing strategies, evaluating strategies, and assessing consumer trends that will affect strategies in the future.
2. Consumer behavior is useful for implementing strategies. It can assist in fully understanding the sources of any market response problems, gauging response to prospective product, price, promotion, and distribution changes, planning the marketing program, and evaluating the marketing program.
3. Three major sources of influence are social, situational, and informational.
4. *Social influences* have to do with the people associated with a consumer. Three major categories of social influences include societal, demographic, and personality.
5. Societal influences from geography, government, history, and culture can be dramatic and intense, but often they are in the background and overlooked.
6. Demographic influences include peer and social roles, family roles, occupation, education, income, age, and sex. Knowing about demographic patterns and trends can help the marketing manager identify new opportunities or changing circumstances.
7. Personality influences include experiences, self-esteem, lifestyle, attitudes, and values. Careful and thoughtful examination of how per-

sonality influences might relate to a particular product or service will often lead to a better understanding of the nature of sales and of how to service the consumer.

8. *Situational influences* have to do with the context in which a product will be used. Different contexts demand different approaches to product use. The marketing manager must try to understand what each consumer experiences in each situation.

9. *Informational influences* have to do with the facts and beliefs a person has about a product or service.

10. In external search, we are looking beyond ourselves for information. Internal search involves memory scanning and self-analysis.

11. Assimilation is the fusion of a new object to an already established schema. Accommodation is the most direct sense in which the environment acts on the individual's cognitive structure.

12. The joint action of assimilation and accommodation is known as adaptation. Adaptation is the fundamental goal of information processing, as well as of many other human and biological activities.

13. People seek to establish equilibrium with the environment through adaptation. When a person transforms the environment or is transformed by the environment to promote more effective interchanges between the person and the environment, this is known as equilibration through adaptation.

14. Although historically consumer researchers have viewed consumers as rational, computer-like information-processing machines, in recent years the trend has been to realize that emotions also influence consumption.

15. Consumers generally are just not that involved in the decision for certain products. When involvement is low, information processing is turned off more quickly.

16. Satisfaction with product use constitutes a special category of information processing because it includes the consumer's direct experiential evidence about the product.

17. One major reason marketing managers need to understand consumer behavior is for market segmentation.

REVIEW QUESTIONS

4.1. Describe the major elements of the simplified model of consumer behavior presented at the beginning of the chapter.

4.2. What are the three major sources of social influence, and what are the types of influence classified under each? Give an example of how each could be related to consumer behavior.

4.3. Why are families not treated as simply another role group?

4.4. How does age influence consumer behavior?

4.5. What have been the major changes in the roles of women in recent years?

4.6. Describe the multi-attribute attitude model.

4.7. Why are situational influences important?

4.8. Why are informational influences important?

4.9. Define the following:
a. Schema
b. Assimilation
c. Accommodation
d. Adaptation
e. Organization

4.10. Why have consumer behavior researchers recently developed an interest in emotion?

4.11. How do high-involvement and low-involvement marketing differ?

4.12. What were the key decisions faced in the Canadian segmentation study?

DISCUSSION QUESTIONS AND PROBLEMS

4.13. Try to construct an example of coffee-consumption differences related to each demographic variable.

4.14. The beginning of the chapter indicated that consumer behavior research can help us predict the future. Do you agree? How predictable is the future?

4.15. Develop a list of all of the usage situations for soft-drink consumption. Does your list imply any segmentation strategies?

4.16. At least five attempts to market diet beer failed before Miller Lite promoted its beer as "Less filling, tastes great." Why do you think that campaign succeeded where so many others had failed?

4.17. Describe your lifestyle. Describe the lifestyle of your parents. How do the two differ? What implications do the differences have for your behaviors as consumers?

4.18. What changes do you anticipate in your lifestyle in the next five years? How do you anticipate that those changes will influence your behavior as a consumer?

4.19. Work through the multi-attribute attitude model with an example from your most recent purchase of a musical album.

4.20. Consider the changes in values described in Table 4–2. What product categories do you expect will experience the most change as a result of those value changes?

4.21. How would you try to convince consumers to purchase a $200 automatic bed-making machine? What segments might you consider when defining this market?

PROJECTS

4.22. Interview three people who are substantially different from you on at least two demographic variables (for example, if you are 23 years old and white, interview a person of the opposite sex who is black and over 50). Ask them to describe their most recent major purchase. How did they find out about the product? How did they decide where to buy it? How did they decide which brand to buy? Then ask them if they have recently purchased a product based on their lifestyle, again seeking the same type of information. Finally, ask about the most recent low-involvement purchase made by the person, again probing for the same information.

4.23. Obtain the current issues of *Fortune, Playboy, Cosmopolitan, Ms.,* and *Family Circle.* Compare and contrast how women and men are portrayed in ads in each of the publications. Describe the segments each magazine seems to be reaching. Do you think that the feminist movement over the past two decades has changed how men and women are portrayed in each of these magazines?

4.24. Develop an advertisement that would appeal to someone who values self-fulfillment. Then change the advertisement to appeal to a person who values being well respected.

Endnotes

[1] R. Crain and F. Danzig, "Patience and Perspective," *Advertising Age,* August 20, 1987, 148–160.
[2] L. R. Kahle, "The Nine Nations of North America and the Value Basis of Geographic Segmentation," *Journal of Marketing,* April 1986, 37–48.
[3] C. Dugas, "Marketing's New Look: Campbell Leads a Revo-

lution in the Way Consumer Products Are Sold," *Business Week*, January 26, 1987, 64–68.

[4]Ibid.

[5]R. Deshpande, W. D. Hoyer, and N. Donthu, "The Intensity of Ethnic Affiliation: A Study of the Sociology of Hispanic Consumption," *Journal of Consumer Research*, September 1986, 214–220.

[6]M. J. Schlinger and J. T. Plummer, "Advertising in Black and White," *Journal of Marketing Research*, May 1972, 149–153.

[7]D. E. Sexton, "Black Buyer Behavior," *Journal of Marketing*, October 1972, 36–39.

[8]G. J. Glasser and G. D. Metzger, "Radio Usage by Blacks: An Update," *Journal of Advertising Research*, April 1981, 47–52.

[9]R. J. Fisher, *Social Psychology: An Applied Approach*, St. Martin's Press, 1982.

[10]J. B. Kernan, W. P. Dommermuth, and M. S. Sommers, *Promotion: An Introductory Analysis*, McGraw-Hill, 1970.

[11]M. Haire, "Projective Techniques in Marketing Research," *Journal of Marketing*, April 1950, 649–656.

[12]Fisher, *Social Psychology*.

[13]R. L. Moore and G. P. Moschis, "Role of Mass Media and the Family in Development of Consumption Norms," *Journalism Quarterly*, Spring 1983, 67–73; G. P. Moschis, "The Role of Family Communication in Consumer Socialization of Children and Adolescents," *Journal of Consumer Research*, March 1985, 898–913; S. Ward, "Consumer Socialization," *Journal of Consumer Research*, September 1974, 1–14.

[14]W. Wells and G. Gubar, "Life Cycle in Marketing Research," *Journal of Marketing Research*, November 1966, 335–363; P. Murphy and W. Staples, "A Modernized Family Life Cycle," *Journal of Consumer Research*, June 1979.

[15]P. Filiatrault and J. R. B. Ritchie, "Joint Purchase Situations: A Comparison of Influence Structure in Family and Couple Decision-Making Units," *Journal of Consumer Research*, September 1980, 131–140; C. W. Park, "Joint Decisions in Home Purchasing: A Muddling-Through Process," *Journal of Consumer Research*, September 1982, 151–162; R. L. Spiro, "Persuasion in Family Decision-Making," *Journal of Consumer Research*, March 1983, 393–402.

[16]D. I. Hawkins, R. J. Best, and K. A. Coney, *Consumer Behavior: Implications for Marketing Strategy*, Business Publications, 1983.

[17]R. Dardis and M. Sandler, "Shopping Behavior of Discount Store Customers in a Small City," *Journal of Retailing*, Summer 1971, 60–72.

[18]L. H. Matthews and J. W. Slocum, Jr., "Social Class and Commercial Bank Credit Card Usage," *Journal of Marketing*, January 1969, 71–78; K. V. Prasad, "Socioeconomic Product Risk and Patronage Preferences of Retail Shoppers," *Journal of Marketing*, Vol. 39, July, 42–47; C. M. Schanninger, "Social Class versus Income Revisited: An Empirical Investigation," *Journal of Marketing Research*, May 1981, 192–208.

[19]E.g., R. P. Coleman and L. Rainwater, *Social Standing in America: New Dimensions of Class*, Basic Books, 1978.

[20]J. Mager, "Is the Whole More Than the Sum of the Parts? A Reconsideration of Social Class in Consumer Behavior," Ph.D. diss., University of Oregon, 1986.

[21]D. L. Walsh, "Targeting Teens," *American Demographics*, February 1985, 21–41.

[22]M. C. Linn, T. de Benedictis, and K. Delucchi, "Adolescent Reasoning about Advertisements: Preliminary Findings," *Child Development*, December 1982, 1599–1613.

[23]G. W. Shiele, "How to Reach the Young Consumer," *Harvard Business Review*, March–April 1974, 77–86.

[24]H. Assael, *Consumer Behavior and Marketing Action*, 2nd ed., Kent, 1987.

[25]D. Levinson, C. Darrow, E. Klein, M. Levinson, and B. McKee,

The Seasons of a Man's Life, Ballantine, 1978; L. Tamir, *Men in Their Forties: Transition to Middle Age*, Springer, 1982.

[26]M. Scarf, *Unfinished Business: Pressure Points in the Lives of Women*, Doubleday, 1980.

[27]R. Bartos, "Over 49: The Invisible Market," *Harvard Business Review*, January–February 1980, 140–148.

[28]S. G. Timmer and L. R. Kahle, "Birthright Demographic Correlates of Values," in *Social Values and Social Change: Adaptation to Life in America*, Lynn R. Kahle (ed.), Praeger, 1983.

[29]Z. V. Lambert, "An Investigation of Older Consumers' Unmet Needs and Wants at the Retail Level," *Journal of Retailing*, Winter 1979, 35–57; L. W. Phillips and B. Sternthal, "Age Differences in Information Processing: A Perspective on the Aged Consumer," *Journal of Marketing Research*, November 1977, 444–457.

[30]N. Stephens, "The Effectiveness of Time-Compressed Television Advertisements with Older Adults," *Journal of Advertising*, No. 4, 1982, 48–76.

[31]M. C. Gilly and V. A. Zeithaml, "The Elderly Consumer and Adoption of Technologies," *Journal of Consumer Research*, December 1985, 358–362; D. R. John and C. A. Cole, "Age Differences in Information Processing in Young and Elderly Consumers," *Journal of Consumer Research*, December 1986, 297–315.

[32]R. Bartos, "What Every Marketer Should Know about Women," *Harvard Business Review*, May–June 1978, 73–85.

[33]C. M. Schaninger and C. T. Allen, "Wife's Occupational Status as a Consumer Behavior Construct," *Journal of Consumer Research*, September 1981, 189–196.

[34]L. R. Kahle, R. A. Kulka, and D. M. Klingel, "Low Adolescent Self Esteem Leads to Multiple Interpersonal Problems: A Test of Social Adaptation Theory," *Journal of Personality and Social Psychology*, Vol. 39, September 1980, 496–502.

[35]D. C. Eisert and L. R. Kahle, "Self-evaluation and Social Comparison of Physical and Role Change during Adolescence: A Longitudinal Analysis," *Child Development*, Vol. 53, Winter 1982, 98–104.

[36]S. J. Levy, "Symbols for Sales," *Harvard Business Review*, 1959, 117–124; M. J. Sirgy, "Self-concept in Consumer Behavior: A Critical Review," *Journal of Consumer Research*, December 1982, 287–300.

[37]E. L. Grugg and H. L. Grathwohl, "Consumer Self-concept, Symbolism, and Market Behavior: A Theoretical Approach," *Journal of Marketing*, October 1967, 22–27; I. J. Dolich, "Congruence Relationships between Self Images and Product Brands," *Journal of Marketing*, February 1969, 80–84; E. L. Landon, Jr., "Self Concept, Ideal Self Concept, and Consumer Purchase Intentions," *Journal of Consumer Research*, September 1974, 44–51.

[38]Mental representations or beliefs.

[39]L. R. Kahle and P. M. Homer, "Physical Attractiveness of the Celebrity Endorser: A Social Adaptation Perspective," *Journal of Consumer Research*, March 1985, 964–971.

[40]L. R. Kahle, *Attitudes and Social Adaptation: A Person-Situation Interaction Approach*, Pergamon, 1984.

[41]M. J. Ryan and E. H. Bonfield, "Fishbein's Intentions Model and Consumer Behavior," *Journal of Marketing*, Spring 1980, 82–95.

[42]M. Fishbein and A. Ajzen, *Belief, Attitude, Intention, and Behavior*, Addison-Wesley, 1975.

[43]See, for example, P. R. Warshaw, "A New Method for Predicting Behavioral Intentions: An Alternative to Fishbein," *Journal of Marketing Research*, May 1980, 153–172; R. Burnkrant and T. J. Page, Jr., "An Examination of the Convergent, Discriminant, and Predictive Validity of Fishbein's Predictive Validity," *Journal of Marketing Research*, November 1982, 550–561;

M. J. Ryan, "Behavioral Intentions Formation: The Interdependency of Attitudinal and Social Influence," *Journal of Consumer Research*, December 1982, 263–278; L. R. Kahle and S. E. Beatty, "The Task Situation and Habit in the Attitude-Behavior Relationship: A Social Adaptation View," *Journal of Social Behavior and Personality*, 1987, 219–232; L. R. Kahle, "The Relationships among Consumer Attitudes, Self-Concept, and Behaviors: A Social Adaptation Approach," in *Advertising and Consumer Psychology*, J. Olson and K. Sentis (eds.), Vol. 3, Praeger, 121–131.

[44]T. A. Shimp and A. Kavas, "The Theory of Reasoned Action Applied to Coupon Usage," *Journal of Consumer Research*, December 1984, 795–809.

[45]L. R. Kahle and J. J. Berman, "Attitudes Cause Behavior: A Cross-lagged Panel Analysis," *Journal of Personality and Social Psychology*, 1979, 315–321.

[46]J. Wittenbraker, B. L. Gibbs, and L. R. Kahle, "Seat Belt Attitudes, Habits, and Behaviors: An Adaptive Amendment to the Fishbein Model," *Journal of Applied Social Psychology*, 1983, 406–421.

[47]L. R. Kahle, D. M. Klingel, and R. A. Kulka, "A Longitudinal Study of Adolescent Attitude-Behavior Consistency," *Public Opinion Quarterly*, Vol. 45, Fall, 402–414, 1981.

[48]W. D. Wells, "Psychographics: A Critical Review," *Journal of Marketing Research*, May 1975, 196–213.

[49]M. Rokeach, *The Nature of Human Values*, Free Press, 1973, 5.

[50]L. R. Kahle, "Social Values in the Eighties: A Special Issue," *Psychology and Marketing*, Vol. 2, Winter 1985, 231–237.

[51]S. E. Beatty, L. R. Kahle, P. M. Homer, and S. Misra, "Alternative Measurement Approaches to Consumer Values: The List of Values and the Rokeach Value Survey," *Psychology and Marketing*, Fall 1985, 181–200; L. R. Kahle, S. E. Beatty, and P. M. Homer, "Alternative Measurement Approaches to Consumer Values: The List of Values (LOV) and Values and Lifestyle Segmentation (VALS)," *Journal of Consumer Research*, December 1986, 405–409.

[52]L. R. Kahle and S. G. Timmer, "A Theory and a Method for Studying Values," in *Social Values and Social Change: Adaptation to Life in America*, L. R. Kahle (ed.), Praeger, 1983.

[53]L. R. Kahle, "The Values of Americans: Implications for Consumer Adaptation," in *Personal Values and Consumer Psychology*, R. E. Pitts, Jr. and A. G. Woodside (eds.), Lexington Books, 1984; L. R. Kahle, B. Poulos, and A. Sukhdial, "Changes in Social Values in the United States during the Past Decade," *Journal of Advertising Research*, March 1988, 35–41.

[54]H. H. Kassarjian, "Personality and Consumer Behavior: A Review," *Journal of Marketing Research*, November 1971, 409–419.

[55]R. J. Lutz and P. Kakkar, "Situational Influences in Interpersonal Persuasion," in *Advances in Consumer Research*, Vol. 3, B. B. Anderson (ed.), Association for Consumer Research, 1976, 370–378; K. E. Miller and J. L. Ginter, "An Investigation of Situational Variation in Brand Choice Behavior and Attitude," *Journal of Marketing Research*, February 1979, 111–123; P. R. Dickson, "Person-Situation: Segmentation's Missing Link," *Journal of Marketing*, Fall 1982, 56–64; L. R. Kahle and S. E. Beatty, "The Task Situation."

[56]R. W. Belk, "Situational Variables and Consumer Behavior," *Journal of Consumer Research*, December 1975, 157–164.

[57]L. Skenazy, "Heeding the Call," *Advertising Age*, August 20, 1987, 38.

[58]Two of the better books are J. R. Bettman, *An Information Processing Theory of Consumer Choice*, Addison-Wesley, 1979, and M. J. Sirgy, *Social Cognition and Consumer Behavior*, Praeger, 1983.

[59]The discussion here draws from Kahle, *Attitudes and Social Adaptation*. The interested reader may want to consult J. Pi-

aget, "Piaget's Theory," in *Piaget and His School*, B. Inhelder and H. H. Chipman (eds.), Springer-Verlag, 1976.

[60]E.g., G. C. Kiel and R. A. Layton, "Dimensions of Consumer Information Seeking Behavior," *Journal of Marketing Research*, May 1981, 233–239.

[61]C. P. Duncan and R. W. Olshavsky, "External Search: The Role of Consumer Beliefs," *Journal of Marketing Research*, February 1982, 32–43.

[62]W. L. Moore and D. R. Lehmann, "Individual Differences in Search Behavior for a Nondurable," *Journal of Consumer Research*, December 1980, 296–307.

[63]J. R. Bettman, "Memory Factors in Consumer Behavior: A Review," *Journal of Marketing*, Spring 1979, 37–53; J. G. Lynch, Jr. and T. K. Srull, "Memory and Attentional Factors in Consumer Choice: Concepts and Research Methods," *Journal of Consumer Research*, June 1982, 18–37.

[64]Cf. B. Loken and R. Hoverstad, "Relationship between Information Recall and Subsequent Attitudes: Some Exploratory Findings," *Journal of Consumer Research*, September 1985, 155–168.

[65]J. Jacoby and W. D. Hoyer, "Viewer Miscomprehension of Televised Communication: Selected Findings," *Journal of Marketing*, Fall 1982, 12–26.

[66]Kahle and Homer, "Physical Attractiveness."

[67]D. A. Aaker, D. M. Stayman, and M. R. Hagerty, "Warmth in Advertising: Measurement, Impact, and Sequence Effects," *Journal of Consumer Research*, March 1986, 365–380; E. C. Hirschman and M. B. Holbrook, "Hedonic Consumption: Emerging Concepts, Methods, and Propositions," *Journal of Marketing*, Summer 1982, 92–101; R. B. Zajonc, "Feeling and Thinking: Preferences Need No Inferences," *American Psychologist*, February 1978, 151–175; R. B. Zajonc, "On the Primacy of Affect," *American Psychologist*, January 1984, 117–123.

[68]H. H. Kassarjian and W. M. Kassarjian, "Attitudes under Low Commitment Conditions," in *Attitude Research Plays for High Stakes*, J. C. Maloney and B. Silverman (eds.), American Marketing Association, 1979; J. L. Zaichkowsky, "Measuring the Involvement Construct," *Journal of Consumer Research*, September 1985, 341–352.

[69]H. E. Krugman, "The Impact of Television Advertising: Learning without Involvement," *Public Opinion Quarterly*, Fall 1965, 349–356.

[70]G. J. Gorn, "The Effects of Music in Advertising on Choice Behavior: A Classical Conditioning Approach," *Journal of Marketing*, Winter 1982, 94–101; R. E. Petty, J. T. Cacioppo, and D. Schumann, "Central and Peripheral Routes to Advertising Effectiveness: The Moderating Role of Involvement," *Journal of Consumer Research*, September 1983, 135–146.

[71]Assael, *Consumer Behavior*.

[72]W. O. Bearden and J. E. Teel, "Selected Determinants of Consumer Satisfaction and Complaint Reports," *Journal of Marketing Research*, February 1983, 21–28; M. C. Gilly and B. D. Gelb, "Post-Purchase Consumer Processes and the Complaining Consumer," *Journal of Consumer Research*, December 1982, 323–328; R. L. Oliver, "A Cognitive Model of the Antecedents and Consequences of Satisfaction Decisions," *Journal of Marketing Research*, November 1980, 460–469.

[73]M. L. Richins, "Negative Word-of-Mouth by Dissatisfied Consumers: A Pilot Study," *Journal of Marketing*, Winter 1983, 68–78.

[74]Y. Wind, "Issues and Advances in Segmentation Research," *Journal of Marketing Research*, August 1978, 317–337.

[75]S. Young, L. Ott, and B. Feigin, "Some Practical Considerations in Market Segmentation," *Journal of Marketing Research*, August 1978, 405–412.

ORGANIZATIONAL BUYING BEHAVIOR

Consumer buying behavior and organizational buying behavior are quite similar. What we know about consumer behavior is generally also relevant to organizational behavior, but in some cases we may need to bolster the consumer behavior knowledge with information that may be somewhat more common to organizations. The study of this process is known as ***organizational buying behavior***, which may be defined as

> the decision-making process by which formal organizations establish the need for purchasing products and services, and identify, evaluate, and choose among alternative brands and suppliers.[1]

Figure 5–1 illustrates the context in which organizational purchases are made and the steps involved in making purchase decisions. After the question of the degree of similarity of organizational buying to consumer buying behavior is considered, the bulk of the chapter is devoted to a discussion of the factors shown in Figure 5–1. At the end of the chapter we consider the effects of these factors on the management of marketing to organizational buying.

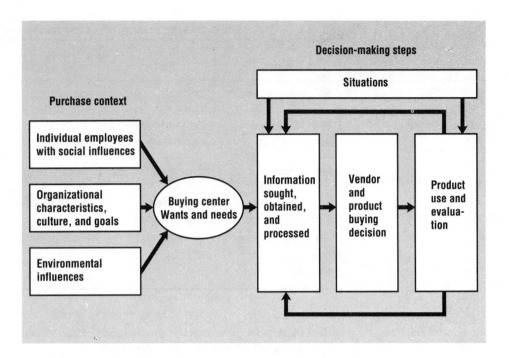

FIGURE 5-1
Simplified model of organizational
buying behavior.

ARE ORGANIZATIONAL PURCHASES UNIQUE?

Although traditionally organizational buying behavior has been considered unique,[2] some people believe organizational buying behavior bears such a similarity to consumer behavior that the distinction is more distracting than enlightening.[3] Certainly, every defining characteristic of industrial buying has a parallel in consumer buying, and the importance of similarities between industrial buying and consumer buying may be more notable than the differences. Table 5–1 presents some commonly held differences between industrial and consumer markets, but all of these dimensions have been disputed as being fundamental to only one type of market.

The key to understanding all of these dimensions is to recognize that none of them are *unique* to organizational buying, but that they may be *more common* in organizational buying, especially in their extreme forms. Consider the following four examples:

1. *Not all consumer demand is primary, nor all industrial demand derived.* Primary demand is demand for a product or service as an end use in and of itself, whereas derived demand is demand for a product or service to help produce some other product or service. Consumers buy sugar to make cookies (derived demand). Likewise, organizations buy light bulbs and typewriters (more primary than derived). But organizations do have a tendency to focus more on derived demand than do consumers.

Table 5–1 Presumed Differences between Industrial and Consumer Markets[4]

Market	Product	Organization of Operation Setup	Other
Derived versus primary demand	Technical complexity	Channel length	Message appeal
Demand elasticity	Purchase frequency	Promotion mix	Delivery importance
Demand fluctuation	Classification	Reciprocity	Sales force compensation
Number of buyers	Amount of information search	Degree of integration	Sales force training
Number of suppliers	Service needs	Supply adequacy	Leasing
Number of influencers	Negotiated prices		Make-or-buy decisions
Geographic concentration	Dollar volume		Instability of markets
Knowledgeability	Riskiness		
Rationality			

2. *Organizations, in contrast to consumers, tend to buy products that are more technologically complex, but counterexamples readily come to mind* (industrial steel versus a consumer car, switches and wiring versus a home television set).
3. *Negotiated prices are more common in organizational buying, but certainly some consumer purchases are negotiated* (cars, homes), *and many organizational purchases are not* (office supplies, utilities).
4. *Groups of people are often involved in organizational purchase decisions, yet for some small items this may not be the case.* And consumers sometimes make group decisions, for example, as families.

Consider the factor of ***rationality***. Most theory of organizational buying implies that organizational buying is always rational. Often it is. For example, loyalty may be an example of irrational behavior, yet some studies have shown that loyalty is most often driven by rational considerations. Certainly, economic considerations are rational. Wind[5] found that loyalty occurs when the dollar value of a transaction is small, past cost savings from a particular vendor are high, the favored vendor has a stable or declining price, and a specific brand is recommended by a vendor. All of these factors make economic sense. Other research, however, has shown that rationality is not the only driving force in organizational buying loyalty. Reluctance to change, desire for the familiar, persistence, and reciprocity have all been cited as irrational motives for organizations' buyer loyalty.[6] One study estimated that only about 30 percent of managers rely on a rational decision style.[7] Given that many consumer purchase decisions are rational, then, clearly rationality does not always distinguish between organizational buying behavior and consumer behavior.

Or consider the importance of personal selling. Many selling situations require entry into complex organizational contexts. In many senses, organizational buying behavior is to personal selling what consumer buying behavior is to advertising. Organizations often buy products after learning about them from salespeople, just as consumers often buy products after learning about them from ads. Marketing managers therefore need to understand how organizations decide what to buy, just as advertisers need to understand consumer decision processes. But one can identify situations in which consumers buy from personal selling (Avon) or organizations buy from retail outlets (The Computer Store).

In general, there is greater instability in industrial than in consumer markets. The variability of sales and profits of manufacturers selling to other manufacturers or industrial service companies is greater than that of manufacturers of consumer products. This is a result of two factors: (1) for *nondurable producer goods*, the effects of accumulation and depletion swings that the customer uses to balance inventories in response to fluctuations in forecast and actual sales; and (2) for *durable producer goods*, acceleration principle effects, whose workings are illustrated in Exhibit 5–1. Still, variation in sales and profit levels is no stranger to consumer goods manufacturers—the difference is one of degree rather than of kind.

At the most extreme cases, differences between organizations and consumers are observable. When a consumer buys a source of power (e.g., a flashlight battery) versus when an organization buys a source of power (e.g., a utility company buying a coal-driven generator), the organization will tend to focus

EXHIBIT **5-1**

The Acceleration Principle—A Cause of Greater Instability in the Industrial Goods Than in the Consumer Goods Market

The acceleration principle is a theoretical explanation of how small increases or decreases in consumer demand can result in large increases or decreases in the industrial durable products used to produce the consumer goods experiencing the shift in demand.

As an illustration of this principle, consider the following (simplified) example of the markets for wine and for the vats used to make it. Assume the following:

1. Vats with a capacity of 1,000 gallons each are used in winemaking in the United States.
2. Each vat lasts, on average, 10 years.
3. Demand for domestic wine in the United States is stable and requires 1 million vats to produce each year.
4. Since the market is stable, the demand for vats is only for replacement. Since vats last 10 years, on average, one-tenth of the vats have to be replaced each year, resulting in an annual market for one-tenth of a million vats, or 100,000 vats per year.

Now, assume that the market for domestic wine in the United States goes up by 10 percent this year. Grapes that would otherwise have been sold for raisins will now be used for wine. To produce the extra wine the number of vats has to be increased by one-tenth, or 100,000 vats. This will result in the market for vats this year becoming

Vats for replacement	100,000
+ Vats for increase in wine demanded	100,000
	200,000

Thus, a 10 percent increase in the demand for the consumer good (wine) will have resulted in a 100 percent increase in the demand for the industrial good (vats).

(A decline of 10 percent in the demand for wine would eliminate the need to replace any of the worn-out vats, and thus cause a 100 percent decline in the demand for vats.)

The real world is never quite as neat and as orderly as the contrived examples used to illustrate it. For example, if we extend our wine example out another year, estimating the market for vats becomes complicated by the fact that 100,000 "extra" new vats were put into service the year before.

However, despite the fact that the application becomes more complex, there can be no doubt that the acceleration principle works, and that it works essentially in the way shown in the example.

more on derived demand, technological complexity, price negotiation, competitive bidding, and group decision making. The same argument could be made for all of the other categories in the table. Many mid-range decisions overlap between consumers and organizations, but extreme cases usually differentiate the two. All of the differences are tendencies rather than laws, are continuums rather than fixed points.

But perhaps the single most important lesson to learn from a comparison of organizational buying versus consumer buying is that in both cases the marketing concept applies. In both cases it is crucial to listen to the customer, to determine what the customer wants and needs, and to develop marketing plans around the customer. Unsatisfied customers detract from the success of both. Adjustments and forms of applications may vary from one situation to the next, but the overriding concern for the customer must always be present. As Peters and Waterman state it,

> A simple summary of what our research uncovered on the customer attribute is this: the excellent companies really are close to their customers. That's it. The other companies talk about it; the excellent companies do it.[8]

CAUSES OF ORGANIZATIONAL PURCHASE DECISIONS

Webster and Wind[9] have identified four classes of causes or influences on organizational decision making: individual factors, organizational factors, environmental factors, and interpersonal or social factors. These factors are quite similar to the factors that influence consumer behavior, discussed in Chapter 4.

Figure 5–1 illustrates one way of conceptualizing the relationship among these factors within a framework that is similar for organizational buying behavior to that presented in Chapter 4 for consumer buying behavior. The *purchase context* includes individual influences (as in Figure 4–1), but it also includes organizational effects and environmental factors that coalesce into the social context of the buying center. Interpersonal interactions within the buying center establish organizational wants and needs, which in turn activate the decision-making steps on the right side of the graphic. The right side of the graphic is quite similar to the right side of Figure 4–1, except that vendor selection requires explicit mention and the buying center is the decision-making entity rather than the single individual considered in Figure 4–1. The next few sections of this chapter describe the purchase context and the decision-making steps, the left and right sides of Figure 5–1, respectively.

PURCHASE CONTEXT

Individual Employees with Social Influences

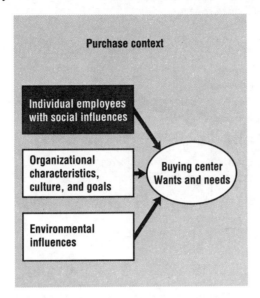

All purchase decisions and, indeed, all human behaviors eventually reduce to the behavior of individuals. In an organization, individuals are called employees (or perhaps volunteers). The steps used to characterize consumer decision making described in Chapter 4 on consumer behavior also provide the building blocks of organizational buying behavior because employees are also consumers, and both employees and consumers are human beings. Just as consumers have societal, demographic, and personality influences, likewise employees also have these social influences. The individuals who come together to make organizational decisions all bring with them societal influences such as the geography of where they live, the government under which they live, the history of their lives, and their culture. They likewise bring together each individual's demographic influences of peer and social roles, family roles, occupation, education, income, age, and sex. Finally, the personality of individuals as dictated by such influences as experiences, self-esteem, lifestyle, attitudes, and values of individuals will impinge on their organizational activities.

Any analysis of purchasing activity must begin with understanding the individual players. All of the analysis and conceptualization in the world does not detract from the fact that buyers and sellers are people dealing with one another. If "bad chemistry" characterizes the relationship between buyers and sellers, one can safely predict suboptimal exchange.

Organizational Characteristics, Culture, and Goals

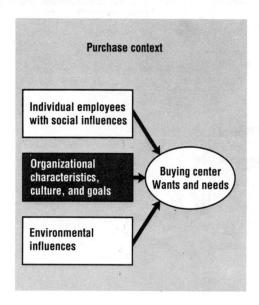

Characteristics: Every organization consists of unique individuals and therefore is a unique organization. Depending on the nature of the organization, its purchasing priorities will differ. Consider the different classes of (1) industry, (2) wholesalers and retailers, and (3) government and other institutions. Industrial purchasers constitute one large class of organizational consumers. Wholesalers and retailers of course purchase products as organizations. Government and other institutions also warrant consideration.

Industrial purchasers seek to acquire goods and services in order to produce other goods and services. They need to purchase raw materials, such as steel to make cars, as well as all of the support materials necessary to run a business, such as audit services or paper clips. The goal of all purchases is to facilitate earning more money.

Wholesalers and retailers purchase materials in order to operate channels of distribution. They resell products. They need to purchase the products, such as manufactured cars, as well as all of the support materials to run a business. They tend to make decisions in much the same way as industrial buyers, also seeking to operate at a profit.

Governments and other institutions, such as nonprofit organizations, also purchase billions of dollars worth of goods and services each year.[10] One estimate is that these purchases constitute 20 percent of the gross national product.[11] The state, federal, and local governments all have a number of needs, as do institutions such as hospitals and private schools. The General Services Administration helps standardize many federal government purchase decisions for nonmilitary needs, but no one agency is responsible for all purchases, even within the federal nonmilitary sector. The Defense Supply Agency regulates most military supply procurement, but each branch of the military also purchases a number of its own supplies. Each state, local, and institutional customer has its own procedure, and the successful marketer will have to learn about each situation.

Government purchases generally receive more public scrutiny than private purchases; hence, the rules and procedures tend to be somewhat more complicated than for other organizational purchases. Paperwork can be complex, and many purchase decisions are made based on various social goals—such as supporting small businesses, depressed areas, and minorities—rather than simply price. Most buyers view the government as a difficult customer, citing as common difficulties excessive paperwork, bureaucracy, too many regulations, too many delays, and too many policy revisions.[12] Yet many agencies actively seek to help interested vendors. The Small Business Administration, General Accounting Office, and Government Printing Office all help describe how to fathom the depth of bureaucracy. For example, the Small Business Administration publishes *U.S. Purchasing, Specifications, and Sales Directory*, which explains how to make and sell to the government, in hopes of promoting competition for government contracts. Many requests for bids, contracts, and proposals can be found in *Commerce Business Daily*.

Different organizations have different characteristics that drive organizational purchasing. Without an adequate understanding of the sources and nature of organizational characteristics, it will be difficult to fathom the purchasing behavior.

Culture: Corporate culture is described in more detail in other sections of this book. At this point, it is necessary to mention only that corporate culture influences buying behavior as much as other activities. Different organizations have styles that dictate different directions. The organization will seek to emulate the ideals of the founder and the norms and traditions of behavior prevalent in the company.

Goals: Above all else, the specific goals of a company will drive purchase decisions. If a corporation seeks to build the best computer for businesses, its purchases will differ from a company that wants to produce a low-cost tire. What business an organization is in and how it wants to operate will nearly always be evident in purchasing activities because purchase activities must be coordinated with the overall organizational goals.

Environmental Influences

If the economy is weak or strong, organizational purchasers know it. If the government of a particular country is about to collapse, one would hope that organizational purchasers know it. Any facts that are important as a source of influence on organizational activity ought to be known and considered in the context of organizational buying behavior. Organizational buyers must understand current events as well as possible.

McKenna has developed a theory of the infrastructure and how it relates to organizational marketing.[13] In his theory, which has found the most propo-

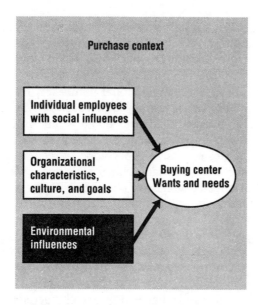

Purchase context

Individual employees with social influences

Organizational characteristics, culture, and goals

Environmental influences

Buying center
Wants and needs

nents in high-technology industries, all of the elements of the marketing infrastructure warrant attention.

Figure 5–2 gives an example of the infrastructure in the personal computer industry. In essence, the *infrastructure* is

> everyone who can influence perceptions of a product, including the financial community, industry watchers and luminaries, the press, and the distribution channels members.

Marketing relationships with infrastructure members are essential to product and market development in dynamic marketing environments of rapid change. It is important to form strategic relationships with members of the infrastructure in order to promote word-of-mouth reports about perceptions of the prod-

FIGURE 5-2
The infrastructure development of the personal computer industry.

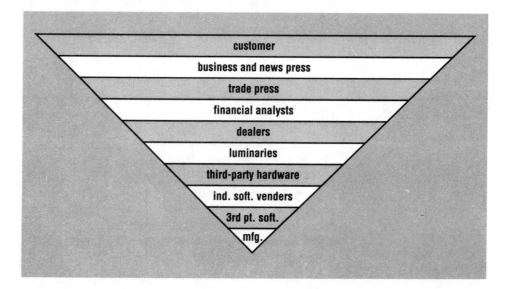

customer
business and news press
trade press
financial analysts
dealers
luminaries
third-party hardware
ind. soft. venders
3rd pt. soft.
mfg.

uct. Marketers should make certain that the press and the financial community understand the virtues of a product. A breakdown anywhere in the infrastructure can hurt marketing efforts. Organizational purchasers know what the infrastructure members think about many potential purchases, directing attention to this aspect of the environment. This theory has been referred to as the "cocktail party theory of marketing" because it implies that cocktail party chatter often directs important decisions.

THE BUYING CENTER

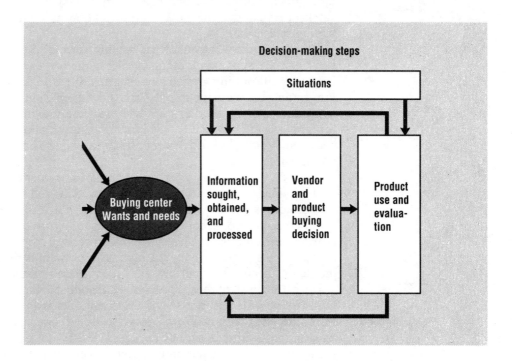

One important concept in organizational buying behavior is that of the buying center.[14] The **buying center** is

> all of those individuals who share in the purchase decision-making process, including the goals and risks of that purchase.

Different people may play different organizational roles, such as user, influencer, gatekeeper, decision maker, and buyer. Although analogous roles exist in families, these roles tend to be more complex in organizations and tend to provide for longer, more detailed dramas than typically occur in families. Often role assignment is more official and formal in organizations, especially for more complex purchases.[15] Often a variety of types of information sources, ranging from scientific to word-of-mouth, will influence activity in the buying center.[16]

Consider how each role might interact in the decision to purchase a new minicomputer for accounting: *Users* would be the accounting department staff who would actually work with the new computer once it is purchased. Their input will of course influence any ultimate decision.

Influencers may provide critical information in spite of having no direct participation in the decision process. Engineers or computing specialists may know much about computers and share that knowledge before any final decision is reached. The views of those people often are received with respect and appreciation.

Gatekeepers control the flow of information within an organization. Perhaps a certain secretary or assistant controls who talks to a key decider. A salesperson who offends or intrigues a gatekeeper may discover quite a different level of influence from competitors. Sellers rarely know before approaching a sales task which people in a particular company will guide decisions. Sometimes gatekeepers control the flow of information as a strategy for advocacy of a particular decision.[17]

Decision makers formulate the actual choice of the computer. For an expensive piece of capital equipment, probably the top executives in the firm will at least sign off. But in a dozen similar firms, the true decider may vary from one firm to another. Perhaps in one firm the vice-president for finance will decide, in another the engineering staff will exert the maximum influence, in another firm the accountants will decide by consensus, in another a top accountant will decide autocratically, and in yet another the purchasing department will control the decision.

Buyers are purchasing agents or purchasing professionals who have specialized knowledge about procurement. Often they will specialize in dealings with certain companies or with certain types of purchases. They may know little about computers or accounting, but they will work to ensure that routine precautions are followed sufficiently to avoid serious mistakes as much as possible. As purchasing professionals, the purchase for them is the focus, rather than the product or need. Their performance is evaluated based on the purchase.

The actors in all of these roles will contribute to the eventual purchase drama. Each person will help define the organizational wants and needs according to his or her role, and each will play the role-related part during the decision-making steps. Often many of the characteristics of political environments and coalition formation will manifest themselves in the buying center.[18] Of course, in any given organization each of these roles may differ somewhat, and even within an organization the roles may vary from one purchase decision to the next.[19]

DECISION-MAKING STEPS

Situations

To understand how organizational purchasing operates, it is necessary to consider the situational dimension of *buy classes*,[20] of which there are three.

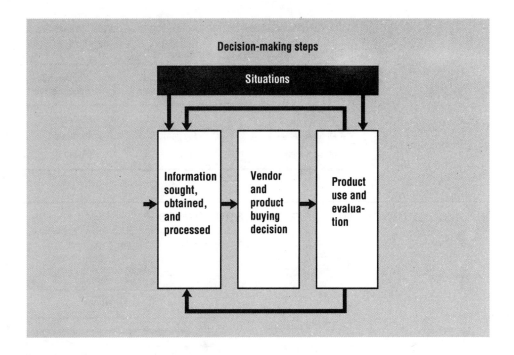

Decision-making steps

Situations

| Information sought, obtained, and processed | Vendor and product buying decision | Product use and evaluation |

1. The ***new task purchase*** invokes problem solving related to a need that has not arisen before. Perhaps the company has decided to market a new product line and needs the supplies to develop it. Perhaps the company wants new employee safety equipment. Because the problem is new and experience cannot help make the decision, a great deal of information is needed. Alternatives will be considered in depth. This stage is especially important because it sets the pattern for future purchases. It also provides the greatest marketing opportunity.

2. The ***straight rebuy*** fills a recurring requirement. Perhaps the company has run out of computer paper. Perhaps the supply of raw materials used for manufacturing has run low. The decision is usually handled by the purchasing department. A list of acceptable suppliers provides the only source of potential vendors. Because buyers have much experience with this common type of purchase, they need little new information. Minor variations in the purchase agreement will not disrupt a straight-rebuy situation, as long as they do not stimulate the purchasing agents to look for a new supplier.

3. The ***modified rebuy*** is one in which alternatives are known but the situation has changed. It may develop from either of the two other types of buy classes. Management wants to reevaluate its purchasing pattern, to gather more information before making a final decision. Perhaps cost savings are necessary. Perhaps a threatened strike raises questions about supplier reliability. Marketers who are not currently suppliers want to convert straight rebuys into modified rebuys.

The main attributes of each of the buy classes are described in Table 5–2.

Table 5–2 Crucial Buy Class Attributes[21]

Type of Buying Situation (Buy Class)	Newness of the Problem	Information Requirements	Consideration of New Alternatives
New task	High	Maximum	Important
Modified rebuy	Medium	Moderate	Low
Straight rebuy	Low	Minimal	None

Information Sought, Obtained, and Processed

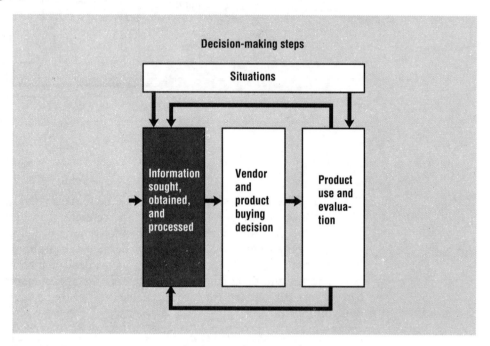

In addition to buy classes, one must also consider **buy phases**. Each organizational purchase goes through eight phases in the procurement process. The nature of the buy phases will depend on the buy class. Thus, a **buy grid** has been developed to describe the 24 combinations of buy classes with buy phases, as described in Table 5–3. This buy grid has been difficult to study because members of buying centers are usually reluctant to discuss their decision processes with outsiders. An independent study of 750 senior sales managers from large companies, however, has shown that the model is essentially valid.[22]

Each of these stages is sufficiently important to discuss in more detail.

1. *Anticipation or recognition of a problem (need) and a general solution.* The anticipation or recognition of a need or problem triggers the purchasing process. The subparts of this phase include recognizing that a problem exists and that a purchase may be the solution to the problem. For a straight rebuy the shelf space may look empty or the inventory computer may flag an impending

Table 5-3   The Buy Grid Framework for Organizational Buying Situations[23]

Buy Phases (Stages)	Buy Classes		
	New Task	Modified Rebuy	Straight Rebuy
1. Anticipation or recognition of a problem (need) and a general solution			
2. Determination of characteristics and quantity of needed item			
3. Description of characteristics and quantity of needed item			
4. Search for and qualification of potential sources			
5. Acquisition and analysis of proposals			
6. Evaluation of proposals and selection of supplier(s)			
7. Selection of an order routine			
8. Performance feedback and evaluation			

shortage. For a new task purchase a change in corporate direction or a breakdown may lead to the recognition of a problem.

2. *Determination of characteristics and quantity of needed item.* Generally, the using group will have the major influence on this phase of the process. The major task here is to define how the problem will be solved by narrowing down the options. In a straight-rebuy situation, this task will be simple. In a new task, engineers and high-level executives may participate in the problem analysis.

3. *Description of characteristics and quantity of needed item.* In this phase, attributes are specified in a manner that can be communicated to all interested parties.[24] Initially this phase extends phase 2, but as it proceeds, it becomes ever more detailed. If possible, marketers should try to become involved at this phase. For some complex products, the specification phase may limit participation. Indeed, some accusations of corruption in government purchasing have resulted from setting specifications that only a crony's company could meet.

4. *Search for and qualification of potential sources.* In simple cases, this phase may merely involve consulting a list. In other cases, the search for suppliers may be long, tedious, and complex. At this point, potential suppliers are identified and the list of players reduced to a few in most cases. Capacity to deliver the product punctually and reputation for quality may influence thinking at this phase. Typically this process of first narrowing down choices of vendors and, later, selecting a vendor receives more attention in organizational purchases than in individual consumer purchases. Because most buyers and sellers interact with one another over a long period of time,[25] social communication can influence this stage significantly.

Recently some companies have oriented themselves toward using fewer vendors with more cooperative and intense relationships. These relationships are known as "just-in-time" relationships because they require delivery of exactly the correct number of units at exactly the correct time.[26] Companies such as Boeing, Harley-Davidson, Hewlett-Packard, and Xerox have used this method, although the auto industry is where these relationships are best known. Typically the companies share design and planning information, link computers, and strive to minimize waste and warehousing through very efficient ordering processes.

EXHIBIT **5-2**

"Just-in-Time" Vendor Exchanges in the U.S. Automobile Industry

Traditionally the U.S. automobile manufacturers have kept their suppliers on edge by demanding the best price and, more recently, the best quality on short notice. Most contracts have been one-year and multiple-sourced. Tough competition from foreign auto makers has forced Detroit companies to reconsider, however.

Today the norm is for auto makers to announce their desires to suppliers as soon as possible—sometimes several years in advance. Then the automobile companies work with suppliers to develop the most efficient supplies and supply network possible, usually for only one supplier. Suppliers actually contribute to the engineering of the overall vehicle in such a way as to optimize quality and minimize price. The selected supplier receives a long-term contract, often for five or more years, that allows security and efficiency to prevail. Modern warehousing and computer-driven ordering allow "just-in-time" exchanges that benefit both the supplier and the auto maker.[27] The overall result benefits supplier, auto company, and consumer with a less costly and more efficient production process.

5. *Acquisition and analysis of proposals.* In straight rebuys, often phases 4 and 5 are indistinguishable, but as a process becomes more complex, the importance of phase 5 becomes more obvious. Sometimes a mere telephone call may measure costs, but at other times the bidding process may involve counterproposals and detailed negotiations lasting for months.

Vendor and Product Buying Decision

The previous process leads to the position where the actual buying decisions are formulated.

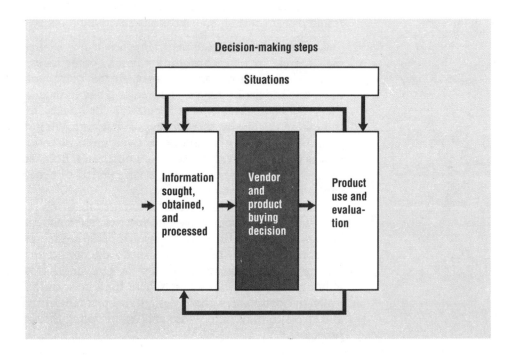

6. *Evaluation of proposals and selection of supplier(s).* During this phase, additional negotiation may occur. Three factors tend to dominate the vendor side of the decision: price, supplier reputation, and service.[28] The process of selecting products, on the other hand, emphasizes quality and performance.[29] Finally, the buying organization decides how to proceed. Even after the selection, additional negotiation may occur.

7. *Selection of an order routine.* Once a product has been purchased, it still must be delivered and installed satisfactorily. Until then, the initial problem has not been solved. This phase is more than simply postpurchase trivia because it provides evidence that will influence future rebuys.

Product Use and Evaluation

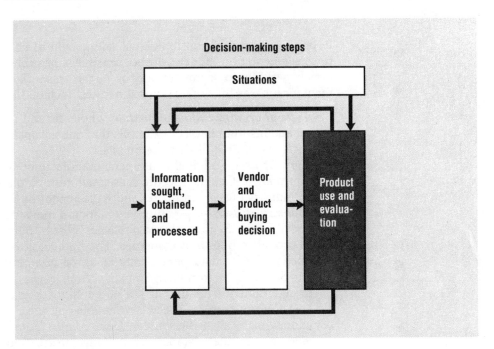

Finally the product is in place. The marketing effort and the purchasing effort both continue, however, due to the potential for future business transactions between the two parties.

8. *Performance feedback and evaluation.* Whether formally or informally, users will notice and comment on product quality and general satisfaction with the purchase. This phase is also important for determining how the next rebuy will proceed. Just as consumer satisfaction and postpurchase evaluation are important in consumer behavior, performance evaluation also guides organizational activities.

Marketing strategy will vary depending on where in the buy grid the particular purchase process stands. Marketers who want to sell in a new-task buy class need to understand and anticipate the problems of the buying company.

Some sales will be made (e.g., in military and high-technology markets) based on a company's reputation for innovativeness and problem-solving capacity. For straight rebuys, current suppliers want to reinforce the routine rebuy and to increase market share. Potential suppliers, as much as possible, want to transform the situation into a modified rebuy. In a modified rebuy, current suppliers again seek to increase market share, although the posture may now be more defensive. They want to transform the modified rebuy into a straight rebuy. Potential suppliers want to establish their viability as suppliers during modified rebuys.[30]

ORGANIZATIONAL SEGMENTATION

In one sense, sending an individual salesperson to an individual client constitutes segmentation. But in another sense it is possible to divide the organizational market into segments, just as in the consumer market. Common segmentation bases for organizational markets include the following:

- *Type of organization*—industrial, wholesale and retail, and governmental and institutional. For example, du Pont sells paints and Rockwell sells tools to all three of these segments.
- *Type of user*—original-equipment manufacturer (OEM), end user, and aftermarket. General Electric sells small motors to appliance makers and to industrial users, and parts and replacement in the aftermarket.
- *Industry of user*—segmenting by Standard Industrial Classification (SIC) codes. The U.S. government publishes a list of numerical codes assigned to product groups and industries. The Bureau of the Census collects and publishes sales data periodically by these groupings down to the state and Standard Metropolitan Statistical Area levels. These data can be used to determine the relative size of potential markets by using industries by area. Information on specific companies by area can be obtained from commercially available sources. *Dun's Market Identifiers*, for example, provides a computer database containing information on up to 3 million U.S. and Canadian companies classified by SIC code of major product or service.
- *Common buying factors*—quality, price, performance, delivery, and service. Most industrial sales turn on one or more of these attributes of the offering, and therefore it may be desirable to segment on one or more of them. An example is a semiconductor manufacturer that sells high-quality, high-price, high-mean-time-to-failure transistors and diodes to producers of military electronic gear, and lower-quality, lower-price semiconductors to microcomputer manufacturers.
- *Geographic area*. Manufacturers of heavy materials and equipment are typically forced to segment by area because of freight costs. The effect of such segmentation is a higher price in areas that are distant from the plant.

Table 5–4   Criteria for Evaluating Segments in Organizational Markets[32]

1. Is each identified segment characterized by a set of common user requirements?
2. Does each identified segment have characteristics (e.g., customer size, growth rate, location) that can be measured at least every year?
3. Does each identified segment have identifiable competitors?
4. Can each identified segment be served by common sales or distribution channels?
5. Is each identified segment large enough that it represents a significant business opportunity?
6. Is each identified segment small enough to allow protection against competition?

- *Size of account.* A prevalent practice for manufacturers that sell through middlemen to organizational accounts is to reserve large "key accounts" to be called on by the company's own sales force. Michelin does this with sales of original-equipment tires to automobile manufacturers, for example.

These six bases for segmentation are the most common ones in use for organizational markets. They are not exhaustive of all possible means of segmentation, however. A more theoretically elegant classification system for bases for organizational segmentation has been proposed that includes the ones just described plus others such as organizational structure, technology used, and purchasing decision rules and procedures.[31]

Which, if any, of these measures is appropriate for segmentation depends on the specific context and goals of segmentation. Each ought to be assessed for relevance before being applied. In addition, cost and profitability are always major concerns. Table 5–4 provides a list of criteria useful for evaluating segmentation strategies.

MANAGING MARKETING TO ORGANIZATIONS

At the beginning of the chapter we argued—we hope persuasively— that, broadly speaking, organizational and consumer buying behaviors are quite similar. Does this mean that marketing programs to organizational and to consumer markets are also quite similar?

Again, the answer is, in general, affirmative. The same elements are present in the marketing mix—product, price, promotion, and distribution —and marketing programs have similar patterns and structures in the two fields.

In the section on marketing programs (Chapters 11 through 18), the principles discussed are generally applicable for both.

Some differences between the two do exist, of course. The more important of them for each of the mix elements are as follows.

Product: Technical requirements are more demanding. A bolt sold to a manufacturer (usually) must meet such specifications as type of material from which it is made, an exact size, tolerances on threads, and type of nut; passenger vehicles sold to the U.S. military must satisfy many performance criteria and construction standards plus pass road tests on durability and handling. The average consumer doesn't even care whether the bolt is metric or not as long as it is the right size; consumer car buying is often influenced considerably by image and styling as well as by performance characteristics.

Pricing: Competitive bidding is used extensively in organizational buying. Competitive bidding occurs when a buying organization announces that it will let a procurement or construction contract on the basis of bids submitted by interested parties. It is a common method of choosing vendors by federal, state, and local governments; by organizations contracting for a building to be constructed; by companies acquiring fleets of cars, oil and gas well drilling, and for food service contracts.

One of the more successful applications of research methods to marketing is the development of competitive bidding models to determine the bid price. Competitive bidding is discussed in the chapter on pricing decisions (Chapter 13).

Promotion: Personal selling assumes a more important role, and advertising a more subsidiary role, in organizational than in consumer marketing. Organizational customers are fewer in number and tend to buy in larger quantities than consumers. As a result, it becomes economically feasible to do more direct selling. With the opportunity for personal communication provided by face-to-face (or telephone-to-telephone) meetings, advertising becomes less important.

Distribution: Rapid delivery and prompt response to service requests are more important to organizational customers than to consumers. Rapid delivery has become increasingly important as the "just-in-time" delivery system has been adopted by organizational buyers to keep inventory costs down. In such a system, a delay of one or two days in the delivery of a key part by a vendor may cause an entire assembly plant to become idle. The same is true of service requirements; a machine tool that is down or a measuring instrument that is off calibration can result in down time to a manufacturer that is costly until the cause is corrected. Consumers also desire quick delivery and prompt service calls, but the economic consequences of delays are generally substantially less to them than to the organizational buyer.

SUMMARY OF IMPORTANT POINTS

1. *Organizational buying behavior* may be defined as "the decision-making process by which formal organizations establish the need for purchased products and services, and identify, evaluate, and choose among alternative brands and suppliers."
2. What we know about consumer behavior is generally also relevant to organizational behavior, but in some cases we need to bolster the consumer behavior knowledge with information that may be somewhat more common to organizations.

3. The *acceleration principle* is a theoretical explanation of how small increases or decreases in consumer demand can result in large increases or decreases in the industrial durable products used to produce the consumer goods experiencing the shift in demand.

4. The *purchase context* includes individual employees who have social influences on them and who work in organizations with characteristics, culture, and goals, all of which experience environmental influences. These come together in the buying center. Webster and Wind have identified four corresponding classes of causes or influence on organizational decision making: individual factors, organizational factors, environmental factors, and interpersonal or social factors.

5. Categories in the organizational market include industrial purchasers, wholesalers and retailers, and governments and other institutions.

6. The *infrastructure* is everyone in the environment who can influence perceptions of a product.

7. The *buying center* is all those individuals who share in the purchase decision-making process, including purchase goals and risks.

8. Different people may play different organizational roles in the buying center, such as user, influencer, gatekeeper, decision maker, and buyer.

9. The *decision-making steps* in organizational buying include (1) situational characteristics, (2) information sought, obtained, and processed, (3) vendor and product buying decision, and (4) product use and evaluation.

10. The major *situational buy classes* are new task, straight rebuy, and modified rebuy.

11. Each organizational purchase goes through eight phases in the procurement process, known as *buy phases*:
    a. Anticipation or recognition of a problem (need) and a general solution.
    b. Determination of characteristics and quantity of needed item.
    c. Description of characteristics and quantity of needed item.
    d. Search for and qualification of potential sources.
    e. Acquisition and analysis of proposals.
    f. Evaluation of proposals and selection of supplier(s).
    g. Selection of an order routine.
    h. Performance feedback and evaluation.

12. Organizational markets can be segmented. The most commonly used bases for segmentation are type of organization, type of user, industry of user, common buying factors, geographic area, and size of account.

13. Among the differences between consumer and organizational marketing the more important are
    a. *Product.* Technical requirements are more demanding in organizational marketing.
    b. *Pricing.* Competitive bidding is used extensively in organizational buying, whereas it is rarely used in consumer buying.
    c. *Promotion.* Personal selling assumes a more important role, and advertising a more subsidiary role, in organizational than in consumer marketing.
    d. *Distribution.* Rapid delivery and prompt response to service requests are more important to organizational customers than to consumers.

REVIEW QUESTIONS

5.1. Describe the major differences between consumer markets and organizational markets.

5.2. What is the *acceleration principle*?

5.3. How do individual employees with their own social influences affect organizational purchases?

5.4. How do organizational characteristics, culture, and goals influence organizational purchasing?

5.5. How do environmental influences affect organizational purchasing?

5.6. What is the *buying center*? What roles exist there?

5.7. Describe the following:
   a. Buy class
   b. Buy phase
   c. Buy grid

5.8. What is an infrastructure?

5.9. Describe the decision-making steps in organizational buying behavior.

5.10. How can organizational markets be segmented?

DISCUSSION QUESTIONS AND PROBLEMS

5.11. An author of a management textbook* lists the following examples of organizational purchasing policies:
   a. Deciding if established suppliers will be used exclusively, or if orders will be placed with any available vendor.
   b. Determining how much should be bought on each order.
   c. Determining the minimum inventory size of each item in computing the reorder point.
   d. Making use of purchase discounts.
   Do consumers have counterpart buying "policies"? Explain.

*A. D. Szilagyi, Jr., *Management and Performance*, 3rd ed., Scott, Foresman, and Company, 1988, 210.

5.12. Why is the paperwork greater for government marketing than for other types of marketing?

5.13. Why do high-technology firms show such a strong preference for infrastructure theory?

5.14. Infrastructure theory has been called the "cocktail party" approach to marketing. Is that characterization fair? Explain.

5.15. How could a salesperson use knowledge of the roles in a buying center to structure a sales approach?

5.16. The marketing manager of a company manufacturing and marketing machine tools wanted to learn more about the factors that influence the choice of machine tools in a buying situation. Accordingly, the person responsible for marketing research in the company was asked to do a survey of a random sample of 100 companies that use machine tools. A questionnaire was prepared and a telephone survey was conducted of the purchasing agent(s) responsible for machine tool purchases for each of the sample companies.

   Was this an appropriate research design for this purpose? Why or why not?

5.17. Why has so little work been done in organizational segmentation?

5.18. It has been argued that in a firm that manufactures and markets industrial products, the Marketing Department is necessarily more interdependent with the R&D, Engineering, and Manufacturing departments than it is in a firm that manufactures and sells consumer products. Do you agree or disagree with this assertion? Explain.

5.19. If marketing to consumers and marketing to organizations are similar in nature, are there any advantages of working in one versus the other? Explain.

5.20. Assume the following:

   - A molding machine used in making skis has a useful life of five years.
   - Five thousand such machines are now in existence.
   - The machines are evenly distributed in age from brand new to five years old.
   - When run at capacity, each machine can make molds for 1,000 pairs of skis per year.
   - The market for skis during the coming year is forecast to be 5 million pairs.

   a. What would be the market for molding machines of this type for the coming year if the market forecast for skis is correct?
   b. What would be the market for molding machines of this type for the coming year if the market forecast for skis is 10 percent too low?

What percentage increase would this be over the market size if the forecast had been correct?

 c. What would be the market for molding machines of this type for the coming year if the market forecast for skis is 20 percent too high? What percentage decrease would this be over the market size if the forecast had been correct?

 d. What do you conclude from this example about the relative volatility of the market for molding machines for making skis (producer good) versus that for skis themselves (consumer good)?

5.21. A stamping machine for bicycle wheel rims has an average useful life of 10 years. Each machine has a capacity of 20,000 rims a year. There are 1,000 such machines now in use. The age of these machines is evenly distributed by years from 1 through 10. The market for bicycles during the coming year is forecast to be 10 million units.

 a. What would be the market for stamping machines of this type for the coming year if the market forecast for bicycles is correct?

 b. What would be the market for stamping machines of this type for the coming year if the market forecast for bicycles is 10 percent too low? What percentage increase would this be over the market size if the forecast had been correct?

 c. What would be the market for stamping machines of this type for the coming year if the market forecast for bicycles is 10 percent too high? What percentage decrease would this be over the market size if the forecast had been correct?

 d. What do you conclude from this example about the relative volatility of the market for stamping machines for making bicycle rims (producer good) versus that for bicycles themselves (consumer good)?

PROJECTS

5.22. Develop a skit in which the actors and actresses play each of the roles in an industrial buying center about to acquire 50 new personal computers.

5.23. Interview a purchasing agent from a local manufacturing company and one from a local government agency about the steps necessary to purchase something. Compare the steps in the decision processes that each describes.

Endnotes

1. F. E. Webster, Jr. and Y. Wind, *Organizational Buying Behavior*, Prentice-Hall, 1972.

2. Industrial Marketing Committee Review Board, "Fundamental Differences between Industrial and Consumer Marketing," *Journal of Marketing*, October 1954, 152–158.

3. E. F. Fern and J. R. Brown, "The Industrial/Consumer Marketing Dichotomy: A Case of Insufficient Justification," *Journal of Marketing*, Spring 1984, 68–77.

4. Ibid.

5. Y. Wind, "Industrial Source Loyalty," *Journal of Marketing Research*, November 1970, 450–457.

6. P. L. Bubb and D. J. van Rest, "Loyalty as a Component of the Industrial Buying Decision," *Industrial Marketing Management*, Vol. 3, 1973, 25–32; H. Assael, *Consumer Behavior and Marketing Action*, 2nd ed., Kent, 1984.

7. Ibid.

8. T. J. Peters and R. H. Waterman, Jr., *In Search of Excellence: Lessons from America's Best-Run Companies*, Harper & Row, 1982, 157.

9. Ibid.

10. S. E. Cohen, "Looking in the U.S. Government Market," *Industrial Marketing*, September 1964, 129–138.

11. P. Kotler, *Marketing Management: Analysis, Planning, and Control*, 6th ed., Prentice-Hall, 1984.

12. "Out of the Maze," *Sales & Marketing Management*, April 9, 1979.

13. R. McKenna, *The Regis Touch: Million Dollar Advice from America's Top Marketing Consultant*, Addison-Wesley, 1985.

14. Webster and Wind, *Organizational Buying Behavior*.

15. L. E. Crow and R. E. Spekman, "Impact of Organizational and Buyer Characteristics on the Buying Center," *Industrial Marketing Management*, Vol. 14, 1985, 49–58.

16. R. T. Moriarty, Jr. and R. E. Spekman, "An Empirical Investigation of the Information Sources Used during the Industrial Buying Process," *Journal of Marketing Research*, May 1984, 137–147.

17. R. E. Krapfel, Jr., "An Advocacy Behavior Model of Organizational Buyers' Vendor Choice," *Journal of Marketing*, Fall 1985, 51–59.

18. M. H. Morris and S. M. Freeman, "Coalitions in Organizational Buying," *Industrial Marketing Management*, 1984, 123–132.

19. D. W. Jackson, Jr., J. E. Keith, and R. K. Burdick, "Purchasing Agents' Perceptions of Industrial Buying Center Influence: A Situational Approach," *Journal of Marketing*, Fall 1984, 75–83.

20. P. J. Robinson, C. W. Faris, and Y. Wind, *Industrial Buying and Creative Marketing*, Allyn & Bacon, 1967.

21. Ibid.

22. E. Anderson, W. Chu, and B. Weitz, "Industrial Purchasing: An Empirical Exploration of the Buy Class Framework," *Journal of Marketing*, July 1987, 71–86.

23. Robinson, Faris, and Wind, *Industrial Buying*.

24. D. R. Lehmann and J. O'Shaughnessy, "Difference in Attribute Importance for Different Industrial Products," *Journal of Marketing*, April 1974, 36–42.

25. F. R. Dwyer, P. H. Schurr, and S. Oh, "Developing Buyer-Seller Relationships," *Journal of Marketing*, April 1987, 11–27.

26. G. L. Frazier, R. E. Spekman, and C. R. O'Neal, "Just-in-Time Exchange Relationships in Industrial Markets," *Journal of Marketing*, October 1988, 52–67.

27. W. J. Hampton and D. Cook, "Detroit Raises the Ante for Parts Suppliers," *Business Week*, October 14, 1985.

28. C. P. Puto, W. E. Patton III, and R. H. King, "Risk Handling Strategies in Industrial Vendor Selection Decisions," *Journal of Marketing*, Winter 1985, 89–98.

29. H. Assael, *Consumer Behavior and Marketing Action*, 2nd ed., Kent, 1983.

30. Robinson, Faris, and Wind, *Industrial Buying*.

31. R. E. Frank, W. F. Massy, and Y. Wind, *Market Segmentation*, Prentice-Hall, 1971.

32. B. C. Ames and J. D. Hlavacek, *Managerial Marketing for Industrial Firms*, Random House, 1984.

CHAPTER 6

THE ETHICAL, POLITICAL, AND LEGAL ENVIRONMENTS

Ethical values are the social glue that enables groups of people to live and work together. They are an important predictor of how people will act in a specific situation and, if the culture is a closely knit one, a crucial determinant of how the members of the society will say they should act. In democratic societies, ethical consensuses tend to become legal statutes through the workings of the political process.

In this chapter we discuss the ethical, political, and legal environments as they affect marketing.

ETHICS AND MARKETING

Ethics are

principles of right or good conduct, or a body of such principles.[1]

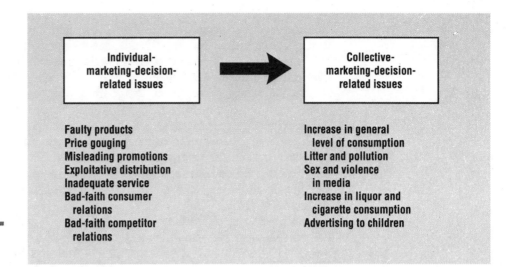

FIGURE 6-1
Categories of ethical issues in marketing.

When applied to marketing, ethical issues can be categorized as falling in one of two areas: individual-marketing-decision-related and collective-marketing-decision-related issues.

Ethical Issues Arising from Individual Marketing Decisions

Most decisions made by the marketer, and an even greater proportion of the decisions made by the consumer, are honorable and responsible. However, there are enough exceptions that ethical problems persist. Consider the following situations:

A children's pool sold by Sears is described on the box as measuring 8 feet by 18 inches. Its actual dimensions are 7 feet 3 inches by 17 inches. The smaller size saves 17 percent on the material used on the circular bottom, 9 percent in the length of the sidewall, and 6 percent in the height of the sidewall.[2]

In October 1945, Gimbels Department Store in New York City offered the first ballpoint pens for sale. As a result of the publicity the pen had received from the claims by its manufacturer (the Reynolds International Pen Company) that it was "a miraculous pen that will revolutionize writing" and that "it writes under water," 5,000 people were waiting outside for the store to open so that they could buy one. The retail price of $12.50 was the ceiling price allowed by the Office of Price Administration (the wartime price control agency in Washington) after Reynolds successfully argued that $10.00 per pen was not enough to make a decent profit. The cost of the pen to Reynolds at that time was 80 cents apiece.[3]

Ratings of radio audiences based on surveys of listeners typically are done each quarter for a four-week "sweep" period. The audience ratings are used by advertisers for deciding with which stations to place ads. Radio stations in some cities (San Diego, for instance) have aired commercial-free programs ("100 hours of commercial-free music," "91 hours of non-stop music") during the sweep periods to try to boost their ratings.[4]

Medical testing laboratories frequently pay rebates to doctors who send in blood and other specimens from patients for testing. The payments are made by a variety of methods ranging from cash commissions to the rental (at high rates) of specimen collection space in doctors' offices. The doctors who accept such payments assert that they are legitimate compensation for the cost of collecting samples to forward to the labs. Such rebates are illegal under the law governing the federal Medicare and Medicaid programs.[5]

Campbell Soup Company was cited by the Federal Trade Commission for placing clear glass marbles in the bottom of a bowl of vegetable soup about to be photographed for an ad. The marbles were used to push the vegetables to the surface and thus create an impression of greater vegetable content.[6]

One study of requests by consumers for replacement of or reimbursement for products under warranty showed that more than 22 percent of them had "virtually no honest basis for recovery."[7]

How can unethical practices in marketing be reduced? The methods that are in use include (1) ethical codes and seminars for employees by companies; (2) ethical codes and self-policing by industries; (3) state and federal legislation for consumer protection requiring disclosure of more information on labels, truth in advertising, truth in lending, safety standards for products, and better warranties; and (4) issuance of federal "trade practices" to help reduce misleading or fraudulent practices in specific industries. (A description of these laws is given later in this chapter.) The code of ethics adopted by the American Marketing Association in 1987 is shown as Exhibit 6–1.

The ultimate way to reduce the number of unethical decisions made by either the marketer or the buyer is of course for the ethically marginal decision makers to begin to "clean up their acts." Aside from any threat of legal sanctions, there is a self-serving reason for doing this, at least with problems of product quality and pricing. As cited in Chapter 1, a study of PIMS data for some 3,000 units of American businesses indicates that the higher the relative value (product quality and service in relation to price) provided the customer, the higher the market share and gross margin for the product line. One cannot provide higher relative value by putting out flawed products, giving shoddy service, or gouging on price.

But in most ethical systems the argument is made that virtue should be practiced for reasons other than material reward. Kant, for example, in his categorical imperative, argues that persons should act in such a way that their principle for action could become a universal law. Although it is not always easy to arrive at a maxim for action that would meet this standard,[8] to attempt to follow such a precept would result in a significant reduction in ethical problems in marketing—and raise the level of professionalism of the field.[9]

EXHIBIT **6-1**

American Marketing Association Code of Ethics

Members of the American Marketing Association (AMA) are committed to ethical professional conduct. They have joined together in subscribing to this Code of Ethics embracing the following topics:

RESPONSIBILITIES OF THE MARKETER

Marketers must accept responsibility for the consequences of their activities and make every effort to ensure that their decisions, recommendations, and actions function to identify, serve, and satisfy all relevant publics: customers, organizations, and society.

Marketers' professional conduct must be guided by:

1. The basic rule of professional ethics: not knowingly to do harm;
2. The adherence to all applicable laws and regulations;
3. The accurate representation of their education, training, and experience; and
4. The active support, practice, and promotion of this Code of Ethics.

HONESTY AND FAIRNESS

Marketers shall uphold and advance the integrity, honor, and dignity of the marketing profession by:

1. Being honest in serving consumers, clients, employees, suppliers, distributors, and the public;
2. Not knowingly participating in conflict of interest without prior notice to all parties involved; and
3. Establishing equitable fee schedules including the payment or receipt of usual, customary, and/or legal compensation for marketing exchanges.

RIGHTS AND DUTIES OF PARTIES IN THE MARKETING EXCHANGE PROCESS

Participants in the marketing exchange process should be able to expect that:

1. Participants and services offered are safe and fit for their intended uses;
2. Communications about offered products and services are not deceptive;
3. All parties intend to discharge their obligations, financial and otherwise, in good faith; and
4. Appropriate internal methods exist for equitable adjustment and/or redress of grievances concerning purchases.

It is understood that the above would include, but is not limited to, the following responsibilities of the marketers:
In the area of product development and management,

- Disclosure of all substantial risks associated with product or service usage;
- Identification of any product component substitution

that might materially change the product or impact on the buyer's purchase decision;
- Identification of extra-cost added features;

In the area of promotions,

- Avoidance of false and misleading advertising;
- Rejection of high-pressure manipulations or misleading sales tactics;
- Avoidance of sales promotions that use deception or manipulation.

In the area of distribution,

- Not manipulating the availability of a product for purpose of exploitation;
- Not using coercion in the marketing channel;
- Not exerting undue influence over the reseller's choice to handle a product.

In the area of pricing,

- Not engaging in price fixing;
- Not practicing predatory pricing;
- Disclosing the full price associated with any purchase.

In the area of marketing research,

- Prohibiting selling or fundraising under the guise of conducting research;
- Maintaining research integrity by avoiding misrepresentation and omission of pertinent research data;
- Treating outside clients and suppliers fairly.

ORGANIZATIONAL RELATIONSHIPS

Marketers should be aware of how their behavior may influence or impact on the behavior of others in organizational relationships. They should not demand, encourage, or apply coercion to obtain unethical behavior in their relationships with others, such as employees, suppliers, or customers. Marketers should:

1. Apply confidentiality and anonymity in professional relationships with regard to privileged information;
2. Meet their obligations and responsibilities in contracts and mutual agreements in a timely manner;
3. Avoid taking the work of others, in whole, or in part, and represent this work as their own or directly benefit from it without compensation or consent of the originator or owner;
4. Avoid manipulation to take advantage of situations to maximize personal welfare in a way that unfairly deprives or damages their organization or others.

Any AMA member found to be in violation of any provision of this Code of Ethics may have his or her Association membership suspended or revoked.

Ethical Issues Arising from Collective Marketing Decisions

Some individual marketing decisions result in no ethical infraction in and of themselves, but contribute to problems in combination with similar decisions over time or by other marketers. Consider the following examples of perceived and actual problems stemming from collective marketing decisions:

> Pope John Paul II, in an eight-page letter in the official newspaper of the Holy See, warned the world's young people: "You are threatened, dear young people, by the evil use of advertising techniques that stimulate the natural inclination to avoid hard work by promising the immediate satisfaction of every desire, while the consumerism that is linked to it suggests that man should seek self-fulfillment above all in the fiction of material goods."[10]
>
> Ozone in the earth's atmosphere acts as a barrier to ultraviolet rays. The rays are an important cause of skin cancer in humans. Fluorocarbons used in spray cans (paint, shaving cream, hair spray) have reduced the level of ozone significantly during the 30 or so years they have been in general use.
>
> Throwaway and non-biodegradable containers have contributed significantly to litter and refuse management problems.
>
> A survey of 500,000 grade school students by the Institute of Social Research indicates that about one-quarter (26 percent) believe other students their age are drinking wine coolers. The executive director of the National Council on Alcoholism says that advertising of wine coolers often uses images attractive to children (for example, one ad shows a polar bear singing and dancing) and wine coolers usually are packaged in boxes that look like soda pop containers.[11]

The ethical problems that compound from the marketing decisions of many firms do not lend themselves well to corrective action at the individual firm level. One company that stops advertising will not significantly ameliorate the problem perceived by the Pope (other observers do not agree that materialism is in fact promulgated by advertising, however),[12] nor will one manufacturer of shaving cream that stops using a fluorocarbon in its product measurably slow the erosion of the ozone level. Problems such as these call for either collective action at the industry level or legislative remedy.

THE POLITICAL ENVIRONMENT

Government affects marketing in a variety of ways. It is at once

A *customer* More than 20 percent of all goods and services produced in the United States each year are purchased by government at the local, state, and federal levels.

A ***marketer and competitor*** (for some companies)   The government of Canada spends more than $1\frac{1}{2}$ times as much on advertising per year as the largest commercial advertiser in Canada, and in the United States the government is one of the leading advertisers. In the United States the government owns and operates such enterprises as the U.S. Postal Service, ComSat, the Tennessee Valley Authority, and the National Service Life Insurance program.

A ***provider of information***   Through the activities of the Bureau of the Census and other agencies that collect and dispense information of use to marketers, and through regulations that require disclosure of information to consumers through labeling and by other means, government is actively involved in the generation and dissemination of marketing information.

A ***source of "legislated markets"***   Markets are often created by legislative acts for products and services that are required to comply with them. Recent examples of large markets resulting from legislation are the antipollution devices for automobiles and industrial plants, now required by the Clean Air Act, and the safety and noise abatement equipment of the Occupational Safety and Health Act.

A ***source of control***   The laws that regulate marketing activities and the enforcement of them originate in one or more units of government.

These are the major ways in which government directly affects marketing. It also has many indirect effects, however, some of which are far-reaching. Examples include changes in monetary and fiscal policy, the levying of taxes, the setting of tariffs, entering and withholding trade agreements as an instrument of foreign policy, changing postal rates, and granting subsidies for selected agricultural products.

The political environment is the chief determinant of how marketing is controlled in the economy. More specifically, the political environment determines (1) what legislation gets passed and what regulations get established, (2) how and to what extent these laws and regulations get enforced, and (3) what changes, if any, will be made in them.

Changing Political Environments

The Revere Copper and Brass Company is the direct descendent of the business founded and operated by Paul Revere in colonial times. During its over-200-year history, the political environment in which it has operated has undergone substantial changes, even though the form of the U.S. government has remained stable and essentially unchanged. Five different political climates as they relate to the economy can be identified in the United States dating back to the time when the colonies decided to form a confederation:

> **The founding period—1776 to 1789.** This period began with the Continental Congress' authorizing work to begin on the Articles of Confederation, and it continued through the calling of the Constitutional Convention, the writing of the Constitution, and its adop-

tion. During this period the principles that were to govern business in the United States were developed, and the institutions established that were necessary to implement them. The system of property rights, the monetary system, the standard of weights and measures, the judicial system, and the patent office were all established then.

The antitrust period—1890 to 1914. It is a testament to the wisdom and judgment of our founding fathers that the system they devised worked with very little change for a hundred years. The only problem of any real consequence that arose was the development of a form of organization that centralized control of companies incorporated in each of a number of different states. The excesses and arrogance of the leading industrialists and financiers in the 1870s and 1880s in the use of trusts led to reaction and a perceived need for increased regulation. The first of the antitrust measures, the Sherman Antitrust Act, was passed in 1890 and was later amended and enlarged in scope by the Clayton Act and the Federal Trade Commission Act, both passed in 1914. The Clayton Act was in turn amended by the Antimerger Act in 1950.

The period of crisis and protectionism—1929 to 1938. The great depression that began in 1929 resulted in a program of massive intervention in the economy by the federal government. Through the National Industrial Recovery Act, codes were established that reduced competition and, for a brief period, effectively legalized price collusion in participating industries. The Agricultural Adjustment Act went even further—prices for agricultural products were controlled by direct governmental actions. The Robinson-Patman Act, legislation designed specifically to protect independent wholesalers and retailers from price discrimination by competitors that were also selling to chains but which became applicable to all businesses, was passed in 1936. The Miller-Tydings Act was passed in 1937 to exempt from antitrust prosecution price-fixing agreements between manufacturers and the resellers of their products.

The consumerist and environmentalist period—1958 to 1978. During the late 1950s, Congress recognized that most of the legislation and common law that concerned seller–buyer relations provided the seller with unwarranted advantages. It also became concerned about preventing abuses and preserving the environment. For the next 20 years a series of laws were passed for the protection of consumers and the environment. They include laws requiring a more complete disclosure of information on products and credit terms, establishing safety standards for products, preventing discrimination in the granting of credit and harassment in the collection of debts, and establishing a national policy on treatment of the environment. It also rescinded the Miller-Tydings Act; the Consumer Goods Pricing Act of 1975 makes it illegal for manufacturers to make price maintenance agreements with their resellers in interstate commerce.

The period of deregulation—1978 to present. Many of the laws passed by Congress established a regulatory commission (or agency) to enforce them. For example, the Federal Trade Commission came into being as a result of the Federal Trade Commission Act, the Consumer Product Safety Commission resulted from the Consumer Product Safety Act, and the Environmental Protection Agency was authorized by the National Environmental Policy Act. Bureaucracies are commonly noted for their attempts to increase their range of authority and responsibility; surprisingly, a movement started in 1978 among several of the agencies to actually *decrease* the amount of regulating they were doing. Airline fares, freight rates, oil and natural gas pricing, and interest rates paid by financial institutions were all freed of regulation in the late 1970s and early 1980s.[13]

This summary of changes in the political climates faced by business over the long term suggests that the only constant is change. The Revere Copper and Brass Company, as indeed can all other companies, can confidently expect still more changes in the political environment that will have substantial effects on the company's marketing and other operations.

THE LEGAL ENVIRONMENT

There are five major ways through which social control in the economic sphere is exercised: "free" markets, ethical constraints, persuasion, tradition, and coercion. If the combination of a free-market system, ethical constraints, and cultural traditions, aided where necessary by governmental persuasion, were adequate to prevent market shortcomings, governmental coercion would not be required. But free-market economies are not perfect, and persuasion, ethics, and tradition have not always been sufficient to correct these imperfections. Monopolies develop, collusion occurs, income does not get equitably distributed, inadequate or misleading information is provided, bills do not get paid, and discriminatory and predatory actions are taken by firms for their benefit at the cost of others. To correct these, and other, failures of the market, governmental coercion is required.

This coercion is exercised through laws and regulations that are passed and enforced at the local, state, and federal levels that affect the operation of firms. The laws and regulations at each level of government are of course only applicable to the territory governed—local laws are applicable only to commerce conducted within the city or county concerned, state laws to state commerce.

The discussion that follows centers mainly on federal laws and regulations because they are the most widely applicable of the three and because in a text on marketing management in general, it is neither practical nor desirable to attempt the level of detail that a recounting of state and local laws would require. Where generalizations can be made about state or local laws and regulations that apply to marketing, they will be stated, however.

Laws and Regulations Affecting Products and Services

In this section, *products and services* should be interpreted to include patents, copyrights, and trademarks, warranties and labeling, and the form, features, and attributes that collectively make up the product.

A summary of the U.S. federal laws that relate to products and services is given in Table 6–1. Their intended and actual effects are discussed in the answers to the questions that follow.

> **Note to the reader.** The discussion of legislation affecting marketing that follows is in a question-and-answer format rather than in the standard format used in the rest of the book. When marketing managers seek legal counsel, it is generally for the purpose of getting answers to questions concerning the legality of current or anticipated practices of their own company or of competitors. The question-and-answer format simulates this process, and so should be more useful for reference. It also should be a more interesting way of presenting legal stipulations and constraints than simply a list of them.

Patents, Trademarks, and Copyrights

1. *What legal rights are conferred to the holder of a patent in the United States? the holder of a trademark? the holder of a copyright?* The general answer to these questions is that it confers legal ownership of functional features and design aspects or written and artistic features for a given period of time.

Central to the motivation of inventors and authors is the ability to protect the results of their efforts from exploitation by others. This protection was considered important enough by the drafters of the Constitution of the United States to include the provision that "the Congress shall have power . . . to promote the progress of science and useful arts, by securing for limited times to authors and inventors the exclusive right to their respective writings and discoveries."[14] The laws resulting from this provision enable the inventor or author to apply for, and to receive when warranted, one or more of the following recognitions of ownership backed by the U.S. legal system:

> **Patent.** An official document that confers ownership of a product's unique functional or design aspects, but not its artistic features, for a limited time (currently 17 years). The presses on which this book was printed and the equipment on which it was bound are both patented.

> **Trademark.** A term connoting legal ownership of a word, symbol, or device for a limited time (currently 20 years, with renewal possible) by reasons either of prior usage or by registration with the U.S. Patent Office. The name of the publisher of this book is a legal trademark, as is (very likely) the name of the bookstore from which you bought it. Brand names are also trademarks, as are the shape of the original Coke bottle and the Playboy bunny logo.

Table 6–1 Federal Legislation Concerning Products

Year Passed	Act
1790	*Federal Patent Act (HR41) and Federal Copyright and Trademark Act (HR43)*. Established a federal patent office and the procedures for issuing patents for innovative functional design features of products, registration of copyrights for literary and artistic works, and registration of trademarks for names, brands, logotypes, and certain artistic design features of products. These acts have been amended several times, the most notable being the 1793 and 1836 amendments to the Federal Patent Act and the 1978 amendment to the Copyright and Trademark Act.
1906	*Federal Food and Drug Act*. Established a Federal Food and Drug Administration charged with the testing of drugs and preventing the "manufacture, sale, or transport of adulterated or fraudulently labeled food or drugs in interstate commerce." This act was amended later to include cosmetics (1938) and food additives (1958).
1958	*National Traffic and Safety Act*. Requires that safety standards for automobiles and tires be created and enforced.
1958	*Automobile Information Disclosure Act*. Prohibits automobile dealers from misrepresenting the factory price of new cars.
1966	*Child Protection Act*. Prohibits the sale of toys, clothing, and other articles used by children that may be hazardous. Amended later (1969) to ban the sale of articles that may pose electrical, mechanical, or thermal hazards to children.
1966	*Fair Packaging and Labeling Act*. Requires information on packages specifying contents, quantity, and manufacturer.
1967	*Federal Cigarette Labeling and Advertising Act*. Requires the statement "Warning: The Surgeon General Has Determined That Smoking Is Dangerous to Your Health" to be printed on all cigarette packages.
1972	*Consumer Product Safety Act*. Created the Consumer Product Safety Commission and authorized it to set safety standards for consumer products and to ensure that they are observed.
1975	*Magnusson-Moss Warranty Act/Federal Trade Commission Improvement Act*. Provides for minimum disclosure and content standards for written consumer product warranties. It also provides the Federal Trade Commission with wider power for defining and preventing "unfair or deceptive practices" harmful to consumers.

Copyright. A term connoting legal ownership of a literary or artistic work for a limited time (currently 50 years) by reason either of a proper copyright notice or registration with the U.S. Patent Office. The word-processing program used for writing this text and the text itself are both copyrighted.

Without these laws, new-product development and the creation of new literary and artistic works no doubt would have been severely curtailed.

Product Safety

2. *Does the U. S. government have the right to require changes in products to improve their safety in use even though the manufacturers of the products hold patents on them?*

Yes. A number of acts passed between 1906 and 1966 (described in Table 6–1) enabled the government to set and enforce standards relating to the safety of consuming foods and drugs, and the safety of using automobiles and children's toys.

In 1972, this piecemeal-legislative approach was abandoned in favor of a general product safety law (the Consumer Product Safety Act). It established a Consumer Product Safety Commission and charged it with setting and enforcing safety standards for consumer products.

3. *Are there state laws that are concerned with product safety?* Yes. Thirty-two states have product liability laws. Their provisions are often different and, in some cases, inconsistent, so a manufacturer designing and selling products in interstate commerce faces difficult problems. For example:

> In Nebraska, a product design will be found acceptable by a state court if it is found to be based on "the best technology reasonably available." In a Pennsylvania court, however, the product will be judged defective if it is found "lacking any element to make it safe for its intended use, or any feature that renders it safe for the intended use." In Arizona, a state court will find the product acceptable if it conforms with "the technical, mechanical and scientific knowledge of designing in existence." Across the border in California, however, the same design will be found defective unless it "performs as safely as an ordinary consumer would expect it to when used in an intended or reasonably foreseeable manner."[15]

4. *What have been the effects of the consumer product safety laws?* There have been two general effects: (1) to save lives and reduce injuries; (2) to increase costs to producers and consumers.

There can be no doubt that the legislation passed on product safety has reduced injuries and saved lives. Studies conducted by the Consumer Product Safety Commission indicate that in the first seven years of its being required, the child-resistant packaging of drug and household toxic substances alone prevented 300 deaths and 200,000 poisonings. This is the highly positive kind of effect that was the intent of this and the other product safety legislation.

When a life is saved because a child cannot open a bottle of tranquilizers, or an adult is in an automobile accident with the seatbelt buckled, this is a *direct* effect of a product safety law. There are *indirect* effects as well. Knowing that the manufacturer is often found to be liable for injuries or deaths resulting from poorly designed or defective products, companies have given increased attention to safety in the design and manufacture of their products. Many companies have also recalled products voluntarily when found to be potentially unsafe. The by-now familiar recall of all automobiles of a particular model that has been found to have a defect is an example.

These cost increases tend to get passed on to consumers in higher prices. It has been estimated, for example, that "federally mandated safety and environmental features increased the price of the average passenger car by $666 in 1978. Compliance with these regulations thus cost American consumers $7 billion dollars a year."[16]

EXHIBIT **6-2**

Product Liability and Insurance Costs

Football Helmets. There are seven football helmet manufacturers in the United States. In the mid 1970s in one year they were collectively faced with lawsuits exceeding $110 million—an amount more than 100 times their reported profits. As a result of the extensive product liability coverage required, about $6 of the $40 to $50 retail price of a helmet was for insurance costs.*

Trampolines. In 1976 most of the 450 school districts in California had at least one trampoline. A year later, only three of the school districts had trampolines because of extremely high insurance costs.*

Die-Cutting Presses. The new owner of a die-cutting press company found that he became liable for injuries sustained by persons using presses that had been produced and sold by the company under its former owner. The company was faced with more than 20 lawsuits during the 10 years between 1972 and 1981 on machines it didn't make. One of the machines was made before the 69-year-old new owner was born.

For 3 of those 10 years the company had to self-insure because the insurance premiums were so high it could not afford to pay them.†

Children's Carseats. In two years, the cost of insurance for each manufacturer of children's carseats rose from $50,000 (1984) to $750,000 (1986).‡

---

*Marketing News, December 2, 1977.
†"Changes in Products' Liabilities Jeopardize Small Companies," *The Wall Street Journal,* November 30, 1981, 29.
‡"Marketers Feel Product Liability Pressure: Risks Crimp Launch of New Items," *Advertising Age,* May 12, 1986, 77.

There are other hidden costs of the product safety laws as well. Product liability insurance rates have risen dramatically; they rose over 200 percent on the average in one year shortly after the Consumer Product Safety Commission began operations.[17] Specific examples of the higher insurance costs are described in Exhibit 6–2.

The threat of liability suits by injured users of products has inhibited new product development in many industries, most notably perhaps in the chemical, pharmaceutical, and medical fields.[18]

5. *What kinds of information are manufacturers required to provide on the labels of products?* Three laws have been passed by Congress to ensure that consumers receive the information they need to make reasonable buying and use decisions. Two of these refer to specific products—automobiles and cigarettes—and were passed to correct what Congress viewed as informational problems specific to each.

The stickers one sees on new car windows displaying pricing information are the result of the act concerning automobiles (the Automobile Information Disclosure Act of 1958). The act concerning cigarettes (the Federal Cigarette Labeling and Advertising Act) was passed to require that the surgeon general's warning be printed on each cigarette package and appear in each advertisement.

The third piece of legislation is an omnibus act for consumer goods (the Fair Packaging and Labeling Act of 1966) in that it requires manufacturers of all packaged consumer goods to state (on the package) what and how much it contains, and who the manufacturer is.

Legislation Affecting Warranties of Products and Services

6. *What kinds of provisions are required for warranties of products and services?* Have you ever bought a product, found it was defective or did not perform satisfactorily, and after writing the company, (1) never received a reply, (2) were informed the warranty had expired, or (3) were told the problem you were having was not covered under the warranty, or the product was no longer being manufactured or serviced by the company, or that you should send the product to the company where it would be repaired (at an exorbitant price) and returned (after an extensive period)?

The Magnuson-Moss Warranty Act/Federal Trade Commission Improvement Act was passed in 1975 to help solve these kinds of problems for consumers. It also provides the Federal Trade Commission with broader powers for defining and preventing acts by companies that are "unfair or deceptive" and thus harmful to consumers.

Legislation Affecting Pricing of Products and Services

7. *What has been the underlying philosophy of federal pricing legislation in the United States?* Congress has had one basic philosophic approach to pricing—that of preserving competition. It has implemented this approach by passing antitrust legislation. The primary purpose of the legislation was to prevent monopoly pricing by making monopolies and collusive agreements between suppliers illegal. It consisted of the Sherman Antitrust Act (1890) as amended by the Clayton Act (1950). Whereas monopolies and cartels have been allowed (even encouraged) in many countries, one of the foundations of domestic economic policy in the United States for the last 100 years has been to prevent them.

EXHIBIT **6-3**

American Airlines: Attempt to Fix Airline Fares with a Competitor

American Airlines President Robert L. Crandall is reported to have called Howard Putman, then president of Braniff, and said, "Howard, I have a suggestion for you. Raise your goddamn fares 20 percent. I'll raise mine the next morning." "We can't talk about pricing," Putnam replied. "Its illegal." "Oh, bullshit, Howard, we can talk about any goddamn thing we want to talk about," Crandall said.*

The first critical error made by Crandall was to make the call—and the second was not to recognize that it was being taped. As a result, he and American Airlines were charged with attempting to monopolize airline routes into and out of the Dallas-Fort Worth "hub" area in violation of Section 2 of the Sherman Act.

The government won the case in District Court. Mr. Crandall and American Airlines signed a consent decree barring them from any further discussions with competitors concerning fares under penalty of Crandall's being required to step down from the airline presidency.

*United States v. American Airlines, CCH 45,083 (D.C., N. TX, March 1983), and "Legal Development in Marketing," Journal of Marketing, Fall 1983, 127.

(As an example of enforcement of this policy, see Exhibit 6–3.) Output has no doubt been expanded and prices lowered as a result.

Congress has strayed from this basic philosophy of preserving competition to one preserving competitors on three occasions. The first was the passing of the National Industrial Recovery Act (NIRA) of 1933. This act made some types of industry-wide pricing agreements legal. (The Supreme Court declared the NIRA unconstitutional in 1935.)

Two other pieces of legislation helpful to some competitors but harmful to competition were also passed in the 1930s. Congress passed the Robinson-Patman Act in 1936 to help wholesale and retail grocers compete with chains. In recent years it has not been enforced very often, however. (See Exhibit 6–4 for a description of the circumstances under which the Robinson-Patman Act was passed—an example of the workings of the political environment.) And the Miller-Tydings Act was passed in 1937 to exempt vertical price-fixing agreements, the so-called fair-trade pricing arrangements, from the antitrust laws.

The "fair-trade" price agreements that were legalized were between manufacturers and retailers of consumer goods, wherein the manufacturer estab-

EXHIBIT **6-4**

The Robinson-Patman Act: An Example of the Political and the Legal Environments at Work

Although the supermarket and the chain store form of organization eventually would have come to the grocery and drug field anyway, they were ushered in by the depression that began in 1929. They were a more efficient and less expensive way of marketing groceries and drugs to customers, to whom the need to save money had suddenly become more important than in the past.

By the mid 1930s the chain had become a growing marketing force in both the grocery and drug fields. The independent wholesalers and retailers of both groceries and drugs were feeling the adverse effects of competition from the chains. As a result of their size, the chains had been able to merge wholesaling and retailing and to effect substantial economies as a result. They also had been able to extract price concessions from suppliers that the traditional wholesaler could not obtain.

The threat to the independent wholesalers and retailers was so great that their associations began lobbying Congress for legislative relief. The National Wholesale Druggists Association was especially active in this campaign. No doubt in part because of the lobbying, the Robinson-Patman Act was passed in 1936. Whereas it did not make the chain form of organization illegal per se, it sought to outlaw the special price concessions the chains were receiving from suppliers. It did this by specifying that it was illegal "to discriminate in price between buyers of products of like quality or grade,"

unless there were savings equal to the amount of the difference in price arising from the manner in which the product is "manufactured, delivered or sold" to the buyer receiving the lower price.

This legislation was enforced vigorously for the next 20 years, not only in the grocery and drug fields, but in such other industries as steel and cement. It was the law of the land, and the Federal Trade Commission (FTC), the agency responsible for enforcing the act, did not shirk its duty.

Gradually, however, economists in the FTC came around to the view that the Commission's primary responsibility is to help preserve competition rather than to help preserve competitors. The Robinson-Patman Act clearly was passed to help preserve a selected group of competitors—the independent wholesalers and retailers. The view that the Commission's higher duty is to preserve competition has come to prevail and, as a result, enforcement actions by the FTC in recent years have become almost nil.

The law has not fallen entirely into disuse because of nonenforcement, however. Far from it. It is the basis for private-party legal actions of the sort in which Wholesaler A sues Supplier B because it (B) is giving lower prices to Chain Store C for the same product (with like quality and grade) than it gives to A. Many such suits are brought every year. The law is still an active force, therefore, in the shaping of pricing policies.

lished the retail price at which the product was to be sold to the consumer and which the retailer agreed to charge. The retailer "agreed" by one of two means to set that price. Direct agreements between the manufacturer and the retailer were used initially. This proved cumbersome, however, and enabling legislation was passed in many states to permit "nonsigners" clauses to be used. This permitted the manufacturer to require all retailers who carried its products in a nonsigners clause state to uphold the fair-trade price after (1) a minimum number of retailers in that state (as few as six in some states) had signed a contract stipulating they would maintain the fair-trade price and (2) all the other retailers handling the product(s) had been notified that the legally required number of signers had signed. The McGuire Act (1952) stipulated that the nonsigners clause could be used legally by manufacturers.

Congress rescinded its support of fair-trade pricing with the Consumer Goods Pricing Act (1975). This act prohibits the use of fair-trade pricing agreements in interstate commerce. A list of these pricing laws with a brief description of them is given in Table 6–2.

8. *What has been the underlying philosophy of pricing legislation passed by the states of the United States?* Most states have legislation for *intra*state commerce that parallels the federal antitrust, price discrimination, and consumer credit legislation for *inter*state commerce. These laws are often referred to within the state as the "little" Sherman Act, the "little" Robinson-Patman Act, and so on.

Most states also have "sales below cost" acts that, as the name suggests, prohibit pricing below cost. The purpose of these laws is to prevent "predatory" pricing—pricing below cost to harm or to drive a competitor out of business.

Table 6–2 Federal Legislation Concerning Pricing

Year Passed	Act
1890	*Sherman Antitrust Act.* Prohibits monopolies and collusive agreements between companies in interstate and foreign commerce.
1914	*Clayton Act.* Amends and extends the Sherman Act to prohibit price discrimination and certain other specific (nonpricing) practices where their effect may be to "lessen competition or tend to create a monopoly."
1914	*Federal Trade Commission Act.* The heart of the act insofar as pricing and other marketing actions are concerned is Section 5, which declares that "unfair methods of competition in commerce are unlawful." A commission was established whose members are empowered to develop descriptions of specific unfair methods of competition, to investigate methods of companies that may be unfair, and to issue cease-and-desist orders of those methods they find in fact to be unfair.
1933	*National Industrial Recovery Act.* Established the National Recovery Administration with power to draw up codes of fair competition by industry. These codes often made it possible to restrict price cutting and to apportion or to limit output. Such actions were exempted from the antitrust laws as long as they did not lead to a monopoly or oppress small enterprises. The National Industrial Recovery Act was declared unconstitutional in 1935.
1937	*Miller-Tydings Act.* Exempts price-fixing agreements between the manufacturer and resellers in interstate commerce from prosecution under the Sherman Act.
1975	*Consumer Goods Pricing Act.* Prohibits "fair-trade" pricing agreements in interstate commerce.

It is not enough, then, for marketing managers to be conversant with only the federal legislation applicable to pricing. They must also be familiar with the pricing legislation within each of the states in which the company operates.

Legislation Concerning Credit

9. *What are the major provisions of U.S. federal legislation concerning the granting of credit?* During the consumers period for legislation, three federal acts were passed concerning the granting of credit. They were the Truth-in-Lending Act (1968), the Equal Credit Opportunity Act (1975), and the Fair Debt Collection Practices Act (1978). The thrust of each act is apparent from the name. A brief description of each is provided in Table 6–3.

Credit arrangements are closely allied to, if not actually a part of, the price of most consumer and industrial durable products. As any car dealer can attest to (and is demonstrated in Exhibit 6–5), various combinations of higher interest rates with lower selling prices and lower interest rates with higher selling prices can result in the same exact return to the seller.

EXHIBIT **6-5**

The "Pricing" of Automobiles: The Trade-off Between Credit Terms and Sales Price

In setting sales prices for a model of a new car, every dealer recognizes that he or she can trade off higher interest rates for lower sales prices, and lower interest rates for higher sales prices, for cars bought on credit without affecting the net amount received for the car.

Suppose the dealer wants to net $10,000 on the car. Further, suppose the dealer plans to sell the credit contract to a bank that requires a net return of 15 percent per annum over the four-year life of the contract.

There are many combinations of interest rates and sales prices that will net the dealer $10,000 (present value) for the car under these circumstances. Here are two of them:

Combination 1: Price of $10,000, interest rates of 15% per annum

Sales price	$10,000

At interest rate of 15% per annum for a 4-year loan (48 monthly payments of $278.30 with no down payment) to net 15% per annum to the bank, the discount amount is

	0
Net to dealer	$10,000

Combination 2: Price of $11,075, interest rate of 8.9% per annum

Sales price	$11,075

At interest rate of 8.9% per annum for a 4-year loan (48 monthly payments of $248.38 with no down payment) to net 15% per annum to the bank, the discount amount is

	1,075
Net to dealer	$10,000

The dealer can choose from among these and many other combinations to decide which is the most attractive combination to the buyer.

Table 6–3   Federal Legislation on Consumer Credit and Collection

Year Passed	Act
1968	*Truth-in-Lending Act.* Requires lenders to state, in writing, the interest costs of a loan. Made provisions for a National Commission on Consumer Finance.
1970	*Fair Credit Reporting Act.* Stipulates that only relevant, recent, and accurate information is contained in a consumer's credit report. Prohibits dissemination of the report to other than persons with a need to know for an appropriate reason.
1975	*Equal Credit Opportunity Act.* Prohibits discrimination in granting credit on the basis of sex, age, marital status, ethnic origin, religion, or receipt of public assistance.
1978	*Fair Debt Collection Practices Act.* Makes it illegal to harass, abuse, or otherwise use unfair methods to collect a debt.

Laws and Regulations Affecting Advertising and Promotion

10. *How is advertising regulated in the United States?* The regulation of advertising in the United States began with a law for postal fraud passed over a hundred years ago. One of the effects of the law was to ensure that farm families ordering items through a mail order catalog got what the catalog promised they would get. The confidence this provided to prospective mail order customers was a major reason for the rapid growth of companies like Montgomery Ward and Sears-Roebuck. These companies soon became two of the largest retailers in the United States.

Since the Federal Trade Commission was formed in 1914, it has been the agency charged with federal regulation of advertising and promotion. It acquired that responsibility under the provision of Section 5 of the original FTC Act, which declares that "unfair methods of competition in (interstate) commerce are unlawful." It was given specific powers to regulate food and drug advertising by the Wheeler-Lea Act of 1938.

The FTC has followed the custom of developing *"commercial practices"* to describe what is unfair or deceptive advertising. These rules apply to a specific product or product line and are developed in consultation with representatives from the industry concerned. For example, the rule that governs how the size of a television receiving screen can be advertised is given in Exhibit 6–6.

Commercial practices rules have been developed for only a small fraction of the products advertised, however. When a rule is not available, it is not always an easy task to determine when an advertisement is "unfair" or "deceptive." As cases in point, consider the following situations:

Wonder Bread has been advertised as being "high in nutrition." This is a true claim, but it is not necessarily higher in nutrition than competing breads. Is it "unfair" to competitors when Wonder Bread is advertised as high in nutrition without giving comparative nutritional data for other brands?

A tire company that markets Champion tires used the brand name Safety Champion for a new tire. The choice of the brand name was not based

EXHIBIT **6-6**

Deceptive Advertising as to Sizes of Viewable Pictures Shown by Television Receiving Sets*

410.1 THE RULE

The commercial sale of televisions, as "commerce" is defined in the Federal Trade Commission Act, cannot be helped along by misrepresenting picture size. It is an unfair method of competition, and an unfair and deceptive act or practice, to use any figure or size designation to refer to the size of the picture shown by a television receiving set or the picture tube contained therein, unless such indicated size is the actual size of the viewable picture area measured on a single plane basis. If the indicated size is other than the horizontal dimension of the actual viewable picture area, such size designation shall be accompanied by a statement, in close connection and conjuction therewith, clearly and conspicuously showing the manner of measurement.

NOTE 1: For the purposes of this part, measurement of the picture area on a single plane basis refers to a measurement of the distance between the outer extremities (sides) of the picture area which does not take into account the curvature of the tube.

NOTE 2: Any referenced or footnote disclosure of the manner of measurement by means of the asterisk or some similar symbol does not satisfy the "close connection and conjunction" requirement of this part.

Examples of proper size descriptions when a television receiving set shows a 20-inch picture measured diagonally, a 19-inch picture measured horizontally, a 15-inch picture measured vertically, and a picture area of 262 square inches include:

"20 inch picture measured diagonally" or
"19 inch × 15 inch picture" or
"19 inch picture" or
"262 square inch picture."

Examples of improper size descriptions of a television set showing a picture of the size described above include:

"21 inch set" or
"21 inch diagonal set" or
"21 inch over-all diagonal–262 square inch picture" or
"Brand Name 21."

*Code of Federal Regulations: Commercial Practices Title 16, Parts 150 to 999, Rev. January 1, 1984, U.S. Government Printing Office, 222–223.

on any objective comparative evidence that this tire was safer than high-quality tires of competitors. Was the use of this brand name in advertising the tire deceptive?

Radio and print ads promised that brushing with Ipana toothpaste would help prevent "pink toothbrush." That is true since the act of brushing teeth itself exercises the gums and reduces the effectiveness of bacteria that form acids in the mouth, both of which reduce bleeding of the gums. However, brushing without any dentifrice at all would be just as effective in reducing bleeding as would brushing with Ipana. Was this advertising deceptive?

You will have already formed preliminary opinions as to whether the claims in these instances were "deceptive" or "unfair." Suppose you believe that the Ipana ads may in fact be deceptive and, if so, should be stopped. If you were on the staff of the Federal Trade Commission and were investigating the ads, what kind of evidence would you develop to establish (legally) that they were deceptive?

The Commission has used essentially two kinds of evidence to demonstrate unfairness or deceptiveness of advertising. The first is evidence that is internal to the Commission. This is "evidence" that relies on the expertise of the Federal Trade Commission to determine falseness or deceptiveness of claims without reference to any evidence from outside the Commission. In the first 3,300 cases on deception ruled on by the Commission from the time of its founding, more than 2,900 of them (87 percent) were decided solely on the basis of this kind of evidence.

The other type of evidence is that which is external to the Commission and includes such sources as expert testimony, consumer testimony, and consumer surveys. This type of evidence has been used to an increasing extent in recent years, a development that most advertisers have welcomed.[19]

Laws and Regulations Concerning Distribution of Products

The federal laws that affect distribution of products are primarily the Sherman Antitrust Act, the Clayton Act, the Federal Trade Commission Act, and the Robinson-Patman Act. We have already discussed these laws as they affect pricing; all of them have provisions that affect distribution as well, however. For ease of reference, we repeat (in Table 6–4) the earlier table summarizing these provisions.

The effects that these laws have on distribution are essentially answers to the following questions:

11. *Is it legal to require a dealer to handle only one's own products and not those of competitors?* This policy is known as one of **exclusive dealing**. On the basis of provisions in the Clayton and Federal Trade Commission acts, such a policy is illegal if it can be found to lessen competition substantially.

12. *Is it legal to force a dealer to carry one's entire line of products if the dealer carries any of the line at all?* This policy is known as **full-line forcing**. It is illegal if it can be shown to lessen competition substantially (Section 3 of the Clayton Act).

13. *Is it legal for a seller to require a dealer to take other products (but not necessarily the full line) in addition to the one(s) that the dealer desires?* This is known as a **tie-in contract**. (For an example, see Exhibit 6–7.) The same restrictions apply to

Table 6–4 Federal Legislation Affecting Distribution of Products

Year Passed	Act
1890	*Sherman Antitrust Act.* Section 1 prohibits "contracts or combinations in restraint of interstate or foreign commerce." This includes contracts between suppliers and resellers as well as contracts or combinations between two or more suppliers or between two or more resellers.
1914	*Clayton Act.* If competition is substantially lessened, it prohibits (1) exclusive dealing and (2) tie-in contracts.
1914	*Federal Trade Commission Act.* Section 5 stipulates that "unfair methods of competition . . . are unlawful." The FTC establishes "Trade Practice Rules" for a large number of industries which define "unfair methods of competition" for each industry.
1936	*Robinson-Patman Act.* Permits brokerage allowances only if they are earned by an independent broker. Requires (1) that promotional allowances and services be offered proportionately to all buyers and (2) that they be used for their intended purpose.

EXHIBIT **6-7**

Chicken Delight: Tie-in Sales to Franchises

A stipulation in the contract for a Chicken Delight franchise was that the franchisees must buy specified equipment (such as cookers), packaging items, and food-preparation mixes only from Chicken Delight. Several of the franchisees believed that the prices charged for these items were higher than those charged for items of a similar quality available from other suppliers. Based on this belief, they sued Chicken Delight under Section 1 of the Sherman Act charging that the agreements were unlawful tie-in arrangements and asking for triple damages.*

In a previous case, the Court had ruled that tie-in sale agreements were not illegal when there was a justifiable need for quality control on the part of the franchiser.† In this case, Chicken Delight contended that it had a right to require the purchases of the cookers, packaging items, and food-preparation mixes for that same purpose—to ensure that the quality of the franchisees' prepared foods would be up to the Chicken Delight standard.

The Court rejected the quality-control defense insofar as the packaging supplies were concerned. However, it recognized that the dips, spices, and cookers that Chicken Delight required of the franchisees might be necessary to ensure the quality level that Chicken Delight demanded. The Court therefore instructed the jury to accept the quality-control defense if "specifications for a substitute would be so detailed that they could not practically be supplied."‡

The jury decided that Chicken Delight could have ensured the quality of its franchisees' foods by means other than requiring tie-in purchases. The franchisees therefore won their suit.

Siegel v. *Chicken Delight*, 448 F. 2d 43 (1971).
†*Susser* v. *Carvel*, 332 F. 2nd 505 (1964).
‡*In re Siegel* v. *Chicken Delight*, BNA ATRR No. 467 (June 23, 1970), B-1, B-4.

tie-in contracts (they cannot substantially lessen competition) as to full-line forcing.

14. *Is it legal for a seller to prohibit a buyer from reselling the seller's products to specified types of other buyers?* For example, could Calvin Klein prevent a department store from selling its jeans to discounters? Again, this policy is illegal if it can be shown to lessen competition substantially.

15. *Is it legal for a company to require that those companies from whom it buys must also buy from it?* This is known as a **policy of reciprocity**. It is prohibited by Section 5 of the Federal Trade Commission Act when it (a) is substantial and (b) is highly systemized.

16. *Is is legal for a seller to grant a dealer an exclusive territory for resale of its product or brand?* The Supreme Court has, in effect, reversed its position on this question since its ruling on the Schwinn (bicycle) case in 1967.[20] In that case, the Court ruled that territorial restriction was a violation of the Sherman Act unless the company sold on a consignment basis.[21] Ten years later, the Court decided (in the Sylvania case) that territorial restrictions are not violations of the Sherman Act unless they have a seriously adverse affect on competition "without redeeming value."[22] The Court seemed to conclude that the increased marketing efficiency realized through territorial restrictions favored the promotion of interbrand competition (even though it might reduce intrabrand competition), and that this increased level of interbrand competition was in itself of "redeeming value."[23]

17. *Is it legal for a seller to offer incentives to the buyer's sales representatives to resell the product?* This practice is commonly called the offering of *"push-money."* It is not illegal, but it may be prohibited by a Federal Trade Commission trade practices rule for that industry. It may also be illegal under the Robinson-Patman Act if it can be shown to injure competition substantially.

18. *Is it illegal for a seller to provide promotional allowances or services to a reseller?* An example of promotional allowances and services is the practice of a packaged food manufacturer. It provides cooperative advertising allowances as well as the mats for the advertisements used by food retailers who handle their products. This is not illegal under the Robinson-Patman Act as long as the allowances and services are offered to all resellers on proportionately equal terms and are used for the stated purpose. (Such allowance cannot be used as a means of providing a hidden price reduction—the receiver must actually use the allowance for its intended purpose.)

Conclusions Concerning Legislation Affecting Marketing

With some defections along the way, the U.S. Congress and the state legislatures have attempted to preserve competition rather than to preserve competitors, and to favor neither consumers nor marketers at the expense of the other. To anyone favoring a free-market system, and this no doubt includes the great majority of marketers, these are laudable objectives as long as the benefits outweigh the costs.

The costs to the government of regulating have been high and the costs to firms of complying have been even higher.[24] The move toward deregulation in the last decade suggests either that governmental policy makers decided that the level of regulation was too high, or that the costs of regulation for the benefits it was providing were excessive, or both. Correction of market imperfections clearly makes some level of regulation desirable. Continuing deregulation can be viewed as a social experiment to determine the level at which benefits and costs are in a reasonable balance.[25]

SUMMARY OF IMPORTANT POINTS

1. *Ethics* are principles of right or good conduct, or a body of such principles.
2. When applied to marketing, ethical issues can be categorized as falling in one of two areas: individual-marketing-decision-related and collective-marketing-decision-related issues.
3. The methods that are in use to reduce unethical marketing practices include (a) ethical codes and seminars for employees by companies; (b) ethical codes and self-policing by industries; (c) state and federal legislation for consumer protection requiring disclosure of more in-

formation on labels, truth in advertising, truth in lending, safety standards for products, and better warranties; and (d) issuance of federal "trade practices" to help reduce misleading or fraudulent practices in specific industries.

4. Kant's *categorical imperative* can be paraphrased as saying that persons should act in such a way that their principle for action could become a universal law.

5. In addition to being a source of regulation, government affects marketing by being a customer, a provider of information, a source of legislated markets, a marketer, and, for some companies, a competitor.

6. There are five major methods of social control: (a) "free" markets, (b) ethical constraints, (c) persuasion, (d) tradition, and (e) coercion.

7. The political environment of marketing determines (a) what legislation get passed and what regulations get established, (b) how and to what extent these laws and regulations get enforced, and (c) what changes, if any, will be made in them.

8. The legal environment of marketing consists of the legislation and regulations that apply to one or more aspects of marketing.

9. The five different political climates that can be identified in the United States dating back to 1776 are
    a. The founding period (1776 to 1789)
    b. The antitrust period (1890 to 1914)
    c. The period of crises and protectionism (1929 to 1938)
    d. The period of consumerism and environmentalism (1958 to 1978)
    e. The period of deregulation (1978 to present).

10. A *patent* is an official document that confers ownership of a product's unique functional or design aspects, but not its artistic features, for a limited time (currently 17 years).

11. A *trademark* is a term connoting legal ownership of a word, symbol, or device for a limited time (currently 20 years, with renewal possible) by reason either of prior usage or by registration with the U.S. Patent Office.

12. A *copyright* is a term connoting legal ownership or a literary or artistic work for a limited time (currently 50 years) by reason either of a proper copyright notice or registration with the U.S. Patent Office.

13. The major federal laws affecting products and services are

    - Federal Patent Act and Federal Copyright Act (1790)
    - Federal Food and Drug Act (1906)
    - National Traffic and Safety Act (1958)
    - Automobile Information Disclosure Act (1958)
    - Child Protection Act (1966)
    - Fair Packaging and Labeling Act (1967)
    - Federal Cigarette Labeling and Advertising Act (1967)
    - Consumer Product Safety Act (1972)
    - Magnuson-Moss Warranty Act/Federal Trade Commission Improvement Act (1975)

14. The basic philosophic approach to pricing legislation by Congress has been to preserve competition. This is the driving force that led to the series of antitrust laws.

15. Congress strayed from its philosophy of preserving competition to one of preserving (selected) competitors with the passage of the National Industrial Recovery Act (NIRA, 1933), the Robinson-Patman Act (1936), and the Miller-Tydings Act (1937).

16. The major federal laws affecting pricing are

- Sherman Antitrust Act (1890)
- Clayton Act (1914)
- Federal Trade Commission Act (1914)
- National Industrial Recovery Act (1933)
- Robinson-Patman Act (1936)
- Miller-Tydings Act (1937)
- Consumer Goods Pricing Act (1975)

17. The major federal legislation on consumer credit and collection are

- Truth-in-Lending Act (1968)
- Fair Credit Reporting Act (1970)
- Equal Credit Opportunity Act (1975)
- Fair Debt Collection Act (1978)

18. The major federal laws affecting advertising and promotion are

- Federal Trade Commission Act (1914)
- Wheeler-Lea Act (1938)

19. The federal laws that affect distribution are primarily

- Sherman Antitrust Act (1890)
- Clayton Act (1914)
- Federal Trade Commission Act (1914)
- Robinson-Patman Act

20. Many states have laws that parallel, for intrastate commerce, the provisions of the federal laws that apply to interstate commerce.

REVIEW QUESTIONS

6.1. What are the ways being used to reduce unethical practices in marketing?

6.2. What is Kant's *categorical imperative*?

6.3. What are the ways in which government affects marketing?

6.4. What is the distinction between the political environment and the legal environment?

6.5. What are the five different (peacetime) political climates that have existed in the United States since 1776?

6.6. What are the major laws that affect the design and use of products and services?

6.7. What is a patent? a copyright? a trademark?

6.8. What are the major laws that affect the pricing of products and services?

6.9. What are the major laws that affect the granting and administration of credit?

6.10. How is an ad determined to be "deceptive" or "unfair" by the Federal Trade Commission?

6.11. What are the major laws affecting advertising and promotion?

6.12. Is it legal under federal law to
   a. Use exclusive dealing?
   b. Use full-line forcing?
   c. Use tie-in contracts?
   d. Prohibit a buyer from reselling to certain other types of buyers?
   e. Use a policy of reciprocity?
   f. Grant exclusive territories?
   g. Use "push-money"?
   h. Provide promotional allowances or services to a reseller?

6.13. What are the major laws affecting distribution of products?

DISCUSSION QUESTIONS AND PROBLEMS

6.14. Since 1984, the R. J. Reynolds Company has run a series of print ads with the question "Can we have an open debate about smoking?" and that includes such statements as "Studies which conclude that smoking causes disease have regularly ignored significant evidence to the contrary." Is this ethical behavior on the company's part? Why or why not?

6.15. One of the conclusions in the Federal Trade Commission's *Staff Report on Television Advertising to Children* is that "... [last year] the average American child aged 2 through 11 was exposed to more than 20,000 television commercials. This came as a result of watching an average of $3\frac{2}{3}$ hours of television per day throughout the year. The children who attended school spent, on the average, more time watching television over the course of the year than they did in the classroom."
   It has been argued* that advertising on children's television is bene-

*"What's Good about Ads to Kids? Three Ad Groups Tell Their Side," *Advertising Age*, November 27, 1978.

ficial (to children) for four reasons: (a) the information advertising provides about children's products allows children to begin to make decisions about them based on their own personal wants or preferences; (b) advertising makes possible the broad array of products marketed for children, matching the fast-changing preferences of the child; (c) child advertising helps prepare children for adult roles by helping to teach them how to make decisions; and (4) without the $500 million or so spent annually on children's advertising in the United States, the incentive to carry and to improve children's programming would weaken.

England and the United States are the only countries that permit programming and advertising on television intended for children. Is commercial advertising for children an ethically defensible practice? Explain.

6.16. Are the following practices unethical? Explain.
   a. A "2 by 4" is actually 1½ inches by 3½ inches.
   b. The Libby-Owens-Ford Co. makes "glare proof" windshields for cars. In making a commercial for the product, the photographer's lights produced glare on the company's windshield in the car being photographed. This problem was solved by taking the windshield out of the car before continuing the photographing.
   c. A major department store installed the message "I am honest. I will not steal" in a Muzak-like background in such a way that the shopper heard it subliminally (heard it but wasn't aware of having heard it). In the first nine months of use shoplifting decreased by about 30 percent.
   d. "Nude Beer" is marketed in some western states. It has labels with photos of models in bikini tops. The tops can be scratched off, showing a topless woman.
   e. A leading manufacturer of radar-detection devices sells about 400,000 units (at nearly $300 each) to drivers seeking protection from being caught and ticketed for exceeding speed limits.

6.17. The following statement appears in the preface to a book on the history of American patent and copyright law:*

> Thanks in large part to the United States Patent and Copyright laws, the American people enjoy unparalleled material and cultural benefits. The incentive furnished by these laws to inventors, authors, and composers has fostered a flood of creativity; on every hand one encounters innovations or works which have enriched society while their originators have been encouraged to continue their efforts.

   a. Do you agree or disagree with the assertion that "the American people enjoy unparalleled material and cultural benefits . . . [due] in large part to the United States Patent and Copyright laws"? Why?

*Bruce W. Bugbee, *Genesis of American Patent and Copyright Law*, Public Affairs Press, 1967, v.

b. Can you think of any way(s) in which patent and copyright laws may have inhibited the "material and cultural benefits" of the United States? If so, what is it (are they)?

6.18. Do you believe it is fair for the U.S. government to be a competitor to such companies as the United Parcel Service (through the U.S. Postal Service) and Metropolitan Life Insurance Co. (through the National Service Life Insurance program)? Why or why not?

6.19. Do you believe a legal environment that is protective of competition (as in the United States) is better than, or not as good as, one that allows monopolies and cartels (such as in the major countries of Europe)? What is the basis for your opinion?

6.20. What is likely to bring the period of deregulation to an end? Why?

6.21. It is generally agreed that product safety laws have saved many lives and prevented countless injuries since they were passed. There also have been disadvantages to consumers resulting from these laws. What are these disadvantages?

6.22. Should the new owner of a machine tool company be liable for injuries sustained on machine tools produced and sold by its former owner? Why or why not?

6.23. In the 1930s many states passed "anti-chain-store" legislation that imposed high (and graduated) taxes on chain-store organizations that had more than a few stores in the state. Should independent retailers be protected from chain retailers? Why or why not?

6.24. a. Give as many reasons as you can in support of reviving federal "fair-trade" legislation.
b. Give as many reasons as you can why new federal "fair-trade" legislation should not be passed.
c. State your conclusion as to whether new federal "fair-trade" legislation should or should not be passed.

6.25. The First Amendment of the U.S. Constitution states that "Congress shall make no law . . . abridging the freedom of speech, or of the press. . . ." Should "freedom of speech, or of the press" be interpreted to apply to commercial speech? That is, should commercial advertising have the protection of the First Amendment?

6.26. Is the use of the trade name "Aspercreme" (for a pain-relieving creme) misleading if the product does not contain aspirin in therapeutically significant quantities? Why or why not?

6.27. Can Apple Computer prohibit its dealers from selling its computers by mail order? Why or why not?

6.28. The Federal Trade Commission has ruled that it does not have to conduct a survey of the public exposed to an ad before determining that the ad has a tendency to deceive. Is this a sound procedural ruling? Why or why not?

6.29. Should an employee who is fired for refusing to take part in illegal acts (fix prices, rig bids, etc.) be able to sue the former employer for damages? Why or why not?

6.30. Seven-Up licensed a bottler to distribute its Like caffeine-free cola. The bottler had an exclusive dealership contract with Royal Crown Cola to distribute cola beverages. Royal Crown moved to terminate the contract and license another bottler. The first bottler sued to prevent Royal Crown from dropping it. Who should win the suit? Why?

Endnotes

[1] *American Heritage Dictionary of the English Language*, Houghton-Mifflin, 1979.

[2] "Maybe the Secret Here Is That You Have to Use a Sears Tape Measure," *The Wall Street Journal*, July 29, 1988, 15.

[3] T. Whiteside, "Where Are They Now? The Amphibious Pen," *The New Yorker*, February 17, 1951, 39.

[4] "San Diego Group Protests No-Ad Radio Gimmick," *Advertising Age*, December 3, 1979, 95.

[5] "Laboratory Kickbacks to Doctors Persist Despite Federal and State Investigations," *The Wall Street Journal*, September 26, 1978.

[6] "Freewheeling Freberg," *Advertising Age*, September 12, 1988, 70.

[7] "Market Must Balance 'Crooked Buyer' Effect," *Marketing News*, September 23, 1977, 1, 9.

[8] A series of questions that, if answered before making a decision with substantial ethical implications, will be a considerable aid toward reaching this goal is given in L. L. Nash, "Ethics without the Sermon," *Harvard Business Review*, November–December 1981, 79–90.

[9] A useful review of ethical issues in marketing is given in P. E. Murphy and G. R. Laczniak, "Marketing Ethics: A Review with Implications for Managers, Educators, and Researchers," in *Review of Marketing*, B. M. Enis and K. J. Roering (eds.), JAI Press, 1981, 251–266. More extensive coverage is given in G. R. Laczniak and P. E. Murphy, *Marketing Ethics: Guidelines for Managers*, Lexington Books, 1985.

[10] T. Shugaar, "Pope Warns Youth about Perverse Ads," *Advertising Age*, April 1, 1985, 3.

[11] D. Schneidman, "Marketing Seen as Factor in Kid Drinking," *Marketing News*, December 4, 1987, 24.

[12] "Marketing and advertising don't really induce people to buy things they don't need, according to Theodore Levitt, Professor, Harvard Business School." From "Advertising, Marketing Don't Cause Unneeded Buying: Levitt," *Marketing News*, May 5, 1978, 6.

[13] Most of the regulations were phased out over a long enough time to give the companies involved the opportunity to make the changes necessary to deal with the coming deregulation.

[14] The so-called intellectual property provision of the Constitution contained in Article I, Section 8.

[15] "Product Liability: Should There Be a Federal Law," *At Home with Consumers*, The Direct Selling Education Foundation, March 1984.

[16] M. C. Weidenbaum, *The Costs of Government Regulation of Business*, U.S. Government Printing Office, 1978.

[17] *Final Report of the Interagency Task Force on Product Liability*, U.S. Government Printing Office, 1978.

[18] R. Rothwell, "Some Indirect Impacts of Government Regulation on Industrial Innovation in the United States," *Technological Forecasting and Social Change*, Vol. 19, 1981, 57–80; "Marketers Feel Product Liability Pressure: Risks Crimp Launch of New Items," *Advertising Age*, May 12, 1986, 3, 75, 78–79; "The Costs of Lawsuits, Growing Ever Larger, Disrupt the Economy," *The Wall Street Journal*, May 16, 1986, 1.

[19] For a definitive discussion of this topic, see M. T. Brandt and I. C. Preston, "The Federal Trade Commission's Use of Evidence to Determine Deception," *Journal of Marketing*, January 1977, 54–62.

[20] *U.S. v. Arnold Schwinn and Co., et al.*, 388 U.S. 365 (1967).

[21] Retained title to the product and had the seller act only as an agent.

[22] *Continental T.V., Inc. v. GTE Sylvania, Inc.*, 433 U.S. 36 (1977).

[23] Of course, territorial restrictions might still be held to be an unreasonable restraint of competition or an unfair method of competition under Section 1 of the Sherman Act or Section 5 of the FTC Act. The burden of proof will be on the plaintiff to demonstrate that these allegations are true, however.

[24] Weidenbaum, *The Costs of Government Regulation*.

[25] For a thoughtful and carefully done examination of regulation as it relates to marketing in the United States, see the three-part series by J. M. Carman and R. G. Harris, "Public Regulation of Marketing Activity," all in the *Journal of Macromarketing*, "Part I: Institutional Typologies of Market Failure," Spring 1983, 49–58; "Part II: Regulatory Responses to Market Failures," Spring 1984, 41–52; and "Part III: A Typology of Regulatory Failures and Implications for Marketing and Public Policy," Spring 1986, 51–64.

MINICASES

Telecommuting: A Trend with Marketing Implications?

It has been estimated that in 1986 more than 5 million persons, or about 5 percent of the workforce, were working at home at least a part of each workweek. This percentage is expected to rise to about 18 percent by the early 1990s.

Working at a location other than a workplace supplied by an employer is known as "telecommuting." The widespread availability of personal computers has made telecommuting a practical reality. A personal computer can be linked by telephone to a computer at the office, so location is often constrained only by the availability of a telephone.

Assume that the prediction that 18 percent of the workforce (about 20 million people) is working at home part of each week by the early 1990s.

1. What opportunities could this have for marketers of consumer products and services?
2. What problems could this present to marketers of other consumer products and services?

The Corporate Culture of an Advertising Agency

David Ogilvy, founder of Ogilvy & Mather, a major advertising agency, described the culture of the company in a dinner address to company executives in 1985. With the exception of the opening remarks, the address is reproduced below.*

Corporate culture is a compound of many things—*tradition, mythology, ritual, customs, habits, heroes, peculiarities, and values*.

Here is how I see *our* culture.

A NICE PLACE TO WORK. Some of our people spend their entire working lives in our agency. We do our damnedest to make it a *happy* experience. I put this first, believing that superior service to our clients, and profits for our stockholders, depends on it.

We treat our people like human beings. We help them when they are in trouble—with their jobs, with illness, with alcoholism, and so on.

We help our people make the best of their talents. We invest an awful lot of time and money in training—perhaps more than any of our competitors.

Our system of management is singularly democratic. We don't like hierarchical bureaucracy or rigid pecking orders.

We abhor ruthlessness.

We give our executives an extraordinary degree of freedom and independence.

We like people with *gentle manners*. Our New York office goes so far as to give an annual award for "professionalism combined with *civility*." The Jules Fine Award, named after the first winner.

We like people who are *honest*. Honest in argument, honest with clients, honest with suppliers, honest with the company—and above all, honest with consumers.

We admire people who work hard, who are objective and thorough.

We do *not* admire superficial people.

We despise office politicians, toadies, bullies and pompous asses.

We discourage paper warfare. The way up the ladder is open to everybody. We are free from prejudice of any kind—religious prejudice, racial prejudice or sexual prejudice.

We detest nepotism and every other form of favouritism.

(Continued on next page)

Minicase II-2 (*Continued*)

In promoting people to top jobs, we are influenced as much by their *character* as anything else.

Like all companies with a strong culture, we have our *heroes*—the Old Guard who have woven our culture. By no means have all of them been members of top management. They include people like Borgie, our immortal Danish typographer. Shelby Page, who was our Treasurer and Chief Iconoclast in New York for 34 years. Arthur Wilson, the roving English art director who is the funniest man in our history. Paul Biklen, who has shepherded thousands of us through training programs. And Joel Raphaelson, editor of *Viewpoint*, veteran copywriter, lanternist, and ghost writer extraordinary.

ATTITUDE TOWARDS CLIENTS. The recommendations we make to clients are the recommendations we would make if we owned their companies, without regard to our own short-term interest. This earns their *respect*, which is the greatest asset an agency can have.

What most clients want most from agencies is *superior creative work*. We put the creative function at the top of our priorities.

The line between *pride in our work* and *neurotic obstinacy* is a narrow one. We do not grudge clients the right to decide what advertising to run. It is their money.

Many of our clients employ us in several countries. It is important for them to know that they can expect the same standards of behavior in all our offices. That is one reason why we want our culture to be more or less the same everywhere.

We try to sell our clients' products without offending the mores of the countries where we do business. And without cheating the consumer.

We attach importance to *discretion*. Clients don't appreciate agencies which leak their secrets. Nor do they like it when an agency takes credit for *their* success. To get between a client and the footlights is bad manners.

We take new business very seriously, and have a passion for winning. But we play fair vis-à-vis our competitors.

PECULIARITIES. We have a habit of divine discontent with our performance. It is an antidote to smugness.

Our far-flung enterprise is held together by a network of personal friendships. We all belong to the same club.

We like reports and correspondence to be well written, easy to read—and *short*.

We are revolted by pseudo-academic jargon like attitudinal, paradigms, demassification, reconceptualise, suboptimal, symbiotic linkage, splinterisation, dimensionalisation.

Some of us write books.

We use the word *partner* in referring to each other. This says a mouthful.

We take our Christmas get-togethers seriously. On these elaborate occasions we take our entire staff into our confidence—and give them a rollicking good time.

When we opened the New York office in 1948, I had it painted battleship grey. The result was depressing, so I changed to white walls and red carpets. Most of our offices are still white and red.

EX CATHEDRA. Through maddening repetition, some of my *obiter dicta* have been woven into our culture. Here are ten of them:

1. "Ogilvy & Mather—one agency indivisible."
2. "We sell—or else."
3. "You cannot *bore* people into buying your product; you can only *interest* them in buying it."
4. "Raise your sights! Blaze new trails! Compete with the immortals!!!"
5. "I prefer the discipline of knowledge to the anarchy of ignorance. We pursue knowledge the way a pig pursues truffles."
6. "We hire gentlemen with brains."
7. "The consumer is not a moron. She is your wife. Don't insult her intelligence."
8. "Unless your campaign contains a Big Idea, it will pass like a ship in the night."
9. "Only First Class business, and that in a First Class way."
10. "Never run an advertisement you would not want your own family to see."

AS OTHERS SEE US. This letter describes our culture as I see it. How do outsiders see it? A recent survey among advertisers and other agencies revealed that our New York office is seen as "sophisticated, imaginative, disciplined, objective and exciting." This describes exactly the culture I have devoted 36 years to cultivating.

The head of another agency recently told us, "You are not only the leaders of our industry, you are gentlemen, you are teachers and you make us proud to be in the advertising business."

Suppose that a cultural anthropologist from your university were commissioned to do a study of the Ogilvy and Mather corporate culture. In what respects, if any, would his or her report be likely to differ from the description provided by Mr. Ogilvy?

---

*"Corporate Culture," *Viewpoint*, Ogilvy & Mather, January–February 1986, 2–3.

The Kellogg Company

[This is a case involving a managerial decision on the social and ethical implications of an action rather than its effects on market share and/or contribution. As such, the objectives to be attained, and the alternatives for attaining them, will differ from those of the other cases presented in the class.]

Nineteen eighty-five was a banner year for Kellogg. The company increased its overall U.S. sales by 17 percent (to $2.1 billion), and its sales in the U.S. cereal market by almost 22 percent (to $1.9 billion), compared with the 1984 levels. Kellogg's share of the domestic cereal market also rose by a little more than 1 percentage point, reaching 42 percent by the end of the year.

Analysts attributed most of these gains to the sizable incease in advertising expenditures in 1985. The U.S. advertising budget that year totaled $364 million, an increase of over $60 million from the amount spent in 1984. This budget increase elevated Kellogg to the position of being the twenty-fifth largest advertiser in the United States in that year.

More than $210 million was spent on television. Since children constitute a substantial consuming segment of the cereal market, and they are influential in brand choice decisions as well, much of the TV advertising was on children's programs. Children also grow up to be adults, and some of them transfer their childhood brand preferences to their own children.

An analyst of advertising and its social effects offers the following observations about advertising in general and advertising to children in particular:*

The significance of the existence and role of communication systems has not been fully recognized by advertisers. A communication system is a conceptual framework within which specific purposes, activities, and relationships may be established. Advertising with the intent to change these purposes, activities and/or relationships is a violation of the system it is attempting to change.

Much of the advertising aimed at children represents an example of such violations. Like all communication systems, a family depends for its viability and integrity on the existence and maintenance of certain structural and functional characteristics. These characteristics may be deduced from the fact that all communication systems ultimately are logical frameworks serving as contexts and bases for the development and maintenance of human knowledge and behavior. They are:

1. Boundary. A family must create and sustain a set of boundaries around itself and its situation to permit it to exert a degree of control over its own development.
2. Purpose(s). A family must serve some identifiable purposes for the individuals involved—purposes not served by some other communication system of which these same individuals are part.
3. Ways of Behaving. A family must develop and sustain ways of behaving and interacting which are appropriate for carrying out its purpose and for sustaining its boundary.
4. Roles and Role Relations. A family must assign particular roles and role relations to each of its members. Each member must know substantially who he or she is in the family.

Insofar as advertising inserts itself into family relations (e.g., by encouraging children to adopt roles not assigned to them in the family), it violates one or more boundaries as well as the integrity of the family. It matters not whether the results of such violations generally will be considered good or bad. What matters is that the family's communication system is violated and that its potential for development is changed or distorted in some way. In short, advertising to children which does not take into account and respect the basic characteristics and dynamics of the family is effectively subversive.

1. Is the advertising of brands of Kellogg breakfast cereals a violation and subversion of the familial communications system? Explain.
2. Should actions be taken by
   a. The Kellogg Company acting individually,
   b. The Kellogg Company and its major competitors acting jointly or
   c. The U.S. Federal Trade Commission
   to
3. a. Allow advertising of cereals on children's programs but in a reduced or altered format?
   b. Stop the advertising of cereals on children's programs altogether?

Explain your answer.

---

*Adapted from Bent Stidsen, "Market Segmentation, Advertising and the Concept of Communication Systems," *Journal of the Academy of Marketing Science*, Vol. 3, no. 1, Winter 1975, 69–84.

Can Marketing Be Used to Change the Environments in Which It Must Operate?

The implicit central questions of the chapter on the marketing environment are:

1. What is the nature of the environments within the firm, the industry, the state of technology, and the economy in which marketing must operate?
2. How can marketing best operate within them?

The second question implies that marketing should take only a *reactive* stance in dealing with the environments it faces. Granted that this may be the major way in which marketing deals with its environments, but is this the *only* way it can deal with them? Can it take a *proactive* stance and try to change the environments within which it must operate?

Answer the following questions for each of the environments of (a) the *firm* itself, (b) the *industry*, (c) the *state of the relevant technology*, and (d) the *economy*:

1. Can marketing be used to change the environment in such a way that it will be more favorable for the marketing program?
2. If your answer to question 1 is yes, what action(s) could it take and what change(s) would likely result?
3. If your answer to question 1 is no, why do you believe marketing cannot change that environment?

University "Culture" and Marketing the University to Prospective Students

Universities as well as corporations have distinctive "cultures." These cultures are affected by such demographic factors as location (southern California versus upstate New York, Philadelphia versus Iowa City, for example), reason for founding (church-related versus public universities), history and tradition (Ivy League schools that are two or three hundred years old versus post–World War II universities), nature of program (a school that offers evening programs predominantly versus one whose programs are primarily offered during the day, schools that tend to specialize in a small number of subject areas versus those that offer a broad range of programs), and by sex of students (schools for women or men only versus coeducational schools). And there are "managed" cultural differences

as well; some schools are very demanding academically and others are not, for example.

Form a two- or three-person team with one or two other students in your class. Be sure that at least one of you has attended another college or university for a minimum of one year. For both your present school and the one previously attended:

1. Prepare a description of the "culture" of each.
2. Describe the student population segment(s) to which each school appeals.
3. Prepare a marketing plan for your school to be used for attracting applications from students in the segments you believe it should target.

Honda Motor Company: Requirement of Repair or Replacement of Rusted Fenders

In a consent decree directed to the American Honda Motor Company, the Federal Trade Commission asserted that Honda knew, or should have known, that the fenders on some Civic and Accord cars were designed in such a way that they would rust prematurely. Honda was also charged by the FTC as not having informed buyers of how to prevent or to repair rust on the fenders.*

The consent order requires Honda to send a letter to all buyers of the relevant Honda models in 24 "salt belt" states (the states in which salt is used on roads in the winter, which results in severe rusting problems) and the District of Columbia informing them of the problem and the fact that they can receive free repair or replacement of rusted fenders. Posters announcing the program are to be placed in all Honda dealerships. Owners outside the 24 states and the District of Columbia are also to receive free repair or replacement of rusted fenders but will not be notified directly.

The fenders and bodies of all cars rust eventually in the "salt belt" states unless exceptional measures are taken to undercoat them and to wash them frequently. What standards should be applied by the Federal Trade Commission to determine when an automobile manufacturer such as Honda is at fault and should make restitution, and when the problem is one that is common to all makes?

*American Honda Motor Co., Inc. CCH 21, 846, FTC File No. 802–3106 (February 1982).

Prescription Drugs by Mail: Should Federal Legislation Prohibiting This Practice Be Passed?

About one-half of 1 percent of the prescription drugs sold in the United States each year are sold by mail, and the share is growing. Mail order drugs typically are priced at a substantial discount compared with drugs purchased in person at a pharmacy. The mail order druggists maintain they can sell prescription drugs at lower prices than many local druggists can because of volume purchasing, low overhead, and the use of generic drugs when possible. The drugs are delivered in the same way they are ordered—through the mail.

Even though a prescription signed by a physician is required for an order, as it is when prescription drugs are purchased locally, and all mail order pharmacists must be registered in the state in which they work, the National Association of Retail Druggists (NARD) maintains that buying drugs by mail is not in the best interest of consumers. The Association published a pamphlet in 1985 that asked consumers, "When you buy prescription drugs by mail, do you really want to bargain away your health?"

How might buying prescription drugs by mail result in "bargaining away" one's health? Should federal legislation be passed outlawing the selling of prescription drugs by mail? Why or why not?

Claims in Advertising

In determining what kind of substantiation is required for claims in advertising, the Federal Trade Commission places them into one of three types. They are:

1. *A puffing claim* A claim that no consumer would take seriously and that does not require substantiation. Example: an imported sports car is referred to as the "sexiest European car."
2. *A nonestablishment claim* A claim that *suggests* that some desirable feature of the product is true but does not *assert* that it is true. Only "a reasonable basis" is required for this kind of claim. Example: "We believe this is the fastest acting pain reliever you can buy."

3. *An establishment claim* A claim in which either an explicit or an implicit assertion is made that something is true. This kind of claim must have substantiation of the type and to the extent that will satisfy the relevant scientific community of its validity. Examples: Ads that contain the statement "here's proof" or "medically proven," or television ads that include a white-coated technician even if no verbal claims are made.

View 10 television ads and record a brief description of the claim(s) made in each of them. Classify each claim into one of the above three categories.

When a Customer Orders a Coca-Cola or a "Coke," Can a Pepsi-Cola Be Served Legally without Verbal Notification of the Substitution?

Overland, Inc. operates a restaurant in which Pepsi-Cola is the only cola drink served. There are signs in the restaurant that state that only Pepsi-Cola is served and Overland has instructed its help to inform customers who order a "Coke" or a Coca-Cola that only Pepsi-Cola is available. Such verbal notification is not always given, however.

The Coca-Cola Company has brought a trademark suit against Overland requesting an injunction to prevent Overland from serving Pepsi-Cola to customers who order a "Coke" or a Coca-Cola.

On what basis should the court make its decision? How should it rule?

Did the Temple University Bookstore Engage in Predatory Pricing by Selling below "Cost"?

The Temple University Bookstore held a one-week sale of textbooks that resulted in sales amounting to $118,427. This brought a net return of $2,932 above average variable costs (AVC), where AVC was defined to

include   invoice cost, freight, bad-check expense, and advertising and payroll expense;

but to

exclude   theft, management expenses, depreciation, interest in debt, property taxes, and other irreducible overhead.

Sunshine Books, Ltd. brought a suit charging that the Temple Bookstore management had engaged in "predatory" pricing for the purpose of attempting to monopolize the sale of textbooks to students by selling below "cost."

The court ruled that AVC, as defined above, was the appropriate definition of "cost" and since the total of the costs so defined was less than the total sales volume, predatory pricing had not occurred.

1. Should average variable cost or incremental (marginal) costs be the definition of "cost" used in such a case? Why?
2. Was the definition of average variable cost used by the court consistent with the usual (accounting) definition of "average variable cost"? Why or why not?

In answering these questions, you may want to refer to the case itself and to a reference used by the court in justifying the inclusions and exclusions. The case citation is *Sunshine Books, Ltd.* v. *Temple University*, CCH 64m356 (D.C.E. PA, November 1981), and the reference is Arreda and Turner, "Predatory Pricing," 88 *Harvard Law Review* 697, 1975.

Telemarketing from the Cell Block: The Cons Become Pros

The Minnesota Department of Corrections has set up a telemarketing program at a maximum-security facility in which 25 inmates place calls to purchasers of a variety of items. A women's correctional facility in Arizona has had its inmates taking inbound "800" number reservations for Best Western Hotels for several years.

Both ventures have been highly successful from both a business and an inmate morale standpoint. A market rate is charged so that private businesses are not being competed with unfairly. Inmates are given an opportunity to earn money for current expenses and for (forced) saving for when they are released. They are learning a marketable skill for when they get out. Their enthusiasm and performance have

been high—considerably higher, in fact, than those of the employees of private companies on the outside.

One of the reasons for the high performance of inmates is the desirability of this job relative to that of other possible jobs that are available to them (the prison laundry, for example). Once they are selected for it, they work hard to keep it. Inmates also don't have the distractions that are found in a typical office, nor are they late for work or do they take long lunches.

Do you think such programs should be continued? Why or why not?

Adapted from L. G. Reiling, "Not Just Audience Captive in Telemarketing Operation," *Marketing News*, August 1, 1986, 8.

Naturally Thin Wafers

Naturally Thin Wafers was a safe, effective diet aid whose main ingredient was ordinary clay. The clay had been compressed into a wafer, dried, and coated with a sugar substitute. One wafer was to be taken 30 minutes before each meal, along with a glass of water. This gave the clay in the wafer time to expand in the user's stomach and to reduce feelings of hunger before the meal.

Naturally Thin was originally introduced in 1948 at a suggested retail price of $1 per package of 25 wafers. Sales were so low that it was soon necessary to withdraw it from the market. It was subsequently reintroduced at $4.95 per package of 50 wafers, with 50 cents being given to the clerk who sold each package. (This practice was known as using "push-money.") It was an immediate success and remained so until content labeling laws destroyed its popularity.

1. Was the increase in price ethically justifiable?
2. Was the use of "push-money" ethically justifiable? Explain.
3. Was the effect of the labeling law in this case a desirable one from a societal viewpoint? Explain.

The TV Woman: Hausfrau and Aphrodite

Everyone knows her. Her clothes are clean, her shoes sensible, her floors shiny, her Formica spotless. She has two children, one helpful friend, one nosy neighbor, and a dog who occasionally tracks dirt into her kitchen. Unfortunately, her husband's shirts are not as clean as they should be and she does not realize he would choose stuffing over potatoes. With the exception of these two things, her daytime life is worry-free. She can see her own face in her dishes.*

Ah, but the evenings! A touch of the right perfume, a touch-up with the proper lip gloss, and a change into softly clinging lounge pajamas and she is wife-mistress, looking lovingly into the firelit face of husband-lover. The day has left her refreshed and rejuvenated and looking forward to enjoying the eight-track tape of the world's great light classics, and whatever else the evening may bring.

Do TV ads that portray women in one of these two stereotypical ways contribute to

1. Popular acceptance of suburban middle-class lifestyles and values? Explain.
2. Discriminatory attitudes toward women in our culture? Explain.
3. Psychological problems for women arising from a perceived failure to successfully assume one or both of these roles? Explain.

---

*Adapted from Anna Quindlen, "Women in TV Ads Changeless," *New York Times News Service*, August 1978.

DECISION MAKING, MARKET MEASURE- III
MENT, AND MARKETING
PLANNING AND
FORECASTING

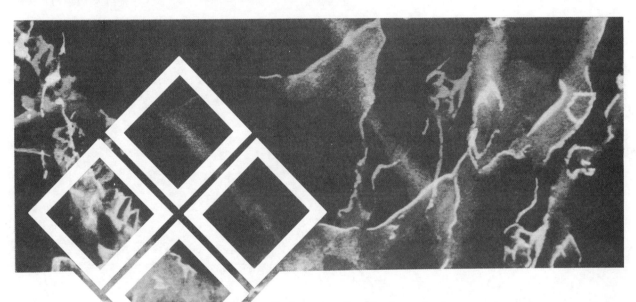

Earlier we described marketing management as consisting primarily of making decisions about marketing strategies and programs for carrying them out. In this section we deal with how decisions are made and how information is acquired for making them.

A formal discussion of the types of decisions that are made in marketing and the techniques for making them is given in Chapter 7. The methods of marketing research as formal means of acquiring information for making marketing decisions are described in Chapter 8. The techniques of measuring markets to provide information for financial evaluation of product markets are discussed in Chapter 9. The section ends with a description of the methods of marketing planning and sales forecasting (Chapter 10).

The emphasis in the treatment of information acquisition in this section is from the standpoint of the manager rather than the researcher. Managers need to know what general methods and sources are available for getting information to help them make better decisions. but they do not need to know all the technical details involved in conducting the research to obtain it.

DECISION MAKING
IN MARKETING

If one were looking for a single phrase to describe the essence of what it is that marketing managers do, the most appropriate choice would be ***decision making***. The decisions made concern marketing problems, of course, and are wide ranging. They involve the planning, organizing, staffing, and controlling of marketing activities, developing marketing strategies, and the solving of the day-to-day problems that arise in the marketing operations of the firm.

Consider the following situations:

> The staff of the Bureau of the Census designed the most recent Census of Population and Housing to be taken primarily by means of a mail out, mail back census questionnaire. Personal interviews were to be conducted of households that did not respond.
>
> An extensive advertising campaign was planned to be put into effect just before the questionnaires were mailed. For each additional 1 percent of the population responding to the mail questionnaire, it was estimated that $2.3 million in personal interviewing costs would be saved.

The U-Haul Company discovered that as a result of population migration to the southern, southwestern, and western states, an excess of one-way rental trailers was accumulating there with shortages developing in the northern and northeastern areas.

The management of the Bradford Instrument Company[1] was considering changing the distribution channels currently being used for the company's electronic and electromechanical instruments. For many years, these products had been marketed through full-service wholesalers supplemented by manufacturers' representatives in the less important market areas. The management believed that the quality and the amount of both sales effort and service the instruments were receiving needed to be increased, however.

How should the managers have gone about making the decisions involved in each of these situations?

Decision making is in part an art as well as a science. Therefore, the manner in which the managers went about making the decisions required to solve the problems described above no doubt varied somewhat. However, there are certain underlying tasks that need to be performed regardless of personal decision-making artistry or style. These tasks are depicted in Figure 7–1.

Identifying the Problem

Problems arise when objectives are not being met. If the response rate to the census questionnaire was forecast to be less than desired, the average usage rate of U-Haul trailers was judged to be too low, or the sales effort and service

FIGURE 7-1
Steps in decision making.

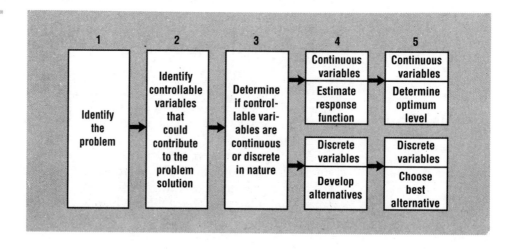

provided to Bradford was inadequate, a decision needed to be made. In each case, one or more objectives of the organizations were not being met.

As illustrated in Figure 7–2, problems are identified, and the need for decisions is recognized by the processes of (1) establishing corporate objectives, (2) setting marketing performance standards based on the objectives, (3) measuring actual marketing performance, and (4) comparing actual performance with performance standards. When performance is not up to the standard, corrective action is indicated—one or more decisions need to be made.

Establishing Corporate Objectives

It is reasonable to suppose that a well-managed company would have a set of explicit, well-defined objectives. The stated objectives of a major corporation headquartered in the midwestern part of the United States are an example of what one might expect, with some necessary variations and additions, from firms in general:

Economic Objectives

- Obtain a return on equity of 18 percent per year.
- Establish our presence in selected new markets.
- Increase worldwide exports to adjust to demand peaks and to achieve more sales in developing and less-developed countries.
- Add businesses that will lessen vulnerability to short-term declines in the world economy.
- Achieve a steady reduction in the assets required to generate sales.

Social Objectives

- Operate as a concerned, enlightened, and socially responsible corporate citizen of the world community.
- Strengthen programs to identify and develop tomorrow's management talent, increasing the depth behind each management position.
- Achieve increased productivity through innovative employee relations practices that encourage and develop employee involvement.

As illustrated by this statement, the economic objectives of the company relate primarily to the interests of the stockholder and include an *identification*

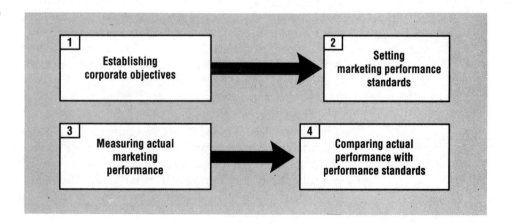

FIGURE 7-2
Recognizing marketing problems.

of the markets to be served and the *rate of return on equity* (ROE) to be made. Additional economic objectives not stated in the above list, but which nonetheless are important ones, are those of *level of sales* and of *market share*.

Social objectives relate to the *employees,* the *customers served* by the company, the *public at large,* and the *environment.*

In practice, most companies fall far short of the expectation that such a set of objectives would be formulated and stated. Research indicates that no more than 5 to 10 percent of even large corporations prepare and maintain formal sets of objectives.[2]

Setting
Performance
Standards

Performance standards are the yardsticks by which the degree of accomplishment of the corporation's objective is measured. A *marketing performance standard*

> is a statement of a specific goal to be met by a stipulated part of the firm in a designated market for a specified period of time.

For the corporation whose objectives are stated above, for example, hypothetical economic performance standards similar to the following might be set:

For the Exemplar product line for the period January 1 through June 30, 1995, the following operating results should be accomplished:

Domestic market:	
Sales	$10.5 M
Market share	16.3%
Foreign markets:	
Sales	$ 3.2 M
Market share	1.7%
Contribution to profit and fixed costs as a percentage of sales (foreign and domestic)	23.9%
ROE (foreign and domestic)	18.0%

Logically, performance standards should be derived from and be supportive of corporate objectives. This is generally not the case, however, since, as we have already seen, few companies have established corporate objectives. Marketing managers have therefore often been forced to set sales, market share, and contribution to profit and fixed-cost performance standards on their own for planning and control purposes.

Measuring
Performance

The third step in identifying a marketing problem—determining when a marketing decision is needed—is measuring the performance actually achieved. This determination may occur as a by-product of the everyday routine of conducting business—the accounting department's recording of sales, for example. For other than sales performance standards, however, special means of measuring performance will usually have to be devised. To determine the level of contribution to profit and fixed costs by product line, for example, special accounting procedures normally have to be established. To ascertain what market share was realized in each of several market segments usually requires that marketing research studies have to be conducted to determine what industry sales were to each segment.

These and other aspects of the measurement of performance are discussed in detail in the chapter on control of marketing activities (Chapter 21).

Comparing Actual Performances with Performance Standards

The final step in identifying problems is to compare the actual performance with the performance standard. By this procedure, performances that are not up to standard are flagged as problems. The attention of the manager can therefore be directed toward bringing results in these areas up to standard. (This is sometimes called **management by exception**, the "exceptions" being the low performing areas. It is also known as "management by objectives" [MBO].)

Identifying Controllable Variables That Could Contribute to the Problem Solution

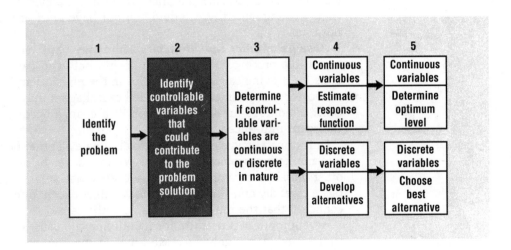

In the language of decision making, corporate objectives and departmental performance standards are set as desired levels of **objective variables**. The level of the objective variable(s) achieved is a function of **causal variables**. A decision is called for only if at least one of the causal variables is controllable; if all of the causal variables are uncontrollable (a result of an adverse economic situation, legal constraints, competitors, or other such causes) nothing can be done to help solve the problem.

In marketing decisions, the principal controllable variables are the product, price, promotion, and distribution of the product for the markets chosen and market segments targeted. Thus,

The level of the objective variable(s) = f (product, price, promotion, and distribution for the markets chosen and segments targeted given the levels of the uncontrollable variables)

The search for the culprit variable(s) is therefore confined to a limited number. The determination of which variable, or variables, is not necessarily an easy task, however.

Three types of evidence can be used to make inferences about the contributory causes to a problem. They are *associative variation, sequence of occurrence,* and *absence of other potential causal factors.*

Associative variation occurs when two or more changes accompany each other. Suppose we have set differing prices by regions and later we observe that sales are lower in the higher-price regions than they are in the lower-price regions. We may infer from this observation that the higher prices *caused* the lower sales. We have only *inferred* that the price differences are the cause of the sales differences, however; we have not *proven* that this is the case. The associative variation only provides circumstantial evidence that the price variations caused sales variations.

Sequence of occurrence can also provide evidence of causation. If the sales variations occurred *after* the price variations, the evidence of a causal relationship is strengthened. We would still not have *proof* of the causal relationship, however.

Absence of other causal factors is the only basis we have to provide incontrovertible proof of a causal relationship between two variables. This is the basis for proving causal relationships in the physical and biological sciences. In a laboratory experiment, a presumed causal agent may be introduced while all other conditions are kept the same. If a change occurs, it can be ascribed to the agent introduced.

Unfortunately, it is not possible to eliminate all other possible causal variables in a marketing problem situation. We can never be sure that there were not other variables at work of which we were not aware. However, if we investigate carefully and eliminate all the variables except one, we can be reasonably confident that the remaining variable is the cause.

An appropriate procedure for identifying the causes of marketing problems is one used by a highly successful management consulting firm and is known as the ***narrowing principle***. The steps used are as follows:

1. Conduct an investigation using available secondary data (sales analysis, available data on competitors' actions, analysis of sales representative reports, etc.) to generate a list of as many potential causes as possible.
2. Use the criteria of associative variation and sequence of occurrence to narrow the list as much as possible.
3. If the degree of remaining doubt and the importance of the problem warrant it, use one or more marketing research projects (such as surveys, laboratory experiments, field experiments, etc.) to help isolate the

cause(s) of the problem. These projects may also be designed to determine the extent of the changes that ought to be made—how much price should be changed, to what extent the advertising budget should be raised or lowered, and so forth.

Determining If Controllable Variables Are Continuous or Discrete in Nature

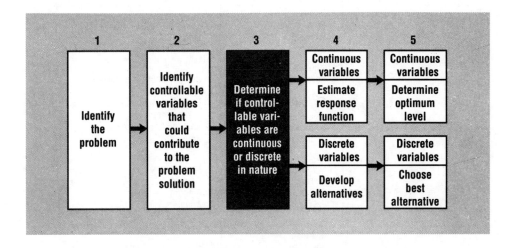

Although decisions can be classified in many different ways, an important way to categorize them is whether they have *continuous* or *discrete alternatives*.

A decision with **continuous alternatives** is one in which the alternatives differ only by degree.

How much to charge for a product, the level of inventory to carry, and the number of sales representatives to hire are examples of continuous alternative marketing decisions.

Recall the problem situations discussed at the beginning of the chapter. The decision faced by the Director of the Bureau of the Census—how much to spend on advertising in an attempt to increase the response rate to the Census of Population and Housing mail questionnaire—is an example of a continuous alternative decision. In general, any decision involving the *level* of the price to charge or the amount of expenditure on product quality, advertising, or distribution is a continuous alternative decision. A detailed listing of marketing decisions that involve choosing among continuous alternatives is given in column 1 of Table 7-1.

Other marketing decisions involve a choice among alternatives that are discrete in nature.

A decision with **discrete alternatives** is one in which the alternatives differ in kind from one another.

Table 7–1 Continuous Alternative and Discrete Alternative Marketing Decisions

Mix Variable	Nature of Alternatives	
	Continuous (column 1)	Discrete (column 2)
Product		
Design		Functions, form, color, texture, etc.
Quality	Degree of durability	Materials used
Features and options		Include or not
Brand name		Which one to use
Packaging	Degree of durability	Materials used, styling, form, color, etc.
Product line		Functions of each product
Warranty	Length	Conditions
Service	Level, number of service personnel	Services provided, conditions
Promotion		
Advertising	Budget, length of campaign	Markets, segments, theme, copy, media
Personal selling	Budget, number of sales representatives	Markets, segments
Sales promotion	Amount, frequency, duration	Type of promotions
Publicity	Amount	Type of publicity
Price		
Level	Amount	
Discounts	Amount	Include or not, conditions
Allowances	Amount	Include or not
Payment terms	Amount	Conditions
Distribution		
Channels		Which one(s) to use
Coverage	Number of outlets	
Outlet locations		Where
Sales representatives	Number	Compensation method
Sales territories	Number, size	Where
Inventories	Level	Locations
Transportation	Size of shipments	Carriers

Examples of discrete alternative decisions include which of several versions of a new product to adopt, which medium to use in an advertising campaign, and what distribution channel(s) to select.

The imbalance in destinations of one-way U-Haul trailer rentals described at the beginning of the chapter is an example of a marketing problem with discrete alternatives. There were many solutions possible, all differing in kind. The possible actions ranged from not renting trailers to go to surplus trailer areas to shipping trailers from surplus to deficit areas.

A more complete list of continuous alternative decisions is given in column 2 of Table 7–1.

You will recognize from Table 7–1 that many marketing problems involve both continuous and discrete alternatives. The Bradford Instrument case described earlier is an example. Many alternatives were available, varying from using other kinds of middlemen to direct sales using the company's own sales and service staff. A glance at the "Distribution" section of Table 7–1 will indicate that several discrete and continuous alternative decisions had to be made before Bradford's distribution problem was fully solved.

Decision models have been developed for making continuous and discrete decisions. They are described in the sections that follow.

Estimating Response Functions for Continuous Alternative Decisions

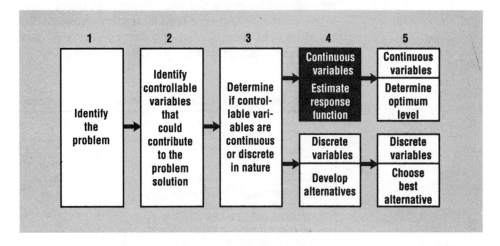

There are both sales and profit response functions. As defined in Chapter 1, the ***sales response function*** for a particular marketing mix element for a given product or service is the relationship between the level of that element and the sales of the product for a specified period. Some examples of sales response functions are shown in the figures below.

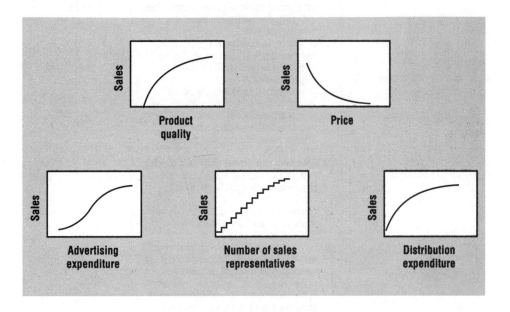

The profit response function is derived from the one for sales by subtracting from sales revenues all relevant costs (including the expenditures on the marketing mix element itself).

Estimating sales response functions accurately is arguably the most difficult task in marketing decision making. Informed choices on the appropriate level of product quality, varying levels of prices, differing amounts of advertising, alternative numbers of sales representatives, and various budgets for distribution cannot be made without first estimating the sales response functions.

Informal management judgment is the most commonly used method of estimation. The formal methods that can be used include statistical analysis of sales data, analysis of case histories, surveys, value analysis, laboratory sales

Table 7–2 Methods of Estimating Sales Response Functions for Continuous Marketing Mix Variables

Method	Applications			
	Product Quality	Price	Advertisement Expenditure	Distribution Expenditure
1. *Informal management judgment.* Unaided estimates of sales response.	X	X	X	X
2. *Statistical analysis of sales data.* Formal analyses (econometric analyses) of sales data to determine the effects of past changes in marketing variables.	X	X	X	X
3. *Analysis of case histories.* Studying the effects of similar changes in other companies.	X	X	X	X
4. *Surveys.* Determining consumer and industrial reaction to possible changes.	X	X	X	X
5. *Value analysis.* Assigning dollar values to the worth of quality differences versus competitors' products to buyers so that a net differential relative to competitor prices can be established (used primarily for industrial products).	X	X		
6. *Laboratory sales experiments.* Simulating an actual purchase situation and testing the sales effects of various marketing mix variable changes.	X	X	X	
7. *On-line sales experiments.* Deliberate changes in one or more mix variables in a sample of areas during the course of regular business operations for the purpose of determining what the sales effects will be.	X	X	X	X
8. *Field sales experiments* (for new products). Selecting a sample of markets and testing sales effects of various levels of the mix variables.	X	X	X	X
9. *Marketing models.* Experimenting with a model of the market rather than with the market itself.	X	X	X	X
10. *Delphi technique.* Obtaining the combined judgments of management of the effects of specified changes of mix variables on sales. (This can be used either before any of the above methods or after one or more of them are used. Judgments are given anonymously, so biases caused by management rank are avoided.)	X	X	X	X

Source: Adapted from D. S. Tull, "Estimating Sales Response Functions for Price and Advertising," *Werbeforschung & Praxis: Werbewissenschaftliche Gesellschaften Wien/Bonn,* May 1985, 165–168.

experiments, on-line sales experiments, field sales experiments, marketing models, and the Delphi technique. These methods are briefly described and their applications shown in Table 7–2.

Surveys and laboratory and on-line sales experiments are discussed in the next chapter. Field sales experiments are discussed in Chapter 9. For descriptions of the other methods, and a more detailed discussion of surveys and experimental methods, see any standard marketing research text.

Determining the Optimum Level of Continuous Variables

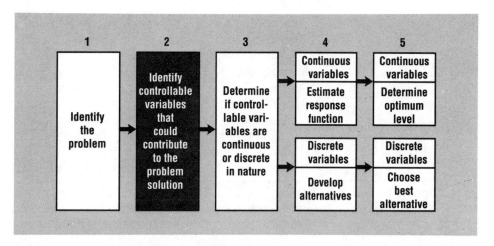

The "Brute Force" Model

Remember the problems in elementary economics in which the solution was found by computing *marginal revenue* and *marginal cost* and finding the point where they were equal? The "brute force" model is a simplified version of the marginal cost = marginal revenue model. It gives the same solution but without the need to calculate the marginal values for revenues and cost. Rather than describe the brute force model here, we first show how it works by use of an example and then describe it in general terms afterward.

Single-Mix Variable Form of the Model: The simplest form of the model is when the level of only a single causal variable (say, the price to charge or the amount to spend on advertising) is to be decided. The assumptions of the model when there is only one mix variable and their implications in an actual situation (the U.S. Bureau of the Census advertising decision) are as follows:

Assumption 1. *There is a single, continuous objective variable, such as profit or costs, whose value is to be optimized.* In the census situation, the objective was to minimize the combined costs of advertising to increase mail questionnaire returns and the personal interviewing of nonrespondents.

Assumption 2. *There is one continuous causal variable (marketing mix variable) that for purposes of making the decision is assumed to be the only controllable variable affecting the outcome.* Advertising is the controllable

Table 7–3 Estimated Effects of Advertising on Response Rate for Census of Population and Housing*

Advertising Expenditure (millions)	Response Rate	Advertising Expenditure (millions)	Response Rate
$0.0	82.8%	$3.5	85.4%
0.5	82.9	4.0	85.6
1.0	83.0	4.5	85.9
1.5	83.2	5.0	86.0
2.0	83.6	5.5	86.0
2.5	84.1	6.0	86.1
3.0	84.7	6.5	86.1

*Hypothetical data

variable in the census case. The effects of variables other than advertising were assumed in the analysis to be constant.

Assumption 3. *The effects of a change in the controllable variable on the value of the objective variable can be predicted reliably.* In order to solve for the optimum expenditure for advertising by the Census Bureau, the effect of advertising on response rate, and response rate on personal interviewing costs, had to be known. The estimated effect of advertising on response rate is given in Table 7–3, and the estimated cost of personal interviewing was $2.3 million for each percentage point of nonresponse.

Given these assumptions and the information on response effects in Assumption 3, an optimum value for the marketing mix variable can be found.

The objective variable in this case is the sum of the advertising and personal interviewing costs required to get a 100 percent response rate. The optimum expenditure for advertising will therefore be the expenditure that, when added to the personal interviewing costs required to obtain a 100 percent response, will give overall costs that are at a *minimum*.

Now it will become clear from where the name "brute force" is derived. In using the model on a problem with a single controllable variable, one is required to calculate the value of the objective variable for each level of the single controllable variable (or set of levels if there is more than one controllable variable) to find the value(s) at which the objective variable is optimized. In our example, we are obliged to calculate the total of the advertising cost plus the personal interviewing cost for every level of advertising expenditure we are considering to find the point at which the sum of these costs is the lowest.

The solution is shown in Table 7–4 by the bracketed values in the table. By use of the equation given at the bottom of the table, the combined lowest cost of advertising plus interviewing is found to be $37.1 million, which results from an advertising expenditure of either $3.5 or $4.0 million.

We can now define this method of solution for a single objective variable, single controllable causal variable as follows:

The *"brute force" solution* involves calculating the value of the objective variable that results from each level of the controllable causal variable being considered, and choosing the level of the controllable variable that results in the optimum value of the objective variable.

Table 7–4 Combined Costs of Advertising and Interviewing at Various Levels of Advertising Expenditures, U.S. Census Bureau*

1 Advertising Expenditure ($M)	2 Response Rate (%)	3a Costs of Advertising and Interviewing Advertising ($M)	3b Interviewing ($M)	3c Total ($M)
0.0	82.8	0.0	39.6†	39.6
0.5	82.9	0.5	39.3	39.8
1.0	83.0	1.0	39.1	40.1
1.5	83.2	1.5	38.6	40.1
2.0	83.6	2.0	37.7	40.7
2.5	84.1	2.5	36.6	39.1
3.0	84.7	3.0	35.2	38.2
[3.5]	85.4	3.5	33.6	[37.1]
[4.0]	85.6	4.0	33.1	[37.1]
4.5	85.8	4.5	32.7	37.2
5.0	85.9	5.0	32.4	37.4
5.5	86.0	5.5	32.2	37.7
6.0	86.1	6.0	32.0	38.0
6.5	86.1	6.5	32.0	38.5

*Hypothetical data

$$\dagger \text{Column 3c} = \text{Column 1} + (100.0 - \text{column 2}) \times \$2.3\ M$$
$$= 0 \qquad\quad + (100.0 - 82.8) \qquad \times \$2.3\ M = \$39.6\ M$$

Precision, Errors of Estimation, and the Flat Maximum Principle

Why shouldn't the analysis be extended to get a more precise answer? The solution arrived at in the table was for the Census Bureau to spend either $3.5 or $4.0 million. Couldn't the optimal amount of advertising be, say, $3.7 or $3.8 million? If so, isn't the amount of a $200,000 or $300,000 difference from spending $3.5 or $4.0. million potentially worth further analysis?

The answer, of course, is that it might be. At some point in problems of this type, however, it is not worthwhile to increase the number of the alternative levels of the controllable variable being considered. There are two reasons that this is the case.

The first is the uncertainties involved in estimating the effects of change in the level of the mix variable on the level of the objective variable. Even the most accurate estimates of response effects that can be expected are likely to be off by a few percentage points. There is no point in arriving at wrong answers in a highly precise way.

The second reason is that after a certain point in continuous alternative problems, added precision does not contribute very much to the quality of the decision. Note in Table 7–4 that there is a maximum difference of $0.3 million in the combined costs of advertising and interviewing when advertising is varied from $3.5 to $5.0 million (columns 3a and 3c). That is, the combined costs of advertising and personal interviewing change from only $37.1 to $37.4 million (a change of less than 1 percent) when advertising expenditures are increased from $3.5 to $5.0 million (a change of about 40 percent).

This is an illustration of the flat maximum principle developed by von Winterfeldt and Edwards[3] and Rasmussen.[4] The principle can be defined as follows. The *flat maximum principle* is that

> small errors can be made in continuous alternative decisions without incurring high costs.

For making decisions about marketing mix variables that have continuous alternatives (the kinds of decisions shown in column 1 of Table 7–1), the marketing manager can, therefore, afford to make some error without incurring a high cost.[5]

Multiple Controllable Variable Problems: Many marketing problems involve more than one controllable variable. For example, in the last Census of Population and Housing, the Bureau of the Census had a special promotional program that it conducted in public schools and with civic groups to encourage response to the mail questionnaire. How would the brute force model have been applied in such a situation?

Finding the optimum level for each variable does *not* give an optimum joint solution. Rather, it would have been necessary to calculate costs for each *set* of advertising and promotional costs being considered. (The response rates for each of 14 levels of advertising expenditures were estimated and given in Table 7–4.) Suppose that a similar table had been prepared for seven levels of (non-advertising) promotional expenditures. Then the combined costs of advertising + promotion + personal interviewing for 14 × 7 = 98 *sets* of advertising and promotion alternatives would have had to be calculated to find the lowest-cost joint program.

MAKING DISCRETE VARIABLE DECISIONS

Developing Alternatives for Discrete Variable Problems

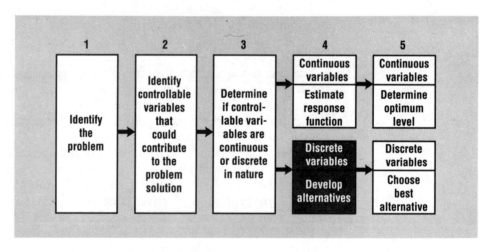

There are many marketing decisions that have discrete alternatives, perhaps even more than involve continuous decisions. Virtually all strategic marketing decisions are discrete in nature—which objectives to choose, what business(es) to be in, which markets to enter. Many operational decisions also involve discrete choices. Examples include which product(s) to introduce, what market segments to choose as targets, which medium (media) to use for advertising, what discounts and allowances to offer, and what distribution channel(s) to use.

Consider the problem faced by the U-Haul marketing manager with respect to maintaining the desired levels of inventories of trailers by area. The migration of population in the United States in recent years had resulted in surplus inventories in the southern, southwestern, and western states with corresponding deficits in the inventories in the northern and northeastern states. It was necessary to do something to correct these inventory imbalances. What alternative actions could have been taken?

Alternative 1   *Balancing inventories of trailers by constraints on rentals by destination.* If no more trailers are permitted to be rented with destinations to net in-migration areas than are rented with destinations from the same areas, after a period of adjustment, inventories will remain at the desired levels in all areas.

Alternative 2   *Balancing inventories by shipping trailers from net in-migrations to net out-migration areas.* Employing, in effect, the methods used by railroads and trucking companies of returning empty vehicles from surplus to deficit areas.

Alternative 3   *Balancing inventories by selling surplus trailers in net in-migration areas.* Just as car lessors sell the automobiles they lease after a period of time, U-Haul could sell surplus trailers in net in-migration areas.

Alternative 4   *Balancing inventories of trailers by providing containerized shipping services from net out-migration to net in-migration areas.* Sell low-cost lockable containers to the shipper and provide the vehicles at both the origin and destination for self pick-up and delivery. Special shipping arrangements could be worked out by U-Haul with common carriers (truck lines and railroads) involving shipping charges and delivery times. The container can be used by the shipper for general storage or future shipments.

Alternative 5   *Balancing inventories by setting rental price differentials by destination.* At some set of price differentials—prices that were higher to net in-migration than to net out-migration areas—the flows between the two sets of areas would have been balanced.

Several observations that are appropriate concerning sets of alternatives in general are illustrated by this set. First, *one can never be sure that the best alternative has been generated.* You no doubt can think of alternatives other than those listed above. Still, after those you have thought of have been added, it is still possible that the *best* solution is not included in the combined list.

This is a major reason that marketing managers have to be psychologically able to handle uncertainty well.

Second, *it is not always necessary to develop alternatives such that only one can be adopted.* Multiple potential solutions, or partial solutions, exist to many marketing problems because demand is affected by all of the mix variables. Note that all five of the alternatives stated above could have been adopted by U-Haul.

Third, since demand is affected by all of the mix variables, *in generating alternatives, one should attempt to think of potential solutions involving each of the product, price, promotion, and distribution variables, rather than potential solutions involving only the variable(s) that seem to have been the cause of the problem.* The U-Haul problem is one of maintaining the proper *distribution* of trailers by area. Although in the first and second alternatives it is treated as a distribution problem only, in the third it is dealt with as a promotion (sales) problem, in the fourth as a product (and service) problem, and in the last as a pricing problem.

Fourth, *generating alternatives is a creative act; choosing from among them is a judgmental one.* This requires that decision makers exercise creative skills as well as judgmental ones. Even the worst of a good set of alternatives may be better than the best of a poor set.

Since people vary in creative abilities, it is usually appropriate to involve several persons in the development of alternatives even if the choice among them is to be done only by the manager.

Choosing among Alternatives in Discrete Variable Problems

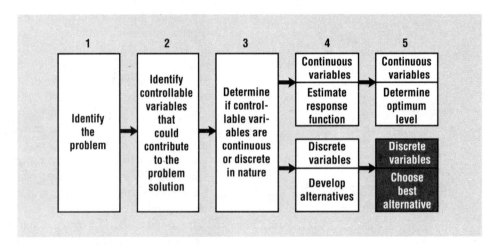

The choice of alternatives is based on predictions of how each would affect the accomplishment of the objective(s) of the firm if it were adopted. The predictions are made either as quantitative estimates of the effects of each alternative on the objective(s) or, if this estimation is not feasible, by a weighing of the advantages and disadvantages of each alternative.

Evaluating
Alternatives
Using
Quantitative
Estimates

In the U-Haul case, the choice among the alternatives considered was based on quantitative estimates of the effects on profit and market share. If possible, management wanted to find a solution that would result in both contribution to profit and fixed costs and market share not falling below their then-current levels.

Given the objective of maintaining market share, limiting trailer rentals to net in-migration areas (Alternative 1) was ruled out because it would necessarily have reduced U-Haul's share of rentals to in-migration destinations; shipping trailers from surplus to deficit areas (Alternative 2) or selling trailers in deficit areas (Alternative 3) would have had little or no effect on market share, but would have affected contribution. Depending on how one defines market share, developing a computerized shipping program (Alternative 4) might have resulted in either a higher or lower market share, and no doubt would have resulted in changes in the level of profits.

Balancing inventories by setting price differentials by destination (Alternative 5) would also no doubt have had both market share and profit effects, although the direction of either is not intuitively apparent.

In this situation, therefore, if only these alternatives were being considered, estimates would have been necessary of the effects on contribution to profits and fixed costs of the shipping trailers and selling trailers alternatives (Alternatives 2 and 3), and of the effects on both market share and profits of the containerized shipping (Alternative 4) and price differential (Alternative 5) alternatives. Predictions would have been necessary in each case of the effects on demand and on costs if that alternative were adopted and, from these, estimates of changes in market share or profits would have been made. The predictions about demand effects would have been made using one or more of the methods described in Table 7-2.

In the actual case, the decision was made to balance inventories by imposing price differentials by area.

A common error that is made in evaluating alternatives using quantitative estimates of financial effects is *to include sunk costs in the estimates*. Suppose that U-Haul had only recently developed an expensive program of computerized pricing from each departure point to each destination using uniform nationwide per-mile charges. Further suppose that it had been argued by some of the persons involved in the decision that if price differentials were used, it would result in wasting the money spent on the uniform computerized pricing software, and that therefore the company should not adopt price differentials.

Such reasoning is flawed by the fact that the computerized software expenditures had already been made and nothing could be done to retrieve them. In making estimates of financial effects of alternatives, the *only costs that are relevant are those that will be affected by choosing that alternative*. By definition, sunk costs are always irrelevant.

Evaluating Alternatives Using Advantage– Disadvantage Analysis

In many cases, it is not feasible to make summary quantitative estimates of the outcomes from choosing each of the alternatives. In such instances, it is necessary to resort to considering the advantages and disadvantages of each of the alternatives and to make the choice among the alternatives on the basis of this evaluation. These are the types of decisions that are generally considered to be the most difficult.

These types of decisions are sometimes referred to as **multi-attribute** decisions. Each alternative has to be judged with respect to a number of attributes—effect on demand, cost, and other—for each of which a favorable rating is an advantage, and an unfavorable rating a disadvantage.

An example is the case of the Bradford Instrument Company. As described earlier, the electronic and electromechanical instruments produced and mar-

**Table 7–5   Advantages and Disadvantages of Distribution
Channel Alternatives—Bradford Instrument Company**

Attribute	Importance*	Alternative 1 Full-service Wholesalers + Manufacturers' Representatives	Alternative 2 Full-service Wholesalers + Own Sales Staff	Alternative 3 Own Sales Staff Only
Control of sales effort	10	Least (3)†	Medium (4)	Most (5)
Coverage of geographic markets	8	More (4)	More (4)	Less (3)
Average inventory investment	7	$1.15 M (5)	$1.37 M (4)	$1.54 M (3)
Control of prices	4	Least (3)	Medium (3)	Most (5)
Control of services provided	9	Least (2)	Medium (3)	Most (5)
Selling costs	8	$0.88 M (5) per year	$0.94 M (4) per year	$1.22 M (2)

*10 is the most important.
†Values in parentheses are ratings. A rating of 5 is the best rating.

keted by the company had for many years been sold through full-service wholesalers supplemented (in the less important markets) by manufacturers' representation. The marketing vice-president had recently become dissatisfied with both the quality and the amount of the sales effort and the service Bradford instruments were receiving, however. He had considered two alternative methods of distributing the company's instruments: (1) replacing the manufacturers' representatives with Bradford's own sales staff and (2) replacing both the full-service wholesalers and the manufacturers' representatives with the company's own sales staff.

The pertinent attributes for evaluating each channel with its associated importance weight and rating as perceived by the marketing vice-president are shown in Table 7–5.

Informal Judgment, Conjunctive, Disjunctive, Lexicographic, Compensatory, and Dominance Models

There are several models that can be used to evaluate alternatives with multiple attributes. Included are the *informal judgment, conjunctive, disjunctive, lexicographic,* and *compensatory models,* and the principle of dominance. We discuss the informal judgment method below and describe the decision rules and their applications for the other models in Table 7–6.

Informal Judgment Model: The most common way of choosing among alternatives involving advantage–disadvantage analysis is to weigh subjectively the advantages and disadvantages of each alternative relative to those of the others, and to arrive at a judgment as to which is the most preferred.

Presumably, weights and ratings get assigned in informal ways to the attributes and whatever means of evaluation is used. The model used is informal in nature and so necessarily remains at least partly unexplicated (and probably only partly understood, even by the decision maker).

We do know, however, that in this kind of decisional situation, the person making the decision tends to use several models en route to a decision. These include the conjunctive, disjunctive, lexicographic, compensatory, and dominance models described in Table 7–6.[6]

Table 7–6   Decision Rules for Models for Choosing among Alternatives

Model	Decision Rule
INFORMAL JUDGMENT	Weigh subjectively the importance and advantages and disadvantages of each alternative relative to the others, and arrive at a judgment as to which is the most preferred.

It is not possible to predict which alternative the vice-president would have chosen in the Bradford Instrument case.

CONJUNCTIVE	Assign importance weights and ratings to each attribute. Set minimum levels of desirability for the more important advantages or disadvantages, and reject any alternatives for which one or more minima are not met. (If only one alternative meets all of the minima, that is the one that will be chosen.)

The vice-president could have decided that the channel chosen would have to have a rating of at least 3 for each of the attributes considered. This would have eliminated Alternative 1 (control of services provided had a rating of 2) and Alternative 3 (selling costs had a rating of 2). Thus, Alternative 2 (keep the full-service wholesalers but replace the manufacturers' representatives with their own sales staff) would have been the choice.

DISJUNCTIVE	Assign importance weights and ratings to each attribute. Set superior levels of desirability for one or more of the attributes, and reject any alternative that does not meet or exceed all of these levels. (If only one alternative meets all of the superior ratings required, that is the one that will be chosen.)

The vice-president could have decided to consider only channels with ratings for control of sales effort and control of services that were 4 or better. In this case, both Alternatives 1 and 2 would have been eliminated, and Alternative 3 (using their own sales staff only) would have been selected.

LEXICOGRAPHIC	Assign importance weights and ratings to each attribute. Arrange the attributes in order of importance, and compare the ratings for the alternatives on each attribute beginning with the most important. On each successive comparison, keep only those alternatives whose ratings tie for high. (When one alternative has the highest rating on an advantage or disadvantage, that is the one that will be chosen.)

From Table 7-5, we see that control of sales effort was the most important consideration, and control of services provided was next in importance. Using this model, Alternative 3 (using own sales staff only) would have been chosen since it had the highest rating of the three on sales effort control.

COMPENSATORY	Assign importance weights and ratings to each attribute. For each alternative, multiply the rating by the weight assigned each attribute and sum over all attributes. The alternative with the highest total score will be the one that is chosen. This is similar to the Fishbein model discussed in Chapter 4.

As indicated by the table that follows, Alternative 3 would be chosen using the compensatory model.

	Alternative 1	Alternative 2	Alternative 3
Control of sales effort	$10 \times 3 = 30$	$10 \times 4 = 40$	$10 \times 5 = 50$
Coverage of geographic markets	$8 \times 4 = 32$	$8 \times 4 = 32$	$8 \times 3 = 24$
Average inventory investment	$7 \times 5 = 35$	$7 \times 4 = 28$	$7 \times 3 = 21$
Control of prices	$4 \times 3 = 12$	$4 \times 4 = 16$	$4 \times 5 = 20$
Control of services provided	$9 \times 2 = 18$	$9 \times 3 = 27$	$9 \times 5 = 45$
Selling costs	$8 \times 5 = \underline{40}$	$8 \times 4 = \underline{32}$	$8 \times 2 = \underline{16}$
Total score	167	175	176

(Continued on page 210)

Table 7–6 (*continued*)

Model	Decision Rule
DOMINANCE	Assign importance weights and ratings to each attribute. Reject any alternative that has a lower rating on one or more attributes than some other rating. (If one alternative has ratings that are all equal to or greater than those of any other alternative, and at least one rating that is higher than that of any other alternative, that will be the one that is chosen.)

Reference to Table 7–5 indicates that none of the alternatives in the Bradford case was dominant.

Results:
A review of the results shows that all but one model making a definitive choice chose Alternative 3 (using own sales staff only).

Model	Alternative Chosen
Conjunctive	2
Disjunctive	3
Lexicographic	3
Compensatory	3

In the actual case, this was the distribution channel that was selected.

DEALING WITH UNCERTAINTY

In the foregoing discussion of decision making, we have assumed (implicitly in most instances) that the outcomes that would result from adopting a particular alternative could be predicted accurately. In the Census case, specific levels of response were assumed to be known for given levels of advertising expenditures. It was assumed that the effects on profit and market share could be predicted accurately for each of the alternatives in the U-Haul decision, and that specific outcomes for each of the attributes being considered in the Bradford Instrument decision could be anticipated.

The actual situation in marketing, of course, is that there is always uncertainty in predicting outcomes. The extent of the uncertainties inherent in marketing decisions compared with other areas of the company has been aptly described as follows:

Marketing remains one of the most difficult areas of analysis and decision making for the company. Marketing problems do not exhibit the neat quantitative properties of many of the problems in production, accounting, or finance. Psychological variables play a larger role: Marketing expenditures affect demand and costs simultaneously: Marketing plans shape and interact with other corporate plans. Marketing decisions must be made in the face of insufficient information about processes that are dynamic, nonlinear, lagged, stochastic, interactive, and downright difficult.[7]

But recognizing that there are more uncertainties associated with marketing decisions than most other decisions made in the firm doesn't make them any less real. It serves only to emphasize that there is a greater need for evaluating and devising methods of dealing with them in marketing than in other areas.

Uncertainties translate into risks. For a given amount of money that is to be gained or lost, the greater the uncertainty about the outcome, the greater the risk involved. From the standpoint of the uncertainties involved, and in many cases the size of the stakes as well, marketing managers are faced with more risky decisions than managers in the other functional areas of the firm.

Propensities of Companies to Assume Risks

There is a kind of strategic choice involved in how to deal with risk in making decisions. Should the company be *risk seeking*, and so look for potentially highly profitable markets, product lines, or products, even though the risks involved may be relatively high? Or should it be *risk averse* and so look for stable and low-risk markets and products, even though by so doing it may forgo more profitable alternatives? Or should it be *risk neutral* and try to balance the prospect of gain with the probability of loss in choosing among markets and products? The basic stance of the firm toward these questions will have a pronounced effect on the marketing strategies adopted.

Contrary to the myth that executive offices are occupied predominantly by hard-driving, entrepreneurially inclined, risk-taking individuals, the evidence indicates that most executives are risk averse. Swalm found this to be the case, and similar findings have been reported by Green and by Barnes.[8] One of the present authors has obtained measures of the propensity to assume risk of approximately 300 middle and upper middle management marketing executives over the past decade. Most of them were found to be risk averse. A small percentage were risk neutral and a very small percentage risk seeking.

> If you would like to get an approximate measure of your own propensity to assume risk, work through Problem 7.26 at the end of this chapter.

The stance of the company toward taking risks is a part of the corporate culture. Whereas there are no known studies on the relative frequencies of risk-seeking, risk-neutral, and risk-averse firms, observation suggests that more companies are risk averse than the combined number that are risk neutral or risk seeking. Although it is rare for a company to have an explicit policy on risk taking, one can infer an implicit policy by the decisions that are made. The example below will illustrate this point.

Suppose we have a new-product-introduction decision that involves deciding whether we should introduce product version A or product version B, or not introduce either. Further, suppose that the consequences of each of these alternatives, conditioned on whether the market situation turns out to be "favorable" or "unfavorable," are as indicated in the table below, which alternative should be chosen?

Alternatives	Favorable Market		Unfavorable Market	
	Probability	Payoff	Probability	Payoff
1. Introduce version A	.6	$100,000	.4	($25,000)
2. Introduce version B	.6	50,000	.4	($10,000)
3. Do not introduce either version A or version B	.6	0	.4	0

By definition, a ***risk neutral company*** is

one that is indifferent between a certain monetary sum and a gamble with an expected monetary value of that same amount.

(The term *expected* is used here in its mathematical sense, that is, the sum of the products of all of the possible outcomes of a decision times their respective probabilities of occurring.) A logical choice for such individuals for choosing among alternatives with uncertain outcomes is, then, a rule that stipulates that the alternative should be chosen with the highest **expected monetary value** (*expected* is again used in its mathematical sense).

In the new-product example, the expected monetary values of the alternatives are as follows:

$$\text{Expected monetary value of Alternative 1} = .6 \times \$100,000 + .4 \langle\$25,000\rangle = \$50,000$$

$$\text{Expected monetary value of Alternative 2} = .6 \times \$50,000 + .4 \langle\$10,000\rangle = \$26,000$$

$$\text{Expected monetary value of Alternative 3} = .6 \times \$0 + .4 \times \$0 = \$0$$

The choice for risk-neutral companies in this example is, then, Alternative 1 (introduce version A).

Risk-neutral companies will often choose an alternative whose expected monetary outcome is not the highest because that alternative has a higher conditional loss than the alternative chosen. The conditional losses of Alternative 2 ($10,000) and Alternative 3 ($0) are both less than that of Alternative 1 ($25,000). A moderately risk-averse company would very likely choose Alternative 2 (introduce version B), whereas a company more tenaciously risk averse might choose Alternative 3 (introduce neither version.)[9]

The expected monetary value rule is widely used in marketing and other functional area texts in business schools. It has the virtues of forcing thought to be given to identifying the various "states of nature" that might affect the outcome of the decision, and of requiring assessments of the probabilities of each state and the payoffs that would result if it turned out to be the actual state.

It is easy for students to draw the inference from their wide exposure to it that this is the rule that one *should* use in making decisions. Such is the case, however, *only* if the company is a risk-neutral decision maker.

As an employee of the firm, the stance of the marketing manager toward assuming risk should be the same, or close to the same, as that of the company's. This should be a consideration of both the company and of applicants for the position of marketing manager for it. If there is a mismatch in this respect, neither party is likely to be happy with the other's performance.

WHAT WE KNOW ABOUT DECISION MAKERS AND THE DECISIONS THEY MAKE

Although research in the processes we use and the competencies we have for decision making has been going on for most of this century, both the extent and the degree of sophistication of such research have accelerated rapidly since the early 1970s. The result has been a rapidly growing mosaic of evidence that, although neither complete nor fully definitive, points toward some conclusions that are useful to know. The findings are summarized below.

1. *Most decision makers are overconfident concerning their abilities to make decisions.* In general, all of the outcomes that could occur from choosing a particular alternative are not anticipated,[10] probability of outcomes are assessed inaccurately, and judgmental rules-of-thumb are used that do not predict well. Yet, persons making decisions consistently overestimate their abilities in all three of these areas.[11] Since marketing executives tend to be confident persons, it seems probable that they as a group are as overconfident of their decision-making abilities as are people in general.

A major contributing "reason" for such overconfidence is that all of the possible outcomes of a decision never occur, actual probabilities are seldom known, and the feedback received is not such as to allow decision makers to judge how good—or how bad—their decision making really is.

2. *New information affecting judgments on outcomes of alternatives is generally not assimilated well.* To illustrate this problem, assume that there is a potential new product about which the executives concerned agree that there is a better-than-average chance (say, a 60 percent chance) of its being successful if it is introduced. Further assume that a market test is conducted that shows that the product would be successful if introduced. The test was of a standard design which past experience has indicated gives a correct indication about six times out of seven (85 percent of the time).

Given the market test indication, is the probability of success (if introduced) closest to 60 percent, 70 percent, 80 percent, or 90 percent? Decide which you think is the correct answer, then check it by looking at the box in the middle of the next page. If your answer was wrong, or you were uncertain about it even if it was correct, an illustration is provided of our limitations in assimilating new information on the likelihood of outcomes.

One of the biases that is present in most people's assimilation of new information is to place undue reliance on the results of small samples.[12] This is true even if the samples are randomly selected, but it is compounded if they are not. For example, if in three instances over the past year or so revenues for different products for a company have increased after prices were raised, there is a tendency for those observing the revenue increases to conclude that a prospective price increase for still another of the company's products will be more likely to result in a revenue increase than is actually the case.

3. *In using informal judgment to choose among multi-attribute, discrete alternatives, various choice models are used, often in different sequences for different problems.* As described earlier, the conjunctive, disjunctive, lexicographic, compensatory, and dominance models are used, along with perhaps some others,[13] in multi-attribute, discrete alternative decisional situations.[14]

Although this could be interpreted as a negative observation about decision makers, that is not necessarily the case. Differing decisional situations may call for differing models. More than one model may need to be used because the earlier one(s) did not result in eliminating a sufficient number of alternatives.

4. *When sunk costs are involved in a situation calling for a decision, many (most?) decision makers will consider them in their decision. They shouldn't.* One should consider only those costs that will change as a result of the decision. Sunk costs will not change.

5. *Most executives, including those in marketing, are risk averse.* As reported earlier, in the studies that have been done on the willingness of executives to assume risk, most of those studied, including marketing executives, have been found to be risk averse. In terms of the relative degree of risk aversion between marketing and other functional-area executives, in one study it was found that marketing executives as a group were slightly more cautious than the average for general administrative, financial, engineering, and production executives.[15]

6. *Riskier decisions tend to be made by a group of decision makers than would be made individually by the persons who make up the group.* It is commonly believed that committees tend to make decisions that are compromises of the views held by the members. When applied to the area of risk assumption, this belief would suggest that the decisions made by committees would be no more risky than the average of those that would have been made by the individuals making up the committee. The rather surprising finding from an analysis of the findings of all the studies on this subject reported in the literature is that the committee decisions tend to be more risky than those of the individuals made in isolation.[16]

A number of possible explanations have been suggested for this "risky shift," including a reduction in the sense of individual responsibility and greater familiarization with the problem gained through an interchange of information. The best explanation may be that we have a cultural value for riskiness that groups bring out. Certain types of decisions, such as decisions about marriage, may bring out cultural values for conservative decisions, but most decisions in marketing and business tend to be ones for which our culture values riskiness.[17]

Most new-product decisions are made by committee, and a sizable proportion (more than half) of them fail. A partial explanation for the high failure rate might be with the "risky shift."

For the situation described on the previous page, the revised probability of the product's being successful is

$$\frac{.85 \times .60}{.85 \times .60 + .15 \times .40} = .895 = 89.5 \text{ percent.}$$

SUMMARY OF IMPORTANT POINTS

1. Decision making in marketing requires (a) *establishing corporate objectives(s)*, (b) *setting marketing performance standard(s)*, (c) *measuring actual performance*, (d) *comparing actual performance with performance standard(s)*, and (e) *taking corrective action when required.*
2. Objectives may be *economic* or *social* in nature.
3. Economic objectives relate primarily to the interests of the stockholders and include contribution to profits and fixed costs, rate-of-return on equity (ROE), level of sales, and market share.
4. Social objectives relate to employees, customers, the public at large, and the environment.
5. Three types of evidence can be used to make inferences about the contributory causes to a problem. They are (a) *associative variation*, (b) *sequence of occurrence*, and (c) *absence of other potential causal* factors.
6. The *narrowing principle* can be used to identify the causes of marketing problems. It consists of the following steps:
   a. Conduct an investigation using available secondary data (sales analysis, available data on competitors' actions, analysis of sales representative reports, etc.) to generate a list of as many potential causes as possible.
   b. Use the criteria of associative variation and sequence of occurrence to narrow the list as much as possible.
   c. If the degree of remaining doubt and the importance of the problem warrants it, use one or more marketing research projects (such as surveys, laboratory experiments, field experiments) to help isolate the cause(s) of the problem.

7. Marketing problems always are concerned with one or more of the mix variables—product, price, promotion, or distribution—and may involve either continuous alternative or discrete alternative decisions.

8. A decision with continuous alternatives is one in which the alternatives differ only by *degree*.

    Examples: the price to charge, the amount to budget for advertising, the number of sales representatives to have.

9. A decision with discrete alternatives is one in which the alternatives differ in *kind*.

    Examples: which market segment(s) to target, which distribution channel(s) to use, which of several versions of a product to adopt.

10. A *sales response function* for a particular marketing mix element for a given product or service is the relationship between the level of that element and the sales of the product for a specified period.

11. Informal management judgment is the most commonly used method of estimation of sales response functions. The formal methods that can be used include statistical analysis of sales data, analysis of case histories, surveys, value analysis, laboratory sales experiments, on-line sales experiments, field sales experiments, marketing models, and the Delphi technique.

12. The optimum level for single-mix variable decisions with continuous alternatives—setting price or determining the advertising budget, for example—can be solved using the *brute force model* (variation of marginal revenue = marginal cost model of elementary economics).

13. The *principle of the flat maximum* is that small errors can be made in continuous alternative decisions without incurring high costs.

14. Most strategic and many operational marketing decisions have discrete rather than continuous alternatives.

15. Generating discrete alternatives is a *creative* act, whereas choosing from among them is a *judgmental* one.

16. In generating alternatives, one should attempt to think of potential solutions that involve each of the product, price, promotion, and distribution variables, rather than for just the variable(s) that seems to have been the cause of the problem.

17. The choice of alternatives is based on predictions of how each would affect the accomplishment of the objective(s) of the firm if it were adopted. The predictions are made either as:
    a. Quantitative estimates of the effects of each alternative on the objective(s), or if this estimation is not feasible,
    b. By a weighing of the advantages and disadvantages of each alternative.

18. In making estimates of financial effects of alternatives, the only costs that are relevant are those that will be affected by choosing that alternative. (By definition, sunk costs are always irrelevant.)

19. The models used for choosing among discrete alternatives include *informal judgment, conjunctive, disjunctive, lexicographic, compensatory,* and the *principle of dominance*.

20. The *conjunctive model* involves rating the attributes associated with each alternative and setting minimum acceptable ratings for some, or all,

of them. Alternatives with attributes with ratings less than the acceptable level are then rejected.

21. The *disjunctive model* involves rating the attributes associated with each alternative and choosing alternatives that have superior ratings on selected attributes.

22. The *lexicographic model* requires arranging the attributes in order of importance, rating each attribute for each alternative that has the highest rating (following any ties) on the most important attribute.

23. The *compensatory model* involves weighting the attributes, rating each one for each alternative, and choosing the alternative with the highest weighted average attribute rating.

24. The *principle of dominance* requires rating the attributes for each alternative and rejecting any alternative that has no ratings that are any better than and at least one rating that is worse than those of one or more other alternatives.

25. Marketing managers generally have to deal with greater uncertainties and associated risks in making decisions than do managers of other functional areas in the firm.

26. Most executives, including marketing executives, are risk averse.

27. The *expected monetary value* decision rule requires the decision maker to choose the alternative that has the highest (mathematically) expected monetary value.

28. Most decision makers are overconfident regarding their abilities to make decisions.

29. Decision makers generally do not assimilate new information affecting judgments on outcomes of alternatives very well.

30. In using informal judgment to choose among multi-attribute, discrete alternatives, various choice models are used, often in different sequences for different problems.

31. Most executives, including those in marketing, are risk averse.

32. Riskier decisions tend to be made by a group of decision makers than would be made individually by the persons who make up the group. This phenomenon is known as the *risky shift*.

REVIEW QUESTIONS

7.1. How is the need for a marketing decision recognized?

7.2. What is a *performance standard*?

7.3. What are some examples of decisions in marketing with continuous alternatives? with discrete alternatives?

7.4. What are the two methods of solving for the optimum level of the marketing-mix variable using the marginal model?

7.5. What is the *flat maximum principle*?

7.6. In developing alternatives, should one attempt to think of potential solutions involving only the variable(s) that seems to have been the cause of the problem? Why or why not?

7.7. Describe the (a) informal judgment model, (b) conjunctive model, (c) disjunctive model, (d) lexicographic model, (e) compensatory model, and (f) principle of dominance.

7.8. What are the conclusions that can be drawn about the abilities and characteristics of decision makers?

7.9. If companies in general do not have "well-defined statements dealing with corporate objectives," how can performance standards be established? And, if marketing performance standards are not set, how can marketing problems be identified?

7.10. Identify the markets being served by the companies providing the indicated products or services:

Product or Service Provided	Market Served
Television programs	entertainment
Airline travel	
Oil company	
Computer company	
Trucking company	
Junkyard	

7.11. What are the performance standards, if any, that are set by your college or university? How is actual performance measured?

7.12. What are the implications of the flat maximum principle for pricing? setting advertising budgets? marketing research?

7.13. Does the flat maximum principle work for discrete alternative problems? Explain.

7.14. "Most business schools emphasize the judgmental process of choosing from among alternatives rather than the creative process of generating them."
   a. Do you agree or disagree with this statement? Why?
   b. Regardless of how you answered (a), should business schools be more concerned with developing the ability to exercise good judgment than to be creative? Explain.

7.15. It is usually the case that applying the conjunctive, disjunctive, lexicographic, and compensatory models to discrete, multi-attribute alternative problems results in differing alternatives being indicated. (This was so in the Bradford Instrument case.) Does this mean that some of the models are inferior to the others? Why or why not?

7.16. Can how "good" or how "bad" a decision is be measured solely by the outcome? Explain.

7.17. Do you believe that the way corporations reward executives for "good" decision making and punish them for "bad" decision making has anything to do with their propensity to assume risk? Explain.

7.18. What possible explanations can you give as to why research findings indicate that committees make riskier decisions than do the individuals composing them?

DISCUSSION QUESTIONS AND PROBLEMS

7.19. In the Bureau of the Census advertising budgeting decision, the total cost of obtaining responses consisted of the cost of advertising and the cost of personally interviewing the nonrespondents. Over the effective-advertising range, as advertising expenditures increased, personal interviewing costs fell. Since the objective was to have the lowest total cost of advertising and personal selling, one would want to continue advertising as long as the reduction in the cost of personal interviewing—the marginal cost of interviewing—was less than the added cost of advertising. At the point where the reduction in interviewing cost was the same as the increase in advertising cost, no more should be spent on advertising. At this point, the two marginal costs are equal.

Using the data in Table 7–4, solve for the optimum amount that the Census Bureau should have spent on advertising by calculating the marginal costs and determining where they are equal. Check your answer against that given in the table.

7.20. Suppose the response rate to various levels of advertising for the Census of Population and Housing had been estimated to be as follows:

Advertising Expenditure ($M)	Response Rate (%)	Advertising Expenditure ($M)	Response Rate (%)
0.0	76.4	3.5	79.9
0.5	76.5	4.0	80.6
1.0	76.7	4.5	81.2
1.5	77.1	5.0	81.6
2.0	77.6	5.5	81.8
2.5	78.2	6.0	81.9
3.0	79.0	6.5	82.0

Solve by finding the lowest combined cost of advertising and personal interviewing (the brute force method). What is the optimum advertising expenditure?

7.21. The Marketing Committee (a committee composed of the president, the executive vice-president, and the vice-presidents of marketing, finance, and production and logistics) of a western industrial equipment company agreed to the following estimates of quantities that would be sold of one of the company's products during the coming six months at the indicated prices:

Price per Unit	Estimated Quantities That Would Be Sold (000)
$19.00	121.0
19.50	118.0
20.00	114.5
20.50	111.0
21.00	107.0
21.50	102.5
22.00	98.0
22.50	95.0

Assume that the company's objectives were to maximize the contribution to overhead and profit during the coming six months and that the average production costs were estimated to be constant at $10 per unit.

a. Solve for the optimum price by finding the level that provides the greatest contribution to overhead and profit (the brute force method).

b. Solve for the optimum price by equating marginal revenue and marginal cost.

7.22. The sales manager for a manufacturer of drug sundries has prepared estimates of the sales volume that would be generated next year given different sizes of the sales force. The estimates are as follows:

Number of Full-time Sales Representatives for the Year	Estimated Annual Sales (000)
25	$5,625
26	5,825
27	6,000
28	6,150
29	6,270
30	6,380
31	6,475
32	6,560
33	6,630
34	6,690

The company averages a mark-up of 100 percent on cost. The estimated cost per sales representative is $60,000 per year, inclusive of salary, travel, and expenses.

Assume that the objective of the company is to maximize the contribution to overhead and profits and that overhead costs do not change with the volume of sales.

    a. Solve for the optimum number of sales representatives by finding the number that results in the greatest contribution to overhead and profits (the brute force method).

    b. Solve for the optimum number of sales representatives by equating marginal revenue and marginal cost.

7.23. What means other than paid advertising might the Bureau of the Census have used in promoting a higher response rate for the mail out, mail back questionnaires used in the 1980 Census of Population and Housing?

7.24. Suppose a shopper has a buying rule-of-thumb for canned vegetables that allows choices to be made between different brands of the same product with varying prices and qualities. The rule is that if the price difference between two brands is five cents or less, buy the brand with the higher quality; if the price difference between the two brands is more than five cents, buy the brand with the lower price.

    a. Is this a disjunctive, conjunctive, lexicographic, or compensatory rule? Why?

    b. Suppose the shopper has the following choices in buying canned peas:

	Price	Quality
Brand X	$1.00/8-oz.can	High
Brand Y	.95/8-oz.can	Medium
Brand Z	.90/8-oz.can	Low

Which brand should be bought?

7.25. The table on the following page has been used for evaluating screening models for new products. Assume that a company's management has decided that any product passed should have a minimum rating of "moderate" or better on all evaluative criteria. Would this be an example of a conjunctive, disjunctive, lexicographic, or linear compensatory choice model?

Ratings and Weights of Evaluative Criteria for Screening Models

Screening Models				Evaluative Criteria	Weight
Conjunctive	Disjunctive	Lexicographic	Linear Compensatory		
E (5)	E (5)	M (3)	M (3)	Ease of obtaining data	.08
H (5)	H (5)	H (5)	H (5)	Computerization potential	.02
E (5)	E (5)	E (5)	E (5)	Ease of updating	.06
L (1)	L (1)	L (1)	M (3)	Necessary operator proficiency level	.04
L (1)	L (1)	L (1)	L (1)	Need for outside help	.03
L (1)	L (1)	L (1)	L (1)	Cost to set up or maintain	.01
L (1)	L (1)	L (1)	L (1)	Needed time to reach proficiency	.05
L (1)	L (1)	L (1)	L (1)	Time required for use	.07
M (3)	M (3)	M (3)	M (3)	Specificity of evaluation	.08
M (3)	M (3)	M (3)	M (3)	Variety of applications	.07
H (5)	H (5)	H (5)	H (5)	Communicability of results	.09
L (1)	L (1)	L (1)	L (1)	Educational potential	.10
H (5)	H (5)	H (5)	H (5)	Use of quantitative and qualitative data	.07
M (3)	M (3)	H (5)	H (5)	Current acceptance and usage	.11
H (5)	H (5)	H (5)	H (5)	Risk factors incorporated	.12

SYMBOLS: H = High· M = Moderate   L = Low   E = Easy   D = Difficult
SCORING: H = E = 5 points
          M = 3 points
          L = D = 1 point
Source: Adapted from Kenneth G. Baker, "The Comparative Analysis of Models for Use in Product Screening Decisions," Ph.D. diss., University of Oregon, 1980, 21.

7.26. Say you have a cash balance of $1,000 above your living costs for the rest of the term. This $1,000 is money you have earned and for which you are not accountable to anyone else. Further suppose that you are faced with the situations described here.

    a. You are forced either to accept a gamble with an equal chance of winning $50 or losing $250 or else making an immediate payment to avoid the gamble.

        (1) Would you accept the gamble?   Yes ____   No ____

If your answer is yes, make a dot at the intersection of the zero payment and the #1 lines in the diagram on page 224. Then go to question b.
   If your answer is no, answer part (2) of this question.

        (2) What is the maximum amount you would pay to avoid the gamble? $_____

Enter this amount in the diagram by making a dot at the appropriate point on line #1.

b. You are forced either to pay an immediate sum to obtain a gamble with an equal chance of winning $400 and losing $200 or else to turn it down at no cost.

    (1) Would you turn it down at no cost?   Yes ____   No ____

If your answer is yes, make a dot at the intersection of the zero payment and the #2 line in the diagram. Then go to question c.
  If your answer is no, answer part (2) of this question.

    (2) What is the maximum amount you would pay for the gamble? $_____

Enter this amount in the diagram by making a dot at the appropriate point on line #2.

c. You are forced either to accept a gamble with an equal chance of winning $100 or losing $200 or else making an immediate payment to avoid the gamble.

    (1) Would you accept the gamble?   Yes ____   No ____

If your answer is yes, make a dot at the intersection of the zero payment and the #3 lines in the diagram. Then go to question d.
  If your answer is no, answer part (2) of this question.

    (2) What is the maximum amount you would pay to avoid the gamble? $_____

Enter this amount in the diagram by making a dot at the appropriate point on line #3.

d. You are forced either to pay an immediate sum to obtain a gamble with an equal chance of winning $200 and losing $100 or else to turn it down at no cost.

    (1) Would you turn it down at no cost?   Yes ____   No ____

If your answer is yes, make a dot at the intersection of the zero payment and the #4 lines in the diagram.
  If your answer is no, answer part (2) of this question.

    (2) What is the maximum amount you would pay for the gamble? $_____

Enter this amount in the diagram by making a dot at the appropriate point on line #4.

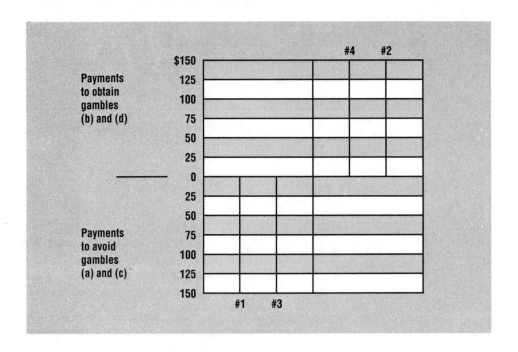

1. Connect the four points you filled in as you read this question with a smoothed-in line.
2. If the line is straight, you are risk neutral; if the line is concave downward (‿) you are risk averse; if the line is concave upward (⁀) you are risk seeking.

(This exercise is taken from D. S. Tull and D. I. Hawkins, *Marketing Research: Measurement and Method*, 4th ed., Macmillan, 1987, 762–764. Used with permission.)

7.27. Assume that the following probabilities, payoffs, and utilities apply to a decision by a developer concerning building a tract of houses:

Alternatives	Favorable Market State			Unfavorable Market State		
	Probability	Payoff	Utilities	Probability	Payoff	Utilities
Build tract	.50	$500,000	100	.50	($400,000)	(200)
Do not build tract	.50	0	0	.50	0	0

a. What decision would be made if an expected monetary value decision rule is used?
b. What decision would be made if an expected utility decision rule is used?

7.28. Assume that the following probabilities, payoffs, and utilities apply to a decision by a department store on opening a branch store in a suburban location:

Alternatives	Favorable Market State			Unfavorable Market State		
	Probability	Payoff	Utilities	Probability	Payoff	Utilities
Open branch	.60	$500,000	150	.40	($400,000)	(250)
Do not open branch	.60	0	0	.40	0	0

a. What decision would be made if an expected monetary value decision rule is used?

b. What decision would be made if an expected utility decision rule is used?

Endnotes

[1]"Bradford Instrument Company" is a fictitious name, but the situation is an actual one.

[2]H. W. Boyd, Jr., and S. H. Britt, "Making Marketing Research More Effective by Using the Administrative Process," *Journal of Marketing Research*, February 1965, 15; V. Wadesman, "Setting Corporate Objectives," *Financial Executive*, January 1976, 44–47; C. P. Edmonds III and J. W. Hand, "What Are the Real Long-run Objectives of Business?" *Business Horizons*, December 1976, 75–81.

[3]D. von Winterfeldt and W. Edwards, "Flat Maxima in Linear Optimization Models," Engineering Psychology Laboratory Technical Report 011313-4-T, University of Michigan, 1973. The principle is discussed in P. Slovic, B. Fischoff, and S. Lichtenstein, "Behavioral Decision Theory," in *Annual Review of Psychology*, Vol. 28, M. R. Rosenzweig and L. W. Porter (eds.), Annual Reviews, 1977, 27.

[4]A. Rasmussen, "How Critical Are Optimal Points in Marketing?" *Det Danske Marked*, March 1963, 125. An illustration of the principle is also given in W. J. Baumol and R. E. Quandt, "Rules of Thumb and Optimally Imperfect Decisions," *The American Economic Review*, March 1964, 23–46.

[5]For an application of this principle to advertising, see D. S. Tull et al., "Leveraged Decision Making in Advertising: The Flat Maximum Principle and Its Implications," *The Journal of Marketing Research*, February 1986, 25–32.

[6]O. Svenson and H. Montgomery, "On Decision Rules and Information Processing Strategies for Choice among Multiattribute Alternatives," *Scandinavian Journal of Psychology*, December 1976, 283–291.

[7]P. Kotler, *Marketing Management: Analysis, Planning, and Control*, Prentice-Hall, 1980.

[8]R. O. Swalm, "Utility Theory—Insights into Risk Taking," *Harvard Business Review*, November–December 1966, 133; P. E. Green, "Risk Attitudes and Chemical Investment Decisions," *Chemical Engineering Progress*, January 1963, 35–40; J. D. Barnes, "A Strategic Competitive Bidding Approach to Pricing Decisions for Petroleum Drilling Contractors," Ph.D. diss., University of Oregon, 1972.

[9]The *maximin, minimax regret*, and *expected utility* decision rules are appropriate for risk-averse decision makers. They are discussed in P. E. Green, D. S. Tull, and G. S. Albaum, *Research for Marketing Decisions*, 5th ed., Prentice-Hall, 1987, 25–26, 77–81.

[10]B. Fischoff, P. Slovic, and S. Lichtenstein, "Fault Trees: Sensitivity of Estimated Failure Probabilities to Problem Representation," *Journal of Experimental Psychology: Human Perception and Performance*, Vol. 4, no. 2, 1978, 330–344.

[11]See Slovic et al., "Behavioral Decision Theory," 5–6, for a general discussion of overconfidence with respect to decision-making abilities. See also W. C. Howell, "Compounding Uncertainty from Internal Sources," *Journal of Experimental Psychology*, Vol. 95, no. 1, September 1972, 6–13; D. Kahneman and A. Tversky, "Subjective Probability: A Judgment of Representativeness," *Cognitive Psychology*, Vol. 3, no. 3, July 1972, 430–454; D. Kahneman and A. Tversky, "On the Psychology of Prediction," *Psychological Review*, July 1973, 237–251; P. Slovic, B. Fischoff, and S. Lichtenstein, "The Certainty Illusion," *ORT Research Bulletin*, Vol. 16, no. 4, 1976; H. J. Einhorn, "Overconfidence in Judgment," in *New Directions for Methodology of Behavioral Research: Fallible Judgment in Behavioral Research*, R. A. Shweder and D. W. Fiske (eds.), Jossey-Bass, 1980.

[12]A. Tversky and D. Kahneman, "The Belief in the Law of Small Numbers," *Psychological Bulletin*, Vol. 76, no. 2, 1971, 105–110.

[13]A. Tversky, "Elimination by Aspects: A Theory of Choice," *Psychological Review*, Vol. 79, no. 4, July 1972, 281–299.

[14]Svenson and Montgomery, "On Decision Rules."

[15]R. W. Rider, Jr., "The Marketing Executive: A Profile," Ph.D. diss., University of Oregon, 1972, 125.

[16]J. H. Barnes, Jr., D. E. Gunerson, and J.G.P. Paolillo, "The Phenomena of Risky Shift," unpublished paper, 1988.

[17]R. Brown, *Social Psychology*, Free Press, 1965; D. G. Pruitt, "Choice Shifts in Group Discussions: An Introductory Review," *Journal of Personality and Social Psychology*, 1971, 339–360. A competing explanation is that groups make persuasive arguments salient. See, for example, D. A. Myers and H. Lamb, "The Group Polarization Phenomenon," *Psychological Bulletin*, 1976, 602–627; and A. Vinokur and E. Burnstein, "Depolarization of Attitudes in Groups," *Journal of Personality and Social Psychology*, 1978, 872–885.

INFORMATION
FOR MARKETING
DECISION MAKING

Although marketing executives differ widely in their decision-making style — some tend to be short term and others long term in orientation, some are deliberate and others decide quickly, some consult co-workers frequently and others prefer to keep their own counsel, and so forth — there is necessarily an element they all share. That is their recognition of the need for sound information on which to base marketing decisions.

Marketing executives require extensive amounts of information. Other than the controller, who has a unique responsibility for dealing with data to measure the investments and divestments, costs, and revenues of the firm, marketing managers probably require more information to carry out their responsibilities than any of the other managers of major functions of the company.

For what uses is the information required? It is needed to

Forecast market levels. Predict trends and levels in the market.

Make plans. Set objectives and decide on the means of attaining them.

Identify problems. Ascertain where objectives are not being met.

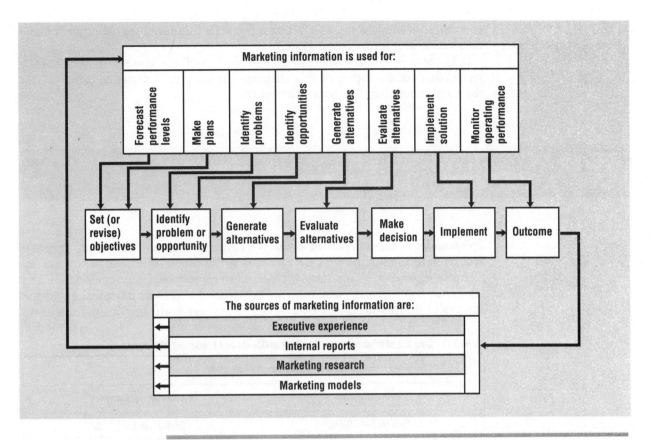

Marketing information is used for:

| Forecast performance levels | Make plans | Identify problems | Identify opportunities | Generate alternatives | Evaluate alternatives | Implement solution | Monitor operating performance |

Set (or revise) objectives → Identify problem or opportunity → Generate alternatives → Evaluate alternatives → Make decision → Implement → Outcome

The sources of marketing information are:

Executive experience

Internal reports

Marketing research

Marketing models

FIGURE 8-1
Uses and sources of information for making marketing decisions.

Identify opportunities. Determine where objectives could be exceeded.

Generate alternatives. Develop alternative solutions for a problem or opportunity.

Evaluate alternatives. Decide which alternative(s) to use.

Implement solutions. Carry out planned means of solving problems or taking advantage of opportunities.

Monitor operating performance. Determine whether actual performance is up to the planned level.

How is the information needed for these purposes obtained? It perhaps will come as no surprise to learn that marketing managers obtain information from the same generic sources that we as individuals use. The methods used are generally more formalized, however, and the sources are named differently. The general sources of marketing information used by marketing managers are *executive experience, internal reports, marketing research* (including secondary data sources), and *marketing models.* When integrated, these sources collectively make up a marketing information system.

It is these marketing information sources, and the system in which they result, that are the topics of this chapter. The chapter is designed primarily for the user rather than the doer of research.

EPISTEMOLOGY AND THE SOURCES OF MARKETING INFORMATION

Epistemology, the science of how we come to "know," indicates that we acquire information by one or more of six different methods. They are by (1) *casual experience,* (2) *authority,* (3) *inquiry,* (4) *observation,* (5) *experimentation,* and (6) *theoretical inference.*[1] These sources are defined and their relationships to the sources of information used by marketing managers are shown in Table 8–1.

Table 8–1 Sources of Information—Private Individuals and Marketing Managers

Sources of Information	
Private Individuals	**Marketing Managers**
1. *CASUAL EXPERIENCE* The cumulative everyday experiences of social interaction, work, school, play, and other miscellaneous sources.	EXECUTIVE EXPERIENCE "Heuristics" learned from outcomes of past marketing programs. Acquiring information through contacts with customers, distributors, competitors, other managers, news sources (general and trade), and miscellaneous sources.
2. *AUTHORITY* Hearing, reading, or viewing something from a source we regard as authoritative.	INTERNAL REPORTS Sales call reports, accounting reports, financial statements, consultants' reports, and other miscellaneous reports.
3. *INQUIRY* Asking persons whom we don't necessarily view as being individually authoritative to obtain a broadly based consensus or measurement. **4. *OBSERVATION*** Observing persons engaged in some activity to learn the ways by which it is performed and the results that tend to correspond to each method. **5. *EXPERIMENTATION*** Manipulating a presumed causal variable to see what effect it has on one or more other variables.	MARKETING RESEARCH Ongoing forecasts, market-share measurements, market-potential measurements, sales analysis, and other. Special studies, market-characteristics studies, plant and warehouse location studies, new-product studies, existing-product studies, pricing studies, advertising studies, promotional studies, distribution-channel studies, export and international studies, and other.
6. *THEORETICAL INFERENCE* Constructing a conceptual model of the system of interest and drawing inferences about the relationships between elements of the system.	MARKETING MODELS Plant and warehouse location models, new-product penetration and repeat purchase models, pricing models, advertising budgeting models, media models, sales call models, and other.

As shown in the table, there is a direct translation of the private individual's sources to those used by marketers:

Executive experience is the direct counterpart of the casual experience that we accumulate from the process of everyday living.

Internal reports come from authorities who work as specialists for the firm (accountants, financial people, consultants).

Marketing research studies are conducted using the methods of inquiry (surveys), observation, and experimentation, and by using available internal reports and published external data by persons and agencies in authority.

Marketing models are only more formalized versions of the models we use to make theoretical inferences for the everyday decisions we make.

THE MARKETING INFORMATION SYSTEM

As shown in Figure 8–2, when these marketing information sources are integrated, and a systematic procedure for disseminating the information provided is added, they make up a marketing information system (MIS).

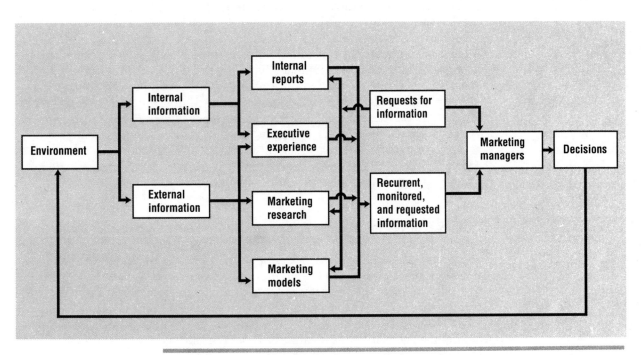

FIGURE 8-2
The workings of a marketing information system (MIS).

A *marketing information* system is a system designed to generate, store, and disseminate an orderly flow of pertinent and timely information to marketing managers.[2]

Note that the MIS makes provision not only for generating pertinent and timely information, but for disseminating it as well.

Figure 8–2 portrays a complete marketing information system. Pertinent information from the environment is obtained and analyzed, as appropriate, through one of the four information sources (executive experience, internal reports, marketing research, and marketing models) and distributed to designated marketing executives for their further analysis and use.

Note from the figure that three kinds of information come out of the system. Some of it is *recurrent information*, such as regular accounting reports, reports from syndicated data agencies giving tabulations from store audits or consumer panels, and Census Bureau reports. A second type is *monitored information*, which includes such items as news of a competitor closing one of its plants, a ruling by the Federal Trade Commission on trademarks, or a new scientific development that may have application to the company's products. The last type is *requested information*, such as a study made by the Marketing Research Department at the request of a particular executive.

The J. C. Penney Company has a broadly based MIS that provides a variety of information of each of these three types that relates to consumer awareness and attitudes, and present and forecast purchase behavior. It involves collecting, analyzing, and disseminating the following kinds of information:

> The marketing research department monitors government and trade association data (monitored information) along with subscribing to consumer spending forecasts from outside agencies (recurrent information). The company participates in a consumer purchase panel that provides detailed data on the consumer purchases made by seven thousand U.S. households each month (recurrent, requested information). The marketing research department also conducts periodic surveys to track consumer awareness and attitudes on each major merchandise category (requested information). This information permits the early identification of spending patterns as well as the efficient management of inventories. In addition, the marketing research department conducts tailored consumer research studies to help develop merchandising and marketing plans.[3]

All executives must have the opportunity to select the specific categories of information they want routed to them to ensure that there is orderly and appropriate dissemination. For example, the manager in charge of buying for Penney's may want to receive all information that pertains to products, prices, and sales by merchandise category, but is not interested in any data on advertising media, whereas the person in charge of advertising may elect to receive all product, price, and sales data, but have no interest at all in data on costs.

The managers at Penney's are asked periodically what kinds of information they need, and how often they need it, as a means of determining what is to be collected and who is to receive it.

Effect of the Computer on the Marketing Information System

It is no coincidence that formalized marketing informations systems came into use in the 1960s—a few years after the companies that initiated MISs had installed computers and learned to use them. The effect of the computer on the MIS has become even more pronounced since the advent of minicomputers in the early 1980s.

Computers have affected the MIS substantially in four different ways. Computers provide:

1. *An improved means of storing and retrieving information.* To be effective, marketing information systems have to have large amounts of information that can be stored and retrieved quickly and inexpensively. Computers are very good for this purpose.

2. *An efficient means of analysis.* Computers can process and analyze large amounts of information to identify changes, trends, and exceptions; make forecasts; maintain perpetual inventories; manipulate marketing models; and perform myriad other analytic tasks.

3. *A stimulus for the commercial development of computerized bibliographic and numeric databases highly useful to the MIS.* The large number of these databases available and the many uses to which they can be put (market analysis, site location analysis, and quota setting, to name just a few) have made the MIS a more efficient and effective decision-making aid, thus promoting its growth. (Computerized databases are discussed on page 238 in more detail.)

4. *An efficient means of marketing model development and manipulation.* Computers and commercially available software (spreadsheets, for example) have made it much easier to develop and to use marketing models as a part of the MIS. (Marketing models as a source of information are discussed on pages 251–253.)

EXECUTIVE EXPERIENCE AS A SOURCE OF MARKETING INFORMATION

The sources of marketing information are:
Executive experience
Internal reports
Marketing research
Marketing models

A certain amount of service as an apprentice is required by the law in most states before a craftsman (such as a plumber) can be licensed, as an accountant before receiving a certified public accountant (CPA) certificate, or as an intern before being allowed to practice medicine. The business school graduate without experience is also usually expected to work for a few years before being promoted to managerial rank. These requirements are clearly the result, at least in part, of the belief that the experience so gained will impart necessary knowledge and skills that previous training or education failed to provide.

What does one learn from experience that is thought to be so valuable? In the case of the marketing executive, two types of knowledge can be identified. They are *heuristic learning* and the *acquiring of information from industry sources.*

Heuristic learning is learning through discovery.[4] We note the outcomes of what we, or other people, do and form judgments about what causes them. By this process we construct conceptual models of whatever process it is we are observing. We also develop rules of thumb—sometimes called "heuristics" because of their origin—to guide actions we need to take in that area.

Through experience, competent executives in marketing develop both models and rule-of-thumb solutions for use in managing marketing programs. As an example, consider the model and a rule-of-thumb solution of one packaged-food-products marketing manager that relate to the introduction of a new product:

> **Model.** In order to have a successful introduction, one must have the product in at least 90 percent of the possible distribution outlets and, through advertising, couponing, providing samples, deals, or other means, generate enough trial purchasers that if 30 percent of them become repeat purchasers, company objectives for market share will be met.

> **Rule of thumb.** When introducing a new product, it will take one and one-half times as much advertising to generate an additional percentage point of market share as it would to generate an extra point of share for a similar established product.

Executives who are highly competent develop models that are generally sound ones. General Foods, a company that has a "brand manager" form of organization, became concerned about the turnover among the more competent brand managers who were, in effect, taking with them when they left the company the models and the rules of thumb they had developed while at General Foods. As a means of retaining some of this acquired expertise, the company began a regular debriefing program. It has since developed a training program for assistant brand managers that uses these (plus other) materials.[5]

Acquiring information from industry sources. It is apparent that executives who spend as much time in the field as marketing executives do will necessarily have the opportunity to learn much about what is happening in the industry from the persons with whom they come in contact. Sales representatives, distributors, competitors, trade association and trade journal personnel, and customers are all ready sources of information. The competent manager will not only take advantage of these opportunities, but will cultivate sources to learn more.

How does executive experience fit into a marketing information system? At first thought, it might seem as if executive experience is external to the MIS, at least to the formal system that is set up and operated. This is not the case. Executives often contribute information to the MIS that they obtain through their day-to-day operations, and they participate in both the development and the evaluation of the marketing models that are a part of the system. They also rely on their experience to determine what information ought to be collected and to whom it should be disseminated.

INTERNAL REPORTS AS SOURCES OF MARKETING INFORMATION

The sources of marketing information are:
Executive experience
Internal reports
Marketing research
Marketing models

Every company routinely compiles and distributes internal reports on such matters as sales calls, sales forecasts, production schedules, inventories, research and development schedules and progress, budgets, legal matters, and financial statements. The purpose of the reports, of course, is to inform top management and the managers of concerned departments (including the department issuing the report) of the status of the items covered.

The assortment of reports typically received by the marketing manager is shown in Table 8–2. A scanning of the exhibit (which is the way it should be read, rather than giving it a detailed reading) indicates the broad range of topics covered and the fact that marketing receives reports from every major department of the company.

Marketing uses the information contained in these reports for analysis and planning, and for making decisions concerning implementation and control.

Table 8–2 Internal Reports Typically Received by the Marketing Manager

Report (frequency)	Information Provided (and Originating Department)
Regular reports	
1. Sales call (after each call is made)	Customer, location, date, whether sale was made, end use, news of company, competitors, industry developments, etc. (Marketing)
2. Sales invoice (when each sale is made)	Customer, location, date, item(s) sold, price, discount(s), industry, sales representative (Accounting)
3. Sales (weekly or biweekly)	Amount sold by item, time period, and sales territory (Accounting)
4. Sales forecast (depends on company—weekly, monthly, quarterly, or annually)	Item, amount forecast to be sold by time period and (in some cases) by geographic region (Marketing)
5. Inventories (daily, weekly, or monthly)	Amount of each item (by model number and size) by warehouse (Marketing, Production, or Traffic and Logistics, depending on how the company is organized)
6. Production schedules (weekly or biweekly)	Amount of each item to be produced by time period, and by plant if appropriate (Production)
7. Production costs (monthly)	Costs of production by item for a specified lot or time period (Accounting)
8. Research and development reports (monthly)	Schedule, progress, and (perhaps) expenditures by project (R&D or Engineering)
9. Marketing budget (monthly, quarterly, semiannually, or annually)	Amount budgeted by line item (advertising, sales, marketing research, and distribution plus special line items such as market tests, new product introductions) by time period (Marketing)
10. Marketing expenditures versus budget (monthly)	Amount expended by line item for each time period versus amount budgeted (Accounting)
11. Income statement (monthly or quarterly)	Sales, expenses, and profit or loss by product line, or strategic business unit or market, depending on how the company is organized (Accounting)
12. Accounts receivable (monthly)	Accounts receivable by age of the account and by customer (Accounting)
13. Quality control	Quality levels of each product by time period (Quality Control or Engineering)
14. Field service	Number of items serviced by model, location, and time period (Field Service or Engineering)
Special reports	
14. Long-range strategic plan	Description of strategic directories and schedule of major events for implementing it/them (Chief Planning Office)
15. Annual operating plan	Description and schedule of major events in the planned operations of the various departments of the company (Chief Planning Office)
16. Marketing research	Depending on the study, it may provide information on a market, a marketing program, or a development that may affect one or both of those (Marketing)
17. Legal	Reports on patent and trademark applications, an assessment of the legality of competitor practices, legal risks associated with current or proposed company practices, etc. (Legal)
18. Production	Reports on potential new production processes, experience curve effects on costs, etc. (Production)
19. Research and development	Assessment of competitor products, the state of the art, etc. (R&D or Engineering)
20. Consultants	Various

Consider the analyses that can be made from the data contained on call reports and sales invoices, for example:

Report	Analyses
Sales call (contains data on customer, location, date, whether sale was made, end use, news of company, competitors, industry developments, etc.)	Efficiency of routing of sales representative Warranted frequency of calls by customer class Appropriate sales territory boundaries Allocation of sales representatives by territory Appropriate level of selling expenses (budget) by territory Effectiveness of sales representatives Competitor activities Industry developments
Sales invoice (contains data on customer, location, date, items ordered, quantities ordered, quantities shipped, back orders, prices, discounts, date shipped, method of shipment, sales representative)	Sales by customer Sales by sales representative Sales by product Sales by territory Sales by customer class Sales by industry Sales by sales representative Appropriate sales quotas by territory Discounts by type Warehouse of shipment
Sales call and sales invoice	Sales by end use Appropriate plan for and level of sales compensation

The usefulness of sales call reports can be extended by making the reporting of items of customer and industry news a requirement, and by training sales representatives actively to seek such information. Without taking such steps, substantially less information may be acquired and fed back through the system. For example, by "planting" items of news with sales representatives and waiting to see what was reported back, Albaum[6] found untrained salespersons to be relatively poor sources of information.

Marketing managers should take care that they receive the internal reports they need, but *only* those reports. Being on the distribution list for large numbers of internal reports may be ego assuaging, but it is a waste of time and company resources to receive any that are unnecessary.

MARKETING RESEARCH AS AN INFORMATION SOURCE

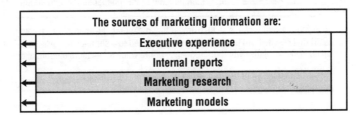

The sources of marketing information are:		
Executive experience		
Internal reports		
Marketing research		
Marketing models		

Companies in the United States collectively spend on the order of $2 billion per year for marketing research.[7] This expenditure is for a single purpose—to provide information to help make better marketing decisions. In fact, an appropriate definition is

> **Marketing research** is a formalized means of obtaining information to be used in making marketing decisions.[8]

In order to gain a basic understanding of what marketing research is and what it does, it is first necessary to understand the "formalized means of obtaining information" it uses—the data collection methods it employs.

Methods Used in Marketing Research

Marketing research uses four basic methods of collecting data. They are *secondary research, survey research, observation,* and *experimentation.* These methods are described briefly in Table 8–3 and more fully in the sections that follow.

Table 8–3   Major Data Collection Methods

I. *Secondary data research*   Utilization of data that were developed for some purpose other than the marketing research project for which they are now being used.
   A. *Internal secondary data*   Data generated within the organization itself, such as salesperson call reports, sales invoices, accounting records, and financial statements.
   B. *External secondary data*   Data generated by sources outside the organization, such as government reports, trade association data, and data collected by market research agencies and sold on a syndicated basis.

II. *Survey research*   Systematic collection of information from respondents.
   A. *Telephone interviews*   Collection of information from respondents via telephone.
   B. *Mail interviews*   Collection of information from respondents by mail or telegraph.
   C. *Personal interviews*   Collection of information in a face-to-face situation.
      1. *Home interviews*   Personal interviews in the respondent's home or office.
      2. *Central location interview*   Personal interviews in a shopping mall or other central location.

III. *Observation*   Systematic observation of shoppers, users, distributors, or competitors.
   A. *Human observation*   Observation by one or more persons, rather than by a recording device.
   B. *Mechanical (or electromechanical) observation*   Observation using a recording device such as a camera or tape recorder, or a physiological measuring instrument such as a psychogalvanometer or voice-pitch analysis.*

IV. *Experimental research*   Manipulation of one or more (independent) variables in such a way that the effect on one or more other (dependent) variables can be measured.
   A. *Laboratory experiments*   Manipulation of the independent variable(s) in an artificial situation.
   B. *Field experiments*   Manipulation of the independent variable(s) in a natural situation.

*A *psychogalvanometer* is an instrument that measures the amount of perspiration (usually in the palm of the hand) that results from the subject's being exposed to a stimulus of some sort. *Voice-pitch analysis* records changes in the relative vibration frequency of the voice to measure emotional changes resulting from exposure to a stimulus.
Source: Adapted from D. S. Tull and D. I. Hawkins, *Marketing Research: Measurement and Method*, 3rd ed., Macmillan, 1984, 31.

Secondary Data Research as a Data Collection Method

Secondary data are data that were developed for some purpose other than helping to solve the problem for which the research project is being conducted.

This is as opposed to primary data, which are data developed specifically to help solve the problem at hand.

Since they are almost always less expensive and can be obtained faster than primary data, a search for secondary data is usually the proper starting point for a marketing research project. Useful secondary data may be found either internally or externally to the company, or both. An illustration of the use of both internal and external secondary data by a well-known direct marketing firm is given in the box below.

> For a firm such as L. L. Bean, the catalog marketer of sporting goods equipment and apparel, having the right mailing lists and using them correctly is the essence of successful marketing. The company rents and exchanges mailing lists that contain 10 to 12 million names per year. The lists come from competitors, magazine subscription lists, and mailing list companies that compile them. Bean keeps extensive records of the frequency and dollar value of purchases its customers make. The company's market research staff analyzes customer penetration down to the zip code level. These zip code penetration rates are used to determine to which names on a mailing list catalogs should be sent, and how many catalogs should go out before a purchase is made.*

*Adapted from *American Demographics*, February 1985, 18–19.

Internal Secondary Data: It is a rare marketing research study that doesn't employ at least some internal secondary data. We have already described internal reports at some length as an information source that is helpful in making marketing decisions. In addition, there are data that have been collected but never reported that may be of substantial value in a marketing research project.

Data collected by the Accounting and Production departments are examples of data that are collected in great detail, but usually reported only after they have been aggregated and averaged. When analysts from the marketing research department of Bell and Howell began a study to determine the level of the company's experience curve for videotape recorders, for example, they found that the reports from the Accounting and Production departments did not provide the data to the level of specificity they required. It was necessary to obtain the detailed accounting records of costs and match them with the specific quantities of VTRs produced in each time period in order to develop a valid measure of the experience curve level.

External Secondary Data: External data of potential value to marketing managers are available from many sources. Five general categories of external data sources are (1) associations, (2) government agencies, (3) computerized bibliographies, (4) other published sources, and (5) syndicated research services.

With the exception of syndicated services, these sources are each described extensively in the following publications:

H. W. Johnson, A. J. Faria, and E. L. Maier, *How to Use the Business Library—With Sources of Business Information*, South-Western, 1984.

J. S. Mulutinovich, "Business Facts for Decision Makers: Where to Find Them," *Business Horizons*, March–April 1985, 64–80.

We describe external data sources briefly in Table 8–4. Since syndicated research services are so widely used in the marketing of consumer packaged products (the marketing of grocery and drug sundry items primarily), we discuss them in the section that follows.

Syndicated Research Services

A syndicated service is one that is sold on a subscription basis. A large number of independent research agencies collect and sell to subscribing companies data of relevance to marketers. The three basic types of data they supply to consumer goods marketers are movement of products through wholesalers, movement of products through retailers, and consumer response (purchases, usage, coupons redeemed, and exposure to advertising) to elements of the marketing mix. For industrial goods marketers, services are available that provide information on a plant-by-plant, area-by-area basis.

Syndicated Data for Consumer Products: For packaged grocery and drug sundry products, syndicated reports are especially useful in determining both the current size of markets and the share held by each brand. Depending on the service, these result from measurements of sales by brand at the wholesale or retail level, and measurements of purchases by brand by consumers.

At the wholesale level in the food industry, SAMI (Selling Areas–Marketing, Inc.) provides data on the shipments of products to retail food stores. It contracts with wholesalers and chains to provide data on shipments by brands every four weeks by agreeing to pay them a percentage of the revenue it receives from selling the reports. It also agrees to provide these organizations with the data on shipments by their competitors, a considerable payment in kind. SAMI provides data on the movement of brands in 425 product categories in 36 television market areas for the most recent 4-week and 52-week periods.

At the retail level in the food and drug industries, two kinds of services are available that measure sales. They are store audits and checkout scanner services. As the name implies, data on sales provided by research organizations conducting store audits are obtained by auditing the movement of products through a sample of retail stores. The best-known and most widely used store audit service is the Nielsen Retail Index. The reports are based on audits every 60 days of a sample of 1,600 food stores, 750 drugstores, and 150 mass merchandisers in 600 counties. They provide sales data on all the major product lines carried by these stores.

Several organizations offer a reporting service based on collecting and aggregating sales data from the checkout scanner tapes of a sample of supermarkets that use electronic scanning systems. National Scanning Services is one of the companies that provide such a service. Scanner tapes are collected weekly from

Table 8–4 Sources of External Secondary Data Relevant to Marketing

Source	Description
1. Associations	Associations of companies involved in the manufacture, delivery, or sale of similar lines of products. Each association typically collects, maintains, and publishes data on industry sales, operating characteristics, growth patterns, etc. See the latest edition of the *Encyclopedia of Associations* by Gale Research for a list of associations by line of trade, descriptions, addresses, and telephone numbers.
2. Government	Federal, state, and local government agencies produce large amounts of data useful to marketers. There are five broad types of data that are helpful: (1) population, housing, and income; (2) industrial and commercial product sales of manufacturers, wholesalers, retailers, and service organizations; (3) sales of agricultural products; (4) employment; and (5) miscellaneous reports. For specific sources, see the latest edition of T. A. Nelson, *Measuring Markets: A Guide to the Use of Federal and State Statistical Data*, U.S. Department of Commerce.
3. Computerized bibliographic and numeric databases	There are more than 200 on-line databases in the United States with a combined total of over 1,200 separate data files. Among them are databases that are useful in bibliographic search, site location, media planning, forecasting, and many other purposes. Two of them that are broadly applicable for marketing are ABI/Inform and the PREDICAST Terminal System.
4. Other published sources	There is a virtually endless assortment of periodicals, books, theses and dissertations, special reports, newspapers, and the like that contain information of value to marketers. Consulting a librarian at your local library, followed, if needed, by a computerized bibliographic search, is a sound procedure for locating such sources.
5. Syndicated research services	A large number of firms regularly collect and sell to subscribers data on one of three types for consumer goods: (1) movement of products at the wholesale level, (2) movement of products at the retail level, and (3) consumer response to elements of the marketing mix (purchases, usage, coupon redemption, and exposure to advertising). Other firms also sell data to industrial subscribers that provide information on a plant-by-plant, area-by-area basis. (For a description of these services, see pages 238–240.)

a national sample of 900 supermarkets and the data on them aggregated and analyzed to provide information on sales by brand, size, price, and flavor or formulation. A. C. Nielsen and Information Resources also provide data based on checkout scanning tapes.

At the consumer level, purchase data are collected from diary panels. The panel consists of a sample of families who are provided with purchase diaries in which they record their purchases of selected products (primarily food, household, and personal care products). Each family turns in its diary periodically (every two weeks or each month, depending on the service) and the data are aggregated and analyzed, and reports prepared by category of product. National Purchase Diary Panel, Inc. (NPD) is the largest supplier of consumer panel data in the United States. It maintains two national panels of 6,500 families each. (A sample page from the consumer purchase diary used by NPD is shown as Exhibit 8–1.)

EXHIBIT **8-1**

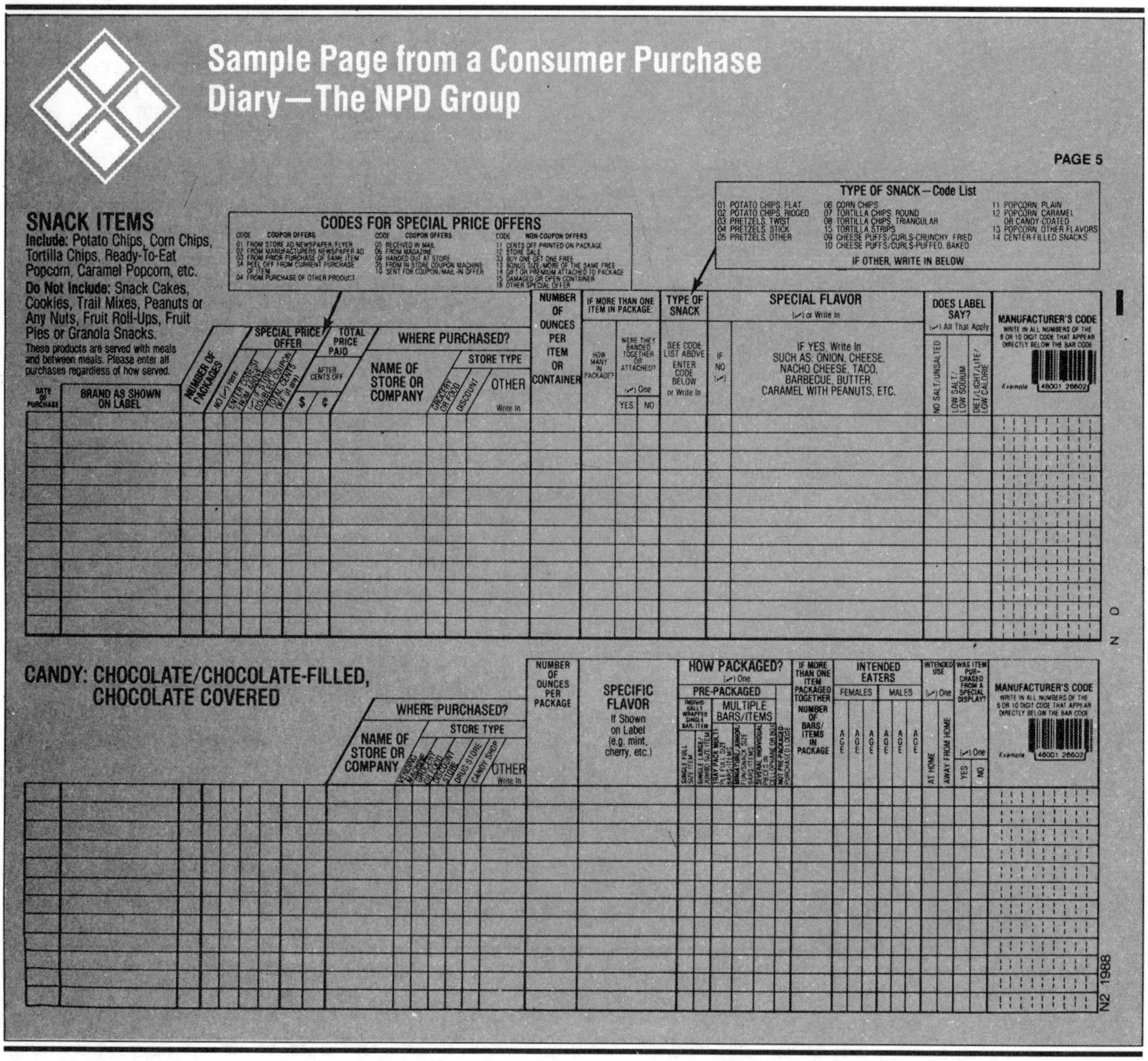

Sample Page from a Consumer Purchase Diary—The NPD Group

PAGE 5

SNACK ITEMS

Include: Potato Chips, Corn Chips, Tortilla Chips, Ready-To-Eat Popcorn, Caramel Popcorn, etc.

Do Not Include: Snack Cakes, Cookies, Trail Mixes, Peanuts or Any Nuts, Fruit Roll-Ups, Fruit Pies or Granola Snacks.

These products are served with meals and between meals. Please enter all purchases regardless of how served.

CODES FOR SPECIAL PRICE OFFERS

TYPE OF SNACK—Code List

01 POTATO CHIPS, FLAT
02 POTATO CHIPS, RIDGED
03 PRETZELS, TWIST
04 PRETZELS, STICK
05 PRETZELS, OTHER
06 CORN CHIPS
07 TORTILLA CHIPS, ROUND
08 TORTILLA CHIPS, TRIANGULAR
09 TORTILLA STRIPS
09 CHEESE PUFFS/CURLS-CRUNCHY, FRIED
10 CHEESE PUFFS/CURLS-PUFFED, BAKED
11 POPCORN, PLAIN
12 POPCORN, CARAMEL OR CANDY-COATED
13 POPCORN, OTHER FLAVORS
14 CENTER-FILLED SNACKS

IF OTHER, WRITE IN BELOW

CANDY: CHOCOLATE/CHOCOLATE-FILLED, CHOCOLATE COVERED

There are several services available that measure the audiences of the electronic (television and radio) and print (newspaper and magazine) media. Television audiences are measured by "people meters" in a national sample of households. The meter records when a TV is on and to what channel it is tuned. The viewer(s) in the household "log on" and "log off" by pushing the buttons individually assigned to them on a remote control device. The recorded information for each household is sent to a central computer, where it is analyzed and ratings for programs calculated. A. C. Nielsen provides metered data from a sample of 2,000 households.[9]

The Arbitron and Radar reports provide data on radio audiences that are derived from a sample of participating households that record station choices in diaries. The Simmons Market Research Bureau provides data on magazine and newspaper readership.

In addition to its store auditing, checkout scanning tape, and audience measurement services, the A. C. Nielsen Company maintains a coupon clearinghouse where grocery and drug store operators can send coupons for reimbursement.

Syndicated Data on Industrial Markets: Both Dun & Bradstreet and the Economic Information Service maintain databanks on manufacturing establishments in the United States and Canada. The information on each establishment includes its location, the SIC (Standard Industrial Classification) codes of the products it manufactures, its estimated sales volume, and the number of its employees. These data are kept current through inquiring directly of the company, clipping services, and corporate reports.

The information provided by these organizations is useful to industrial marketers for such purposes as estimating market potential by geographic area, defining sales territories, developing sales prospect lists, setting sales quotas, and allocating advertising budgets.

Survey Research as a Data Collection Method

Survey research involves the systematic collection of data directly from respondents for the purpose of understanding or predicting some aspect of the behavior of the population of interest.

Depending on the circumstances of the problem being researched, the data may be collected by telephone, by mail, by personal interview, or by some combination of these methods. The consumer purchase diary panels described earlier are a form of survey research, for example, and the purchase data they provide are collected by mail.

After secondary data research, surveys are the most frequently used method of collecting data in marketing research. They are a valuable research tool for determining buying and using behaviors, and the reasons for them, in selected markets and market segments.

A useful, if somewhat overly simplified, way of categorizing survey research studies is by whether they are "qualitative" or "quantitative" in nature. An essential difference between the two is that

Qualitative research tends to be exploratory and done to provide plausible verbal explanations of the "whys" and "hows" of market dynamics.

Whereas

Quantitative research is primarily descriptive or causal in intent and so is done to provide numerical data that collectively describe or test hypotheses about the market and its workings.

A brief discussion of these two types of research will be helpful in understanding the options the manager has in obtaining information from market participants through surveys.

Qualitative Survey Research: Qualitative research typically involves asking respondents open-ended questions or using nondirective methods of inducing verbal reactions to the issues being researched. The kinds of issues explored and questions raised include "How is the buying decision made?" "Why do you prefer your brand to its principal competitor brands?" "What does quality in this type of product mean?" and the like. The samples of respondents used in qualitative research are usually nonrandom in nature, so the resulting data are not statistically projectable.

Perhaps the most common technique employed in qualitative research is the focus group. *Focus groups* are group discussions held with a sample of 8–12 persons knowledgeable about the product class. The discussion is moderated in an unobtrusive way by a researcher and averages 1½ to 2 hours in length. The results are often videotaped and may even be viewed by client executives through a one-way mirror.

Another common technique is the individual "depth" interview. Depth interviews usually take 30 to 45 minutes and are conducted by interviewers with a topic checklist but without a set of prespecified questions. The interviewer is free to ask questions and to probe in such a way as to elicit relevant responses as long as the questions posed do not bias the responses.

Quantitative Survey Research: Quantitative survey research usually involves constructing a standardized questionnaire of prespecified questions to be asked in a specified order and administering it to a sample of respondents selected as nearly at random as the situation and its economics allow. The kinds of questions for which answers are sought include "How large is the market?" "What are the pertinent demographics of the buyers?" "How often and in what quantities is the product typically bought?" and the like. The results are projectable and are usually analyzed to provide cross-tabulations, means, correlations, and other statistical measures.

Qualitative versus Quantitative Survey Research: Qualitative research studies cost less, use smaller samples, may provide more insights into purchase and use decisions, and require more skilled interviewers. The results are more investigator-dependent than for quantitative research studies.

The two general approaches to obtaining information from respondents are not necessarily noncomplementary and mutually exclusive. A not-uncommon approach is to use qualitative research to explore the problem involved to suggest issues and hypotheses to be examined in a later, structured, quantitative research project.[10]

Errors in Survey Research Data: Regardless of the survey research method chosen, the data must be collected and interpreted with care as there are errors—sometimes in substantial amounts—that can be present. Three types of errors in particular must be guarded against. They are sampling error, nonresponse error, and response error.

1. *Sampling error.* Usually, but not always, it is necessary to take a sample rather than a census of the population to be studied in a marketing research project. If the population of interest is companies that make checkout scanners for supermarkets, there are only eight of them worldwide, and so all of them could be surveyed at a relatively low cost (especially if a mail or telephone survey were used). However, if the population of interest is all the shoppers in supermarkets in the country, it would be prohibitive for reasons of time and cost to take a census. A sample of some sort would therefore have to be taken.

If a researcher wanted a sample of 100 people who were representative of supermarket shoppers in the country, and he or she were to go out to the nearest street corner to interview the first hundred people who came by, the chances are that an unrepresentative sample would be obtained. The degree of unrepresentativeness would of course depend on many things—the city in which the researcher was working, the location within the city, whether it was a weekday or a weekend, the time of the day, and the weather that day would each affect how different the sample actually obtained was from a cross section of the general population of supermarket shoppers. The data that he or she obtained from that sample might give a highly misleading view of the topics asked about.

To avoid the errors that can result from having a bad sample, researchers would like to have a complete listing of the population to be sampled—called a *sampling frame*—and to select sample members from the list in such a way that they can draw inferences about the population with no expected sampling error. One of the problems in most marketing research studies involving consumers is that there is no complete list of them available. Researchers therefore have to use sampling frames that themselves are subject to error, and to use ingenious methods to reduce the errors that are otherwise likely to result. Two examples are sampling using *telephone books* and *points and times in shopping malls* as sampling frames.

Sampling using telephone books. Telephone books are often used as sampling frames, obviously so for telephone surveys, but also for personal interviews in the home or for mail surveys. There are some serious problems with telephone books as sample frames, however. Even when the book is first issued, it does not contain persons who do not have telephones, persons who have telephones but who received service after the book went to press, and persons who have voluntarily unlisted numbers. The listings in the book therefore tend to underrepresent segments of the population that are poorer (those without telephones), the geographically mobile (those who received service after the telephone directory went to press), and those who have voluntarily unlisted numbers (young women living alone, policemen, teachers, and others).

Estimates of the percentage of households not listed in current telephone directories in the United States are close to 25 percent as a national average, and have a median for large metropolitan areas of about 30 percent.[11]

A method of ensuring a more representative sample is to use some form of **random digit dialing**. This involves generating, at random, some or all of the digits of the telephone numbers used. If the survey is to be conducted by telephone, these numbers are the ones that are called for purposes of interviewing. If the survey is to be conducted using personal interviews, these numbers can be called to arrange appointments and, not so incidentally, to obtain addresses.

Using this technique for telephone surveys has been shown to eliminate much, but not all, of the bias of using a telephone book as the sampling frame.[12]

Sampling using locations and times in shopping malls. Sampling and interviewing persons in shopping malls has become a very common method of conducting surveys. It has the advantage of being relatively inexpensive and of yielding a higher proportion of persons being willing to be interviewed than they would be in their homes. In addition, if research facilities are located in the mall (and several market research agencies do maintain permanent facilities in a sample of malls around the United States), studies such as taste tests, testing of television commercials, and the like can be conducted that could not be done at all in telephone interviews and would be very difficult to do in the home.

There are obvious problems in getting a representative sample of the population in a shopping mall survey, however. Not everyone shops at a mall—especially those who live long distances from malls, the aged, and the infirm—and there is a problem in getting a valid cross section of those who do.

The only remedy for including nonmall shoppers in the sample is to supplement the mall sample with one taken outside. However, for those segments of the population who do (at least occasionally) shop in malls, procedures have been worked out to ensure that a reasonably close approximation of a random sample is taken. These procedures include the following:

Using probability sampling methods to select the shopping malls at which the sample is to be taken.

Allowing for the unrepresentative demographic composition of shoppers by asking potential respondents their age, level of education, approximate annual income, and so forth and selecting them to ensure that these characteristics are represented in the sample in the same proportions they are represented in the population.

Allowing for frequency of visit to the mall by weighting of responses.

Allowing for location in the mall by stationing interviewers at every entrance with instructions to select every *k*th person.

Allowing for the time of day and the day of the week differences in shoppers by interviewing at randomly selected times.[13]

Evaluating research project samples. Before using the findings of a research study, one should always consider how the sample was taken. Most of the serious errors that occur in sampling are intuitively obvious once they are thought about, and so one does not have to be a sampling expert to discover them.[14] The critical question that one needs to raise is always, "Does this sample, after allowing for the adjustments made in the analysis of the findings from it, represent fairly the population in which we are interested?" If the answer is either "no" or "I am not sure," a warning flag is raised about using the findings.

2. *Nonresponse error.* An error that is closely allied to sampling error is that of **nonresponse**. Nonresponse errors arise when one or more of the characteristics of the respondents are different from those of the population. It will do little good to select an excellent sample initially if there is a large rate of nonresponse that results in the achieved samples not being a good representation of the population.

Bias results from nonresponse when the characteristics of interest of the nonrespondents differ from those of the respondents. In general, nonrespondents are less interested in the subject matter of the survey than are respondents. If the survey concerns usage of a product, for example, it is probable that the nonrespondents use less than the respondents, and therefore have less interest in spending the time and effort to report on their usage than do the respondents. If the nonresponse effects are not allowed for, the result may be an estimate of usage that is too high.

The ways of dealing with nonresponse include the following:

1. Keep nonresponse as low as is economically feasible. Design the survey to include successive mailings or callbacks; use preliminary notification; offer money, nonmonetary gifts, or other incentives to respond.
2. Measure the effects of the nonresponse by taking a subsample of the nonrespondents. This is a particularly effective strategy when the original survey was conducted by mail and the subsample is interviewed either personally or by telephone.
3. Estimate the effects of the nonresponse. The methods that can be used to assist in the estimation include:
   a. *IMPUTATION* Assigning the same responses to nonrespondents as those from respondents with similar demographic characteristics.
   b. *TREND ANALYSIS* Recording responses on successive mailings or callbacks and projecting any resulting trend to the remaining nonrespondents.
   c. *POLITZ-SIMMONS METHOD* A method for estimating the characteristics of not-at-home nonrespondents in telephone and personal interview surveys from the responses of respondents with a known frequency of being at home at that time.[15]

Evaluating nonresponse in a research project. Marketing managers should always raise the question, "Is the nonresponse in this survey likely to affect the findings significantly?" If the answer is "yes," the question, "In which direction?" should be raised. Then the question, "Would a sizable shift of the findings in that direction affect the decision for which I am using the data?" should be asked. If the answer is in the affirmative, appropriate caution in using the data is indicated.

3. *Response error.* The most difficult of the potential errors in surveys with which to deal effectively is response error. Errors in the recorded responses to a survey can occur for the following reasons:

1. *The respondent does not understand the question to mean what it was intended to mean.* In one study, for example, the question was asked of housewives, "Do you like tomato juice?" The question was intended to mean, "Do you like the taste of tomato juice?" Some respondents answered "yes" without actually liking its taste, however, because they interpreted the question to mean "Do you like to cook with tomato juice?" and they liked to cook with it because it helps tenderize meat, their family liked recipes with tomato juice in them, and so forth.
2. *The interviewer does not understand the response to mean what it was intended to mean.* In the same study the question was asked, "What suggestions could you make for improving tomato juice?" and the following answer was given:

> I really don't know. I never thought much about it. I suppose that it would be nice if you could buy it in bottles because the can turns

black where you pour the juice out after it has been open for a day or two. Bottles break, though.

Should the interpretation be made that she had "no suggestion," "suggested packaging in a glass container," or "suggested some way should be found to keep the can from turning black around the opening"?[16]

3. *The respondent does not tell the (whole) truth.* There are two major reasons for respondent inaccuracies:

a. The respondent does not know all the reasons for the behavior being asked about, but gives a definitive reply anyway. Q. "Why did you buy a Honda?" A. "Because it gets better gasoline mileage" is almost certainly only a partial answer.

b. The respondent deliberately lies to avoid embarrassment or to increase his or her perceived prestige. In a study for TWA on flying, interviewers asked, "Are you afraid to fly?" and discovered that practically no one had any fear at all about flying. When the question was rephrased to ask, "Do you think your neighbor is afraid to fly?" a high percentage of neighbors turned out to have fears concerning flying.

4. *The interviewer "cheats" either by not interviewing the respondent at all or by not asking difficult or potentially embarrassing questions, and by making up and recording fictitious responses.* This is known as "curbstoning" and is prevalent in studies in which the pay is based on the number of completed interviews or requires interviewing in neighorhoods with high crime rates.

Because we ask questions and receive answers in everyday conversation, and do so with what usually seems to be a satisfactory level of communication, we tend to believe that asking questions of and receiving valid answers from respondents in surveys should pose no particular problem. That turns out all too often not to be true. We discount the facts that in our everyday conversations we are usually talking with friends or acquaintances (not total strangers); we rephrase questions if the listeners indicate they do not understand them (interviewers are usually not allowed to do this because of the likelihood of biasing the response); and we usually are not asking difficult, time-consuming, or potentially embarrassing questions ("About what was the income of your family last year?").

The best remedy for response errors is to have experienced professionals prepare and administer the questionnaire. There are methods that are available to reduce response errors (the third-person technique used in the TWA study on flying described above is one), and to measure those that are present. The professional will know these methods and employ them when they are needed.

Observation Research as a Data Collection Method

In some situations, an alternative to asking questions is to observe. The marketing manager does not need to ask competitors what their prices are—they can be observed where they are being sold. Purchase behavior (Do children really affect cereal purchase decisions?), service support (What kinds of service facilities do our distributors have?), and traffic patterns (Is it really better to put the milk cases in the back of the supermarket?) are examples of informational items that can be observed. (The findings by an observational study to one of these questions is given in the box that follows.)

> Observation of slightly more than 500 parent–child cereal purchase situations in 20 supermarkets in two Michigan cities indicates that children play a central role in cereal selection decisions.
>
> Children initiated the request (or demand) for a specific brand of cereal in two-thirds (66 percent) of the purchase situations. In all purchases at which they were present (child-initiated + parent-initiated purchases), the brand specified by the child was purchased almost two-thirds of the time (63 percent).*

*Source: C. K. Atkin, "Observation of Parent–Child Interaction in Supermarket Decision Making," *Journal of Marketing*, October 1978, 41–45.

Marketing managers routinely obtain information relating to questions such as the above through casual observation. This is a part of the executive experience discussed earlier and is a valuable part of the total information available to help solve marketing problems. However, casual observation is different from **observation as a research method**. We can define the latter as

> Observation that serves a specifically formulated purpose, is planned systematically, is recorded systematically, and is subjected to checks and controls on its overall accuracy.[17]

Not all of the information needed can be obtained through observation, however. In order to observe an item successfully and efficiently, it must be (1) accessible; (2) repetitive, frequent, or otherwise predictable; and (3) observed in a reasonably short time span. Attitudes cannot be observed, for example, as they are not directly accessible. And it would not be efficient to observe, during use and until they failed, a sample of the products of a company that makes home appliances, since time-to-failure is neither easily predictable nor likely to be short.

When it is feasible to conduct an observational study, there are two circumstances in which it may be preferable to other methods. The first is the obvious one, in which observation is the only means available for collecting accurate information. If Gerber's wanted to determine which of several alternative pablum formulations was preferred by infants, for example, observation would be the only means of getting the information. In terms of accuracy, observational studies of garbage have indicated that persons in the households from which it came tend to underreport beer consumption and overreport milk and beef consumption when surveyed.[18]

The second circumstance for using observation in preference to other methods is when the cost for observational data of a desired level of accuracy is less than that for alternative methods. As an example, the meters used by the A. C. Nielsen and the Arbitron research agencies to record the stations to which the TV sets in a sample of households are tuned, and the times during which they are being used, are a form of (mechanical) observation that is both more accurate and less expensive than diary methods and coincidental telephone calls.

Experimental Research as a Data Collection Method

Experimental research is the fourth of the general methods used by researchers to obtain information to help solve marketing problems. We can define experimentation as follows:

> *Experimentation* involves the manipulation of one or more (independent) variables by the experimenter in such a way that the effect on one or more other (dependent) variables can be measured.

Marketing experiments, then, are designed so that the researcher can change one or more variables—product design and price, for example—in such a way that the effect on one or more other variables—sales, market share—can be measured.

Experiments in marketing are of two general types, laboratory and field. *Laboratory experiments* are not necessarily conducted in a laboratory as such, but they are carried out in an artificial environment. As the name implies, *field experiments* are conducted under actual market conditions.

Laboratory Experiments: Laboratory experiments are widely used in marketing in testing new product designs, package designs, and advertising themes and copy. They are used to a lesser extent to test prices and promotions involving "deals." Some examples of commonly conducted laboratory experiments are:

Blind taste tests. A laboratory experiment in which consumers are asked to taste and to evaluate various formulations of a food product or drink without knowing the brand name. The conditions that are controlled in the typical taste test include the time of day and the absence of any accompanying foods or individually added flavors.

Tachistoscopic tests of package designs, and print and outdoor media and point-of-purchase ads. A tachistoscope is a slide projector that permits images to be projected for various lengths of time (down to a minute fraction of a second) and at various levels of illumination. Package designs and ads are tested to determine at what speeds product, brand, and logo (headline in the case of ads) are recognized. For ads, it has been found that there is a correlation between readership and speed of recognition of the various elements.

Price testing in a simulated "store." The type of "store" most often used is a trailer fitted out as a section of a supermarket or drugstore. Prices on the products under test are changed experimentally, and the amounts purchased at each price are recorded.

Unlike field experiments, laboratory experiments permit a substantial degree of control over the conditions under which the experiment is to be conducted.

They therefore provide assurance that the same results will be obtained if the experiment is replicated with a similar group of subjects. They have the added virtues of not being visible to competitors and, in general, of being much less expensive than field experiments.

Given these positive features, why aren't laboratory experiments used exclusively in preference to field experiments? The answer is not difficult to guess: There is always at least some question of how generalizable the results of a laboratory experiment are to an actual market situation. One can never be quite sure that all of the relevant variables have been introduced or controlled in the laboratory experiment, or that persons will act the same in the laboratory as they will in the marketplace.

An example of the lack of generalizability of a laboratory test is a taste test run by Green Giant on a highly flavored version of baked beans with pork. They ran blind taste tests and found preferences for the flavored beans over unflavored pork and beans to be on the order of three or four to one. When it was test marketed, however, it was a "disaster." Surveys showed that people preferred to buy unflavored beans and add their own flavorings. This option had not been available to the subjects in the laboratory experiment.[19]

Field Experiments: Field experiments can be either a form of a test market for a new product or an on-line experiment for an existing product.

Market tests involve introducing the new product to a part of the market. If the part of the market to which it is introduced is a sample of consumers directly in their homes, it is known as a **simulated market test**. If it is introduced directly to a sample of retail stores, it is called a **controlled market test**. If it is introduced in a small number of cities or metropolitan areas (one to five), it is known as a **standard market test**. The standard market test is sometimes expanded into a regional introduction that is part continuing market test, part introduction.

In general, both the accuracy and the costs of the market tests increase progressively from the home to the retail store to the city as the experimental introductory area. The decisions about which, if any, of these types of market tests to use is therefore partially one of accuracy versus cost. Considerations of time and (as we shall see below) security of information also become involved in the decision. These types of market tests are discussed in greater detail in the next chapter.

On-line field experiments involve experimentally changing price, or the level of advertising or promotion, in a part of the market for an existing product and measuring the sales changes that result. When it is feasible to do so, this is often an effective way to obtain information for decisions on changes in the levels of the variables included in the experiment.

The term *on-line* is used here as an abbreviated way of referring to "during the course of regular business operations." The term *on-line sales experiment* should then be understood as follows:

> **On-line experiments** consist of deliberate changes in one or more marketing variables made during the course of regular business operations in such a way that the effects on sales can be measured.

Consider the following example of such an experiment:

The Florists' Telegraph Delivery Association (FTDA) management was uncertain about the media that should be used to advertise the FTDA services. Accordingly, an experiment was designed to compare the sales effects of using radio, newspapers, TV, and outdoor advertising with their regular media mix. Each of these media was used exclusively in a different group of three markets. The choice of which medium to give each group of markets was made at random. Sales could be measured accurately since all FTDA orders had to clear through a central clearinghouse. The groups of markets were similar in population, income, and FTDA activity and business.

The experiment ran for six months, with virtually identical advertising budgets for each medium tested. Setting the U.S. rate of annual increase in sales at 100, the increases were

Outdoor	131
Radio	101
Regular media mix	95
Newspapers	63
Television	46

The Florists' Association is one of the few television advertisers ever to abandon that medium.[20]

When (1) there is uncertainty about the appropriate action to take (as there was by the Florists' Association), and (2) an on-line experiment will not disrupt the normal course of business (as this experiment did not), and (3) an on-line experiment can be conducted at little or no extra cost (as this experiment was), it makes sound managerial sense to collect information by this means. In fact, on-line experiments always ought to be considered when planning the marketing program to obtain information on the sales effects of price and alternative levels of advertising, sales promotion, sales force, and distribution expenditures.

The fact that they always ought to be *considered* does not mean that they ought always to be *used*, however. On-line experiments with price can run afoul of the Robinson-Patman and Clayton acts, for example, and so they should be checked carefully for their legality before being used. Dealers sometimes object strongly when advertising is decreased in their areas, especially if it becomes known that it has been increased in other areas. Sales managers voice the same kinds of objections to advertising or sales force reductions in their territories, particularly when they are on an incentive salary system. For these and other reasons, along with the out-of-pocket expenses involved in collecting data for some experiments, the cost of an on-line experiment may be higher than the value of the information gained, and therefore it should not be conducted.

The point remains, however, that on-line experiments always ought to be considered when planning the marketing program. They should be used when it is appropriate to do so.

Whether they are test markets or on-line in nature, field experiments when compared with laboratory experiments are characterized by a high degree of realism, are highly visible, have a low level of control, and are relatively expensive. A cost of the high degree of realism of experiments under actual market conditions is their visibility. Prospective actions are often disclosed to competitors who know the field experiments are being conducted, and, in some cases, competitors can even monitor the results through subscribing to the same syndicated data services that the experimenting company is using for the experiment. There is, of course, no control at all over the actions of competitors, who can, if they so desire, even "jam" the results by changing price, or the level of advertising or promotion, in the test market areas.

MARKETING MODELS AS AN INFORMATION SOURCE

The sources of marketing information are:	
Executive experience	
Internal reports	
Marketing research	
Marketing models	

A useful definition of a marketing model is as follows:

A *marketing model* is a specification of a set of variables and their interrelationships relevant to a marketing situation.

An example of a marketing model that relates to pricing is

The price per unit should be set at the point where estimated total contribution to profit and fixed costs is at a maximum.

Even though this is a very simple model, note that it conforms to the above definition in that (1) it is a specification of a set of variables (price per unit and estimated total contribution to profit and fixed costs), (2) it reflects their interrelationships (the price per unit should be such that it maximizes estimated total contribution to profit and fixed costs), and (3) it relates to a marketing situation (pricing).

Models can be used to describe, to explain, to predict, or to help make decisions. Descriptive, explanatory, and predictive models provide information, and decisional models process information to help in decision making. Examples of the four types of models are given in Table 8–5.

Even though the end result of the manager's consideration of a problem area will be a decision (even if the decision is to do nothing about it), explanatory, descriptive, and predictive models are always used in the deliberations leading

Table 8–5 Examples of Descriptive, Explanatory, Predictive, and Decisional Models

Descriptive	Repeat-purchase behavior is such that a (roughly) constant proportion of the persons who buy a brand in one period also buy it in the next period.
Explanatory	Repeat purchases are made by persons to whom the product is available, who are satisfied with the product and its price, and who may be habit prone.
Predictive	If we were to lower the price of our brand by 10 percent at the beginning of the next period and our competitors do not lower their price, we would retain our repeat purchasers and attract some of the buyers who have been repeat purchasers of our competitors' brands.
Decisional	After estimating total contribution to profits and fixed costs for the period at each price by multiplying the margin per unit times the estimated number of units sold, set the price at the level that maximizes the estimated contribution to profits and fixed costs.

up to the decision. The reason for this is straightforward—managers have to understand the situation surrounding the problem, and be able to predict the effects of potential actions, before they can make an informed decision.

The use of explicit models in marketing clearly affects the kinds and the extent of the information the marketing manager needs. Little makes the prediction that, as a result of the increased use of model-based decision making in marketing, there will be a shift from "market status reporting to market response reporting."[21] Lilien and Kotler point out the implications of such a trend:

> Whereas manager A (without models) gets reports on what things are—data points for sales, shares, prices, advertising expenditures—manager B, using models to interpret the data, gets reports on how things react—price elasticities, advertising responses, promotional effectiveness indicators. Manager B is clearly in a better position to make informed decisions.[22]

Explicit models exist and are used in market planning, in understanding and predicting consumer behavior and organizational buying, for market segmentation and forecasting, and for making decisions in the areas of product planning, pricing, advertising, personal selling, sales promotion, and distribution. We have already discussed some of the applicable models in market planning, consumer behavior, and organizational buying, and we discuss models in each of the other areas in the appropriate chapters.

The Role of the Requesting Executive in the Research Project

It is not unusual for line marketing executives to be critical of the marketing research reports they receive and, by implication, if not directly, of the researchers who did the research they contain. In particular, one hears comments about research as being "impractical," "taking too long," and "costing too much."

When these comments are raised within a company, they may, of course, be an indication that the marketing research department is not doing a competent job. At least as often, however, they are the result of a lack of coordination and close working relationship between the marketing executives who request research projects and the researchers who do them.

A tradition of sorts has grown up in some companies that a line executive requests a research study, the researcher goes off to conduct it, and the two do not meet until it is finished. This lack of communication and coordination between manager and researcher is often justified on the grounds of not wanting to risk compromising the objectivity of the researcher. Although no one would argue with the desirability of the researcher's remaining as objective as possible while conducting a study, the manager must necessarily be a contributor to it if it is to be as successful as it could be. Specifically, the requesting executive needs to participate in the following ways:

1. *The manager should explain the management problem to the researcher.* The project is being requested to provide information that will help the requestor (and perhaps others) solve a particular problem or set of problems. The manager needs to inform the researcher about the problem so that he or she understands it fully.

2. *The manager should relate to the researcher opinions and estimates (even hunches) that are concerned with the solution to the problem.* This is necessary to help the researcher translate the management problem into a research problem. The research problem is to decide what information is needed and, within the constraints of time and budget, how best to obtain it. The researcher needs to understand fully what the management problem is, and the current best judgments about how it should be solved, in order to formulate the research problem properly.

3. *The manager should review a statement of the research problem and, in conjunction with the researcher, revise it as necessary until both agree on the information that will be obtained and the time required to obtain it.*

4. *The manager should review progress and preliminary findings with the researcher at appropriate intervals while the study is being done.*

5. *The manager should go over the final report very carefully and ask any questions of clarification necessary to a complete understanding of what was done, and what the findings and their implications are.*

Commissioning a research project involves a purchase of information. The requesting manager, like the careful buyer of anything else, should act to ensure that full value is received for the money and time spent.

SUMMARY OF IMPORTANT POINTS

1. Marketing managers need information to
   forecast market levels
   make plans
   identify problems
   identify opportunities
   generate alternatives
   evaluate alternatives
   implement solutions
   monitor operating performance

2. The general sources of marketing information used by marketing managers are executive experience, internal reports, marketing research, and marketing models.

3. Epistemology, the science of how we come to "know," indicates that we acquire information by one or more of six different methods. They are by casual experience, authority, inquiry, observation, experimentation, and theoretical inference.

4. A *marketing information system* (MIS) is a system designed to generate, store, and disseminate an orderly flow of pertinent and timely information to marketing managers.

5. Computers have affected the marketing information system in four different ways. Computers provide:

   a. An improved means of storing and retrieving information.

   b. An efficient means of analysis.

   c. A stimulus for the commercial development of computerized bibliographic and numeric databases highly useful to the MIS.

   d. An efficient means of marketing model development and manipulation.

6. *Marketing research* is a formalized means of obtaining information to be used in making marketing decisions.

7. Marketing research uses four basic methods of collecting data. They are secondary research, survey research, observation, and experimentation.

8. *Secondary data* are data that were developed for some purpose other than helping to solve the problem for which the research project is being conducted. This is as opposed to *primary data*, which are data developed specifically to help solve the problem at hand.

9. The three basic types of data that *syndicated research services* supply to consumer goods marketers are movement of products through wholesalers, movement of products through retailers, and consumer response (purchases, usage, coupons redeemed, and exposure to advertising) to elements of the marketing mix.

10. The *people meter* is an electronic device that records when a TV set is on, to what channel it is tuned, and the viewer(s) in the household who have "logged on" for viewing.

11. *Survey research* is defined as the systematic collection of data directly from respondents for the purpose of understanding or predicting some aspect of the behavior of the population of interest.

12. *Qualitative survey research* is exploratory research done to provide plausible verbal explanations of the "whys" and "hows" of market dynamics. *Quantitative survey research* is usually descriptive or causal in intent and so is done to provide numerical data that collectively describe or test hypotheses about the market and its workings.

13. *Focus groups* are group discussions held with a sample of 8–12 persons knowledgeable about the product class. The discussion is moderated in an unobtrusive way by a researcher and averages 1½ to 2 hours in length. The results are often videotaped and may even be viewed by client executives through a one-way mirror.

14. *Qualitative research studies* cost less, use smaller samples, may provide more insights into purchase and use decisions, and require more

skilled interviewers. The results are more investigator-dependent than for *quantitative research studies*.

15. The appropriate procedures for taking a *mall intercept sample* include the following:

Using probability sampling methods to select the shopping malls at which the sample is to be taken.

Allowing for the unrepresentative demographic composition of shoppers by asking potential respondents their age, level of education, approximate annual income, and so forth and selecting them to ensure that these characteristics are represented in the sample in the same proportions they are represented in the population.

Allowing for frequency of visit to the mall by weighting of responses.

Allowing for location in the mall by stationing interviewers at every entrance with instructions to select every *k*th person.

Allowing for the time of day and the day of the week differences in shoppers by interviewing at randomly selected times.

16. The ways of dealing with *nonresponse* in surveys include the following:
   a. Keep it as low as is economically feasible. Design the survey to include successive mailings or callbacks; use preliminary notification; offer money, nonmonetary gifts, or other incentives to respond.
   b. Measure the effects of the nonresponse by taking a subsample of the nonrespondents. This is a particularly effective strategy when the original survey was conducted by mail and the subsample is interviewed either personally or by telephone.
   c. Estimate the effects of the nonresponse. The methods that can be used to assist in the estimation include:
   Imputation   Assigning the same responses to nonrespondents as those from respondents with similar demographic characteristics.
   Trend analysis   Recording responses on successive mailings or callbacks and projecting any resulting trend to the remaining nonrespondents.
   Politz-Simmons method   A method for estimating the characteristics of not-at-home nonrespondents in telephone and personal interview surveys from the responses of respondents with a known frequency of being at home at that time.

17. Errors in the recorded responses to a survey can occur for the following reasons:
   a. The respondent does not understand the question to mean what it was intended to mean.
   b. The interviewer does not understand the response to mean what it was intended to mean.
   c. The respondent does not tell the (whole) truth.
   d. The interviewer "cheats" either by not interviewing the respondent at all or by not asking difficult or potentially embarrassing questions and making up and recording fictitious responses.

18. *Observation* as a research method is observation that serves a specifi-cally formulated purpose, is planned systematically, is recorded sys-tematically, and is subjected to checks and controls on its overall accuracy.

19. *Experimentation* involves the manipulation of one or more (inde-pendent) variables by the experimenter in such a way that the effect on one or more other (dependent) variables can be measured.

20. *On-line experiments* consist of deliberate changes in one or more mar-keting variables made during the course of regular business operations in such a way that the effects on sales can be measured.

21. A *marketing model* is a specification of a set of variables and their interrelationships relevant to a marketing situation.

22. The requesting executive should participate in a research project in the following ways:

    a. The manager should explain the management problem to the re-searcher.

    b. The manager should relate to the researcher opinions and estimates (even hunches) that are concerned with the solution to the problem.

    c. The manager should review a statement of the research problem and, with the researcher, revise it as necessary until both agree on the information that will be obtained and the time required to obtain it.

    d. The manager should review progress and preliminary findings with the researcher at appropriate intervals while the study is being done.

    e. The manager should go over the final report very carefully and ask any questions of clarification necessary to a complete understand-ing of what was done, and what the findings and their implications are.

REVIEW QUESTIONS

8.1. For what uses is information required by marketing managers?

8.2. What are the general sources of marketing information used by mar-keting managers?

8.3. What are the methods that *epistemology*, the science of how we come to know, indicates we use to acquire knowledge?

8.4. What is a *marketing information system*?

8.5. How have computers affected the marketing information system?

8.6. What is *marketing research*?

8.7. What are the four basic methods used in marketing research for collecting data?

8.8. What are the three basic types of data that syndicated research services supply to consumer goods marketers?

8.9. a. What is *qualitative* survey research?
b. What is *quantitative* survey research?

8.10. What is a *focus group*?

8.11. In general, how do qualitative research studies compare with quantitative studies in terms of
a. Cost
b. Sample size
c. Skill of interviewers required
d. Degree that results are investigator-dependent

8.12. What is *observation* as a research method?

8.13. What is *experimentation* as a research method?

8.14. What is an *on-line* experiment?

8.15. What is a *marketing model*?

8.16. In what ways should the requesting executive participate in a research project?

DISCUSSION QUESTIONS AND PROBLEMS

8.17. What internal secondary data might be useful in helping to predict:
a. Cash flows from the introduction of a new product.
b. The potential range of error of a sales forecast.
c. The appropriate inventory levels for various times of the year.
d. The number of sales representatives that will resign during the next 12 months.

8.18. Suppose that the marketing manager of a company receives all of the internal reports described in Table 8–2. What kinds of internal information, if any, of importance to managing the marketing program for the company would not necessarily be received?

8.19. As a marketing manager, assume that you meet with a researcher to define the problem on which you want a study conducted. After asking questions, the researcher suggests that maybe the problem might be stated somewhat differently from the way in which you defined it. What should your reaction be?

8.20. Some companies that are planning to have a research project conducted by an outside agency think it is desirable to solicit proposals from a large number of potential suppliers. Do you agree with this practice? Why or why not?

8.21. It has been suggested that selecting the best outside research firm to conduct a *qualitative* research study is probably more difficult than selecting the best outside firm to do a *quantitative* research study. Do you agree or disagree with this suggestion? Why?

8.22. Store audits are conducted for each brand of each product class in each sample store by obtaining information on (1) inventory at the beginning of the period, (2) shipments received during the period, and (3) ending inventory.
   a. What is the accounting arithmetic that could be applied to these data to obtain an estimate of sales for the period?
   b. If this estimate of sales were not adjusted, would you expect it to be biased in one direction or the other? Why?

8.23. The data provided by store audits, consumer diary panels, and checkout scanner tapes for the same products and time periods should be closely comparable. Often they are not, however. What reasons can you give that might explain the differences?

8.24. Suppose you are a marketing manager who is discussing the proposal by a research agency for conducting a national survey of 500 households. Suppose that the topic of the survey is to determine what the eating habits of a cross section of the population are with respect to Mexican food.
   You find that the sampling plan recommended is to interview 100 shoppers each at the entrances nearest the bus stops in shopping malls in Seattle, Minneapolis, Chicago, Cleveland, and Philadelphia between 10 AM and 1 PM on weekdays. What questions might you raise as to the probable validity of the findings from such a sample? Why?

8.25. Considering both cost and keeping sampling error to a low level, how should a representative national sample of supermarket shoppers be designed?

8.26. Suppose that your company sells packaged dry groceries and is considering a plan to pay supermarkets for giving them a "preferred" shelf position. What would be an appropriate design for a research project to determine (a) what the "preferred" shelf position would be and (b) how much it would be worth paying the supermarket to obtain it?

8.27. Suppose you are the marketing manager for Mattel, Inc., a manufacturer of children's toys. A toy being developed for two- to three-year-olds has three different versions. A decision has to be made concerning which version(s) to introduce. What would be an appropriate design for a research project to provide information to help in making this decision?

8.28. For what purposes can the weekly data from a checkout scanning syndicated service with a nationwide sample of supermarkets (such as National Scanning Services, Inc.) be used?

8.29. What are the strengths and weaknesses of field experiments?

8.30. What are the strengths and weaknesses of laboratory experiments?

8.31. If you had decided that you had to use a standard market test, what steps could you take to minimize disruption by competitors?

8.32. If you were managing an airline, what observational studies, if any, would you want to have conducted on a
a. regular basis?
b. occasional basis?

8.33. Suppose you were interested in starting a new business. What is the management problem? What is the research problem?

8.34. What considerations are involved in choosing between a laboratory test, a controlled store test, and a market test for testing four possible prices for an existing product? Which method is the most and which method is the least desirable with respect to each consideration?

8.35. An analyst for a pharmaceutical company did an analysis of the company's sales data by sales territory. One of the analyses made was the relationship of the number of sales representatives per territory to sales in that territory. A plot of results is shown below.

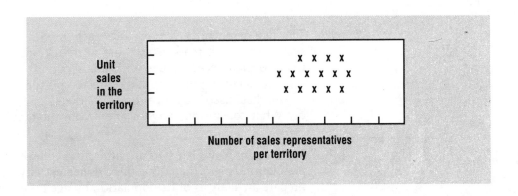

a. What tentative conclusion(s) should be reached?
b. How could it (they) be tested?

8.36. It has been suggested that for articles sold both through vending machines and over the counter (candy, cigarettes, food items, etc.), package designs should be sales tested by first trying the new designs in vending machines.

   a. What method of measuring sales response would this involve?
   b. What assumptions are involved in this design?

8.37. Companies that subscribe to the same consumer panel or store audit services as a company conducting a market test often have the same sales data from the test as does the testing company. Why might a competitor in this situation want to make a reactive price change in the test markets that would be the same as would be made if the test price were an actual price change?

8.38. Industrial Supplies, Inc. distributes a line of industrial supplies throughout the United States. It is divided into 75 geographic sales divisions. Each sales division is headed by a division manager who supervises 10 sales representatives. The divisions produce roughly equivalent sales levels. All sales representatives are paid a straight salary. The firm's management would like to determine the sales and profits effect of shifting to either a straight commission plan or a base salary plus a commission.

   a. Design a field sales experiment change that would allow you to test the effects of the two proposed plans.
   b. How would your experiment change, if at all, if 10 percent of the territories generated 40 percent of the total sales, 30 percent generated another 30 percent of the sales, and 60 percent of the territories generated only 30 percent of the total sales?

PROJECTS

8.39. The first issue of *Advertising Age* each month has a "New Products" section in which market tests and introductions are described. Consult the two most recent issues with this section.

   a. Tabulate the products market tested by type of product, number of markets used, and location of markets.
   b. What conclusions do you draw from the tabulations?

8.40. For the city in which you are attending college or university (or, if its population is less than 150,000, the nearest city of that size or larger), prepare an analysis of its population by age group, population by ethnic origin, and income by income class as they compare with the entire United States.

In your judgment, and based only on these three criteria, would the city be a good one to use as a test market for
a. Planter's Peanut Butter
b. An Armstrong Flooring design
c. Heublein's Ortega Tacos
All new products to be marketed nationally if introduced? Explain.

Endnotes

[1]See W. Churchman, *The Theory of Experimental Inference*, Macmillan, 1961, for a discussion of these sources.

[2]Taken from D. S. Tull and D. I. Hawkins, *Marketing Research: Measurement and Method*, 4th ed., Macmillan, 1987, 12.

[3]Adapted from ibid., 13–14. The original sources were private correspondence and "Penney's Sees 'Fairly Good' Retail Gains," *Advertising Age*, November 2, 1982, 20.

[4]According to *Webster's Ninth New Collegiate Dictionary*, heuristic learning is "discovery or problem solving by experimental and especially trial-and-error methods."

[5]See Chapter 19, "Marketing Organization," for a discussion of brand management.

[6]G. S. Albaum, "Horizontal Information Flow: An Exploratory Study," *Journal of the Academy of Management*, March 1964, 21–33.

[7]Based in part on J. Honomichl, in "How Much Was Spent on Research? Follow Me," *Advertising Age*, June 21, 1982, 48.

[8]Tull and Hawkins, *Marketing Research*, 5.

[9]"A Revolution in TV Audience Measurement," *Changing Media*, Ogilvy & Mather, November 1986; "People Meters to Be Sole Tool for '87 Nielsen TV Ratings," *Marketing News*, January 30, 1987, 1.

[10]For further discussion of these two types of research and the techniques they employ, see Tull and Hawkins, *Marketing Research*, Chaps. 7, 8, and 9; G. Grenway and G. deGroot, "The Qualitative–Quantitative Dilemma," *Journal of the Market Research Society*, April 1983, 147–164; and K. M. Wallace, "The Use and Value of Qualitative Research Studies," *Industrial Marketing Management*, August 1984, 181–185.

[11]G. J. Glasser and G. D. Metzger, "National Estimates of Non-listed Telephone Households and Their Characteristics," *Journal of Marketing Research*, August 1975, 359–361.

[12]W. R. Klecka and A. J. Tuchfarber, "Random Digit Dialing: A Comparison to Personal Surveys," *Public Opinion Quarterly*, Spring 1978; and D. S. Tull and G. S. Albaum, "Bias in Random Digit Dialed Surveys," *Public Opinion Quarterly*, Fall 1977, 389–395.

[13]See S. Sudman, "Improving the Quality of Shopping Center Sampling," *Journal of Marketing Research*, November 1980, 423–431, for an excellent description of these procedures.

[14]The methods of good sampling are not *always* intuitively obvious, however. For example, it is not obvious that it is often better to have strata represented in the population disproportionately rather than proportionately in the sample.

[15]For a more extensive discussion, see Tull and Hawkins, *Marketing Research*, 130.

[16]P. E. Green and D. S. Tull, *Research for Marketing Decisions*, 4th ed., Prentice-Hall, 1978, 120–121.

[17]C. Selltiz, M. Jahoda, M. Deutsch, and S. W. Cook, *Research Methods in Social Relations*, Holt, Rinehart, & Winston, 1959, 200.

[18]W. L. Rathje, W. W. Hughes, and S. L. Jernigan, "The Science of Garbage: Following the Consumer through His Garbage Can," in *1976 Business Proceedings*, W. Locander (ed.), American Marketing Association, 1976, 56–64.

[19]L. Ingoassia, "A Matter of Taste," *The Wall Street Journal*, February 26, 1980, 23.

[20]Adapted from C. T. Ramond, *Advertising Research: The State of the Art*, Association of National Advertisers, 1976, 102–103.

[21]J. D. C. Little, "Decision Support Systems for Marketing Managers," *Journal of Marketing*, Summer 1979, 25.

[22]G. L. Lilien and P. Kotler, *Marketing Decision Making: A Model Building Approach*, Harper & Row, 1983, 14.

CHAPTER 9

FINANCIAL EVALUATION OF PRODUCT MARKETS

Of all the decisions that must be made in the management of the marketing program, the most crucial are those concerned with the selection of the products to offer and the markets in which to sell them. In fact, these decisions are so critical to the success of the company that those involving major products and markets ordinarily are made by the top management of the company. The marketing manager typically recommends which product markets to enter, or to abandon, but the chief executive officer and the board of directors are usually involved in the final decision on entry and exit for all important products and markets.

In the chapter on marketing strategy (Chapter 2) we discussed the general strategies involved in selecting product markets. The strategies were categorized as being based on *market, engineering or production, risk, management preference,* or *financial* considerations. We stated in the discussion of these strategies that the financial consideration of estimated *size, profitability,* and *cash flows* was of such importance in the choice of product markets that an entire chapter would be devoted to it later. This is that chapter.

The flow diagram in Figure 9–1 shows the topics covered in the chapter and how they combine to provide estimates of the size, profitability, and cash flows of prospective product markets. The three steps shown there for making these financial estimates are

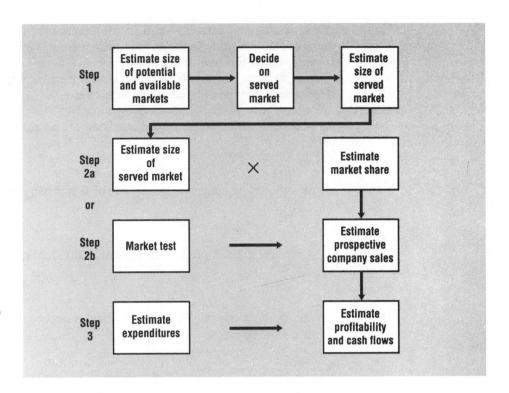

FIGURE 9-1
Flow diagram of methods of
estimating the size, profitability,
and cash flows for candidate
product markets.

Step 1   Estimating the size of the potential, available, and served markets
Step 2   Estimating prospective company sales
Step 3   Estimating profitability and cash flows.

They are discussed in turn in the sections that follow.

STEP 1. ESTIMATING THE SIZE OF THE POTENTIAL, AVAILABLE, AND SERVED MARKETS

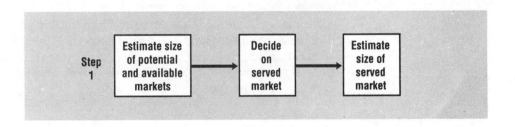

The Meaning of Market Size

The *size* of a physical object, such as a box, is a straightforward concept that provides little chance for misunderstanding. There are three dimensions—

length, width, and breadth—and (if the object is not irregular in shape) once we know the measurements of each dimension, we know all that is possible to know about the size of the object.

When we speak of market size, however, the meaning is not nearly so clear. *Market size* may be defined as the size of the

potential, available, or served markets, or the amount of actual sales

for

an industry, a company, a subunit of a company, or an organization

for

a product class, a product line, or an individual product

for

the world, a country, a region, a state, a county, a metropolitan area, or a sales territory

for

a short period, a period of medium length, or a long-range period

in terms of

monetary or unit sales, or leases.

Hence, there are six dimensions for market size: those of (1) *type of market of interest*, (2) *for what commercial or organizational entity*, (3) *for what product(s)*, (4) *for what area*, (5) *for what period*, and (6) *in what unit of measurement*.

With the exception of the type of market of interest, the meaning of each of these dimensions is clear. An example will help to clarify the meaning of *potential*, *available*, and *served markets*.

The management of the Container Corp., a company that manufactures and sells corrugated and solid fiber boxes in California, was considering marketing its products in Fresno county (coextensive with the Fresno Standard Metropolitan Statistical Area). Before making that decision, it needed to know the "size of the market."

Potential Market: If the market of interest were the potential market, it would be defined as follows:

The **potential market** is the potential total *industry sales* (or leases) *to all possible market segments* for a specified *product class* for an indicated *area* for an identified *time period* expressed in a stipulated *unit of measurement* under conditions of optimum market development.

Note that the six dimensions of market size are stipulated in the definition. When applied to the example, these dimensions can be described as follows:

Industry. All companies manufacturing and selling industrial containers.

All possible market segments. All possible user industries including food and kindred products, chemicals, stone, clay, and glass products, and others.

Product class. All industrial containers, whether they are boxes, bags, barrels, crates, or other, solid or corrugated, and made from fiber, plastic, glass, wood, steel, or other materials.

Area. Fresno county.

Period. A year.

Unit of measurement. Monetary sales.

Note also that the amount of industry monetary sales is defined under conditions of "optimum market development" by the industry. This is necessarily the case if the full economic potential of the market is to be realized.

Available Market: Some parts of the potential market may not have the *interest* to buy containers from an outside supplier such as the Container Corp., or they may be interested but lack the *resources* to buy the containers at the prices offered. When either of these situations occurs, the available market is less than the potential market. An appropriate definition is then

The ***available market*** is that portion of the potential market that has both the *interest* and the *resources* to buy the product(s) at the prices offered.

It is obvious that both promotion and price have a great deal to do with determining what portion of the potential market is available. A prospective buyer may be a part of the *potential* market for an automobile but have no interest in a Maserati because he never heard of it. He would therefore not be a part of the *available* market. An advertising campaign for Maseratis might generate interest on his part, but he still would not be a part of the available market unless he could afford an automobile in that price range.

Served Market: Container Corp. management might be interested in serving only the food and kindred products, chemical and allied products, and stone, clay, and glass products industries because the company had specialized in selling to those industries in its other marketing areas. The *served* market for the company would therefore be less than the *available* market. More generally, it follows that

the ***served market*** is that portion of the potential market that is available and from which business is sought.

It is obvious that the served market cannot be decided on intelligently without first knowing what segments are included in the available market, and the size and composition of each.

The relationship among these three different types of markets is shown graphically in Figure 9–2.

These differing concepts of a market and the measurements of them are useful for management purposes. If sales are not at a satisfactory level in a product market, for example, the following actions can be considered:

The company can increase its marketing efforts in the served market.

The company can expand the available market, and those segments of it that it is serving, by lowering price, increasing access through more intensive distribution or addition of new territories, or both.

Increase the potential market, and by so doing, the available and served markets, by promotional campaigns designed to attract new consumers.

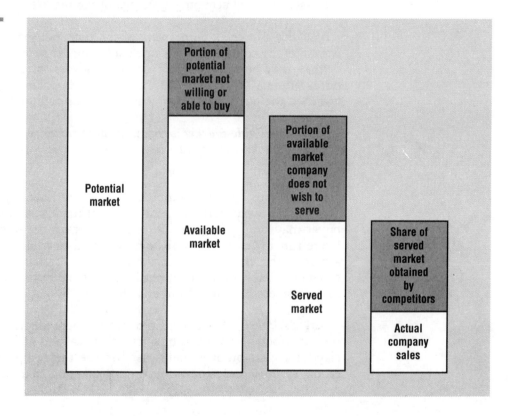

FIGURE 9-2
The relationship among the potential, available, and served markets and actual sales for a company.

Table 9–1 Methods of Estimating Product Market Size

Method	Type of Market
1. Adjusted industry sales	Available market
2. Market buildup	Potential market Available market Served market
3. Substitution potential	Potential market
4. Analogous location	Available market Served market
5. Market indexes	Potential market Available market
6. Surveys	Available market Served market
7. Market tests.	Prospective company sales

Methods of Estimating the "Size" of a Prospective Product Market

Seven major methods are available for estimating the "size" of a product market. They are (1) adjusted industry sales, (2) market buildup, (3) substitution potential, (4) analogous location, (5) market indexes, (6) surveys, and (7) market tests. As shown in Table 9–1, these methods provide estimates for varying definitions of markets; some give estimates of the potential market, some of the available market, and still others of the served market and of prospective company sales.

Estimation Method 1— Adjusted Industry Sales

A straightforward method of measuring the *available* market is to obtain a measurement of industry sales and to make any necessary adjustments. The potential market for corrugated and solid fiber boxes, for example, could be measured as the aggregated industry sales for various kinds of industrial containers, adjusted for any difference in the time period for which the data were collected and the one period for which the available market estimate is required.

The sources of sales data most frequently used are trade associations, syndicated data services, and government agencies.

Sales Data from Trade Associations: Most trade associations collect sales data (by product line) from their members and publish them in an aggregated form. There are more than 2,000 trade associations in the United States. As noted in the last chapter, they are listed in the *Encyclopedia of Associations* (Gale Research) along with their lines of trade, descriptions, addresses, and telephone numbers.

Sales of corrugated and solid fiber boxes are compiled by state by the Fiber Box Association and reported in the *Fiber Box Industry Annual Report*, for example. Similarly, data on the sales of steel containers are available from the American Iron and Steel Institute. Neither source collects or publishes data by industry at the county level, however, nor is it likely that the trade associations to which producers of plastic, wood, rubber, and glass containers belong would have such data by county either.

If the size for market areas smaller than states is desired, trade association data for the state usually have to be allocated by some procedure. One method of doing this is illustrated in Exhibit 9–1 in the "Market Buildup" section later in the chapter.

Sales Data from Syndicated Data Services: Syndicated data services report sales data by area for each of the major product classes, and the brands they contain for grocery and drug sundry products. Those that are based on consumer diaries also report sales by the demographics of the buyer. Therefore, if a company is interested in targeting a particular set of demographic groups, it is possible to single them out for an estimate of the size of the *served*, as well as the *available*, market for its brand.

Syndicated data services are a particularly useful basis for estimating the size of the available market for products that are essentially copies of grocery and drug sundry products that are already on the market. This method of estimation is illustrated in the example that follows.

> The new-products director of a Sterling Drug subsidiary was astounded when he first saw Airwick's Carpet Fresh, a carpet-cleaning product, and learned how it was to be used. A white powder, it is first sprinkled on the carpeting and then vacuumed up. The whole idea seemed wrong—who would first dirty the carpet before cleaning it?
>
> Tracking Carpet Fresh sales from syndicated data service reports convinced him otherwise, however. Based on the sales data reported by the service, he estimated that sales would reach $40 million per year, a large enough market to make it profitable for a second product to enter.
>
> Six months after work on the new product got under way, it was introduced with the name Love My Carpet. Sales built as expected after introduction, and it is now a successful product.

Although there are syndicated data services for industrial products, none of them collects and reports sales data. (See Chapter 8, pages 238–241, for a detailed description of syndicated data services.)

Sales Data from Government Agencies: Federal, state, and local government agencies provide an extensive amount of sales data. The most important source of such data for the United States is published by the federal government. Sales statistics are available for each of the levels of distribution—manufacturers, wholesalers, and retailers for products, and the suppliers for services. The principal sources of sales data for each of these levels are the censuses conducted for each. A Census of Manufacturers, a Census of Wholesale Trade, a Census of Retail Trade, and a Census of Selected Services are conducted every five years (years ending in 2 and 7). The data in the censuses are provided for the country as a whole and by state, Standard Metropolitan Statistical Areas, counties, and cities that are of an indicated size.

The *Current Industrial Reports, Current Wholesale Trade, Current Retail Trade,* and *Monthly Selected Services* series update the related censuses at least annually. The extent of the geographic breakdown for the data provided in these reports varies, but in all cases is less than that for the censuses.

The government frequently collects data in greater detail and for smaller geographic areas than it publishes. In these instances it is often possible to obtain a special tabulation (for which one must pay) from the collecting agency. This turns out to be the case with the sales data for industrial containers at the county level. If the marketing manager for the manufacturer of fiberboard boxes had wanted to do so, a computer run from the data collected for the last Census of Manufacturers would have provided data on sales of industrial containers in Fresno county.

Estimation Method 2 — Market Buildup

Market buildup is a method of estimating the sizes of the *potential, available,* or *served* markets, depending on how it is applied. The underlying logic of the method is simple and straightforward. If one knows:

n the number of buyers in a market

and

q the average number of units each will buy during a given time period,

then

Q the total quantity bought in units, is found by

$$Q = nq$$

If we add to the equation:

p the average price paid per unit,

then

PQ the total quantity bought in dollars, is obtained as

$$PQ = npq$$

Note that if n is defined as the number of buyers potentially in the market, then an estimate of the size of the *potential* market results. If n is defined as the number of buyers actually in the market, an estimate of the *available* market is provided. And if n is defined as the number of buyers whom the company wants to serve from among those available, an estimate of the *served* market is obtained.

Because of the smaller number of buyers involved, this method is used primarily by industrial goods companies. A variation of it is an appropriate method to use to estimate the size of the market for industrial containers in Fresno county, for example. To estimate the *served* market size, the procedure is as follows:

1. Determine the amount of the product used *per employee* in each industry of interest at the national level.
2. Determine the *number of employees* in each industry of interest in the area for which the estimate of market size is to be made.

EXHIBIT **9-1**

Estimate of Dollar Sales of Corrugated and Solid Fiber Boxes in Fresno County

Col. 1 Value of Box Shipments by Industry Nationwide[a] (000s)	Col. 2 Number of Employees by Industry Nationwide[b] (000s)	Col. 3 Usage per Employee by Industry (col. #2/col. #3)	Col. 4 Number of Employees by Industry— Fresno County[c]	Col. 5 Estimated Shipments by Industry (000s)	Col. 6 Industry and SIC Number
SIC 20 Food and kindred products	$4,181,206	1,487.7	$2,810	7,900	$22,199
SIC 28 Chemicals and allied products	896,000[d]	872.6	1,027	900	924
SIC 32 Stone, clay, and glass products	896,000[d]	531.5	1,200	1,200	2,023
				Total	$25,146

[a]Based on data reported in *Fiber Box Industry 1985 Report*, Fibre Box Association.
[b]*1983 Census of Manufacturers, U.S. Summary*, U.S. Bureau of the Census.
[c]*1983 Census of Manufacturers, California*, U.S. Bureau of the Census.
[d]No error is involved; the value of shipments for the two industries was the same.

3. Multiply (1) by (2) for each industry.
4. Sum over the industries of interest.

This procedure is illustrated in estimating the size of the served market for corrugated and solid fiber boxes in the food, chemical, and stone, clay, and glass products industries in Fresno county in Exhibit 9–1. As shown there, the estimated annual market for corrugated and solid fiber boxes in the three indicated industries in Fresno county is about $25 million.

There is evidence that this method is widely used.[1] There is also evidence that in some applications it gives inaccurate results.[2] It should therefore be used with care.

Estimation
Method 3—
Substitution
Potential

Any new product, or existing product newly introduced into a market, is to some extent intended to be a substitute for existing products. Thus the computer served as a substitute for calculators and files, a new arthritis drug as a replacement for existing remedies, and low-calorie wines for standard-calorie wines.

A method of estimating the potential market from secondary data is therefore to determine the *substitution potential*. The estimates made for an automatic milling machine in Exhibit 9–2 are an example.

This method can be applied to both consumer and industrial durable products. However, it works better for industrial than for consumer durables.

EXHIBIT **9-2**

Estimating the Market for a Machine Tool Control Through Substitution Potential

A manufacturer of machine tools developed a control mechanism that would permit the automatic machining of any part. The principle involved was to have an expert machinist make the part on a machine that was equipped to accurately measure and record the movements of the cutting head. The tape could then be played back through the control which, when mounted on a machine of the same type, would automatically reproduce the movements of the cutting head and thus machine the part.

Estimates were made of the average savings in machinists' time that would accrue from using the control on various types of machine tools. From these, it was determined that it would be economical to use the control only on milling machines.

Two methods of marketing the control were considered; as an attachment to an existing machine and as an integral part of a new milling machine produced by the manufacturer. Investigation revealed that it was difficult to ensure the necessary level of accuracy on existing machines, however, so it was decided that if it were marketed, it would be only as a part of a new machine.

Cost estimates indicated that users could economically replace milling machines that were 10 years of age or older with the new machines. From secondary data, an estimate was made of the number of machines that were of that age or older. After adding an estimate for growth, the resulting figure was used as an estimate of the potential market for new machines.

Estimation Method 4— Analogous Location

The method of analogous location is used primarily in determining the size of *available* markets for locating outlets of retail chains, financial institutions, and franchise operations. However, in some situations, and especially so in retail site location, the decision may be to serve all of the available market. In these cases, the method provides an estimate of the size of the *served* market as well.

The method involves plotting the area around the potential site in terms of traffic patterns, residential neighborhoods, income levels, and competitors.[3] The map so obtained (an example is given as Exhibit 9-3) is then compared with maps of other outlets *whose sales levels are known* until a similar one is found. The sales level of the analog outlet is then used as a predictor of the new outlet. This is the estimated size of the *available* (and perhaps the *served*) market.

Since to use this method it is necessary to have maps of a sizable number of locations of outlets whose sales are known, it is best suited for use by chain organizations.

Estimation Method 5— Market Indexes

A **market index** number is a measure of the proportion of the total market for a product contained in a specified marketing area.

For example, if a market researcher for the Clorox Company, the manufacturer and national marketer of Clorox bleach, were to estimate that the market index number for the Phoenix (Arizona) Metropolitan Statistical Area is 0.007, that would be an estimate that the proportion in the Phoenix MSA of the total U.S. market for household bleach is 0.007 (0.7%).

Market indexes can be *general* or *specific* in nature. General market indexes are used to provide estimates of the size of *potential* markets, whereas specific market indexes are used to give measures of the size of *available* markets.

EXHIBIT **9-3**

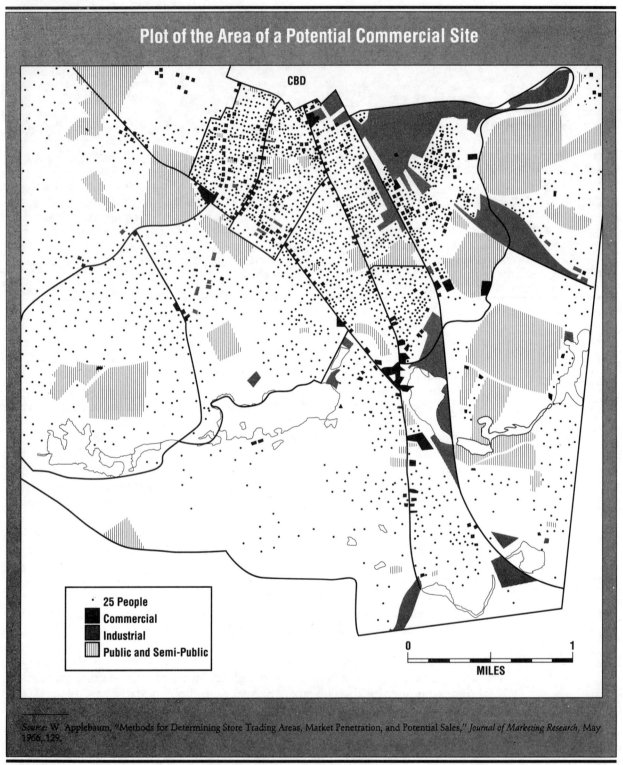

Plot of the Area of a Potential Commercial Site

CBD

Legend:
- · 25 People
- ■ Commercial
- ■ Industrial
- ▨ Public and Semi-Public

0   1

MILES

Source: W. Applebaum, "Methods for Determining Store Trading Areas, Market Penetration, and Potential Sales," *Journal of Marketing Research*, May 1966, 129.

General Market Indexes: The principle underlying the construction of market indexes is that *when one series is correlated with a second series, the first series may be used to predict the second one.* For example, if population is correlated with sales of household bleach, then the population in the Phoenix MSA ought to be useful as a predictor of the potential market for household bleach in that area.

In addition to market indexes being either general or specific, they can be either *single* or *multiple factor* in nature. If the researcher for Clorox were to use only population as a predictor of market potential, the market index that would result would be a **single-factor** index. One might expect, however, that by adding other factors—income, retail sales, and perhaps others—the performance of the index would be improved. **Multiple-factor** indexes generally do outperform single-factor indexes, and so are used much more frequently.

A multiple-factor market index that is widely used for estimating potential market size for consumer products in the United States is the "Buying Power Index" published by *Sales and Marketing Management* magazine. Each year the magazine publishes a "Survey of Buying Power" issue that contains data on population, income, and retail sales in the United States down to the metropolitan area, county, and city levels. Similar data are also provided for Canada at the province and metropolitan area levels. For each geographic area, it combines these three data points into a "buying power index" that is an indicator of the size of the potential market in that area for an "average" low-priced, mass-marketed consumer product.

The same magazine also publishes an annual "Survey of Industrial Buying Power."

Multiple-factor indexes usually take the form:

$$MP_i = W_1 F_{1,i} + W_2 F_{2,i} + \cdots + W_n F_{n,i}$$

where

$$MP_i = \text{measure of market potential in area } i$$
$$W_1 = \text{the weight assigned factor 1}$$
$$F_{1,i} = \text{a measure of factor 1 in area } i$$

The **buying power index** is a three-factor index of this form. The factors for the Phoenix MSA and the factor weights are as follows:[4]

$$F_{1,i} = \text{percentage of population in area}$$
$$= 0.788\,\%$$
$$W_1 = 0.2$$
$$F_{2,i} = \text{percentage of retail sales in area}$$
$$= 0.836\,\%$$
$$W_2 = 0.3$$
$$F_{3,i} = \text{percentage of effective buying income}$$
$$\text{(disposable personal income) in area}$$
$$= 0.820\,\%$$
$$W_3 = 0.5$$

We can therefore calculate the buying power index for the Phoenix area (= market potential for the Phoenix area) as

$$BP\text{Phoenix} = MP\text{Phoenix}$$
$$= 0.788(0.2) + 0.836(0.3) + 0.820(0.5)$$
$$= 0.818.$$

Thus, using this market index, the estimated market potential in the Phoenix area as a proportion of the total U.S. market for household bleach is 0.00797 (= 0.797 percent).

How accurate is this estimate? One appraisal of the general accuracy of the index is that it is "quite adequate for the needs of its users."[5] For specific areas, however, one must consider whether there are special circumstances that invalidate the assumption that the product will sell there at the same rate as it does in the total market area. For example, bleach probably does not sell at the national average rate in Phoenix. Because clothes there are more often dried in the sun than they are in other areas, it seems likely that less bleach per capita is used than on the average for the rest of the country. If that is true, the market index for bleach could be improved by adding another factor—one involving the relative number of days of sunshine per year in each area.

Specific Market Indexes: Suppose the market analyst for Clorox wanted to devise a market index that would be specific for household bleach. How could this be done?

A market index equation for estimating the size of the *available* market for a specific product or product line can be formulated through the use of **regression analysis**. Data on the factors that are assumed to affect sales of bleach are regressed against actual sales of bleach for a set of sample areas. The resulting equation then provides the basis for estimating the available market for bleach, given data on the factors that affect sales, for areas for which industry sales are not known. The procedure for constructing such a specific market index is given in Exhibit 9–4.

Estimation Method 6— Surveys

Consumer product syndicated data services are an example of how the survey method is used to estimate market size (along with information about the products bought and, for the services that use consumer purchase diaries, the demographic characteristics of the buyers). The estimate provided by these services is the size of the *available* market.

Some industrial products companies routinely conduct a survey of all known users of their product(s) in their current sales territories each quarter or each year. USX (formerly the United States Steel Corporation) conducts a survey each quarter of companies in each of 13 steel-using industries to determine their expected purchases of steel during the next quarter and the next 12 months. A company that manufactures bearings for railroad cars conducts a similar survey among railroad car builders each quarter. These surveys typically are conducted by the sales force, and establish the size and composition of the available market to provide better information for marketing planning and control.

In our example, a survey of users of packaging materials and containers in Fresno county could be taken to estimate the available market size. Information could be obtained from such a survey on both (1) the amount of these products

EXHIBIT **9-4**

Procedure for Constructing a Specific Index of the Available Market for a Product

The steps to use in developing a specific index of the size of the available market for a product are as follows:

1. *Decide what factors are going to be used.* The decision on the factors to include turns on the researcher's belief about which variables are highly correlated with the sales of the product. For example, population is no doubt a correlate of sales of household bleach, and income probably is as well. But are retail sales? number of days of sunshine per year? A sound rule to follow when it is believed that a factor *might* be correlated with sales of the product is "when in doubt, include it."

2. *Decide in what form the values of the factors are going to be expressed.* Such questions as "Should the factors for each area be expressed as a percentage of the total market area?" and "Should retail sales be defined as sales of grocery products only?" need to be raised and answered at this stage.

3. *Determine for what areas sales data are available for the product, or line of products, for which the index is being constructed, and for each of the factors.* Sales data are usually available to the state level (from the trade association), but availability of data on the factors will of course depend on the factors chosen. If they are demographic in nature, or climatic (as in the case of the "days of sunshine" variable), they will almost always be available at least to the state level.

4. *Choose the areas to be used and compile the sales and factor data for each area.* The same areas will have to be used for both the sales and the factor data. The sales and factor data should also be compiled on the same basis (e.g., if the values of the factors for each area are expressed as a percentage of the total for the entire market area, the sales data for each area should also be expressed as a percentage).

5. *Run a regression analysis of the data with sales as the dependent variable and the factors as the independent variables.* [*] (A stepwise regression program should be used if there are questionable factors included.) The resulting equation will be of the form

$$AM_i = a + b_1 f_{1,i} + b_2 f_{2,i} + \cdots + b_n f_{n,i}$$

where

AM_i = an estimate of the available market of area i
a = a constant
b_1 = the weight for factor 1
$f_{1,i}$ = the value of factor 1 for area i

If such a regression equation were actually run for the sales of household bleach, the factors and their weights might be as follows:

$f_{1,i}$ = the value for the number of people in area i
b_1 = the weight for the population factor
$f_{2,i}$ = the value for retail sales in area i
b_2 = the weight for the retail sales factor
$f_{3,i}$ = the value for disposable personal income in area i
b_3 = weight for the disposable personal income factor
$f_{4,i}$ = average days of sunshine per year in area i
b_4 = weight for the days of sunshine factor

Although the example we have used is a consumer product, market index equations can also be derived for specific industrial products using a similar procedure.[†]

---

[*]For a discussion of regression analysis, see P. E. Green, D. S. Tull, and G. S. Albaum, *Research for Marketing Decisions*, 5th ed., Prentice-Hall, 1987, 425–463.
[†]For an example, see W. E. Cox, Jr., and G. N. Havens, "Determination of Sales Potential and Performance for an Industrial Goods Manufacturer," *Journal of Marketing Research*, November 1977, 574–578.

used over, say, the past 12 months and (2) the amount that is forecast to be used during the next 12 months.

A survey of all known users (a **census**) to estimate market size is expensive, especially if there are a large number of users and the amount purchased by each is low. A survey of a *sample* of users is often a more practical approach, particularly for consumer products.

Seven methods of estimating market size were given in Table 9–1, and so far we have described six of them. The seventh, market tests, is the only one of the seven from which estimates of prospective company sales can be obtained directly. It therefore is discussed in the next section.

STEP 2. ESTIMATING PROSPECTIVE COMPANY SALES

As shown in the flow diagram below, two methods of estimating prospective company sales are available. The first is to multiply an estimate of the sales in the served market (obtained by one of the methods discussed in Step 1) by an estimate of the *market share* the company would obtain if it were to enter that product market. The second is to conduct a **market test** and obtain a direct estimate of the prospective company sales.

Estimating Market Share for a New Product Market

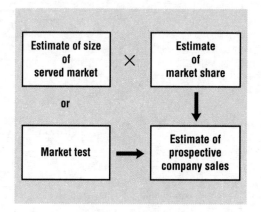

The **market share** of a firm is the proportion of its sales to the total sales of the industry in the served market for a specified period.

If the measurement of market share is made in reference to the served market, the market share is then

$$s_i = PQ_i/PQ_s$$

where

$$PQ_i = \text{the firm's sales}$$
$$s_i = \text{firm } i\text{'s share of the served market}$$
$$PQ_s = \text{the size of the served market}$$

We can easily rewrite the above equation as

$$PQ_i = s_i \times PQ_s$$

and so, if we have an estimate of market share and the size of the served market, we can estimate the level of sales.

How does one estimate what the market share will be in a new product market? There are four estimation methods. The underlying basis for estimation is given in the fundamental market share theorem. A second method is to conduct an intention-to-purchase survey. The third method is make to an estimate based on a judgmental adjustment of the company's share in an analogous market area. The fourth (and usually the most accurate) method is the use of a market test.

The Fundamental Market Share Theorem: The fundamental market share theorem states that:

> Other things being equal, the market share of a company in a product market will be equal to the share of the "attraction" resulting from its marketing effort to the total "attraction" resulting from the marketing efforts of all firms in the industry operating in that product market.[6]

Put more simply, this model essentially says that

our market share = our attraction/(our + their attraction)

where the attraction of a brand depends on its marketing mix. Expressed mathematically the model is

$$s_i = a_i/\Sigma a_i$$

where

s_i = the expected market share of firm i

a_i = the "attraction" resulting from the marketing effort of firm i

Σa_i = the "attraction" resulting from the marketing efforts of the total industry

There is nothing very surprising about this theorem—it is an explicit statement of what each of us would expect intuitively to be the case. Applying it to obtain an accurate estimate of market share calls for a substantial amount of information and liberal doses of good judgment, however.

To make an estimate of market share using the theorem in a new product market, one first has to determine what the relative attraction is of the levels of each of the marketing variables spelled out in the marketing plan for the product market (product characteristics, price, advertising and promotion, distribution, service, and so forth) vis-à-vis those of the industry as a whole. For example, the planned amount of advertising to total industry advertising is known as **share of voice**. If it is believed that the company's advertising will, on the average, be as effective as that of the industry, then the relative attraction resulting from advertising would be equal to the share of voice. Similar evaluations of the relative attraction resulting from the other planned levels of the variables in the marketing plan need also to be made.

The second step is to form an overall judgment of the relative attraction of the company's marketing program versus the total of those of the industry in the product market. This of course requires a weighting for each of the marketing variables. How important will our relative product quality be in determining market share? the relative number of points of distribution we expect to have? our price? our planned advertising and promotion level?

A special consideration in the effectiveness of the marketing program for a new marketing area is the **absence of lagged effects** of past marketing efforts. For example, although it is difficult to measure accurately, there is little doubt that advertising has a lagged effect—that is, that a part of present-period sales are the result of past-period advertising. The same is very likely true for past efforts of the sales force. In beginning a marketing program in a new marketing area, there are of course no lagged effects for past marketing efforts. This has to be allowed for in the estimate of market share.

Several mathematical functions have been proposed that allow estimation of attraction by brand. They have not been used very much, however, because of problems of statistical estimation of the terms they contain.[7]

This method of estimating market share is essentially a by-product of the planning for entry into a new product market, and so should ordinarily be used whenever such planning is carried out. If no formal plan has been prepared, its use will, in effect, result in one being developed.

Intention-to-Purchase Survey: A survey of consumers or industrial users can be conducted to obtain intention-to-purchase data. Depending on whether it is a new product or not, the intention-to-purchase question can be asked after the respondent has read a concept statement, seen a print or TV ad, been shown a package of the product, or participated in a use test of the product. Usually the intention-to-purchase question is phrased using a probabilistic scale of the following general form:

> After having (read the concept statement, seen the ad, looked at the product, used the product), if this product were available at your (supermarket, drugstore, industrial supply store) would you say that you:
>
> - would definitely buy it?
> - would probably buy it?
> - might or might not buy it?
> - would probably not buy it?
> - would definitely not buy it?

Biases exist in the answers to intention-to-purchase questions, and so the answers have to be interpreted with care. (Making estimates of purchases that will actually be made by respondents to such questions is discussed in Chapter 11.)

Share in Analogous Market Area(s): If the firm plans to use approximately the same marketing program in the new area as it does in existing areas and if the number and the perceived effectiveness of competitors is approximately the same, then the market share in the analogous area(s) can be used to estimate the share in the new area. A reduction should be made in the estimates of the market shares for the first few periods that allows for the absence of lagged effects of past marketing efforts, however.

Market Test(s): We are about to discuss market tests as a method of estimating prospective company sales. This is the primary use for such tests. However, if we have an estimate of the size of the served market (obtained from using one or more of the methods discussed earlier) and we estimate prospective company sales using a market test, we can of course make an estimate of market share. Such an estimate is nearly always made when a market test is run.

Using Market Tests to Estimate Prospective Company Sales

Marketing being the art or inexact science that it is, the closest approach to learning how a product would fare if it were introduced in *all* of a market is to introduce it in a *part* of the market. When this is done, a **market test** is being conducted. Market tests are essentially of two types, either a *field market test* or a *simulated market test.*

Field Market Tests: Field market tests are also primarily of two types. They are either a controlled store test, in which the basic test unit is retail stores or industrial distributors, or a standard market test, in which the basic test unit is a market area.

If the test is to be a **controlled store test** for a consumer product, it is introduced directly into a sample of 30–100 retail stores. Ordinarily these stores will have been selected purposely (rather than randomly) to ensure that the managements will cooperate with the test, and that they are of the size and type (independent, chain) and in the locations desired. The managers of the sample stores agree (in return for a fee paid the store) to stock the product(s) involved at the prices stipulated and to use the in-store advertising provided.

Data on sales are obtained through store audits, also agreed to in advance by the store managers. A panel of households that report purchases via consumer diaries is also ordinarily set up and operated at each store location to determine initial- and repeat-purchase rates. From these data, projections can be made to estimate the size of the penetrated market.

If the test is for an industrial product, a sample of industrial distributors is selected (usually 30 or fewer) and the product placed with them. The arrangements made for the test are very similar to those for consumer products, except there is no counterpart of the consumer panel.

Although the controlled store test is not nearly as expensive as a standard market test, it does not provide as much information. Since the product is placed directly in the sample stores, no information is gained on the percentage of stores that would handle the product (the *distribution points*) if it were distributed through the normal trade channels. There is also no information generated on the effects of advertising other than in-store advertising and cooperative advertising with the store.

The **standard market test** is an actual introduction of the product into a sample of cities or metropolitan areas. In each test area, it is introduced through the trade channels and at one of the price and advertising levels that are being considered for the full-scale introduction. For example, the Reggie candy bar was test marketed in Chicago, New York, Philadelphia, Los Angeles, and San Francisco at a retail price of 25 cents and with an advertising-budget equivalent of $3.5 million nationally at an annual rate.[8]

In one study it was found that the "typical" market test (1) used three test areas, (2) lasted about 10 months, (3) used both store audits and consumer surveys to obtain data on the results, (4) tested different levels of one or more marketing mix variables, and (5) was conducted in a "normal" marketing environment.[9]

A list of frequently used market test cities is given in Table 9–2. That there is considerable artistry involved in both the number and choice of cities used in standard market tests is illustrated by tests of two similar products conducted at the same time:

> Market tests were conducted on barbecue fire starters by the Clorox Company and Mobil Chemical. The product tested by Clorox was Match Light, a product consisting of charcoal briquets soaked with fluid. It was market tested in Dallas, Denver, Omaha, and San Diego. Mobil Chemical's product was Get Glowin', a solid rectangular fire starter. It was tested in Minneapolis and Houston.*

*Advertising Age, July 3, 1978, 45.

The advantage of the standard market test vis-à-vis other means of testing is the range of information that comes from marketing the product under close-to-actual market conditions. Data can be obtained on both the trial- and repeat-purchase rates and on the sales effects of different prices and promotional levels.

Standard market tests are not without problems, however. The relatively high cost of conducting them has already been alluded to. In addition, they have the disadvantage of requiring a considerable amount of time, and necessarily disclose not only the fact that the new product is being tested but the test price(s) and advertising level(s) as well. Competitors can disrupt the tests and distort the results through changing prices and promotional levels. (For example, McDonald's "blew us away with promotion" when Wendy's tested a breakfast menu of biscuit-and-egg sandwiches.)[10] Alternatively, the competitors can decide not to disrupt the test and, by using a syndicated store audit service, can obtain the same data as the company sponsoring the market test. This allows the competitors to begin to prepare countering strategies, including

Table 9–2 Frequently Used Test Market Cities in the United States

Albany, New York	Minneapolis, Minnesota
Atlanta, Georgia	Nashville, Tennessee
Cincinnati, Ohio	New Orleans, Louisiana
Columbus, Ohio	New York City, New York*
Davenport, Iowa	Oklahoma City, Oklahoma
Dayton, Ohio	Omaha, Nebraska
Erie, Pennsylvania	Orlando, Florida
Fort Wayne, Indiana	Peoria, Illinois
Fresno, California	Phoenix, Arizona
Grand Rapids, Michigan	Portland, Oregon
Indianapolis, Indiana	Salt Lake City, Utah
Kansas City, Kansas	Spokane, Washington
Los Angeles, California*	Tucson, Arizona
Milwaukee, Wisconsin	Wichita, Kansas

*New York City is the most frequently used test market city and Los Angeles is second, per a study by Selling Areas Marketing, Inc. (SAMI). *Marketing News*, September 12, 1986, 47. Compiled from trade sources. Each city appeared on at least three different lists.

introducing similar products. Examples of testing companies being beaten to market include:

1. Helene Curtis' Arm in Arm deodorant was beaten by Church & Dwight's Arm & Hammer.
2. Hills Bros.' High Yield coffee was introduced nationally after Procter & Gamble's Folger's Flakes.
3. Hunt-Wesson's Prima Salsa tomato sauce was beaten nationally by Chesebrough-Pond's Ragu Extra Thick & Zesty.[11]

Simulated Market Tests: Simulated market tests have gained rapidly in popularity in recent years because of the problems, and the expense, of field market tests.

Simulated market tests are conducted to measure consumer attitudes and purchase rates for a proposed new product in a purchase situation other than an actual store (usually at home). The consumer is exposed to advertisements for the new product, and is given the opportunity to purchase and to use it, after which he or she is interviewed to obtain information on rating of attributes and on attitudes toward the product. The estimates of continuing trial, repeat purchases, and usage rate, coupled with assumptions about distribution and advertising, are then used to estimate market share. The steps involved in a typical simulated test market are shown in Figure 9–3.

A number of consulting firms and advertising agencies offer simulated test marketing services. (Elrick and Lavidge, Yankelovich, Skelly, and White, BBDO, and N. W. Ayer are examples.) In addition, several private companies (Pillsbury, for one) have their own simulated market test systems.

Simulated market test systems have a significant cost advantage over standard market tests. A simulated market test typically costs no more than $100,000, whereas the cost of a standard market test will usually be more than $1 million. Simulated market tests also have the advantage of little risk of disclosure to competitors.

A major problem with simulated market test systems is that they cannot forecast directly what the effects will be of competitive actions such as promotions, price changes, or introductions of another new product. They are also not very effective for evaluating alternative levels of price, advertising, and promotion for the new product itself.

Intuitively one would not expect simulated market tests to give a very accurate estimate of prospective company sales. However, the evidence of the actual accuracy suggests that it is better than one might predict. An advertisement for Elrick and Lavidge's COMP simulated test marketing program claims "correct to the nearest market share point more than 95 percent of the time"[12] for predicted versus first-year-actual market share, and an advertisement for NPD's ESP claims "forecasts of year one volume within 9.9 percent of in-market results."[13] The average absolute error in first-year-predicted versus actual market share for 44 products pretested with Management Decision Systems' ASSESSOR was 1.54 points.[14] Moreover, client companies (such as S. C. Johnson & Co.)[15] consistently report good results. And perhaps the most convincing evidence of an acceptable level of accuracy is the rapidly increasing rate of usage.

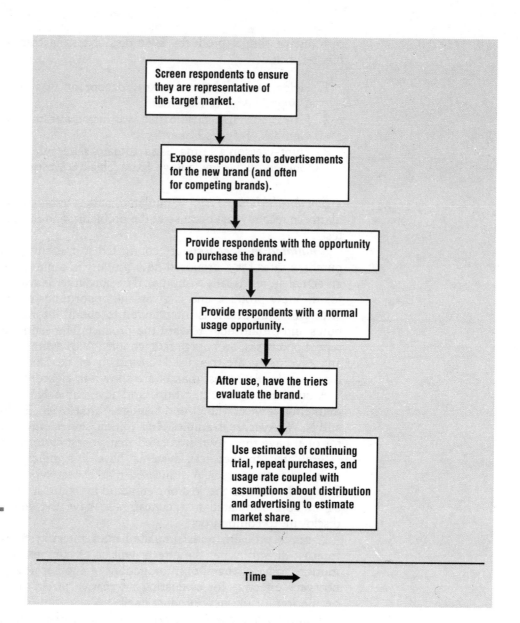

FIGURE 9-3
Steps in simulated market tests.

Source: Adapted from D. S. Tull and D. I. Hawkins, *Marketing Research: Measurement and Method,* 4th ed., Macmillan Publishing Co., 1987, 180.

STEP 3. ESTIMATING PROFITABILITY AND CASH FLOWS

For for-profit concerns, financial forecasts overrule all other considerations over the long term as to whether to enter a new product market or to exit one the company is now in.

Having an estimate of the size of the market, and of the market share that would be obtained, provides the basis for making projections of the *revenues* that could be expected if the decision were made to enter (or remain in) it. These, when combined with *expenditure* projections, provide the basis for estimates of the financial implications of the move.

Forecasting Investment and Operating Expenditures

Although investments and operating expenditures cannot be forecast with certainty, the range of error in the estimates of them is usually substantially less than that for sales.

Development Cost Estimates: If a new market is to be entered with an existing product "as is," no development costs will be incurred. If an altered or a new product is to be introduced, however, development costs will be involved. Development costs may even be involved if the pending decision is whether or not to drop out of a product market, as one of the necessary conditions for competing successfully may be a product-improvement program.

Development costs are incurred from physical development of the product and use testing and market testing. Research & Development must design, produce prototypes, and physically test the new product. Marketing must conduct use tests, package tests, and, after pilot production runs have been made, a market test of the new product if that is appropriate. Typically, the costs of physically developing the product will be estimated by Engineering or Research & Development, and the marketing research costs by Marketing.

Plant and Equipment Expenditure Estimates: Unless the new product is an adaptive one, new plant or production equipment investments are likely to be required. Such estimates are usually made by the Industrial Engineering or the Production department. Even the decision of whether to remain in a product market may require estimates of plant and expenditure estimates as new, more-efficient manufacturing facilities may be one of the requirements of staying in.

Marketing Cost Estimates: The preliminary strategic marketing plans settled on earlier must be translated into tentative operating marketing plans for each year and the annual costs estimated. Estimates have to be made of all the elements of the marketing plan: Advertising, promotion, personal selling, storage, transportation, service, and marketing research each must be estimated if applicable. These estimates are ordinarily made by Marketing Research.

Costs of Goods Sold Estimates: These estimates will ordinarily be made by Manufacturing.

General and Administrative Expense Estimates: These expenses are for allocated overhead to cover the cost of executive salaries, space, utilities, and other indirect costs. The Accounting Department is the usual source of such estimates.

Projected Cash Flow Statements for Entering or Exiting a Product Market

The financial basis that most financial analysts recommend for a decision such as entering or exiting a product market center on the projected *revenues* and *expenditures* by time period, the resulting *cash flows* by period, and their *net present value*. Managers will usually be interested in the maximum investment at risk, the return on investment, and the payback period for product market decisions as well.

Before proceeding, defining these terms and describing how their values are determined will be useful:

Cash flow (CF) is the difference in the inflows and outflows of cash for a firm, or in this case for a venture, during a specified period.

Discounted cash flow (DCF) is the present value of the cash flow for a given future period using a specified discount rate. It is calculated as

$$DCF = \frac{CF}{(i + r)^t}$$

where

r = the discount rate
t = the number of periods for which the cash flow is to be discounted

Net present value (NPV) is the sum of the discounted cash flows over a specified number of periods.

Maximum investment at risk is the highest amount of negative cash flow the company will encounter in a project or venture.

Return on investment (ROI) is the discount rate (calculated as the internal rate of return [IRR]) that will result in a net present value of zero for a given number of periods. The internal rate of return is calculated using successive trial discount rates until the one that gives an NPV of zero is found.

The **payback period** is the length of time until the cumulative DCFs become positive.

The projected "most likely" cash flow statement for a prospective new product for a six-year planning period is shown in Table 9–3a. The "most likely" statement is the one that contains the best estimates of revenues and expenditures that those involved in the forecasting can make.

Looking at the cash flow estimates in that statement (the last three lines), management could draw the following conclusions, given that the product market was entered and the projections were accurate:

1. The company would have a total out-of-pocket investment of $1,058,000 over a period of two years of development and introduction of the product (from annual cash flow projections). This represents the *maximum investment at risk* for the company.

Table 9–3a   Projected "Most Likely" Cash Flow Statement for Six Years for a Prospective New Product (in thousands of dollars)

	Year 1	Year 2	Year 3	Year 4	Year 5	Year 6
Sales revenue	$ 0	$873	$1,745	$2,871	$3,245	$3,438
Cost of goods sold	0	440	710	1,017	1,023	1,015
Gross margin	0	433	1,035	1,854	2,222	2,423
Development costs	325	35	0	0	0	0
Production equipment	115	0	70	0	0	0
Marketing costs	0	880	735	985	1,065	1,073
General and administrative expenses	45	91	209	345	389	413
Annual cash flow	(485)	(573)	21	524	768	937
Cumulative cash flow	(485)	(1,058)	(1,037)	(513)	255	1,192

Net present value = $85 (20.0 percent discount rate)

Return on investment (IRR) = 23.47 percent

Outlays for working capital and taxes, and the adding back of depreciation charged in cost of goods sold, the salvage value of fixed assets, and working capital at the end of the planning period have not been included in the statement to reduce its complexity.

2. Although it would begin to recoup its investment in the third year, it would not have all of its investment back until about the last quarter of the fifth year (from cumulative cash flow projections).

   The *payback period* would then be approximately 4¾ years.
3. If the discount rate the company uses for projects with this degree of riskiness (the *hurdle* rate) is 20 percent, this venture would provide a positive net present value at the end of the six-year period.
4. Through year six the *return on investment* for the company is 23.5 percent.

"What-If" Projected Cash Flow Statements

Given the uncertainties in the forecasts, it is desirable to prepare a series of cash flow statements based on forecasts of revenues and outlays that differ from those used in the "most likely" statement. These are commonly called "what-if" statements and take their name from the terminology used in the computer spreadsheet programs that are normally used to prepare the statements.

A useful assortment of "what-if" cash flow statements consists of the following:

1. A *most likely* statement.   A statement that contains the best estimates of revenues and expenditures that those involved in the forecasting can make.
2. An *optimistic* statement.   A statement that reflects the "what-if" assumption that revenues will be 25 percent higher and outlays will be 25 percent lower each year than those in the "most likely" statement.
3. A *pessimistic* statement.   A statement that reflects a "what-if" assumption that revenues will be 25 percent lower and outlay estimates will be 25 percent higher each year than those in the "most likely" statement.
4. *Mixed* statements.   Statements that include the estimates of revenues and outlays that result from specific "what-if" assumptions. (The revenue estimates in the "most likely" statement are high by 25 percent

**Table 9–3b Projected "Optimistic" Cash Flow Statement for Six Years
for a Prospective New Product (in thousands of dollars)**

	Year 1	Year 2	Year 3	Year 4	Year 5	Year 6
Sales revenue	$ 0	$1,091	$2,181	$3,589	$4,056	$4,298
Cost of goods sold	0	330	532	763	767	761
Gross margin	0	761	1,649	2,826	3,289	3,537
Development costs	244	26	0	0	0	0
Production equipment	86	0	52	0	0	0
Marketing costs	0	660	551	739	799	805
General and administrative expenses	34	68	157	259	292	310
Annual cash flow	(364)	7	889	1,828	2,198	2,422
Cumulative cash flow	(364)	(357)	532	2,360	4,558	6,980

Net present value = $2,790 (20.0 percent discount rate)

Return on investment (IRR) = 145 percent

but the expenditure estimates [other than cost of goods sold] are correct, we increase our planned advertising budget $250,000 per year which will increase sales by 15 percent per year, manufacturing will be able to produce the product on a 75 rather than an 85 percent experience curve, and the like.)

The "what-if" statements provide management with the opportunity to see the financial consequences of the potential errors in the forecasts and of the contingencies that might arise. By this means, management is able to make a better assessment of financial risks and rewards than it could if only a single, "most likely" statement were prepared.

The "optimistic" and "pessimistic" statements for the new product are shown in Tables 9–3b and c. Observe what a dramatic difference a 25 percent adverse error in both revenue and expenditure makes in the projected financial outcome of the venture. The swing is from a maximum investment at risk of less than $400,000 to one of almost $4.6 million, a payback period of approximately two years to well over six years, a positive net present value of about

**Table 9–3c Projected "Pessimistic" Cash Flow Statement for Six Years
for a Prospective New Product (in thousands of dollars)**

	Year 1	Year 2	Year 3	Year 4	Year 5	Year 6
Sales revenue	$ 0	$ 655	$1,309	$2,153	$2,434	$2,578
Cost of goods sold	0	550	888	1,271	1,279	1,269
Gross margin	0	105	421	882	1,155	1,309
Development costs	406	44	0	0	0	0
Production equipment	144	0	88	0	0	0
Marketing costs	0	1,100	919	1,231	1,331	1,341
General and administrative expenses	56	114	261	431	486	516
Annual cash flow	(606)	(1,153)	(847)	(780)	(662)	(548)
Cumulative cash flow	(606)	(1,759)	(2,606)	(3,386)	(4,048)	(4,596)

Net present value = ($2,684) (20.0 percent discount rate)

Return on investment (IRR) is negative.

$2.8 million to a negative value of close to that same amount, and an ROI of 145 percent (!) to one that is negative. Clearly, if management could be assured of the optimistic outcome it would introduce the product, whereas if the pessimistic outcome were certain it would drop the product.

These differences illustrate an important principle in projected cash flow analyses: Since cash flow is the small difference between revenues and expenditures, a *small* error in the estimate of either, or both, of these values can result in a *large* error in the estimate of cash flow.

"What-if" (pro forma) financial statements for a proposed venture are almost universally required by prospective lenders for purposes of deciding whether to make the loan. (The loan officer also needs to have something in the file in case the loan goes bad and the judgment to grant it has to be defended.) But the central reason for doing financial analyses of these kinds is to assist management in making the decision of whether to go ahead with the venture—in this context, whether to enter or exit a particular product market.

SUMMARY OF IMPORTANT POINTS

1. A *product market* can be defined as the potential, available, or served market:

   for an industry, a company, a subunit of a company, or an organization

   for a product class, a product line, or an individual product

   for the world, a country, a region, a state, a county, a metropolitan area, or a sales territory

   for a short period, a period of medium length, or a long-range period in terms of monetary or unit sales, or leases.

   Hence, there are six dimensions for market size: those of (1) type of market of interest, (2) for what commercial or organizational entity, (3) for what product(s), (4) for what area, (5) for what period, and (6) in what units of measurement.

2. The *potential market* for a product is the potential total industry sales (or leases) to all possible market segments for a specified product class for a specified area for a specified time period expressed in a specified unit of measurement under conditions of optimum market development.

3. The *available market* for a product is that portion of the potential market that has both the *interest* and the *resources* to buy the product(s) at the prices offered.

4. The *served market* for a product is that portion of the potential market that is available and from which business is sought.

5. Seven major methods are available for estimating the "size" of a product market. They are (1) adjusted industry sales, (2) market buildup, (3) substitution potential, (4) analogous location, (5) market indexes, (6) surveys, and (7) market tests.

6. A *market index* number is a measure of the proportion of the total market for a product contained in a specified marketing area.

7. The *buying power index* is a three-factor (population, income, and retail sales) market index.

8. In a *controlled store test*, the product is introduced directly into a sample of 30–100 retail stores or industrial supply houses.

9. The methods that can be used to estimate what *market share* will be in a new product market are:

   a. The fundamental market share theorem

   b. An intention-to-purchase survey

   c. Judgmental adjustment of the company's share in an analogous market area

   d. A market test

10. The *fundamental market share theorem* states is that:

    Other things being equal, the market share of a company in a product market will be equal to the share of the "attraction" resulting from its marketing effort to the total "attraction" resulting from the marketing efforts of all firms in the industry operating in that product market.

11. In a *standard market test*, there is an actual introduction of the product into a sample of cities or metropolitan areas.

12. In a *simulated market test*, measurements of consumer attitudes and purchase rates for a proposed new product are made in a purchase situation other than an actual store (usually at home).

13. Financial concepts that are relevant to product-market choice are:

    Cash flow (CF) is the difference in the inflows and outflows of cash for a firm or venture during a specified period.

    Discounted cash flow (DCF) is the present value of the cash flow for a given future period using a specified discount rate.

    Net present value (NPV) is the sum of the discounted cash flows over a specified number of periods.

    Maximum investment at risk is the highest amount of negative cash flow the company will encounter in a project or venture.

    Return on investment (ROI) is the discount rate (calculated as the internal rate of return [IRR]) that will result in a net present value of zero for a given number of periods.

    The *payback period* is the length of time until the cumulative DCFs become positive.

14. Since cash flow is the small difference between revenues and expenditures, a *small* error in the estimate of either, or both, of these values can result in a *large* error in the estimate of cash flow.

REVIEW QUESTIONS

9.1. What dimensions need to be included in the definition of *market size*?

9.2. What is the *potential market* for a product?

9.3. What is the *available market* for a product?

9.4. What is the *served market* for a product?

9.5. What are the major methods available for estimating the size of a product market?

9.6. What is a *market index number*?

9.7. What is the *buying power index*?

9.8. a. What is a *standard market test*?
     b. What is a *simulated market test*?
     c. What is a *controlled store test*?

9.9. What are the methods that can be used to estimate what market share will be in a new product market?

9.10. What is the *fundamental market share theorem*?

9.11. What is:
     a. Cash flow (CF)?
     b. Discounted cash flow (DCF)?
     c. Net present value (NPV)?
     d. Maximum investment at risk?
     e. Return on investment (ROI)?
     f. The payback period?

DISCUSSION QUESTIONS AND PROBLEMS

9.12. In general, which is better: a single- or a multiple-factor index of market size? Why?

9.13. Seven methods of estimating the size of a product market are described in the text. In estimating the size of a prospective product market, one marketing manager requests estimates based on at least three of these methods, and more than three when appropriate. Does this seem to be a reasonable request? Explain.

9.14. Should market share be routinely calculated on the basis of the potential market, the available market, the served market, or all three of these markets? Explain.

9.15. Companies that subscribe to the same consumer panel or store audit services as the company conducting a market test often get the same sales data from the test of a prospective new product as does the testing company. Why might a competitor decide to make the same changes in its marketing program in the *test areas* that it would make in *all areas the new product would be in competition* in if it were introduced?

9.16. Union Carbide, the maker of Glad plastic bags, has an agreement with a Danish company to market in the United States a disposable plastic bag that can be filled with water and frozen to make ice cubes. It was test marketed in Tulsa, Oklahoma; Dallas, Texas; and Tucson, Arizona, where it was advertised as "an easy way to have extra ice on hand."
   a. How did the choice of these test markets likely affect the estimated size of the market for the product?
   b. What does the choice of these test market cities suggest about the error that Union Carbide management most wanted to avoid with respect to introducing or not introducing the product? Why?

9.17. Despite the fact that media costs are much higher in New York City, in 1987–1988 there were more than four times as many standard market tests conducted there as in Milwaukee. Why do you suppose this was the case?

9.18. Suppose you are a marketing manager who is making a decision concerning the test marketing of a new product. Suppose you are considering using a simulated test market, a controlled store test, or a standard market test, or some combination of the three. How would you go about making the decision?

9.19. Using the projected cash flow statement given on page 291, determine
   a. The maximum investment at risk
   b. When the company would break even, not including imputed earnings
   c. When the company would break even, including imputed earnings of 18 percent

Projected Cash Flow Statement ($000)

	Year −1	Year 1	Year 2	Year 3	Year 4
Sales revenue	$ 0	$340	$815	$1,490	$1,735
Cost of goods sold	0	225	405	550	610
Gross margin	0	115	410	940	1,125
Development costs	145	25	0	0	0
Plant and equipment	75	35	0	105	0
Marketing costs	0	375	320	385	420
G & A	30	40	95	180	210
Annual cash flow	(250)	(360)	(5)	270	495

9.20. From the projected cash flow statement below, determine
   a. The payback period
   b. ROI (using IRR). You should have access to either a hand-held calculator that is programmed to make IRR calculations or to a computer for making the IRR calculation.
   c. The cumulative discounted cash flow at the end of year 5 using an 18% discount rate.

Projected Cash Flow Statement ($000)

	Year −1	Year 1	Year 2	Year 3	Year 4	Year 5
Sales revenue	$ 0	$817	$2,432	$3,863	$4,757	$5,512
Cost of goods sold	0	512	1,047	1,406	1,645	1,815
Gross margin	0	305	1,385	2,457	3,112	3,697
Development costs	1,116	0	0	0	47	0
Plant and equipment	347	0	0	296	0	0
Marketing costs	105	576	923	1,152	1,315	1,585
G & A	167	97	288	456	564	660
Annual cash flow	(1,735)	(368)	174	553	1,186	1,452

9.21. Assume that for a particular new product introduction, it is estimated that after capital expenditures are made:

> Variable manufacturing costs will be 50 percent of sales, and fixed costs will be 35 percent of sales.

Suppose variable manufacturing costs turn out to be 55 percent of sales rather than 50 percent, and fixed costs as a percentage of sales are as estimated. What percentage change will this make in cash flow?
(*Note:* Give your answer as the percentage change in the original estimate of cash flow rather than the change in percentage points.)

9.22. Suppose you were considering opening a retail store to sell a product line of your choice (choose the product line that would be of the greatest interest to you) in one of five cities within a 100-mile radius of your home.
   a. How would you determine which city would be the best choice?

b. How would you determine the amount of capital you would need to open the store?

9.23. Using the "Buying Power Index" (an annual issue of the Survey of Buying Power is published by *Sales and Marketing Management* magazine and should be available in your university library), determine:
a. The relative "buying power" of your home city (or the nearest city listed in the Survey of Buying Power if your home city is not).
b. The ratio of the "buying power" for the city used in (a) to that of
(1) New York City
(2) Milwaukee
(3) Springfield, Missouri
(4) The Davenport–Rock Island–Moline metropolitan area

The problems described in 9.24 through 9.26 are intended to be solved using the "What-If" worksheet program. The program and instructions for its use will be made available by your professor.

9.24. Assume that you are the marketing manager for Atmospherics, Inc., a small pneumatic equipment company that is considering adding a new line of high-pressure air compressors. Much of the research and development on the compressors has already been done; $300,000 has been spent for this purpose to date. You have worked with an assistant to develop the following estimates based on information from the industry trade association and other sources:

Item	Year Zero	Most Likely	Most Favorable	Least Favorable	Mixed
Market size/year (units)		10,000	12,500	8,000	10,000
Market growth/year		8%	12%	5%	12%
Market share year 1		10%	14%	7%	10%
Market share growth (decline)		1%	3%	0%	1%
Price		$1,500	first year		
Price growth (decline)/year		$50	$100	0	$50
Cost of goods sold—AVC		$500	$450	$600	$550
Growth (decline)—AVC					
Marketing expenses		$50,000 initial outlay			
		$100 per unit			
Discount rate		25%	25%	25%	25%
General and administrative expenses		25% sales			
Depreciation		15% capital			
Working capital		15% sales			
R&D	$100,000				
Capital expense	$125,000				
Taxes after depreciation		38%			
Market research	$15,000				

You decide to prepare a "mixed" cash flow statement because one of you thinks the market will grow substantially faster than does the other one.

The company management bases its decisions on whether to introduce new products on a one-year projection of "start-up" costs plus the results of five years of operations after introduction.

a. Should the $300,000 the company has spent to date on R&D be one of the factors considered in the decision concerning whether or not to introduce the new compressor line? Explain.

b. Using the "most likely" cash flow statement, what is:
   (1) The maximum investment at risk?
   (2) The payback period?
   (3) The net present value at the end of year 5?

c. Suppose the company has set a "hurdle rate" of 25 percent (that is, the internal rate of return has to be at least 25 percent) for new products. Based on this criterion, should the new air compressor line be introduced?

d. Does the difference in the estimated rate of growth in the market in any way change the decision?

e. Using the "most likely" cash flow statement, what is the return on investment (the internal rate of return) for introducing the new line?

9.25. Magna Sound, an electronics audio equipment manufacturer, has been losing money on its car stereo line for the past three years. The company that is now its principal competitor entered the market four years ago with a superior unit at a lower price. The Magna Sound management has decided that it needs to do one of two things—either to design and market a competitively priced product that is at least as good as that of the chief competitor or else to drop out of the business.

Research and development for a new unit will take about a year and cost an estimated $350,000, and new work stations to build it efficiently will run another $245,000. Other estimates relating to revenues, expenses, and capital items and the discount rate (hurdle rate) the company management has set are as follows:

Item	Year Zero	Most Likely	Most Favorable	Least Favorable	Mixed
Market size/year (units)		200,000	250,000	175,000	200,000
Market growth/year		5%	8%	2%	6%
Market share year 1		20%	25%	14%	20%
Market share growth (decline)		4%	6%	0	6%
Price		$375	first year		
Price growth (decline)/year		$15	$35	0	$35
Cost of goods sold—AVC		$200 per unit			
Growth (decline)—AVC		(3%) per year			
Marketing expenses		$300,000 introductory campaign			
Discount rate		30%	30%	30%	30%
General and administrative expenses		35% sales			
Depreciation		20% capital			
Working capital		12% sales			
R&D	$300,000				
Capital expense	$245,000				
Taxes after depreciation		38%			
Market research	$40,000				

The company management uses estimates of "start-up" costs plus estimated operating results for five years in making decisions of this kind.

The venture being considered must clear a 30 percent "hurdle rate" (that is, the internal rate of return has to be at least 30 percent).

a. Using the "most likely" cash flow statement, what is:
   (1) The maximum investment at risk?
   (2) The payback period?
   (3) The net present value at the end of year 5?

b. The company management has set a "hurdle rate" of 30 percent for all new ventures. Based on this criterion, should the new stereo line be redesigned and marketed?

9.26. The chief designer and the manufacturing superintendent of WindandSea Sailboats, Inc. were considering a leveraged buyout of the company. Despite producing what was generally acknowledged as one of the outstanding lines of 16- to 36-foot sailboats, the company had been only marginally profitable. The two employees were convinced that this was because the company had not marketed the boats properly. They believed that with a sound marketing program the company could become highly profitable.

The owners of the company were willing to sell it for $4 million, with $1 million down and $1 million plus interest at the end of each of the next three years. Interest was set at 14 percent per annum. The annual payments to the former owners would therefore be

End of year 1 $1 million plus $420,000 interest
                = $1,420,000
End of year 2 $1 million plus $280,000 interest
                = $1,280,000
End of year 3 $1 million plus $140,000 interest
                = $1,140,000.

The two employees between them were able to finance only $100,000 of the down payment. They talked with a local venture capitalist, who agreed to put up the remaining $900,000, but only on condition that he be paid back in three annual installments of $300,000 plus dividends equal to $300,000 more each year. He agreed to have his interest in the company bought out at the end of the fourth year for $4 million.

They also recognized that they would need funds for working capital. They talked to a local bank and arranged for a line of credit of up to $2 million at 13 percent interest. It was to be paid off at no less than one-third of the maximum balance each year and all to be repaid by the end of the third year.

Ignoring the principal and interest payments for the working capital, the payments that they would be committed to if they bought out the company would be:

End of year 1 $1 million plus $420,000 interest to former owners
                plus $600,000 to venture capitalist
                = $2,020,000
End of year 2 $1 million plus $280,000 interest to former owners
                plus $600,000 to venture capitalist
                = $1,880,000

End of year 3 $1 million plus $140,000 interest to former owners
                 plus $600,000 to venture capitalist
               = $1,740,000
End of year 4 $4 million (if they purchased the venture capitalist's
                 share of the firm)

To help in determining whether they could make these payments plus the principal and interest payments to the bank, the two prepared a series of cash flow statements. The estimates they used in preparing them were as follows:

Item	Year Zero	Most Likely	Most Favorable	Least Favorable	Mixed
Market size/year (units)		10,000	12,500	8,000	10,000
Market growth/year		3%	5%	(3)%	3%
Market share year 1		6%	8%	5%	6%
Market share growth (decline)		3%	5%	0%	
Average price		$27,000 first year			
Price growth (decline)/year		$1,200	$2,400	0	$24,000
Cost of goods sold—AVC		$13,000			
Growth (decline)—AVC		(2)%			
Marketing expenses		$100,000 initial outlay 400 per unit			
Discount rate		20%	20%	20%	20%
General and administrative expenses		21% sales			
Depreciation		15% capital			
Working capital		10% sales			
R&D	$0				
Capital expenses	$100,000				
Taxes after depreciation	38%				
Market research	$25,000				

a. Do you think the two employees should buy the company? Explain.
b. If they were to buy the company and the operating results were reasonably close to the "most likely" projection:
   (1) Could they buy out the venture capitalist at the end of year 4? Explain.
   (2) If they could, would this be a wise thing to do? Why or why not?
c. As shown in the table above, they left the "mixed" estimates the same as the "most likely" estimates with the exceptions of reducing the market share each year in response to a larger price growth amount. They did this to see if it would be a sound strategy. Given that their estimate of annual loss in share was correct, would it be a sound strategy? Why or why not?

Endnotes

[1] R. J. Piersol, "Accuracy of Estimating Markets for Industrial Products by Size of Consuming Industries," *Journal of Marketing Research*, May 1968, 148.

[2] Ibid., 149–153.

[3] W. Appelbaum, "Methods for Determining Store Trade Areas, Market Penetration, and Potential Sales," *Journal of Marketing Research*, May 1966, 127–141.

[4] Given in the "1987 Survey of Buying Power," *Sales and Marketing Management*, July 27, 1987, Sections B, C.

[5] C. Waldo and D. Fuller, "Just How Good Is the Survey of Buying Power?" *Journal of Marketing*, October 1977, 64–66.

[6] D. E. Bell, R. L. Keeney, and J. D. C. Little, "A Market Share Theorem," *Journal of Marketing Research*, May 1975, 136–141.

[7] G. L. Lilien and P. Kotler, *Marketing Decision Making: A Model Building Approach*, Harper & Row, 1983, 94–96.

[8] *Advertising Age*, March 6, 1978, 64.

[9] V. B. Churchill, Jr., "New Product Test Marketing—An Overview of the Current Scene," an address to the Midwest Conference on Successful New Marketing Research Techniques, March 3, 1971.

[10] R. Kreisman, "Wendy's Ready to Roll with Breakfast," *Advertising Age*, March 3, 1981, 3.

[11] B. G. Yorovich, "Competition Jumps the Gun," *Advertising Age*, February 9, 1981, 8–20.

[12] *Marketing News*, November 27, 1981, Sections 2, 13.

[13] Ibid., Sections 2, 5.

[14] G. L. Urban and G. M. Katz, "How Accurate Are Simulated Market Tests and How Should Managers Use Them?" *Analytic Approaches to Product and Marketing Planning: The Second Conference*, Proceedings of Conference co-sponsored by the Management Science Institute and Vanderbilt University, November 1981, 350.

[15] "What's in Store," *Sales and Marketing Management*, March 15, 1982, 60.

CHAPTER 10

MARKETING PLANNING AND FORECASTING

Marketing planning is necessarily practiced in all economies, but the location and the nature of the planning organizations vary widely by country.

It is ironic that both the earliest and the greatest amount of systematic marketing planning have been done in a country in which marketing does not officially exist. The country of reference is, of course, the Soviet Union. Central planning for the economy was begun there in 1917. Planning in the USSR, carried out by both the federal government and the individual republics, involves decisions on the kinds of products to be produced, the prices to be charged, the amount of advertising to be done, and the manner in which distribution is to be effected. But, in the past at least, virtually no marketing planning is done at the level of the individual firm. (Whether this will change significantly under Gorbachev and his move toward restructuring the Soviet economy remains to be seen.)

By contrast, almost all marketing planning in the United States is done by individual companies rather than by the federal or state governments. Levi-Strauss is an example of a company that engages in extensive strategic and operational planning. The management believes that its successful transition from a symbol of the counterculture to the world's largest apparel company is in large measure due to the company's having "one of the most sophisticated planning processes in the United States."[1]

Forecasting is an integral part of marketing planning. One cannot plan for the future successfully if he or she cannot forecast the probable conditions to be faced and the outcomes of alternative actions being considered. In this chapter we describe the marketing planning process and discuss the steps involved in carrying it out.

MARKETING PLANNING

What Is Marketing Planning?

As Ackoff has stated, "planning is the design of a desired future and of effective ways of bringing it about."[2] In a marketing context, a useful definition is

Marketing planning involves the setting of marketing objectives, choice of products, selection of markets, and designing of marketing programs for each product market for a specified future period.

This definition intentionally has been left broad enough to cover both strategic and operational marketing planning.

Strategic marketing planning is concerned with the planning of the fundamental means for achieving the company's objectives through the markets entered and the marketing programs used to serve them.

An example of strategic marketing planning is given in the box below.

> Home sewing reached a peak in the late 1960s and demand for over-the-counter fabrics has declined since then. Having observed this trend, the Strategic Planning Department of Montgomery Ward did a study to determine why this was the case. The answers were not hard to find: More married women in the workforce, changing lifestyles for women across the country, and more out-of-home interest and activities (active sports involvement, going back to school, and other) all had contributed to less time for sewing. Since the forecast was for these trends to continue, the outlook was for a flat or declining demand for over-the-counter fabrics.
>
> As a result, the management of Ward's reduced the space for piece goods in many of its stores and made the decision to phase out of the business in the early 1980s.

Operational marketing planning is concerned with the implementation of the strategic plan. It involves the planning of marketing programs that are designed to effect the strategies decided on.

An example of operational marketing planning is that carried out by a major food products manufacturer:

One of the forecasts prepared for use in marketing planning for the coming year was that there would be a sharp increase in corn and wheat prices. A computer model was used to determine the effect these price increases would have on the margins for each product in which one or both of these products was used.

For breakfast cereals, three main alternatives for maintaining profit margins were identified: reduce advertising, reformulate to substitute less-expensive grains for a part of the corn or wheat in the current formulation, or raise prices. As a result of trying the first two alternatives in the model, it became evident that they, either singly or in combination, would not provide the desired margin. After using the model to determine what price increase was needed, an evaluation was made of the effects an increase of that magnitude would have on customer purchases and on competitors.

The decision was to begin R&D in the reformulation and to change it subject to no noticeable taste difference. A slight price increase and a reduction of advertising were planned at the time grain prices increased.

The stages involved in strategic and operational marketing planning, and the relationship of the two, are shown in Figure 10–1. Each stage is disscussed in detail in later sections of this chapter.

FIGURE 10-1
The marketing planning process.

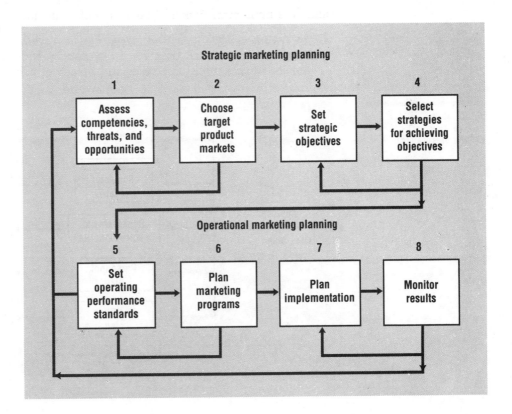

Why Do Marketing Planning?

No purposeful ongoing activity can be carried out without planning. The question is not whether the manager should plan, but rather how it should be done and how much to do.

Marketing planning is central to both the marketing function itself and the company as a whole. An orderly and effective marketing program cannot be carried on without it. Moreover, the operations of other functional areas of the firm cannot be planned until the marketing plan has been prepared. As shown in Figure 10–2, the planning of production, finance, research and development, personnel, and facilities is directly dependent on the marketing plan. The planned quantities and revenues of sales by product are direct determinants of production, financial, personnel, and facilities requirements for the time period of the plan.

Sound planning in any area of a business is difficult because one is dealing with an uncertain future. Planning in marketing is the most difficult area of all because many of the factors critical to the success of the plan are outside the control of the firm. Consumer needs and wants change, often rapidly and in ways that are difficult to predict. Competitors introduce new products, raise or lower prices, and change promotional programs and methods of distribution without advance warning. Government agencies change existing controls and impose new ones. Given all these uncertainties, it might be concluded that marketing planning is not worth the effort.

The experience of companies in which planning is done, however, indicates that if sound procedures are used, formal planning of the marketing operation results in a number of benefits. These benefits include:

1. *Encourages systematic thinking ahead by management.* In formal planning, careful thought must be given to objectives and how they can be realized. Further, both objectives and means of achieving them must be

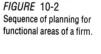

FIGURE 10-2
Sequence of planning for functional areas of a firm.

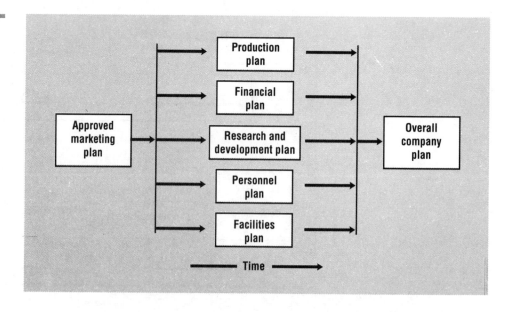

made explicit and communicated to others, a process that discourages uninformed analysis and careless reasoning.

2. *Helps identify possible developments facing the company.* Rapid change has been the hallmark of most of the world's economies in the post–World War II period. A systematic look at these changes can help identify the opportunities and the problems they may bring for the firm.

3. *Results in better preparations to meet changes when they occur.* Through the process of planning, management will have thought through what actions or counteractions it will take when opportunities arise and problems occur.

4. *Results in better communication between departments.* The dissemination of the marketing plan alerts the other departments to the forecasts and developments anticipated by Marketing.

5. *Results in better coordination of actions among departments.* The coordination of production schedules with inventory and customer shipment requirements, the provision of working capital to finance inventories, the orderly development and commercializations of new products, and the matching of facilities and levels of personnel with requirements are examples of areas requiring interdepartmental coordination that are fostered by planning.

The Evolution of Marketing Planning

The Development of Operational Marketing Planning

Formal operational planning began with budgeting. A **budget** is a plan concerning expenditures. Prudently managed firms have had budgets as long as they have existed. When budgets were set for the sales force, for advertising, and for distribution, planning necessarily was involved. Since budgets are concerned only with costs, however, it is only this aspect of these activities that was being planned.

Operational planning beyond budgeting began to be commonly used in the 1950s. It is significant that operational planning in general, and operational *marketing* planning in particular, burgeoned at a time when war-induced shortages had been overcome and surplus production capacity had begun to appear. The ratio of manufacturing output to capacity reached a postwar peak in 1951–1953 and declined thereafter. Managements of firms began to look for ways to deal with the uncertainties brought about by surplus capacities. Planning was the commonly adopted answer.

Operational marketing plans are usually for a period of one year and coincide with the company's financial year. Some exceptions to this rule exist: A few firms, such as some of those in the fashion apparel industry, divide the year into two or more selling seasons and have separate marketing plans prepared for each, whereas other companies prepare plans for periods longer than one year. This latter practice is most prevalent in industries in which marketing of products or services is a more lengthy process: The heavy equipment and construction industries are examples.

| The Development | The development of strategic planning in marketing has been strongly affected |

The Development of Strategic Marketing Planning

The development of strategic planning in marketing has been strongly affected by organizational changes that have occurred in companies. The emergence of the product market portfolio concept in the early 1970s has resulted in a growing acceptance that divisions, product lines, or even market segments may have different roles in achieving overall corporate objectives. The recognition that the rates of growth of different units may be different and that the profitability levels may vary has led to differing objectives being set and levels of performance being planned.

The realization that those units of the company dealing with different product markets needed to be managed differently has led to changes in organization. **Strategic business units** (SBUs) have emerged that are defined with reference to the product markets which they serve. A business unit may be a division, a department, a product line, or a market segment. Usually it is set up as a separate profit center, with the manager in charge of it responsible for its profit performance. Product departments in companies such as General Foods and Procter & Gamble are two examples. The General Electric Company is also organized into a number of clearly defined business units.

Both the organization and the planning of the marketing efforts of the firms so organized have undergone a concomitant change. Instead of a single marketing department in a company, many larger firms have decentralized the responsibility for marketing to the division or business unit level. This has resulted in operational marketing planning also being decentralized, with the planning being done at and for each specific unit.

It has also resulted in strategic marketing planning becoming a part of the business unit strategic plan. An essential part of the managing of a business unit is defining the business it is in—the product market(s) it is to serve. A second requisite is decisions concerning the role each product market is to play with respect to growth, profits, and market share.

Both of these requirements are strategic marketing considerations. However, the way in which they are resolved has such important effects on the business unit as a whole that their planning logically should include the top management of the unit, as well as the chief marketing executive.

Strategic marketing planning has therefore evolved as an integral part of strategic business planning.

The Marketing Planning Process

The central element in planning, as in every other managerial activity, is **decision making**. Marketing planning, be it strategic or operational in nature, consists of a series of decisions made today that deal with future events that are considered likely or attainable. As Peter Drucker observed 30 years ago, planning does not involve decisions to be made in the future; rather, it deals with the futurity of present decisions.[3]

As we have already seen, the planning decisions made can be classified by whether they are strategic or operational in nature. Logically, the strategic marketing decisions need to be made first, since they are to be implemented through the planned marketing operations. A cycle of marketing planning results such that:

- Strategic marketing plans are made.
- Operating plans designed to carry out the strategies are devised.
- The operational plans are put into effect.
- The outcomes are monitored.
- The results are fed back into both the strategic and the operating marketing planning processes for making any necessary modifications.

A new cycle is then ready to begin. The cyclical nature of marketing planning and the stages involved in each cycle were shown earlier in Figure 10–1.

The success or failure of any planning function hinges in large part on the ability of the planner(s) to ask critical questions about the operation being planned. It is only by asking the right questions that one identifies potential problems and ways to solve them, and recognizes opportunities and ways to take advantage of them.

Although it is not possible to list all the relevant questions for all marketing planning situations, at the end of this chapter we list illustrative critical questions for planning and state how they might be answered in the marketing plan for a particular company.

Strategic Planning Process

Strategy formulation essentially involves the matching of competencies with threats and opportunities. As shown in the portion of Figure 10–1 reproduced below, four steps are involved in strategic marketing planning. They are to (1) assess competencies, threats, and opportunities; (2) choose target product markets; (3) set strategic objectives; and (4) select the strategies for achieving the objectives. These steps are discussed in turn below.

1. Assessing Competencies, Threats, and Opportunities

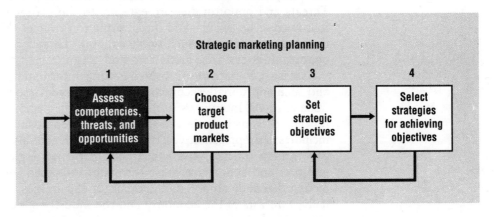

The assessment of competencies, threats, and opportunities for the company and the choices of product markets have to be jointly made. One cannot choose a product market intelligently without considering the company's competencies, but one cannot assess the company's competencies fully without reference to the product markets they are called on to serve. This same interdependency applies to the threats and opportunities faced by the company. Stages 1 and 2 in the above figure could therefore be interchanged without doing violence to the planning process.

If done well, assessing the competencies, threats, and opportunities of a company is a sizable task, and especially so if the company is large and diversified. For example, consider the extent of such an assessment for the businesses operated by the R. J. Reynolds Industries Corporation (now RJR/Nabisco):

> R. J. Reynolds Industries, Inc. is a highly profitable, diversified company whose core businesses are tobacco, foods, and beverages. It has also established an entrepreneurial subsidiary to acquire and manage emerging businesses (including packaging, mail-order retailing, and the management of dental services) that it believes might have the potential to become a core business.

The assessment would have to be done for each of the three core and the three emerging businesses, covering such diverse areas as the marketing of tobacco products and of dental services.

There are five primary areas in which the competencies of a company need to be assessed. They are:

1. The quality of its management
2. Its marketing
3. Its manufacturing
4. Its engineering capabilities
5. Its financial strength

Although assessing competencies may not be an easy task, its focus is the company itself, and so the sources of information are largely internal to it. Threats and opportunities are external to the company, and so the questions that need to be asked—and the information sources that need to be consulted to answer them—are much wider ranging. Threats can take many forms, and opportunities can arise from a myriad of sources.

Assessing a company involves getting information from company records and such appropriate secondary sources as trade associations, census data, and trade journals. Interviews with knowledgeable persons are also generally helpful. The persons interviewed should include company executives and may also include sales representatives, trade association officials, editors of trade journals, government officials, and consumers. Armchair logic should be exercised to interpret and synthesize the information obtained with respect to trends affecting demand, supply, and competitor capabilities, intentions, and plans. Finally, forecasts of the economy and the industry should be made for the planning period.

A schedule of critical questions for each category and references for how to obtain answers to them are given in Table 10–1 at the end of this chapter.

An illustration of the critical nature of these questions for strategic marke planning is afforded by the attempt of planners at the du Pont Company answer one of them (question 7 in Table 10–1) for one of the company's product lines:

> Among its many product lines, du Pont produces and sells synthetic fabrics (nylon, Orlon, and others). Recently its planners attempted to forecast if, and when, Occupational Safety and Health Administration (OSHA) officials would issue a ruling that the use of looms with a noise level in excess of a stated level of decibels would have to be discontinued. The noise level was believed to be injurious to the aural health of employees working near them. (Earplugs are not permitted because of the increased risk of accidents to workers wearing them.) As a major producer of synthetic fabrics, du Pont would be required to replace large numbers of looms that could not meet the noise standard. This would result in temporary reductions in supply, higher production costs, and consequent higher prices.

2. Choosing Product Markets

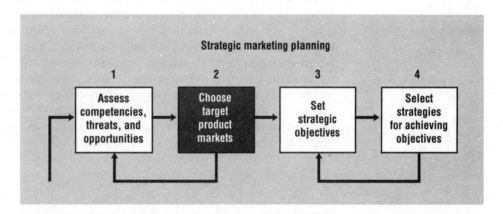

Perhaps the single most important set of decisions made during the strategic planning process is the choice of the target product markets of the company. These decisions require both a review of existing markets and an examination of prospective markets that might be entered.

Review of Existing Product Markets

Before the decision was made by Montgomery Ward to phase out the selling of over-the-counter fabrics, a series of questions were raised by management concerning trends that were affecting sales. These questions included the following:

1. Who is our customer?
2. Where does he or she live now? In the future?

3. What is his or her lifestyle?
4. Is it changing? How?
5. Which age groups are growing? Which are static? Which are declining?
6. How many women are in the workforce? How many will there be in 5 years? 10 years?
7. What effect(s) will all of these factors have on over-the-counter fabric sales in 5 years?
8. How much floor space is currently being used for fabrics? What is its probable opportunity cost?
9. What effects would dropping the over-the-counter fabrics line have on women shopping at Ward's?

Note that these questions focus on the two areas of the prospects and the requirements for the product market and the portfolio effects of dropping the product line. In considering the phasing out of any product or product line, information needs to be obtained and judgments made with respect to these same two areas. Critical questions relating to them are given in Table 10–2 at the end of the chapter.

Review of Potential Product Markets

The Nike Corporation is an example of a company that recently considered adding a new product. The decision concerned a line of walking shoes to add to the jogging, court sport, aerobic, and field sport shoes it already was marketing. After a careful investigation, the company decided to add the new line.

When set within the context of conditional entry, many of the same questions that need to be asked about phasing out a product market need to be raised for each potential product market to be added. The Nike management, for example, had to consider the level of present and prospective demand, trends with respect to the supply of materials necessary for producing the product, the competitive situation, the financial prospects, and the portfolio effects of product markets. These are all considerations that, singly or in combination, cause diversifying moves to either fail or succeed.

Level of Present and Prospective Demand

A crucial factor in adding a product market is, of course, the present and prospective demand. The critical questions concerning product market demand are given in Table 10–2.

Analysis of Trends Affecting Supply

Another area of importance is an analysis of trends affecting supply. It is evident that such trends can be critical in the long-term success or failure of a company. An oil company could not develop useful marketing plans without careful attention being given to the prospects for long-term supplies of oil, for example. The future supplies of oil were even a relevant question to the Montgomery Ward planners involved in the planning concerning the over-the-counter fabric business. Since many synthetic fabrics are made from petroleum derivatives, a forecast of continuing oil shortages and increasing prices indicates probably relative increases in the price of synthetic fabrics and the possibility of shortages.

Some critical questions that should be raised about long-range supply prospects are given in Table 10–2.

Competitor Analyses

An analysis of competitor capabilities, intentions, and plans is another essential part of the information needed to make an informed decision on entry into a product market. The examples in the box below illustrate strategic entry into product markets to counter the moves of competitors.

> The primary aim of Caterpillar's joint venture into Mitsubishi in Japan in the mid 1960s was to pressure its major competitor, Komatsu, in the latter's home market where Komatsu derived 80 percent of its worldwide cash flow. Although Caterpillar's joint venture was a distant second in the market for construction equipment in Japan and was not highly profitable, it served as a strategic brake on Komatsu's international expansion, since Komatsu was faced constantly with a need to defend itself in its key home market.
>
> Clorox's introduction of Wave into the U. S. bleach market was to deflect Procter & Gamble's attack on Clorox's market leader, Clorox, by creating a second front in the market rather than to generate substantial profits from Wave.*

*B. G. James, "SMR Forum: Strategic Planning under Fire," *Sloan Management Review*, Summer 1984, 59.

Getting the information to assess accurately the intentions and plans of competitors is a difficult task if conducted ethically. As a consequence, resorting to industrial espionage for this purpose is an all-too-frequent occurrence. This temptation is, of course, to be avoided because it is not only unethical but illegal as well.

Some critical questions that need to be raised about competitors are given in Table 10–2.

Financial Prospects

In a for-profit enterprise, the forecast financial returns for a venture are crucial to the decision to undertake it. Revenues must be forecast and both capital and operating expenditures estimated to provide the cash flow estimates required for an informed decision.

The methods of making such forecasts are described in some detail in the chapter on financial evalution of product markets (Chapter 9).

Portfolio Effects

Essentially the same portfolio-effect questions arise when considering adding a new product market as they do when weighing the dropping of an old one. The central question concerning the portfolio effect of adding a new product or entering a new market is whether there are synergies to be realized by doing so. Some specific questions that should be raised about portfolio effects are given in Table 10–2.

3. Setting Strategic Objectives

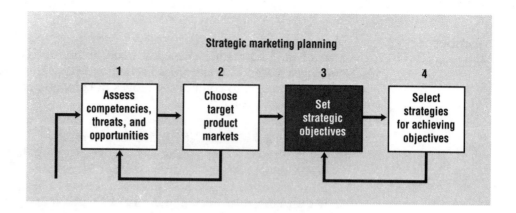

Strategic marketing planning

1. **Assess competencies, threats, and opportunities** → 2. **Choose target product markets** → 3. **Set strategic objectives** → 4. **Select strategies for achieving objectives**

The chairman and chief executive officer describes the strategic objectives set at R. J. Reynolds Industries:

> RJR's mission is the achievement of acceptable, orderly growth of shareholder value over time. And to accomplish this mission of increasing shareholder value, RJR must maintain predictable and sustainable quality earnings growth. Clear numerical goals [are] set in terms of earnings growth, dividend payout, and return on equity. Expectations from each subsidiary company [are] quantified so that their progress [can] be charted.[4]

The strategic objectives for each product market have to be set individually. In the case of the R. J. Reynolds Company, for example, it would not be reasonable to expect the same performance levels with respect to, say, growth and return on investment for the food and for the beverage business, or even for industries within one of the businesses.

Some critical questions that need to be raised in setting strategic objectives for each product market are given in Table 10–3 at the end of the chapter.

If you look again at the figure depicting the stages in strategic marketing planning, you will note that there is a loop between the "set strategic objectives" and the "select strategies for achieving objectives" boxes. This means that strategies to be employed need to be considered concurrently with the setting of strategic objectives. One cannot conclude that market share should be expected to be increased by X percent over the planning period, for example, without considering the strategies that will be used to bring it about.

The steps that should be taken in setting strategic objectives are:

1. *Make a reference sales forecast.* A **reference sales forecast** is one that is made with the assumption that no change will be made in the present marketing program. If the reference forecast gives results that, when translated into market share, ROI, cash flow, or other corporate goals, will be satisfactory as corporate objectives, no further steps need be taken. If the results are not satisfactory:

2. *Move to stage 4, select a different strategy that promises to improve performance, and make a conditional sales forecast.* A **conditional sales forecast** is made

with the assumption that one or more specified changes will be made in the marketing program as a result of the strategy change. Translate the results into market share, ROI, cash flow, and or other corporate goals. If these forecast results are satisfactory as corporate objectives, stop here. If not:

3. *Repeat step 1 until satisfactory results are obtained.* Reference and conditional forecasts are discussed later in the chapter.

Strategic objectives should be stated clearly and in measurable terms. Not to do so is to invite confusion and controversy. Examples of unclear and nonmeasurable strategic objectives are not difficult to find, however. One company's management has stated that its objective is to "increase sales by 50 percent over the next 5 years." (It is not clear whether the desired increase refers to unit or dollar sales. In a period of inflation, the difference could be dramatic.)

It was appropriate for R. J. Reynolds' management not to state its objectives solely as "[to] maintain predictable and sustainable quality earnings growth." (One can determine whether a particular year's earnings "sustained" previous earnings, but how does one measure whether earnings qualify as having "quality growth" or not?)

The strategic objectives should be grounded in reality. It is all right to set operating objectives high enough to be challenging, but they should not be so high that they will be nearly impossible to achieve. One observer believes that the cause of many of the problems that Texas Instruments experienced in the early 1980s was "planning sessions that generated false hopes, not realistic goals."[5]

4. Selecting Strategies for Achieving Objectives

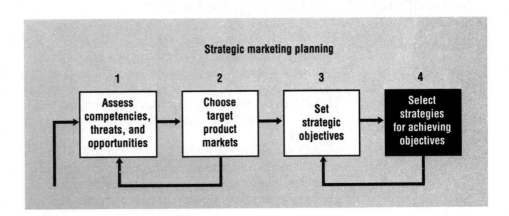

Commonly used marketing strategies were discussed in Chapter 2. Other viable strategies are possible, however—both those that are new and original and those that are variations of the ones discussed there.

Although generation of successful strategies finally must rest with the knowledge, the experience, the imagination, the effort put forth, and the innate abilities of the person(s) involved, there are critical questions that need to be raised. These questions include those shown in the first section of Table 10–4 at the end of the chapter.

Devising new alternative strategies is a creative act; choosing from among an existing set is a judgmental one. The decision as to which strategic alternatives to adopt is made in the same way as other decisions are made—that is, by one or more of the methods described in the chapter on decision making (Chapter 7).

These decisions are among the most difficult decisions made in a business. The planning horizon for marketing strategies is almost always longer than for the programs to implement them, the uncertainties are usually substantial, they are frequently difficult to reverse, and the economic stakes are often high. For these reasons, a series of "tough" questions need to be raised concerning each potential strategy. These questions are given in the second section of Table 10–4.

The comments of the chairman and CEO of R. J. Reynolds concerning the importance of flexibility in plans underscores the importance of one of the questions (question 11 in Table 10.4):[5]

> It is always a mistake to follow any plan slavishly, with no room for adjustment. In fact, this is the most common cause of all for planning failures, and not just in business. The Soviets have provided us with the classic example: their endless five year plans. Because of the forbidding bureaucracy that was in charge, these plans could never be changed, so they never worked. In planning, flexibility is absolutely vital. Any plan that can't be changed will surely turn out to be a bad plan.

The Operating Marketing Planning Process

Through strategic planning, the "grand design" is set; in operational marketing planning, the ways it is to be achieved are devised.

In the discussion that follows, we shall assume that the operational marketing planning period is one year. This is not a necessary period for operational plans to cover, of course, but it is a convenient one. As noted earlier, it is also the typical length of time for which companies do operational marketing planning.

As illustrated in the figure that follows, four steps (the fifth through the eighth steps in preparing the marketing plan) are involved in operational marketing planning. They are to (5) set performance standards, (6) plan marketing programs, (7) plan the implementation of them, and (8) monitor results.

5. Setting Operating Performance Standards

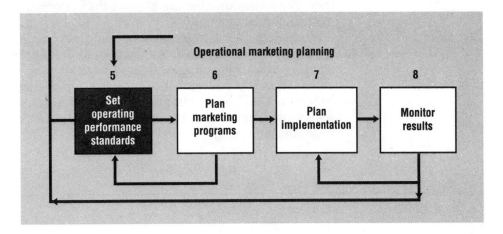

A marketing performance standard is an objective for the operational marketing program. The most commonly used marketing performance standards relate to sales volume and market share on the sales side and to marketing budgets on the cost side. Depending on how the company is organized and the degree of control desired, these may be broken down by territory, market, or product, and by individual sales representative.

The point of departure for setting marketing performance standards is the strategic objectives. The performance standards should be the operational translation of the strategic objectives. This does not mean that the sets of objectives and standards necessarily should be congruent, however. The performance standards set for marketing may differ in two respects from the strategic objectives. First, some performance standards may be set that are operational extensions of but have no direct counterparts in strategic objectives (gross margin budgets, level of awareness for brands, quotas for sales representatives, level of points of distribution). Second, where direct counterparts do exist, the marketing performance standard may be higher, but never lower, than its strategic equivalent. For example, a higher market share might be called for in the marketing performance standard than in the strategic objective for a particular product market, but a lower market share should not be indicated. If

strategic objective > marketing performance standard

either the objective ought to be lowered or the performance standard ought to be raised.

The critical questions that apply to the setting of marketing performance standards are given in Table 10–5 at the end of the chapter.

It will be recalled from the discussions of setting strategic objectives that it is necessary to set objectives and select strategies concurrently; one cannot reasonably set objectives for a strategic marketing program without knowing what strategies the program is going to employ, and one cannot rationally select strategies without knowing what the objectives are. The same logical interdependence applies in operational marketing planning in setting performance standards. One needs to set the performance standards and plan the marketing program jointly.

Practice does not always follow logic. Sales volume standards are sometimes set and profit performance standards may be imposed before the marketing planning process even begins. In such cases it is up to the marketing planner to determine if the performance standards can be met and, if so, the minimum budget that will be required to meet them. If not, he or she is obligated to advise management that the performance standards cannot be met and to try to get them changed.

6. Planning the Marketing Program

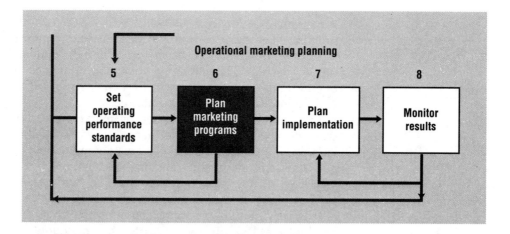

There are essentially two orientations to operational marketing planning—profit planning and sales volume planning. Profit-oriented planning results from attaching more importance to profits than to increased sales (or market share), and sales-volume-oriented planning is a consequence of the reverse ordering of these objectives.

These two approaches result in different marketing plans. Generally speaking, profit-oriented operational plans will have higher prices or lower levels of expenditure for advertising, sales promotion, personal selling, and distribution than will sales-volume-oriented plans. The emphasis in profit-oriented planning is to realize profits now; that of sales volume planning is to build market share now in the expectation that higher profits will be realized in future periods. Despite this difference in objectives and results, the two types of plans are closely interrelated.

Conditional sales forecasts are necessary in order to plan the level of price and expenditures on the promotional and distributional variables that will be necessary to meet the marketing performance standards for existing products. They are discussed in the forecasting section of this chapter.

7. Planning the Implementation of the Marketing Program

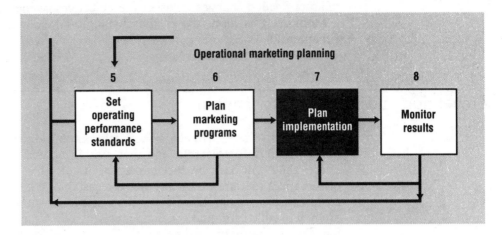

It is not enough to plan what price changes will be made—decisions also have to be made as to how and when they will be announced and when they are to become effective. The same kinds of decisions are necessary for each of the other variables.

Considerations involving the implementation of changes with respect to each of the marketing variables are discussed in the chapters dealing with the individual variables.

8. Monitoring the Results

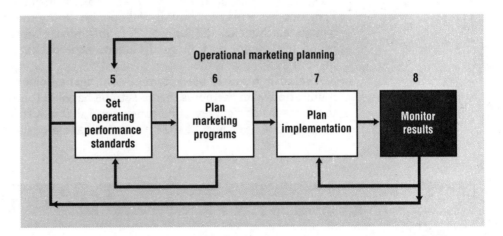

The results of a well-planned monitoring and control system are invaluable to the ongoing planning function. The measurements of sales, market share, and profit by product, territory, or market segment and comparison with the planned levels indicate how well (or how poorly) the plans are being met.

Variances from the plan are signals of problems that exist or of previously unrecognized opportunities that ought to be exploited. In either case, they indicate needed changes in either the objectives or the marketing program.

Monitoring is discussed in the chapter on marketing audits and controls (Chapter 20).

Prevention and Contingency Planning

To this point there has been an implicit assumption that the events affecting the market are forecastable, and that, within acceptable bounds of error, the effects they will have on the market are predictable. But what about market disturbances that are essentially not forecastable, but that, if they did happen, could cause severe problems? We refer to events such as possible natural disasters (a sizable earthquake in San Francisco, a devastating hurricane in Florida), a major disruption in production (the Union Carbide tragedy in Bhopal, India, the Three Mile Island near-nuclear meltdown in Pennsylvania), actions by terrorists or psychopathic personalities (airliner hijackings, the lacing of Tylenol tablets with cyanide), and unanticipated health problems with products (toxic shock syndrome with a Procter & Gamble tampon, contamination of Red Cross blood supplies with AIDS). Can planning be utilized for such potentially severe market disturbances?

The answer to this question is a qualified "yes." For preventable events, ***prevention planning*** can be used to try to ensure that they do not in fact occur. The x-raying of baggage before boarding aircraft and tamper-proof packaging of drug sundries are evidences of such planning.

For events outside the control of the company, ***contingency planning*** can be employed. Plans for dealing with crises can be made that outline in advance how they should be handled. For example, a major financial concern in San Francisco has a plan for how it will operate during the three months following a major earthquake, and Johnson & Johnson has plans for dealing with another round of Tylenol poisonings should its new packaging prove inadequate to prevent such an episode.

A relatively widely used form of contingency planning concerns how communication with the news media is to be handled following a crisis. According to the results of a survey of Fortune's top 1,000 industrial and 500 service firms, about half (47 percent) of the companies have a crisis communication plan.[8]

FORECASTING

Early in 1984, the Houston-based COMPAQ Computer Corporation, manufacturer of IBM-compatible microcomputers, faced a decision that would profoundly affect its future. Recognizing that IBM would soon introduce its version of the portable computer and threaten COMPAQ's dominance in this profitable market, the company had two options: It could elect to specialize in this product line and continue to market its highly regarded portables aggressively, or it could expand market offerings to include desktop microcomputers. The latter move would force the year-old company to confront IBM on its home ground.

COMPAQ Computer's quandary was further complicated because new techniques, competitors, and products were already transforming a market that had only recently been established. COMPAQ's forecast of the size, direction, and price trends of the 1984 microcomputer market was confounded by uncertainties about the market's response to several vital factors:

The entry of IBM's new portable computer

IBM's price cut in June 1984 and its potential erosion of margins

The entry of lap portables introduced by Hewlett-Packard and Data General

The launch of IBM's new PC AT, complicated by unexpected delivery delays and compatibility problems

The introduction of desktop computers by Sperry, NCR, ITT, and AT&T

Despite the difficulty, the vice-president of marketing and the CEO—the two executives most directly involved with the decision—demonstrated what can be done. They used an extended series of consumer and dealer surveys coupled with periodic evaluations of the technology to assess the future market and to guide the development of products and programs to accommodate the industry's fluid and evolving needs.

COMPAQ entered the desktop segment of the market, even though 1984 was unforgiving and rampageous. Several large competitors restricted their programs; many smaller companies went into—or to the edge of—receivership. Financially and competitively, COMPAQ succeeded. During 1984 sales rose from $111 million to $329 million, and earnings increased from $4.7 million to $12.8 million.

Managers *can* use forecasting techniques to help them reach important decisions.*

*D. M. Georgoff and R. G. Murdick, "Manager's Guide to Forecasting," *Harvard Business Review*, January–February 1986, 110–111.

In the earlier section of the chapter, references were made to the need for reference and for conditional sales forecasts. As indicated there,

A *reference sales forecast* is made with the assumption that no change will be made in the present marketing program.

And:

A *conditional sales forecast* is made with the assumption that one or more specified changes will be made in the marketing program.

In this section we discuss the methods that can be used for making these types of forecasts.

METHODS FOR MAKING REFERENCE SALES FORECASTS

There are seven methods in use for making reference sales forecasts: (1) aggregate of individual sales forecasts, (2) executive judgment, (3) Delphi, (4) survey of buyer intentions, (5) exponential smoothing, (6) statistical trend analysis, and the (7) Box-Jenkins methods.

Aggregate of Individual Sales Forecasts

Many, if not most, marketing managers require their sales representatives to forecast sales of each product in their territories for the next quarter, or the next two quarters. When aggregated, these forecasts provide an overall sales forecast for the company by product for the period covered.

The logic of this technique of forecasting is, on its face, persuasive: The sales representative should know his or her customers and their requirements over the next few months better than anyone else, and thus should be able to forecast sales for his or her territory better than anyone else.

There are problems with this technique, however. First, sales representatives are generally not favorably disposed toward "paperwork." They have to fill out a report each time they make a call, and they invariably resent this as an intrusion on time that otherwise could be spent making sales calls. To add the quarterly requirement of forecasting requirements for each product for their territory is usually viewed in this same light. Motivating them properly is therefore a necessity if one is to be sure that they are to be conscientious about their forecasts.

Second, many companies compensate their sales representatives at least partially by percentage of a sales "quota" that is achieved. Since the sales forecasts that they make for the next quarter are almost certainly going to be used in helping establish their quotas for the next quarter, there may be an understandable tendency to err on the low side.[9]

Third, optimistic or pessimistic biases about future sales periodically develop within companies and are often contagious. The company management may believe that "we are going to have a great year next year" and that optimism may spread to, and get reflected in, the sales force forecasts.[10]

It is usually desirable to introduce supplementary procedures to help improve the accuracy of sales representatives' forecasts. These include (1) making a general economic forecast for the forecast period available to the sales force, (2) giving each salesperson a record of his or her past forecasts compared with actual sales, and (3) having each sales representative's forecast reviewed by the immediate supervisor before it is turned in. Some companies also pay a bonus if the forecast's accuracy for the sales territory meets or exceeds a stipulated level.

Sales representative forecasts are usually not very accurate beyond one or two quarters out. They are only useful in short-term planning of the marketing program, therefore, and are generally not used in strategic marketing planning at all.

Average or Consensus of Individual Executives' Forecasts

Methods of Obtaining and Processing Executive Forecasts

Another common method of forecasting is to have a number of executives in the company each make a forecast and then either average them or else try to reach a consensus in the course of one or more meetings.

Averaging is usually preferable to trying to reach a consensus. The problem with trying to reach a consensus is that the more persuasive the person, or the higher the rank, the more weight his or her forecast is likely to have in the process of reaching agreement on what the final forecast should be. Since there is no evidence that forecasting ability is positively correlated with either persuasiveness of personality or executive rank, this procedure may lead to biased forecasts.

There is a method of reaching consensus (or a degree of consensus that can be reached if full agreement is not possible) that does not involve meetings. It is the Delphi method.

The Delphi Method: This technique, developed at the Rand Corporation in the early 1960s,[11] consists of the following series of steps:

1. Each participant is asked to make a separate prediction and to describe the important considerations taken into account in making the prediction.
2. Both the predictions and the statements of considerations are given to an analyst.
3. The analyst combines the predictions and summarizes the statements in such a way that no individual prediction or statement can be associated with the person making it.
4. The analyst then returns them to the participants.
5. The participants make a new round of predictions and supporting statements.

This process continues until it appears that there will be no appreciable added degree of consensus from another round.[12]

Step 3 in this process ensures that both forecasts and information will be exchanged among the participants but that anonymity will be preserved. This prevents any senior manager biases from being injected into the joint forecast.

Reported examples of companies that use (or have used) the Delphi method for sales forecasting include American Hoist and Derrick,[13] Corning Glass, and IBM.

Accuracy of Executive Forecasts	As reported later in the chapter, a series of studies have been done comparing individual executive forecasts (usually of sales) with forecasts using nonjudgmental, quantitative methods. Quantitative techniques consistently outperform the executives. As the authors of one of the studies conclude concerning executive forecasting, ". . . .too much reliance on judgment is not advisable."[14]

Survey of Buying Intentions

One might reasonably expect that accurate forecasts, at least to the product class if not to the brand level, could be obtained for industrial and consumer durables by asking a sample of prospective buyers how many units, if any, they intend to buy during the forecast period.

As reasonable as this approach sounds, available evidence suggests that its forecasting record has been uneven. Buying-intention surveys for consumer durables have been conducted during the past on a regular basis by both private companies and U.S. and Canadian governmental agencies. Although there is no evidence about the forecasting accuracy of those conducted by companies, the accuracy of the forecasts prepared from the surveys by the governmental agencies has been so low as to cause the surveys to be discontinued. The U.S. Bureau of the Census discontinued its Consumer Buying Expectations Survey in the early 1970s because it forecast no better than the naive model of "purchases this period will be the same as purchases last period." The conclusion of one analyst concerning the continuing results of the Canadian Buying Intentions Survey is that "buying intentions, when used alone, have limited predictive ability for sales of [consumer] durable goods over time."[15]

The record of buyer-intentions surveys for new plant and equipment expenditures has been a somewhat better one. The U.S. Bureau of Economic Analysis survey of new plant and equipment expenditures for 1987, for example, had an error of 5.9% for manufacturing companies—low by the standards of other methods of forecasting.

Exponential Smoothing

One of the more accurate short-term sales forecasting methods is **exponential smoothing**. It is a method of averaging past-period sales in which sales for the more recent periods are weighted more heavily than those for an earlier period.

Assume that it is July 1, 1989, and that we want to make a reference sales forecast for the summer quarter for a product whose sales for the preceding eight quarters had been as follows:

	1987	1988	1989
January–March		120	130
April–June		110	120
July–September	90	100	
October–December	100	110	

An inspection of the data indicates an apparent seasonal decline in sales in the spring and summer, with an upturn in the fall and winter. One can adjust sales data for seasonal effects by using a seasonal index.[16] For making sales forecasts for periods of less than a year, such seasonal adjustments are often needed.

The simplest exponential smoothing model is

$$\hat{Y}_{t+1(\text{desea.})} = \alpha\,\overline{Y}_{t(\text{desea.})} + (1 - \alpha)Y_t$$

where

$\hat{Y}_{t+1(\text{desea.})}$ = deseasonalized forecast sales for next period (the summer quarter in this example)

α = the weight for the present-period sales with a value between 0 and +1

$\overline{Y}_t$ = present-period (spring quarter) smoothed sales.

The first time the model is used, the value for $\overline{Y}_t$ can be the average for two (or three) past years' sales. (If full years of data are used for the average, one does not have to worry about deseasonalizing them.) For succeeding forecasting periods, the value for smoothed sales for the (then) present period is the exponentially smoothed model forecast for that period.

Assume that the seasonal index for the spring quarter is $S_t = 1.05$. The seasonally adjusted value for spring quarter sales is then

$$\hat{Y}_{t(\text{desea.})} = Y_t/S_t$$
$$= 120/1.05$$
$$= 114.3 \text{ units}$$

The average of 110 units for the preceding eight quarters becomes the initial smoothed value of sales, or $\overline{Y}_t = 110$. If we use a value for α of 0.40, the forecast becomes:

$$\hat{Y}_{t+1(\text{desea.})} = \alpha\overline{Y}_{t(\text{desea.})} + (1 - \alpha)\overline{Y}_t$$
$$= 0.40(114.3) + (1 - 0.40)110$$
$$= 111.7 \text{ units}$$

If we assume that the seasonal index for the summer quarter is 0.85, the seasonally unadjusted forecast will be:

$$\hat{Y}_{t+1} = 0.85\,(111.7)$$
$$= 94.9 \text{ units}$$

There are more-complicated exponential smoothing models used in forecasting. For example, one version uses double exponential smoothing, which, as the name implies, involves the smoothing of smoothed data.[17]

Statistical Trend Analysis

If you examine the sales data just used for making the exponential smoothing forecast (repeated here for convenience), you can see that the sales for four quarters later are in each instance higher than for the earlier corresponding quarter: July–September sales for 1988 are higher than July–September sales for 1987; October–December sales for 1988 are higher than October–December sales for 1987, and so forth. This indicates that there is an upward trend in sales over the two-year period.

	1987	1988	1989
January–March		120	130
April–June		110	120
July–September	90	100	
October–December	100	110	

If we have reason to believe that this trend is going to continue, we can make use of it in forecasting. We can fit a line, or a curve, to the data and project it out for the next period (or for as many periods as we would like, for that matter). The result is shown in Figure 10–3.

As shown by the figure, the two variables involved in the trend analysis are sales and time. The line that indicates the relationship between the two can be fitted either by hand or by the use of regression analysis. If linear regression analysis is used, the equation of the trend line obtained from the analysis is of the form:

$$\overline{Y}_{t+1} = \alpha + b(t + 1)$$

where

$$\overline{Y}_{t+1} = \text{a forecast of next period's sales}$$
$$\alpha = \text{a constant}$$
$$b = \text{the slope of the trend line}$$
$$t + 1 = \text{the number of periods in the regression plus 1}$$

FIGURE 10-3
Forecast using statistical trend analysis.

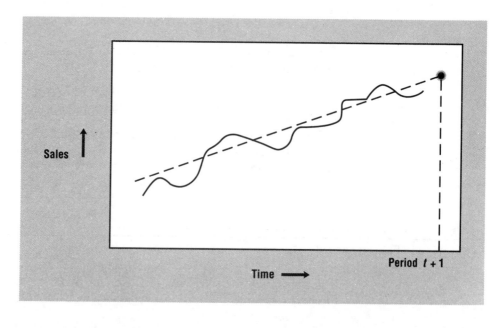

Sales

Time ⟶

Period *t* + 1

If there is much of a seasonal effect in sales, one is well advised to run the trend analysis using seasonally adjusted sales data and then to seasonally adjust the resulting forecast. The result of following this procedure for the eight quarters of sales data given above is the trend line:

$$\overline{Y}_{t+1(\text{deseas.})} = 98.01 + 2.63(t + 1)$$

and a seasonally unadjusted forecast for the summer quarter of 1989 of:

$$\overline{Y}_{t+1} = 110.10$$

Statistical trend analysis can be used on data for any time period. Quarterly data are appropriate for short-term reference forecasts for operational marketing planning. Semiannual or annual data should be used for longer-term reference forecasts for either operational or strategic marketing planning.

Box-Jenkins

In the general case, time series data are assumed to be composed of random, seasonal, trend, and cyclical components. A (hypothetical) time series composed of these four elements is shown in Figure 10–4.

The nature of random movements in time series prevents any forecasting model from predicting them. Seasonal patterns can be identified and forecast reasonably effectively through seasonal indexes, which can be used in conjunction with any forecasting model. Trend (sometimes called *secular* trend to indicate that it is long-term, rather than short-term, in duration) can be handled with increasing degrees of effectiveness using the exponential smoothing and statistical trend analysis models, respectively.

Cyclical movements are the most troublesome, and when they are at all pronounced or rapid, also the most important of the time series components

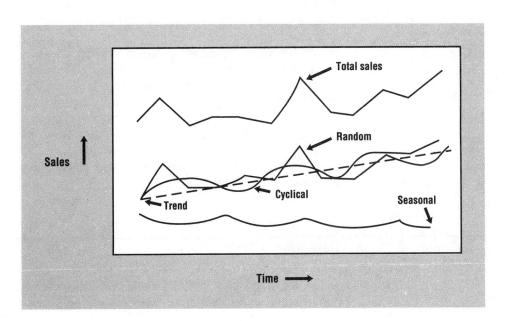

FIGURE 10-4
Random, seasonal, trend, and cyclical components of sales over time.

to forecast accurately. It is especially important for a company to know when a turning point is about to occur—when a sales decline is about to be reversed, or when sales are going to start to decline after a series of increases. Accurate forecasting of turning points allows the appropriate marketing programs to be planned, and the accompanying changes in production schedules and financial arrangements to be made.

Neither exponential smoothing nor statistical trend analysis can identify turning points. They may do an excellent job of forecasting when cycles are not present, but when they are, large errors may occur at turning points.

Box-Jenkins is the best known of a number of quantitative methods that have the capability to identify turning points. It is an interactive computerized method in which the forecaster first identifies a tentative model for describing and forecasting from the set of data at hand and then enters it and the data into the computer. The Box-Jenkins program then estimates values for the parameters of the model and runs a diagnostic analysis to determine how well the model describes the data. If it is an adequate description, the model is used to make the forecast. If not, the program provides diagnostic information to assist the forecaster·in revising the model. This procedure is continued until an acceptable model is obtained and the forecast is made.[18]

A minimum of 45 (and preferably no fewer than 75) observations are required for any time series from which a forecast is to be made using the Box-Jenkins method.

METHODS FOR MAKING CONDITIONAL SALES FORECASTS

You will remember that a conditional sales forecast is made with the assumption that one or more specified changes will be made in the marketing program. The change(s) may be in adding a new product, changing a price, increasing or decreasing the advertising budget, adding a new distribution channel, or in any of the other elements of the marketing program.

The methods that are used most often for making conditional sales forecasts are (1) executive judgment, (2) the Delphi method, (3) Box-Jenkins, (4) surveys, (5) on-line sales experiments, (6) simulated market tests, (7) standard market tests, (8) analysis of case histories, and (9) causal regression analysis. All but the last two of these methods have been discussed in this or another chapter. To avoid repetition, only analysis of case histories and causal regression analysis will be described here.

Analysis of Case Histories

When the publisher of the Tallahassee *Democrat*, the only daily newspaper published in Florida's capital, was considering switching from afternoon to morning publication, he authorized a "study of afternoon newspapers that had converted to morning publication, as well as newspapers that publish all day and newspapers that had changed from morning to afternoon."[19] As a result of the findings of the study, after 73 years of being published in the afternoon, the decision was made to convert the *Democrat* to a morning paper. The change turned out to be a successful one.

Case histories are a step removed from on-line experiments in that they involve studying the sales effects of similar changes in marketing variables in other companies. The analogy to the present change clearly cannot, then, be as close as for an on-line experiment. Still, when used with the appropriate caution, they can be a valuable source of information. (An on-line experiment could not have been run by the management of the *Democrat* for obvious reasons.) Case histories are most widely used for estimating the sales effects of changes in products and in distribution channels.

Causal Regression Models

A causal forecasting model is one in which changes in the level of sales are the result of changes in the level of variables other than time. A study of ski area sales in northern New York State and New England, for example, determined that a highly accurate forecast of sales for each ski area during the coming year could be made using an equation that related sales with the planned advertising budget; the percentage of it spent on radio, televison, and magazine advertising, and the average of the distances the area was from New York, Boston, Hartford, and Albany.[20] This is an example of the use of a causal regression model in forecasting.

The American Can Company forecasts the demand for beer cans by using a causal regression equation of the following form:

$$\overline{Y}_{t+1} = \alpha + b_1 I_{t+1} + b_2 D_t + b_3 A_t$$

where

$\overline{Y}_{t+1}$ = forecast sales for the coming year
α = a constant
I_{t+1} = estimated disposable income for the coming year
D_t = estimated number of drinking establishments in the current year
A_t = age distribution in the current year
b_1, b_2, b_3 = coefficients derived from the regression analysis.[21]

This functional form and the values for α, b_1, b_2, and b_3 were arrived at by the forecaster using the following procedure:

1. Considering what variables represented in what forms are likely to be determinants of beer can sales.
2. Obtaining data on past levels of both these variables and the sales of beer cans.

3. Running a multiple regression analysis of these variables against beer can sales to obtain values for the α and b values in the equation.
4. Conducting an analysis to see if the resulting equation provides forecasts of acceptable accuracy on historical data.
5. If the accuracy level is a satisfactory one, use the equation for forecasting; if it is not, repeat steps 1 through 4 until it is.

This is a particularly useful form of forecasting model for allowing the effects of key marketing variables to be included in the forecast. The relative price, promotion, and distributional variables can be quantified and examined using historical data in the regression analysis. Those that are found to contribute significantly to forecasting accuracy can then be included in the forecasting equation. Values for each in the forecast period can be included as they have been set forth in the marketing plan.

CONSIDERATIONS FOR CHOOSING FORECASTING METHODS

In the usual case, more than one forecasting method should be used. The reasons for this are (1) to improve accuracy and (2) to obtain a better idea of the range of possible error. Three methods are probably best; if two are used and the forecasts differ, it may not be clear which one is the more accurate. However, if three are used and two of the forecasts are similar, there is some assurance that the two are more likely to be closer to the actual value than the third one is.

There is evidence to suggest that an *average* of the forecasts from two or more methods is generally more accurate than using one of the constituent forecasts. In a review of accuracies of various forecasting methods, 21 studies of combined versus individual forecasting accuracies are cited, and the combined forecast emerges as the winner in 18 of them.[22] The theoretical basis for combining sales forecasts is that the different methods employ different characteristics of the sales data being used for the forecast and so, in a sense, provide different information on the probable market.

The use of multiple methods of forecasting is the rule in actual practice. A study of 175 midwestern U.S. firms indicates that they use, on the average, 2.6 sales forecasting methods "regularly" and another 1.8 methods "occasionally."[23]

But how should one go about choosing the methods to use? There are four critical considerations involved in choosing a forecasting method: (1) the applications for which the method is best suited compared with the application for which it would be used, (2) its accuracy, (3) the data availability and time required, and (4) cost.

One of the conclusions that emerge from the literature is that forecasts made using quantitative techniques generally outperform those based on judgment.

For example, Mabert compared forecasts based on executive consensus, the aggregate of individual sales representative forecasts, and those using various quantitative techniques, and found that three of the quantitative techniques (Box-Jenkins, exponential smoothing, and another form of smoothing) yielded superior forecasts.[24]

In general, exponential smoothing (after seasonally adjusting the data), seems to provide the most accurate forecasts, with Box-Jenkins a close second. For example, exponential smoothing was found to be more accurate, on the average, in forecasting 111 different time series than 13 other time series analysis and projection models (including Box-Jenkins).[25]

The relative accuracies of the various quantitative forecasting models are partially dependent on the time series being forecast. For example, Box-Jenkins is likely to outperform exponential smoothing for a company with a pattern of sales that is strongly cyclical in nature. This is because the exponential smoothing model can only *react* to turning points after they occur, not *predict* them.

A useful source for helping to select forecasting methods is D. M. Georgoff and R. G. Murdick, "Manager's Guide to Forecasting," *Harvard Business Review*, January–February 1986, 110–122.

Keeping a Forecasting "Track" Record

Observation suggests that few companies keep records of forecasts compared with the actual sales made. If any systematic attempt is to be made to determine, and to improve, the accuracy of a company's sales forecasting, such a record is a necessity. If more than one method of forecasting is used, a record should be kept for each so that comparative accuracies can be determined. One should also record any assumptions made in the forecast.

Table 10–1 Schedule of Critical Questions and References for the Assessment of Competencies, Threats, and Opportunities

	Text References
ASSESSMENT OF COMPETENCIES 1. Compared with our competitors, what are our (a) strengths, (b) weaknesses, in (i) overall management skills, (ii) marketing, (iii) manufacturing, (iv) engineering, and (iv) financial capabilities? 2. What are the costs and amounts of time required to correct weaknesses?	Judgments based on company-specific information. Same as above.
ASSESSMENTS OF THREATS AND OPPORTUNITIES Trends in the Economy and Industry 3. What changes, if any, have taken place in the economy in the past three years (such as increases or decreases in the rate of inflation, rising or falling interest rates, ranges in dollar exchange rates, booms or recessions) that are likely to have significant future effects on marketing in the industry?	Analysis of economic changes, Chapter 3, pp. 80–87.
4. What changes, if any, likely to take place in the economy in the next five years that will have significant effects on marketing in the industry?	Forecasting, Chapter 10, pp. 314–325.
5. What major changes are occurring that have their origin within the industry (such as new manufacturing methods, material shortages, influx of foreign competition) that are likely to have significant effects on marketing in the industry?	Analysis of industry changes, Chapter 3, pp. 73–77.
6. What steps have been taken to counter or take advantage of these economic and industry changes? What steps could be taken?	Judgments based on company-specific information.
The Political and Legal Context 7. Are there laws that are being proposed (in such areas as product safety, advertising, protective tariffs, consumer credit) that will affect the firm's marketing program significantly?	Secondary information, Chapter 8, pp. 237–238.
8. Are there rulings that may be made by a regulatory agency (such as the Federal Trade Commission, the Antitrust Division of the Department of Justice, the Food and Drug Administration, the Occupational Safety and Health Administration, the Consumer Product Safety Commission) that might seriously affect the cost or availability of the critical raw materials or the product itself?	Same as above.
Technological Developments 9. What major changes, if any, are occurring in the technology of the product? in packaging? in storage and transportation? in communication?	Industry-specific information.
10. What generic substitutes, if any, pose threats as replacements to company products? What is the earliest that each potential replacement could occur?	Judgments based on industry-specific information.
Demographic and Social Changes 11. What effects will projected changes in the size, age distribution, geographic distribution, and income and educational levels of the population have on the marketing of the product?	Secondary data sources, Chapter 8, pp. 236–241; forecasting, this chapter, pp. 314–325.
12. What changes in the lifestyles and attitudes of consumers will likely affect the marketing of the product? What marketing changes will be required?	Chapter 4, pp. 107–111.

Table 10–1 Schedule of Critical Questions and References for the Assessment of Competencies, Threats, and Opportunities (*continued*)

	Text References
Generic and Brand Demand	
Generic Demand	
13. What changes are likely to occur over the next five years in market size, growth or decline, profitability, and geographic distribution?	Forecasting, Chapter 10, pp. 314–325.
14. At what stage is the product class in the product life cycle?	Product life cycle, Chapter 12, pp. 413–415.
15. What market segments for the product class have been entered?	Segmenting the market, Chapter 2, pp. 41–44.
16. What markets and market segments have yet to be entered?	Same as above.
17. How large are these untapped markets and how expensive would it be to enter them?	Product market selection, Chapter 2, pp. 48–52.
Brand Demand	
18. What share of the overall market does our product have? by market? by market segment?	Syndicated research services, Chapter 8, pp. 238–241.
a. What will be the probable rate of increase or decrease for each?	Forecasting, this chapter, pp. 314–325
b. Which are the higher profit segments? the lower profit segments?	
c. What percentage of the buyers in each market segment are aware of our brand? have tried it? have repurchased it? think it is of the highest quality?	Survey research, Chapter 8, pp. 241–246.
d. What changes in customer needs and desires are taking place in each segment?	Chapter 4, pp. 120–122.
e. How do the customers in each segment make buying decisions?	Chapter 4, pp. 95–122.
19. What percentage of the total desired distribution outlets carry our sources, brand (each brand)?	Secondary sources, Chapter 8, pp. 238–241.
20. Is the brand (each brand) correctly positioned in each market segment?	Chapter 2, p. 44.
21. How could our brand be improved?	Concept generation and testing, Chapter 11, pp. 361–365.
Suppliers	
22. What raw materials are required to produce the product? What is the long-term availability of these raw materials?	Judgment based on company-specific information.
23. How stable are our present suppliers? What alternative sources are available?	Same as above.
Competitors	
24. What are the objectives and strategies of each of the leading competitors?	Competitor analysis, Chapter 3, pp. 74–77.
25. How do the customers rate the company versus each of its competitors in terms of product quality, service, price, and reputation?	Competitor analysis, Chapter 3, pp. 74–77.
26. What are the market shares of each of the competitors? Which are growing and which are declining?	Competitor analysis, Chapter 3, pp. 74–77.
27. What are the production costs of the competitor with the highest market share? the lowest market share?	Estimating competitor costs, Appendix A.
28. How likely is it that new competitors will enter, and who are they likely to be?	Judgments based on company-specific information.
29. How are our competitors likely to react to changes in our strategies?	Same as above.

Table 10–2   Schedule of Critical Questions and References for the Choice of Product Markets for Strategic Marketing Planning

	Text References
REVIEW OF EXISTING PRODUCT MARKETS Prospects and Requirements	
1. At what stage of the product life cycle is the product?	Chapter 12, pp. 413–415.
2. What share of the market does it have? What is the market share of each of our competitors?	Syndicated data, Chapter 8, pp. 238–241.
3. Do we have the necessary technical and marketing expertise to remain competitive?	Judgment based on company-specific information.
4. What are the forecast cash flows for the planning period?	Chapter 9, pp. 284–287.
Portfolio Effects	
5. Is the product complementary with one or more of our other products with respect to marketing or production?	Judgment based on company-specific information.
6. Does it serve to balance other product markets with respect to cyclical or seasonal fluctuations?	Same as above.
7. Does it protect the supply or provide a market for another product (vertical integration)?	Same as above.
REVIEW OF POTENTIAL PRODUCT MARKETS Present and Prospective Demand	
8. What market segments for the product class have been entered?	Segmenting the market, Chapter 2, pp. 41–44.
9. What markets and market segments have yet to be entered?	Same as above.
10. How large are these markets and how expensive would it be to enter them?	Product market selection, Chapter 9, pp. 263–276.
11. At what stage is the product class in the product life cycle?	Product life cycle, Chapter 12, pp. 413–415.
12. What changes are likely to occur over the next five years in market size and geographic distribution?	Forecasting, this chapter, pp. 314–325.
13. What are forecast sales over the next five years if we were to enter the product market?	Same as above.
Trends Affecting Supply	
14. What is the probable long-term availability of the raw materials required to produce the product?	Judgment based on company-specific situation.
15. What are the prospects for technological developments that will significantly improve the quality or reduce the cost of the product?	Same as above.
16. How likely is it that actions by one or more governmental agencies will seriously affect the cost or availability of critical raw materials, or the product itself?	Judgment based on company-specific situation.
The Competitive Situation	
17. What are the market shares of the principal competitors in the product market? Are they increasing, decreasing, or remaining the same?	Chapter 3, pp. 74–77.
18. What is the productive capacity of each competitor?	Chapter 3, pp. 74–77.
19. What are the probable plans of each competitor with respect to production capability?	Chapter 3, pp. 74–77.
20. What are the prospects for significant technological improvements in (a) the product, (b) manufacturing tooling and equipment by each competitor?	Judgment based on company-specific situation.
21. How probable is it that new competitors will enter, and who are they likely to be?	Same as above.
22. What are the marketing strategies of companies now in the industry?	Chapter 3, pp. 74–77.
23. What strategies should we adopt if we were to enter the product market? How would competitors likely react to our strategies?	Chapter 10, pp. 303–307.
Financial Prospects	
24. What investment in R&D and production and distribution facilities is required to enter the product market?	Estimate based on company-specific situation.
25. What are the estimated cash flows for the planning period?	This chapter, pp. 308–309; Chapter 9, pp. 284–287.
Portfolio Effects (The same as questions 5, 6, and 7 above.)	

Table 10–3 Schedule of Critical Questions and References for the Setting of Objectives in Strategic Marketing Planning

	Text References
1. What are the criteria by which we want to measure performance in this product market—sales volume? market share? return on sales? return on investment? net present value of cash flow? return on equity? other?	Company choice.
2. What has the performance been in the past with respect to these criteria?	Company-specific information.
3. With no change in marketing strategies, what are the performance levels for these same criteria likely to be in the future?	Reference forecasts, this chapter, pp. 316–322.
4. Considering the strategies we plan to employ, what performance levels of these criteria is it reasonable to expect?	Conditional forecasts, this chapter, pp. 322–324.

Table 10–4 Schedule of Critical Questions and References for Devising and Choosing Strategies in Strategic Marketing Planning

	Text References
GENERATING A SET OF ALTERNATIVE STRATEGIES TO CHOOSE FROM	
1. What are the crucial factors that will (a) permit us to, (b) prevent us from achieving the objectives set?	Depends on the specific situation.
2. Which of these factors are controllable by us?	Same as above.
3. What strategies are commonly used in the industry?	Same as above.
4. What variations of these might be viable?	Same as above.
5. Given the product markets we have decided to be in and the objectives we have set, what are viable strategic alternatives for pricing? advertising and promotion? distribution? personal selling?	Same as above.
CHOOSING AMONG STRATEGIC ALTERNATIVES	
For each alternative being considered, the following questions should be raised:	
6. How would competition react? Do we have a sustainable advantage?	Same as above.
7. What are the critical assumptions on which the success of the strategy rests? Are they realistic?	Same as above.
8. Does the business possess the necessary skills and resources? Do the key operating managers understand the strategy, and will they be committed to making it a success?	Same as above.
9. Is the strategy internally consistent?	Same as above.
10. What are the risks and contingencies?	Same as above.
11. If the strategy is adopted and needs to be changed, how flexible is it? What are the "bail-out" costs?	Same as above.
12. What are the forecast economic consequences?	Same as above.

Table 10–5 Schedule of Critical Questions and References for the Setting of Marketing Performance Standards in Operational Marketing Planning

	Text References
1. What are the strategic objectives for this product market—sales volume? market share? return on sales? return on investment? net present value of cash flow? return on equity? other?	Company choice.
2. For which of these objectives do we need to set up directly related performance standards? indirectly related standards?	Company-specific information.
3. With no change in marketing programs, what are the performance levels for these same criteria likely to be during the next year?	Reference forecasts, this chapter, pp. 316–322.
4. Considering the marketing program we plan to employ, what performance levels is it reasonable to expect?	Conditional forecasts, this chapter, pp. 322–324.

1. *Marketing planning* involves the setting of marketing objectives, choice of products, selection of markets, and designing of marketing programs for each product market for a specified future period.
2. Marketing planning comprises strategic and operational planning:
   a. *Strategic marketing planning* is concerned with the planning of the fundamental means for achieving the company's objectives through the markets entered and the marketing programs used to serve them.
   b. *Operational marketing planning* is concerned with the implementation of the strategic plan.
3. The benefits of planning are that it
   a. Encourages systematic thinking ahead by management
   b. Helps identify possible developments facing the company
   c. Results in better preparations to meet changes when they occur
   d. Results in better communication between departments
   e. Results in better coordination of actions among departments
4. The steps in the marketing planning cycle are:
   a. Strategic marketing plans are made.
   b. Operating plans designed to carry out the strategies are devised.
   c. The operational plans are put into effect.
   d. The outcomes are monitored.
   e. The results are fed back into both the strategic and operating marketing planning processes for making any necessary modifications.
5. The steps involved in strategic planning are to:
   a. Assess competencies, threats, and opportunities
   b. Choose target product markets
   c. Set strategic objectives
   d. Select the strategies for achieving the objectives
6. It is necessary to set objectives and select strategies concurrently; one cannot reasonably set objectives for a strategic marketing program without knowing what strategies the program is going to employ, and one cannot rationally select strategies without knowing what the objectives are.
7. The five primary areas in which the competencies of a company need to be assessed for strategic planning purposes are:
   a. The quality of its management
   b. Its marketing
   c. Its manufacturing
   d. Its engineering capabilities
   e. Its financial strength
8. A *reference sales forecast* is made with the assumption that no change will be made in the present marketing program. A *conditional sales forecast* is made with the assumption that one or more specified changes will be made in the marketing program.

9. The steps involved in operational marketing planning are to:
   a. Set performance standards
   b. Plan marketing programs
   c. Plan the implementation of them
   d. Monitor results
10. There are seven methods in use for making reference sales forecasts:
    a. Aggregate of individual sales forecasts
    b. Executive judgment
    c. Delphi
    d. Survey of buyer intentions
    e. Exponential smoothing
    f. Statistical trend analysis
    g. Box-Jenkins
11. The methods that can be used for making conditional sales forecasts are:
    a. Executive judgment
    b. The Delphi method
    c. Box-Jenkins
    d. Surveys
    e. On-line sales experiments
    f. Simulated market tests
    g. Standard market tests
    h. Analysis of case histories
    i. Causal regression analysis
12. There is evidence to suggest that an average of the forecasts from two or more methods is generally more accurate than using one of the constituent forecasts.

REVIEW QUESTIONS

10.1. What is
       a. marketing planning?
       b. strategic marketing planning?
       c. operational marketing planning?

10.2. What are the benefits of planning?

10.3. What are the steps in the marketing planning cycle?

10.4. What are the steps involved in strategic marketing planning?

10.5. What are the five primary areas in which the competencies of a company need to be assessed for strategic planning purposes?

10.6. What is
a. a reference sales forecast?
b. a conditional sales forecast?

10.7. What steps are involved in operational marketing planning?

10.8. What is
a. prevention planning?
b. contingency planning?

10.9. What are the methods of making a reference sales forecast?

10.10. What are the methods of making a conditional sales forecast?

10.11. How is the Delphi method used in forecasting?

10.12. Should more than one method of forecasting be used? Why or why not?

DISCUSSION QUESTIONS AND PROBLEMS

10.13. Would you say that the federal agricultural price support and subsidy programs that have been in place since the 1930s are a form of market planning? Why or why not?

10.14. Is the definition *"planning* is purposeful, future-oriented decision making" a useful one? Why or why not?

10.15. Since in most businesses a limited number of strategic marketing strategies are used during the professional lifetime of the top executives, there may be little in the way of experience that they will be able to call on in deciding which strategy (or strategies) to adopt. A marketing consultant, however, may have participated in the choice of strategies by a large number of firms and so may be able to give advice that is more firmly rooted in experience. Does this suggest that consultants ought routinely to be used when strategy decisions are to be made? Explain.

10.16. The sales pattern of black-and-white television sets for the first few years after they were introduced by RCA was used by analysts for that company to predict the pattern for its color-set sales when it was introduced. The growth in sales of color sets (RCA and the industry) actually was much slower than for black-and-white sets.
a. What method of making a conditional sales forecast is this?

b. Why do you think the black-and-white set sales pattern was not a good predictor of color-set sales?

10.17. Why do you think that quantitative methods (such as exponential smoothing) consistently outperform executives' reliance on their judgment in making sales forecasts?

10.18. In the discussion on page 319, why would the seasonal index for S_{t+1} be very close to 0.85, given the sales data assumed in the example?

10.19. "Forecasts made using a simple moving average over a two-year period will tend to be high, or low, by an amount equal to slightly more than one-half of any increases, or decreases, that result from a linear trend in sales over the two years." Demonstrate that this statement is true mathematically:
a. By use of an example
b. In the general case

10.20. Assume that a company that has no discernible seasonal pattern to its sales has had the following amounts of dollar sales (in thousands) for the past eight quarters:

$$Y_{t-7} = \$110.5, \quad Y_{t-5} = \$101.6, \quad Y_{t-3} = \$97.8, \quad Y_{t-1} = \$87.1,$$
$$Y_{t-6} = \$104.6, \quad Y_{t-4} = \$94.2, \quad Y_{t-2} = \$82.7, \quad Y_{t} = \$76.9.$$

Make a forecast for the next period (Y_{t+1}) using:
a. Your judgment
b. The naive model ($Y_{t+1} = Y_t$)
c. The simple moving average model
d. The exponential smoothing model with $\alpha = 0.40$
e. The exponential smoothing model with $\alpha = 0.50$
f. Statistical trend analysis

10.21. Assume that the company in problem 10.20, instead of having the sales over the past eight quarters shown there, had had the following dollar sales (in thousands) for those quarters:

$$Y_{t-7} = \$76.9, \quad Y_{t-5} = \$82.7, \quad Y_{t-3} = \$ 94.2, \quad Y_{t-1} = \$104.6,$$
$$Y_{t-6} = \$87.1, \quad Y_{t-4} = \$97.8, \quad Y_{t-2} = \$101.6, \quad Y_{t} = \$110.5.$$

Make a forecast for the next period (Y_{t+1}) using:
a. Your judgment
b. The naive model ($Y_{t+1} = Y_t$)
c. The simple moving average model
d. The exponential smoothing model with $\alpha = 0.40$
e. The exponential smoothing model with $\alpha = 0.50$
f. Statistical trend analysis

10.22. The sales data in problems 10.20 and 10.21 were the same except that they were reversed with respect to time. Having worked both prob-

lems, what conclusions do you draw from the relative levels of forecasts of each of the methods with regard to:
a. Past sales data that have a downward trend
b. Past sales data that have an upward trend

10.23. In the discussion on the choice of forecasting methods (p. 324), it was argued that a minimum of three methods should be used. The reasoning went that "if two are used and the forecasts differ, it may not be clear which one is the more accurate whereas, if three are used and two of the forecasts are similar, there is some assurance that the two are more likely to be closer to the actual value than the third one is." What happens if three methods are used and the forecasts from all three are different?

10.24. Which, if any, of the following quantitative forecasting methods—moving average, exponential smoothing, statistical trend analysis, or Box-Jenkins—allow for cyclical effects in the forecast?

Endnotes

[1]"Levi-Strauss' Success Due to Coordination of Marketing, Strategic Planning: Grohman," *Marketing News*, July 10, 1981, 1, 6.

[2]R. L. Ackoff, *A Concept of Corporate Planning*, Wiley-Interscience, 1978, 1.

[3]P. Drucker, "Long-Range Planning: Challenge to Management Science," *Management Science*, April 1959, 239.

[4]J. T. Wilson, Chairman and CEO of R. J. Reynolds Industries, "Strategic Planning at R. J. Reynolds Industries," *The Journal of Business Strategy*, Fall 1985, 27.

[5]B. Uttal, "Texas Instruments Regroups," *Fortune*, August 9, 1982, 40–45.

[6]Adapted from G. S. Day, "Tough Questions for Developing Strategies," *The Journal of Business Strategy*, Winter 1986, 63–68.

[7]Wilson, "Strategic Planning," 26.

[8]"Advance Planning Needed to Cope with Crises," *Marketing News*, April 26, 1985, 14.

[9]The evidence from one study indicates that this was not the case, however. See T. R. Wotruba and M. L. Thurlow, "Sales Force Participation in Quota Setting and Sales Forecasting," *Journal of Marketing*, February 1973, 11–16.

[10]See R. Staelin and R. E. Turner, "Error in Judgmental Sales Forecasts: Theory and Results," *Journal of Marketing Research*, February 1973, 10–16, for a discussion of this kind of pervasive bias.

[11]First described in N. Dalkey and O. Helmer, "An Experimental Application of the Delphi Method to the Use of Experts," *Management Science*, April 1963, 458–460.

[12]A description of how to use the method is given in R. J. Tersine and W. E. Riggs, "The Delphi Technique: A Long-Range Planning Tool," *Business Horizons*, April 1976, 51–56. An application of it is given in R. J. Best, "An Experiment in Delphi Estimation in Marketing Decision Making," *Journal of Marketing Research*, November 1974, 447–452.

[13]S. Basu and R. G. Schroeder, "Incorporating Judgments in Sales Forecasts: Applications of the Delphi Method at American Hoist and Derrick," *Interfaces*, May 1977, 10–23.

[14]R. Carbone and W. L. Gorr, "Accuracy of Judgmental Forecasting of Time Series," *Decision Sciences*, Vol. 16, Spring 1985, 153–160.

[15]J. Murray, "Canadian Consumer Expectational Data: An Evaluation," *Journal of Marketing Research*, February 1969, 60.

[16]See D. S. Tull and D. I. Hawkins, *Marketing Research: Measurement and Method*, 4th ed., Macmillan, 1987, 585–589, for a discussion of how to determine seasonal indexes.

[17]For a more technical and comprehensive discussion of exponential smoothing, see S. C. Wheelwright and S. Makridakis, *Forecasting Methods for Management*, 3rd ed., John Wiley & Sons, 1980, 54–80.

[18]See G. E. P. Box and G. M. Jenkins, *Time Series Analysis, Forecasting, and Control*, Holden-Day, 1970, for a complete description of the method.

[19]Reported in the 1979 annual report, 6.

[20]H. E. Echelberger and E. L. Shofer, Jr., "Snow + (X) = Use of Ski Slopes," *Journal of Marketing Research*, August 1970, 388–392.

[21]G. E. S. Parker, "How to Get a Better Forecast," *Harvard Business Review*, March–April 1971, 101.

[22]E. Mahmoud, "Accuracy of Forecasting: A Survey," *Journal of Forecasting*, April–June 1984, 141. See also S. Makridakis and R. L. Winkler, "Averages of Forecasts: Some Empirical Results," *Management Science*, September 1983, 977–986.

[23]D. J. Dalrymple, "Sales Forecasting Methods and Accuracy," *Business Horizons*, December 1975, 71.

[24]V. A. Mabert, "Statistical versus Sales Force—Executive Opinion Short Range Forecasts: A Times Series Analysis Study," Krannert Graduate School, Purdue University Working Paper, 1975.

[25]S. Makridakis and M. Hidon, "Accuracy of Forecasting: An Empirical Investigation," *Journal of the Royal Statistical Society*, February 1979, 97–145.

MINICASES

Kansas City Royals Baseball Club

The marketing program for the Kansas City Royals has been an aggressive one over the past few years. With a budget of approximately $200,000 per year, the director of marketing and special events has developed a program of good coverage of the games on radio and television networks, separate radio, TV, and bumper sticker advertising, special event nights, wide distribution of pocket-sized game schedules, and a ticket reservation center that has WATS lines to more than 100 local ticket-selling locations within the team's marketing area.

One area of concern has been how the Royals should be positioned. In the mid 1970s, for example, the advertising emphasized winning—"all the way to the World Series"—and the management was embarrassed when the team lost in the American League playoffs to the New York Yankees in two succeeding years.

a. What alternatives are available for positioning the Royals?

b. Which do you believe should be chosen?

Seven-Up Advertising Theme

In the two years before the Seven-Up Company was acquired by Phillip Morris, Inc., its advertising had been based on the "uncola" theme. As the term implies, the ads had concentrated on the differences between Seven-Up and cola drinks, and the better taste of Seven-Up.

At the time of the acquisition, Seven-Up had about a 7 percent market share of the U.S. market. The market share of all cola drinks was then about 65 percent of the domestic market, with Coca-Cola having about 34 percent and Pepsi-Cola approximately 22 percent. In the previous year, about $17 million had been spent on Seven-Up advertising, whereas PepsiCo. had spent almost $25 million and Coca-Cola more that $34 million.

a. What are the assumptions, implicit or explicit, involved in the move from the "uncola" to the "America's turning 7-Up" campaign?

b. Did the change from the "uncola" to the "America's turning 7-Up" theme represent a strategic or an operating decision? Explain.

MINICASE III-3

Wisconsin Electric Power Company

The Wisconsin Electric Power Company, like most of the utilities in the United States, is faced with attempting to control the growth in peak demand. Effective management of peak demand plays an important role in determining the success of a utility's operation because of environmental constraints and high construction costs for additional generating capacity.

Wisconsin Electric serves about 800,000 electric customers, including residential, commercial, and industrial accounts.

a. What alternative means of controlling peak demand might Wisconsin Electric consider?
b. What are the advantages and disadvantages of each?

MINICASE III-4

North American Aviation: The Minuteman Missile

The 1956, the Department of Defense (DOD) was to accept bids for the manufacturing and installation of the Minuteman intercontinental ballistic missile. There was to be a major contractor for assembling the rocket engine and the guidance and control systems in the shell of the missile along with the necessary electronics for operation of the missile. The rocket engine and the guidance and control systems were to be supplied by subcontractors.

There were 19 companies that were known to be planning to bid on the guidance and control system, but only 4 of them were believed to have any real chance of winning the award: General Motors, which had the subcontract on the guidance and control for the Titan missile; Sperry-Rand, which was manufacturing the guidance and control for the Skybolt; General Electric, which was supplying the guidance and control for the Polaris missile; and North American Aviation (now a part of the Rockwell Corporation), with no major subcontracts for guidance and control equipment, but with a strong engineering and manufacturing capability in the field.

A year before the date on which proposals were to be submitted for the Minuteman, North American prepared and submitted proposals to DOD to replace each of the current guidance and control systems on the Titan, Skybolt, and Polaris with a higher-performance, less-expensive system that would be delivered faster than the schedule given by the subcontractors for each. General Motors, Sperry-Rand, and General Electric each reacted to this threat by renegotiating their subcontracts with DOD at lower unit prices and with a faster delivery schedule.

A year later, when the Minuteman guidance and control systems proposals were submitted, only North American was able to provide satisfactory delivery dates. The three other major potential suppliers were so committed on their present contracts that Minuteman equipment could not be delivered for an extended period.

Assuming that the earlier proposals by North American had been a ploy to get its major competitors effectively to remove themselves as serious contenders for the Minuteman award:

a. Was this a marketing strategy? Explain.
b. Was it an ethical strategy? Explain.

The Edsel

After catching up with the post–World War II backlog of demand, in the early 1950s the Ford Motor Company turned to a program of developing and introducing new cars. One of the first of the new cars was the Edsel, a mid-price car named after the father of Henry Ford II, the then-president of Ford.

Research on the Edsel concept was carried out in 1951. The results were promising. Consumers reported that they liked the distinctive design and the automatic transmission that was planned for it. Go-ahead was given by Henry Ford II, and the design was completed and tooling manufactured. Marketing plans were made that targeted the Edsel to compete with General Motors' Buick for the middle-class, above-average income, 35–55 age group segment.

Some final research was done for Ford by Market Facts, a Chicago marketing research agency, just before the car was introduced in 1957. The president of Market Facts at that time, David Hardin, has described the results as follows:

The findings were very negative. The car had no style appeal. The horse-collar grill and all just didn't go over.

The automatic transmission buttons on the steering wheel made it awkward. But the company had already sunk, I don't know, perhaps $200 million into the car.

It had convinced a lot of dealers all over the country to switch from Oldsmobile and Buick to the Edsel. A lot of people were banking on the Edsel. When we came back with a very poor product appeal test, it was ignored. In all honesty, you have to give the company credit for going ahead and producing the car because a lot of people were counting on it even though the research was negative. They had sunk too much money into it to back off.*

a. Was "they had sunk too much money into it to back off" a valid reason for introducing the Edsel? Explain.

b. Were there other reasons for introduction that were potentially valid ones? Explain.

---

*As reported in "Past AMA President Hardin, Head of Market Facts, Looks Back at the Early Days of Marketing Research," *Marketing News*, December 19, 1986, 24.

Safeway Stores, Inc.: Shopping Habit Forecast

Planners for the major supermarket chains have forecast that a global gasoline scarcity will begin by the year 2000 and will worsen as the new century continues. They anticipate an accompanying continuing increase in gasoline prices that will make the previous highs of $1.50 to $1.75 per gallon (in the United States) look inexpensive.

They are concerned about changes in shopping habits that declining supplies of gasoline will bring about. Will customers make fewer shopping trips, but buy more each trip? If so, the hypermarkets popular in France, England, and Germany, where gasoline prices are already much higher than in the United States, may be the desirable direction to go. Hypermarkets are extremely large supermarkets (100,000 square feet or more) that carry not only a full line of foods but clothing, housewares, garden supplies, automotive accessories, and sporting goods as well (100,000 or more items in total). Customers might prefer to walk to stores conveniently located in their neighborhood, however. In this case small,

limited-line food stores might be an appropriate answer. Some might want to return to telephone orders and home delivery of groceries, a method of shopping popular before most households had cars.

As of the mid 1980s, Safeway Stores, the country's largest supermarket chain, was following a policy of enlarging present stores and building larger new ones in locations where the demand warranted such action. The floor space of the remodeled and new stores was about 30,000 square feet, not nearly as large as a hypermarket but about 50 percent larger than conventional-sized supermarkets. Some limited-line food stores had been built and were operating profitably. (Profits per square foot were not up to the level of the larger stores, however.)

a. What actions *could* Safeway take to forecast the direction future shopping habits are likely to take?

b. What actions *should* Safeway take? Explain.

Burlington Industries and Westinghouse Electric: Selection of Test Market Areas

An interview was conducted on test marketing by a senior editor of *Sales and Marketing Management* magazine of the marketing managers for the Burlington Socks division of Burlington Industries and the Turtle-Lite group of the Westinghouse Electric Corporation.* Following is a (partial) report of the questions asked and answers given:

S&MM: Why do you test market—to see if you have a viable product, or to develop the most profitable plan for your rollout?

Westinghouse Electric: For our Turtle-Lite long-life light bulbs, we had to find out if, by spending the advertising and promotion dollars we were budgeting, we would have a viable program and a respectable payout.

Burlington Socks: In a recent test marketing situation we were in at Burlington Socks, we knew we had a quality product—a sock carrying the Levi's brand name from Levi-Strauss. (Levi-Strauss has a licensing agreement with Burlington Industries allowing socks to be marketed by Burlington using the Levi's brand.) We wanted to determine the best way to display it, advertise it, and promote it in department stores and specialty apparel stores. We picked three markets. In one we had no advertising. In another we used print and radio. In the third we used print alone. We gave away a display fixture with a minimum order, then tracked product

movement by personal contact with store owner or manager and with consumers, both at the point of sale and in follow-up telephone interviews. That gave us the information to say, let's roll it out using this mix of advertising and display.

S&MM: Where did you test it?

Burlington Socks: In three markets on the West coast, which is a fairly good area for the Burlington brand and is Levi-Strauss' stronghold.

Westinghouse Electric: If you did well in your strong market, how would you project the results into your weaker markets? We felt that if we could sell in an area in which Westinghouse had a smaller distribution base, we could sell where we had a better franchise, so we tested in our weakest markets.

a. Do you think that the choice of test markets may reflect different attitudes toward risk by Burlington Industries and Westinghouse Electric? Explain.
b. Do you believe that the intentional choice of weak, strong, or average test market areas provides the most valuable information from a market test? Explain.

---

*"The True Test of Test Marketing," *Sales and Marketing Management,* March 1979, 55–58.

The Callison Company: How Many Test Markets to Use?

Suppose you are the newly appointed marketing manager for Callison, Inc.,* a company that produces and markets packaged drug sundry products. Further suppose that you have a potential new product that is about to go into test market. It is a product that is an extension of an existing company brand. The "mother" product will be left on the market regardless of whether this one is introduced or not. A simulated market test and a controlled store test have given highly favorable results for the prospective new product.

You know that the conventional wisdom in the industry is that two to four test markets should be used, and that the company has always used four test markets in testing products in the past. You also know that for a nine-month test, each additional market adds about $500,000 in cost. You wonder if it is worth an extra million dollars to have the data from four test markets instead of two, or an extra half million to get data from four markets instead of three.

It occurs to you that you could simulate the results of a market test by using data from a sample of SAMI† markets. Each month SAMI provides data on warehouse withdrawals of products in 54 market areas. The market areas include most of the cities or metropolitan areas that are commonly used for market testing. If random samples of two, three, and four SAMI areas were taken and the data on warehouse withdrawals for a current company brand recorded for each, the results would simulate a market test using those market areas. If the samples were replicated a large number of times (say, 50), one would expect that the means of the replications for share and volume estimates would be very close to the actual means for all 54 SAMI areas. One could then measure the variation around the replication means and so obtain information on the expected relative accuracy of two-, three-, and four-market standard market tests for this type of product.

You decide to do this for two of the company's current brands, one of which is the mother product for the potential new brand extension. As expected, the means of the 50 samples taken for each brand for each of the measures of interest are very close to the mean for that brand for all 54 SAMI areas. The results on the variations around the means are as follows:

Standard Deviation of Estimates of National Share and Volume Based on 50 Drawings

	2 Areas Randomly Drawn	3 Areas Randomly Drawn	4 Areas Randomly Drawn
BRAND 1 (mother product for the potential brand extension)			
Share of market	14.7%	14.0%	13.0%
Share of market per retail outlet	15.3	12.4	10.6
Sales per capita	22.0	15.0	14.6
Ratio of test brand to key competition	18.0	17.7	15.1
BRAND 2			
Share of market	15.5	12.8	8.4
Share of market per retail outlet	9.2	9.2	7.4
Sales per capita	13.7	11.4	9.1
Ratio of test brand to key competition	16.8	15.1	12.5

a. How do you interpret the above data in terms of the relative accuracies of the predicted share and volume measures for the two-, three-, and four-market tests?

b. What characteristics of the product and its market would influence the choice of number of markets to use in the standard market test? Explain.

c. Which do you think is the most important of the four measures shown for the two brands in the table? Why?

d. From what you are told in the case, how many market areas do you think should be used for this product? Explain.

---

*A fictitious name for an actual company that manufactures and markets drug sundries. The data in this case were developed by the company using the method described and have not been disguised or altered in any way.

†See p. 239 for a description of SAMI and its method of operating.

MINICASE III-9

The Trailblazers and Broadcasting

In recent years, sporting events have become bigger business than ever. Many companies have event specialists that concentrate on sports for promoting products, and some of the major advertising agencies have developed special departments in sports marketing. Advertisers see linkages to sporting events as a method of improved communication. Products associated with popular teams may rise above the advertising clutter, and sports broadcasts do draw some audience members who are among the demographic groups that are most elusive for other programming.

The National Basketball Association (NBA) has the third largest following among professional team sports in the United States, trailing football and baseball but well ahead of the others. In a typical year, the 23 teams in the NBA draw over 10 million fans to their games and generate around $200 million in revenue.[*]

Historically most NBA teams have earned the bulk of their money from ticket sales. At one time, teams sold broadcast rights for a small fee, viewing the broadcast as a public relations tool aimed at maintaining interest among ticket buyers. The station controlled production of the broadcast and sold advertising to earn its profit. As the popularity of basketball has spread, however, broadcasts have increasingly entered the profit picture. Teams are now more interested in obtaining a share of the profits from advertising revenue associated with the broadcast. And the growth of cable television has also presented opportunities for increasing revenue from spectators.

Recently the Portland Trailblazers were faced with a decision of whether they should enter the television broadcast business. They had taken over the radio broadcast of their games just that year, but television was an entirely new territory. Some baseball teams produced their own broadcast and sold advertising, thus taking the risks and difficulties of production in-house, but also increasing profit potential by controlling the fees charged for the advertising. But in basketball the idea was new.

The key marketing personnel were widely regarded as capable. In a player trade with the Indiana Pacers during the 1982–1983 season, the Pacers asked for 40 hours of consulting time from the vice-president of marketing for the Trailblazers, Jon Spoelstra, as partial compensation. This request was quite unusual in that most trades involve other players, draft choices, and money rather than marketing advice. (The request paid off for the Pacers, whose home attendance went from 4,500 to over 10,000 the following year, in spite of having the worst win–loss record in basketball that year.)[†]

a. In spite of this skill, the decision was not an easy one. Could a group whose main specialty was basketball succeed at television production and television media sales?

b. Would it be wise to enter these two new businesses based only on experience with basketball and on very limited experience with radio?

c. What are the potential communication advantages and risks?

d. What are the potential business advantages and risks?

---

[*]B. Welling, J. Tasini, and D. Cook, "Basketball Business Is Booming," *Business Week*, October 28, 1985, 73–82.
[†]E. A Schwartz, "Marketing Is Everything," *Oregon Business*, December 1984.

Guidelines for the Public Use of Market and Opinion Research

In 1981 the Advertising Research Foundation published a report prepared by the Public Affairs Council titled *Guidelines for the Public Use of Market and Opinion Research*. Its stated purpose was:

An effort to state a professional consensus on how market and opinion research for public use should be assessed and what determines how useful, sound, and credible research may be in such applications. . . . It was written because research is being used increasingly for public purposes:

- as evidence in legal cases;
- as evidence in government and other public hearings;
- in support of advertising or publicity claims for products, candidates, or causes;
- as support for news stories and features which appear in the press and other media.

These public purposes can and do affect our lives and our institutions. They are creating a new role for research and a need of new ways to assess its soundness and value.*

The report provides guidelines for evaluation in seven areas. They are:

1. ORIGIN. What is behind the research
2. DESIGN. The concept and the plan
3. EXECUTION.Collecting and handling the information
4. STABILITY. Sample size and reliability
5. APPLICABILITY. Generalizing the findings
6. MEANING. Interpretations and conclusions
7. CANDOR. Open reporting and disclosure

Each section contains a set of guidelines relevant to that topic area. The guidelines identify major issues and state the research principles that should be applied in each area. They are followed by a list of two sets of questions:

Key Questions. Questions that "are so basic that the usefulness of the research must be open to serious challenge if they cannot all be answered affirmatively from the information provided."†

Quality Checkpoints. Questions that "are designed to provide further indications of the value of a piece of research for public use."‡

The guidelines, key questions, and quality checkpoints for Section II follow.

SECTION II DESIGN—THE CONCEPT AND THE PLAN**

Guidelines

The research approach, the sample and the analysis should be clearly described, and they should conform to the requirements of objective and scientific study, and to the purpose for which the research was conducted.

The universe—which is the population of people, facilities or occurrences to be studied—should be carefully specified, and the sample should be designed to represent that universe.

A plan for the research, covering the kinds of measurements to be made, the method of data collection and a proposal for analyzing the findings, should be set up and agreed to before the research is undertaken.

The research should be designed to produce fair measurements and honest information. It should not try to mislead its users. It should not pretend to an objectivity or a significance it does not merit.

In planning, the time, money and skills to be invested in the research should be balanced against the impact of the expected information. Important decisions ought not to be based on poorly conceived and grossly inadequate studies, nor should great efforts be invested to produce trivial data.

Key Questions

B-1. Is there a full description, in non-technical language, of the research design, including a definition of what is measured and how the data are collected? _____

---

*Advertising Research Foundation, *Guidelines for the Public Use of Market and Opinion Research*, 1981, 5.
†Ibid., 6.
‡Ibid., 6.
**Ibid., 7–8.

Guidelines for the Public Use of Market and Opinion Research (*continued*)

B-2. Is the design consistent with the stated purpose for which the research was conducted? _____

B-3. Is the design evenhanded, that is, is it free of leading questions and other bias; does it address questions of fact and opinion without inducing answers that unfairly benefit the study sponsors? _____

B-4. Have precautions been taken to avoid or equalize patterns of sequence or timing or other factors that might prejudice or distort the findings? _____

B-5. Does it address questions which respondents are capable of answering? _____

B-6. Is there a precise statement of the universe or population the research is meant to represent? _____

B-7. Does the sampling source or frame fairly represent the population under study? _____

B-8. Does the report specify the kind of sample used, and clearly describe the method of sample selection? _____

B-9. Does the report describe the plan for analysis of the data? _____

B-10. Are copies of all questionnaire forms, field and sampling instructions and other study materials available to anyone with a legitimate interest in the research? _____

Quality Checkpoints

B-11. Does the study use a random sample—that is, one which gives every member of the sampling frame an equal or known chance of selection? _____

B-12. Does the research use procedures for the selection of respondents that are not subject to the orientation or convenience of the interviewers? _____

B-13. If the research calls for continuing panels or repeated studies are there unbiased ways to update or rotate the original sample? _____

B-14. In field use, would the questionnaire hold the interest and attention of the respondents and the interviewer? _____

B-15. Is the information asked for limited to what people can supply and can reasonably be expected to give openly and accurately? _____

B-16. Are study or test conditions or responses relevant to the situation to which the findings are supposed to relate? _____

B-17. Where controls or other products are involved, are they the appropriate ones to be included? _____

B-18. Was the plan for analysis set up and agreed to before the data were collected? _____

a. Do you think the criteria given above in the guidelines, key questions, and quality checkpoints for the design of research for public use are also applicable to evaluating a proposal for research to be used in decision making in a company? Why or why not?

b. Do you think there are criteria that are applicable for evaluating the design of research projects for the private use of a company that are not stated in the guidelines, key questions, or quality checkpoints listed above? Explain.

MARKETING PROGRAMS: MANAGING THE MARKETING MIX

IV

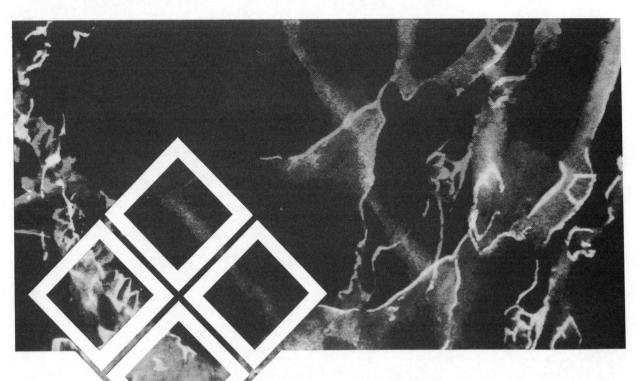

Developing well-chosen marketing strategies and making appropriate marketing plans to implement them are obviously critically important parts of the marketing manager's job. The most carefully formulated marketing strategies and the best-laid marketing plans will be effective only if the day-by-day management of the marketing mix elements is carried out properly, however.

The continuing decisions made with respect to products, prices, promotion, and distribution occupy most of the marketing manager's time. Reasoned choices between alternatives can only be based on assessments of the likely effects each would have on the behavior of one or more market participants—distributors, customers, competitors, or others. Since the accuracy of predictions concerning human behavior is always suspect, the decisions are difficult to make and subject to error. Managing the marketing program effectively is therefore not an easy task.

The chapters in this section begin with product management (Chapter 11) and product line management, brand management, and the product life cycle (Chapter 12). From there the progression is through pricing decisions (Chapter 13), communication planning (Chapter 14), advertising, sales promotion, and public relations management (Chapter 15), and personal selling and sales management (Chapter 16). The section ends with chapters on distribution management (Chapter 17) and retailing and wholesaling management (Chapter 18).

CHAPTER 11

PRODUCT MANAGEMENT

The products or services offered by a company are the economic reasons for its existence. They are the central variables in the company's marketing efforts. They limit the markets that can be entered, the range of prices that can be charged, the kinds of advertising that can be used, and the distribution channels that can be employed. Without sound decisions concerning the products or services it is to offer, the company will ultimately fail regardless of how well it carries out the remainder of its marketing program and its finance and production functions.

In a dynamic, competitive economy, the products and services offered by the companies in an industry are in a constant state of flux. Consumers are provided with a choice of products that change continuously in number, quality, functions, features, form, color, and size. Industrial buyers are faced with a similarly changing set of products to serve their companies' needs. Users of services—be it transportation, financial, medical, or any of the myriad other services available—are likewise presented with an ever-varying set of offerings from which to choose. Although these changes add variety to and extend the range of customer choice, they complicate the lives of the managers whose jobs are concerned with the development or acquisition of new products and services for a company.

In this chapter we consider the management decisions concerned with the *addition* of new products and services. Since we agree with Wind that the "general product concepts and methods discussed in the context of frequently purchased products are equally applicable to services,"[1] we do not discuss the

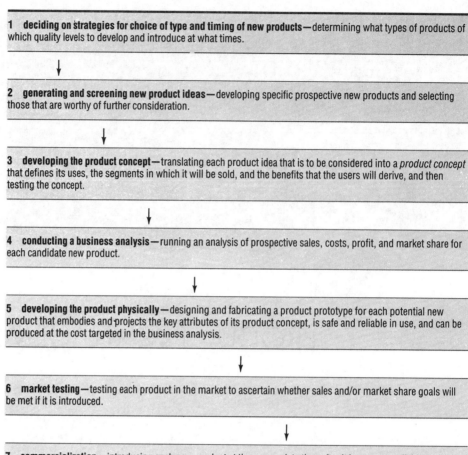

1 deciding on strategies for choice of type and timing of new products—determining what types of products of which quality levels to develop and introduce at what times.

2 generating and screening new product ideas—developing specific prospective new products and selecting those that are worthy of further consideration.

3 developing the product concept—translating each product idea that is to be considered into a *product concept* that defines its uses, the segments in which it will be sold, and the benefits that the users will derive, and then testing the concept.

4 conducting a business analysis—running an analysis of prospective sales, costs, profit, and market share for each candidate new product.

5 developing the product physically—designing and fabricating a product prototype for each potential new product that embodies and projects the key attributes of its product concept, is safe and reliable in use, and can be produced at the cost targeted in the business analysis.

6 market testing—testing each product in the market to ascertain whether sales and/or market share goals will be met if it is introduced.

7 commercialization—introducing each new product at the appropriate time after it becomes available to the market.

FIGURE 11-1
Management decision areas
for new products.

addition of services per se. Product *elimination* decisions are discussed in the next chapter.

The management decisions concerning new products center on the steps of (1) the strategies for choice of type and timing of new products; (2) generation and screening of new product ideas; (3) development and choice of concepts; (4) analysis of prospective company sales, costs, profits, and cash flows; (5) physical development of the product; (6) market testing; and (7) commercialization. These decision areas are shown in Figure 11–1 and are discussed in order in the succeeding sections of the chapter.

STRATEGIC CONSIDERATIONS IN ADDING NEW PRODUCTS

Underlying Business Strategies That Define New Product Roles

Before development is begun, the management of a company should identify the strategic role(s) that a new product will be expected to satisfy.[2] As described in Chapter 2, these roles can be defined in terms of the underlying strategies of the company. Other than financial strategies, they include the following:

Market-Related Strategies

1. Offset seasonal or cyclical sales lulls
2. Round out a product line
3. Realize marketing efficiencies
4. Combat competitive entry
5. Exploration
6. Defend market share position
7. Increase market share

Engineering or Production-Related Strategies

8. Utilize technical capability
9. Use production expertise or excess capacity
10. Use by-products of existing products

Risk-Related Strategies

11. Diversification to reduce risk

Management Preference

12. Owner/manager preference

How well these strategic roles are carried out is dependent in part on the type of new product introduced.

Types of "New" Products

What constitutes "newness" in a product? When does a product have enough of these newness attributes to be called a *new* product? What are the types of *new* products?

> **The Handheld Kodak Camera—A "New" Product?**
>
> The first camera was sold commercially in the United States in 1839. It was a "wet-plate" camera that required sensitizing of a glass plate with a nitrate emulsion. The plate had to be developed in a darkroom, or in a dark tent if the picture was taken in the field, immediately after the picture was taken.
>
> In 1888 the Eastman Dry Plate and Film Company—the predecessor of Eastman Kodak—introduced the first Kodak camera. It was a handheld camera loaded with enough film for 100 pictures. The camera and the exposed film were returned to the company to have the film developed, prints made, and the camera reloaded.
>
> Most would agree that the wet-plate camera was a "new" product. For the first time, images could be made by a process other than drawing,

tracing, carving, or sculpting. Both the image and the process by which it was created were sufficiently different from the earlier ones to qualify the camera as a new product. But was the handheld Kodak introduced by Eastman almost 50 years later also a "new" product?

In answering the questions raised above, it is useful to define a "new" product as falling into one of three different categories. These are:

Innovative new products. Products that involve a substantial amount of innovation in function, features, or form. The original camera is an example of this type of new product.

Emulative new products. Products that are copied (with some variation) from existing products of one or more other companies by a company that does not have a product in the same line. IBM's first computer, which followed the Univac 1 of the Sperry Co., is an example.

Adaptive new products. Products that involve adaptations in function, features, or form from another product of the same company that are perceived by the consumer as being new. The adaptation by Kodak of the "wet plate" to the handheld camera is an example.

Note that the characteristic making the product "new" in each of three categories is different. The innovative product is technologically new in important respects and so is *new to the economy*. The emulative product is not new technologically but is *new to the company*. The adaptive product is neither new to the economy nor to the company and so, when they perceive it to be so, is only *new to the consumer*.

The differences in the marketing implications of these three types of "new" products are substantial. They involve differing risks and potential rewards for differing time periods. The strategies involved in the **development** and **introduction** of the three kinds of new products are therefore necessarily different also.

Strategic Considerations Concerning Innovative versus Emulative Products

Whereas all companies adapt their existing products more or less regularly, most of them tend to be predominantly either innovators or emulators with respect to developing other new products. These two approaches to product development and the characteristics often associated with each have been described as follows:

The *innovator* typically establishes competitive new product leadership by building on technological advantages, undertakes preemptive marketing strategies, and invests heavily in the development and launching of new products. In contrast, the *follower* (emulator) often maintains a low risk profile, seeks low manufacturing costs, and reacts to competition by generating "second but better" new products.[3]

There is no evidence to indicate that one of these strategies is necessarily better than the other. Either can yield satisfactory results. The innovator strategy is a higher-cost one and therefore requires more resources to implement it. Beyond this requirement, the choice between the two is largely a matter of management preference.

Strategic Considerations for Adaptive Products

Although emulative and innovative products can potentially be developed (or acquired) that will meet any of the strategic roles required of them, it is apparent that adaptive products are much better suited to meeting some of them than others. For example, an adaptive product might be well suited to *help round out a product line*, to *increase marketing efficiency*, to *utilize excess production capacity*, or to *capitalize on distribution strengths*. However, it is not likely to be effective in offsetting seasonal sales declines, in using by-products from the production of existing products, or in reducing risk through diversification.

Acquisition versus Internal Development of New Products

It is not uncommon for a merger or an acquisition decision to be made primarily on the basis of financial decisions with little consideration being given to the product additions that accompany it. Yet virtually every acquisition or merger of one manufacturing or service company by or with another is accompanied by the addition of products that are "new" to the surviving organization. Licensing and joint ventures are other external sources of new products.

An alert management will keep external sources in mind as a potentially viable alternative to the internal development of new products. An external source may be faster and less expensive while, in the case of a merger or acquisition, having the added benefit of reducing competition as well. Wind provides an excellent discussion of this method of adding new products.[4]

Strategy Regarding Product Quality

What quality level(s) should the product have? Should it be a low-quality product that is to be sold at a low price, a high-quality product with a high price, or a range of products of varying qualities and prices?

The general relationship between product quality and profitability as determined from analysis of data for more than 500 businesses in the PIMS (Profit Impact of Marketing Strategy) project is shown in Figure 11–2. As indicated

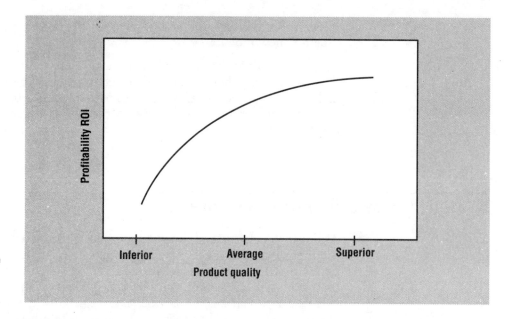

FIGURE 11-2
The relationship of product quality
and profitability.

there, profits tend to increase with an increase in quality over a wide quality range. However, profitability does not increase at the same rate as quality and eventually levels off and may then decline. This suggests that if a single quality level is to be chosen and profitability is a major consideration in the choice, a superior (but not extremely high) quality product will generally be the best choice.[5]

The strategic choice of developing more than one version of the product, each with a different quality level, turns on how the market is segmented:

If there are identifiable segments at differing price-quality levels and each of these segments is accessible and of a sufficient size to make entering it worthwhile, then multiple quality levels may be appropriate.

If a low-quality, low-price segment is entered, the PIMS data show clearly that marketing expenditures should be kept low.

For products of inferior quality, even average marketing expenditures decrease profitability somewhat, and high marketing expenses depress it severely.

One must therefore depend on price to carry the bulk of the marketing effort for low-quality products rather than advertising, promotion, and personal selling.[6]

Strategies of Timing of Introducing New Products

In for-profit companies, the driving concern in introducing new products is to maximize profits for the relevant planning period. This does not always mean that introducing a new product sooner, rather than later, is to be preferred, however.

Products often either cannot or should not be introduced as soon as the decision to do so has been made. There may not be adequate production capability immediately available to support an introduction; market test quantities are often produced in a pilot plant with the expenditures for a full-scale production facility delayed until the test results are known, or the condition of the market may not be propitious. If the product sales are seasonal or cyclical in nature, it may be appropriate to wait until the appropriate stage before introducing. If the product is an adaptive one, it may be desirable to wait until present inventories of the parent product are exhausted, or nearly so, before replacing it with the new product. (Publishers sometimes delay the introduction of a new textbook until the inventory of a book that is likely to be replaced is depleted, for example.)

It may be desirable to wait to introduce a new adaptive product even if inventories of the parent product are already low for reasons of an expected high cannibalization rate of parent product sales. *Cannibalization* occurs when part of the sales of the new product come at the expense of sales of the parent product. (The opposite, *complementary sales*, occur when a new product complements an existing one and results in increased sales of the existing product.) Since there are additional costs of having both the parent and the adaptive product on the market—two production lines, two inventories, and two sets of shipping costs rather than one—if the cannibalization rate is expected to be very high it may be preferable to wait to introduce the new product until sales of the product susceptible to being cannibalized begin to falter. (This practice was followed routinely by IBM in the 1960s and 1970s, for example, to avoid making its mainframe computers on lease obsolete.)

IDEA GENERATION

Generating Product Ideas

Ideas for new products can come from a variety of sources, both those that are incidental to and those that are organized for product-idea-generating purposes. The incidental or unsolicited sources include customers, company sales representatives and dealers, competitors, employee suggestions, and patent disclosures. The formally organized or solicited sources include consumer research projects, research and development departments, and such idea-generating techniques as brainstorming, reverse brainstorming, synectics, attribute listing, and problem inventory analysis.

One should always be alert to unsolicited suggestions for new products, as they can be creative and worthwhile. Legend has it that the founder of the Coca-Cola Company paid five dollars for a slip of paper on which were written two words of advice on how the business of selling syrup to soda fountains could be changed profitably. (The words were, of course, "bottle it.")[7] For most of its corporate life, however, the Coca-Cola Company appropriately has maintained a corporate research and development department and has carried out an active and continuing program of consumer research. Unsolicited sources are neither systematic nor dependable sources of new product ideas.

Solicited Sources of New Product Ideas: Consumer Research Projects

Since customers are the users and the ultimate arbiters of what "good" products should be, they are a logical group from which to solicit new product ideas and on which to test proposed new products before they are introduced.

There are several methods in general use to identify consumer needs and desires. These include (1) conducting **surveys of consumers** in which they are asked directly about problems with existing products and ideas for new products; (2) holding **focus group sessions** in which 8 to 12 people are asked to talk about a line of products, what they think of them, how they use them, and how they could be improved; (3) obtaining information on product dimensions and ratings so that **preference maps** of existing products can be prepared and analyzed to find product configurations not now on the market; and (4) using new-product-idea generating techniques such as **attribute listing** and **problem inventory analysis** (described below).

Some companies have gone one step further in formalizing the process of obtaining product information from consumers by setting up **consumer panels**. These are groups of users of the product(s) of interest that provide reactions and information at the company's request. General Electric and General Foods are examples of companies that maintain such panels.

Solicited Sources of New Project Ideas: Company Research Projects

Research and Development Departments: The activities of "research" and of "development" are important sources of new product ideas. In one survey conducted by the consulting firm of Booz, Allen, and Hamilton, it was found that slightly more than one-half of all new product ideas come from the R&D departments of the companies surveyed. Although there may have been some confusion in this study of the original and the proximate source of the idea for the new product, the fact remains that a well-managed R&D department is a critically important source of new product ideas as well as the means of developing them into viable products.

Brainstorming: This is the term applied to a process developed by Osborn[8] by which a group generates potential answers for a problem that is posed. The

Table 11–1 Sources of New Product Ideas

Sources	Description
Unsolicited	
Customers	Customer letters and telephone calls
Employees	Unsolicited suggestions from service and sales representatives, other employees
Competitors	New products market tested, introduced by competitors
Dealers	Letters, telephone calls, casual mention to sales representatives
Patent disclosures	Independent inventors, other companies filing for patents
Solicited	
Consumer research projects	Surveys, focus groups, problem inventory analysis, preference maps, consumer panels, attribute listing, other types of research
Research and development	Ideas based on technological development developments
Employee suggestion programs	Employee suggestion boxes, programs providing monetary awards for usable product ideas
Employee research projects	Focus groups, analysis, brainstorming, synectics attribute listing, problem inventory analysis, other techniques

group is convened, the problem is stated (in this case, to suggest possible new products for the company that are related to the present product lines), and the following ground rules for the meeting are given:

1. *There is to be no criticism.* No evaluative statements, either with respect to one's own suggestions or to those of others, are to be made.
2. *Unusual solutions are encouraged.* Participants are told that they should try to think of solutions that may seem impractical or even ridiculous at the time, as well as those that seem more sensible.
3. *As many answers as possible are desired.* The greater the number of possible solutions, the more likely it will be that one or more of them will be useful.
4. *Combinations and variations are sought.* Participants are encouraged to combine the ideas of others and to suggest variations of them, as well as to generate suggestions of their own.[9]

The technique is easy to use and typically results in large numbers of product ideas being suggested. An example of its use is described in the box below.

One brainstorming session concerned finding new uses for and product variations of a kitchen cleaning pad. It is made of colored nylon mesh and is roughly the size and shape of a bar of soap. Seventy-eight suggestions for new uses or variations were made in the course of a 45-minute session including enlarging it and selling it as a beanbag chair; and coloring the mesh red and green, making it round and somewhat smaller, and marketing it as an unbreakable Christmas tree ornament.

Reverse Brainstorming: For generating new product ideas, the participants in a reverse brainstorming session start with a particular product concept and try to identify as many shortcomings of it as possible. The resulting list of negative attributes then provides a starting point for discussion of mutations or improvements.

Although reverse brainstorming was not used in the case of the nylon mesh cleaning pad, had it been it no doubt would have resulted in a number of significant shortcomings of the product being recognized. Included among these would have been such negative attributes as the fact that it has no soap incorporated in it and so it must rely on the (limited) abrasiveness of the nylon mesh for cleaning, and it has no sponging capability. These negative features of the product would have sparked some obvious ideas for variations of the product.

Synectics: Synectics is a variation of the brainstorming technique. Its originator, William J. J. Gordon, believed that specifying the problem at the outset of a session reduces the range of alternative solutions suggested and that creativity is higher among persons who are moderately fatigued. His adaptation of brainstorming was then to start the session with a very general problem statement and to narrow it only when the discussion at that stage indicated that additional alternatives were not likely to be forthcoming. Through a series of successively more specifically derived problem descriptions (and suggested alternative solutions for them), an opportunity was presented both for wider-ranging alternatives to be generated and for greater creativity to be developed through the fatigue induced by the added time required.

If this technique had been employed for generating ideas for improving the nylon mesh cleaning pad, for example, the moderator might have started the session with a statement that the problem was that of "cleaning." That might have resulted in evoking a discussion of cleaning agents such as soaps, detergents, abrasives, ultrasonic sound, solvents, bleaches, water, and steam, and cleaning methods such as scrubbing, vibrating, beating, rubbing, tumbling, and soaking. The problem might then gradually have been narrowed through successive specifications of it as household cleaning, cleaning in the kitchen, cleaning of dishes and cookware, and, finally, cleaning of those articles using a handheld pad. By this point, the session might have lasted as long as three hours, the minimum time that Gordon believes is necessary to allow the creative potential of the group to be reached.

The Campbell Soup Company makes regular use of synectics. As a result of a synectics session on how chicken could be used, three new products containing chicken were developed and introduced.[10]

Attribute Listing: This technique involves listing the attributes of an actual or potential product and then modifying one or more of them to improve the product. An example of the use of attribute listing is in the improvement of the design of the pallets (portable wooden platforms used for storing and moving materials and products in factories and warehouses) manufactured by a small company:

> The company . . . listed the attributes that defined the existing pallets, such as wood composition, rectangular runners, and accessible on two sides by a fork lift. Then each of these attributes was examined for any change(s) that would improve the satisfaction of the user's need, for example, the wood composition could be changed to plastic, resulting in a cheaper price; the rectangular wooden runners could be replaced by cups for easier storing, and the cups would allow the new pallet to be accessible on all four sides for ease of pick-up.*

*R. D. Hisrich and M. P. Peters, *Marketing a New Product: Its Planning, Development, and Control,* Benjamin/Cummings Publishing, 1978, 58.

In this case, a **substitution** was used to change one attribute (plastic for wood), and a **modification** was made in another (cups for runners). Osborn lists nine potential ways of changing attributes or uses of products that should be considered when using this technique: put to other uses, adapt, modify, minify, magnify, substitute, rearrange, reverse, and combine.[12]

Problem Inventory Analysis: Users of a product may be generally unsatisfied with it but, if approached and asked directly how it could be improved, may not be able to offer useful suggestions. For example, you very likely have used rubber cement and you may not be entirely satisfied with it as a product. Yet if asked how it should be improved, you might well have trouble giving a useful response.

A technique for assisting users in identifying problems with products, and thus helping them make suggestions for improvements, is problem inventory analysis. The use of this technique involves first developing a list of problems that are associated with the product class in general. Such a list is usually developed initially within the company manufacturing the product and then augmented by focus group sessions of distributors and users. The inventory is then presented to a sample of users, and each is asked to identify the problems associated with using the particular product of interest.

An example of the use of this technique is by a manufacturer of rubber cement. The inventory of problems associated with using adhesives in general, shown in Table 11–2, was first developed. It was then shown to a sample of consumers and office workers and to a sample of distributors, who were each asked to identify any problems they had had with rubber cement. The principal problems turned out to be associated with the container. A glass bottle that was used for the product was tall relative to the size of the base and had a brush attached to the inside of the lid. Most users indicated that they had had problems with the bottle tipping over, the bottle breaking when dropped, the brush breaking off the lid, and the cement drying in the container. The problems identified by the distributors were primarily those of breakage and of the cement drying out before it was sold.

As a result, the company decided to redesign the container. Plastic was used instead of glass, and the bottle was made shorter and wider. A smaller lid was

Table 11–2 Problem Inventory Analysis for Adhesives

Adhesive quality	Application
Not strong initially	Must clean surfaces
Weakens over time	Must mix two or more ingredients
Will not make bonds of	Have to supply multiple coats
Metal to metal	Can only be applied within restricted temperature
Low metal to metal	range
Plastic to plastic	Must use clamps due to drying too slowly
Nonplastic to plastic	Difficult to apply
Fabric to fabric	Difficult to remove excess
Nonfabric to fabric	
Nonwood to wood	Use effects
Paper to paper	Shows through wood stains
Nonpaper to paper	Causes bubbles when painted over
Not waterproof	Discolors papers and fabrics
Can only be used on articles that later will be	Difficult to remove from clothing
subject to a restricted temperature range	
	Marketing
Physiological effects	Not sold in bulk
Toxic fumes	Not widely available
Toxic if swallowed	Expensive
Bad for skin	
Bad for eyes	
Difficult to remove from person	
Container	
Dries in container	
Bottle breaks	
Brush breaks off bottle lid	
Bottle tips easily	
Tube cracks	
Tube top becomes cemented to tube	
No applicator	
Not reusable	

used that was especially designed to provide a tighter seal and to be molded with the brush as an integral unit.[12]

SCREENING NEW PRODUCT IDEAS

If the company has been at all systematic about the way in which new product ideas were generated, the result will be that more—usually *many* more—potential new products will have been suggested than could reasonably be developed and marketed. The task at this stage is to select from among the ideas developed those that are worthy of further consideration.

The percentage of ideas discarded in the screening stage is quite high. One study of the experience of 700 manufacturing companies indicates that approximately 70 percent of all new product ideas were dropped during the screening process.[13]

Product idea should be	Product idea is actually	
	Retained	Dropped
Retained	Good decision	DROP error
Dropped	RETAIN error	Good decision

The potential for error is large in the screening process. Two types of errors can be made: to retain an idea when it should be dropped (RETAIN error), and to drop an idea that should be retained (DROP error).

The relatively high rates of new product failures following introduction attest to the fact the RETAIN errors are made all too frequently. And corporate folklore is full of stories about missed opportunities because of DROP errors. One concerns the Coca-Cola Company in its early years:

In 1899 Asa Chandler . . . disposed of the right to bottle Coke throughout practically the entire United States for one dollar, which he didn't bother to collect. The recipients of this largess were two young Chattanooga lawyers, and it is no fable that for their unpaid dollar they obtained a franchise that came to be worth hundreds of millions.*

*E. J. Kahn, Jr. *The Big Drink: The Story of Coca-Cola,* Random House, 1950, p. 69.

Approaches to Screening New Product Ideas

The Uniwrench, an adjustable combination wrench, is a new concept that integrates desirable features of adjustable wrenches and combination wrenches in a single tool. It has both an open end and a box end which simultaneously fit a wide range of metric and standard sizes. If produced in quantity, the estimated cost per wrench is approximately $3. It is expected to be directly competitive with adjustable wrenches having an annual market in excess of $25 million.[14]

Suppose you were given the assignment of setting up the screening procedure for the Uniwrench. What alternative methods should you consider? How should you go about choosing the procedure to be used for this product?

Alternative Product Screening Procedures

The alternative methods you could choose from range from the use of unaided executive judgment up through highly formal procedures requiring each person involved to rate the prospective product on a number of different attributes.[15] Examples of these two contrasting approaches are given below by the procedures that could be used by a committee concerned with the screening of new products.

Assume that a New Product Idea Screening Committee is to be used that consists of the president (who will chair it); the vice-presidents of finance, production, engineering, and marketing; the directors of research and development and of marketing research; and the corporate counsel. If the committee is informally operated, a decision on the Uniwrench might be reached as follows:

> A meeting of the Committee is called to consider the Uniwrench. The research and development director distributes drawings of the prospective product and discusses its technical features. The marketing research director then presents the results of a preliminary market study for the product. Questions are asked as appropriate. The president then asks for comments from each of the vice-presidents and the corporate counsel. Members again raise any questions that they have. When there are no more questions, a vote is taken to retain or discard the Uniwrench product idea.

A formally operated New Product Idea Screening Committee might operate in the same way through the information-gathering-and-dissemination phase. The decision would be made differently, however. One commonly used method is as follows:

> After a meeting of the Committee to provide information on the Uniwrench and prospects for its commercialization, each member is asked to rate it on a form such as the one on page 360. (An example of a set of ratings is given on the form.) The product idea is then retained or dropped depending on whether the average ratings exceed a prescribed minimum value.

New Product Idea Rating Form

Please rate the proposed new product on a scale of 1 to 10 (10 is the most favorable) on each of the attributes listed below*:

Weight	Attribute	Rating	Weighted Rating
.25	*Market demand* (potential market, potential sales, trend and stability of demand, length of product life cycle)	5	1.25
.25	*Market acceptance* (need, ease of use, promotion, distribution effectiveness)	4	1.00
.20	*Social considerations* (legality, safety, environmental and social effects)	10	2.00
.15	*Competition* (level of present and prospective competition, relative quality and price, prospects for patent protection)	4	0.60
.15	*Risk* (engineering and production capability, investment required, estimated profitability, payback period)	3	0.45
	Total		<u>5.30</u>

*These attributes and their descriptions are adapted from K. G. Baker, "The Comparative Analysis of Models for Use in New Product Screening Decisions," Ph.D. diss., University of Oregon, 1980, 145.

You will recognize that if your choice is to use a formal rating procedure such as the one described above, your task of developing a screening procedure would not be complete until you had decided on a method of translating ratings into a RETAIN or DROP decision. At least two decision rules could be used for this purpose, the compensatory and the conjunctive rules.

If the **compensatory rule** were applied, it would involve (1) assigning weights to each attribute, (2) multiplying each attribute rating by its assigned weight, (3) summing the weighting ratings over all attributes, and (4) establishing a cut-off point such that new product ideas with total weighted ratings equal to or higher than it are retained and those lower than it are discarded. If the cut-off had been higher than 5.30 in the example, the Uniwrench product idea would not have been retained for further consideration.

The **conjunctive rule** requires (1) assigning a minimum required rating to each attribute and (2) discarding any product idea that has a rating below the minimum for any attribute. In the example above, if the minimum rating for each attribute had been set at any value above 3, the product idea would have been rejected.

The one study that has been done that allows a comparison of these two rules for a new product idea screening indicates that the conjunctive rule is superior.[16] Intuitively, it is reasonable that some minimum level of performance on each attribute is required for commercial success; a strong market demand cannot compensate for the fact that the proposed new product would not fare well against the established competition, for example.

Choosing the Screening Method

This section began with your supposed assignment to the task of selecting a screening method for a specific new product idea. How would you go about making such a choice?

A systematic method of choosing the screening method would involve (1) setting up the criteria that you would like the chosen procedure to meet, (2) examining how well or poorly each alternative procedure meets each criterion, and (3) choosing the procedure that most nearly meets the criteria.

The appropriate criteria include the following:

1. Low cost
2. Fast
3. Adaptable
4. Easily understood
5. Easily carried out
6. Requires explicit consideration of all relevant criteria
7. Easily communicable results
8. Provides learning potential
9. Acceptance by management

The first five of these criteria are tilted slightly in favor of an informal procedure. Such a procedure costs less, is somewhat faster, can be more easily adapted, is more readily understood, and is more easily implemented. The advantages of informality stop there, however. A formal system is more likely to require consideration of all relevant variables, and so provides an easier and more assured form of communication about them. In addition, the requirement for all evaluators to consider all the variables permits the discovery of areas in which there are differences in evaluator judgments and so makes for greater interchange of information. Over the course of several evaluations, learning will take place, and better evaluations on the part of the participants are likely to result.

A critical factor in choosing a screening procedure is to ensure that it will be acceptable to those who are to use it. If it is not fully accepted, it is likely to be bypassed and eventually dropped. An inferior procedure that will be used is better than a superior one that is not used. One investigator has concluded that, given that an existing formal model is used, it will probably be satisfactory since "... the common decision criteria used by all managers far outweigh the firm specific criteria in importance."[17] However, another researcher has concluded that managers are more likely to use formal models and make better decisions if the managers have participated in their development and the models reflect their specific problem and mode of decision making.[18] This suggests that limited customizing of an existing formal model might be an appropriate method of developing a screening model.

CONCEPT DEVELOPMENT AND TESTING

A *product concept* is a product idea that has been defined in terms of the uses, the segments in which it will be sold, and the benefits that the users will derive.

Consider the following alternative product concepts for some well-known products:

Arm & Hammer Baking Soda
Concept 1:
  Application: An ingredient for baking.
  Benefit: A reliable product with a low level of impurities that does not cause baking failures.
Concept 2:
  Application: Refrigerator odor absorbent.
  Benefit: Results in a "sweeter, cleaner, fresher-smelling" refrigerator.

Apple Computers
Concept 1:
  Application: Home computer.
  Benefit: Provides a word processor, home amusement center for playing computerized games, record keeping, and home security systems.
Concept 2:
  Application: Small business computer.
  Benefit: Record keeping and invoicing.
Concept 3:
  Application: Educational computer.
  Benefit: Provides a means of training students in the use of computers, allows researchers to have a personal computer for analysis of data.

General Motors "J" Car
Concept 1:
  Application: Family second car.
  Benefit: Designed to make transporting children and carrying groceries easy, low-priced, economical.
Concept 2:
  Application: Commuter car.
  Benefit: Designed for comfortably transporting four adults, low-priced, economical.

It is clear from these examples that the same products, even in the same physical form, can have different product concepts. When Church and Dwight (manufacturers of Arm & Hammer) began advertising its baking soda for use in deodorizing refrigerators, for example, it was employing a different concept of the product. Yet no changes were made in the package or its contents.

Concept Testing Techniques

Once candidate product concepts are developed, a screening of them must be made. There are several questions for which answers are required before a sound choice of concepts can be made. They include:[19]

1. Is the concept fully understandable? The concept of a home computer as a family amusement center may not be readily understandable by many potential customers.
2. Does this product solve a problem or meet a need for you or other members of your family that other products on the market do not satisfy? (If "yes," what is the problem or need? How important is it that it be taken care of?) There was no other refrigerator deodorizer on the market at the time the Arm & Hammer management first considered advertising their baking soda as one. But was there a perceived

need for such a product? And, if so, was it important that it be taken care of?

3. What improvements can you suggest for the product? Should the commuter car have reduced trunk space to provide more room for passengers? Should the family car have special safety features for children, a hatchback for easier loading and unloading of groceries?
4. What would you expect this product's price to be?
5. Would you buy it if it were available at that price?

Describing the Concept

These questions have to be answered by potential buyers and users, not company personnel. To get such answers, one must first find a satisfactory way of describing or depicting the product concept and then devise a method of obtaining and analyzing answers that is as reliable and as valid as possible.

Some product concepts are easy to convey. The use of an open box of baking soda as a refrigerator deodorizer is easily understood from a short, simple description, for example. Adequately describing other product concepts may pose some severe problems, however. In automobile design, for example, it is difficult to describe space in terms of comfort: How comfortable the car would be with respect to seating, leg, and head room and ease of getting in and out are not readily describable in easy-to-understand terms. General Motors has used both **pictorial representations** and full-scale clay **mock-ups** as means of conveying information on space and comfort factors to the respondent. (The use of full-scale mock-ups of course required that the respondents be brought to a showroom before they were questioned.)[20]

Questioning Consumers

Care must also be taken in how one asks questions and interprets responses. The testing of the baking soda-for-refrigerators concept provides an example:

> Church and Dwight, makers of Arm & Hammer baking soda, had known for years that its product, left open in a refrigerator, would absorb food odors. However, a marketing research company, using prestructured questionnaires, had asked hundreds of women, "Do you have an odor problem in your refrigerator?" Virtually all had replied, "No, I do not."
>
> There was some indication that, although the respondents didn't think they had a food-odor problem, they would like protection against the possibility of such a problem. Another round of research was authorized in which housewives were presented with a rough ad that said, "Here's a nice little secret for your refrigerator. An open box of Arm & Hammer Baking Soda actually absorbs food odors . . . keeps your refrigerator sweeter, cleaner, and fresher smelling."
>
> The women who saw the ad reacted very favorably. Church and Dwight decided to disregard the earlier research and advertise this new use for baking soda. The results were immediate and almost overwhelming. Within months, there were literally millions of open boxes of Arm & Hammer baking soda in the refrigerators.*

*Edited excerpt from E. Potischman, "How to Breathe New Life into Your Old Brand," *Advertising Age,* July 16, 1973, 39, 40, 44.

A widely used evaluative technique is to present the concept in a written, pictorial, or finished print or television ad form to each of a sample of 200–400 persons and then to ask an intention-to-buy question. The question is often asked using a five-point scale, such as the following:

> After having (read the concept statement, seen the ad), if this product were available at your (supermarket, drugstore, department store), how likely would you be to buy it? Would you say that you:
>
> - would definitely buy it?
> - would probably buy it?
> - might or might not buy it?
> - would probably not buy it?
> - would definitely not buy it?[21]

The percentage of respondents who give the most favorable answer is often used for predictive purposes. Once a company has used this technique on a number of products that were subsequently introduced, it is possible to set up a cut-off score for separating the predicted "winning" from the "losing" concepts. For example, if at least 35 percent of the respondents marked the top choice for products that were introduced and turned out to be successful, this cut-off score can be established to determine which concepts are to undergo further product development.[22]

An alternative is to use the score obtained from the percentage who mark one of the two top choices. Taylor[23] studied the predictive accuracy of intention-to-buy questions with respect to branded grocery products and concluded, based on experience with over 100 brands in several product categories, that subsequent development work should not proceed unless 80–90 percent of the respondents give "definitely would buy" or "probably would buy" answers at the concept testing stage. With a prototype product that the respondents can use before answering the buying intention question, the "definitely would buy" responses should be at the 70–80 percent level to warrant continuing development, according to these researchers.

A technique that has rapidly gained acceptance and usage for concept testing since the early 1970s is **_conjoint analysis_**. It enables one to test several alternative configurations of a product (various levels of quality features, package designs, brand names, and piece combinations, for example) by obtaining rank-ordered preferences from respondents. Measures of consumer utilities are obtained for each level of each attribute tested, as well as overall consumer preferences for the various product configurations.[24]

Other questions are also asked of respondents during the tests. They include questions to determine how well the concept is understood, whether it meets a need felt by the respondent, to what extent the respondent now uses brands in the product class, and what the respondent thinks the price ought to be, and questions to determine demographic and psychographic characteristics for segmentation purposes.

Once an acceptable product concept has evolved, a tentative marketing program needs to be devised. The questions that need to be addressed at this stage include:

1. What are the target market segments for the product?
2. How will it be positioned within those segments?
3. What ranges of sizes or models will be offered?
4. What will the introductory price be for each of these product versions? How will they be priced after the introductory period?
5. How will we distribute the product?
6. How will we advertise and promote it? How much do we expect to budget for advertising and promotion for each of the first five years after introduction?
7. What is our target sales volume for each of the first five years after introduction?
8. What is our target market share for each of the first five years?
9. What is the expected development period for the product? What is our expected cash flow for the development period and each of the first five years after introduction?

The answers to these questions are of course subject to change at later stages of the product development process. The Research and Development department may come up with new configurations of the product, cost estimates may be revised due to different production methods being planned, the market situation may change—all of these and many other changes may take place before introduction that will necessitate later strategy revisions. However, answers to the questions listed above, however tentative they may be, are needed for two reasons: to allow management to decide whether a full-fledged business analysis should be conducted, and to provide the information on the marketing mix variables that is necessary for conducting the business analysis.

BUSINESS ANALYSIS

Unless the product idea originated in the Research and Development department as a result of research being conducted there, relatively limited amounts will have been spent on the typical product idea to this point. It will have been originated, screened, and developed into a product concept, will have undergone a program of consumer testing, and will have had a tentative marketing strategy devised for it. The large expenditures are still to come, however; product development, market testing, and introduction all normally require sizable expenditures.

For this reason, it is important to conduct a business analysis at this time. The results of the business analysis will be used to make the decision on investing in the physical development of the product. The principal feature of the business analysis at this stage consists of projected cash flow statements. For this purpose, forecasts of the revenues, investment, and expenditures resulting from the introduction of the new product have to be made.

Forecasting Sales of New Products

Sales forecasts for *existing* products are used primarily to make operating decisions; those for *new* products are used to make investment as well as operating decisions. Operating decisions are usually made for a quarter or a year; investment decisions are almost always made for more than a year. A sales forecast for an existing product ordinarily may be made for the next year by quarter; a forecast by year for several years may be required for a new product. Sales forecasts for new products are therefore usually for longer periods than those for existing products. Although there is considerable variation among companies, and even among products within companies, as to the length of the forecast period, casual observation suggests that three to five years is the median period for new product sales forecasts.

The length of the period complicates the forecasting problem for new products for two reasons. The first is the obvious one that the farther out one has to forecast, the more difficult it becomes. The second complication arises from the need to forecast both **trial** and **repeat** (first and subsequent) purchases of the product.

Other than unaided judgment, there are two methods of making forecasts of trial purchases only. They are to:

1. Use the top choice ratings from the concept test Estimate the percentage of those who marked the top choice who will try the product by allowing for product category biases, seasonality, distribution buildup, and level of advertising and promotion.

2. Use the conjoint analysis results from the concept test Estimate the percentage of respondents who rated the concept as having the highest utility who will buy the product after allowing for seasonality, distribution buildup, and level of advertising and promotion.

Two other methods can be used to make estimates of both trial and repeat purchases. They are to:

3. Use the sales of analogous products that have been introduced Estimate the percentage of sales that this product will attain compared with those of a similar product in a similar market by allowing for product and marketing program differences.

4. Use of a historical data regression model Models developed by using a sample of past new products and employing regression to identify the effects of relative price, advertising and promotion levels, points of distribution obtained, and so forth. The planned levels of these variables are used in the model to predict the levels of trial and repeat purchases. Two of the better known examples are the N. W. Ayer and the National Purchase Diary models.[25]

The forecasting record of these methods is mixed. One observer has concluded that they can be used to predict the sales of adaptive and emulative products reasonably well, but they do not provide reliable forecasts for innovative products.[26]

Forecasting Investment and Operating Expenditures

Although investments and operating expenditures cannot be forecast with certainty, the range of error in the estimates of them is usually substantially less than that for sales. Forecasts have to be made of physical development costs, estimates, plant and equipment, marketing costs, costs of goods sold, and general and administrative expenses.

Methods of making these estimates were discussed in the chapter on financial evaluation of product markets (Chapter 9).

Preparation of Cash Flow Statements

The overall financial implications of these estimates of revenues and investment and operating expenditures are determined through the cash flow statement. The preparation of cash flow statements was discussed in Chapter 9. As described there, a series of statements consisting of "most likely," "optimistic," "pessimistic," and "mixed" are desirable. This assortment of statements gives management an understanding of the financial consequences of varying forecasts of revenues and expenditures, and permits a sounder assessment of rewards and risks of introducing the new product than does a single, "most likely" cash flow statement.

PHYSICAL DEVELOPMENT OF THE PRODUCT

We have been using the term *product development* to include all the stages involved in getting a new product on the market, beginning with generating the product idea and ending with its introduction. One of those stages is the *physical development* of the product, and it is with that connotation that we use the term here.

Effectively translating the product concept into an existing physical product requires the combined talents and efforts of R&D and of Marketing, and usually calls for a considerable amount of money and time. The effective coordination of R&D and Marketing is required because the final product design has to reflect user needs and perceptions as well as provide functional efficiency. Substantial expenditures of money and of time are typically necessary to allow for

(1) alternative designs to be drawn up and evaluated, (2) prototypes to be made and tested, (3) a brand name to be selected, and (4) a package to be developed.

Designing the Prototype

A *prototype* in product development is one of the early models of the product. It will not necessarily be identical to the final product (although it sometimes is), but it is expected that it will have its essential features.

The critical concern in the design of the prototype is that it meet user needs and perceptions. The product concept has to be translated into the physical product in such a way not only that essential specifications are met, but that the user also will *perceive* them as being met well.

Examples abound of product designs that actually meet desired specifications but are not perceived by the users as doing so. For example, the Chevrolet car of the mid 1930s was just as speedy as the newly introduced Ford V-8, but was not thought to be so because its accelerator was harder to depress (had a stiffer spring) than that of the Ford. Pringles, processed potato chips marketed by Proctor & Gamble, are uniform in size and shape, whereas consumers perceive "real" potato chips as having different shapes and sizes. The L-1011 airplane has a very good safety record, but many passengers believe it is unsafe because interior fittings rattle when it takes off and lands.

By reason of their training in engineering, R&D personnel are prone to concentrate on functional design specifications. Marketing must collaborate closely with R&D during the prototype design to ensure that user considerations get incorporated into the design as well.

Testing the Prototype

Once the prototype is designed and a sample of sufficient size is produced to do so, testing begins. Both **technical** and **use tests** normally are conducted.

Technical testing consists of both analysis tests and performance tests. **Analysis tests** are conducted to determine if the product meets the design specifications. Such tests are similar to the tests on units of the manufactured products that are conducted for quality-control purposes when the product is in production. **Performance tests** are carried out to determine how the product performs under actual use conditions—to answer such questions as "Does it wear as long as it should?" "Does its appearance hold up with continued use?" and the like.

Use tests are a critically important part of the testing program. One can never be sure how well consumers will receive the product or what problems may develop in using it until it has actually been used by a representative sample of consumers. The examples of bleach that caused fabrics to disintegrate when too much was used, lawnmowers that threw pebbles like projectiles when used on gravelly lawns, and canned dog food that exploded on pantry shelves are too many and too serious to allow one to assume that there "won't be any trouble with our product."

Use tests are best conducted on a representative sample of consumers. In general, in carrying out the tests it is desirable, when appropriate, to (1) not disclose the brand or the identity of the sponsor, (2) have different versions or formulations of your product used, (3) have your product used along with competitive products (whose identities also are not disclosed), and (4) interview the users to determine patterns of use, problems encountered (if any) attitudes toward the product, and purchase intention.

Naming and Branding

Choosing the brand name for the product is an important part of the product development process. If a family brand is used by the company to identify a product line within which this product could fall, should that same brand be used? If so, how is the new product to be distinguished from the other products carrying the same family brand? If not, what "stand-alone" brand name should be used? These and other questions deserve careful attention.

Since naming and branding are aspects of the overall management of the product line, they are discussed in the next chapter.

Packaging

The package is at once a part of the product sold and a communications medium. As a part of the product, the package should:

1. Protect the contents from breakage or spillage
2. Be easy to open, dispense from, and close
3. Be safe to use
4. Keep the product from deteriorating
5. Be of the proper size and shape for storage
6. Be reusable, able to be recycled, or biodegradable
7. Not be deceptive in size
8. Be available in the sizes appropriate to the market segments served
9. Be economical

These are the attributes that an *ideal* package for a product would have insofar as the use characteristics and its cost are concerned. It should be recognized, however, that realization of some of these characteristics may come at the partial expense of others. To design an aspirin bottle that is safe in homes with young children means that it must be difficult for them to open; if it is difficult for them to open, it will probably be somewhat difficult for their parents to open as well. To have a biodegradable package may require using more-expensive cardboard rather than less-expensive plastic. An ideal package—one that is perfect with respect to all criteria—may therefore not be possible for some products.

One that approaches that rare status is the plastic tub in which margarine typically is sold. An evaluation and rating of it, along with that of two less successfully packaged household products, is given in Exhibit 11–1.

EXHIBIT **11-1**

	Evaluation of Cereal, Soft Drink, and Margarine Containers in Terms of Their Use, Characteristics, and Cost					
	Cardboard Breakfast Cereal Box		Glass Soft Drink Bottle w/Screw Cap		Plastic Margarine Tub	
Use Characteristic	Verbal Evaluation	Rating*	Verbal Evaluation	Rating*	Verbal Evaluation	Rating*
1. Protects the contents from breakage, spillage	Tips easily	4	Breaks when dropped, tips easily	2	Gets a high mark	10
2. Easy to open, dispense from, close	Neither opens nor closes very easily, frequent spills when dispensing	2	Gets a high mark	10	Gets a high mark	10
3. Safe to use	Gets a high mark	10	Unsafe when dropped	5	Gets a high mark	10
4. Keeps the product from deteriorating	Gets a high mark before opening, average after opening	7	Gets a high mark before opening, average after	8	Does well as long as product is refrigerated	8
5. Proper size and shape for storing	Tips easily, requires especially high shelf space	1	Tips easily	6	Gets a high mark	10
6. Reusable or able to be recycled	Very limited reusage potential for consumer, not recyclable	1	Very limited reusage potential for consumer, not recyclable	6	Designed for reuse as food container	10
7. Biodegradable	Gets a high mark	10	Gets a low mark for states without bottle laws	4	Designed for reuse (so not applicable)	NA
8. Available in sizes appropriate to market segments served	Gets a high mark	10	Gets a high mark	10	Gets a high mark	10
9. Economical	Gets a high mark	10	Gets an average mark	6.1	Gets a high mark	10
Overall	An average package	5	A somewhat above average package	6.1	An excellent package	9.8

*On a scale of 1 to 10, with 10 the most favorable score.

The other function of packaging is to serve as a communications medium. In this capacity, the ideal package will:

1. Be attractive
2. Project a favorable image of the product
3. Be readily identifiable in a shopping situation
4. Have a clearly readable description of the contents

5. Provide information on assembly, preparation, and use when appropriate
6. Communicate the benefits that the product provides to the targeted market segment
7. Not be deceptive in size

Newly redesigned packages for packaged goods are normally use-tested if there is any significant departure from the physical design that has been used. The image of the product that it projects, its identifiability in a shopping situation, and the extent to which it communicates product benefits are also typically researched before it is adopted. Techniques that are used in consumer package tests for these purposes include focus groups, mall intercept and in-home surveys, and laboratory tests. In the laboratory tests, instruments such as tachistoscopes (a high, variable-speed slide projector) and eye cameras are used. These techniques and instruments are described in all standard marketing research tests.

MARKET TESTING

As described in Chapter 9, there are two kinds of market tests, simulated and field market tests.

A *simulated market test* is one in which a sample of consumers is exposed to advertising for the product and is given an opportunity to purchase it, and the purchasers asked to evaluate the brand and answer intention-to-purchase questions. One source reports that they provide an estimate of first-year sales of "plus or minus 20 percent (of actual sales) at an 80 percent confidence level."[27] For reasons of accuracy at low expense and to avoid the disclosure problems of standard market tests, simulated market tests have gained popularity rapidly in recent years.

Field market tests are divided into two types, controlled store tests and standard market tests. A *controlled store test* is one in which a new product is introduced directly into a sample of retail stores (or industrial distributor supply houses if the product is not a consumer product). In return for a fee paid to the store, the manager agrees to stock the product, to price it at the level set by the sponsor, and to display point-of-sale promotional materials. Controlled store tests are inexpensive and unobtrusive, and provide estimates of sales per point of distribution. They do not, however, give estimates of how successful the distribution program will be or the effectiveness of media advertising for the brand.

A *standard market test*, if one is carried out, is typically the last of the marketing research projects that are conducted for a new product. Standard market tests involve the actual introduction of the product into two to four cities or metropolitan areas. A full-scale marketing program is carried out within each test area. That is, in each area the brand is introduced through the channel of distribution and at one of the price and advertising levels that is being considered for the actual introduction.

Standard market tests are generally the most accurate of the means available for determining whether a product is going to succeed or fail. However, they are expensive, and they disclose to competitors not only the fact that a new product is being considered, but what it is and what marketing program is being considered for it as well. At the competitors' option, they can get the same data as the testing company (through a syndicated data service), or they can "jam" the test by not taking normal retaliatory action when a new product is introduced (either no action at all or by excessive promotional campaigns or price cutting). Standard market tests also typically require a substantial amount of time.

Standard market tests commonly last long enough (the extremes are from a few months to a year and a half) to measure trial and initial repeat purchase rates, but do not last long enough to determine brand loyalty patterns and decay rates. These latter patterns and overall sales for the product typically are projected using one of a number of mathematical models.[28] (A short description of two of the simpler models are given in Minicases IV-6 and IV-7 at the end of this section.)

Once the data from the test(s) that are run are collected and analyzed, all the information that was planned to be obtained has been obtained. It is then time for the decision on introducing the product.

COMMERCIALIZATION

The Decision to Introduce

The ideal situation, of course, is that all of the research that has been conducted—from concept test through the final market test—will have indicated a high probability that the product will be a success. This makes the decision to introduce a relatively easy one, given that no major unfavorable changes in market conditions are forecast for the near future.

If the research results have been uniformly discouraging, the "don't introduce now" decision may also be an easy one to make. However, that decision raises the issue of what should be done with the product idea. Should it be abandoned? Or should the product development process start over with changes in the concept, the product design, or the marketing plan, or some combination of these factors?

It is when there are mixed indications coming out of marketing research for the product that the risks and the difficulties of making a sound decision are the greatest. An "introduce" decision made in error can be costly in terms of out-of-pocket costs; a "do not introduce decision" that is the wrong one can cost several times more in terms of forgone profits.

The failure rate of new products is high; exactly how high is not clear, however. The results that have been reported for new product failure rates in studies conducted since 1960 are shown in Exhibit 11–2.

The studies whose results are reported there have varied considerably in the nature of the sample, the time and area for which they were conducted, and the definition of what "failure" means.

EXHIBIT 11-2

New-Product Failure Rates

New food and drug items
  Nielsen: 53% failed in 1971 versus 46% in 1962[a]
  Nielsen: 61% failed[b]
  Business Week: 50–80% failed[c]
  Rosen: over 80% failed[d]
  Dodd: over 80% failed[e]
  Helene Curtis: 43% failed[f]
  United Kingdom: over 40% failed[g]
  Dancer-Fitzgerald-Sample: 98% failed[h]
New consumer goods (primarily packaged)
  Angelus: over 80% failed[i]
  Booz, Allen, and Hamilton (1968): 37% failed[j]
  The Conference Board (1971): 33% failed[k]
  The Conference Board (1980): 42% failed[l]
  Ross Federal Research Corp.: 80% failed[m]
  Gallagher: 36% failed[n]
New industrial goods
  The Conference Board (1971): 20% failed[k]
  The Conference Board (1980): 38% failed[l]
  Booz, Allen, and Hamilton (1968): 30 to 40% failed[j]
  Cooper: 24% failed[o]
New consumer and industrial goods
  Booz, Allen, and Hamilton (1982): 35% failed[p]
  Association of National Advertisers: 39% failed[q]
New "products"
  U.S. Dept. of Commerce: 90% failed[r]

Those who are interested in reading further about new product failure rates should see C. M. Crawford, "New Product Failure Rates: A Reprise," Research Management, July–August 1987, 20–24.

---

[a]"New Product Success Ratio," *The Nielsen Researcher*, No. 5, 1971, 2–10.
[b]"Which Type of Product Is More Successful—New or Me Too," *Nielsen Researcher*, No. 2, 1980, 16–17.
[c]"An Outside Job Fills the Product Gap," *Business Week*, May 16, 1970, 48.
[d]C. E. Rosen, "New Product Decisions—Creative Measurements and Realistic Applications," *New Products: Concepts Development and Strategy*, in R. Scrace (ed.), U. of Michigan, Graduate School of Business Administration, 1967, 11–17.
[e]J. W. Dodd, Jr., "New Products—Policy, Strategy, and Sense of Direction," in Scrace, *New Products*, 18–24.
[f]"Helene Curtis Comeback Move," *Advertising Age*, May 13, 1974, 1ff.
[g]"New Products in the Grocery Trade," *The Grocer*, Kranshar, Andrews, and Eassie (London), 1971.
[h]Reported in "Study of New Product Failure Rates Refutes Basic Premise of Growth," *The Wall Street Journal*, June 20, 1980, 23.
[i]T. L. Angelus, "Why Do Most New Products Fail?" *Advertising Age*, March 24, 1969, 85–86.
[j]Booz, Allen, and Hamilton, "Management of New Products," 1968, especially 11–12.
[k]D. S. Hopkins and E. L. Bailey, "New Product Pressures," *The Conference Board Record*, Vol. 8, June 1971, 16–24.
[l]D. S. Hopkins, "New Product Winners and Losers," *Conference Board Report no. 773*, 1980, 4–5.
[m]J. T. O'Meara, "Selecting Profitable Products," *Harvard Business Review*, January–February 1961, 80–88.
[n]*The Gallagher Report*, February 17, 1981, 1.
[o]R. G. Cooper, "New Product Success in Industrial Firms," Vol. 2, 1982, 215–223.
[p]Booz, Allen, and Hamilton, "New Product Management for the 1980's," 1981.
[q]Association of National Advertisers, *Prescription for New Product Success*, 1984, 47 pp.
[r]S. J. Shaw, "Behavioral Session Offers Fresh Insights into New Product Acceptance," *Journal of Marketing*, January 1965, 9–13.

There no doubt are many reasons for about one-half of the decisions to introduce new consumer products and one-third of the decisions to introduce new industrial products being wrong. Three seem to be especially important, however: emotional involvement replacing objective judgment, poor forecasting, and expected value decision making.

Emotional Involvement in the Introduction Decision

Anyone who has been involved in the introduction of a new product will recognize the favorable bias that develops among at least some of those who are working on it. For whatever reason—the need to generate new sales, the mystique of being involved in a new venture, a positive propensity for change, or a need to be associated with a winning effort—research analysts and management persons alike tend to make emotional investments in the product. One observer has commented on this behavioral pattern as follows:

> I have been disappointed at a number of cases in which enthusiasm for the product has caused normally rational people to become more salesmen than analysts. The result—they become selectively inattentive to negative feedback. . . . They shirk their basic responsibility to remain objective.[29]

Obviously, a general favorable biasing of judgments is to be guarded against. Having a champion for each prospective new product—a kind of self-appointed ombudsman—may be desirable, however. This ensures that the product will not quietly die as a result of no real decision—either positive or negative—being made about it.

Poor Forecasting: Forecasting of any kind is fraught with problems; those of forecasting the sales and costs and the resulting cash flows and profits for new products are perhaps as severe as one can encounter.

The one study that is available on forecasting errors for new products indicates that, indeed, the errors are large.[30] For 63 industrial and consumer products introduced by large companies, the *mean error in the sales forecasts was 65 percent* (over the period for which the forecasts were made). A better measure is the *median error*: that was *26 percent*. The errors in profit forecasts for 53 of these same products were even much higher—a *mean error of 128 percent* and a *median error of 46 percent*. Given these levels of error, it is understandable why bad new-product introduction decisions might be made.

Expected Value Decision Making: We should not be too hasty about concluding that high new-product failure rates are evidence per se of bad forecasting compounded by biased decision making, however. If the probability of a successful introduction is greater than of a failure and if the profits that are to be made from the introduction of a successful product are greater than the losses that will be incurred from an unsuccessful one, even a company management that is essentially risk averse should introduce risky new products—and have a substantial failure rate as a result.

By way of example, assume that the actual profits and losses (no forecast errors) and their probabilities for all the potential new products considered by a company are the following:

Action	Product will be a Success		Product will be a Failure	
	Probability	Estimated Profits	Probability	Estimated Losses
Introduce	.7	$10M	.3	($5M)
Do not Introduce	.7	0	.3	0

In this case, a company that wants to maximize its profits and is financially strong enough to survive a failure or two should introduce *all* of the products being considered. Why? Because the expected value of a successful introduction, the probability of a success × the profits of a success

$$= .70 \times \$10M = \$7M,$$

is almost five times that of the expected value of a failure:

$$= .30 \times (\$5M) = (\$1.5M).$$

These kinds of odds would appeal to even a very conservative, risk-averse management. But note that while the company was prospering from its new product program, it would have a new-product failure rate of 30 percent.

Essentially this reasoning has been expressed by a vice-president of marketing as follows:

> To target a new product development program to expect a 100 percent success rate would be counterproductive—extreme conservatism would rule with very few, if any, projects reaching fruition. The rational approach is to set goals, determined by marketing and financial with the approval of corporate management, that would include an "acceptable percentage" in the range from limited success to total failure.[31]

A favorable decision for the product is the beginning, not the end, of the commercialization process. It triggers the requirement for new decisions on the timing, the area, and the marketing program for the introduction.

The Timing of the Introduction

For reasons described earlier—availability of sufficient inventory, the market for the product is seasonal or cyclical in nature, expected excessive cannibalization of the parent by an adaptive product—it may be desirable not to introduce at the time the development of the product is completed. Waiting for a more propitious time to introduce may actually result in higher profits.

The Area of the Introduction

Either for reasons of limited production capability or for purposes of confirming forecasts before a full-scale introduction is made, or both, test market introductions are often expanded into regional rather than national introductions. This is a means of reducing risks and at the same time gaining market experience.

The Marketing Program

Decisions also have to be made about the introductory versus the sustaining levels of the marketing mix variables. These decisions are based in part on the frequency of purchase of the product.

For a frequently purchased product, success ultimately is determined by the level of repeat purchases. Since one cannot be a repeat purchaser without first having been an initial purchaser, the major thrust of the marketing program during the introductory period is to induce trial by as much of the potential market as possible. This in turn requires higher introductory advertising and promotion budgets than will normally be used to sustain sales after the introductory period is over. (For example, conventional marketing wisdom indicates that the share of all the advertising done should be about twice that of the market share desired for the new consumer product.) Sampling of the product, comparing, and price "deals" at the consumer level to encourage stocking of inventory by wholesalers and retailers may also be required. Careful monitoring of the penetration rate will allow adjustments to be made in these variables, as required.

Although high sales during the introductory period of an infrequently purchased product are clearly desirable, they are less critical than for frequently purchased products. Therefore, introductory and sustaining levels of the mix variables do not need to vary as much for the infrequently purchased product.

SUMMARY OF IMPORTANT POINTS

1. The new-product development and introduction process typically consists of seven phases. These are:
   a. Deciding on strategies for choice of type and timing of new products
   b. Idea generation and screening
   c. Concept development
   d. Business analysis
   e. Physical development of the product
   f. Market tests
   g. Commercialization
2. A product can be one of three different kinds:
   a. An *innovative* new product involves a substantial amount of innovation in function, features, or form.
   b. An *emulative* new product is copied (with some variation) from existing products of one or more other companies.
   c. An *adaptive* new product involves adaptations in function, features, or form from another product of the same company that are perceived by the consumer as being new.
3. Innovative new products are new to the economy, the company, and the consumer. Emulative new products are not new to the economy, but are new to the company and to the consumer. Adaptive new products are not new to the economy or the company, but are (perceived as being) new to the consumer.
4. An analysis of PIMS (Profit Impact of Marketing Strategy) data for approximately 500 businesses indicates that of the three quality levels of inferior, average, and superior, a superior-quality product yields the highest level of profit, on the average.
5. The PIMS data show that if product quality is inferior, marketing expenses should be kept low. Average expenditures on marketing for an inferior-quality product decreases profitability somewhat, and high marketing expenditures depresses it severely.
6. *Cannibalization* results when an existing product loses sales to a new product within the same company. *Complementary sales* occur when a new product results in increased sales of the existing product.
7. Ideas for new products can come from both *incidental* and *solicited* sources. Incidental sources include customers, company sales representatives and dealers, competitors, employee suggestions, and patent disclosures. Solicited sources include consumer research projects, re-

search and development departments, and the use of idea-generating techniques such as brainstorming, reverse brainstorming, synectics, attribute listing, and problem inventory analysis.

8. The ground rules for the standard *brainstorming* session stipulate that:
   a. There is to be no criticism.
   b. Unusual solutions are encouraged.
   c. As many answers as possible are desired.
   d. Combinations and variations are sought.

9. *Synectics* is a variation of brainstorming in which the problem is only generally defined at the beginning and more specifically defined in stages as the session progresses. The typical synectics session is much longer than the usual brainstorming session because of the belief that fatigue leads to added creativity.

10. *Attribute listing* involves listing the attributes of an actual or potential product and then modifying one or more of them to improve the product.

11. *Problem inventory analysis* involves developing a list of problems associated with using products in the product class and then asking a sample of users to identify the problems with using the specific product of interest.

12. Two types of errors can be made in screening new product ideas: a RETAIN error when the idea should have been dropped and a DROP error when the idea should have been retained.

13. Screening procedures range from informal ad hoc judgment through the use of formal rating and scoring on specific attributes.

14. One of two decision rules, compensatory or conjunctive, is ordinarily used in formal rating procedures to translate the ratings into a RETAIN or DROP decision. Of the two, available evidence indicates that the conjunctive rule results in better decisions.

15. The appropriate criteria for choosing a screening method include the following:
    a. Low cost
    b. Fast
    c. Adaptable
    d. Easily understood
    e. Easily carried out
    f. Requires explicit consideration of all relevant criteria
    g. Easily communicable results
    h. Provides learning potential
    i. Acceptance by management

16. A *product concept* is a product idea that has been defined in terms of the application(s) for which it will be marketed and the benefits it will provide.

17. Once an acceptable product concept has evolved, a tentative strategy for marketing it needs to be devised. The questions that need to be raised and answered for this purpose include
    a. What are the target market segments for the product?
    b. How will it be positioned within those segments?
    c. What ranges of sizes or models will be offered?

d. What will the introductory price be for each of the product versions? How will they be priced after the introductory period?

e. How will we distribute the product?

f. How will we advertise and promote it? How much do we expect to budget for advertising and promotion for each of the first five years after introduction?

g. What is our target sales volume for each of the first five years after introduction?

h. What is our target market share for each of the first five years?

i. What is the expected development period for the product? What is our expected cash flow for the development period and each of the first five years after introduction?

18. An important financial measure that managements use in making the decision of whether to proceed with the development of the product is the *cash flow* expected to be generated by the product over the planning period.

19. A product *prototype* is one of the early models of the product. It is not necessarily identical to the final product (although it sometimes is), but it is expected that it will have its essential features.

20. In terms of use characteristics, a good package:

a. Protects the contents from breakage or spillage

b. Is easy to open, dispense from, and close

c. Is safe to use

d. Keeps the product from deteriorating

e. Is of the proper size and shape for storage

f. Is reusable, able to be recycled, or biodegradable

g. Is not deceptive in size

h. Is available in the sizes appropriate to the market segments served

i. Is economical

21. As a communication medium, a good package

a. Is attractive

b. Projects a favorable image of the product

c. Is readily identifiable in a shopping situation

d. Has a clearly readable description of the contents

e. Provides information on assembly, preparation, and use when appropriate

f. Communicates the benefits that the product provides to the targeted market segment

g. Is not deceptive in size

22. Market tests may be *simulated, controlled,* or *standard* in nature.

23. *Simulated market tests* use consumer attitudes or purchase rates in a purchase situation other than an actual store as a predictor of initial sales and market share.

24. *Controlled market tests* are test introductions of a prospective new product into a sample of retail stores.

25. *Standard market tests* are actual introductions of products into a sample of cities or metropolitan areas.

26. Failure rates for new products are high. A simple average of the reported failure rates from 15 studies indicates that about 50 percent of

new consumer products and 30 percent of new industrial products fail.

27. Three factors seem to be important in explaining the relatively high failure rates: emotional involvement of the decision makers, poor forecasting, and expected value decision making.

28. If the payoffs for success average several times the costs of failure, even a risk-averse management can afford to expect—even plan— to have at least one new product failure for every success.

29. The introduction of new products often has to be delayed for reasons of limited production capability, the seasonal or cyclical nature of sales, and high inventories of the existing product that is being replaced.

REVIEW QUESTIONS

11.1. How do "innovative," "emulative," and "adaptive" new products differ?

11.2. What are the underlying business strategies that define the role of the new product?

11.3. What are the phases of the product development process?

11.4. What is:
  a. Brainstorming?
  b. Synectics?
  c. Attribute listing?
  d. Problem inventory analysis?

11.5. What is a product concept?

11.6. How does one determine for a new product the:
  a. Maximum investment at risk?
  b. Payback period?
  c. Internal rate of return?

11.7. What do the PIMS data show with respect to the relationship of product quality and profitability?

11.8. What is a:
  a. Simulated market test?
  b. Controlled market test?
  c. Standard market test?

11.9. Under what conditions, if any, would it be appropriate for a company intentionally to have a new product failure rate of 50 percent?

DISCUSSION QUESTIONS AND PROBLEMS

11.10. Classify the following products as to whether they were innovative, emulative, or adaptive at the time they were introduced:
   a. The first motion picture camera (Assume that the French company that introduced it had not marketed any other camera prior to the introduction of the motion picture camera.)
   b. The first self-developing picture camera (This camera was introduced initially by the Polaroid Company, which was then marketing other cameras.)
   c. The second self-developing picture camera (This camera was introduced by the Kodak Company.)
   d. The first camera with an automatic lens adjustment for light conditions (Assume this camera was introduced originally by a company that was then marketing other cameras.)
   e. A camera developed by Bell & Howell with a built-in telephoto lens (At the time it was developed the company had another camera with a telephoto lens available as an attachment.)
   f. The first videocamera
   g. The hand-held camera (first developed by Sony Corp.) that takes a still picture by recording electronic signals on a small magnetic disk. The pictures can be projected from the disk to a television screen.

11.11. The Fulton Corporation (Fulton, Illinois) manufactures and markets an aluminum mailbox to be mounted on a support at the side of the street or road. The mailbox is lockable, moisture resistant, and rustproof, and meets the size specifications of the U.S. Postal Service. For what other applications might it be used?

11.12. When the Gillette Company introduced Dry Idea, a roll-on antiperspirant, the company conceded that it would not stop perspiration any better than at least five products already on the market. But, the company said, the product "goes on dry and feels better, and thus leads the user to feel it is more effective." A budget of $18 million was allocated by Gillette for a 10-month introductory period.
   From a societal point of view, was Dry Idea a waste of resources? Explain.

11.13. Other things being equal, are sales forecasts for new products with high purchase frequencies likely to be more or less accurate than those for products with low purchase frequencies? Explain.

11.14. For which of the following products, if any, might a standard market test have been appropriate prior to making the introduce/do not introduce decision? Why?
   a. RCA portable color TV set
   b. A Peugot 10-speed bicycle
   c. An Alberto-Culver shampoo
   d. Dupont exterior house paint
   e. Quaker Oats Natural cereal

11.15. The Pontiac division of General Motors recently developed specifications for three different high-performance sports cars. They were rated on the attributes listed below with an excellent rating being 5 points, very good 4 points, good 3 points, fair 2 points, poor 1 point, and very poor 0 points. The weights for each of the criteria are also shown below.

   Which design, if any, should have been selected from a screening process that used
   a. Informal judgment (in this case, your judgment)
   b. A compensatory rule with a cut-off of 3.75
   c. A conjunctive rule with a minimum rating of 2 (fair)

Attribute	Weight	Ratings		
		Design 1	Design 2	Design 3
Acceleration	.15	5	5	5
Appearance	.15	5	4	4
Braking	.15	4	3	4
Fuel economy	.10	2	4	3
Handling	.10	4	5	2
Maneuverability	.10	5	5	4
Entry/exit ease	.05	3	2	2
Ride comfort	.05	3	2	2
Roominess	.05	3	2	2
Quietness	.05	0	1	2
Visibility	.05	2	5	2

11.16. Outline the step-by-step program that you would recommend for Sears, Roebuck to use in testing the concept of an electric car as a
   a. Second family car
   b. Commuter car
   c. Delivery vehicle

11.17. Calculate the average cost for units 10,000 to 20,000 of a new product that has an initial unit cost of $1,000 and is on an experience curve of 85 percent. (The *b* value for an 85 percent curve is 0.234.)

11.18. Assume that a competitor is producing a similar new product to the one in question 11–17. You assume that the first unit cost might also have been about $1,000 but, since the competitor's plant is less automated than yours, you believe its product is on about a 90 percent experience curve. If these estimates are correct, what is the advantage you will have in average cost per unit for units 10,000 to 20,000?

11.19. Suppose that the estimated profits and losses and their probabilities for each of the potential new products being considered by the Campbell Soup Company are the following:

Action	Product will be a Success		Product will be a Failure	
	Probability	Estimated Profits	Probability	Estimated Losses
Introduce	.50	$18M	.50	($8M)
Do not introduce	.50	0	.50	0

a. Should the Campbell Soup management authorize introducing all of these products if it is
   (1) Risk neutral? Explain.
   (2) Risk averse? Explain.
b. What would the expected failure rate be on this group of products if it did introduce all of them?

11.20. Suppose that the estimated profits and losses and their probabilities for each of the potential new products being considered by the Campbell Soup Company are the following:

Action	Product will be a Success		Product will be a Failure	
	Probability	Estimated Profits	Probability	Estimated Losses
Introduce	.65	$18M	.35	($8M)
Do not introduce	.65	0	.35	0

a. Should the Campbell Soup management authorize introducing all of these products if it is
   (1) Risk neutral? Explain.
   (2) Risk averse? Explain.
b. What would the expected failure rate be on this group of products if it did introduce all of them?

11.21. An average of new consumer product failure rates in the United States in 15 studies is about 50 percent. Under what conditions, if any, would it be appropriate for a company to plan on having a new-product failure rate of 50 percent? Explain.

11.22. Dart & Kraft introduces several new products each year. Suppose that Dart & Kraft is a risk-neutral company that is attempting to maximize cash flows, and so all of its new product decisions are based on the net present value of five-year cash flow projections. Further suppose that they are now considering three products for introduction that have the following characteristics:

	Product A	Product B	Product C
Net present value of cash flows for five-year planning period conditional on product's achieving a market share of 15 percent or more by the end of the fifth year	$10M	$8M*	$5M
Net present value of cash flows for five-year planning period conditional on product's achieving a market share of less than 15 percent by the end of the fifth year	$(10M)	$(6M)	$(4M)
The probability of achieving a market share of 15 percent or more by the end of the fifth year	.60	.50	.40
The probability of achieving a market share of less than 15 percent by the end of the fifth year	.40	.50	.60

a. Should Product A be introduced? Explain.
b. Should Product B be introduced? Explain.
c. Should Product C be introduced? Explain.

11.23. Name three pairs of products you consider to be complementary. Explain why you think they have this characteristic.

PROJECTS

11.24. In cooperation with three other persons, develop suggestions for improving the design of one of the coin-operated copy machines located in your school library using
a. Brainstorming
b. Attribute listing
c. Problem inventory analysis

11.25. An issue of *Advertising Age* each month reports on products in market test in the United States. From the latest issue, determine
a. The lowest, highest, and average number of cities being used for market testing
b. The most popular test cities
c. What mix variables are being tested

Endnotes

[1]Y. J. Wind, *Product Policy: Concepts, Methods, and Strategy,* Addison-Wesley, 1982, 551.

[2]For a discussion of the roles of strategy in product additions, see R. G. Cooper, "How New Product Strategies Impact on Performance," *Journal of Product Innovation Management,* Vol. 1, 1984, 5–18, and "New Product Strategies: What Distinguishes the Top Performers," *Journal of Product Innovation Management,* Vol. 1, No. 3, September 1984, 151–164.

[3]Booz, Allen, and Hamilton, Inc., "New Product Management of the 1980s: Phase 1," 1981, 3. For an expanded view of the emulator's strategic options, see P. J. Flatow, "No. 2 Can Be More Innovative Than the Forerunner," *Marketing News,* November 21, 1986, 17, 31.

[4]Wind, *Product Policy,* 211–218, 264.

[5]S. Schoeffler, R. D. Buzzell, and D. F. Heany, "Impact of Strategic Planning on Profit Performance," *Harvard Business Review,* March–April 1974, 141.

[6]Ibid., 142.

[7]E. J. Kahn, Jr., *The Big Drink: The Story of Coca-Cola,* Random House, 1950, 69.

[8]A. F. Osborn, *Applied Imagination,* 3rd ed., Charles Scribner's Sons, 1963.

[9]Ibid., 156.

[10]" 'Synectics' Helps to Capitalize on Consumer Trends," *Marketing News,* January 2, 1987, 41.

[11]Osborn, *Applied Imagination,* 213–214.

[12]For a more detailed discussion of the use of problem inventory analysis in generating new product ideas, see E. M. Tauber, "Discovering New Product Opportunities with Problem Inventory Analysis," *Journal of Marketing,* January 1975, 67–70.

[13]Booz, Allen, and Hamilton, Inc., "New Product Mangement," 3.

[14]Described in K. G. Baker, "The Comparative Analysis of Models for Use in New Product Screening Decisions," Ph.D. diss., University of Oregon, 1980, 145.

[15]For a discussion of screening criteria and screening methods, see R. G. Cooper and U. de Brentani, "Criteria for Screening New Products," *Industrial Marketing Management,* February 13, 1984, 149–156; R. G. Cooper, "Selecting Winning New Product Projects: Using the NewProd System," *Journal of Product Innovation Management,* Vol. 2, No. 1, March 1985, 34–44; and K. G. Baker and G. S. Albaum, "Modelling New Product Screening Decisions," *Journal of Product Innovation Management,* Vol. 3, No. 1, March 1986, 32–39.

[16]Baker and Albaum, "Modelling New Product Screening Decisions."

[17]U. de Bretani, "Do Firms Need a Custom-Designed New Product Screening Model?" *Journal of Product Innovation Management,* Vol. 3, No. 2, June 1986, 108–119.

[18]J. D. C. Little, "Models and Managers: The Concept of a Decision Calculus," *Management Science,* April 1970, 628–655.

[19]This series of questions is adapted from E. M. Tauber, "Reduce New Product Failures: Measure Needs as Well as Purchase Interests," *Journal of Marketing,* July 1973, 61–64.

[20]Described in P. E. Green and D. S. Tull, *Research for Marketing Decisions,* 4th ed., Prentice-Hall, 1978, 487–498.

[21]D. S. Tull and D. I. Hawkins, *Marketing Research: Measurement and Method,* 4th ed., Macmillan, 1987, 632.

[22]This procedure does not always work, however. For an example in which it did not apply, see R. C. Harbicht, "Testing Concept Is Not Enough," *Marketing News,* January 3, 1986, 48.

[23]J. W. Taylor, J. J. Houlahan, and A. C. Gabriel, "The Purchase Intention Question in New Product Development: A Field Test," *Journal of Marketing,* January 1975, 90.

[24]For a discussion of conjoint analysis, see P. E. Green, D. S. Tull, and G. S. Albaum, *Research for Marketing Decisions,* 5th ed., Macmillan, 1988, 615–631.

[25]H. J. Claycamp and L. E. Liddy, "Prediction of New Product Performance: An Analytical Approach," *Journal of Marketing Research,* November 1969, 414–420; and "ESP—A New Way to Predict New Product Performance before Test Marketing," National Purchase Diary, 1976.

[26]E. M. Tauber, "Forecasting Sales Prior to Test Market," *Journal of Marketing,* January 1977, 81.

[27]J. R. Rhodes, "Using Predictive Models to Reduce the Costs and Risks of New Product Development," *Proceedings of the Marketing Educators' Conference, 1980,* American Marketing Association, 158.

[28]For a description and an evaluation of nine of these models, see C. Narasimhan and S. K. Sen, "New Product Models for Test Market Data," *Journal of Marketing,* Winter 1983, 11–24.

[29]Ibid., 58.

[30]D. S. Tull, "The Relationship of Actual and Predicted Sales and Profits in New Product Introductions," *Journal of Business,* July 1967, 233–250.

[31]D. S. Hopkins, "New Product Winners and Losers," *Conference Board,* 1980, 11.

12

PRODUCT LINE MANAGEMENT, BRAND MANAGEMENT, AND THE PRODUCT LIFE CYCLE

For one or more of several reasons—product sales complementarity, customer preference, economies of manufacturing, economies of marketing, distribution channel influence, management expertise—companies, be they manufacturer, wholesaler, industrial distributor, or retailer, typically offer product lines rather than unrelated assortments of products for sale.

The choice and maintenance of product lines require a set of continuing decisions. The lines the company offers have to be chosen; the individual products that make up the lines must be selected; brand strategy needs to be decided on, and specific brands, trademarks, and names have to be designated or designed. These decisions require periodic review as changes in the market and the competitive situation occur. In particular, evaluations of product line, individual product, and brand strategy decisions need to be made at each of the stages of the product life cycle.

These decisions are shown in Table 12–1. The addition of new products was discussed in the last chapter. The remaining decisions concerning product line choice and maintenance are the subject of the first half of this chapter. In the second half we discuss the product life cycle.

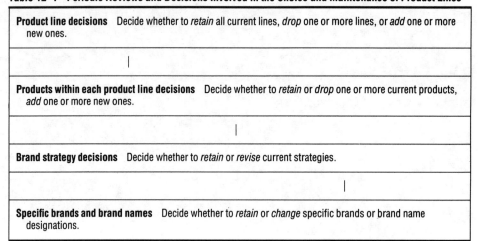

Table 12-1 Periodic Reviews and Decisions Involved in the Choice and Maintenance of Product Lines

Product line decisions	Decide whether to *retain* all current lines, *drop* one or more lines, or *add* one or more new ones.
Products within each product line decisions	Decide whether to *retain* or *drop* one or more current products, *add* one or more new ones.
Brand strategy decisions	Decide whether to *retain* or *revise* current strategies.
Specific brands and brand names	Decide whether to *retain* or *change* specific brands or brand name designations.

PRODUCT LINE DECISIONS

Examples of product lines are **sporting goods, industrial fasteners, office supplies**, and **household appliances**. Note that the groups of products that one would expect to make up a "line" in each of these categories would tend to:

PERFORM THE SAME GENERAL FUNCTIONS

Sporting goods—used in recreational activities
Industrial fasteners—used to fasten two or more materials or parts together
Office supplies—used in the daily operation of an office
Household appliances—perform or assist in performing a household task

BE SOLD THROUGH THE SAME OUTLETS

Sporting goods—sporting goods stores
Industrial fasteners—industrial supply houses
Office supplies—office supply houses
Household appliances—appliance stores, department stores

BE SOLD TO THE SAME MARKET SEGMENTS

Sporting goods—sports enthusiasts
Industrial fasteners—manufacturers, construction companies
Office supplies—organizations with offices
Household appliances—homeowners, landlords, builders of dwelling units

The products in a product line should meet at least one of these criteria. Accordingly, we can define it as follows:

A **product line** is a group of products that are related in the functions they perform, the outlets through which they are sold, or the segment(s) of the market to which they are sold.

Classes of Products

From this definition it should follow that product lines consist of products from the same general class. This usually is the case. Product lines tend to have products that are either consumer *or* industrial goods, but normally not a mixture of the two. (This tendency is not without exception, however. For example, AT&T sells telephones to both homeowners and office managers, IBM markets microcomputers to both private individuals and companies, and General Mills sells flour to both homemakers and bakeries.)

An example of the product lines of one (predominantly) consumer goods company, General Mills, is given in Table 12–2.

Table 12–2 Consumer Food Product Lines and Brand Names and Generic Terms of the General Mills Company

Baking Mix *Bisquick*	*Honey Buc*wheat Crisp* *Honey Nut Cheerios* *Ice Cream Cones*

Biscuit Mixes
  Gold Medal
  Robin Hood
	Kaboom
	Kix
	Lucky Charms

Brownie Mixes
  Betty Crocker
  Betty Crocker Bake Shop
  Gold Medal
  Robin Hood
	Nature Valley 100% Natural Cereal
	Pac Man
	S'Mores Grahams
	Total
	Total Corn Flakes
	Trix

Betty Crocker Cake Mixes
  Angel Food
  Chiffon
  Microwave
  Snackin' Cake
  Stir 'N Frost
  Supermoist
	Wheaties
	
	Betty Crocker Cookie Mix
	  Big Batch
	
	Corn Bread Mixes
	  Gold Medal
	  Robin Hood

Cereals
  Total Oatmeal
  Wheat Hearts
  Body Buddies
  Booberry
  Cheerios
  Cinnamon Toast Crunch
  Circus Fun
  Clusters
  Cocoa Puffs
  Count Chocula
  Country Corn Flakes
  Crispy Wheats 'N Raisins
  Fiber One
  Frankenberry
  Golden Grahams
	Betty Crocker Dessert Mixes
	  Classics
	
	Fish and Seafoods
	  Gorton's
	    Clam Chowder
	    Clams
	    Codfish Cakes
	    Crispy Batter
	    Crunchy
	    Fishmarket Fresh
	    Light Recipe Entrees
	    Light Recipe Fillets
	    Microwave Crunchy
	
	(Continued on page 388)

Table 12–2 Consumer Food Product Lines and Brand Names and Generic Terms of the General Mills Company (*continued*)

Fish and Seafoods (*continued*)
  Microwave Fillets
    Potato Crisp
  Shrimp
  Specialty
  Value Pack

Flours
  Big Jo
  Drifted Snow
  Gold Medal
    Better for Bread
    Wondra
    Wondra Pour 'N Shake
  La Pina
  Red Band
  Robin Hood
  Softasilk
  Velvet

Betty Crocker Frostings
  Frosting Mixes
  Creamy Deluxe Ready-to-Spread Frostings
  MiniMorsels Ready-to-Spread Frostings

Frozen Novelties
  Betty Crocker Brownie Sundae
  Betty Crocker Soft Sundae
  Goldrush Ice Cream Candy Bars
  Goldrush Nuggets
  Goo Goo Cluster
  Great American Chilly Pops
  Tropical Pops

Betty Crocker Main Dish Mixes
  Chicken Helper
  Hamburger Helper
    Pizzabake
    Sloppy Joe Bake
    Tacobake
  Hamburger Helper Deluxe
    Oriental Classics
    Presto Pasta!
    Tuna Helper

Muffin Mixes
  Betty Crocker
  Betty Crocker Bake Shop
  Gold Medal
  Robin Hood

Pancake Mixes
  Betty Crocker
  Gold Medal
  Robin Hood

Betty Crocker Pie Crust Mix/Sticks

Pizza Crust Mixes
  Gold Medal
  Robin Hood

Potato Mixes
  Betty Crocker Potato Buds
  Betty Crocker Potato Medleys
  Betty Crocker Twice Baked

Salad Mixes
  Suddenly Salad

Salad Toppings
  Bac∗os

Snacks
  Bugles
  Pop Secret

Specialty Snacks
  Betty Crocker Fruit Bars
  Betty Crocker Fruit Roll-Ups
  Betty Crocker Fruit Swirl Bars
  Betty Crocker Fruit Wrinkles
  Betty Crocker Pudding Roll-Ups
  Nature Valley Chewy Granola Bars
  Nature Valley Granola Bars

Betty Crocker Stuffing Mixes

Yogurts
  Yoplait
  Breakfast Yogurt
  Custard Style
  Original
  Soft Frozen Yogurt
  Yoplait 150

Restaurants
  Red Lobster
  The Olive Garden
  York's/Leann Chin's

Specialty Retailing
  Talbot's
  Eddie Bauer

Italicized brand names and trademarks are either registered by General Mills or else licensed by it from another company.

Source: General Mills, Inc.—Brand Names and Generic Terms, July 1988. Provided through the courtesy of General Mills.

Within the **consumer goods category** product lines typically consist of convenience, shopping, or specialty goods, but usually not a mixture of them. (See Figure 12–1 for definitions and examples of these classes of consumer products, and the classes of industrial products.)

The same general rule applies to industrial products. As shown in Figure 12–1, the classes of **industrial products** are installations, accessory equipment, materials, fabricated parts, and supplies. Here again, product lines ordinarily consist of products belonging to only one of these classes.

FIGURE 12-1
Types of consumer and industrial products.

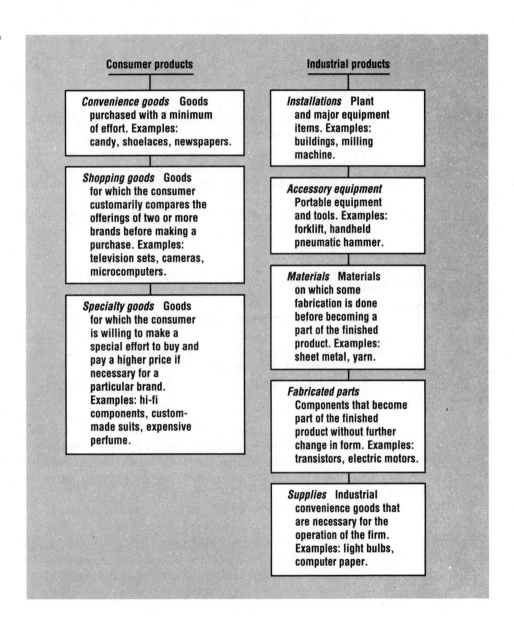

Consumer products

Convenience goods Goods purchased with a minimum of effort. Examples: candy, shoelaces, newspapers.

Shopping goods Goods for which the consumer customarily compares the offerings of two or more brands before making a purchase. Examples: television sets, cameras, microcomputers.

Specialty goods Goods for which the consumer is willing to make a special effort to buy and pay a higher price if necessary for a particular brand. Examples: hi-fi components, custom-made suits, expensive perfume.

Industrial products

Installations Plant and major equipment items. Examples: buildings, milling machine.

Accessory equipment Portable equipment and tools. Examples: forklift, handheld pneumatic hammer.

Materials Materials on which some fabrication is done before becoming a part of the finished product. Examples: sheet metal, yarn.

Fabricated parts Components that become part of the finished product without further change in form. Examples: transistors, electric motors.

Supplies Industrial convenience goods that are necessary for the operation of the firm. Examples: light bulbs, computer paper.

Decision on Product Lines to Offer

Choice of Initial
Product Line(s)

Traditionally the initial choice of product line(s) for the American manufacturer, wholesaler, and retailer has been made on an ad hoc, opportune basis. John D. Rockefeller heard about the discovery of oil in Pennsylvania and wondered if there was a future in refining the gooey liquid to make "coal" oil to burn in lamps. Richard Sears became bored during the night shift of his railroad telegrapher's job and began to sell watches to the other telegraphers on the line. Henry Ford put one of the newfangled gasoline engines on a modified wagon and decided to see if he could sell such a "horseless carriage." More recently, a physical education professor named William Bowerman experimented with molding rubber in the household waffle iron to develop the "waffle" sole for running shoes, and the Nike Company was born.

Casual observation suggests that opportunism still prevails among start-up small businesses in the initial choice of product lines. A trend toward corporate entrepreneurship and the growth of venture capitalism, accompanied by an increase in the size of founded businesses in which they are involved, has put the choice of initial product lines on a more reasoned basis, however. Research has begun to precede, and to an extent replace, the "tryout" as the primary source of information.

When research is used in the choice of an initial product line, the choice almost always turns on the prospective size and projected profits and cash flows of the line. The appropriate methods for estimating the levels of these variables are the same as those discussed in Chapter 9 for estimating the size of the potential, available, and served markets; prospective company sales; and profitability and cash flows for individual products.

Choice of Product
Lines to Add

Before deciding whether to add a product line, consideration should be given to a number of factors. These considerations include customer preference, company expertise, marketing efficiency, product line complementarity, effect on distribution channel influence, lines carried by competitors, diversification, financial requirements, and projected profitability and cash flows. They apply to manufacturers, wholesalers, and retailers alike. These considerations are shown in Figure 12–2. A brief discussion of each follows.

Customer Preference: If the present customers tend to buy products in the line being considered and, if so, it is likely that they would buy them from your company, a strong plus is registered for the prospective line. It is useful to have salespersons routinely report on all products that present customers ask for that the company currently does not offer.

Company Expertise: It is a cardinal rule in adding a new product line that the company have (or be willing to make the necessary investment to acquire) the knowledge to market it properly. In addition, if postpurchase service is required, the company should commit to acquiring the ability to do a first-rate job in this area. If the customers are not likely to be served competently, the line should not be added.

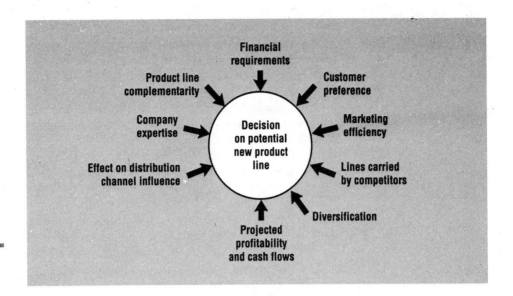

FIGURE 12-2
Considerations in adding a new product line.

Marketing Efficiency: Adding a line that is related to those already being offered can increase marketing efficiency as long as two conditions are met: (1) excess marketing capacity exists (the existing marketing force is not being utilized fully), and (2) the extent of its utilization can be increased through selling the new line to the same customers, using the same physical distribution facilities, advertising the new line jointly with existing lines, and the like.

Product Line Complementarity: In some cases it is possible to add product lines that actually increase the sales of existing lines. An example is the convenience-type food markets that ARCO and some other gasoline retailers added next to their stations beginning in the early 1980s. Gasoline sales have increased at the locations with convenience markets because stopping by for a bottle of milk or a loaf of bread often results in the purchase of gasoline while there.

Complementarity of sales can also be affected by matching, or exceeding, the lines carried by competitors.

Effect on Distribution Channel Influence: The more product lines a manufacturer can offer to wholesalers or retailers that carry them, the more influence that manufacturer will have with the wholesalers and retailers in the distribution channel. Procter & Gamble, for example, has a considerable influence on retailers in part because of the number of product lines (e.g., detergents, bar soaps, toothpaste, coffee, and disposable diapers) the company offers.

Lines Carried by Competitors: Suppose a major competitor (or competitors) offers lines your company does not carry that are sold to the same customers that your company serves. By adding one or more of these lines, sales of your company's existing lines might increase.

The reasons why are not difficult to guess. Potential purchasing economies are provided to the customer by making the wider assortment of goods available. A shopping trip or a purchase order made primarily for an item or items in the newly added line may include items in other lines. And the added convenience of being able to buy from the wider assortment may generate purchases that otherwise might not have been made.

Diversification: If, in the judgment of the management, there is undue dependence on a line (or lines) of products in a narrow set of industries, diversifying to reduce risk may be a desirable move. General Mills, for example, acquired the Red Lobster, Olive Garden, and York's/Leann Chin restaurants as a means of reducing its dependence on grocery products.[1]

Financial Requirements: One cannot, of course, intelligently proceed with adding a new line without considering the out-of-pocket costs involved. Inventory requirements, storage facilities, training of marketing staff, and servicing demands all can result in sizable outlays for some products.

Projected Profitability and Cash Flows: The summary measures of the effect of the above considerations are the projected profitability and cash flows that would result if the new product line were added. Preparing the statements that give these estimates of course requires a sales forecast for the new line (and its net effects on sales of existing lines) and estimates of the costs that will be incurred as a result of adding the new line.

BRAND STRATEGIES AND CHOOSING BRAND NAMES

Brand Strategies

Once the decisions concerning product line and the products that make them up have been made, it is necessary to choose the brand strategy (or strategies) that will be used.

A **brand** is a name, term, sign, symbol, or design, or a combination of them, which is intended to identify the goods or services of one seller or group of sellers and to differentiate them from their competitors.[2]

There are seven brand strategies that can be used:

1. *NO BRAND.* Used primarily for commodities (agricultural products, unfinished lumber, ores) and generic products. Producing a product for sale with a "generic" label is, in effect, not branding it, and so falls in this category.
2. *PASSIVE BRANDING.* The product is branded but the brand is not promoted. The purpose of the brand is only to identify the seller. Passive branding typically is used for semicommodity-type products (steel, finished lumber and woods, cement, basic chemicals) and other products that are bought primarily on a price basis. For example, both Boise Cascade and Weyerhauser brand the plywood they manufacture.

3. *PRIVATE BRANDING.* The manufacturer puts the brand of the buyer (another manufacturer, wholesaler, or retailer) on the product (for example, the Whirlpool Corp. placing the Kenmore brand on washers and dryers it sells to Sears, Roebuck).
4. *INDIVIDUAL PRODUCT BRANDING.* The manufacturer gives a different brand name to each product it produces (for example, Procter & Gamble Crisco, Pampers, and Tide).
5. *PRODUCT LINE BRANDING.* The manufacturer (or retailer) gives a different brand name to each product line it produces (or sells at retail) (for example, Sears' Kenmore appliances and Craftsman tools).
6. *FAMILY BRANDING.* The manufacturer (or retailer) uses the corporate name (or some other brand name) along with an identifying name or symbol for each of its products (for example, Campbell tomato, chicken . . . soup; Boeing 727, 737 . . . 767 airplanes).
7. *COMBINATIONS.* Combinations of two or more of the above.

There are a number of considerations involved in choosing which of these brand strategies to use, including the nature of the products, the financial situation of the company, the marketing strength of the company, and to what extent the products are related in terms of use and quality levels. The effects of these factors on the choice of brand strategy are shown in Table 12–3.

Choosing the Brand Name

A ***brand name*** is that part of a brand that can be vocalized.[3]

A good brand name has a number of characteristics. These include:

1. *PHONETIC AND MNEMONIC CHARACTERISTICS.* How easily and accurately can it be read? pronounced and understood when heard? remembered?
2. *PSYCHOLOGICAL CHARACTERISTICS.* How appropriate is the name for the product? What message does the name communicate? How well is the message communicated? What positive or negative images are associated with the name? How unique is it? What are the aesthetics associated with it?
3. *PROMOTIONAL AND PERFORMANCE CHARACTERISTICS.* Does the name offer opportunities for generating associated advertising themes or graphic designs? Is it unlikely to become the generic name for the product (and thus be lost to the holder—examples are the once brand names aspirin, cellophane, escalator, linoleum, trampoline, yo-yo, and brassiere, which are now generic names for those products)?[4]

There can be little question that the imagery associated with brand names affects our perceptions of products. For example, one study has shown that persons asked to taste a jelly labeled as *Welsh's Grape Jelly* significantly preferred its taste to the same jelly with a *Generic Grape Jelly* label.[5]

Brand names have a variety of origins. For example, the following nine names were the final ones considered for a new Ford car:

Aurora	Falcon	Spectra
Bearcat	Flair	Swan
Contessa	Futura	Thunderbolt

Table 12–3 Factors Affecting Choice of Brand Strategy

Brand Strategy	Situational Factors	Accrued Benefits	Costs and Risks
1. No brand	Commodity-type product Low-cost producer Limited financial strength Limited marketing strength	Only option Inexpensive	No market power Low return Must match lower price or suffer sales, share loss Vulnerable to successful competitor product differentiation, cost breakthrough
2. Passive branding	Semicommodity-type product Purchased primarily on the basis of specification, price	Inexpensive	Limited market power Limited return Must match specifications, price Vulnerable to competitor product specification improvements, cost breakthroughs
3. Private branding	Differentiated product Excess capacity	Inexpensive Helps move down the experience curve Preempts competitor sales	Buyers can become dominant Vulnerable to competitor cost breakthroughs
4. Individual product branding	Moderate to high financial strength Moderate to high in marketing strength Unrelated products or need for differentiated product images	Brand loyalty reduces price competition and permits higher margins Can be used in segmenting, positioning Producer gains shelf space Producer gains channel power Consumer risk is reduced	Expensive Brand name may become generic
5. Product line branding	Moderate to high financial strength Moderate to high in marketing strength Distinct product groups that are unrelated by function, quality, price, market segment	Can be used in segmenting, positioning More efficient advertising, distribution Eases new-product introductions Producer gains channel power	Moderately expensive Failure of one product may put product line at risk Reduces ability to differentiate items within the product line
6. Family branding	Moderate to high in strength Moderate to high in marketing strength Products that are related by function, quality, price, market segment	More efficient advertising, distribution Eases new-product introductions Producer gains channel power	Moderately expensive Failure of one product may put all products at risk Reduces ability to differentiate products
7. Combinations	Permits fit of brand strategy to individual product or product line situation	Benefits listed above for each brand strategy used	More expensive than pure product line or family branding Costs and risks listed above for each brand strategy used

Source: Adapted from a table in a manuscript privately circulated by D. I. Hawkins.

Note that there are seven origins of names represented: weather phenomena (2), an animal, fowls (2), a Spanish noblewoman's title, a noun connoting natural aptitude, a coined word containing a morpheme, and the plural of the noun describing the full range of a phenomenon. The name selected was, of course, *Falcon*.

The name *Futura* contains a morpheme. A morpheme is the core semantic unit within a word, in this case *futur* from the word *future*. Several consulting firms specializing in brand and company name selection try to use morphemes from words with desirable connotations in the names they recommend. (Ex-

EXHIBIT **12-1**

Origins of Brand Names

Origin	Examples
1. Acronym	*IBM, ARCO*
2. Animal or fowl	*Camel* cigarettes, *Swan* soap
3. Application	*Dentu-Creme* denture cleanser, *Windex* window cleaner
4. Area or place	*American Airlines, Manhattan* shirts
5. Astrological name or symbol	*Aries* automobile, *Ram* golf equipment
6. Celestial	*Starkist* tuna, *Sunbeam* appliances
7. Coined word	*Kodak* cameras, *Nylon* synthetic fabric
8. Derived from other ventures	*Flintstone* vitamins, *Star Wars* toys
9. Family name	*Hershey* chocolate, *Bic* pens
10. Famous person	*Lincoln* automobile, *Reggie* candy bar
11. Favorable attribute	*Sunkist* oranges, *Rayban* glasses
12. Foreign	*Dutch Boy* paints, *English Leather* men's cologne
13. Fruit	*Apple* computer, *Pear* soap
14. Gems	*Diamond* matches, *Ruby's Brand—Jewel of Footwear* shoes
15. Homonyn with favorable attribute	*Lite* beer, *Sun-Maid* raisins
16. Imputed benefit	*Beautyrest* mattress, *Wynn's Friction Proofing* oil additive
17. Ingredient	*Clorox* bleach, *Wheaties* cereal
18. Letters and numbers	*SX-70* camera, *V8* vegetable juice
19. Macho	*Yukon Jack* whiskey, *Rebel* four-wheel-drive vehicle
20. Military	*Commando* pup tents, *Warrior* bicycles
21. Mood	*Magic Mountain* tea, *Zest* soap
22. Morpheme	*Compaq* computer, *Oxydol* soap and detergent
23. Mythological	*Aphrodite* perfume, *Mercury* automobile
24. Nonsense	*Poppycock* snack, *Whatchamacallit* candy bar
25. Palindrome	*Lozol* drug for high blood pressure, *Seres* vaccines
26. Occupation	*Lamplighter* mobile homes, *Professor* spoons
27. Seasons	*Autumn* grape juice, *Spring Maid* sheets
28. Spoonerism	*Tanfastic* tanning lotion
29. Superlative	*Acme* scales, *Super* explosives
30. Technological feature	*On-tap* root beer, *Polaroid* sunglasses
31. Trees	*Royal Oak* briquettes, *Pine-Sol* cleaner
32. Weather	*Cyclone* fence, *Rain-Maker* Sprinklers
33. Word spelled backward	*Ak-Sar-Ben* race track, *Serutan* laxative

ample: *Compaq* was the name selected for a company that then manufactured only portable computers. The morpheme is *pak*, meaning a small object. It was changed to *paq* to make the name more memorable.) One of them has entered in a computer each of the 6,200 or so morphemes in the English language for use in helping to coin brand names.[6]

Thirty-three generic origins of names of brands are listed and illustrated in Exhibit 12–1.

Methods of generating candidate brand names range from casual suggestions through brainstorming, search of thesauruses and dictionaries, computer runs (to coin words), naming contests, and the *U.S. Trademark Directory*. (In the four years between 1981 and 1985, more than 150,000 brand names were registered with the U.S. Patent and Trademark Office. It is not illegal to adopt a brand name already in use as long as it is for a product in a different product class.) The Marketing Research Department of the Ford Motor Company generated more than 10,000 names for the car that was finally named the Falcon. It is not unusual for as many as 50 to 100,000 candidate names to be developed for a new product.

After preliminary screening to a workable number of names, those remaining are tested using such methods as paired comparisons, ranking, rating scales, word association, and conjoint analysis. (See any standard marketing research textbook for à description of these techniques.[7]) The surviving 5–15 names ordinarily are tested in a consumer survey before the final choice is made.[8]

MARKETING OVER THE PRODUCT LIFE CYCLE

A three-week-old infant, a three-year-old toddler, a twenty-three-year-old young adult, a fifty-three-year-old empty nester, and a ninety-three-year-old elderly person with a terminal disease all require special types of attention and nurturing to flourish as their stages allow. How best to service and interact with each depends on the stage of the life cycle. Just as humans have different needs and capacities at different stages of the human life cycle, products also require attention to different needs and capacities at different stages in the product life cycle.

Products, like people, vary in terms of life stage and life expectancy. Some products exist only in the imagination of a forward-thinking engineer or an eccentric inventor. Other products, such as the most recently announced personal computer innovation or the most recently released popular song, hardly have been available long enough for us even to know their names. Several relatively new products, such as Stouffer's Lean Cuisine (upscale frozen entree) or universal life insurance, have achieved considerable success and may expect a long period of market dominance. Some products, such as Crisco shortening and Ivory soap, have maintained a share of the market for decades. Black-and-white televisions and soft drinks sweetened with saccharin may still be purchased, but they no longer occupy the prominent place in the market that they did in their earlier years. And, of course, many products have essentially died.

Covered wagons, celluloid collars, hoola hoops, the slide rule, and the manual typewriter, if available at all, are difficult to find now.

The astute marketing manager must deal with the product within the context of its life cycle stage. To avoid advertising a completely new product could be as serious a mistake as to withhold milk from a newborn child. At the other end of the cycle, heroic efforts to save a product with no life left could also be futile and expensive. The difficulty is estimating life expectancy, because products differ from people in that they have no built-in biological clock.

STAGES OF THE LIFE CYCLE

The stages of the product life cycle are product development, market development, rapid sales growth, competitive turbulence, mature market, declining market, and death.[9] Figure 12–3 depicts these stages in a simple, idealized case of a successful product introduction, using the classic "S-shaped" curve. It shows what might be expected to happen to sales and profits during each phase.[10]

During product development and market development, many costs are incurred that cannot be regained until rapid sales growth. The exact point at which a product becomes profitable and how that profitability relates to sales will depend on several factors, such as the nature of the manufacturing process, the competitive environment, and consumer demand. At some point the market will become mature and saturated, and no new demand will fuel the growth that characterized the introduction of the product. Most sales will be repurchases. Eventually the demand for the product will decline and then die, although the exact time of death can rarely be predicted with certainty very far into the future.

FIGURE 12-3
An example of sales and profits across a product life cycle.

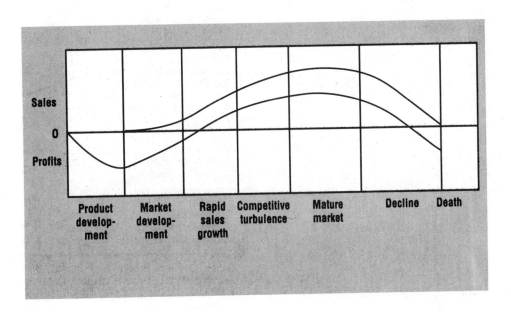

WHY PRODUCTS MOVE THROUGH LIFE CYCLE STAGES

Why do products move through the life cycle stages? The reasons are varied and complex but can be divided into five causal categories: (1) fundamental market changes, (2) technical developments, (3) company or competitor decisions, (4) complementary product or service changes, and (5) regulatory changes.

Market Changes

Why is it that the brands shown in Table 12–4 have retained a high level of sales and have remained at or near the leading market position for their product categories for 60 years? A major reason for the continuing success of most of these products is that there has been strong continuing demand for the product

Table 12–4   How Brand Leaders from 1923 Stood in 1983

Product or Brand Leader in 1923	1983 Ranking
Swift Premium bacon	1
Kellogg's corn flakes	3
Eastman Kodak cameras	1
Del Monte canned fruit	1
Hershey's chocolates	among top 5
Crisco shortening	2
Carnation canned milk	1
Wrigley chewing gum	1
Nabisco biscuits (including Uneeda)	1
Eveready flashlight batteries	1
Gold Medal flour	1
Life Savers mint candy	1
Sherwin-Williams paints	1
Hammermill paper	1
Prince Albert pipe tobacco	1
Gillette razors	1
Singer sewing machines	1
Manhattan shirts	among top 5
Coca-Cola soft drinks	1
Campbell's soups	1
Ivory soap	1
Lipton tea	1
Goodyear tires	1
Palmolive toilet soap	2
Colgate toothpaste	2

Source: "Study: Majority of 25 Leaders in 1923 Still on Top: 'Old Standbys' Hold Their Own," *Advertising Age,* September 19, 1983, 32.

category. This is not to detract from the obvious competence of the management of these brands over that period—many other brands of the same products came and went during that time—but the stability in the market for those products made it easier to maintain their success.

This success is, of course, not the case for many product categories. As shown in Figure 12–4, there are products that turn out to have long-term patterns of growth, and others that go through a lengthy period of decline. There are also products that are the result of fads and of fashions that suffer from more rapid change, both increases and decreases in demand.

Products with Long-Term per Capita Growth in Demand

Some product and service categories seem to grow steadily and consistently over time. There are at least two types of product categories in which this occurs.

The first such product category consists of **products that have long-term demand but purchase is highly income-elastic**. Owning a house of your own, having a college education, owning appliances such as air conditioners, traveling to exotic destinations, and purchasing recreational equipment are illustrations of products in this category. As per capita income has risen, per capita market demand has also increased. If the product is one to which the experience curve applies, the continuing growth in demand reduces production costs, thereby lowering the price and making it accessible to more consumers. By this process, growth fuels itself for more growth. The early years of the videocassette recorder are an example of this occurring.

A second category of products or services for which long-term growth occurs includes those **products for which a continuing, positive educational process takes place**. Vitamin pills, dental services, airline travel, and birth control devices are illustrative of growth for this reason.

Products with Stable per Capita Market Demand

Products in this category most often fulfill some basic continuing human need. Soap and shoes are examples of such products, as are basic food products.

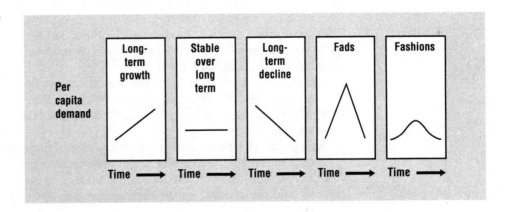

FIGURE 12-4
Changes in market demand that affect product life cycles.

Products with a Declining Long-Term per Capita Demand

These products or services are usually of one of two categories: either inferior goods or products or services for which there has been a long-term negative educational program.

"Inferior" goods are products whose purchase declines as incomes rise, or when the prices of superior products in the same class decline. Hamburger is such a product, for example—less will be bought when income goes up or as the price of steak falls. Long-distance travel by train or bus declines when people can afford to fly, and home-remedy sales decline as people can afford to get professional medical help.

Examples of *products whose sales have suffered from long-term negative educational programs* include nuclear power plants, fatty meats, and cigarettes.

Fads: Fads move through life cycle stages very quickly. A typical movie or popular song recording may move from market development to decline in a matter of months or even weeks. Fads succeed or fail primarily based on their entertainment value and on their ability to provide an opportunity for consumer self-expression. If a movie or product has potential widespread entertainment appeal, media coverage may quickly spread information about it. If a movie or product provides an opportunity for self-expression for a particular segment of consumers, word-of-mouth communication may disseminate information rapidly. People who bought Rubik's Cube, Cabbage Patch dolls, or Statue of Liberty paraphernalia— fads that have run, or nearly run, their course—were telling their worlds who they are and what entertains them.

Fads are relatively difficult for marketers to predict, influence, and service, but they are not totally arbitrary. Investors in *Friday the Thirteenth: Part V* must have had some idea that they would make money based on the successes of parts I–IV. But for every Trivial Pursuit that sweeps the nation, hundreds of products whose sponsors hope will become fads die at birth. Market development fails because underlying demand fails to develop, declines sharply, or even disappears.

Fashions: Fashion occupies an intermediate position between fads and technical changes in predictability and endurance. Although clothing first comes to mind when discussing fashion, virtually any product or service can at least in part be dominated by fashion trends, including cars, toilets, politicians, vacation destinations, and snack foods.

During the product development phase, fashion ideas about what is aesthetically pleasing come from many sources: subcultures, art movements, new ideals of beauty, historical resurrection or evolution, creative consumers, or creative entrepreneurs.[11] Market development can be traced to fashion leaders who want to be unique and whom others observe using the fashion, whether in person or through mass media. The leaders imbue the fashion with symbolic meaning.[12] Advertising may propel the diffusion of the fashion leader image. When adopting the fashion appears to be easy, convenient, affordable, attractive, and pleasant, people will be likely to follow leaders whom they admire or want to emulate.

As a fashion becomes more popular and it moves through rapid sales growth to a mature market, conformity rather than uniqueness dominates motivations for the new consumers' adopting the fashion. Social acceptance becomes widespread, and the product approaches saturation. The fashion cycle then begins again with leaders who desire uniqueness modeling new fashions, which will eventually lead to the first fashion's decline and death.[13] The whole process revolves around consumers' desire to communicate an image to others publicly, whether that image be rigid conformist, outlandish individualist, or something in between.[14]

Technical Development Effects on the Life Cycle

Technical developments affect product life cycles in two ways. The first effect is in the products themselves. Technical changes can usher in new products (innovative products) and can result in changes in existing products (adaptive products). Technical changes can also alter production processes and result in quality improvements or price reductions, both of which may affect the life cycle.

Changes in the Life Cycle Resulting from Product Changes

Life cycle changes often occur when technological advances are discovered or developed. A product that functions to solve some problem more efficiently or effectively than previous products may create a new life cycle situation. For the new product, the stage of market development begins. For the old product, the period of decline begins.

Technical change is an especially useful concept about product life cycle when a product is defined as:

1. the application of a distinct technology
2. to the provision of a particular function
3. for a specific segment of consumers.[15]

When any one of these three aspects of this definition changes, a whole new life cycle applies. (1) The microwave oven may be in the stage of competitive turbulence in the United States, market development in Norway, and product development in Nigeria. (2) The use of microcomputer technology for arcade games by junior high school students may be declining, for bookkeeping by accountants may be a mature market, and for desktop publishing by hobbyists may be rapidly growing. (3) The use of nylon as a material for hosiery has no necessary life cycle connection to the use of nylon for carpeting or tire cord.

Note that none of these limitations applies strictly to a brand. Often competition can quickly alter brand market shares of similar products serving similar needs for a similar segment without any life cycle shift.

Changes in the Life Cycle Resulting from Production Process Changes

Technical change in production processes can also bring about dramatic change in the stage and nature of the life cycle for a product. The automobile had been around for some 20 years before Henry Ford changed the way it was manufactured from customized units to standardized units produced on a production line. The resulting dramatic decreases in costs transformed the automotive life cycle from the "market development" to the "rapid growth" stage very quickly.[16]

Company or Competitor Decisions Effects on the Life Cycle

The decisions of the companies in the industry clearly affect the life cycle of the product. The increase in the use of minicomputers in business applications has been affected substantially by the development of network and graphics capabilities, for example. The decline in per capita consumption of cigarettes has no doubt been slowed appreciably by the introduction of filter tips and low-tar versions.

Complementary Product or Service Change Effects on the Life Cycle

Often events in a related field influence a product's sales. The example that is typically used for an out-of-date product—the buggy whip—became outdated when gasoline engines replaced horses as the primary source of power. College textbook sales in specific disciplines are closely tied to enrollments in those fields. Computer sales have been heavily dependent on software quality, availability, and prices. The decline phase of the full-size automobile was initiated by the rise in gasoline prices.

Regulatory Change Effects on the Life Cycle

Governmental regulatory changes can affect the life cycles of products greatly through either requiring or prohibiting products. When the Eighteenth Amendment to the U.S. Constitution was ratified on January 6, 1919, the resulting prohibition of sale produced major life cycle changes in the alcoholic beverage industry in the United States. Similarly, when Prohibition was repealed on December 5, 1933, liquor marketing again experienced a radical shift. The mandating of safety devices and emission standards for automobiles has had an effect of similar scale on the production and sale of seatbelts and lead additives for gasoline.

Degree of Control of the Product Life Cycle

For the most part, these causes of change in the product life cycle are not controllable by the companies in the industry. As shown in Table 12–5, market and regulatory changes are minimally controllable, if at all. Technical changes and company or competitor decisions are partially controllable insofar as brand sales are concerned (but not the industry sales or life cycle stage), and complementary product changes are only controllable through vertical or horizontal integration by the company.

Table 12–5 Degree of Company Control of the Product Life Cycle, by Change Agent

Change Agent	Degree of Company Control
Market changes	Minimally controllable. Through advertising, public relations
Technical changes	Partially controllable. Can control to some extent the degree of technical change developed in own company through size of R&D budget
Company or competitor decisions	Partially controllable. Can control only company decisions
Complementary product changes	Conditionally partially controllable. Can control own complementary products if horizontally integrated
Regulatory changes	Minimally controllable. Can influence regulatory changes only through lobbying

If one can't control, one has to try to predict. The measurement and prediction of the life cycle is discussed in the section at the end of the chapter.

NATURE OF THE STAGES

We turn now to a more-detailed consideration of the nature of each stage of the product life cycle. Because Chapter 11 gives a detailed consideration of product development, we will omit discussion of that stage here and begin with market development.

Market Development

Market development follows product development. Once management identifies an excellent product for a particular target market and has completed preparation for production and distribution, the next job is to develop a market. How can the product be diffused throughout the target marketplace?

During the period of market development, spreading product information is the primary goal. Here publicity is more important than at any other period in the product life cycle. The success or failure of a fad product depends almost entirely on the publicity early in market development. Fashion and technical products also benefit from publicity for rapid diffusion. Consumers must learn about the product and its advantages.

For technical changes where advantages cannot be conveyed through conventional media, distribution of product samples may spread the word about a product more effectively than any other method. When Procter & Gamble introduced Duncan Hines chocolate chip cookies, sampling proved to be an effective mechanism for telling consumers how close to homemade the cookies tasted. Words and pictures depicting a rich-tasting cookie, crispy on the outside and chewy on the inside, are no match for the sensory experience of eating the actual product.

Advertising also alerts consumers to a new product. Credibility is the largest problem for advertisements promoting new products and developing new markets.[17] Consumers must be convinced that some new attribute or virtue exists through a medium—the advertisement—that has less-than-optimal credibility. Credible spokespersons, convincing demonstrations, and objective information should all enhance credibility.

New-product advertisements do not need to provide total information about a product. Too often ads try to accomplish too much and end up cluttered and confusing. If consumers learn about one major advantage, that often will arouse enough curiosity for them to seek additional details from retailers or other sources.

> Conventional wisdom among marketers of packaged consumer goods is that for the advertising program, for the introductory period for a new product a budget should be planned that will result in one and one-half to two times as much being spent in terms of advertising dollar share being spent during the period as is desired in terms of market share by the end of the introductory period.[18]

For example, suppose RJR/Nabisco is planning to introduce a new brand of cigarette with the objective of achieving a market share of 1.0 percent within two years after introduction. Applying the rule of thumb just described, the company would have to spend on advertising an amount equal to 1.5 to 2.0 × 1.0% = 1.5 to 2.0 % of the total dollars spent in advertising of all brands of cigarettes during each of the two years.

Note the clear implication in such an action that there is a *lagged* or *carryover effect* of advertising—that advertising in this period will result not only in sales for this period but in sales for future periods as well. Virtually everyone knowledgeable about advertising agrees that lagged effects of advertising exist. Determining the extent of the lag accurately for a given product is one of the more difficult problems of measurement in marketing, however.[19]

Personal selling also is important during this phase for most types of products. Sales calls to the trade to build distribution will help spread information about the product through the distribution system.

The manager must also quickly resolve any distribution or production problems that may plague consumer satisfaction later during rapid growth. If a consumer learns about a product but cannot obtain it, the learning may result in a lost and forgone sale. One year Schick advertised a product on the Super Bowl before distribution to retailers was complete, with the result that consumers with aroused curiosity could not satisfy their desires for the product. Often establishing the channels of distribution requires a great deal of attention in this stage since retailers may be cautious about pushing an unknown product.

Zaltman and Stiff suggest several factors that influence the rate of diffusion of a new product:[20]

Comparative advantage. The better the product appears when contrasted with the closest alternative, the more quickly it will diffuse. A car that improves gas mileage to 200 miles per gallon with no loss of power will attract more consumer interest than one that improves mileage by 1 percent over current models but sacrifices 40 percent of power.

Perceived risk. The less likely consumers are to view purchasing a new product as potentially an expensive mistake, the more quickly it will diffuse. If *Consumer Reports* has judged our 200-mpg car as an example of superior engineering, it will diffuse more quickly than if no trusted sources can attest to the car's quality. Likewise, if the car costs $100,000, the risk will be perceived as greater than if the cost is $5,000.

Barriers to adoption. The fewer barriers to adoption of the new product, the more quickly it will diffuse. For example, an industrial corporation that has just spent a large sum of money on one type of assembly plant may be unwilling to purchase a new robot-based assembly system that performs the assembly more efficiently and inexpensively because the old technology has not yet been depreciated and because the unions may object to a shift to robotics.

Information and availability. The more people have access to information about a product and the product itself, the more quickly it will diffuse. If consumers do not know about the new 200-mpg car or the robot, they certainly will not buy.

Exogenous factors. A severe recession may stifle sales of all products, even promising ones that otherwise would experience rapid market growth. Legislative, regulatory, and judicial decisions can also revise growth patterns quickly. Videocassette recording materials diffused rapidly after the U.S. Supreme Court ruling clarified how copyright laws apply to them. Many food and drug products live and die by Food and Drug Administration rulings. Once gambling became legal in Atlantic City, that new industry grew there very quickly.

Should a company rush to develop a new market, or should it wait until others have succeeded and failed through costly trial and error, only to move in later? Pioneers, at least in consumer goods industries, usually enjoy an advantage over later arrivals to the marketplace and usually have a larger market share.[21] This generalization is true, although one can think both of examples (Hallmark, Kleenex, Wrigley, Apple personal computers) and of counterexamples (IBM personal computers). Pioneers have the first crack at establishing barriers to entry for competitors, such as copyrights, patents, and control of necessary-but-obscure natural resources. Pioneers usually have better products and a wider variety of products than later entries, especially at first. Pioneers may race down the experience curve more quickly than later entrants, thus arriving more quickly at manufacturing savings due to experience-based efficiency and scale economies. These savings may enable pioneers to maintain a superior marketing mix. Finally, consumers know more about pioneers. This last advantage evaporates, however, in industries with heavy advertising.

Rapid Sales Growth

During the period of rapid growth, distribution floodgates should be opened for most products. Sales tend to increase exponentially. At this point a manager wants to establish a long-term contact with enough consumers to approach market share goals. Competitors hoping to emulate market pioneers arise during this phase because uncertainty about the product's future tends to decline here. The manager must work to ensure a marketing mix that will allow achieving market share goals without the emulating competitors overtaking the goodwill that started during market development.

The major objectives of the advertising program during the growth stage of the cycle are to strengthen ties with dealers and to reinforce awareness and continue to induce trial by consumers. During this stage, modifications of the product may be made to improve it or to appeal to new market segments. Informing potential buyers of these changes is, of course, an important part of the advertising program.

Different consumers will adopt a product during the stage of rapid sales growth than adopted it during the market development stage. The shape of the normal curve depicted in Figure 12–5 may look familiar. Many human traits and tendencies—height, friendliness, and intelligence to name but a few—have a distribution similar to that curve. The figure indicates that this same pattern of distribution characterizes when people adopt an innovation. A few people adopt the innovation quickly during the phase of market development, and then the percentage of new adopters first accelerates, and then decelerates, until the market is saturated.

This description is more than a statistical characterization. It describes specific types of consumers who differ in response to new offerings within a particular product domain.[22]

Innovators first discover the new offering. They tend to accept risks gladly if they can find a better solution to a problem and perhaps be viewed as an expert. They are usually relatively young, well educated, and looking upward. Although these people constitute a small percentage of the eventual consumers one desires, they are quite important in that they are more knowledgeable, cosmopolitan, and visible than other consumers. Their negative response to a

FIGURE 12-5
Frequency and type of consumers adopting an innovation as a function of how long the product has been on the market.

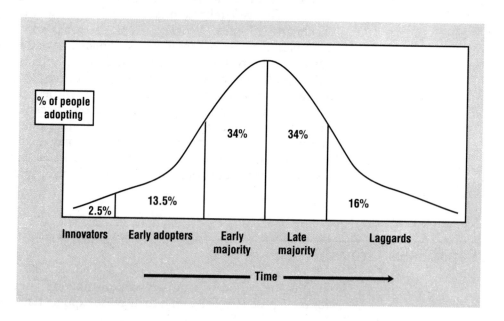

product may lead to a product's early death; their acceptance may lead to rapid growth. The first marketing information about an innovation should be directed to them, not to the "average" consumer. Commercial and professional sources of information interest innovators.

Early adopters are quite similar to innovators in temperament and importance. These opinion leaders may fear failure more than innovators and may be slightly more cautious than innovators, but in other notable ways they are quite similar to the young, educated, ambitious innovators. Because friends and colleagues look to these experts for advice and information, this group also can accelerate or kill a new product's sales.

The *early and late majority* adopt a new product or innovation at the average time, neither too quickly nor too late. They may be older and less educated than the earlier adopters, but they are social and modern people willing to try change eventually. They are somewhat less able financially to risk purchasing breakthrough products, but eventually an innovation will reach them.

Laggards tend to doubt other people. They socialize less and have a more skeptical outlook toward new ideas and new things. And they are the last to adopt an innovation.

Competitive Turbulence

Not all scholars identify this stage as important, but some evidence suggests that at least sometimes this unique stage has considerable importance.[23] The rate of growth slows as maturity approaches, and many competitors may have excess manufacturing capacity. The fight for market share intensifies, and weak competitors may fade.

During this phase, managers must carefully attend to the needs and desires of dealers, lest competitors lure the better dealers into exclusive agreements. The free-for-all of rapid growth shifts to a phase of subtle adjustment and fine tuning. The market mix must be revised slightly to serve each profitable niche as well as possible. Price will influence a greater number of consumers as all competitors have increasingly similar products. Advertising will emphasize product attributes that differentiate a product from competitors.

Mature Market

If the product ceases to evolve very much, the competitive structure of the market may stabilize as the sales data stabilize. Most marketing efforts are *defensive* rather than *expansive*. Demographic factors and economic condition changes could alter sales, but the main source of profit will come from reduced manufacturing costs rather than from luring large new blocks of customers. The maturity stage is usually longer than any other stage. This is the "cash cow stage" in which, even though market share does not change substantially, profits are at their highest.

Advertising continues to emphasize product differentiation. Most consumers already know about the product, and most uses have already been explored. The role of advertising during the maturity stage is essentially that of defending the product from incursions by competing brands, maintaining good dealer relationships, and informing buyers and potential buyers about product and price changes. Flanker products (e.g., different models, sizes, or colors) are often introduced during the maturity stage, and advertising must inform potential customers about them as well.

The major source of sales shifts from first purchases to replacement purchases. Consumers making repeat purchases have quite different reasons for buying and quite different purchase processes than first-time buyers. Prior experience with the product will weigh heavily in repurchase decisions. Marketing communication is less important, but distribution becomes more important. Pricing will influence consumers without strong brand loyalty.

Midgley has noted that since nondurable products have much quicker repurchase cycles than durables, the graphs of the life cycles of the two types of products will look different.[24] He has suggested that the classic "S-shaped" product life cycle curve shown in Figure 12–4 is the basic cycle pattern for durables. He believes that patterns that others have presented as counterexamples of the product life cycle concept in fact are specialized cases of the durable–nondurable and cycle–recycle distinctions.[25] For example, Figure 12–6a shows the pattern for the cycle–recycle purchases of durables. Figure 12–6b shows cycle–half recycle for nondurables, and Figure 12–6c shows the stable maturity for nondurables.

The Decline Stage

During the period of decline, sales and profits slip as alternative products begin life cycles of their own. New products emerge that fill needs more effectively. Advertising elasticities tend to decline along with sales in this stage, and so advertising becomes less and less profitable as the decline stage progresses. The central objective for the advertising program is to continue to "pull" enough sales through the distribution outlets to maintain the number and quality of dealers at the desired levels. For this reason, the proportion of the advertising budget devoted to cooperative advertising with dealers often rises during the decline phase.

Advertising and promotion eventually are removed as the old product is milked until distribution becomes too expensive relative to sales to justify continued production and supply. If death seems near, pricing may be guided by the desire to liquidate remaining supplies of the product.

As the president of the Procter & Gamble Company observes, however, the death of a product is not necessarily inevitable:

There isn't an inevitable decline. A brand that's in trouble is not inevitably doomed to continue on a downward spiral. Even in what may be seen as the toughest of situations, ones that would lead many people to walk away and say, "we will work on something else," —if you're able, if you have enough people who are able to understand the consumer, understand what your prod-

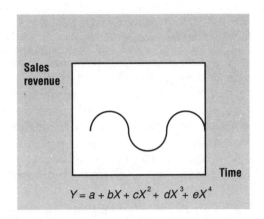

$$Y = a + bX + cX^2 + dX^3 + eX^4$$

FIGURE 12-6a
Cycle/recycle for durables.

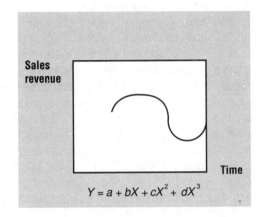

$$Y = a + bX + cX^2 + dX^3$$

FIGURE 12-6b
Cycle–half recycle for nondurables.

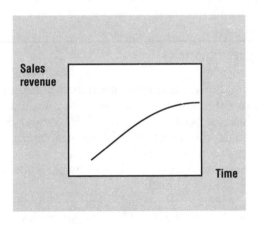

FIGURE 12-6c
Nondurable stable maturity.

uct is doing and not doing ... whether it is an established brand or a new one, it can be turned around. I think it's exciting what you can do on a brand, if you get back and really understand the consumer. It works, it really works.[26]

An example is a P&G laundry detergent, Dash. After 20 years of decline, a new formula and a new package turned the brand around. Sales tripled within six months after these changes were made.

Leavitt has proposed four growth strategies worth considering when it appears that a decline may be starting:[27]

1. *Promote more frequent usage among current users.* Soft-drink marketers went from single bottles to 6-packs, and then to 12-packs to encourage greater consumption. Oregon promoted tourism with the theme, "Stay and play an extra day." Professional sports teams try to sell season's tickets to people who previously bought single-game tickets.
2. *Promote more varied usage among current users.* A-1 encourages consumers to use its steak sauce on hamburgers as well as steaks and at restaurants as well as at home. Arm & Hammer promotes using baking soda to deodorize refrigerators as well as for a cooking ingredient. Q-Tips promotes its product to remove eye make-up as well as being a sanitary probe for treating cuts and abrasions and cleaning ears and noses.
3. *Find new users.* Firms should look for new regions, new markets, new segments, and new countries where their product may have appeal. Coors, for example, sold beer regionally until the middle of the 1970s, at which time it expanded to national marketing. As the Hispanic market has grown, Campbell's Soup Company and other food marketers have flavored their products and tailored their promotion to appeal to this ethnic group. In 1966, Culligan began marketing its water softeners in Belgium and in 1988, AVIA began to sell its sports shoes in Germany.
4. *Make a new product based on the basic materials.* Campbell's introduced Prego spaghetti sauce as an extension of its Franco-American line. Texas Instruments introduced Magic Wand Speaking Reader as an extension of its successful product Speak and Spell.[28] And Puma has introduced lines of walking and aerobic shoes to complement its sports shoe line.

Death: Product-Elimination Decisions

One of the most difficult and least-researched decisions product managers face is a decision to eliminate products. How long should a company stick with a product that has not been performing well? Should the product somehow be redesigned, should the advertising be reformulated, or should the company simply admit that continuing with the product is a bad idea and lay it to rest? In a world oriented toward progress and success, admitting that a product has no future is sometimes difficult.[29]

The primary reasons one would want to eliminate a product are that the causes of change of the product life cycle stages have driven the product to a point where it is no longer likely to make a contribution to profitability or to other company objectives. To review, these causes include (1) fundamental market changes, (2) technical developments and factors that have their origin as technical developments, (3) company or competitor decisions, (4) complementary product or service changes, and (5) regulatory changes. Any product can eventually succumb to adverse changes brought about by one or more of these causes to the point that it no longer contributes to profit or other company objectives.

The process of elimination of a product typically passes through at least four stages. Each stage is essential if a reasoned decision is to be reached.

1. *RECOGNIZE WEAK PRODUCTS.* The first stage in any decision to eliminate a product is determination of whether or not it is contributing adequately to company objectives. Such a determination should have been made as a part of a continuing and systematic monitoring of all company products. Products ought to live up to expectations for profitability, sales growth, market share, and consumers' attitudes. One list of factors to consider in such a review is the one given by Wind in Exhibit 12–2.

2. *ANALYSIS OF WEAK PRODUCTS.* Management must examine the products flagged in Step 1 to determine why they are falling short. Product elimination is only one of the options at this point. It is necessary to consider product modification, repositioning, and improved marketing mix strategies as well. How much will each option cost in resources and executive time, and what are the likely benefits from each?

3. *EVALUATION OF EFFECTS OF ELIMINATING A PRODUCT.* If repositioning, product modification, and improvement of the marketing mix seem unlikely to salvage a product, the next step is to contemplate the implications of product elimination. How will eliminating a product influence the entire company in terms of finance, resources, marketing, and management?[30]

- *Financial considerations* probably will receive the most attention. How will eliminating the product influence the supply of fixed and working capital? Will eliminating this product free resources for other current products? for new products? What will eliminating do to other products' profitability in terms of production and marketing overhead allocation?

    Table 12–6 demonstrates that the question of overhead absorbed by the ailing product is an important one in making the elimination decision. A product can be operating at a substantial loss, and yet if it is dropped, company profits may *fall*.

- *Potential constituency pressures* may influence decision making at this stage. How would other persons involved with the product (employees,

Table 12–6 Effect of Overhead Reallocation of a Product Eliminated Because It Was Operating at a "Loss"

Suppose consideration is being given to dropping a product that is expected to have the following annual sales and costs:

Net sales	$1,500,000
Cost of goods sold	1,000,000
Gross margin	500,000
Direct marketing costs	250,000
Margin after variable costs	250,000
Allocated marketing and production fixed overhead costs	1,000,000
Net profit ⟨loss⟩	($ 750,000)

Even though the product will be operating at a projected "loss" of $750,000, if the product is dropped, company profits will be $250,000 *lower* than they would be if the product were retained.

Why? Because the fixed overhead costs will still be incurred after the product is eliminated, and the $1 million that has been allocated to it will have to be charged to other products.

EXHIBIT **12-2**

Factors to Consider in Product Evaluation*

CATEGORY	ISSUES
Product sales	Absolute product sales Sales volume as percentage of firm's sales Sales growth Sales as percentage of projected growth Expected future sales volume Expected future sales growth
Market share	Current (absolute) share Current relative share Trend of market share Share as percentage of projected share
Industry sales	Sales volume Sales growth
Competitive position	Strength versus major competitive products Superiority versus anticipated new products Product quality (analysis of complaints)
Profit contributions	Profits and return on investments Projected profits and return on investments
Investment requirements for	New plant and equipment Working capital Management time Marketing support
Strategic fit—compatibility with	Desired product portfolio Planned production facilities Distribution outlets Marketing organization Corporate image
Environmental fit—compatibility with	Legal requirements Political climate Ecological standards Changing consumer tastes Technological development
Marketing efficiency	Promotion elasticity Advertising elasticity Price elasticity
Production efficiency	Cost of production Production flexibility

*Y. J. Wind, *Product Policy: Concepts, Methods and Strategy*, Addison-Wesley, 1982.

unions, dealers, shareholders, consumers) respond if the product were dropped? Sometimes the response can be almost overwhelming. When Coca-Cola decided to eliminate what is now known as Classic Coke, the public outcry was so prompt, loud, and prolonged that eventually the product was brought back.

- **Potential marketing effects** are always of concern, especially to marketing managers. If a product is eliminated, how will that affect sales of other products? Is a "full-line" policy a concern? Will relationships with consumers be impaired? Will the corporate image be hurt?
- **Management assignments** will necessarily be affected. Those managers associated with the product will want to know how capital, facilities, and executive time will be reallocated.

4. *IMPLEMENTATION OF THE ELIMINATION DECISION.* Assuming the decision is made after all these steps to drop the product, then the timing and the procedure for elimination must be planned in order to minimize disruption of customers, employees, dealers, and shareholders. One will also want to follow an orderly procedure to keep any adverse effects on company profits to a minimum.

Even at this stage, several options are available. The choice may be to sell the product to some interested party, perhaps including patents and production and distribution facilities. The decision may be a partial discontinuation by cutting back on models or on the area in which the product is marketed. Or the choice may be to run out the inventory and slash all support costs to the absolute minimum.

MEASURING THE PRODUCT LIFE CYCLE STAGE

One problem with product life cycle theory is that product life cycle phases vary in length. Given that a product has entered, say, the mature phase, how can we be certain when it has approached the next phase (decline)? For example, in the early 1970s coal mining seemed like a postmature industry and nuclear power seemed like a rapidly growing industry. Today coal mining appears to have a brighter future than nuclear power. Some fad products may remain mature for only a matter of weeks, and some products may remain mature for generations. As an example of the latter, consider the case of Bon Ami, the powdered cleanser, described in Exhibit 12–3.

Three of the common groups of techniques for measuring life cycle stage are qualitative methods such as the Delphi method, quantitative times series analysis and projection such as the Box-Jenkins method, and quantitative causal methods such as econometric models.[31] (See also Chapter 10.)

These measurement techniques have to be used with reservation, however. The qualitative methods always include an element of subjectivity. And most of the quantitative models that are available have assumptions that may lack validity. For example:

EXHIBIT **12-3**

Bon Ami Cleanser—Into the Second Century

In 1886 John T. Robertson began to manufacture industrial soap for textile companies to use on their spindles. One part of this soap was quartz or silica. In the manufacturing process for his industrial soap, feldspar was separated from the quartz. Robertson discovered that, if he combined this by-product feldspar with liquid soap, he had an effective, nearly nonabrasive cleanser with a market potential. When a local clergyman added the name Bon Ami to the product to provide a classy French touch, a product was born that still thrives today. The product quickly captured market share from Sapolio, the leading soap product at that time.

Bon Ami has had its ups and downs, but it has endured wars, recessions, the Great Depression of the 1930s, and changes in ownership. The positioning statement on the container, "hasn't scratched yet," has persisted from the early days of the product, although new management (Faultless Starch Co.) has stylized the chick shown next to the slogan on the package, and it has revived the product with innovative new promotional techniques. The near death of the product during the 1950s now seems quite distant given recent sales gains.

Many of the methods Bon Ami has used in promotion through the years still have contemporary rings to them. For example, expanding consumers' conceptions of product use situations to increase sales is good advice today. ("Orange juice isn't just for breakfast anymore.") Consider the following copy from a 1911 ad:

Did you think that Bon Ami was only for cleaning windows? No, indeed. It is a favorite for windows and mirrors, but that is simply because it is the only cleaner that cleans perfectly. Such surfaces show every smear or speck plainly. Bon Ami also cleans kitchenware, painted wood work, brass, nickel, copper, oil cloth and porcelain. . . .

More recently, Bon Ami promotion has recommended use on more modern products, such as Corning Ware, Pyrex, CrockPot, and Farberware. How far this strategy will take Bon Ami into the second century of its mature stage remains to be seen.

Source: Adapted from *Advertising Age*, April 30, 1980, 24.

- Most models assume that adoption is an either/or process, yet often intermediate steps such as awareness and knowledge may be important factors in predicting future sales.
- Most models assume that the sales ceiling is constant, yet for an income-sensitive product, economic boom times may result in increasing the number of buyers substantially, and economic downturns may result in sizable market shrinkages.
- Most models assume that only one adoption will occur, yet replacement and repeat sales often occur.
- Most models ignore marketing mix and competitive structure, yet often how well the product does is highly dependent on these factors.
- Most models have parameters (terms) whose values have to be estimated, often with limited information.

Wind has identified five questions to answer when trying to measure life cycle stage:[32]

1. What is the appropriate unit of analysis—product class, product form, product line, individual product, or brand? The individual product seems most susceptible to accurate measurement, but the purpose of a particular analysis will determine the best answer to this question.

2. What is the relevant market? A product sold regionally for a long period of time and then sold nationally (Coors, for example) may be in one stage of the life cycle in its original market, and in an earlier stage in the rest of its current market. Similarly, a product marketed sequentially to different segments (say, specialty stores first, then department stores, then mass merchandising chains) may be in different stages of the life cycle in the different segments.

3. What pattern and which stages are relevant? Some authors consider the stage of *competitive turbulence* important; others do not. Some researchers consider many varieties of fundamental patterns of the life cycle possible; others do not. You may recall Figure 12–6 which illustrated the patterns of customer demand for different types of products. Knowing which type of pattern is appropriate for a particular product type will aid in understanding and measuring life cycle stage.

4. How can one identify the correct stage? One must know what the stage is and how change will be recognized. One theory emphasizes looking at percentage of change in sales from one year to the next.[33] If one plots these changes on a normal curve, the Z score (number of standard deviations) operationally defines the life cycle stage.[34]

5. What is the correct time unit for analysis? The appropriate time unit will vary by the product being investigated. Most published research uses the year as the time unit, but with some fad products the entire trip through all life cycle stages may last less than a year.

Understanding the product life cycle can help a manager formulate strategy for a particular product by providing a context in which to interpret the significance of shifts in sales data and from which plans and policies can be ventured. Many products have demonstrated a tendency to follow something like the product life cycle pattern.[35]

SUMMARY OF IMPORTANT POINTS

1. A *product line* is a group of products that are related in the functions they perform, the outlets through which they are sold, or the segment(s) of the market to which they are sold.

2. *Consumer products* may be classified as:
   a. *Convenience goods*—goods purchased with a minimum of effort
   b. *Shopping goods*—goods for which the consumer typically compares the offerings of two or more stores involving two or more brands
   c. *Specialty goods*—goods for which the consumer is willing to make a special effort to buy and is willing to pay a higher price if necessary for a particular brand

3. *Industrial products* may be classified as:
   a. *Installations*—plant and major equipment items
   b. *Accessory equipment*—portable equipment and tools

    c. *Materials*—materials on which some fabrication is done before becoming a part of the finished product

    d. *Fabricated parts*—components that become part of the finished product without further change in form

    e. *Supplies*—industrial convenience goods that are necessary for the operation of the firm

4. Before deciding whether to add a product line, consideration should be given the factors of customer preference, company expertise, marketing efficiency, product line complementarity, effect on distribution channel influence, lines carried by competitors, diversification, financial requirements, and projected profitability and cash flows.

5. A *brand* is a name, term, sign, symbol, or design, or a combination of them, which is intended to identify the goods or services of one seller or group of sellers and to differentiate them from their competitors.

6. There are seven brand strategies that can be used:

    a. *No brand.* Used primarily for commodities (agricultural products, lumber, ores) and generic products.

    b. *Passive branding.* The product is branded but the brand is not promoted. The purpose of the brand is only to identify the seller. Used primarily for semicommodity-type products (steel, finished lumber and woods, cement, basic chemicals) and other products that typically are bought on a price basis.

    c. *Private branding.* The manufacturer puts the brand of the buyer (another manufacturer, wholesaler, or retailer) on the product.

    d. *Individual product branding.* The manufacturer gives a different brand name to each product it produces.

    e. *Product line branding.* The manufacturer (or retailer) gives a different brand name to each product line it produces (or sells at retail).

    f. *Family branding.* The manufacturer (or retailer) uses the corporate name (or some other brand name) along with an identifying name or symbol for each of its products.

    g. *Combinations.* Combinations of two or more of the above.

7. A good brand name has the appropriate:

    a. Phonetic and mnemonic characteristics

    b. Psychological characteristics

    c. Promotional and performance characteristics

8. The stages of the product life cycle are product development, market development, rapid sales growth, competitive turbulence, mature market, declining market, and death.

9. The reasons that products move through the life cycle stages can be divided into five clusters: (1) fundamental market changes, (2) technical developments and factors that have their origin as technical developments, (3) company or competitor decisions, (4) complementary product or service changes, and (5) regulatory changes.

10. Sales of some product and service categories seem to grow steadily and consistently over time. Sales of many of these products have an underlying long-term demand, but purchase is highly income-elastic. Other products have received steady, long-term, positive educational support.

11. Products with stable long-term demand most often fulfill some basic human need that has not changed in degree or way of solving the need.

12. Products with long-term per capita decline often are *"inferior"* goods. Negative educational programs can also contribute to the decline.

13. *"Inferior"* goods are products whose purchase declines as incomes rise, or when the prices of superior products in the same class decline.

14. *Fads* move through life cycle stages very quickly. Fads succeed or fail primarily based on their entertainment value and on their ability to provide an opportunity for consumer self-expression.

15. *Fashion* occupies an intermediate position between fads and technical changes in predictability and endurance.

16. Fashion ideas about what is aesthetically pleasing come from many sources: subcultures, art movements, new ideals of beauty, historical resurrection or evolution, creative consumers, or creative entrepreneurs.

17. When technological advances are discovered or developed, a product that functions to solve some problem more efficiently or effectively than previous products may create a new life cycle situation.

18. Technological changes can also alter production processes and result in quality improvements or price reductions.

19. Technological change is an especially useful concept about product life cycle when a product is defined as:
    a. the application of a distinct technology
    b. to the provision of a particular function
    c. for a specific segment of consumers

20. Governmental regulatory changes can affect the life cycle stage of products greatly through either requiring or prohibiting products or attributes of products.

21. For the most part, the causes of change in the product life cycle are not controllable by the companies in the industry.

22. During the period of market development, obtaining distribution outlets and spreading product information are the primary marketing goals.

23. At least for packaged goods, a commonly accepted rule of thumb for setting the advertising budget for a new product for the introductory period is that one and one-half to two times as much should be spent in terms of advertising dollar share during the period as is desired in terms of market share by the end of the introductory period.

24. Factors that influence the rate of diffusion of a new product include comparative advantage, perceived risk, barriers to adoption, information and availability, and exogenous factors.

25. Pioneers (at least in consumer goods industries) usually enjoy an advantage over later arrivals to the marketplace and usually have a larger market share.

26. The major objectives of the advertising program during the growth stage of the cycle are to strengthen ties with dealers and to reinforce awareness and continue to induce trial by consumers.

27. The sequence of consumers' adopting innovations is innovators, early adopters, early majority, late majority, and laggards.

28. Not all scholars identify the *competitive turbulence stage* as important. Here the rate of growth slows as maturity approaches, and many competitors may have excess manufacturing capacity. The fight for market share intensifies, and weak competitors may fade.

29. In the *mature market stage* of the life cycle, most marketing efforts should be defensive rather than expansive. The main source of profit will come from reduced manufacturing costs rather than from luring large new blocks of customers. The maturity stage is usually longer than any other stage. This is the "cash cow stage" in which, even though market share does not change substantially, profits are at their highest.

30. During the *period of decline*, sales and profits slip as alternative products begin life cycles of their own. New products emerge that fill needs more effectively.

31. Managers should not assume that every decline in sales implies impending death for a product. Repositioning, product modification, or improvement of the marketing mix may bring resurgence and even the start of a new life cycle.

32. There are five questions to answer when trying to measure product life cycle:
   a. What is the appropriate unit of analysis—product class, product form, product line, individual product, or brand?
   b. What is the relevant market?
   c. What pattern and which stages are relevant?
   d. How can one identify the correct stage?
   e. What is the correct time unit for analysis?

33. In financial evaluations of an ailing product, one should take care to assess the affect of reallocating overhead to other products if the ailing product is dropped.

REVIEW QUESTIONS

12.1.   What is (are):
   a.   A product line?
   b.   Convenience goods?
   c.   Shopping goods?
   d.   Specialty goods?
   e.   Installations?
   f.   Accessory equipment?
   g.   Materials?
   h.   Fabricated parts?
   i.   Supplies?

12.2.   What factors should be given consideration before deciding whether to add a product line?

12.3. What is:
 a. A brand?
 b. A brand name?

12.4. What are the seven brand strategies that can be used?

12.5. What are the characteristics of a good brand name?

12.6. What are the stages of the product life cycle?

12.7. Why do products move through the life cycle stages?

12.8. What are the important managerial concerns during:
 a. New-product development?
 b. Market development?
 c. Rapid sales growth?
 d. Competitive turbulence?
 e. The mature market stage?
 f. Decline and death?

12.9. What are the steps in making a product elimination decision?

12.10. What are the problems in measuring product life cycles?

DISCUSSION QUESTIONS AND PROBLEMS

12.11. The definition for product lines given in the tex.. does not include assortments of products that are sold at prices in the same range (for example, household items that sell for $1 or less). Yet the original "dime stores," and more recently the "dollar stores," offer only items priced within the indicated price ranges. Should the definition be amended to include similarly priced items as potential product lines? Explain.

12.12. The product lines of General Mills and the products they contain are shown in Table 12–2. Would you say the products shown there are *convenience goods, shopping goods, specialty goods,* or a *mixture* of these three types? Explain.

12.13. Some consulting organizations that specialize in helping companies select brand names are named:

 NameSake
 Delano, Goldman, & Young, Inc.
 Namelab
 Interbrand, Inc.

a. If you were to choose one of these companies to assist in naming a brand and you knew nothing about any of them except its name, which would you choose? Why?

b. What does this suggest to you about the importance of a brand or company name?

12.14. Seven-Up has filed applications to register the following brand names for one or more new soft drinks it may introduce:

1. Alumni	13. Inspiration	25. Sunbay
2. Big Bronc	14. Kappa	26. Sunberry
3. Bronc	15. Kemosabe	27. Sunbelt
4. California Gold	16. Laredo	28. Sunbrela
5. Cimarron	17. Lone Cal	29. Suncap
6. Coasta	18. Nat	30. Sunday
7. Colorado	19. Osha	31. Sunpop
8. Cum Laude	20. Phi Beta	32. Sunslim
9. Dakota	21. Phi Beta Kappa	33. Sunspa
10. Excite-Mint	22. Sarge	34. Sun Star
11. Frisco	23. Sunapple	35. Sun Swirl
12. Frucosa	24. Sunatural	36. Suntra
		37. Sunzest

Assume the soft drink will be a low-calorie, fruit-flavored drink. Choose the name you believe to be the best and the one you believe is the worst from this list. Explain why you selected each.

12.15. A recent ranking of the best-selling chocolate bars in the United States is as follows:*

Rank in Terms of Sales	Name	Rank in Terms of Sales	Name
1	Snickers	16	Heath
2	Reese[†]	17	York
3	M&M's[†]	18	Twix
4	M&M's[†]	19	Rollo
5	Hershey	20	Mr. Goodbar
6	Three Musketeers	21	Whatchamacallit
7	Kit Kat	22	$100,000
8	Hershey	23	Marathon
9	Milky Way	24	Toffifay
10	Baby Ruth	25	Clark
11	Butterfinger	26	Junior Mints
12	Nestle Crunch	27	Summit
13	Almond Joy	28	Mars
14	Reese[†]	29	Fifth Avenue
15	Mounds	30	Chunky

*According to DEBS Confectionery Marketing Report.
[†]One of these is the small and the other the large M&M's and Reese's.

a. Which do you think are the three best names for candy bars? the three worst? Explain.

b. What conclusions do you draw about the importance of the-name to the success of the candy bar? Explain.

12.16. The makers of AYDS, the appetite-suppressant chocolates, are considering renaming the product as a result of its now-unfortunate connotation.
a. Given the widespread name familiarity the product has and the sizable advertising costs that will be involved in reaching a comparable level of familiarity for a new name, should the company change the name? Explain.
b. If the name is to be changed, what new name would you suggest? Why?

12.17. Consult the volume of *Thomas Registry of American Manufacturers* in your university library that contains the Brand Name Index (call number T12.T6). From it, determine:
a. If there is an active national brand that is the same as your family name.
b. Two generic origins of brand names other than those listed in Exhibit 12–1. Give two examples of each generic origin.

12.18. a. Identify five products in each of the product life cycle stages.
b. Explain why you believe each is in the stage you assigned it.

12.19. How do you know when a product has moved to the next stage?

12.20. a. What is the product life cycle stage of each of the following products?
1. Frank Sinatra records
2. Designer jeans
3. Light beer
4. Jelly beans
5. Wine coolers
6. Convection ovens
b. What would be your primary concerns if you were a brand manager for each of those products?

12.21. Is it possible to forecast the sales of *fads* accurately? Why or why not?

12.22. a. It has been suggested that an *evolution* metaphor might be more apt than a *life cycle* metaphor to characterize how the sales of products change over time. Do you agree? Explain.
b. How would such a metaphor alter our perception of product sales change?

12.23. Suppose the Smallbusiness Corp. had a net loss of $100,000 last year. As a means of improving the profits of the company, the president is considering dropping a product that operated at a $100,000 loss last year and is expected to incur the same loss this year.

The product is forecast to have the following sales and costs for this year:

Net sales	$500,000
Cost of goods sold	200,000
Gross margin	300,000
Direct marketing costs	150,000
Margin after variable costs	150,000
Allocated fixed overhead costs	250,000
Net profit ⟨loss⟩	($100,000)

Should the company discontinue the product as a step toward returning to profitability? Explain.

12.24. A company that has only two products, Products A and B, forecasts the following sales and costs for each for next year:

	Product A	Product B
Net sales	$800,000	$600,000
Cost of goods sold	500,000	400,000
Gross margin	300,000	200,000
Direct marketing costs	100,000	150,000
Margin after variable costs	200,000	50,000
Allocated fixed overhead costs	100,000	100,000
Net profit ⟨loss⟩	$100,000	($ 50,000)

The overall profit for the company is therefore expected to be $50,000. The management is considering discontinuing Product B to raise the profit to $100,000. Should this step be taken? Explain.

Endnotes

[1] For a means of evaluating the risk involved in a product portfolio and how it will change if products are added or dropped, see S. Rabino and A. Wright, "Financial Evaluation and the Product Line," *Journal of Product Innovation Management*, Vol. 2, March 1985, 56–65.

[2] Given in American Marketing Association, *Marketing Definitions: A Glossary of Marketing Terms*, 1960.

[3] Ibid.

[4] Adapted from W. H. Doyle, "Brand Name Still Crucial, But Now It's 'Manufactured,' Not Dreamed Up," *Marketing News*, February 10, 1978, 12.

[5] J. A. Bellizi and W. S. Martin, "The Influence of National versus Generic Branding on Taste Perceptions," *Journal of Business Research*, Vol. 10, No. 3, 1982, 385–396.

[6] J. A. Trachtenberg, "Name That Brand," *Forbes*, April 8, 1985, 130. See also B. Rehak, "Got a New Product? Need a Name?" *Viewpoint*, September–October 1986, 12–13.

[7] See, for example, D. S. Tull and D. I. Hawkins, *Marketing Research: Measurement and Method*, 4th ed., Macmillan, 1987.

[8] For a procedure of generating and screening names, see Doyle, "Brand Name Still Crucial."

[9] C. H. Wasson, *Dynamic Competitive Strategy and Product Life Cycles*, 3rd ed., Austin Press, 1978; Y. J. Wind, *Product Policy: Concepts, Methods, and Strategy*, Addison-Wesley, 1982.

[10] Ibid.

[11] G. B. Sproles, "Behavioral Science Theories of Fashion," in *The Psychology of Fashion*, M. R. Solomon (ed.), Lexington Books, 1985; G. B. Sproles, "Analyzing Fashion Life Cycles—Principles and Perspectives," *Journal of Marketing*, Fall 1981, 116–124.

[12] S. B. Kaiser, H. G. Schutz, J. L. Chandler, and L. M. Lieder, "Shoes as Sociocultural Symbols: Retailers' versus Consumers' Perceptions," in Solomon, *The Psychology of Fashion*.

[13] Sproles, "Behavioral Science Theories."

[14] M. B. Holbrook and G. Dixon, "Mapping the Market for Fash-

ion: Complementarity in Consumer Preferences," in Solomon, *The Psychology of Fashion.*

[15] D. F. Abell, *Defining the Business: The Starting Point of Strategic Planning*, Prentice-Hall, 1980; G. S. Day, "The Product Life Cycle: Analysis and Applications Issues," *Journal of Marketing*, Fall 1981, 60–67.

[16] For an elaboration on the effect of technical changes on the product life cycle, see C. De Bresson and J. Lampel, "Beyond the Life Cycle: Organizational and Technological Design. I. An Alternative Perspective," and "Beyond the Life Cycle: II. An Illustration," *Journal of Product Innovation Management*, Vol. 2, No. 3, September 1985, 170–187 and 188–195; and R. U. Ayres and W. A. Steger, "Rejuvenating the Life Cycle Concept," *The Journal of Business Strategy*, Summer 1985, 66–76.

[17] D. Olson, M. J. Schillinger, and C. Young, "How Consumers React to New Product Ads: Implications for Copy Development," *Journal of Advertising Research*, June–July 1982, 24–30.

[18] J. O. Peckham, "Can We Relate Advertising Dollars to Market Share Objectives?" *Proceedings, Twelfth Annual Conference of the Advertising Research Foundation*, 1966.

[19] A classic study done in this area is by K. S. Palda, *The Measurement of Cumulative Advertising Effect*, Prentice-Hall, 1964.

[20] G. Zaltman and R. Stiff, "Theories of Diffusion," in *Consumer Behavior: Theoretical Sources*, S. Ward and T. Robinson (eds.), Prentice-Hall, 1972; see also G. S. Day, "The Product Life Cycle."

[21] W. T. Robinson and C. Fornell, "Sources of Market Pioneer Advantages in Consumer Goods Industries," *Journal of Marketing Research*, August 1985, 305–317.

[22] D. Leonard-Barton, "Experts as Negative Opinion Leaders in the Diffusion of a Technological Innovation," *Journal of Consumer Research*, March 1985, 914–926; E. M. Rogers and F. F. Shoemaker, *Communication of Innovations: A Cross-Cultural Approach*, Free Press, 1971.

[23] Wasson, *Dynamic Competitive Strategy.*

[24] D. F. Midgley, "Toward a Theory of the Product Life Cycle: Explaining Diversity," *Journal of Marketing*, Fall 1981, 109–115.

[25] D. R. Rink and J. E. Swan, "Product Life Cycle Research: A Literature Review," *Journal of Business Research*, September 1979, 219–242.

[26] L. Edwards, "Back to the Basics," *Advertising Age*, August 20, 1987.

[27] T. Leavitt, "Exploit the Product Life Cycle," *Harvard Business Review*, November–December 1965, 81–94.

[28] S. Onkvisit and J. J. Shaw, "Competition and Product Management: Can the Product Life Cycle Help?" *Business Horizons*, July–August 1986, 51–62.

[29] R. S. Alexander, "The Death and Burial of Sick Products," *Journal of Marketing*, April 1964, 1–7; P. H. Hemelman and E. M. Mazze, "Improving Product Abandonment Decisions," *Journal of Marketing*, April 1972, 20–26; G. J. Alvonitis, "Industrial Product Elimination: Major Factors to Consider," *Industrial Marketing Management*, May 1984, 77–85.

[30] Alvonitis, "Industrial Product Elimination."

[31] V. Mahajan and Y. Wind, *Innovation Diffusion Models of New Product Acceptance*, Ballinger Publishing, 1986.

[32] Wind, *Product Policy.*

[33] R. Polli and V. Cook, "Validity of the Product Life Cycle," *Journal of Business*, October 1969, 385–400.

[34] If the Z value is larger than $+0.5$, the product is in the growth stage. If it is between $+0.5$ and -0.5, it is in the maturity stage. If it is smaller than -0.5, the product is in decline.

[35] See Polli and Cook, "Validity of the Product Life Cycle"; Day, "The Product Life Cycle."

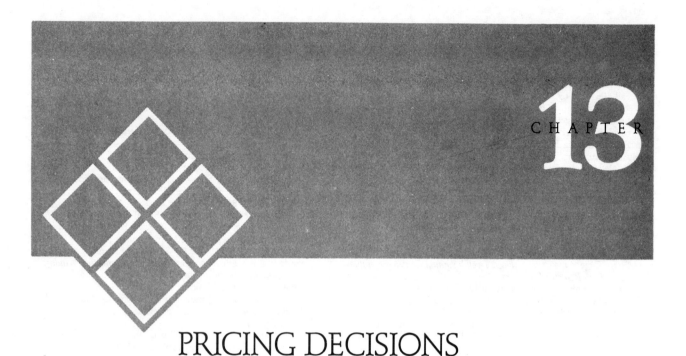

PRICING DECISIONS

Pricing is an important, complex, and interesting part of marketing management. It is at once a critical **strategic** element of the marketing mix, as it affects the perception of quality and thus is an important contributor to the positioning of the product, and a major **tactical** variable, as it can be changed quickly for competitive purposes.

Changes in price can be made much faster than changes in any other mix variable, a characteristic that adds substantially to its tactical value. Competitors can change prices just as quickly—a situation that calls for a rapid decision about what, if anything, is to be done to respond. The frequency and pressure under which reactive pricing decisions have to be made are no doubt important reasons why, according to one study, marketing managers perceive pricing and price competition as being the most stressful of the mix variables with which to deal.[1]

Prices are influenced by many factors, and can be set by a variety of means. The following situations illustrate some of the many considerations involved in pricing:

> The competition between Coca-Cola and Pepsi-Cola has been so intense over the years that the price of Coke in 1985 was 90 percent lower than it was in 1900 (in 1900 dollars).*

*"'Clash of the Cola Titans Keeps Prices Low: Coke," *Advertising Age*, August 25, 1986, 25.

In 1971 it required Pittway Corp. workers an hour to assemble a residential smoke detector and the price was more than $100. Fifteen years later, the assembly time had been reduced to two minutes and the price was less than $12.

When electric clocks were first developed, they cost less to produce than quality spring-wound clocks, and so they were priced to sell for less. They did not sell well, apparently because consumers concluded that a quality clock would not be sold so cheaply. The clocks were withdrawn from the market and reintroduced later at a higher price—after which they sold more successfully.[*]

The contracts for the stations, subways, aerial-line segments, trains, train control equipment, fare collection devices, parking lots, and landscaping for the San Francisco Bay Area Rapid Transit (BART) system were awarded on the basis of competitive bids. A study of the bids submitted has indicated that bid prices were lower, other things being equal, when the bidding was by large firms or by joint ventures with many firms, when the bidders had won few previous BART contracts, when the completion time of the contract was longer, and when the number of bidders was greater.

As a means of diverting the demand for electricity to times when the usage is lower, the Jersey Central Power and Light Company has adopted time-of-day pricing. This is a rate structure under which more is charged for electricity used during the peak daytime hours than for electricity consumed in the off-peak periods, such as weekday nights.

[*]A. Oxenfeldt, D. Miller, A. Shuchman, and C. Winick, *Insights into Pricing*, Wadsworth, 1961, 79.

Prices are influenced by:

Demand of buyers

Availability to buyers

The cost to suppliers

Custom and regulation

Prices are arrived at by:

Barter

Negotiation

Market forces operating through formally organized exchanges

Auction

A system of competitive bids

Cost-plus-fixed-fee

Administration by the seller

Regulation by a government body

All of these methods of setting prices are used in most of the free countries of the world. The method with which marketing managers in domestic markets are most concerned, however, is **administered pricing**, that is, prices set by the seller. A form of administered pricing that has assumed increasing importance as companies have become more divisionalized is **transfer pricing**, the "price" at which manufactured parts, supplies, and equipment are transferred from one business unit to another in the same company.

The methods of setting administered prices are the principal concerns of this chapter. The legal aspects of pricing, always an important and sometimes complex consideration, is not considered here. It is discussed in Chapter 6, "The Ethical, Political and Legal Environments of Marketing."

WHAT DOES *PRICE* MEAN?

An official in the Federal Trade Commission, the agency that administers acts dealing with price discrimination, once remarked that "everyone seems to know what 'price' means except economists and lawyers." *Price* is a term that is subject to many different interpretations. Does it mean only the amount paid directly for the product or service bought by the customer? Should transportation costs be included in the "price" in "delivered pricing" systems? Are warranties and services provided as part of the "price" if they are not quoted separately? What about cash and quantity discounts and other terms and conditions of sale?

It is clear that such questions had to be resolved by the Federal Trade Commission if it were to take effective action in enforcing "price" discrimination laws. A common understanding is also needed here. The definition we shall use is:

> **Price** is the amount charged for the product (or service) including any warranties, guarantees, delivery, discounts, services, or other items that are a part of the conditions of sale and are not paid for separately.

The Objectives of Pricing

To be effective, pricing must be carried out within the context of a set of clearly understood, consistent pricing objectives. The *principal* pricing objectives should be the same as those of the firm itself. In addition, there may need to be *collateral* objectives for pricing.

Principal
Objectives
of Pricing

A number of studies have been made concerning the pricing objectives of companies. The findings of one study are shown in Exhibit 13–1.

An examination of the lists of objectives in Exhibit 13–1 indicates that *profit* and *market share* goals tend to be the dominant ones. The objectives are stated in various ways; profit as an objective, for example, is expressed as a "satis-

EXHIBIT **13-1**

Pricing Objectives of Firms

In a study done on a sample of 202 firms, the objectives that were identified and the rank order of importance attributed to each were as follows:

	Rank		
	First*	Second†	Third‡
1. Satisfactory return on investment	21%	19%	13%
2. Maintaining market share	19	15	20
3. Meeting a specified profit goal	19	14	9
4. Largest possible market share	13	11	11
5. Profit maximization	8	8	14
6. Meeting a specified sales goal	10	17	16
7. Pricing at the high end of the price range	5	5	11
8. Meeting competition	2	0	0
9. Highest return on investment	2	8	5
10. Set prices at a high level initially and lower them later	2	2	2

*Percentage of respondents selecting pricing objectives 1 through 10 as the most important pricing goal in their firms' operations. Approximately 90 percent of respondents selected only one objective.
†Percentage of respondents selecting pricing objectives 1 through 10 as the second pricing goal consideration in their firms' operations.
‡Percentage of respondents selecting pricing objectives 1 through 10 as the third pricing goal consideration in their firms' operations.
Source: S. Samiee, "Pricing Objectives of U.S. Manufacturing Firms," in R. M. Hopkins and A. Toma (eds.), *Proceedings of the Southern Marketing Association,* 1978, 445–447.

factory return on investment," as a "meeting a specified profit goal," or as "profit maximization" or "highest return on investment." Market share goals are also stated variously, including meeting a "specified sales goal" and maintaining or realizing the "largest possible market share."

The other objectives given in Exhibit 13–1 are more properly viewed as pricing *methods* rather than as objectives. To state that one wants to "meet competition," "price at the high end of the price range," or "set prices at a high level initially and lower them later" is more to describe how pricing decisions are made than to specify objectives of pricing.

Since profit and market share goals appear to be the predominant ones,[2] the methods of pricing that are primarily profit oriented and those that are essentially share oriented are described later in the chapter.

Collateral Pricing Objectives

There are other objectives that are collateral, or subsidiary, to those of profit and market share. These include the balancing of demand for individual products in the line, leveling out of demand over time, increasing sales to selected market segments, and meeting the personal objectives of executives.

Balancing of Demand for Products in the Line: Any manufacturer producing a multiproduct line, or wholesaler or retailer carrying more than one model or brand in the line, may find it necessary to balance demand for particular products through adjusting prices.[3] Not to do so may make production or carrying costs so high as to make it uneconomical to continue the product.

A special case of the need to balance sales has arisen as a result of federal regulations concerning the automobile industry:

> To help meet the federal Corporate Average Fuel Economy standard for each company's entire line of cars, automobile manufacturers use price changes to adjust sales of the models with varying fuel efficiencies. The trick is to sell enough of the mini and subcompact models, averaging 28 to 35 mpg, to offset the heavier cars that get 12 to 15 mpg to meet the required overall corporate average.

Leveling Out of Demand Over Time: Many companies that produce and sell goods or services with seasonal or daily patterns of demand use price as a means of reducing peak demand and increasing it when it is low. Examples are lower telephone rates for evenings and weekends, off-season rates at hotels, end-of-model-year sales on automobiles, and lower installation prices for storm windows in the summer and air conditioners in the winter. In the case described earlier, the Jersey Central Power and Light Company has reduced peak (daytime) demand for electricity by the equivalent of $125 million of coal-fired generating capacity by encouraging nighttime use through price incentives.[4]

Increasing Sales to Specific Market Segments: Sales to specific market segments can be increased by charging selectively lower prices. Examples of the use of this kind of pricing include manufacturers' selling products at a discount for private branding; special discounts to employees, club members, or stockholders; different utility rates for homes and factories; different prices for milk for drinking and milk for making dairy products; and different prices for domestic and export sale.

Personal Objectives of Executives: Those executives of a company who are in a position to affect or approve pricing decisions—the chief executive officer and those on a Pricing or Finance Committee, for example—typically have many ties to the industry of which they are a part. Most industries have trade associations in which company officials hold office and serve on committees. Company executives represent the industry on advisory committees to the government and in such other matters as industry-wide negotiations with unions.

While serving in these capacities, the role of the executive is shifted from being primarily concerned with the welfare of the company to the well-being of the industry. The extent to which there is identification with the industry may also increase as a result of social relationships with executives in other firms with whom one used to work, or who belong to the same country club or church.

What are the likely effects on price that result from such associations? In one source it is conjectured that they have contributed to **price stability** through

> A blunting of the competitive urge to injure one's competitors and the creation of a sympathetic understanding and regard for them. It is far easier to steal

the customers of anonymous and faceless rivals than to pirate away business from persons with whom one has recently spent a pleasant social evening and will meet again soon.[5]

Social relationships with customers may also contribute to keeping prices lower than they would otherwise be. In periods of high interest rates, for example, small-town banks typically do not raise interest rates to big-city levels, as the bankers do not want to be perceived by their friends as being Shylocks.

We discuss profit-oriented and share-oriented pricing in the following two sections. Then we consider a method of pricing known as value-based pricing that can be primarily either profit- or share-oriented, or both, depending on the pricing situation.

PROFIT-ORIENTED PRICING

As indicated earlier, the stated objectives of firms predominantly fall into the areas of achieving some desired level of profit, or achieving some target level of market share, or both. Depending on which of these objectives is being pursued, different methods of setting prices will be used, and different prices will be set. A price intended to maximize profit during a given short-term period will be higher, for example, than one aimed at increasing market share during the same period.

Profit-Oriented Pricing for a Single Market Segment

Profit-oriented pricing of a product or service for a single market segment is different from, and simpler than, that for two or more segments. An actual pricing situation in which the objective was to maximize profits over a six-month period is that of the Concord Corporation:[6]

The Concord Corporation manufactures and markets an accessory item for a piece of industrial equipment. The accessory is sold both to the industrial users and to the manufacturers of the original equipment on which it is used.

Concord's management has two policies regarding price: (1) its expectation is that the prices set will be in effect for six months (barring unusual or unforeseen circumstances), and (2) it attempts to set prices that will maximize profits for that period.

The procedures for setting the price that is estimated to yield the maximum profit for a product or service sold in a single market segment are not difficult to specify. They were followed by Concord in arriving at the price for the accessory item to be charged in the industrial user segment. The procedures used were:

1. Estimate the amount that would be sold at each of the prices being considered.
2. Estimate the average variable costs per unit of producing each quantity that would be sold at each price.
3. Calculate the contribution to profit and fixed costs (difference between estimated dollar sales and total variable costs) at each price.
4. Determine the price that results in the greatest contribution to profit and fixed costs.

The Concord Corporation followed these steps in arriving at a price for its equipment accessory item for the industrial user market segment. As shown in Table 13–1, a range of quantities that would be sold at each price was estimated along with a "most likely" quantity. These estimates were made using the Delphi technique. The average variable cost per unit was estimated for the quantities at each end of the range, and for the "most likely" quantity.

Table 13–1 Profit-Oriented Pricing—Concord Corporation

Estimates for next six months:

Col. 1	Col. 2		Col. 3		Col. 4		Col. 5	
Price per Unit	Quantity Sold (000)		Dollar Sales (000)		Total Variable Costs (000)		Contribution to Profit and Fixed Costs (000)	
	Range	Most Likely	Range	Most Likely	Range	Most Likely	Range	Most Likely
$32	11.6–12.4	12.1	$371.2 396.8	$387.2	$170.8 182.2	$178.0	$200.4 214.6	$209.2
$34	11.0–12.0	11.5	$374.0 408.0	$391.0	$162.3 176.5	$169.4	$211.7 231.5	$221.6
$36	10.5–11.5	11.0	$378.0 414.0	$396.0	$155.1 169.4	$162.3	$222.9 244.6	$233.7
$38	10.0–11.0	10.5	$380.0 418.0	$399.0	$147.9 162.3	$155.1	$232.1 255.7	$243.9
$40	9.8–10.5	10.0	$392.0 420.0	$400.0	$145.1 155.1	$147.9	$246.9 264.9	$256.1
$42	9.5–10.0	9.8	$399.0 420.0	$411.6	$140.7 147.9	$145.0	$258.3 272.1	$266.6
$44	8.0–9.0	8.5	$352.0 396.0	$374.0	$119.0 133.5	$126.3	$233.0 262.5	$247.7
$46	6.0–8.0	7.0	$276.0 368.0	$322.0	$ 89.8 119.0	$104.4	$186.2 247.0	$217.6
$48	5.2–7.3	6.0	$249.6 350.4	$288.0	$ 78.0 108.8	$ 89.8	$171.6 241.6	$198.2

The contribution to profit and fixed costs was then calculated for each price, and the price with the highest contribution was determined. As shown in the table, this turned out to be $42 per unit.

It should be noted that Concord arrived at this price without considering fixed costs. Since, by definition, fixed costs will not be affected by the price that is charged or the quantity that is sold, *there is no need to include fixed costs in the costs to be considered in setting profit maximizing prices*. The price at which the greatest contribution to profit and fixed costs is realized will also be the point of maximum profit.

You will have already recognized that the procedure used for finding the price yielding the maximum estimated profit was the brute force method described in Chapter 7. You will also recall from that chapter that this price will be at the point where marginal cost equals marginal revenue, or MR = MC. That is, profit is maximized when the revenue added by the last unit sold is equal to the cost of producing that unit.

A review of how one goes about calculating marginal revenue and marginal costs is given in Figure 13–1. The most likely estimates of quantities to be sold and the cost estimates for the industrial user market segment are used. You should examine the figure to assure yourself that the $42 price is in fact where MR = MC.

Pricing in Two or More Market Segments

If a product is being sold in two or more segments of the market, different prices should be charged in the segments as long as:

1. The price set has a different effect on the quantity demanded in each of the segments.[7]
2. The segments are separated physically in time or by some other means that does not permit buyers in the lower-priced segment to sell to those in the higher-priced segment.
3. It is legal to do so.
4. It is economical to do so.
5. The objective is to maximize profits in each segment.

Charging different prices for the same, or essentially the same, product in two or more market segments is a common practice. It is used in pricing privately branded products, in export sales, for leveling demand over time (the peak-load pricing of utilities described earlier, for example), and for other applications. This practice is referred to in the legal and economics literature as *price discrimination*.

The industrial equipment accessory item produced by the Concord Corporation provides an actual illustration of pricing in two different market segments. Concord charges different prices for the product to the industrial users

The price at which maximum profit is realized is the price at which marginal revenue = marginal cost (MR = MC).

The *marginal revenue* for a price change is calculated by the formula:

$$\text{Marginal revenue} = \frac{\text{total revenue at price 1} - \text{total revenue at price 2}}{\text{quantity sold at price 1} - \text{quantity sold at price 2}}$$

For example, the marginal revenue for the prices $42 and $44 per unit, and the estimated quantities that would be sold at each price (as shown in Table 13–1), is:

$$\text{MR} = \frac{\$411,600 - 374,000}{9,800 - 8,500} = \$28.92 \text{ per unit.}$$

The *marginal cost* for the change in quantities sold at two different prices is calculated similarly, or:

$$\text{marginal cost} = \frac{\text{total costs at price 1} - \text{total costs at price 2}}{\text{quantity sold at price 1} - \text{quantity sold at price 2}}$$

In the calculation, either *total costs* (total fixed plus variable cost) or *total variable costs* may be used.

The marginal cost for the change in quantities sold at $42 and $44 per unit is then

$$\text{MC} = \frac{\$145,000 - 126,300}{9,800 - 8,500} = \$14.38 \text{ per unit.}$$

The graph of the marginal revenues and marginal costs over the appropriate range is shown below. As indicated there, they intersect at the point where price is $42 per unit, the price at which the contribution to profit and fixed costs was shown (Table 13–1) to be maximized.

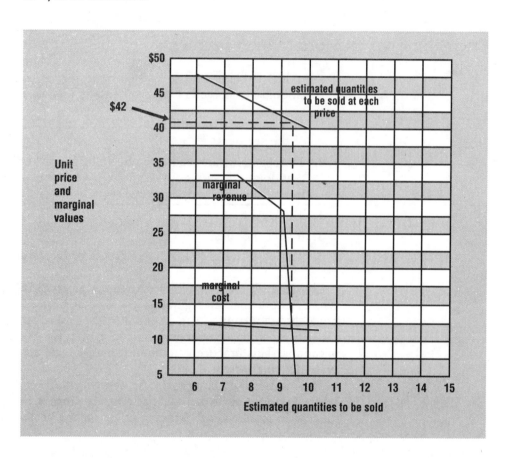

FIGURE 13-1
Marginal revenues and costs for industrial equipment accessory item—Concord Corp.

and to the original equipment manufacturers (OEM segment) for essentially the same product. (There are slight alterations in design, and the Concord brand does not appear on the units sold in the OEM segment.)

In pricing the product for the OEM market, estimates were made of quantities that would be sold in that segment at varying prices. Using the same procedure as described for the industrial users market, the price at which profit was maximized was found to be $38 per unit.

Pricing the product for each segment by ignoring the other one therefore resulted in prices of $42 (industrial user segment) and $38 (OEM segment). Although this procedure *may* give the optimum price in each of the segments, the chances are that it will not. It is always better to arrive at prices for a product or service sold in more than one segment by *considering all segments in combination* rather than one at a time.

To set the optimum price in the combination of segments one uses a **price discrimination model**.[8] This model allows the profit to be maximized jointly rather than by individual segments.

The procedure for applying the price discrimination model, illustrated by the pricing of the accessory item for the two markets to which it is sold, is:

1. For each segment, estimate the amount that would be sold at each of the prices being considered.

2. Estimate the average variable costs per unit of producing the combined quantity (for all segments) that would be sold at all relevant combinations of prices in the segments.

3. Calculate the contribution to profit and fixed costs for each combination of prices.

4. Determine the combination of prices that results in the greatest contribution to profit and fixed costs (difference between estimated combined dollar sales and combined total variable costs).

This procedure was followed by the Concord Corporation in pricing the equipment accessory item for the industrial user and OEM market segments. The contribution to profit and fixed costs was calculated for 28 pairs of prices. (The prices considered ranged from $32 to $44 per unit for the industrial user segment and from $34 to $40 per unit for the OEM market, in increments of $2 per unit.) As shown in Table 13–2, the highest estimated contribution was made at a price of $42 in the industrial user segment and at $36 in the OEM segment.

It is important to note that the profit-maximizing prices were *not* the same when found individually by segment and by combination of segments. Although the price for the industrial user market remained at $42 in both cases, the optimum price in the OEM segment changed from $38, when the product was priced for that market individually, to $36, when it was priced jointly with the industrial user market. (However, the contribution to profits and fixed cost for the $42–38 combination of prices was almost as high.) You will have recognized again that the procedure used in arriving at the prices of the two segments was the brute force technique. A marginal cost = marginal revenue solution exists as well.

Table 13–2   Profit-Oriented Pricing for a Product Sold in Two Market Segments at Different Prices—Concord Corporation

Industrial User Market			OEM Market			Combined Industrial User & OEM Markets				
Col. 1 Price per Unit	Col. 2 Unit Sales* (000)	Col. 3 Dollar Sales (000)	Col. 4 Price per Unit	Col. 5 Unit Sales* (000)	Col. 6 Dollar Sales (000)	Col. 7 Total Unit Sales (000)	Col. 8 Average Variable Costs	Col. 9 Total Dollar Sales (000)	Col. 10 Total Variable Costs (000)	Col. 11 Cont. Profits Fixed Costs (000)
$32	12.1	$387.2	$34	23.8	$809.2	35.9	$13.88	$1196.4	$498.4	$698.0
			36	22.3	802.8	34.4	13.93	1190.0	479.1	710.9
			38	20.5	779.0	32.6	13.98	1166.2	455.8	710.4
			40	18.5	740.0	30.6	14.05	1127.2	429.8	697.4
$34	11.5	$391.0	$34	23.8	$809.2	35.5	$13.89	$1200.2	$493.3	$707.0
			36	22.3	802.8	33.8	13.95	1193.8	471.4	722.4
			38	20.5	779.0	32.0	14.00	1170.0	448.1	721.9
			40	18.5	740.0	30.0	14.07	1131.0	421.9	709.0
$36	11.0	$396.0	$34	23.8	$809.2	34.8	$13.92	$1205.2	$484.3	$720.5
			36	22.3	802.8	33.3	13.96	1198.8	464.9	733.9
			38	20.5	779.0	31.5	14.02	1175.0	441.5	733.5
			40	18.5	740.0	29.5	14.08	1136.0	415.4	720.6
$38	10.5	$399.0	$34	23.8	$809.2	34.3	$13.93	$1208.2	$477.8	$730.4
			36	22.3	802.8	32.8	13.97	1201.8	458.4	743.4
			38	20.5	779.0	31.0	14.03	1178.0	435.0	743.0
			40	18.5	740.0	29.0	14.10	1139.0	408.3	730.2
$40	10.0	$400.0	$34	23.8	$809.2	33.8	$13.95	$1209.2	$471.4	$737.8
			36	22.3	802.8	32.3	13.99	1202.8	451.9	750.9
			38	20.5	779.0	30.5	14.05	1179.0	420.5	750.5
			40	10.5	740.0	28.5	14.11	1140.0	402.2	737.8
$42	9.3	$411.6	$34	23.8	$809.2	33.6	$13.95	$1220.8	$468.8	$752.0
			36	22.3	802.8	32.1	14.00	1214.4	449.4	765.0
			38	20.5	779.0	30.3	14.06	1190.6	425.9	764.7
			40	18.5	740.0	28.3	14.12	1151.6	399.6	757.0
$44	8.5	$374.0	$34	23.8	$809.2	32.3	$13.99	$1183.2	$451.5	$731.3
			36	22.3	802.8	30.8	14.04	1176.8	432.4	744.4
			38	20.5	779.0	29.0	14.10	1153.0	408.9	744.1
			40	18.5	740.0	27.0	14.16	1114.0	382.4	731.6

*"Most likely" sales estimates

Estimating Quantities That Will Be Sold at Varying Prices

The critical element in the practical application of pricing models that are designed to maximize profit, or to achieve a target level of profit or ROI, is the estimates of the quantities that will be sold at each potential price.

The method used by Concord was the Delphi technique. The general methods of estimating the quantities that will be sold at varying levels of the marketing mix variables were described in Chapter 7, and are summarized in Exhibit 13–2. By whatever method is used, it is generally useful to establish a range of estimated quantities, along with a "most likely" quantity. This allows one to gauge the possible risks from lower sales than the level expected, as well as the possible benefits from higher sales than expected. Although not shown in Table 13–2, this was done in the Concord case.

EXHIBIT **13-2**

Methods of Estimating the Quantities That Will Be Sold at Each Potential Price

Executive Judgment. Judgmental estimates by marketing and other knowledgeable executives. The *Delphi* method is a useful procedure for this purpose. Judgment finally has to be exercised regardless of other methods used.

Accuracy: Dependent on the executives concerned.
Cost: Relatively low.

Analysis of Sales Data. A fundamental source of information on the effect that price has on quantity sold, particularly when the price charged has been varied, either by geographic area or over time, or both. When possible, a pattern of deliberate price variation should be established to provide better data.

Accuracy: Can be very good.
Cost: Relatively low.

Value Analysis. Involves assigning dollar values to quality differences, feature differences, and differences in services provided so that a net differential relative to competitors' prices can be established. Used primarily for industrial products.

Accuracy: Good where cost effects of product differences can be assigned accurately, and where the primary selection criterion is an economic one.
Cost: Relatively low.

Surveys. Obtaining information systematically from present or prospective buyers about the prospective effects of price on purchases.

Accuracy: Low for conventional survey techniques. The use of *trade-off* and *conjoint analysis* techniques appears to provide much more reliable and valid results.
Cost: Moderate to high, depending on sample size.

Laboratory Experiments. Involves simulating an actual purchase situation and testing the effect of different prices on the amounts purchased. Such experiments are usually done for consumer rather than industrial products and are typically carried out in a simulated store.

Accuracy: Very good if realism of the purchase situation is high.
Cost: Moderate.

Sales Tests. A field experiment in which a sample of test market units is selected (distributors, stores, cities, sales territories) and prices varied experimentally among them.

Accuracy: Most accurate method available.
Cost: Most expensive method available.

Simulation. Experimentation with a model of the market rather than with the actual market for the product. This method has found little use for administered pricing decisions, but has had considerable use in competitive-bid pricing. (As the name implies, competitive-bid pricing is carried out in situations where bids are submitted by more than one bidder for a contract or project.)

Accuracy: Can be very good for arriving at competitive-bid prices.
Cost: Low to moderate for competitive-bid pricing.

SHARE-ORIENTED PRICING

Whereas profit-oriented pricing is concerned with profits in the short term, share-oriented pricing involves a longer view. In this method of pricing, the objective is to build market share, usually forgoing profits that could have been realized in order to do so, in the expectation that the larger unit sales will produce larger profits later.

You will recall that the strategy of taking profits now versus building market share and realizing profits later was discussed in Chapter 2. The *experience curve* was described there as a central concept involved in the choice between these strategies. It is closely associated with share-oriented pricing.

Pricing Using the Experience Curve

One method of share-oriented pricing is to "price down the experience curve." This involves (1) using the experience curve to forecast costs and (2) after an introductory period (for new products), pricing at a fixed percentage above forecast costs.

You will remember that the **experience curve** is a cost curve such that each time the accumulated output doubles, the total cost per unit is reduced by a fixed percentage.

The experience curve for a kitchen appliance is shown in Figure 13–2. It is an 80 percent curve; that is, every time the cumulative output of the appliance doubles, unit costs are reduced 20 percent. The initial unit cost was $247. By the time the company had produced 100 units, costs had been reduced to about $50 per unit. At 1,000 units of cumulative output, unit costs had dropped to about $27 per unit. At the 10,000 unit mark, unit costs had dropped to slightly less than $13 per unit.[9]

A plot of the prices charged for the appliance is also shown on Figure 13-2. The company could not recover all of its production costs at the time the appliance was introduced because the prices of competitive units were substantially lower. It was introduced at a price of $54 per unit and was reduced over time to $40 per unit to make the offering more competitive. This price was maintained until costs had dropped to $20 per unit. The price was then reduced periodically to follow costs downward and maintain a margin of 85 percent above costs.

FIGURE 13-2
Costs and prices for kitchen appliances

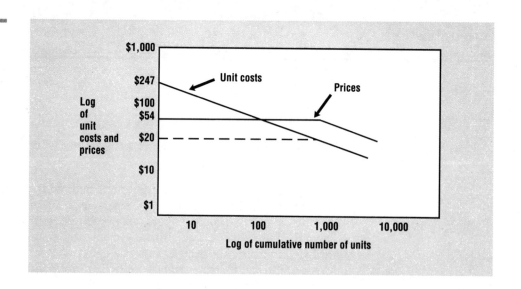

This is not an unusual pricing pattern. Many products have exhibited it over the years, including black-and-white television sets, gas ranges, polyvinyl chloride, semiconductors, and Japanese beer.[10] It is so prevalent in the pricing of Japanese products that it is often called "Japanese pricing."

Forecasting Costs with Experience Curves

In cases where it is applicable, cost forecasts needed for pricing decisions can be made using the applicable experience curve. It will be remembered that a mathematical formula for determining *unit costs* at any point on a given level of experience curve was presented in Chapter 2. A formula is available for calculating *average* unit costs as well. An example of forecasting unit and average costs for the kitchen appliance is given in Exhibit 13–3.

EXHIBIT **13-3**

Forecasting Unit and Average Costs Using the Experience Curve

Suppose the company manufacturing the kitchen appliance wanted to forecast:

i   the *unit cost* of unit number 12,000
ii   the *average cost* of units 10,001 through 12,000

when the first unit produced cost $247 and the applicable experience curve is 80 percent.

i   Forecast of the cost of unit number 12,000.

The formula for the unit cost for a given cumulative number of units produced is

$$UC_i = UC_1/i^b$$

where

   i is the cumulative number of units produced
   UC_i is the cost of the *i*th unit
   UC_1 is the cost of the first unit
   b is a constant

In this problem, UC_1 is $247. The value for *b* for an 80 percent curve is given in Table A-1 of Appendix A and is 0.322. Using a hand-held calculator with a y^x capability, the forecast of cost for unit number 12,000 is found to be:

$$UC_{12,000} = \frac{\$247}{12,000^{0.322}} = \frac{\$247}{20.582} = \$12.$$

ii   Forecast of average cost for units 10,001 through 12,000.

The formula for the average cost over a range of units of cumulative output is:

$$AUC_h^i = \frac{UC_1}{1-b} \frac{[(i + 0.5)^{1-b} - (h + 0.5)^{1-b}]}{i - h}$$

where

   AUC_h^i is the average unit cost over the cumulative output from *h* units to *i* units
   UC_1 is the unit cost for the first unit
   b is the constant for the applicable experience curve

The forecast average unit cost for units 10,001 through 12,000 is then:

$$AUC_h^i = \frac{\$247}{1-0.322}$$

$$\frac{[(12,000 + 0.5)^{1-0.322} - (10,001 + 0.5)^{1-0.322}]}{12,000 - 10,001}$$

$$= \frac{\$247}{0.678} \frac{[(583.038 - 515.281)]}{1,999} = \$12.35.$$

Since prices are visible and objectively measurable, manufacturers are accustomed to competing on price, and customers are used to making buying decisions in which price plays a central role. However, it is *value*, not price, that is our real concern as customers.

For those products for which an objective measure of value can be made and communicated to the prospective customer, it is a sound strategy for the company with the potential value leader to set its price below the **economic value to the customer** (EVC), which can be defined as:

> The maximum price that will be paid by a customer who is fully informed about both the product and the offerings of competitors.[11]

By setting the price below the EVC, the seller provides a **customer inducement**—a price for the product at which the value to the customer will be greater than its cost. An example of the use of value-based pricing is the pricing of the 9-volt lithium battery by the Eastman Kodak Company:

> After a lengthy development period, Eastman Kodak introduced the lithium battery, a battery with a use life of about twice that of alkaline batteries. It was introduced in the 9-volt size.
>
> The principal competition for Kodak was the 9-volt Duracell and Eveready alkaline batteries. At that time, their retail prices averaged about $3.40 per battery. This was the approximate cost to Kodak of producing the lithium battery.*
>
> Since the lithium battery lasts twice as long as the alkaline ones, its economic value to the customer is about twice the price of the alkaline batteries, or approximately $6.80 at the time Kodak introduced it. Kodak priced it to list at $5.80 at retail, however, to provide an inducement to the customer of $1.00 per battery.

*Estimated from data given in "Kodak's Entry into the Battery Business Includes First Mass-Market Lithium Cell," *The Wall Street Journal*, May 23, 1986, 5.

Although this is a legitimate example of value-based pricing, most applications of this form of pricing are more complicated. The complications arise primarily in estimating the EVC of the product. Value-based pricing is used primarily in the pricing of durable industrial goods because a greater degree of objectivity is possible in determining relative value among competing products.

The Steps Involved in Value-Based Pricing

There are five steps involved in value-based pricing:

1. Estimate the present value of the *life cycle cost* of the principal competitor's product.

2. Estimate the *EVC* of your product.
3. Subtract your average variable cost from your EVC to determine the *discretionary margin* you have relative to your principal competitor.
4. Decide how you want to divide that discretionary margin between *customer inducement* and your contribution to profit and fixed cost.
5. Set the value-based price as the sum of your cost plus contribution to profit and fixed costs.

We illustrate these steps with an example involving the sale of a special-purpose computer, software, and printer to be used for the ordering–receiving–shipping–billing–perpetual inventory system of a manufacturing concern.

Step 1. *Estimating the present value of the life cycle cost of the principal competitor's product.* In addition to the purchase price, the buyer of an industrial durable good often incurs costs of installation, training, maintenance, operation, or providing ancillary equipment over the use life of the product. By estimating these costs, discounting those to be incurred in the future back to the present and adding the purchase price, one can arrive at an estimate of the present value of the **life cycle cost** of each competing product.

Suppose that your company is competing for the sale of the hardware and software for the system just described for the manufacturing company. Further suppose that the system is being planned for a 10-year use life, and that an analyst in your company has made the estimates shown in the Step 1 portion of Figure 13–3 for the system being proposed by your chief competitor. As shown there, the present value of the life cycle costs of the competitor's system is $31,404. This represents an estimate, in terms of present value, of what the customer would be committing to pay for the purchase and operation of the competitor's system for 10 years.

Step 2. *Estimating the economic value to the customer (the EVC of your product).* Assume that your company analyst estimated each of your company's life cycle cost items with the exception of the purchase price to be the amounts shown in the Step 2 portion of Figure 13–3. Assume also that your company's system was estimated to have an incremental value of $1,000 to the customer because your company had a superior reputation for service.

Logically the maximum price that an informed buyer would pay for your product is

> Your principal competitor's life cycle costs
> **plus**
>
> Any incremental value your product may have relative to the competitor's product
> **minus**
>
> Your nonpurchase price life cycle costs.

This is the EVC—the economic value to the customer—of your product. As shown in Figure 13–3, the EVC turns out to be $18,484 for your system.

Step 3. *Determining the discretionary margin you have.* Since the EVC is the estimated maximum price that the customer would pay and you presumably would not want to price below average variable cost, the

Discretionary margin = EVC − average variable cost.

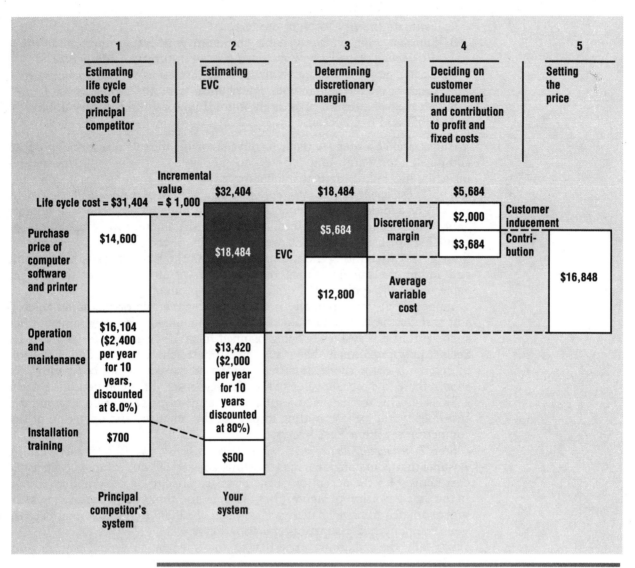

FIGURE 13-3

Steps in value-based pricing—computer system example.

Source: Format adapted from a figure in J. C. Forbis and N. T. Mehta, "Value Based Strategies for Industrial Products," *Business Horizons,* May/June 1981, 33.

Assume that Accounting has estimated the average variable cost of your system to be $12,800. As shown in the Step 3 portion of Figure 13–3, your discretionary margin then turns out to be $18,484 − $12,800 = $5,684.

Step 4. *Dividing the discretionary margin into the inducement to the customer and contribution to profit and fixed costs.* Although "always" is a word that allows no exceptions, we are tempted to use it here and assert that "one should *always* provide an inducement for the customer to buy if one is at all interested in obtaining the order." Giving the customer an inducement to buy while still pricing above costs sets up the "win–win" situation described in Chapter 1. You will recall from the discussion there that the PIMS data show "win–win" offerings to be the most profitable mode of operation.

But how much of an inducement should be given to the customer? The answer depends in part on how firm the estimate of EVC is. The firmer it is, the more persuasive it is likely to be when presented to the customer, and the less the inducement required to make the sale. The amount of the inducement also depends in part on whether the overall pricing strategy is designed for "profit-now" or "market share now, profit later." A market share now strategy will obviously make a larger inducement desirable than will a profit-now strategy.

In the example (Figure 13–3, Step 4), the inducement to the customer was set at $2,000, and the resulting contribution to profit and fixed costs turned out to be $3,684.

Step 5. *Setting the value-based price.* This is the purely mechanical procedure of adding the contribution margin decided on in Step 4 to the average variable cost. In the example, the purchase price of the computer, software, and printer was set at $12,800 + $3,684 = $16,484.

Note that this price is almost $1,900 higher than that of the principal competitor. Yet, if the estimate of EVC is correct, it resulted in a $2,000 better *value* than the competitor's price.

Value-Based Pricing Requires Greater Personal Selling Effort

For value-based pricing to be effective, the customer has to be aware of, and ultimately must believe in the validity of, the estimates that were made to determine EVC. This means that the estimates must be soundly based and a convincing presentation of them made to the buyer(s).

When value-based pricing is first used in a company, it is important that sales representatives, both of the company itself and of distributors if they are being used, should be trained in the type of selling that the method requires. It also is important for the necessary information on the life cycle costs and EVC estimates to be provided to the sales representatives. Unless these steps are taken, value-based pricing is likely to be ineffective, and may even be a failure.

TRANSFER PRICING

Several hundred billions of dollars of products—perhaps as much as one-fourth of the gross national product—are transferred each year between units within a single company in the United States before being sold to another company, or to the final consumer. When the transferring and receiving units of the company have income statement responsibilities, these products have to be transferred at a "price." Determining that "price" is the subject area of **transfer pricing**.

The Industrial Products and Components Division of General Electric makes small electric motors (among other products). Some of these motors are sold to other manufacturers for use in their products. Some of them are also used internally in General Electric's own end products. One of the products in which these motors are used is the General Electric vacuum sweeper, manufactured and sold by the Consumer Products and Components Division. The Consumer Products and Services Division has its own income statements, and its management is responsible for meeting objectives for return on investment.

When a motor is transferred between the two divisions, at what "price" should the transfer be made? Should the transfer be recorded at cost? at cost plus a return on investment? at a "price" that is negotiated between the two divisions? at a market-based "price"?

Although some of these alternatives seem clearly preferable to others, there is no final, clear answer that should be used in all situations. The best transfer-pricing system is one that meets the criteria of (1) encouraging transfers if they increase the profit of the company as a whole and (2) discouraging transfers if they decrease the profit of the company as a whole. The transfer-pricing system that meets these criteria will depend in part on the individual situation of each company.

However, some observations about the choice of internal pricing systems are generally applicable. They are stated below for the four most commonly used transfer-pricing methods.[12]

1. *TRANSFER AT COST.* This is clearly unfair to the management of the transferring division if they are being motivated on the basis of profit and ROI for their division. It will therefore tend to discourage transfers that might be in the best interests of the company as a whole.

There are other complications. If the division is also selling the same product(s) externally and costs vary between production lines or over time, should the lower-cost or the higher-cost units be transferred internally? Or should it be a standard cost? Should overhead be charged?

2. *TRANSFER AT COST PLUS RETURN ON INVESTMENT.* This has most of the problems associated with the cost alternative plus some additional ones. The addition of an arbitrarily determined ROI allowance does not help in the management evaluation process and, depending on the level at which it is set, may tend to encourage undesirable transfers or discourage desirable ones.

3. *NEGOTIATED "PRICE."* Some companies rely on negotiation between the divisions concerned to set "prices" at which the transfer is to be made. This is costly in terms of executive time, and in cases where the buying division takes a large share of the supplying division's output, places the buying division in a highly favorable bargaining position. This is particularly the case if the buying division has top management approval to buy from external sources of supply if a satisfactory agreement is not reached internally.

Some companies have negotiated agreements between divisions that amount to a profit-sharing arrangement. The component products are transferred at cost, but the buying division's profits from the sale of the end product are divided on the basis of the share of the total cost made up by the component product.

4. *MARKET-BASED PRICES.* This is probably the best arrangement when the supplying division is also selling a substantial part of its output externally. An objectively verifiable market price—which presumably is competitive (or else the selling division would be unsuccessful in selling to outside buyers)—is then available. The market price is sometimes reduced by an amount equal to the estimated savings in marketing costs.

The principal problem with market-based prices arises when the supplying division is *not* selling to outside buyers. It then becomes more difficult to establish what the equivalent market price would be. This, in effect, puts the determination of transfer price into the "negotiated price" mode of determination.

A study of transfer-pricing methods in Great Britain indicates that the most commonly used methods are market-based pricing for transfers between domestic divisions and cost-based pricing for transfers between a domestic and an international division.[13]

One always has to be careful to avoid legal complications regardless of what method of setting price is used. This is especially the case when domestic component parts divisions are supplying foreign assembly divisions, as below-cost transfer prices may be interpreted by the host country as a method of escaping import duties or a disguised method of "dumping," and above-cost transfer prices as a method of escaping host country taxes. (These may be contributing reasons for the greater reliance on cost-based pricing in transfers between domestic and international divisions just described.)

PRICING IN PRACTICE

A variety of pricing methods are used in practice.[14] Available evidence indicates that the most prevalent methods are to price at a competitive level and to use cost-based pricing (Table 13–3).

Table 13–3   Use of Various Approaches to Setting Price

Approaches to Setting Prices	Type of Product		
	Industrial	Consumer Durable	Consumer Nondurable
Competitive level	46.7	45.0	46.0
Cost-plus	25.1	28.2	27.1
What the market will bear	13.4	15.8	14.2
Certain percentage above or below competitive level	6.7	8.1	11.1
According to government regulations	8.0	2.7	1.6
Other	0.1	0.1	—
Total	100.0	100.0	100.0

Source: J. G. Udell, *Successful Marketing Strategies in American Industries*, Mimir Publishers, 1972, 152.

A brief review is given here of meeting competition as a pricing policy, cost-based pricing, regional pricing, discounting, and two customer-based pricing approaches—skimming and psychological pricing.

Meeting Competition

The long-standing practice of two department stores in New York City, Gimbel's and Macy's, sending shoppers to each other's stores regularly during each day to ensure that neither is being undersold by the other exemplifies the "meeting competition" method of pricing. Although usually not done with this frequency, many companies use price comparisons as the basis for pricing their own products.

The logic often advanced for pricing at or near the average of competitor prices is that price represents the combined judgments of the industry pricers as to what the price for the product should be. Stated another way, the average of competitor prices is the closest thing to a price as determined on a commodity market, and is thus representative of the "best" price for the product.

There are several problems with this logic. It assumes that the products are perceived by the buyers as being the same, or nearly so. It does not take into account the services offered, or not offered, with the product. Nor is there allowance made for the other elements of the marketing mix; price, advertising, and distribution differences are neglected. There is no consideration given to different prices for different market segments. Finally, cost differences among competitors are ignored.

Not only is meeting competition seemingly a poor way to price theoretically, it also does not appear to be a sound pricing method in practice. An examination of the experience of over 1,600 businesses indicates that companies are usually better off following a policy of either pricing at a premium or pricing at a discount, relative to competitors. That is, "an equivalent-price strategy is usually the worst choice."[15]

Cost-Based Pricing

Cost-based pricing, like pricing to meet competition, is a common pricing method. It may even be the most common pricing method for small firms.[16]

Although cost-based pricing has generally been denounced by marketers and economists, it is understandable why it is so widely used. Cost is a necessary part of the pricing equation regardless of objective. Three reasons account for why cost forecasts may be used alone, and not in conjunction with demand forecasts, for pricing:

1. *A desire to avoid risks may make cost-based pricing desirable.* Even with inflation, cost forecasts usually can be made more accurately than can demand forecasts. Conservatism may dictate a pricing approach that

covers costs and brings an acceptable profit margin, rather than incorporating risky demand forecasts.

During periods when inflation rates are relatively high, there often are "escalator" clauses in contracts in which price increases are automatically made in accordance with a previously stated formula. This is a form of cost-based pricing and is used to avoid inflation-related risks.[17]

2. *For companies with a large number of products (or spare parts), cost-based pricing may be the only practical method of pricing.* It would be uneconomical for the Crane Company, with more than 100,000 products, to attempt to estimate demand for each of them before setting a price. Supermarkets, with more than 10,000 items, have a similar problem.

3. *Companies that are engaged in share-oriented pricing are, by definition, using a cost-based pricing method.* Pricing in such companies is usually done by adding a fixed percentage of cost to cost.

One of the appealing features of cost-based pricing is that prices can be set and updated by computer, using accounting data. A supermarket manager can set gross margins by product category, for example, and a computer can be used to set prices based on invoices. If the margin for dry groceries is to be 28 percent of cost, for example, each item can be priced by multiplying invoice cost by 1.28. This is especially useful if a system of electronic scanning of product code and computerized checkout is being used by the supermarket.

Regional Pricing

"In recent years, consumer product companies have sold a growing portion of their goods at prices set for specific regions."[18] There are at least two reasons for this practice. The first is freight costs; consumer durables manufactured in the East and Midwest have traditionally been higher on the West Coast of the United States, and lumber and plywood produced in the Northwest have been higher in the Midwest and East, both for this reason. The second reason is to gain sales and market share in areas where they are weak.

When the price differentials exceed shipping costs, middlemen known as **diverters** often buy in the lower-price regions and ship to buyers in the higher-price regions. Some multiregional and national retailers do this for themselves in this situation, as well as acting as diverters for other retailers.

Discounting

A list price is one thing; the price paid by many buyers may be quite another. Even though lower average prices may be paid as a result of discounts, the intent (and often the reality) of discounted prices is to increase profits. Airline discount fares are an example:

> . . . TWA has software that enables [it] to create pricing scenarios on a flight-by-flight basis that predict the effect of fare adjustments on TWA's bottom

line. . . . Similarly, at any moment, Continental's computer is monitoring the status of reservations on 495,000 future flights. The computers measure the bookings against expectations and call attention to any flight that is off the normal pace, depending upon the season, flight time, cities being served, day of the week, and whether a predominantly business or leisure market is being served. Fares and advertising can then be revised.[19]

There are five kinds of discounts: (1) trade or functional, (2) trade promotion, (3) cash, (4) consumer promotion, and (5) quantity.

Trade or Functional Discounts: This type of discount is given to middlemen in payment for the functions they perform (storage, personal selling, delivery, and so forth). These discounts are typically expressed as chains of numbers such as 35, 10, 10, 2/10 net 30. The first number refers to the percentage discount the dealer is allowed for the position occupied in the distribution channel, the second and third numbers the percentage discount given for the performance of promotional or other services, and the last the discount for prompt payment.

In calculating the discounted price, the discounts are applied sequentially. If the price is $100, for example, a dealer with a 35, 10, 10, 2/10 net 30 discount chain would pay:

$$\$100.00 - .35(\$100.00) = \$65.00$$
$$\$65.00 - .10(\$65.00) = \$58.50$$
$$\$58.50 - .10(\$58.50) = \$52.70$$

and, if payment is made within 10 days,

$$\$52.70 - .02(\$52.70) = \$51.65.$$

Trade Promotion Discounts: The second and third discounts in the chain described above are for dealers who carry out cooperative advertising of the product with retailers, whose sales forces install special retail displays, or for supplying other specified services.

Cash Discounts: An example of a cash discount is the "2/10 net 30" just shown. This means that if the billed amount is paid within 10 days a 2 percent discount can be taken. If it is not paid within 10 days, the full amount is due within 30 days.

Cash discounts are offered for two reasons: (1) to provide an incentive for early payment and thus to increase cash flow, and (2) to reduce bad debt losses. It also serves as a de facto price decrease to those who take advantage of it, and therefore presumably increases demand.

The "2/10 net 30" discount, a commonly used set of terms for prompt payment, provides an attractive implicit interest rate to the buyer. (The interest rate is a little over 36 percent per annum on a noncompounded basis.) It is even more attractive, however, if the buyer delays payment for 40 or 50 days and still takes the discount. Historically, large companies have always done this. Casual observation suggests that this practice has spread to smaller companies in many industries. When this happens, the vendor has the option of rebilling for the discount taken and running the risk of losing the customer, or ignoring the loss in billed amount. Many suppliers have finessed this problem by raising prices by an amount equal to their cash discount.

A number of large corporations have begun to offer cash discounts for electronic payments (transfer of funds by computer). RJR/Nabisco is an example.[20]

Consumer Promotional Discounts: Although often not thought of as such, such promotions as coupons, rebates, one-cent sales, and senior citizen and children's price reductions are, in every sense of the term, consumer discounts. Such promotions for frequently purchased consumer products have grown in recent years to a point that they now exceed advertising by companies in terms of annual dollar volume.

Their purpose is, of course, to stimulate demand for the product being promoted. They are discussed at some length in the chapter on advertising, sales promotion, and public relations (Chapter 15).

Quantity Discounts: A quantity discount schedule is a list of unit prices at ranges of quantities purchased—as the number of units purchased moves from one quantity range to the next, the price per unit declines. An example is the discount schedule for the IBM-AT computer:[21]

Quantity	Unit Price ($)
1–19	5,795
20–49	5,099
50–149	4,867
150–249	4,636
250–499	4,404
500–999	4,230
1,000 +	4,056

This is a *noncumulative, per-unit price, all-unit prices* schedule, a common type of schedule. That is, only the units bought on each order qualify for the discount, and the buyer pays the same unit price for all units bought on that order.[22]

Quantity discounts may be offered for any of at least three reasons. The principal reason is probably that they offer economies to the seller in the way that the product is manufactured and sold. A second reason is that, used appropriately, they serve as a means of discriminating in price between buyers, and thus as a means of increasing profits. Finally, it has been argued that they serve as a tool for increasing channel cooperation.[23]

Quantity discounts give rise to potential cost savings that are not explicit in the discount schedule itself. One practice is for users of the product to place pooled orders through a group member to take advantage of the lower per-unit cost at the pooled quantity than at the quantity any of the individual group members would buy. This practice is even extended in some cases to the buyer(s) ordering extra units, which are brokered to other users. Some critics argue that this is a major reason for the existence of "gray" markets in which price-discounted goods enter the market through unauthorized channels.[24]

In setting up the quantity discount schedule, decisions obviously have to be made on the breaks between quantity ranges and the amount of the discount for each range. One has to be careful to avoid putting windows into the schedule. A ***window*** occurs when the total price for the last quantity purchased in one range is greater than the total price for the first quantity purchased in the next range. IBM did this in setting up the quantity discount schedule (shown above) for its AT computer. One could order 19 ATs for 19 × $5,795 = $110,105, but a much better buy was to order 20 at 20 × $5,099 = $101,980.

Skimming

Much has been written about "skimming" as a pricing method.[25] It is an approach to pricing a new product that involves setting a high initial price and lowering it by increments over time.

The high initial price may be interpreted as an indicator of high quality of the product, which, if so, is a perception that can be capitalized on both then and when the price is reduced later. Each successive price reduction may also introduce a product to a new price segment of the market. If this is the case, skimming of prices may be viewed as a policy of segmentation over time, rather than across space or between groups.

A classic case of skimming was the pattern of pricing used on the ballpoint pen when it was originally introduced in the United States. As described earlier (Chapter 6), the Reynolds International Pen Company began producing the pens in the fall of 1945. The cost per pen was averaging about 80 cents. Prices were still being controlled (as they had been during all of World War II) by the Office of Price Administration (OPA). A representative of the company went to Washington and negotiated with OPA a ceiling retail price of $12.50 per pen.

This price held until October 1946, by which time "approximately a hundred manufacturers were turning out ball point pens, some of them selling for as little as $2.98. At that time, Reynolds brought out a new model and reduced prices to $3.85. By February 1947 the suggested retail price of Reynolds pens had dropped to 98 cents and by May of 1948, to 39 cents."[26]

The decision by Reynolds to charge as high an introductory price as OPA would allow was based in part on a recognition of the huge pent-up demand for gift and semiluxury type products that had gone unsatisfied during the war years. The subsequent decision to reduce price only when forced to by competitors was the result of an attempt to maximize short-term profits with no evident concern to build—or even retain—market share. (This is in direct contrast to the policies of the BiC Corporation in more recent years, which has priced its pens competitively and promoted them extensively in an attempt to build market share.)

There are a number of conditions that tend to make a skimming policy desirable. Not all of them need be present, however, in order to make a skimming policy a reasonable decision. They are:

1. *The price–quantity relationship is difficult to estimate.* A correct assessment of the market response to a high price was made for the Reynolds pen.
2. *The quantity demanded is relatively insensitive to price.* This was the case with the Reynolds pen.

3. *The market can be segmented on the basis of price.* It is not clear whether new segments were reached by Reynolds as price was lowered for the pen.
4. *The introductory period is to be a relatively long one.* This was not true in the case of the pen.
5. *Competitors cannot imitate the product quickly.* Competitors came in *very* quickly after the Reynolds pen was introduced.
6. *Management desires a fast payout.* This was definitely the case with Reynolds.

Psychological Aspects of Pricing

There are a number of findings from the field of psychology and from marketing studies that relate to pricing practice. These findings, and their implications, are:

Finding 1. *Pricers have a tendency to perceive the price of their product as being more important to the buyer than it is and, as a result, set prices too low.* This stems from the fact that price is very important to the pricer, because it is his or her job. This feeling of importance is projected onto the buyer to a greater degree than is warranted.[27]

Finding 2. *Most buyers believe that prices should move proportionately to costs.*

Finding 3. *Buyers perceive a change in a price only when it exceeds a just-noticeable difference (JND) that is some fixed percentage of the price being charged.*[28] That the applicable JND is a percentage and not an absolute amount is illustrated by the change in the price of a subway token and an automobile. The subway token may be increased in price by 5 cents and every subway rider is immediately aware of the change. The price of an automobile may be increased by $50 and very few buyers will know that it has changed.

Finding 4. *Buyers tend to believe that there is a price–quality relationship such that the higher the price, the better the quality.*[29] This is the basis for the saying "You get what you pay for." It applies particularly to products whose quality is difficult to judge and whose brands are believed to vary widely in quality. For such common products as wine, cosmetics, shampoo, floor wax, and others that cannot be judged easily with respect to quality, and whose quantity of brands varies widely, a higher price, up to some limit, may result in even a higher volume. This was apparently the case with electric clocks when they were introduced (as described in the beginning of the chapter).

Such a relationship leads to an upward-sloping and then, at some point, to a backward-bending price–quantity purchased relationship. The examples on page 450 are for two products whose quality is perceived as being hard to judge and for which higher sales result from higher prices over a part of the price range.

It seems likely that the more frequent price changes that are made during an inflationary period tend to erode the perceived relationship between price and quality.[30]

Finding 5. *For consumer products, price consciousness appears to vary by product class and to be lower for branded items.* In one study it was found that for 60

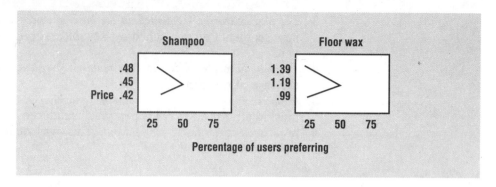

Source: D. S. Tull, R. A. Boring, and M. H. Gonsior, "A Note on the Relationship of Price and Imputed Quality," *Journal of Business*, April 1969, 189.

advertised and price competitive branded items, the percentage of respondents who were able to recall prices correctly varied from 86 percent for Coca-Cola to only 2 percent for shortening. In another study it was found that the ability to remember prices correctly was less for branded than for unbranded items.[31]

Making Price Changes

Price changes need to be made for a variety of reasons. **Price cuts** can become necessary whenever it is judged that profits would be higher at a lower price, competitors cut prices, a price reduction is needed to maintain or increase market share, or there is a need to balance demand for (or to close out) slow-moving items. **Price increases** are needed when costs go up, demand increases, line balancing requires it, production capacity limits have temporarily been reached, or for other reasons.

Whenever a price change is to be made, consideration is needed as to how the change should be implemented. Generally, price increases will often need to be initiated and announced differently than price cuts.

Reducing Prices

Usually, but not always, price reductions are viewed positively by prospective buyers. However, this is not always the case. Buyers may perceive the price reduction as the result of a lowering of quality, an indication that a new formulation or model is about to be introduced, or that prices may come down further and so it will pay to wait.[32]

Care should be taken that the way the price cut is announced will alleviate these concerns. For example, the advertising of a consumer product whose price is being reduced could carry the headline "Same High Quality at a New Low Price."

One should also take care to ensure that the price decrease is either large enough to be perceived as a lower price (the amount of the price cut exceeds the *just noticeable difference*) or is advertised as such. If a series of reductions are to be made over time (as, for example, those resulting from following a share-oriented pricing strategy when costs are reduced from moving down the experience curve), it is preferable to make the cuts with the frequency and in the amount that will permit recognition each time that the price has been reduced.

Raising Prices   When there are high rates of inflation, increases in price are made far more frequently than decreases. Raising prices becomes necessary to protect profit margins that would otherwise be reduced by increasing costs. There is also a persistent fear of government's instituting price controls that contribute to price increases, the reasoning being that "if we raise prices now, any government freeze of prices will allow us to charge the new price rather than the old one."

In one sense, inflation makes the raising of prices easier and more acceptable than during times when price levels are stable. Price increases are always resented, not only by the customer but by the company's sales representatives as well. However, as described earlier, there is widespread acceptance of the belief that prices should move proportionately to costs. The existence of inflation makes it easy for the sales representative to explain, and the customer to understand, why cost-induced price increases are necessary.

The Nature of Price Increases: The standard method of raising price is, of course, simply to raise the price. There are many other methods of increasing prices, however. Included are

1. Revising the discount structure
2. Changing the minimum acceptable order size
3. Changing terms of payment
4. Collecting interest on delinquent accounts receivable
5. Writing escalator clauses into contracts
6. Using delayed quotation pricing
7. Producing less of the lower-price items in the product line
8. Reducing inventories
9. Unbundling (charging separately for parts and accessories previously included, charging for delivery and special services, etc.)
10. Reducing the quality or size, or otherwise redesigning the product to make it less costly to produce

An example of a frequent user of the last of these pricing measures is the Hershey Chocolate Company. From the mid 1950s through the late 1970s, Hershey changed the price of its basic milk chocolate bar 3 times and the weight 15 times.[33]

The Timing of Price Increases: When a sizable price increase is to be made, or when continuing cost increases require frequent review of prices, it is generally preferable to make a series of small increases during a period rather than one or two large ones. Such increases both are less likely to be perceived as such and will be more acceptable when they are.

Some companies have adopted a policy of passing cost increases on directly to the customer by adding surcharges based on the cost of materials as of the day of shipment.[34]

1. Prices are influenced by the demand of buyers, the availability to buyers, the cost to suppliers, and custom and regulation.

2. Prices can be arrived at by barter, negotiation, market forces operating through formally organized exchanges, auction, a system of competitive bids, cost-plus-fixed fee, administration by the seller, and regulation by a government body.

3. The price of a product or service is the amount charged for it including any warranties or guarantees, delivery, discounts, services, or other items that are a part of the conditions of sale and are not paid for separately.

4. Objectives need to be established and communicated clearly to all those involved in administered pricing.

5. The principal objectives of companies are *profit* and *market share*.

6. Collateral pricing objectives include the balancing of demand for individual products in the line, leveling out of demand over time, increasing sales to selected market segments, and meeting the personal objectives of executives.

7. For *profit-oriented pricing*, explicit forecasts need to be made of the quantities that will be sold at each price being considered for each market segment. Forecasts are also required of unit costs for the *total* forecast sales (the sum of the sales forecasts for the various market segments). That price should be set in each market segment that will yield the largest forecast contribution to fixed costs and profits. When prices differ between segments, this is known as *price discrimination*.

8. When pricing in more than one market segment, profit-maximizing prices usually will be different when set jointly than when set individually by segment.

9. For *share-oriented pricing*, explicit forecasts need to be made of the quantities that will be sold, and the market share that will result, at each price being considered for each market segment.

10. Information to help forecast the quantity that would be sold in each market segment at each of the prices being considered can be obtained from

    a. Executive judgment
    b. Analysis of sales data
    c. Value analysis
    d. Surveys
    e. Laboratory experiments
    f. Sales tests
    g. Simulation

11. An *experience curve* is a cost curve such that each time the accumulated output doubles, the total cost per unit is reduced by a fixed percentage.

12. The formula for the *unit cost* for a given cumulative number of units produced on an experience curve of a given level is:

$$UC_i = UC_1/i^b$$

where i is the cumulative number of units produced, UC_i is the cost of the ith unit, UC_1 is the cost of the first unit, and b is a constant determined by the level of the experience curve.

13. The formula for the *average unit cost* over a range of units of cumulative output is:

$$AUC_h^i = \frac{UC_1}{(1-b)} \frac{[(i + 0.5)^{1-b} - (h + 0.5)^{1-b}]}{(i - h)}$$

where AUC_h^i is the average unit cost over the cumulative output from h units to i units, UC_1 is the unit cost for the first unit, and b is the constant for the applicable experience curve.

14. The *economic value to the customer* (EVC) of a product is the maximum price that will be paid by a customer who is fully informed about both the product and the offerings of competitors.

15. There are five steps involved in value-based pricing:
    a. Estimate the present value of the *life cycle cost* of the principal competitor's product.
    b. Estimate the *EVC* of your product.
    c. Subtract your average variable cost from your EVC to determine the *discretionary margin* you have relative to your principal competitor.
    d. Decide how you want to divide that discretionary margin between *customer inducement* and your contribution to profit and fixed cost.
    e. Set the value-based price as the sum of your cost plus contribution to profit and fixed costs.

16. Methods of setting *transfer prices* between supplying and using divisions of a single corporation include transfer at cost, transfer at cost plus return on investment, transfer at a negotiated price, or transfer at a market-based price.

17. *Meeting competition* is a commonly used method of pricing in practice.
    According to available evidence, meeting competition is generally not a good pricing strategy.

18. *Cost-based pricing* is also a commonly used pricing method. Its popularity results from its being (a) perceived as a way of reducing pricing risks, (b) the most practical method of pricing large numbers of items, and (c) the basis for share-oriented pricing.

19. There are five kinds of discounts: trade or functional, trade promotion, cash, consumer promotion, and quantity.

20. The conditions that tend to make a *skimming* price policy desirable for a new product are (a) the price–quantity relationship is difficult to estimate, (b) the quantity demanded is relatively insensitive to price, (c) the market can be segmented on the basis of price, (d) the introductory period is to be a relatively long one, (e) competitors cannot imitate the product quickly, and (f) a fast payout is desired.

21. Findings from the field of psychology and from marketing studies of the psychology of price include:
    a. Pricers have a tendency to perceive the price of the product as being more important to the buyer than it is and, as a result, set prices too low.

b. Most buyers believe that prices should move proportionately to costs.

c. Buyers perceive a change in a price only when it exceeds a just noticeable difference (JND) that is some fixed percentage of the price being charged.

d. Buyers tend to believe that there is a price–quality relationship such that the higher the price, the better the quality.

e. Consumer price consciousness appears to vary by product class and to be lower for branded than for unbranded items.

REVIEW QUESTIONS

13.1.   What does the word *price* mean?

13.2.   How can prices be set?

13.3.   What are the principal pricing objectives of firms? the collateral pricing objectives?

13.4.   How do *profit-oriented* and *share-oriented* pricing differ?

13.5.   What are the general methods of obtaining information to help forecast the quantity that would be sold at each potential price?

13.6.   What is an *experience curve*?

13.7.   What is the *economic value to the customer* (EVC) of a product or service?

13.8.   a.   What is a *transfer price*?
        b.   What are some common methods of setting transfer prices?

13.9.   a.   What is a *skimming* price policy?
        b.   What are the conditions that make it desirable?

13.10. What are the major findings relating to price from the field of psychology and from marketing studies of the psychology of price?

DISCUSSION QUESTIONS AND PROBLEMS

13.11. If you were a member of the Federal Trade Commission, would you want to use the definition of price given on page 426? Why or why not?

13.12. What is your understanding of the word *price* in the Robinson-Patman Act? On what do you base that understanding? (See page 165 for a description of the act.)

13.13. Explain in your own words why the maximum profit (or minimum loss) in the short term is realized by pricing such that MC = MR.

13.14. Explain why for profit-oriented pricing in two or more market segments, prices that result in less than maximum profits may be arrived at if they are set individually by segment.

13.15. Are there differences between the cost data generated for traditional cost accounting purposes and cost data required for pricing purposes? If so, what are the differences? If not, why not?

13.16. Conduct a survey of the members of another class you are in to determine:
   a. How many of them bought a book required for the class.
   b. How many of the books purchased were (1) new, (2) used.
   c. What effect, if any, a 20 percent *increase* in price of the new book would have had on the new-book purchasers.
   d. What effect, if any, a 20 percent price *decrease* in the price of the new book would have had on used book purchases.
   What conclusions do you reach from the survey?

13.17. Suppose you are the marketing manager for a company with 30 sales territories in the United States. You are uncertain whether the $10 unit price being charged in all territories should be left unchanged; raised to $11 in all territories; reduced to $9 in all territories; or left at $10 in some territories, raised to $11 in other territories, and reduced to $9 in still other territories. Design a sales test to get information to help solve these questions.

13.18. Discuss the probable differences, if any, in the level of prices for a product at each stage of the life cycle.

13.19. Are there industries for which experience curves are not likely to forecast costs well? If so, what industries, and why would you expect this to be the case? If not, why not?

13.20. Suggest five products (other than those referred to in the chapter) for which you believe buyers may use price as a cue to quality. Why do you believe these products are susceptible to a perceived price–quality relationship of this kind?

13.21. What effect, if any, do you believe the trend toward organizing companies into strategic business units (organizational units that have income statement responsibility) has had on transfer pricing? Explain.

13.22. Devise a procedure for setting the unit price in each quantity range that will avoid leaving any "windows" in the quantity-discount schedule.

13.23. A consultant who gives pricing seminars for executives has a section in the syllabus for the seminar titled, "Raising 'Prices' without 'Raising' Prices." What do you think this section is likely to contain?

13.24. In 1986, Duquesne University in Pittsburgh offered "tuition futures" to parents with newborn children. The parents could buy the newborn four years of college starting in the year 2004 for $5,082 today. Some 600 parents signed up.

    a. Tuition at Duquesne in 1986 was $4,500 for one year. Inflation in tuition at U.S. colleges and universities in the mid 1980s was running at an annual rate of about 7 percent. Was this a good financial arrangement for the parents? for Duquesne?

    b. What kind of problems could arise in such an arrangement for the parents? for Duquesne?

13.25. In a Florida Agricultural Experiment Station sales test on the price of oranges, the following price–quantity relationships were generated:

Price per Dozen	Mean Sales per Store per 100 Customers (dozens)
$.34	108.5
.39	78.4
.44	56.7
.49	58.5
.54	50.0
.59	44.2
.64	34.6

Assuming a constant cost to the retailer of 31 cents per dozen, what price should be charged in order to maximize the contribution to fixed costs and profit?

13.25. A manufacturer of chain saws has the following estimated demand and cost schedules:

Do-It-Yourselfer Market Estimates		Logging Market Estimates	
Price	Quantity Demanded/Year	Price	Quantity Demanded/Year
$100	20,000	$ 80	5,000
110	19,000	90	4,500
120	17,500	100	4,000
130	15,000	110	3,500
140	13,000	120	2,500
150	11,000	130	1,000
160	8,000		

Additional Quantity Manufactured	Estimated Average Unit Cost	Additional Quantity Manufactured	Estimated Average Unit Cost
5,000	$90.43	15,500	$88.57
5,500	90.34	16,000	88.48
6,000	90.24	16,500	88.40
6,500	90.15	17,000	88.32
7,000	90.06	17,500	88.23
7,500	89.97	18,000	88.15
8,000	89.88	18,500	88.07
8,500	89.79	19,000	87.99
9,000	89.70	19,500	87.90
9,500	89.61	20,000	87.82
10,000	89.52	20,500	87.74
10,500	89.43	21,000	87.66
11,000	89.34	21,500	87.58
11,500	89.25	22,000	87.50
12,000	89.17	22,500	87.42
12,500	89.08	23,000	87.35
13,000	88.99	23,500	87.27
13,500	88.91	24,000	87.19
14,000	88.82	24,500	87.11
14,500	88.74	25,000	87.03
15,000	88.65		

a. If the company wants to maximize jointly the contribution to profits and fixed costs in the two market segments, where should prices be set?

b. If the company wants to build market share in both segments rather than to maximize profits but requires a minimum contribution to fixed costs and profits of $600,000, where should prices be set?

c. Assume that the company has estimated fixed costs of $152,000 for the year, a book value of fixed assets of $425,000, and an average turnover of working capital of 1.5 times. If the objective is to maximize ROI for the period, what prices should be charged in the two market segments?

13.26. If the cost of the first chain saw produced was $4,950 and 81,510 units were manufactured earlier, what is the level of the experience curve for chain saws for the company in problem 13.25?

13.27. Using the formula in Exhibit 13-3, calculate the cost of the second integrated circuit produced if the cost of the first unit was $5,000 and the applicable experience curve was 74 percent. (The value of b for a 74 percent experience curve is 0.434 from Table A-1.)

13.28. The answer you obtained in Problem 13.27 should be equal to $5,000 × 0.74 = $3,700, within rounding error. Why is this the case?

13.29. The formula for the experience curve is

$$UC_i = UC_1/i_b$$

where UC_1 is the unit cost of the first unit, UC_i is the unit cost of the ith unit, and b is a constant whose value depends on the level of the experience curve.

The values for b for 85 percent, 80 percent, and 75 percent experience curves, respectively, are 0.234, 0.322, and 0.415. Solve for these three values of b, letting $i = 2$ and $UC_1 = \$1,000$. (*Note:* You will need a calculator with a yx capability or a log table to work this problem.)

13.30. With the same initial first-unit cost ($UC_1 = \$1,000$) and the same 80 percent experience curve level ($b = 0.322$), what percentage of unit cost advantage would Texas Instruments have had on the last calculator unit produced if the cumulative output of Texas Instruments was 1 million and that of Hewlett-Packard was 500,000? (*Note:* Calculate the unit cost advantage percentage [$UCA\%$] as $UCA\% = \{[UC_{HP} - UC_{TI}]/ UC_{HP}\} \times 100$. Check your calculation with the value given in Table A-3.)

13.31. Repeat problem 13.30 but with:
   a. Cumulative output of Texas Instruments at 100 and of Hewlett-Packard at 50.
   b. Cumulative output of Texas Instruments at 1,000 and of Hewlett-Packard at 500.
   c. Is the cost advantage percentage the same for (a) and (b)?

13.32. a. Explain mathematically why the experience curve is a straight line on log-log paper.
   b. In general mathematical terms, what is the first unit cost? What is the b value?
   c. Solve problem 13.27 graphically using log-log paper.

13.33. Are there *windows* in the IBM quantity discount schedule for its AT computer (shown on p. 447) other than at the 19/20 unit quantity break?

13.34. Assume that the standard Hershey chocolate bar weighs 0.2 ounces and costs 20 cents. Now suppose its weight is reduced by 13 percent and the price remains the same. What percentage increase in price per ounce has taken place?

13.35. It has been suggested that the Delphi method of estimating the "optimistic," "pessimistic," and "most likely" quantities of a product that will be sold at each of a number of prices being considered is appropriate to use before any experimental or survey methods are used for estimating the quantities that will be sold at each price. Further, the suggestion is that if experimental or survey methods are used, the Delphi method should be used again before a price is decided on. Describe the logic that might be used for
   a. The use of the Delphi method *before* the use of other estimating methods.

b. The use of the Delphi method *after* the use of other estimating methods.

The problem statement that follows is to be used for problems 13.36, 13.37, and 13.38.

The General Electric Small Motors Division sells motors both to outside appliance manufacturers and to General Electric's own Appliance Division. The Small Motors Division is operated on the basis of a "profit now" strategy and the division manager has income statement accountability. Accordingly, the marketing manager of the Small Motors Division uses the "brute force" method of pricing the motors sold outside the company.

The Small Motors Division has recently developed and gone into production of a drive motor for tapes in VCRs. It has never produced or sold a motor for this purpose before. The Appliance Division has been producing and selling a VCR for some time.

13.36. a. What methods of pricing motors "sold" to the General Electric Appliances Division might be used? Briefly describe each.
b. Which method do you believe would be preferable? Explain.

13.37. State and briefly describe three different general methods that might reasonably be used to help forecast the quantity of VCR tape-drive motors that would be sold to outside customers at each of a series of prices being considered.

13.38. Given the following cost and revenue estimates for the first three months of production and sales of the VCR tape-drive motor, what price should be charged to outside customers? Show your work.

Price per Unit	Average Variable Cost per Unit	Fixed Cost per Unit	Estimated Number of Units That Would Be Sold at Each Price
$25.00	$16.00	$10.00	50,000
26.00	16.35	10.42	48,000
27.00	16.65	11.35	44,000
28.00	17.05	12.82	39,000
29.00	17.50	15.15	33,000
30.00	18.00	20.00	25,000
			Price = _____/unit

What is the approximate level of the experience curve for the VCR tape-drive motor? _____ % Show your work.

Endnotes

[1]"Segmentation Strategies Create New Pressure among Marketers," *Marketing News*, March 28, 1986.

[2]At least for manufacturing firms. The objectives in Exhibit 13-1 are for manufacturing firms only.

[3]For an example of the determination of optimal prices in a product line, see D. J. Reibstein and H. Gatignon, "Optimal Product Line Pricing: The Influence of Elasticities and Cross Elasticities," *Journal of Marketing Research*, August 1984, 259–267.

[4]As reported in the annual report of the General Public Utilities Corporation, 1977.

[5]A. Oxenfeldt, D. Miller, A. Shuchman, and C. Winick, *Insights into Pricing*, Wadsworth, 1961, 117.

[6]A fictitious name, but an actual pricing situation.

[7]More precisely (and technically) stated, the elasticity of demand over the relevant range of prices is different in each of the segments.

[8]This model is discussed in S. C. Webb, *Managerial Economics*, Houghton-Mifflin, 1976, 329–331.

[9]Data supplied privately.

[10]Boston Consulting Group, *Perspectives on Experience* (n.p., 1972).

[11]Adapted from the definition given in J. L. Fortis and N. T. Mehta, "Value-Based Strategies for Industrial Products," *Business Horizons*, May–June 1981, 32.

[12]For a comprehensive economic analysis of transfer pricing, see Webb, *Managerial Economics*, 341–344. See also the chapter on the "multidimensional structure" (Chap. 8) in O. E. Williamson, *Markets and Hierarchies: Analysis and Antitrust Implications*, The Free Press, 1975; and T. T. Nagle, *The Strategy and Tactics of Pricing*, Prentice-Hall, 1987, 233–234.

[13]A. Mostafa, J. A. Sharp, and K. Howard, "Transfer Pricing—A Survey Using Discriminant Analysis," *Omega*, Vol. 12, no. 5, 1984, 465–474.

[14]For discussions of how prices are set in practice, see R. F. Lanzillotti, *Pricing Production and Marketing Practices of Small Manufacturers*, Washington State University Press, 1964, 12–15; M. I. Alpert, "Pricing in an Era of Rapid Change," in *Review of Marketing*, G. Zaltman and T. Bonoma (eds.), American Marketing Association, 1978, 235; M. R. Schlessel, "Pricing in a Service Industry," *Business Topics*, Spring 1977, 37–48; and B. P. Shapiro and B. B. Jackson, "Industrial Pricing to Meet Customer Needs," *Harvard Business Review*, November–December 1978, 119–127.

[15]S. Land, "How Price Premiums and Discounts Affect Performance," The PIMSLETTER on Business Strategy, No. 7, 1978, 1.

[16]See Lanzillotti, *Pricing Production*; Schlessel, "Pricing in a Service Industry"; and Shapiro and Jackson, "Industrial Pricing."

[17]J. P. Guiltinan, "Risk Aversive Pricing Policies: Problems and Alternatives," *Journal of Marketing*, January 1976, 10–15.

[18]*The Wall Street Journal*, October 21, 1988, B1.

[19]"Computers Permit Airlines to Use Scalpels to Cut Fares," *The Wall Street Journal*, February 2, 1987, 21.

[20]"U.S. Treasury Pays Suppliers Electronically," *The Wall Street Journal*, August 24, 1987, 17.

[21]Taken from J. B. Wilcox, R. D Howell, P. Kuzdrall, and R. Britney, "Price Quantity Discounts: Some Implications for Buyers and Sellers," *Journal of Marketing*, July 1987, 64.

[22]For a discussion of other types of discount schedules, see ibid.

[23]For an exposition of this view, see A. P. Jeuland and S. M. Shugan, "Managing Channel Profits," *Marketing Science*, Summer 1982, 239–272.

[24]W. Litley, "The Graying of the Marketplace," *Canadian Business*, August 1985, 46–54.

[25]See, for example, P. Kotler, *Marketing Management: Analysis, Planning and Control*, 5th ed., Prentice-Hall, 1976, 527; J. Dean, "Pricing Policies for New Products," *Harvard Business Review*, November–December 1976, 141–153; and S. C. Webb, *Managerial Economics*, Houghton-Mifflin, 1976, 345–346.

[26]T. Whiteside, "Where Are They Now? The Amphibious Pen," *The New Yorker*, February 17, 1951, 59.

[27]A. Oxenfeldt, D. Miller, A. Shuchman, and C. Winick, *Insights into Pricing from Operations Research and Behavioral Science*, Wadsworth, 1961, 78.

[28]S. H. Britt, "How Weber's Law Is Applied to Marketing," *Business Horizons*, February 1975, 21–24.

[29]There is a substantial body of evidence to indicate that this is the case. See, for example, H. J. Leavitt, "A Note on Some Experimental Findings on the Meaning of Price," *The Journal of Business*, July 1954, 205–210; D. S. Tull, R. A. Boring, and M. H. Gonsior, "A Note on the Relationship of Price and Imputed Quality," *The Journal of Business*, April 1964, 186–191; B. Shapiro, "The Psychology of Pricing," *Harvard Business Review*, July 1968, 14 ff.; and K. B. Monroe, "Buyers' Subjective Perceptions of Price," *Journal of Marketing Research*, February 1973, 70–80.

[30]Y. Lieberman, "Marketing Consequences of Inflationary Pricing," *The Journal of Consumer Marketing*, Winter 1985, 50.

[31]A. Gabor and C. Granger, "On the Price Consciousness of Consumers," *Applied Statistics*, November 1961, 170–188.

[32]For a very good review of this topic, see Monroe, "Buyers' Subjective Perceptions."

[33]"Consumers Find Firms Are Pacing Quantities to Avoid Price Rises," *The Wall Street Journal*, February 15, 1977, 1; and "Hershey Cuts Weight of Chocolate Bar, Says Operating Net Is Off," *The Wall Street Journal*, July 28, 1977, 6.

[34]"How Price Tactics Feed Inflation," *Business Week*, March 10, 1980, 36–37.

CHAPTER

14

MARKETING COMMUNICATION PLANNING

It is not enough for a product to be designed well, produced efficiently, priced reasonably, and distributed so that it is available to a substantial portion of the target market. The marketing task is not complete without informing the target market of the product and where it is available, persuading as many as possible of its merits, and changing the predisposition to buy to the extent and by a sufficient number of buyers to meet sales objective for the product.

The informing—persuading—changing the predisposition to buy tasks of marketing are carried out through the communications programs of the company. Four major means of communications are employed by companies for these purposes. They are the advertising conducted by the firm, the personal selling by its sales force, and the sales promotion and public relations programs it sponsors. These major means of communications from seller to prospective buyer are defined as follows:

Advertising. Any paid form of nonpersonal presentation and promotion of ideas, goods, or services by an identified sponsor.

Personal selling. Oral presentation in a conversation with one or more prospective purchasers for the purpose of making sales.

461

Sales promotion. Short-term price, prize or gift or product incentives designed to induce purchase when offered to distributors, industrial users, or consumers.

Publicity. Nonpersonal stimulation of demand for a product, service, or business unit by arranging to have commercially significant news about it published, broadcast, telecast, or presented on stage that is not paid for by the sponsor.[1]

All companies have to use one of more of these means of communicating with their market(s), and most companies use all of them, although in differing proportions. Collectively, the extent and the manner in which they are used make up the *communications mix* of a firm. Companies should coordinate all four elements of the communications mix to achieve communications and marketing goals.

In this chapter we consider models of the communications process and of communication planning, and the research findings that relate to the elements of them. Positioning is also discussed. In the next chapter we discuss the management of advertising, sales promotions, and public relations programs. Personal selling is discussed in Chapter 16.

COMMUNICATIONS MODELS AND RESEARCH FINDINGS

Generalized Communications Process Model

To illustrate the process that takes place in any communication—be it personal or impersonal, verbal or visual, commercial or noncommercial, preplanned or unplanned—consider the last television commercial you saw.

There was a *sender* (the sponsoring company) and a *receiver* (you). The sender developed a message (the information that was to be conveyed) and **encoded** it by putting it into the symbols that made up the ad. (The symbols used not only were the words and numbers presented but included the situational context, the spokesperson(s) or characters used, the visual context, and the musical background as well.) The encoded message was transmitted through a *medium* (television). (In all likelihood, some of the people for whom the ad was intended did not see it. Other people were exposed to the ad but did not pay any attention to it. But you did attend to the ad.) It was **decoded** by you as you watched it; that is, the words you heard and the images you saw were translated by you into thoughts and mental images. You probably gained some information about the product, and almost certainly had either a change or affirmation of your attitudes (however slight) toward both the product and the sponsoring company. You may have understood it well, or perhaps not. If you did understand it, you may have agreed with the message, or perhaps not. Attitudinal and opinion changes or reaffirmations constituted your **response** to the ad. Finally, if research were being done to evaluate the effectiveness of the

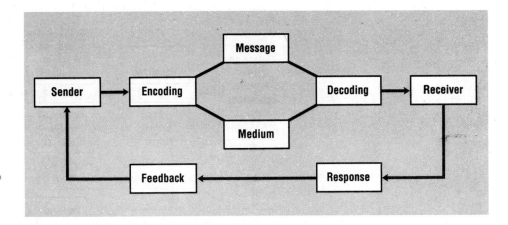

FIGURE 14-1
Generalized communications model.

campaign of which the ad was a part, you may have had the opportunity to provide **feedback** on your response to this and other ads for the product. If you decided to purchase or not purchase the product as a result of the ad, that also resulted in feedback.

The generalized model of the communications process that emerges from an analysis such as this is shown in Figure 14–1. It is useful for helping to understand how communication takes place and where and why difficulties may occur. It has been used for much of the research that has resulted in the findings on communication that are reported later in the chapter.

The model is descriptive of the flow of a communication from sender to receiver and back, and not how a communications program that has specific objectives (such as an advertising campaign) should be planned to achieve them. For our purposes it will be useful to recast the model in that context. Just as a two-way conversation communicates more effectively than a one-way lecture, likewise marketing communication will be more effective when the marketer uses research input to have two-way communication.

Communications Planning Model

The planning model is shown in Figure 14–2. For each market segment, it begins with a decision on who are to be the target receivers and an assessment of their current perceptions of the brand or company, and follows logically through setting objectives and the budget to accomplish them, deciding on the message and the medium (or media) by which it is to be sent, encoding and then transmitting the message, having it received and decoded by the audience, and finally registering responses and obtaining feedback to complete the communications cycle.

It is apparent that although one should consider in the planning of the communication the receiving, decoding, and responding processes, these are carried out solely by the receiver. Once the message is sent, therefore, these elements of communication can no longer be affected by the sender. This fact is indicated in Figure 14–2 by the dotted line that encloses those elements.

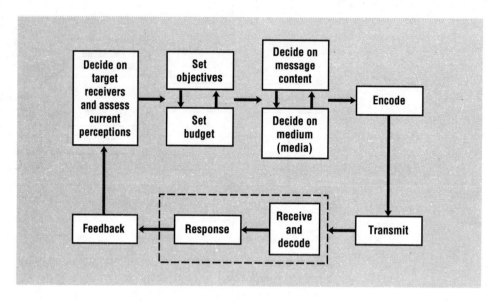

FIGURE 14-2
Communications planning model.

The planning model suggests a series of questions that need to be raised and answered during the development and carrying out of a communications program for a given period of time. These include:

Receivers	Who are the target receivers? What are their current perceptions about the product? the company?
Objectives	Given the receiver perceptions, what objectives should be set concerning the effects of the communications program?
Budget	What budget should be set to accomplish the objectives?
Message	What is the informational content of the message(s) that ought to be sent? what appeals? what order of presentation?
Spokesperson	Should a spokesperson (such as a well-known personality or sports figure) be used?
Medium (media)	What medium (or media) ought to transmit the message(s)?
Transmittal	Should the number and frequency of messages in each time period be about the same, or should there be "flighting" of the messages (some periods with a high number and frequency of messages and some with a lower number and frequency)?
Receipt, Decoding, and Response	The receipt and decoding of and the response to messages are all under the direct control of the receiver rather than the sender. The questions appropriate for these elements of the communications process therefore fall into the area of the feedback obtained.
Feedback	Who received the messages? How were they interpreted? What were the responses?

The research findings that relate to these questions are discussed below.

RESEARCH FINDINGS CONCERNING COMMUNICATIONS

Receivers of Communications

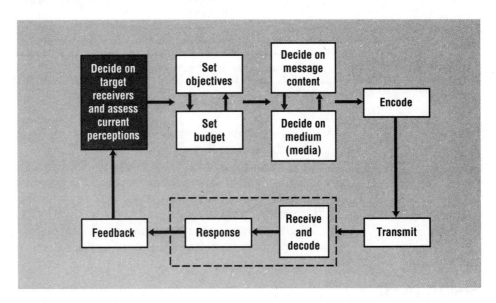

Who Are the Target Receivers?

If the planning of the marketing program in general has been carried out effectively, market segments will have been identified and the target segments already selected. The buyers in each segment therefore become the target audiences for the communications programs for the company.

Different communications may well be needed for each segment. For example, Peugeot, a French manufacturer of automobiles and bicycles, markets its bicycles to the *general amateur, professional tourer,* and *professional racer* segments. Distinctly different messages containing different information and appeals need to be sent to these three segments.

What Are the Perceptions of the Target Receivers about the Product?

Most companies regularly obtain measurements of market share. Changes in market share reflect the composite effects of actions taken by the company and its competitors and changes in the market. It is usually difficult to ascribe a particular change in market share to any one cause, or series of causes, without other information. In particular, tracing market changes to changing perceptions of buyers resulting from the communications programs of a firm and its competitors requires corroborating data from the buyers. To obtain such data, a survey of consumers has to be conducted.

An example is the early surveys conducted by Brown[2] for the purpose of deciding what marketing actions might be indicated for the brands involved. Sponsored by General Mills, they were done for several products, including all-purpose flour, packaged pie mix, ice cream, packaged dry soup, and scouring cleanser. Three primary measurements were made: the percentage of house-

Table 14–1 Awareness, Perception of Quality, and Market Share of Scouring Cleansers

Brand	Percentage of Housewives Aware of the Brand	Percentage of Users Who Give the Brand Top Rating	Market Share*
A	95.1	45.7	41.2
B	62.8	44.9	16.3
C	43.6	29.4	11.0
D	36.0	46.7	10.0
E	65.8	24.6	6.1

*As approximated by the percentage of households using it.
Source: G. H. Brown, "Measuring Consumer Attitudes Toward Products," *Journal of Marketing*, Vol. 14, no. 5, April 1950, 694.

wives who know the brand, the percentage who gave it a top rating, and the market share of the brand.

The results for scouring cleansers are given in Table 14–1. Assume the role of a consultant for a few minutes, and, before you read Exhibit 14–1, decide what actions regarding communications, if any, ought to be taken by the management for each brand.

On the basis of these data, one might reasonably draw the inferences and take the actions concerning communications described in Exhibit 14–1.

EXHIBIT **14-1**

Inferences from Table 14–1 Regarding Appropriate Communications Actions for Each Brand

Brand A. The leading brand with a 41 percent share. The product is perceived as being of high quality and virtually all consumers are aware of it. It is probably priced competitively and must be distributed widely to have obtained the share that it has.

No major changes in marketing actions (including communications) appear to be needed.

Brand B. A distant second to Brand A in market share. The quality of the brand is perceived to be about the same as that of Brand A, but the level of awareness is substantially lower (63 percent as compared with 95 percent). May have some price or distribution problems as well.

Informing more consumers about the brand would very likely raise market share.

Brand C. The brand is third in market share despite a very low level of awareness and a low perception of quality. The brand manager must be doing some things right in pricing and distributing the brand. He or she should investigate whether the quality is actually low or just perceived to be so; if it is actually low, it should be improved.

In either case, there is a need to inform consumers about the existence of the brand and to persuade them of its merits.

Brand D. Fourth in market share, the brand has the highest quality perception and the lowest awareness level of any of the cleansers. The brand may also have pricing and distribution problems.

Consumers will have to be informed about the product if market share is to be increased substantially.

Brand E. Last in market share, the brand has the lowest quality perception of any of the brands and is about average for awareness level. An investigation should be made to determine if the quality is actually low or is just perceived to be so. If it is actually low, steps should be taken to improve it. Comparison with Brand C suggests that there may be a pricing or distribution problem also.

Following resolution of the product quality problem, a program of informing and persuading consumers about the merits of the brand is needed.

In some situations, an assessment of perceptions about the company is necessary, as well as about the product. A retailing firm such as Macy's, for example, needs to know how its stores are perceived compared with competitors' stores with respect to price, service, selection, and friendliness of employees. A company that is attempting to diversify through acquisition via exchange of stock with other companies wants to keep its stock prices high and needs to know how it is perceived by buyers of stock in terms of progressiveness, aggressiveness, management competency, and earnings potential. Companies that have undergone a period of bad public relations, such as McDonnell-Douglas after the failure of the engine mount on the early DC-10s or Chrysler after its near bankruptcy, need to know how their company is perceived in terms of product design and financial viability: Bad perceptions affect sales.

A common method of obtaining perceptions of companies is to conduct a survey using the **semantic differential**. An example of the findings of a study using this technique of two competitive department stores is given in Figure 14-3. Data for the study were collected by having the respondent rate the stores on a series of a seven-point scale, each bounded by one of the sets of bipolar adjectives shown in the figure. The data were then aggregated and presented in the profiles shown.

The differences in perceptions of the two stores are striking. Store A is perceived as being a higher-quality, higher-price store that has decidedly slower service and less helpful and less friendly employees. A change in personnel policies or training is indicated, with a communication to shoppers of the

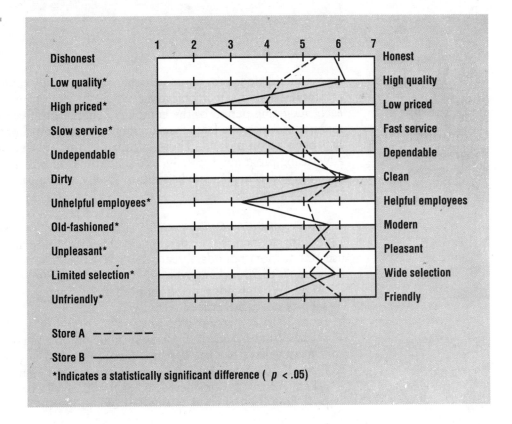

FIGURE 14-3
Profile of perceptions of two department stores using the semantic differential.

store's emphasis on the speed of service and helpfulness and friendliness of its personnel.

Communications Objectives and Budgets

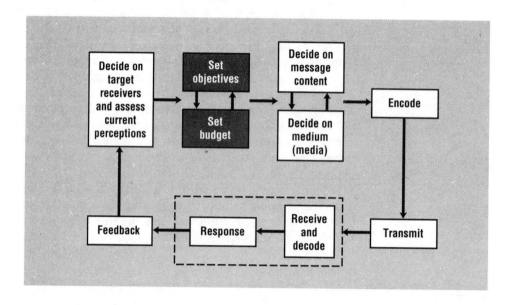

What Objectives Should Be Set for the Communications Program?

If communications programs were managed in a fully rational and explicit way, a carefully stated set of objectives would be drawn up for each program for each budgeting period of the company. These objectives would be stated in a manner that permits later measurement and a determination of whether they had been accomplished. Those companies that do set explicit objectives for advertising programs typically formulate them in terms of the informing, persuading, and changing predisposition to buy communications effects.

Some examples:

1. *COMMUNICATIONS OBJECTIVES OF A MILLING COMPANY.* Within the next 12 months, to increase the percentage of heavy family flour users (families who use 100 or more pounds a year)

a. From 60 to 90 percent who answer our brand when asked: What brands of all-purpose flour have you seen or heard advertised recently? — *Informing* objective

b. From 20 to 25 percent who answer our brand when asked: What brand of all-purpose flour do you personally believe has the best quality? — *Persuasion* objective

c. From 12 to 15 percent who answer our brand when asked: All things considered, what brand of all-purpose flour do you think is the best one to buy?[3] — *Changing predisposition to buy* objective

2. *COMMUNICATIONS OBJECTIVE OF A MANUFACTURER OF OFFICE EQUIPMENT.* The company advertises principally through direct mail, with the aim of obtaining leads for its sales force. The mailing pieces have reply devices which an interested reader can return for literature about the company's products. The company has learned from continuing audits of advertising results about how many leads a given advertising investment will produce. Its communications objective is to generate the number of leads required for efficient follow-up by the sales force.[4]

What Budget Should Be Set to Accomplish the Objectives?

Setting objectives of this kind permits communications budgets to be set on the basis of the estimated amount required to accomplish them. That is, an ***objective and task method*** of setting budgets can be used when a quantifiable objective is first established.

To set a budget that will achieve an objective but will not result in under- or overkill insofar as the objective is concerned requires a knowledge of the response function involved. For example, in order for the management of the flour manufacturer to set an appropriate budget for advertising to accomplish the objective "within the next 12 months to increase the percentage of heavy family flour users from 60 to 90 percent who answer our brand when asked: 'What brands of all-purpose flour have you seen or heard advertised recently?'" requires a knowledge of the relationship between the advertising expenditures for the kind of advertising that will be done in the medium (media) that will carry it and the recall of the advertising that will result. If the objective were in terms of sales, market share, or profits, knowledge of the response function linking the appropriate one of them with the level of advertising expenditures would be necessary in order to set the budget intelligently.

Generally speaking, making reliable estimates of advertising response functions is not an easy task. The response function for the furniture manufacturer's advertising is something of an exception to this rule, however. It also knows from studies of sales representatives' performance how many leads each representative efficiently can follow up over the period of a year. Since the company has learned from past advertising results about how many leads a given advertising investment will produce, it can determine how many leads are needed and estimate with considerable accuracy how much to spend on advertising to get them.

A study by San Augustine and Foley suggests that explicit communications objectives are set by a relatively small percentage of advertisers.[5] There are six major methods of setting advertising budgets: (1) an arbitrary allocation, (2) all-you-can-afford, (3) percentage of last year's sales, (4) percentage of anticipated sales, (5) objective and task, and (6) quantitative models. Only the last two of these methods require the prior formulation of objectives. Yet less than 20 percent of the sample of large consumer and nonconsumer goods advertisers studied by San Augustine and Foley used one or both of these methods. (Although it does not necessarily follow that only these companies formulated objectives for their advertising programs, the presumption is that had other companies done so, they would probably have used a different method of setting the budget.)

Methods of determining response functions were discussed in Chapter 7. Setting budgets for advertising, sales promotion, and public relations are discussed separately in the sections of the next chapter, dealing with each of those methods of communication.

The Message

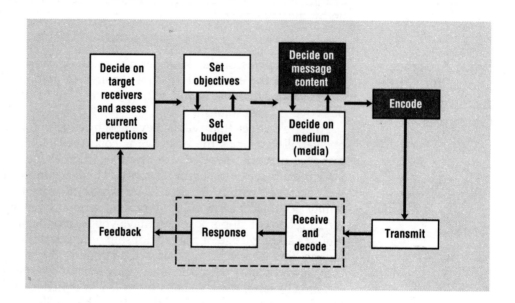

What Is the Informational Content of the Message That Ought to Be Sent?

The sender may want to *inform* potential buyers about the product and its attributes, its price, or where it may be purchased. An attempt to *persuade* potential buyers may focus on attempting to induce trial, to *change evaluations* of the product, or to provide postpurchase reassurance that the purchase was indeed a sound decision.

Communications research has resulted in a number of findings about message content that bear on the effectiveness of the message. The research has tended to concentrate in the areas of fear appeals, use of humor, one-sided versus two-sided messages, order of presentation, and the use of direct comparison.

The Use of Fear Appeals: Should the American Cancer Society attempt to persuade teenagers not to take up smoking because of the higher risk of lung cancer? Should campaigns for promoting the use of safety belts in automobiles use the threat of permanent injury or death to induce people to "buckle up"? Should a brand of mouthwash use advertisements that depict social ostracism for people with bad breath?

The available evidence indicates that if fear appeals are to be successful, they must be used in situations in which the source is credible,[6] the receiver does not already have a high anxiety level about the threatened outcome,[7] avoidance actions are easy to take,[8] and the level of fear induced is not so high as to cause the receiver to distort or reject the message.[9]

Given these findings, it is understandable why the American Cancer Society's initial campaign using an "it can happen to you if you are a smoker" threat delivered by terminally ill cancer patients did not succeed. The requiring of a warning message on all smoking tobacco product packages and advertising that "the Surgeon General has determined that smoking may be injurious to your health" appears to have been similarly unsuccessful; the Federal Trade Commission reported that per capita cigarette consumption did not fall for the first year or so after the warning messages were required.[10]

Fear appeals can be effective in some situations, however. For example, they appear to have been effective for promoting brands of personal-hygiene products that claim to be useful, such as deodorizers (soap, toothpastes, and mouthwashes, as well as deodorants). The reasons for the success of fear appeals for these products may have been that (1) the anxiety level about social ostracism arising from breath or body odor was not high enough to cause most persons to distort or dismiss the message, and (2) it was easy to take corrective action (buy the brand being advertised).

The Use of Humor: Suppose you are participating in a meeting concerning an upcoming advertising campaign. The representatives from your firm's advertising agency have just proposed that the ads that will make up the campaign should have a humorous theme since that will "increase their effectiveness in gaining attention." Should you agree that a humorous theme would be preferable to a serious one?

The evidence about the effectiveness of humor in advertising is mixed, and appears to be highly situation-specific. There is general agreement that humor is effective in gaining attention.[11] However, if not used properly, humor may be distracting and so reduce comprehension.[12] Whereas there is some evidence that humor can be a positive factor in persuasion,[13] other studies comparing the persuasive effects of otherwise similar humorous and serious messages indicate that they are roughly equal in this respect.[14]

If humor is used, care should be used in how it is blended in. A set of prescriptions for the use of humor in advertisements is:[15]

1. The brand must be identified within the opening 10 seconds, or there is a danger of inhibiting recall of important selling points.
2. The type of humor makes a difference. Subtlety is more effective than the bizarre.
3. The humor must be relevant to the brand or key idea. Recall and persuasion are both decreased when the linkage is not made.
4. Humorous commercials that entertain by belittling potential users *do not* perform well.
5. If the advertisement is to be used in other than local media, care must be taken to ensure that the humorous content will be regarded as such in *all* areas where the ad will appear.
6. The humor should have an enduring quality. Few jokes amuse as effectively the fifteenth time you hear them as they did the first.

Does the Red Roof Inns radio ad script reproduced in the box on the next page meet these criteria?

What do the $60-a-night motel chains offer you that you can't get at Red Roof Inns?

Let's add them up and see.

This handy shower cap, 59 cents; shampooette, $2.

Ah, dental floss, always a plus.

Ooh, we're still spending $27 a night more than at Red Roof Inns.

Huh, wait a minute. I forgot the mint.

(*Voice-over*: Don't pay too much. Hit the roof. Red Roof Inns. Call 1-800-THE ROOF.)

It's a good mint.

It's not worth $27, but it's good.*

*"Budget Motels Take to Humor Ads," *Advertising Age*, November 14, 1988, 65.

One-sided versus Two-sided Messages: One-sided marketing messages (that is, messages that present only favorable arguments for buying a product or service), are the norm for advertisements and sales presentations. If an unfavorable argument is presented, it is almost always for the reason of setting up a "straw man" argument that can quickly and effectively be refuted.

One-sided messages are most effective in reinforcing existing attitudes and beliefs. If the objective of the message is to try and change a strongly held attitude, a two-sided message is usually more effective, particularly if the receivers are well educated.[16] When the objective of an advertising campaign is to gain, rather than just hold, market share, two-sided messages might well be more effective.

Order of Presentation: There is evidence to indicate that in low-involvement learning situations there is substantially greater recall of information at the beginning and the end than in the middle of a message.[17]

Most consumer exposures to advertisements and purchasing agent exposures to sales presentations are low-involvement learning situations for them. Accordingly, in preparing such messages care should be taken to present the most important information—brand name and key sales points—at the beginning and at the end of the message.

Direct Comparison: Should Pepsi ads make taste comparisons with Coke? Should Ford make direct comparisons of its cars with those of General Motors in its ads? In general, should comparative ads be used?

The evidence bearing on this issue is both conflicting and inconclusive. However, it suggests an interesting hypothesis—that comparative ads probably should not be used for packaged convenience goods, but may well be effective for shopping goods.

The evidence is as follows:

1. *Packaged convenience goods comparative ads.* An Ogilvy & Mather[18] study found (1) no difference in awareness or persuasiveness with noncomparative ads, and (2) consumers often confuse a sponsor for its competitor.

2. *Shopping goods comparative ads.* Prasad[19] found recall higher than for noncomparative ads.

A potential explanation for the difference in the apparent results of using comparative ads for convenience and shopping goods has to do with the *need* for comparative information. Consumers do not require information from advertising to evaluate the comparative attributes (such as price, quality, style, and so forth) of competitive packaged convenience goods. But they do need it for items such as major appliances, floor coverings, automobiles, and the like. They are therefore likely to view a comparative ad for these products with a higher level of involvement, and thus have a higher level of recall and a lower likelihood of confusing sponsor and competitor. Although it may be appropriate for Ford to use comparative ads relative to GM, Pepsi probably shouldn't do so relative to Coke.

Another factor to consider is that direct comparisons publicize your competitor's name and identify that competitor as a concern of yours. Weeks after an ad has aired, people may not remember the ad but only remember the brands in the message as advertised brands. If nearly all potential customers know your competitor (e.g., Burger King's customers know of McDonald's), this situation probably is not serious. But if increasing name recognition is a communications goal of your competitor, your comparative ad may help your competitor's goal attainment.

The Spokesperson

Should an Identifiable Spokesperson Be Used?

For many years, O. J. Simpson was a prominent part of Hertz Rent-A-Car ads, both in the electronic and the print media. During the same period, no identifiable spokespersons were used by Avis, National, or any of Hertz's other competitors. Are there general reasons, grounded in research findings, that suggest that one of these approaches is preferable to the other?

A spokesperson may be used to present a message for either, or both, of two reasons. The first is **to attract attention to the message**. Since professional football fans and rental car customers are both predominantly male, there was no doubt a high degree of recognition of O. J. Simpson, a star football player, in the ads. (In fact, the Hertz ads featuring Mr. Simpson were often run during televised National Football League games. This virtually assured a high degree of recognition.) The high degree of recognition probably resulted in more attention being paid to the ads by the viewer.

The second reason for using a spokesperson is to increase **source credibility**. Companies that advertise generally are not viewed as being very credible because of their obvious interest in selling the product being advertised. A spokesperson who is believed to be credible may increase the credibility that he or she presents.

There is general agreement in the findings from research that for a source to be considered credible it must be viewed as being both *expert* and *trustworthy*. The credibility of the Hertz ads were therefore partially a function of the extent to which O. J. Simpson was viewed as being both expert and trustworthy (attributions that were no doubt in turn influenced by cues received from his performances over time in the television ads).

The image of a spokesperson ought to match the company's desired product image. The audience will associate the spokesperson and the product. Linda Evans endorsed Crystal Light, a low-calorie drink mix, because Ms. Evans has a healthy appearance and because she plays a fictional character named Crystal.[20] Energetic Mary Lou Retton effectively represented the Energizer. Michael Jordan, well known for his leaping abilities in basketball, conveyed a well-matched image with the Nike line of "Air Jordan" shoes.

The use of an identifiable personality or a spokesperson, however well known and credible he or she may be, is not without potential problems. These problems have been well described as follows:

> Using a company spokesperson creates special risks for the sponsoring organization. Few well-known personalities are admired by everyone. Thus, it is important to be certain that most of the members of the relevant target markets will respond favorably to the spokesperson. An additional risk is that some behavior involving the spokesperson will affect the individual's credibility after he/she is associated with the firm. The American Cancer Society had to stop a series of commercials in which Tony Curtis spoke against cigarette smoking when he was arrested on a marijuana charge. Ideal Toy Corporation apparently lost several million dollars on an Evel Knievel toy line after the stuntman was convicted of beating a reporter with a baseball bat.[21]

One way to deal with this problem is to create a fictional celebrity whose only association is with the product and whose image can be controlled. Often this association can be quite effective. "Ronald McDonald" has virtually total name recognition in the United States. Even "Mr. Clean," who had not been used in cleanser ads for several years, had 93 percent name recognition in 1985, compared with 56 percent for (then) Vice-President George Bush.[22]

We have considered the use of spokespersons thus far only with respect to advertising. In personal selling situations, the sales representative necessarily is the spokesperson for the message. Establishing and maintaining source credibility there is also of obvious importance. Care should be taken to select persons who are trustworthy and to provide sufficient training for them to be experts in the products sold and in their applications.

The Medium

What Medium (Media) Should Be Used?

A wide variety of media can be used for commercial messages. In advertising, one can use one or both of the electronic media (radio, television), can choose among four major print media (newspaper, magazine, direct mail, yellow pages), elect to use point-of-sale displays or outdoor advertising, and, as a final option, distribute samples of the product as well. Even in personal selling, where the choices are much more restricted, the sales representative can call on the customer in person or use the telephone.

A reasoned choice among media requires considerations of capability to deliver the message to the intended audience, the costs of doing so, and the communications and sales effects achieved. We consider media delivery ca-

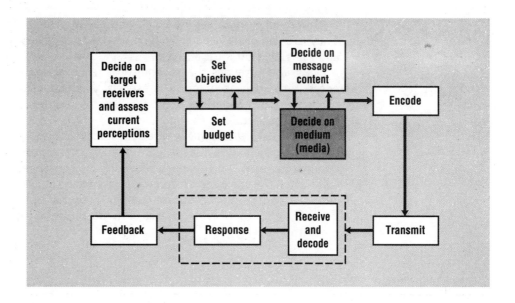

pabilities and costs in the next chapter. Here, we deal with the communications effects of media.

An important distinction among media is the *extent of the involvement* required. The electronic media are relatively *low*-involvement media since the pace of presentation of the information is fixed and cannot be controlled by the listener or viewer.[23] Perhaps for this reason, augmented by the experience we have all received from reading textbooks and other printed sources we regard as authoritative, the printed media have more credibility for most people than the electronic media.[24]

Each medium has special advantages for one or more uses. Although *television* is a low-involvement medium, it is especially good for such products as appliances, automobiles, and fashion goods. It can be used to provide demonstrations of how the product is used and how handsome it appears in use situations. To take advantage of this capability, television ads are often adapted to portray action resulting from using products even when normally no resulting actions would be seen. *Examples*: the playing of a recorded song on a tape that breaks a wine glass, the animated portrayal of the penetration of an ointment into a sore muscle.

Radio is especially effective in situations where the spoken word and other sounds related to the message are important. Political messages, stereo equipment, theatre productions, and announcements of sales and special events are examples of products and services that are well adapted to radio advertising.

Magazines are particularly well suited to the advertising of products whose attributes and special features need more than the ordinary amount of description. Magazines tend to be read more at leisure than newspapers, and depending on the specific magazine being used, may be a more creditable source of information on product attributes.[25] For example, *Tennis World* is viewed as a credible source on tennis equipment and *Road and Track* for automobiles. In general, magazines deliver a more segmented market, except in terms of locality, than television.

Almost all *newspapers* are local, and those of any size are published daily. They are therefore especially well adapted to advertising short-term specials and sales held by local retailers.

Direct mail provides the capability of reaching target market segment audiences with great accuracy. It is especially effective for low-cost specialty and shopping goods and services (books, records, insurance, charitable and political contributions, etc.).

Personal sales presentations offer the greatest opportunities for adapting the message to the specific needs and reactions of the potential buyer. It is the only commercial medium in which feedback is accomplished during and immediately after the message is delivered.[26] This provides the sales representative with the opportunity to ensure that the potential buyer understands the offering fully and to provide answers to objections—capabilities that no other medium has.

Transmittal of Messages

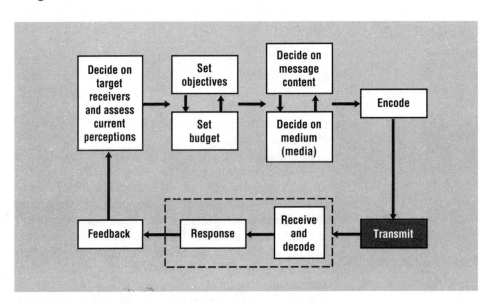

What Should the Frequency of the Messages Be?

A common conception of the proper pattern of sending messages over time is that they should be **evenly spaced**. There are often reasons for varying message frequencies between periods, however. When this is done, it is referred to as **flighting**. Some common flighting patterns are shown in Figures 14–4b, c, and d.

A **concentrated pattern** may be desirable for any one of several reasons. Often there are better prices or discounts to be gained by concentrating expenditures rather than spreading them. There may also be added communications value in such a pattern; consumer awareness thresholds may be crossed which would not be reached at a lower, constant frequency of transmission.

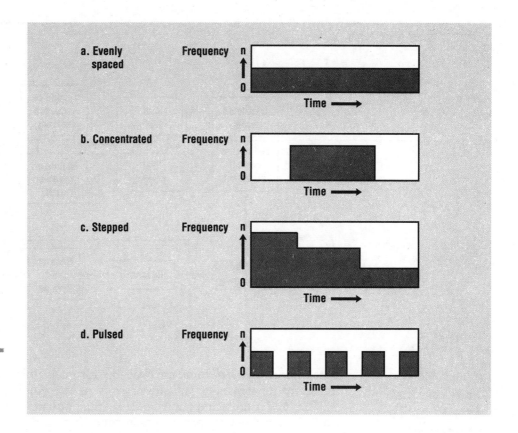

a. Evenly spaced Frequency

b. Concentrated Frequency

c. Stepped Frequency

d. Pulsed Frequency

Time →

FIGURE 14-4
Constant, concentrated, stepped, and pulsed message frequency patterns (frequencies of 0 to n messages per period).

Concentration of expenditures may also open new media strategy possibilities that would otherwise have been unavailable at the planned level of budget.

A ***stepped pattern*** is commonly used in the advertising of a new product. A relatively high frequency is used during the introductory phase and is later reduced to a sustaining level. The reasoning behind such a pattern is to generate a high level of awareness and trial during the introductory period and to sustain the awareness and repeat-purchase levels thereafter. Strong obtained such a pattern for a new product from a computer program he developed based on empirical data linking recall and exposure to newspaper advertisements. He also found stepped schedules of exposures to be more efficient than evenly spaced schedules for products that show seasonality in their sales patterns.[27]

The ***pulsed pattern*** is simply a repeated concentrated pattern. As such, it may be desirable for one or more of the same reasons as for the concentrated pattern, that is, there may be cost savings, new strategic options, or greater efficiencies in advertising in pulses as opposed to a constant frequency. For example, Strong presents evidence that there is a greater effect on average audience recall of grouping newspaper advertising in flights (sets) of two rather than to have them evenly spaced over time.[28] Some other researchers (notably, Herbert Krugman of General Electric) believe that flights of three are the most efficient method of scheduling advertising exposures.

Obtaining Feedback

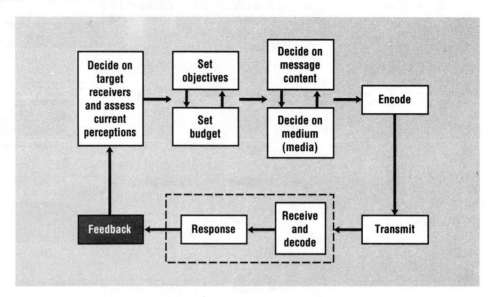

Who Received
the Messages?
How Were They
Interpreted?
What Were the
Responses?

Data on **media distribution** are available for magazines and newspapers. They consist of data from organizations such as the Audit Bureau of Circulation (ABC), which audits and publishes subscriber and newsstand sales. In addition, magazines and newspapers typically conduct periodic surveys and make available reports on the age, income, educational level, and other demographic characteristics of their readers. Since radio stations tend to have formats that appeal to particular demographic groups, they also often commission studies to determine listener profiles.

Such data do not tell the communicator anything about the *audience* for a particular message or set of messages, however, nor how the members of the audience interpreted or responded to them. The only systematic way to do this is to conduct a survey of (a sample of) the potential audience to determine who was actually exposed to the message and what their interpretations and responses were.[29]

Obtaining this kind of feedback serves two purposes: (1) it allows an evaluation of the effectiveness of the communications program since the last survey was conducted to obtain feedback, and (2) it provides an assessment of (the newly obtained) current perceptions of receivers to begin the new communications planning cycle.

POSITIONING

All of the theory about communications discussed in this chapter is used to help establish a product's position as a means of gaining sales.

Positioning was defined earlier (Chapter 2) as:

> The act of designing the company's image and value offer so that the segment's customers understand and appreciate what the company stands for in relation to its competitors.[30]

Once segments have been defined, a product must be positioned in such a way that the target market correctly perceives its relationship to other competing products in the market.

Procter & Gamble, for example, markets several laundry detergents, and it seeks to position each detergent differently for different segments or target markets. Cheer washes clothes at all temperatures; Oxydol "makes whites whiter"; Dash provides concentrated, low-suds cleansing power; Bold has fabric softener. Every aspect of the marketing communications program—indeed, of the entire marketing program—ought to support the position that the company wants to achieve.[31]

Products may be positioned along a number of dimensions, such as benefits, attributes, price, distribution, quality, and image the consumer wants to project. The positioning dictates which image the product shares. Consider the marketplace for jeans: Calvin Klein implies a quite different image than Levi.

The positioning strategy is intimately tied to the entire marketing program. The consumer segments and their desired product attributes will determine what positioning strategy will be most effective, given the current perceptions of a product. The packaging, price, advertisements, sales promotions, selling strategy, and distribution must all then be synchronized to create the desired positioning. If any element is inappropriate, the entire program will be less effective. General Motors is said to be targeting 19 different segments with its cars. Consider what would happen to Pontiac sales—the division positions its cars as sporty and powerful and to be owned and driven predominantly by young adults of average or higher incomes—if next year's TransAm and other Pontiac cars were to come out with boxy designs and low-power, fuel-efficient engines.

Products may also be repositioned or multiply positioned. For example, radio stations often are repositioned by changing the type of music played—rock and roll to country and western, country and western to "top 40," "top 40" to rock and roll. Hunt's Pudding Snack Packs now are not only for dessert but also for after school when the children return home.

A variety of research techniques can be used to determine a product's positioning. Conjoint analysis, multidimensional scaling (used for Figure 14–5), factor analysis, focus groups, in-depth interviews, and the Kelly rep grids are all examples of methods that have been used. The goal of all of these methods in positioning research is to understand consumers' perceptions of products, whether qualitatively or quantitatively. When creating a new product or repositioning an old product, a company may want to ask consumers about their ideal product and about current competitors in a particular market. By comparing the two patterns, the company may be able to identify places where current product offerings fall short.

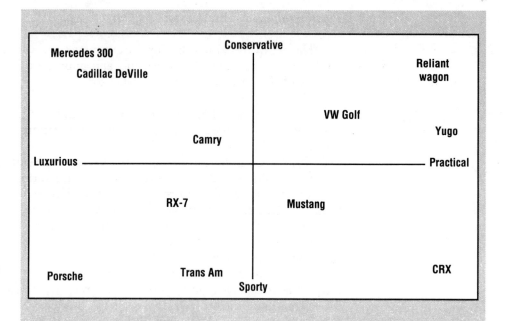

FIGURE 14-5
Positions of cars on
practical–luxurious and
conservative–sporty dimensions.

1. The informing, persuading, and changing the predisposition to buy tasks of marketing are carried out through the *communications mix* of the firm.
2. The communications mix consists of four major elements: advertising, personal selling, sales promotion, and publicity.
3. The definitions of these means of communication are:
   a. *Advertising.* Any paid form of nonpersonal presentation and promotion of ideas, goods, or services by an identified sponsor.
   b. *Personal selling.* Oral presentation in a conversation with one or more prospective purchasers for the purpose of making sales.
   c. *Sales promotion.* Short-term price, prize (or gift), or product incentives designed to induce purchase when offered to distributors, industrial users, or consumers.
   d. *Publicity.* Nonpersonal stimulation of demand for a product, service, or business unit by arranging to have commercially significant news about it published, broadcast, telecast, or presented on stage that is not paid for by the sponsor.

4. *Communication* involves a sender who encodes a message that is sent through a medium to a receiver who decodes it, responds, and provides feedback when appropriate.

5. In planning a communications program to a market segment one should assess the current perceptions of receivers, set the objectives and the budget for the program, decide on the message content and the medium (or media), encode the message(s), transmit it (them), and arrange to obtain feedback.

6. To assess the current perceptions of the target receivers, a *survey* is generally required.

7. The company may elect to use either *communications* or *sales objectives* for its communications program.

8. *Communications objectives* are concerned with informing, persuading, or changing predisposition to buy.

9. *Sales objectives* are concerned with the levels of sales or market share.

10. Regardless of the nature of the objective, it should be stated in a form that permits it to be measured.

11. Setting the communications budget in a rational, systematic way requires that the *response function* between the means of communication being used and the objective(s) to be achieved must be measured or estimated.

12. *Fear appeals* should be used only in situations in which the source is credible, the receiver does not already have a high anxiety level about the threatened outcome, avoidance actions are easy to take, and the level of fear induced is not so high as to cause the receiver to distort or reject the message.

13. The use of *humor* appears to increase the attention to messages, but there is mixed evidence concerning its effects on persuasion.

14. *One-sided messages* are most effective in reinforcing existing attitudes and beliefs; *two-sided messages* are more effective in terms of changing strongly held attitudes or beliefs.

15. In preparing messages in low-involvement learning situations—advertising, for example—care should be taken to present the most important information at the beginning and at the end of the message.

16. Comparative advertisements should probably not be used for packaged convenience goods but may well be effective for shopping goods.

17. A *spokesperson* should be used only if he or she is viewed as being both expert and trustworthy, and so is believed to be credible.

18. A *credible source* is one who is viewed as being both expert and trustworthy.

19. Printed media have more credibility for their audiences than the electronic media have for theirs.

20. Each medium has special advantages for particular uses.
    a. *Television* is good for advertising such products as appliances, automobiles, and fashion goods because it can be used to provide demonstrations of how the product is used and how handsome it appears in use situations.
    b. *Radio* is especially effective in situations where the spoken word and other sounds related to the message are important.

    c. *Magazines* are particularly well suited to the advertising of products whose attributes and special features need more than the ordinary amount of description.

    d. *Newspapers* are well adapted to retail advertising.

    e. *Direct mail* provides the capability of reaching target market segment audiences with great accuracy.

    f. *Personal sales presentations* have the potential of being the most persuasive of all commercial media. It is the only commercial medium that (1) offers the greatest opportunity for adapting the message to the specific needs and reactions of the potential buyer and (2) permits feedback during and immediately after the message is delivered.

21. a. *Flighting* of messages involves varying the frequency of messages between periods.

    b. A *concentrated* frequency pattern may be desirable for reasons of lower media costs, more effective communication, and the opening of new media strategy alternatives.

    c. A *stepped* pattern is commonly used in the advertising of a new product.

    d. A *pulsed* pattern may be desirable for one or more of the reasons given for using a concentrated pattern.

22. *Feedback* should be obtained by a survey to determine who received the messages, how it was interpreted, and what the responses were. In addition to providing data for evaluating the communications program since the last such survey, it provides an assessment of (the now) current perceptions of receivers to begin the new communications planning cycle.

23. *Positioning* is the act of designing the company's image and value offer so the segment's customers understand and appreciate what the company stands for in relation to its competitors.

24. Products may be positioned along a number of dimensions, such as benefits, attributes, price, distribution, quality, and image the consumer wants to project.

25. The product's packaging, price, advertisements, sales promotions, selling strategy, and distribution must all be synchronized to create the desired positioning.

REVIEW QUESTIONS

14.1.   What are the major elements of the communications mix?

14.2.   What are the two major alternatives with respect to objectives for the communications program?

14.3. Under what conditions is (are):
   a. Fear appeals
   b. Humor
   c. One-sided messages
   d. Comparative advertisements
   likely to be effective?

14.4. What are the characteristics that make an information source credible?

14.5. What are the uses or conditions for which:
   a. Televison
   b. Radio
   c. Magazines
   d. Newpapers
   e. Direct mail
   f. Personal sales presentations
   is (are) best adapted?

14.6. What is *flighting* of messages?

14.7. Why might one elect to use a
   a. Concentrated
   b. Stepped
   c. Pulsed
   pattern rather than an evenly spaced pattern of frequency of messages?

14.8. In a pulsed pattern, how many messages should be grouped to form a single pulse? Why?

14.9. What kinds of information should be obtained as feedback from the messages making up a communications program? Why?

14.10. Compare and contrast the *general* and the *planning* communications models.

DISCUSSION QUESTIONS AND PROBLEMS

14.11. Are humorous ads likely to be effective for
   a. Volkswagen?
   b. Tylenol?
   c. Allstate fire insurance?
   d. Huffy bicycles?
   e. *Time* magazine?
   Explain.

14.12. An eminent economist has stated that "persuasion is an insidious form of coercion since persons being persuaded are seldom aware that they are being persuaded."
a. Do you agree with this statement?
b. Suppose that the U.S. Congress passed a law that limits advertising only "to those advertisements that are designed to inform and not to persuade."
1. Would this be desirable from a societal viewpoint?
2. What kinds of criteria could be used to determine when such an edict was being violated?

14.13. Suppose the Department of Health, Education, and Welfare were to decide that it should undertake a national antismoking campaign to offset the (perceived) effects of advertising inducing nonsmokers to smoke and smokers to continue to smoke.
a. If an advertising campaign were to be developed, to whom should it be targeted? What appeals should be used?
b. What appeals should be considered?
c. Could this properly be considered to be a "marketing" problem?

14.14. Buffalo Chips is the name of a brand of potato chips introduced a few years ago. An early TV commercial showed a football fan watching a game and chomping Buffalo Chips. "Hey, Cath," he yells to his wife in the kitchen. "What?" she asks, obviously annoyed and expecting him to ask her to bring a beer. "Love you," he replies. What are the underlying assumptions and rationale of the ad?

14.15. Miller Lite, a low-calorie beer, was the first such national brand of beer on the market and was an almost-overnight success. Its early advertising campaign featured "tastes great" and "not filling" appeals presented by well-known professional athletes in humorous contexts.
What are the underlying assumptions and rationale of the ad?

14.16. In early 1981, American Motors introduced the "old car retirement plan" which provided consumers with a cash bonus ranging from $300 to $500 when they traded in their 1978 or older model cars. (The buyer received such a rebate in addition to the trade-in value of the car.) Trade-in of a 1978 or 1977 received a $300 bonus, a 1976 or 1975 a $400 bonus, and a 1974 or older car a $500 bonus on a new Spirit, Concord, or Eagle model.
The themes for print and TV ads were "Which is going to give out first, your car or your money?" and "Are you still driving a car that was built when gas was 60 cents?"
What are the underlying assumptions and rationale of the campaign?

14.17. It has been asserted that "TV programming is a way of filling in time between commercials." Is this an appropriate description? Explain.

14.18. In the early 1980s, Sears, Roebuck conducted a survey to determine which of six well-known women would be best as a spokesperson and model for the company's line of women's wear. Cheryl Tiegs, a professional model, was the winner by a wide margin. She was signed and her name used on such items as sweaters, blouses, and shirts with an expectation that sales on these items might increase by as much as 5 or 6 percent. To the pleasant surprise of the Sears management, the sales increases were four to five times that level on Cheryl Tiegs items.

Why do you believe the use of a professional model's name and modeling services were so successful?

14.19. DAGMAR (*Determining Advertising Goals, Measuring Advertising Results*) is an approach to advertising management in which communications objectives, rather than sales objectives, are set and measured. It is controversial, the controversy centering primarily on whether communications or sales objectives are preferable.
   a. What are the assumptions underlying the choice of communications objectives rather than sales objectives?
   b. What are the assumptions underlying the choice of sales objectives rather than communications objectives? Which do you believe should be used? Why?

14.20. The evidence obtained by American researchers is that flighting of messages leads to a higher average level of recall than does evenly spaced scheduling. The preponderance of British research supports evenly spaced scheduling as being more efficient, however.
   a. What are the underlying assumptions that would lead to:
      1. Flighting being more efficient than evenly spaced scheduling?
      2. Evenly spaced scheduling being more efficient than flighting?
   b. Could both the American and British research findings be valid? Explain.

14.21. Does the following script for a radio ad for Econo Lodges meet the criteria for effective humor in advertising? Explain.

> Hi, I'm Tim Conway and I'm probing Amazing America for Econo Lodges. Tonight, I'm talking to you from the cavity in a two-ton molar in a health education museum in Cleveland. When I'm done here, I'm going to put the bite on high prices by staying in Econo Lodges, the premier economy motel where you spend a night, not a fortune.
>
> In fact, 40,000 people will sleep in Econo Lodges tonight. . . .Uh, not all the same one, of course. So, for reservations, call 1–800–55-ECONO. And, uh, don't forget to floss.*

*"Budget Motels Take to Humor Ads," *Advertising Age*, November 14, 1988, 65.

14.22. Periodically, suggestions are raised before the Ways and Means Committee of the U.S. House of Representatives to tax advertising. A recurring means that is suggested for doing so is to allow only 60 percent of the expenditures on advertising during the year to be charged off as a company expense during that year, and the remaining 40 percent to be charged off in 10 percent increments for each of the ensuing four years.

a. The rationale usually given for such a bill is that a reasonable estimate is that only about 60 percent of advertising's effect is felt in the first year, and that the full effects are not dissipated for about four more years. There are convincing measurements to demonstrate that advertising has lagged effects, but none to indicate that 60 percent of the total effect of advertising is realized in the first year, or that the remaining 40 percent should be amortized at a rate of 10 percent per year thereafter.

   Should such a bill be passed unless and until definitive measurements of the amount and duration of advertising lagged effects can be made? Explain.

b. If such a bill were passed by Congress, would you expect total advertising expenditures in the United States to (1) remain the same? (2) decline? Explain.

c. Suppose that $100 billion would continue to be spent on advertising by for-profit companies in the United States each year. Further suppose that their average marginal tax rate is 34 percent, and that their relevant cost-of-capital rate is 12 percent per year.
   1. How much additional revenue would be raised for the U.S. government during each of the first four years of such a bill's existence?
   2. By approximately what percentage would average advertising costs to companies be increased in each of these first four years?

14.23. A Los Angeles–based bank is planning to open its first branch in San Francisco. As a means of attracting depositors, a series of 13 full-page ads is planned in the S. F. *Chronicle* during each of the first two years after the opening. Experience in other locations has indicated that there is no one month or part of the year in which new accounts tend to be opened more than at other times. Assuming that the bank is not now known in the San Francisco area:

a. During which weeks (1 through 52) should the ads be scheduled during the first year? Why?

b. During which weeks should they be scheduled during the second year? Why?

14.24. The seasonal pattern of retail champagne sales in France for a recent five-year period is shown in the table on page 487. A French vintner that is introducing a new brand of champagne is planning to run a series of 13 ads in a weekly trade paper. How should the ads be scheduled? Explain.

**Retail Champagne Sales in France
(Five-Year Average)**

Month	Sales as a % of Annual Sales
January	5.86
February	5.39
March	6.32
April	6.63
May	7.24
June	7.24
July	6.16
August	2.62
September	8.01
October	10.48
November	15.10
December	18.95
	100.00

Endnotes

[1] These definitions are adapted from those given in *Marketing Definitions: A Glossary of Marketing Terms*, American Marketing Association, 1960.

[2] G. H. Brown, "Measuring Consumer Attitudes Toward Products," *Journal of Marketing*, April 1950, 691–698.

[3] Adapted from an example in S. S. Sands, *Setting Advertising Objectives*, The Conference Board, 1966, 10.

[4] Ibid., 11.

[5] A. J. San Augustine and W. F. Foley, "How Large Advertisers Set Budgets," *Journal of Advertising Research*, October 1975, 12.

[6] B. Sternthal and C. S. Craig, "Fear Appeals: Revisited and Revised," *Journal of Consumer Research*, December 1974, 22–34.

[7] W. J. McGuire, *Effectiveness of Appeals in Advertising*, Advertising Research Foundation, 1963; and M. R. and W. L. Wilkie, "Fear: The Potential of an Appeal Neglected by Marketing," *Journal of Marketing*, January 1970, 54–62.

[8] J. R. Stuteville, "Psychic Defenses against High Fear Appeals: A Key Marketing Variable," *Journal of Marketing*, April 1970, 39–45.

[9] Ibid.

[10] It began to fall later, however. Federal Trade Commission, *Report to Congress on Cigarettes for 1978*, U.S. Government Printing Office, 1979.

[11] C. Leavitt, "A Multidimensional Set of Rating Scales for Television Commercials," *Journal of Applied Psychology*, August 1970, 427–429. See also B. Sternthal and C. S. Craig, "Humor in Advertising," *Journal of Marketing*, October 1973, 12–18.

[12] J. Walter Thompson Advertising Agency, "Humor in Advertising," memo, 1969.

[13] R. Osterhouse and T. Brock, "Distraction Increases Yielding to Propaganda by Inhibiting Counterarguing," *Journal of Personality and Social Psychology*, August 1970, 344–358; and L. Testinger and N. Maccoby, "On Resistance to Persuasive Communications," *Journal of Abnormal Social Psychology*, April 1964, 359–366.

[14] G. Dokorny and C. Gruner, "An Experimental Study of the Effect of Satire Used as Support in a Persuasive Speech," *Western Speech*, Summer 1969, 204–211; D. Kilpela, "An Experimental Study of the Effects of Humor on Persuasion," Masters thesis, Wayne State University, 1961; and A. Kipela, "An Experimental Study of the Effect of Humorous Message Content upon Ethos and Persuasion," Ph.D. diss., University of Michigan, 1972.

[15] Based on criteria given in D. I. Hawkins, K. A. Coney, and R. J. Best, *Consumer Behavior: Implications for Marketing Strategy*, Business Publications, 1980, 347.

[16] See C. Hovland, A. Lunnsdaine, and F. Sheffield, *Experiments on Mass Communication*, Princeton University Press, 1948, Chap. 8.

[17] H. E. Krugman, "The Impact of Television Advertising: Learning without Involvement," *Public Opinion Quarterly*, July 1965, 349–356; and H. E. Krugman, "Memory without Recall, Exposure without Perception," *Journal of Advertising Research*, August 1977, 7–12.

[18] "The Effects of Comparative Television Advertising That Names Competing Brands," Ogilivy and Mather Research, unpublished report.

[19] V. K. Prasad, "Communications—Effectiveness of Comparative Advertising: A Laboratory Analysis," *Journal of Marketing Research*, May 1976, 128–137.

[20] L. R. Kahle and P. M. Homer, "Physical Attractiveness of the Celebrity Endorser: A Social Adaptation Perspective," *Journal of Consumer Research*, March 1985, 954–961.

[21] Hawkins et al., *Consumer Behavior*, 346.

[22] M. N. Vamos, "New Life for Madison Avenue's Old-Time Stars," *Business Week*, April 1, 1985, 94–95.

[23]H. E. Krugman, "The Measurement of Advertising Involvement," *Public Opinion Quarterly,* Winter 1966–1967, 583–596.

[24]D. A. Fuchs, "Two Source Effects in Magazine Advertising," *Journal of Marketing Research*, August 1964, 59–62.

[25]D. A. Aaker and P. K. Brown, "Evaluating Vehicle Source Effects," *Journal of Advertising Research*, August 1972, 11–16.

[26]With the limited exception of the QUBE system, a system that allows cable television viewers with special equipment to respond directly to questions raised or offers made on a program.

[27]E. C. Strong, "The Spacing and Timing of Advertising," *Journal of Advertising Research*, December 1977, 25–30.

[28]Ibid., 28.

[29]For a good discussion of the measurement of media distribution and audiences, see J. F. Engel, M. R. Warshaw, and T. C. Kinnear, *Promotional Strategy: Managing the Marketing Communications Process*, 4th ed., Richard D. Irwin, 1979, 322–333.

[30]P. Kotler, *Marketing Management: Analysis, Planning, Implementation, and Control*, 6th ed., Prentice-Hall, 1988, 308.

[31]"Positioning Reigns for Consumer *or* Industrial Products," *Marketing News*, May 9, 1986, 14.

ADVERTISING, SALES PROMOTION, AND PUBLIC RELATIONS MANAGEMENT

A set of continuing operating decisions are required to carry out the *informing, persuading,* and *changing the predisposition to buy* tasks of the communications program. These decisions are needed to answer the questions that arise in implementing the program:

How much should we spend for each method of communications during the budgetary period?

What message(s) should be sent? and

What media should be used?

Another important question, that of the frequency with which messages should be sent, was discussed in the last chapter.

In this chapter, we consider the decisions involved in answering these questions with respect to advertising, sales promotion, and public relations.

How Much Should We Spend for Advertising?

The amount that should be spent on advertising depends of course on the strategic objectives of the firm. For example, if the objective is to maximize profits in the present period—a profit-now strategy—very likely the optimal expenditure will be less than it would be if the objective were to build market share now in order to make higher profits later—a share now, profit later strategy.

In general, it is very difficult to determine the optimal budget for a profit-now strategy. The lag between advertising and its effects, the interactive effects of advertising and the other marketing mix variables, the unforeseen actions of competitors, and the vagaries of market demand make the determination of a sound budget for advertising that will maximize present-period profits a difficult and demanding task. (That is the bad news. The good news, as we shall see later, is that it may be that substantial errors in setting the advertising budget may not affect present-period profits very much.)

As difficult as it is to set optimal profit-now advertising budgets, it is still much easier than trying to set optimal share now, profit later budgets. Each of the difficulties just listed that one encounters in the setting of profit-now budgets is compounded by the longer duration—several periods instead of one—of the share now, profit later strategy.

This section confines the discussion to setting profit-now budgets unless otherwise stated.

The Theoretical Basis for Advertising Budgeting

The linkage between advertising and profit (contribution to profits and fixed costs) is shown in Figure 15–1. That is, the level of advertising has a positive relationship with perceived relative quality, and through that to perceived relative value. (The term *relative* as used here refers to the level compared with that of other firms in the same industry.) Perceived relative value is in turn linked to sales and market share, and sales (and the profit margins on them) is the determinant of contribution to profits and fixed costs.

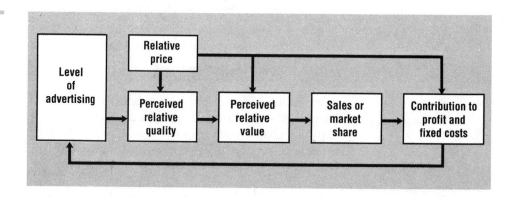

FIGURE 15-1
Linkage between advertising, intervening variables, and profits.

For consumer businesses, these linkages have been verified by the PIMS data.[1] For purposes of setting the advertising budget, however, the direct concern is the relationship between advertising and sales (market share) if the strategy is share now, profit later; or advertising and sales if it is profit-now. In the first instance this is a sales response function for advertising, and in the second a profit response function.

The Sales Response Function for Advertising: Conventional wisdom among advertising theorists and practitioners is that the shape of the sales response function is as shown in Figure 15–2. That is, it is a flat *S*-shaped curve that is more technically known as a growth curve. One statement of the belief by an advertising practitioner that this is the shape of the response function is:

> My own view is that the [sales] response function [for advertising], fully understood, will turn out to be an S curve. . . .[2]

Not all persons knowledgeable about advertising concur, however. Some, notably Simon[3] and Simon and Arndt,[4] have argued that the sales response function is one of ***diminishing returns*** (Figure 15–3), and have reported measurements of the sales and communications effects of advertising to support their view.

The argument of whether the diminishing returns or the growth curve is the actual shape of the sales response function from a practical standpoint is largely moot. Reflection indicates that even if the growth curve is the form the response function actually takes, the reasonably sophisticated firm (if it advertises at all) will be advertising in an amount equal to or greater than that at the inflection point. (The inflection point is the point on the curve where sales stop increasing at an increasing rate and start increasing at a decreasing rate.) The reasoning for this conclusion is simply that if it is worthwhile to advertise at all, it will pay to increase advertising expenditures as long as the return from each increment of advertising is increasing. This brings optimal advertising expenditures at least to the inflection point.

How far onto the diminishing-returns portion of the curve the expenditures should be set depends on how fast the incremental returns decrease. Clearly, one would not want to go out as far as the flat portion of the curve since incremental returns would be zero at that point. On the other hand, it might well be some distance beyond the inflection point before incremental return falls to the point of equaling incremental advertising cost.

FIGURE 15-2
Sales response function for advertising—growth curve.

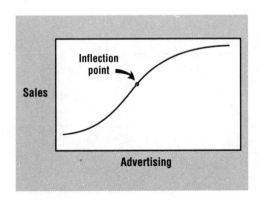

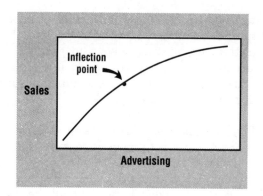

Even if the actual response curve is shaped like the growth curve, then, the effective part of it is the diminishing-returns portion. For the purposes of setting advertising budgets, therefore, we can assume that the response curve is a diminishing-returns curve.

The Profit Response Function for Advertising: If the sales response can be measured or estimated reasonably accurately, the profit response function can be derived from it. The variable costs of advertising and production will be known and can be subtracted from sales revenues to determine the contribution to profit and fixed costs over the appropriate range of the advertising expenditures. Figures 15–4a and 15–4b illustrate the relationship between the sales and profit response functions. The shaded portions of both curves are assumed to be the range of advertising expenditures being considered.

How Are Advertising Budgets Set in Practice?

As indicated in Table 15–1, there are six major methods of setting advertising budgets: (1) percentage of anticipated sales, (2) percentage of past year's sales, (3) all we can afford, (4) setting an arbitrary amount, (5) objective and task, and (6) use of formal decision models.

Percentage of Anticipated Sales and Percentage of Past Year's Sales as a Means of Setting the Advertising Budget: By far the most common method of arriving at advertising budgets is to set them as a percentage of sales. As shown in Table 15–1, 54 percent of the sample companies established budgets as a per-

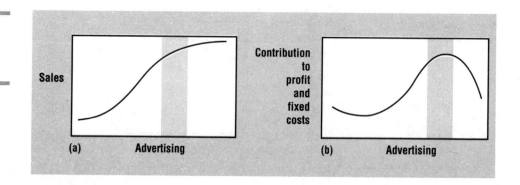

Table 15–1   Method of Setting Advertising Budgets as Reported by Advertising Executives of 25 Large Consumer and 25 Large Nonconsumer Goods Advertisers

Method	Consumer Goods Advertisers		Nonconsumer Goods Advertisers		Total*	
	No.	%	No.	%	No.	%
Percentage of anticipated sales	16	64	11	44	27	54
Percentage of past year's sales	7	28	11	44	18	36
Affordable approach	7	28	7	28	14	28
Arbitrary approach	4	16	6	24	10	20
Objective and task	3	12	5	20	8	16
Formal decision models	1	4	0	0	1	2
All others	5	20	3	12	8	16

*Totals exceed 100 percent because of multiple responses.
Source: A. J. San Augustine and W. F. Foley, "How Large Advertisers Set Budgets," *Journal of Advertising Research*, October 1975, 12.

centage of *anticipated sales*, and another 36 percent set them as a percentage of the *past year's* sales.

Using a percentage of sales can be shown theoretically to be a sound method of setting advertising budgets.[5] However, it is a justifiable method for setting advertising budgets for single products as a percentage only of *anticipated*, and not the *past year's*, sales.

The critical problem with the percentage-of-sales approach to setting advertising budgets in practice is that it is usually applied to last year's (or last period's) sales. If this is the case, the percentage chosen does not rest on the underlying assumption that advertising influences sales. The amount of the budget that results therefore has to be considered to be determined arbitrarily rather than in a theoretically defensible way. This same comment applies to the budgeting methods described next—the all-we-can-afford and the arbitrary-amount approaches.

All-We-Can-Afford and Arbitrary-Amount Methods of Advertising Budget Setting: The San Augustine and Foley study (Table 15–1) indicates that nearly 30 percent of large companies report that the all-we-can-afford approach is one of the methods used for setting advertising budget. Putting all that can be afforded (however that is determined) into advertising involves an implicit assumption that the marginal return from the last dollar spent this period will return, if not this period then eventually, at least one additional dollar in profits. Whether this assumption is correct depends on the sales- and profit-response functions. If the response functions are as shown in Figure 15–5a and b, spending all that could be spared for advertising would be appropriate if it happened to be an amount equal to A1, but would obviously not be very sensible if it turned out to be equal to A2.

Putting as much into the advertising budget as can be afforded without benefit of estimates of the sales return that can be expected is therefore something akin to investing one's savings without bothering to look at the prospects for return. However, there are times when it may be profitable to advertise for purposes other than the expectation of increasing sales; institutional advertising to boost stock prices prior to the floating of a new stock issue or before an

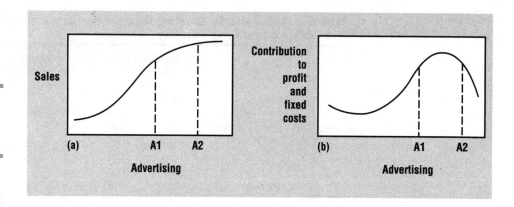

FIGURE 15-5a
Hypothetical sales response
function for advertising.

FIGURE 15-5b
Hypothetical profit response
function for advertising.

acquisition attempt via exchange of stock are examples. The all-we-can afford approach has the redeeming feature of establishing the outer limit for such expenditures. In addition, if management does not believe it can estimate the sales effects of advertising at all reliably, in Dean's words, "it sets a reasonable limit on the gamble."[6]

The San Augustine and Foley study indicates that another 20 percent of large companies report that the selection of an arbitrary amount is one of the methods they use to arrive at an advertising budget. The same observations apply to this method as were made for the all-we-can-afford approach.

Objective-and-Task Method of Setting the Advertising Budget: A reasoned, rational approach to making budget decisions in any area requires as the first step the setting of the objective(s) that the budget is to accomplish. The budget is then set in the amount it is estimated will be required to accomplish the objective(s).

This is known as the objective-and-task approach for setting advertising budgets. As discussed in the last chapter, the objectives set can be either for sales or for communications effects, with communications objectives predominating.

The objective-and-task method of setting budgets in advertising is not widely practiced. As shown in Table 15–1, only approximately one of each six large firms (16 percent) use it as one of the methods for arriving at the advertising budget.

Formal Decision Models as Methods of Setting Advertising Budgets: Mathematical models for setting advertising budgets date back to the mid 1950s.[7] As indicated by Table 15–1, they have been used sparingly. A requirement in the use of any mathematical model is the estimation of one or more of its parameters, and the difficulties involved in making reasonably good estimations are no doubt the major contributing reasons for the low level of use. Some large advertisers have made use of them, however, including Pillsbury and Coca-Cola.

EXHIBIT **15-1**

Diminishing-Returns Model of the Sales Response Function for Advertising

A diminishing-returns sales response function can be described by the equation

$$PQ = k + bA^x$$

where

P = price
Q = quantity sold
k = a constant (the dollar sales that would be realized without advertising)
b = the advertising coefficient
A = the amount of advertising expenditures, and
x = an exponent with a value between 0 and +1.0.

The values for k, b, and x will be dependent on the price P along with the nature and quality of the product and its distribution, and on the marketing mix variable levels of competitors.

Suppose that the objective of the company is to advertise at the level that will return the greatest contribution to profit and fixed costs for the current budgetary period. It can be shown* that the optimum level of advertising is

$$A^* = \frac{[xb(1 - AVC)]^{1/1-x}}{P}.$$

Assume that the following values are appropriate for a particular product whose advertising budget is to be set for the coming year:

k = $36.0 million/yr.
x = 0.60
b = 10.0
AVC = $6.80/unit
P = $9.90/unit

and industry sales are forecast to be $500M

If the advertising budget A were set at $3M for the year, sales would be

$$PQ = k + bA^x = \$36M + (10)(\$3M)^{0.60}$$
$$= \$36M + (10.0)(\$1.93M) = \$55.3M,$$

and contribution to profits and fixed costs would be

$$\text{Cont.} = PQ - Q(AVC) - A$$
$$= \$55.3M - \frac{\$55.3M}{\$9.90}(\$6.80) - \$3.0M$$
$$= \$14.3M$$

The most profitable level of advertising is

$$A^* = \frac{[xb(1 - AVC)]^{1/(1-x)}}{P}$$
$$= \frac{[(0.60) \times (10)(1 - \$6.80)]^{1/(1-0.60)}}{\$9.90}$$
$$= [6.0 \times .313]^{2.5} = \$4.84M$$

where the sales would be

$$S = \$36.0M + 10.0(4.84M)^{0.60}$$
$$= \$61.8M$$

Contribution to profit and fixed cost is

$$\text{Cont.} = \$61.8M - \frac{\$61.8M}{\$9.90}(\$6.80) - \$4.84M$$
$$= \$14.5M$$

The major problem in using the model is obtaining reliable estimates of k, b, and x.

*See D. S. Tull et al., "'Leveraged' Decision Making in Advertising," *Journal of Marketing Research*, February 1986, 28.

The nature and implications of one mathematical model concerning advertising budgeting are presented in Exhibit 15–1.[8]

How Should Advertising Budgets Be Set?

We describe two methods of setting advertising budgets in this section; (1) budgeting based on the response function and (2) a back-up (and perhaps fall-back) method using an adjusted competitive parity approach.

Setting Advertising Budgets Based on Measurements or Estimates of the Response Function: To set budgets based on the response function, one must:

1. Measure or estimate the relevant portion of the sales response function.
2. Translate it into a profit response function.
3. Set the advertising budget at the point that will produce the maximum contribution to sales and fixed costs.

Effective use of this approach of course depends on obtaining a reliable measurement or estimate of the response function.

1. *Measuring the sales response function.* As described in Chapter 7, there are four methods that are the most appropriate ones for measuring sales response functions. These are on-line experiments, statistical analysis of sales data, field sales experiments, and the Delphi method. Only on-line experimentation is elaborated on here.

It will be recalled from Chapter 7 that an on-line experiment to measure sales response functions involves deliberate changes in one or more marketing variables in one more or more geographic areas during the course of the regular marketing program in such a way that the effects on sales can be measured.

In designing on-line experiments for measuring sales response functions for advertising, one should follow the following general guidelines:

- *Number of experimental areas.* From 2 to 30, depending on the number of areas in which the firm markets.
- *Type of experimental areas.* Sales territories or other defined geographic areas that are as nearly self-contained as possible in terms of (a) the coverage of the media that will be used and (b) the distribution area of the middlemen used. If the experimental market areas are not defined to be self-contained in terms of media coverage, it may be difficult to determine exactly how much advertising is done in the area during the experimental period. If an experimental area is not congruent with the area covered by the local distributor(s), the company conducting the on-line experiment may find it necessary to set up special measurement procedures to determine the level of sales. This may be expensive.
- *Number of control areas.* All the rest of the areas in which the "normal" advertising level is used.
- *Levels of advertising in the experimental areas.* +50%, −50% of the normal level of advertising if there are only two experimental areas; +50%, −50%, +25%, and −25% of the normal level if there are four or more experimental areas. The basis for the calculation of the level of advertising is expenditures per capita.
- *Method of selecting experimental areas.* Random selection from among all self-contained media and distribution areas available.
- *Method of assigning level of advertising to each experimental area.* Random assignment.
- *Length of the on-line experiment.* At least a year.

A sample design is shown in Figure 15–6.

The costs of obtaining information on the response function(s) is, of course, an important consideration. As Little points out:

If the parameters were constant over time, the company should put a big effort into measuring them right away, because the extra profit from increased accuracy would extend far into the future. It is difficult to believe that in practice

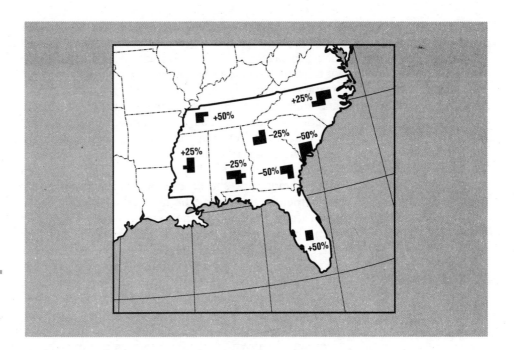

FIGURE 15-6
Design of (hypothetical) on-line
experiment to measure sales
response to advertising—
Southeast Region market areas.

the parameters stay constant. For example, competitive activity, product change, changes in the quality of the promotion, and shifts in economic conditions lead us to expect shifts in response. Consequently, an expensive effort to learn the parameters immediately cannot be justified. On the other hand, the parameters may change slowly with time, in which case some effort is worthwhile and, in fact, quite important.[9]

For this reason, continuing on-line experiments may be more appropriate than more-elaborate, and expensive, occasional field experiments. Out-of-pocket costs and distribution channel problems (especially in areas that receive large advertising appropriation reductions) arise in some instances from on-line experiments, which can make them expensive, however.

If expenses (or other reasons) prevent using on-line experiments, statistical analysis of sales data may be a useful alternative. There are usually some variations among geographic areas in the levels of per capita advertising expenditures that occur in the normal course of media buying. If this is the case, a statistical analysis of the relationship between per capita advertising and sales may provide useful information on the sales-response function.

2. *Estimation of the sales-response function.* In the absence of information from on-line experiments, field experiments, and statistical analysis of advertising and sales data, judgmental estimation of the sales-response function warrants consideration. As Berger points out, this is not an unusual approach in practice:

> The media planners I know best are now explicitly using the response function in planning media. They model the response function on a judgment basis, considering marketing objectives, consumer involvement and behavior, the nature of the advertising, competitive advertising and many other factors. They devise the response function brand by brand and case by case.[10]

Setting Advertising Budgets on an Adjusted-Competitive-Parity Basis: **Competitive parity** in this context is used to mean advertising at the same advertising-to-sales ratio as the average of that of one's competitors. The rationale of this approach has been expressed as follows: "The basic premise is that, on average, market factors will drive competitors to advertise at efficient levels, and that careful study of those norms can be used to guide budget setting practice."[11] Some companies will have a percentage that is too high and others one that is too low, but the industry average (the argument goes) should represent an approximation of the optimum percentage to spend.

However, even granting this, the average of the percentage of sales spent by one's competitors should not be used without adjustment. The need for the adjustment results from the fact (which can be shown both theoretically and empirically) that one of the determinants of the optimum (profit-now) advertising budget is the contribution margin of the product.[12] The contribution margin is the difference between the price and the variable costs of the product. The higher the contribution margin, the higher the advertising-to-sales ratio for the product should be. That this principle is followed by companies in the food industry, for example, is demonstrated in Figure 15–7.

An adjustment for any difference between the average margin of competitive products and one's own product therefore has to be made. If each of the other companies shown in Figure 15–6 were direct competitors of Pillsbury, and Pillsbury were in the process of setting the advertising budget for the coming year, for example, it would not want to use the industry average advertising-to-sales ratio of 5.3 percent. Rather, since its contribution margin is considerably lower, the budget in terms of advertising as a percentage of sales should also be substantially lower.

The procedure for setting the advertising budget using the adjusted-competitive-parity method is:

1. Determine the percentage of sales spent on advertising (by product, if possible) of each of the competitors.

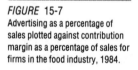

FIGURE 15-7
Advertising as a percentage of sales plotted against contribution margin as a percentage of sales for firms in the food industry, 1984.

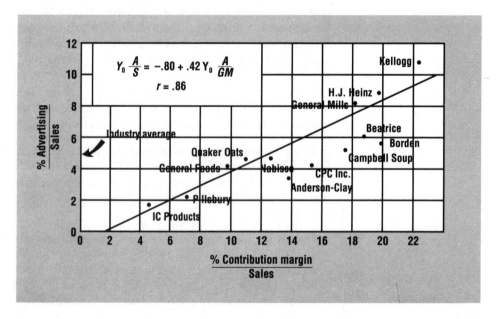

2. Determine the contribution margin as a percentage of sales (again, by product if possible) of each of the competitors.

3. Plot advertising as a percentage of sales against the contribution margin as a percentage of sales (per Figure 15–7).

4. Fit a line (either statistically or visually) to the data.

5. Pick off the percentage of sales that advertising should be from the contribution margin percentage.

6. Forecast sales for the forthcoming period.

7. Multiply forecast sales by the indicated percentage of sales to determine the amount of the advertising budget.

How does one get data on advertising expenditures and contribution margins of competitors? If the competitors are large companies, advertising expenditures by brand and category are supplied by Broadcast Advertisers Reports/ Leading National Advertisers (BAR/LNA) Seven Media Service. Other sources include the Publishers Information Bureau, Outdoor Advertising Association of America, Institute of Outdoor Advertisers, Media Records, Rome Reports, Agricultural Marketing Information Services, and Radio Expenditures Reports. Contribution margins for the firm as a whole can be obtained from company annual reports and 10K reports.

What are the Costs of Errors in Setting the Advertising Budget?

Using the diminishing-returns model given in Exhibit 15–1, one can derive the relationship between the percentage that a profit-now advertising budget is in error (the percentage that it is away from the optimum budget) and the percentage changes in sales and percentage loss of the optimum contribution to profit and fixed costs that result. As shown in Table 15–2, the percentage loss in contribution to profits and fixed costs is less than 1 percent for errors in advertising budgeting of plus or minus 25 percent.[13]

It seems reasonable to assume that the adjusted-competitive-parity method will result in an advertising budget that is within 25 percent of the optimum. If so, this method is an appropriate one to use in setting budgets if the data for competitors can be obtained.

This table suggests that if one is going to err in setting the budget, the error ought to be on the high side. Note that a budget error of +25 percent results in an indicated sales increase of over 3 percent at the cost of less than 1 percent of contribution to profit and fixed costs. If the model predicts accurately, this outcome means that "over" advertising is an inexpensive way of picking up additional sales and market share.

Table 15–2 Percentage Changes in Advertising Period Sales and Contribution to Profits and Fixed Costs Due to Changes in Level of Advertising Expenditures from the Optimum*

Percentage Change In	Percentage Error in Advertising Budget			
	−25%	−10%	+10%	+25%
Sales	−4.2	−1.6	+1.4	+3.4
Contribution	−0.6	−0.1	−0.1	−0.4

*For diminishing-returns sales-response function with advertising elasticity of 0.15.

Some qualifications need to be kept in mind when assessing the predictive validity of the model, however. First, the assumption is made that competitors will not react to the advertising expenditures being made. If the advertising budget were intentionally set at 25 percent over the estimated optimum profit-now level, for example, competitors might raise their budgets as well. Second, the figures in Table 15–2 are based on an advertising elasticity of 0.15, which is, as nearly as we can tell, roughly an "average" elasticity for products. There is considerable variation around this average over the range of durable and nondurable, consumer and industrial products. Third, no allowance is made for the effectiveness, or lack thereof, of the specific advertising campaigns used. Fourth, there is no allowance for lagged effects of advertising (future-period sales that result from present-period advertising). Finally, there is no allowance in the model for reduction in the average unit costs of production due to experience curve effects.

What Messages Should Be Sent?

It costs just as much to send an ineffective message as an effective one, and the results may be dramatically different. It is therefore worthwhile to try to prepare and to select those advertisements that will be effective.

But how to do that? Should the creation and the selection of "effective" ads rest with the copywriters and other "creatives" in the advertising department or agency, fine tuned or overridden by company management when they think it is necessary? Or should there be a continuing program of research to guide and evaluate the work of those who prepare the advertisements? We consider these questions with respect to the two major kinds of research that are used in advertising—developmental and copy-testing research.

Developmental Research

Developmental research is used to develop and evaluate alternative themes of the messages that should be sent. If one were involved in advertising wood-burning stoves, for example, many appeals can be used including warmth (both physically and psychologically), economy, independence, energy conservation, safety, cleanliness, and appearance. Which of these should be used?

A series of focus groups conducted by one wood stove manufacturer indicated that the appeals that were most effective varied by market segments. To white-collar and managerial professionals, the appeals of psychological warmth (coziness), energy conservation, and appearance were the most important. To blue-collar persons, economy, physical and psychological warmth, and independence were the primary reasons given for having or wanting to have a wood stove. A difference in usage patterns also exists between the two segments: white-collar and managerial professionals tend to use wood stoves as a source of heat in a family room, whereas blue-collar families use it as a primary source of heat for the entire house.

These findings were used in preparing ads for the different target market segments. Different appeals were used in ads to be run in *House & Garden* magazine, for example, than in *Farm and Ranch Living*.

There is little dispute about the usefulness of developmental research such as this for preparing ads. Both client company and agency personnel generally agree that it is appropriate and helpful to have this kind of information as long as it is valid and reliable. The dispute arises in the use of copy-testing research.

Copy-Testing Research

As the name implies, **copy-testing research** is used to evaluate the content—the copy—in ads. Pretesting is done to provide answers to the questions "Should we use this ad?" and, if the answer is in the affirmative, "Should we make any changes before we use it?" Posttesting is carried out after the ad is run to determine how effective it actually was.

An example of the pretesting of an ad is given by the research done by Sears, Roebuck on a television ad for girls' dresses:

> [The ad] had gone through the creative strategies and approval processes of management and was ready for concept testing for communication, brand name awareness, and selling thrust.
>
> Audience research indicated the ad lacked stimulation and product feature impact, so close-up footage of the product was added. . . . As it turned out, the ad produced far better research scores.

After the ad was run, a study indicated that it had been successful from a sales standpoint as well.[14]

Sears uses a panel of 225 consumers to whom the ads are shown and from whom opinions are obtained for the pretests the company conducts. There are a variety of ways to carry out pretests. They include the use of consumer juries (the panel of consumers Sears uses is an example), measurements of physiological responses (eye dilation, electrical conductivity of the skin, frequency of electrical waves in the brain, change in voice frequency, eye movement, and others), readability tests, coupon-redemption rates, buying intention, and simulated sales response.

Posttesting procedures involve recognition tests, recall tests (recall of the ad, recall of specific copy items such as the headline or slogan or particular information items contained in the ad), awareness of the brand and its attributes and benefits, attitudes toward the brand, and various forms of sales tests.[15]

Almost irrespective of how it is done, there is a marked difference in attitude toward copy testing between the creative people in advertising departments and agencies and the management of the client companies. The creatives in general distrust and resent copy testing—especially those tests that result in numerical measurements (or "magic numbers," as one person from an agency has called them).[16] They distrust it because convincing evidence of its reliability and validity in terms of predicting actual results has not been developed, and they resent it because they believe it is often an unfair measure of their work. Many feel that it stifles creativity.[17]

The managements of client companies tend to agree that the predictive validity of current testing methods is suspect. However, in general they are unwilling to risk advertising budgets, which in many cases amount to millions of dollars, on the unaided judgments of either the creative director of the advertising agency or themselves. They continue to use data from copy tests because they believe such data, even if flawed, are better than no data at all.[18]

Given this view, copy testing will continue and, given the escalation of production and media costs, may well increase. The resolution of the problem will come only as researchers develop more reliable and valid copy-testing methods.[19]

What Advertising Media Should Be Used?

The major advertising media are print (magazines and newspapers), electronic (radio, broadcast TV, and cable TV), outdoor, and direct mail. These media vary greatly in both effectiveness and cost. The selection of the best media and the proper allocation of the advertising budget among them are therefore important decisions.

Reach, Frequency, and Impact: Gross Rating Points (GRP) and Weighted Exposure (WE)

An idealized allocation among media of a fixed advertising budget would result in the largest number of people being exposed to the messages at the highest frequency with the greatest impact per exposure. The concepts that are involved in these considerations in media allocation are:

Reach (R)   The number (or percentage) of people (or households) that are exposed to the message at least one time during a specified period (usually four weeks)

Frequency (F)   The number of times each person (household) is exposed to the message during the period

Impact (I)   The effectiveness of each exposure in attaining the advertising objective(s)

There are obvious trade-offs among these three elements. If the advertiser wants a wide reach, then a great many media will have to be employed. This will reduce the frequency with which any one person or household will be exposed for a given advertising expenditure. Increasing impact by the size of the ad (print media) or its length (electronic media) will similarly come at a cost to reach or frequency for a fixed budget. Simultaneously maximizing reach, frequency, and impact has therefore been referred to as realizing an "unattainable end."[20]

The effects of the trade-offs involved can be evaluated in part by using the concepts of *gross rating points* and *weighted exposures*.

Gross rating points (GRP) = the product of reach (R) × frequency (F) or GRP = R × F.

Weighted exposures (WE) = the product of reach (R) × frequency (F) × average impact (I); or

$$WE = R \times F \times I$$
$$= GRP \times I.$$

A campaign to introduce a felt-tip pen under the Crayola brand had as an objective to reach 52 percent of the households in the U.S. market for an average of six times during the introductory period.[21] In terms of gross rating points, the objective was

$$GRP = 52\% \times 6 = 312.$$

This is presumably the expected result of the media plan that was judged to be the best among the alternatives considered for the available budget. The plan used and three hypothetical alternatives that might have been used are compared in Exhibit 15–2.

Selection of Media and Specific Media Vehicles

The task of the media planner can be simply stated—it is to select those media and the specific vehicles in each medium that will maximize the total weighted exposure value among a defined target audience for the budget to be spent. Successfully carrying out such a charge is one of the more complex and demanding assignments in the field of marketing, however.

EXHIBIT **15-2**

Crayola Felt-tip Pen—Media Plan Used and Three Hypothetical Alternatives

	Media Plan Used	Alternative 1	Alternative 2	Alternative 3
Reach	52%	60%	44%	60%
Frequency	6.0	5.0	7.0	6.5
Average impact	1.00*	1.00	1.00	0.75

*Assumed.

With the (assumed) value of average impact of $I = 1.00$, the weighted exposure for the plan used is calculated to be:

$$WE = GRP \times I = 312 \times 1.00 = 312.00.$$

In Alternative 1, reach would have been increased (from 52 percent to 60 percent) at the expense of frequency while average impact remained the same (1.00), and so weighted exposures would have been:

$$WE_{ALT\ 1} = (R \times F \times I)$$
$$= (60\% \times 5.00 \times 1.00) = 300.00$$

or less than the value of 312.00 for the plan used. In Alternative 2, reach would have been decreased (from 52 percent to 45 percent) to allow frequency to be increased (from 6.0 to

7.0) and average impact remained unchanged (1.00), giving a weighted exposure of:

$$WE_{ALT\ 2} = 44\% \times 7.0 \times 1.00 = 308.00.$$

Again, this is less than the value for the plan actually used. Finally, in Alternative 3 both reach and frequency are increased (reach from 52 to 60 percent and frequency from 6.5 to 7.0), but at the cost of print ads being made smaller and radio and TV ads being shortened so that average impact would have been decreased (1.00 to 0.75). The resulting weighted exposure value would have been:

$$WE_{ALT\ 3} = 60\% \times 6.5 \times 0.75 = 292.50.$$

This value again is less than that for the plan used.

The complications come (1) in acquiring valid estimates of reach, frequency, and impact by media vehicle, and (2) in combining these estimates with cost data to arrive at an optimum media plan.

Acquiring Estimates of Reach, Frequency, and Impact by Specific Vehicle by Medium

Reach: A specific vehicle in a medium is a particular newpaper, magazine, television or radio time slot, or set of posterboard locations. Audience measurements are available for most vehicles in terms of audience distribution, the number of copies circulated, or television or radio sets carrying the advertisement. (These distribution measurements are made by such organizations as the Audit Bureau of Circulation [ABC] and the Canadian Circulation Audit Board [CCAB] for newspapers and magazines and The Traffic Audit Bureau for outdoor advertising.)

Reach is a measure of the exposed audience, however, and so distribution data are not enough. Exposure measurements for newspapers and magazines are done by several commercial organizations that conduct interviews of readers and prospective readers.

Exposure to the electronic media is measured by having a panel of respondents who keep a diary of programs listened to or watched, by coincidental telephone calls to a sample of households to determine what program (if any) is currently tuned in, or by later interviews in which the respondent is asked to recall the programs listened to or viewed. There is also an electronic recording technique in which an audimeter is attached to the radio and television sets in a sample of homes to record the times that the set is on and the station to which it is tuned. "People meters" expand electronic recording's capabilities for television audience measurement by allowing viewers to "log on" and "log off" electronically.

If there were accurate measurements that were done frequently, media planners would have no difficulty in estimating reach for the media vehicles for which they are available. However, sizable measurement errors can exist, a fact that is dramatized for magazine readership by the substantial differences that occur often in the measurements of the two major magazine readership research firms.[22] Errors arise from sampling and in the measuring process from respondents' not remembering what they read or saw, and misreporting what they remember. (In particular, there is a tendency for people to claim readership of high-prestige magazines or newspapers they do not read and to disclaim readership of low-prestige ones they do read. In one study, for example, the estimate made from the proportion of sample respondents who reported that they were readers of a prestigious magazine was that there were 15 times more readers than there were copies of the magazine sold.)[23]

When the combined reach of a series of ads is to be determined from successive independent measures of exposure, errors can arise in both reach and frequency estimates due to an unknown amount of duplication of exposure.

Frequency: The major problem in the determination of frequency of exposure is estimating the amount of audience duplication. To illustrate this problem, suppose that the circulation of a particular magazine is known to be 750,000. Suppose further that the same ad is run in each of three successive issues and independent readership measurements show that 250,000 persons saw the ad in each issue. What is the average frequency of exposure?

As indicated in Figure 15–8, average frequency varies directly with duplication of readers, going up from 1.0 with no duplication (Figure 15–8a) to 3.0 with complete duplication (Figure 15–8c). Reach of course varies inversely with duplication, going down from 750,000 with no duplication to 250,000 with complete duplication.

Note that the gross rating points in the three situations depicted in Figure 15–8 are all the same. The GRP in Figure 15–8a is equal to reach × frequency, or 100% × 1.0 = 1.0. The GRP for the situations in Figures 15–8b and c, respectively, are 66.7% × 1.5 = 100.0 and 33.3% × 3.0 = 100.0 as well.

Even though the GRP is the same for all three outcomes, it is unlikely that a media planner would be indifferent between them. If the objective for advertising were to increase the awareness of the product, for example, a high reach, low frequency outcome would no doubt be preferred. If, on the other hand, the objective were to change the average predisposition to buy of the readers, the low reach, high frequency outcome would most likely be the preferred one.

Impact: The most difficult to estimate of the reach–frequency–impact components of the weighted exposure formula is impact. Impact obviously varies greatly among ads: A good ad may be several times more effective than a poor one. Depending on the objectives of the campaign, impact for a given message will also vary among media, and among vehicles within each medium.

The factors that affect impact include:

1. *Acceptance and believability.* The ad, the medium, and the vehicle all contribute to credibility. A magazine ad with seemingly reasonable and well-documented claims using Walter Cronkite as a spokesman will have more acceptance and greater believability than an ad with exorbitant, undocumented claims appearing in a sensationalist tabloid.

Newspapers and magazines in general enjoy higher acceptance and believability than the other media. The medium with the lowest credibility is direct mail.

FIGURE 15-8
Reach and frequency variations for three different levels of audience duplication for three ad insertions.

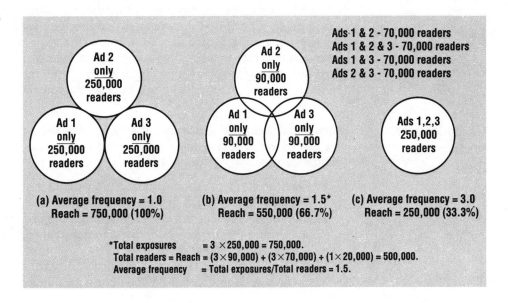

2. *Audience selectivity.* Media, especially vehicles within media, vary greatly in terms of their ability to provide an audience congruent with the target market segment. Ads, by virtue of the symbols used, also vary substantially in terms of this same capability. Thus, an ad for a high-priced perfume that is in color, features a glamorous model, and appears in a fashion magazine is likely to have much greater selectivity in terms of the desired audience than a black-and-white ad in a newspaper.

In general, direct mail has the greatest and outdoor advertising the lowest selectivity of all the media. Television has less selectivity than radio, newspapers, and magazines.

3. *Attention-getting ability.* The ability of an ad to attract attention is a function of the ad, how long it is run, and its placement within the vehicle. The same ad inserted in a relatively clutter-free position in a vehicle will command substantially greater attention than one surrounded by many other ads. An ad that has been run only a limited number of times will have greater attention-getting capability than one ready for "wearout" to set in.

Media become victims of their own success as they attract more advertising and so increase clutter. Television and direct mail are examples of media in which overuse has contributed to reduced attention-getting capability.

4. *Information-providing ability.* Media also vary in terms of their ability to retain attention, as well as to attract it. They also vary in their abilities to communicate specific kinds of information.

Apparently because consumers read newspapers and magazines and expect to spend substantial amounts of time in doing so, greater amounts of information can be conveyed by ads in these media than by those in radio and television. Since it has the advantage of using sight, sound, and motion, television has a unique potential for conveying information on how a product works, how it is used, and how efficient it is in use.

Estimating Impact: Impact estimates for alternative media plans as currently made are largely judgmental in nature. Developmental research to evaluate alternative messages do not involve media evaluations. Copy tests are necessarily made for ads that are prepared for specific media, but not for particular vehicles within each medium. As a former head of the Advertising Research Foundation wrote in 1976, "No acceptable measures of response to advertising [impact] exist for comparing vehicles in different media."[24] Regrettably, measurements of impact have not improved appreciably since then.

Considerations
for Selection
Decisions

Media and media vehicle decisions are complex and difficult to make. Consider, for example, the following options, all to deliver the "same" message, for the Xerox Company:

1. *Direct mail.* Preparation, printing, and mailing at 14.3 cents each third class, 25.4 cents each first class.
2. *Television.* A 30-second commercial on a major network.
   a. During the Super Bowl. Estimated audience of 82 million persons. Cost is $500,000 per commercial.
   b. During a popular prime-time program with an average audience of 36.4 million. Cost is $60,000 per commercial.

3. *Magazine.* A full-page ad in:
  a. *Time* magazine. Circulation is 4,451,800 copies with an average readership of 4.7 persons per copy. Cost is $45,055 per black-and-white ad, $70,285 for four-color.
  b. *Sports Illustrated* magazine. Circulation is 2,343,380 copies with an average readership of 5.3 persons per copy. Cost is $28,880 for a black-and-white ad, $45,050 for four-color.
4. *Radio.* A 30-second commercial on a major network.
  a. During the Super Bowl. Estimated audience of 35 million persons. Cost is $55,000 per commercial.
  b. During the early evening network news program. Estimated audience is 10 million persons. Cost is $10,000 per commercial.

These are only a few of the large number of vehicle options that the Xerox media planner has. Given that the alternatives have been narrowed to these, however, how should the media planner go about deciding which one (or combination of the above) should be selected at what frequency(ies) if the budget for the period is set at 1.2 million?

The considerations that the media planner should take into account include:

I. MEDIA CHARACTERISTICS

  1. Cost of exposures. This is usually calculated on a cost-per-thousand (CPM) basis.
  2. Relative impact. For example, given the choice of a person seeing an ad in *Time* or in *Sports Illustrated*, does the advertiser have any preference and, if so, which is preferred and by how much? It is usual to think of an average media vehicle option as having a value of 1.0 and then assign value for other media options relative to it.
  3. Upper bounds on insertions. The maximum number of times the media option can be used in each period.

II. MARKET CHARACTERISTICS

  4. Population of the target segment.
  5. Sales potential per person in the segment.
  6. The percentage of potential realized with $1, 2, \ldots, n$ average exposures per person.

III. BRAND CHARACTERISTICS

  7. Brand-purchases rate.
  8. Brand switching rate.
  9. Market share.

IV. MEDIA SEGMENT DATA

  10. Target segment coverage. The fraction of the segment population that will be in the audience of the media vehicle.

11. For each pair of candidate media vehicles, the fraction of the population in the segment that will be in the audience of both vehicles.

12. Budget for the period.[25]

After having read this list (which is not necessarily exhaustive), the obvious question to be raised is, "How does one incorporate all of these considerations into an organized framework for arriving at the media plan?"

Making Media and Media Vehicle Selection Decisions

The Cost-per-Thousand (CPM) Criterion: One method of making media and media vehicle decisions is to select those options that give the lowest cost per thousand potential exposures. This is commonly known as the CPM approach. The cost-per-thousand amounts for each of the vehicle options being considered by the Xerox media planner are:

Direct mail	$143.00 for third-class mail
	$234.00 for first-class mail
Television	$6.10 for a Super Bowl commercial
	$1.65 for a prime-time program commercial
Magazine	$2.15 for a black-and-white *Time* ad
	$3.36 for a four-color *Time* ad
	$2.33 for a black-and-white *Sports Illustrated* ad
	$3.63 for a four-color *Sports Illustrated* ad
Radio	$1.57 for a Super Bowl commercial
	$1.00 for a network news program commercial

If the criterion is choosing the vehicle with the lowest CPM, therefore, the Xerox budget for the period would be allocated solely to commercials on the radio network news program.

Clearly, this is a naive basis on which to do media planning. It completely ignores such important considerations as relative impact, target segment coverage, and frequency effects.

Just as clearly, this is not the only criterion used in media planning. If it were, high-cost media, such as direct mail, would never be used. Further, if the CPM criterion were used exclusively, we would expect media vehicle CPMs to be nearly identical.[26] Since we observe both that high CPM media are widely used in practice and that there are large differences across media vehicle CPMs, criteria other than the CPM must be being employed.

Linear Programming: In 1961, the Batton, Barton, Durstine & Osborn advertising agency took full-page ads in the *New York Times* to announce that, through the use of the computer and a program that BBD&O had, it was now possible to do media planning so much more efficiently that one would get "$1.67 worth of advertising for $1.00." The basis for this claim was a linear programming model that could be used to find "optimal" media plans given current costs and the client's marketing objectives.[27]

Linear programming is an analytic method of finding an "optimal" solution subject to a set of constraints. If linear programming were to be used by Xerox as a means of arriving at a media plan, for example, it would be necessary to specify an objective to be maximized given the constraints to be observed. Suppose the objective to be maximized were the weighted exposures (impact) for the period. An objective function would then be set up with weighted exposures being a function of dollars spent, prospects reached per dollar, and relative impact—all for each of the 10 vehicles being considered by the Xerox media planner. The constraints would include the maximum number of insertions that could be made during the period for each vehicle (once per week for *Time* and *Sports Illustrated*, for example), the maximum or minimum to be spent on any vehicle, and the total advertising budget.

In the Xerox example, there are 1,265 possible combinations of the 10 media vehicles being considered by the analyst. Given the specifications just described, the output from the computer run using the linear programming model would specify which one of these combinations would be "optimal" and the amounts to be spent on each of the vehicles included.

The word *optimal* has been framed by quotation marks thus far in this discussion because of the implicit assumptions that are involved in using the linear programming model. If single-stage linear programming models are used, these assumptions are that (1) successive purchases in a vehicle contribute equally to the effectiveness of the advertising, (2) repeated exposures of a prospect contribute equally to the effectiveness of the advertising, (3) audience duplication is not a problem, (4) there are no quantity discounts in media buying, and (5) any schedule of advertisements during the period is as effective as any other schedule. Since these are all unrealistic assumptions, the "optimal" solution provided by single-stage linear programming is at best an approximation of the true optimum.[28]

The BBD&O program was a single-stage program. Sequential linear programming involves breaking the media planning period down into shorter subperiods and applying the single-stage linear programming, or another suitable model, sequentially to the subperiods. Changes in the data entered into the model for the second and subsequent subperiods can allow for most of the problems (described above) in single-stage linear programming. Other, more-sophisticated sequential models can also be used that incorporate such consideration as brand-purchase rates, brand-switching probabilities, and market share in arriving at each successive subperiod media plan.[29]

Comprehensive Analytic Media-Planning Model: One of the better comprehensive models is the MEDIAC.[30] It is designed to deal directly with such media-planning considerations as market segment coverage, audience duplication, repeated exposure effects, sales potentials, and vehicle audience seasonality. It is programmed so that the planner can enter an original data set, receive the "optimal" media plan within a few minutes, and then make changes if desired on one or more of the input variables to determine what effects they have on the media plan.

Although significant progress has been made, it seems fair to say that media models have not fully lived up to their early promise. A major constraining element has been the unavailability of much of the data by media vehicle—audience size, audience duplication, demographic characteristics, geographic location, relative impact by product, brand-purchase rates, brand-switching rates, and so forth—or for the consumer—memory decay rate, sales potential, and so forth—that are required as inputs to the models.

SALES PROMOTION

The primary thrust of advertising programs is to inform, persuade, and change the predisposition to buy. As such, their orientation is both to induce trial and to encourage repeat purchase—objectives that are both short-term and longer-term in nature.

There is a large set of advertising-related marketing activities, however, that are solely designed to stimulate short-term sales. They often incorporate elements of a price reduction as well. They are known as sales promotions.

It will be recalled from the last chapter that **sales promotion** was defined as short-term price, prize (or gift), or product incentives designed to induce purchase when offered to distributors, industrial users, or consumers. Some recent examples for consumer products and services are described in Exhibit 15–3.

Sales promotions are run to the trade—distributors and dealers—and to industrial users, as well as to consumers. A list of the more important types of sales promotions for each of these groups includes:

DISTRIBUTORS AND DEALERS

Catalogs, brochures

Cooperative advertising allowance

Bonuses, contests for sales representatives

Display racks, shelves

Financing assistance

Payment for premium display space

Short-term price discounts

Inventorying assistance

File units of the product

Technical assistance, manuals

Clocks, calendars, etc., with company logo

Tie-in sales

INDUSTRIAL USERS

Catalogs, brochures

Technical assistance, manuals

Gifts for purchasing agents

EXHIBIT **15-3**

Some Typical Sales Promotions

A coupon for Maxwell House coffee was run about every five weeks by General Foods. Its face value averaged 40 cents.

Miller Brewing Company organized and is sponsoring dart leagues and tournaments in taverns on behalf of its Lowenbrau beer.

The RJR/Nabisco Company offered a book-of-days calendar "full of amusing quotes and intriguing anecdotes" about women. It cost $1 with proof of purchase of two packs of Virginia Slims cigarettes.

Arby's fast-food restaurants offered a water glass with a reproduction of one of six of Norman Rockwell's most famous *Saturday Evening Post* covers. A purchase of a minimum amount was necessary to order to receive a glass.

Cracker Jack, which for more than 50 years has given away a free toy in every pack, ran an "instant winner super toy surprise" sweepstakes. A rub-off card was inserted in each pack (along with the free toy) and winners received prizes of Mattel toys.

The Cadillac Division of General Motors offered rebates of as much as $1,000 per car and an interest rate that was substantially lower than that available from lending institutions.

In 1989 two of the regional "Baby Bell" telephone companies delivered coupons, product samples, and other marketing messages in the poly bags containing their telephone books.

Virtually every domestic U.S. airline has a "frequent flyer" club that gives free flights based on the accumulated number of miles flown on the airline.

Inventorying assistance

Short-term price discounts

Delayed payment

Trial-product samples

CONSUMERS

Coupons

Cents-off "deals"

Free samples

Contests

Rebates

Sponsorship of charities, leagues, sports events

Premiums (e.g., dishes) and specialty items (e.g., calendars)

Trading stamps

Delayed payment, reduced interest rate

Games

It is obvious that sales promotions encompass a highly diverse set of activities. This diversity makes it difficult to discuss them as a single, undifferentiated group. Our discussion therefore is limited to setting the sales promotion budget and evaluating results.

Setting the Sales Promotion Budget

It comes as a surprise to most persons not directly involved in advertising or sales promotion that the total annual budget for sales promotion activities in the United States is estimated to be larger than that for advertising. In fact, although overall sales promotion expenditures are not measured, they are "generally estimated at twice the advertising total."[31]

In principle, setting the budget for a specific sales promotion (say, a coupon campaign) is no different from setting the advertising budget for a given period. Intelligent budget determination in both instances requires an estimate of the sales and profit response functions of the proposed actions.

In practice, budgets tend to be set largely on the basis of countering actual and expected competitor promotions rather than on explicit estimates of sales and profit response. If one company in an industry is involved in sales promotion, usually most of them are. Because of the potential of large short-term sales losses from a successful competitor promotion, company brand and marketing managers become sensitized to the need to react quickly to competitor promotional campaigns. Sales promotion budgets then tend to get competitor-driven; a form of competitive parity budget setting results. Setting the budget for the sales promotion program in this way is more difficult than it is for advertising, however, because of the volatility and diversity of competitor promotional programs, and the difficulty of predicting how much they are likely to spend and when they will spend it.

Some companies have established programs of developmental research and of pretesting planned promotions to provide estimates of the likely response to them. The methods used are essentially the same as those for developmental research and for pretesting campaigns in advertising. Focus groups are used to generate ideas for alternative forms of promotions. Consumer surveys, controlled store tests, on-line experiments, and field sales experiments are the major methods for pretesting specific promotions.[32]

Evaluating Sales Promotion Results

Sound management of any ongoing program requires a continuing monitoring and evaluation of results. Yet the indications are that for sales promotion programs it is the exceptional company that systematically attempts to determine how sales and profits were affected.

Although such a lack of attention has to be at least partially attributable to poor management practice, before judging those involved harshly one needs to recognize that sound evaluation of promotions are seldom easy and often expensive. The critical element in the evaluation is of course the estimate of sales that resulted from the promotion. Not only must this estimate be made for the period in which the promotion was run but, if it is believed that a lower price or other inducement may have caused advance buying, it should also be made for at least one purchase cycle following the promotion. The net additional sales provide an evaluation of the sales effects of the promotion. Multiplying the number of additional units sold by the estimated profit per unit and subtracting the costs of the promotion gives an evaluation of the profit effects.

As an example, consider the information required, and the sources from which it can be obtained, for an evaluation of the coupon campaign by General Foods for Maxwell House coffee that was referred to earlier. (See Exhibit 15–4.)

Some comments concerning this example are appropriate. First, the number of coupons redeemed by persons loyal to Maxwell House (item 1b) is highly dependent on how the coupons were distributed.[33] If they were distributed by direct mail or printed in a newspaper, there would have been a much smaller proportion of loyal Maxwell House users redeeming them than if a coupon had been inserted in each can of Maxwell House for a given period. (Although we do not know the method by which General Foods distributed the Maxwell house coupons, the company reportedly "has substantial evidence that it was simply 'buying its own customers' and not reaching new users" with the Maxwell House coupon campaign.)[34] Second, coupon fraud (item 1c) can account for up to one-quarter of redemptions in any given campaign.[35] A reasonably accurate estimate of it can therefore be critical to the evaluation of sales and profit effects of promotions involving coupons. Third, the fact that General Foods was running a coupon campaign every five weeks would have complicated the determination of inventorying effects (item 1d). Fourth, the analysis in the example does not make allowance for subsequent repeat purchase made by persons introduced to Maxwell House as a result of buying it with a coupon. To the extent that such purchases are made, the evaluation of sales and profit effects produced by an analysis such as this is conservative. Finally, there are costs to promotions that do not get reflected in accounting data. Extra man-

EXHIBIT **15-4**

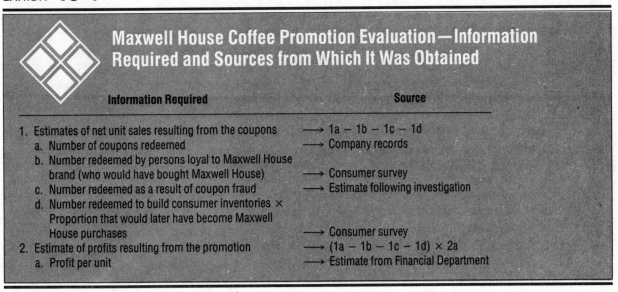

Maxwell House Coffee Promotion Evaluation—Information Required and Sources from Which It Was Obtained

Information Required	Source
1. Estimates of net unit sales resulting from the coupons	→ 1a – 1b – 1c – 1d
a. Number of coupons redeemed	→ Company records
b. Number redeemed by persons loyal to Maxwell House brand (who would have bought Maxwell House)	→ Consumer survey
c. Number redeemed as a result of coupon fraud	→ Estimate following investigation
d. Number redeemed to build consumer inventories × Proportion that would later have become Maxwell House purchases	→ Consumer survey
2. Estimate of profits resulting from the promotion	→ (1a – 1b – 1c – 1d) × 2a
a. Profit per unit	→ Estimate from Financial Department

agement time, incurring ill will from retailers (from forcing them to handle coupons), and the promotion "proneness" generated in purchasers as they become exposed to more and more promotions are examples.

PUBLICITY

Another advertising-related activity is that of obtaining publicity. As defined in the last chapter, **publicity** consists of the nonpersonal stimulation of demand for a product, service, or business unit by arranging to have commercially significant news about it published, broadcast, telecast, or presented on a stage that is not paid for by the sponsor.

Some examples of the effective use of publicity are given in Exhibit 15–5.

EXHIBIT **15-5**

Some Examples of Successful Promotions

For the first 70 years of their existence, Hershey bars were not advertised; rather, the company depended on "word of mouth" advertising to keep Hershey the undisputed leader of the U.S. candy bar business.* Advertising was begun in 1969 because during the late 1960s Hershey had become second in sales to Mars, Inc., the manufacturer of M&M's, Snickers, and other popular candy bars and confections.

Prior to the revolution in Iran in 1979, the Shah of Iran controlled the mass media. This prevented the Ayatollah Khomeini, in exile in Paris, from obtaining publicity for his views. To solve this problem, his supporters made telephone calls to him which they recorded on cassettes and passed from person to person. In addition, printed messages were reproduced in photocopy machines and distributed widely by them.

Former President Richard Nixon's autobiography, *RN Memoirs*, was marketed in 1978 by publisher Grosset and Dunlap with almost no advertising. "The media and all the rest of the publicity is doing our advertising for us," said a marketing executive for the company at the time. "Any advertising we'd do would get absolutely lost in everything else that's being generated."†

In the late 1890s Sapolio, a kitchen cleanser, was the most widely known product in the United States. This was the result of both advertising and extensive public relations efforts. *Spotless Town* was a play written for and distributed by the company in which a liberal number of references was made to Sapolio and which was staged by countless literary societies, schools, and churches around the country. In 1892, a small boat, named the *Sapolio* and manned by only one person, set sail from Bayonne, New Jersey, to Seville, Spain, to retrace the route of Columbus on the four hundredth anniversary of his voyage. It received continuing attention in the press until its safe arrival in Spain and when it was displayed later at the Columbian Exposition in Chicago in 1893. As is no doubt evident without saying, the trip was sponsored by the manufacturers of Sapolio.

On June 2, 1986, *Sports Illustrated* wrote an article on baseball which started with a vivid picture of a Giants base runner and a Mets catcher racing to home plate. Both players were sufficiently airborne that the large letters on the bottom of their shoes spelling Nike dominated the picture. Nike did not pay *Sports Illustrated* anything for the two-page picture, which would have cost over $100,000 to run as an ad. But by signing the players to endorsement contracts, Nike reaped valuable publicity.

---

*J. M. Winski, "Once Holdout Hershey Becomes Big Advertiser," *Advertising Age*, September 7, 1981, 67.
†L. Rogen, "Nixon's Book Sells on Publicity Alone," *Advertising Age*, May 29, 1978, 35.

As is evident from these examples, publicity can be either complementary or supplementary to advertising.

Differences in Publicity and Advertising

Aside from the obvious difference of having to pay for the one and not for the other, the differences in the two include the following:

1. *Control of the message.* In advertising, the advertiser has full control of the message to be sent (within the bounds of media and legal constraints on truthfulness and taste). In using publicity, the public relations firm or company can attempt to control the content of the publicity obtained. The medium providing the coverage is the final determiner of what is written or said, however.

2. *Favorable versus unfavorable messages.* By its very nature, advertising content is always favorable to the sponsor. Publicity received by the Bureau of the Census from its campaign to increase the proportion of questionnaires mailed back and so to reduce both the cost of the 1980 Census and the undercount of the population was uniformly favorable. There was an undercount, however, and a number of cities sued the U.S. government to recover additional revenue for payments stemming from what they believed to be a differentially greater undercount of their populations than for the population as a whole. Much of the publicity resulting from these suits was unfavorable to the Census Bureau.

3. *Credibility.* Usually messages received via publicity are treated as being more credible than those from advertising. The medium containing the message is viewed as authenticating it when it is reported for its news or entertainment value. There is no such expectation of the medium for advertising. Thus, the favorable references to Sapolio contained in the *Spotless Town* play were no doubt given much greater credibility by the audiences than were similar favorable references when contained in the product's advertising.

4. *Use of contrived events.* A frequent ploy of those seeking publicity for a client is to generate a newsworthy event that will include references to the sponsoring person, product, or company. The solo trip across the Atlantic in a boat named the *Sapolio* is an early example of the publicitor's art being practiced through this means. More recently, Mobil Oil and others received publicity by sponsoring the trip of the first airplane to go around the world without refueling (the *Voyager*).

Setting the Budget for Public Relations

Obtaining publicity is usually under the auspices of the department responsible for the firm's public relations. Publicity is only a part of the activities involved in public relations; the latter function usually has the responsibility for maintaining good relationships with stockholders, the financial community in general, and the appropriate agencies and members of the executive and legislative branches of government as well as the general public.

Budget setting for publicity in theory is no different from that for advertising; the budget should be set on the basis of the estimated appropriate response function. In practice, however, the kinds of publicity-seeking activities are so diverse and the occasions for them and the outcomes of publicity campaigns so difficult to predict that estimating response functions is a highly tenuous affair.

As a result, budgets tend to be set as a percentage of sales (usually a small fraction of 1 percent). If the need, or opportunity, arises for a publicity campaign that cannot be covered by the assigned budget, management is approached for a supplementary budget.

In part, therefore, budgeting for publicity is an opportunity-based as well as a planned procedure.

Evaluating the Publicity Program

Measuring the Communications Effects of Publicity

A determination of the communications effects of publicity campaigns is normally carried on in one of two ways. The traditional method of obtaining an evaluation is the **scrap book**; clippings of all print media materials and a record of all electronic media references or news items are assembled, and the number of resulting exposures estimated. In one such evaluation, the conclusion was reached that 235.4 million exposures resulted from the following media coverage:

> . . . 3,500 column inches of news and photographs in 350 publications with a combined circulation of 79.4 million; 2,500 minutes of air time on 290 radio stations and an estimated audience of 65 million; and 660 minutes of air time on 160 television stations with an estimated audience of 91 million. If this time and space had been purchased at advertising rates, it would have amounted to $1,047,000.[36]

This method does not result in a precise measurement because it relies on media distribution data rather than on measurements of actual exposures. Further, there is no indication at all of the effects of the exposures in terms of awareness or attitude change.

The second method of evaluating communications effects is the **tracking study**. This method was discussed earlier as a means of evaluating advertising. It involves measurement of awareness and important dimensions of relevant attitudes toward the brand before and after the campaign. After allowing for the effects of company advertising and competitive marketing efforts, the difference between the before and after measurements is attributed to publicity.

Measuring the Sales Effects of Publicity

The same techniques for measuring the sales effects of advertising can be used for publicity. That is, one can conduct surveys, do statistical analyses of sales data, or carry out on-line or off-line sales experiments. As in advertising, experiments provide by far the best methods of evaluation.

One of the problems in evaluating sales effects of publicity by nonexperimental means is the difficulty of getting a usable measurement of the amount of the publicity. In advertising, the dollars spent during a period is the usual measurement used; for publicity, no such measurement is readily available. Using the estimated number of exposures (as per the illustration above, for example) becomes even a less satisfactory measure of the amount of publicity obtained when there is reason to believe that a substantial amount of word-of-mouth "advertising" is taking place.

Still, nonexperimental evaluations of sales effects can be made, even if they do not always carry great conviction. Consider the change in sales and advertising for Sapolio from 1891 to 1892, the year the boat named the *Sapolio* crossed the Atlantic.[37]

	Sales of Sapolio (units of one-half gross)	Advertising of Sapolio
1891	127,247	$147,191
1892	134,588	117,631

In the absence of persuasive reasons for believing that other factors were major contributors to the sales increase in 1892 (and there do not appear to have been any), one might reasonably conclude that the publicity attendant to the trip contributed to the sales of several thousand units of Sapolio—the increase in sales of over 7,000 units plus whatever loss in sales one wants to estimate from the reduction in advertising.

The total cost of the trip to the company was $98.50.

SUMMARY OF IMPORTANT POINTS

1. There are six major methods of setting advertising budgets. They are (a) percentage of anticipated sales, (b) percentage of past year's sales, (c) all we can afford, (d) setting an arbitrary amount, (e) objective and task, and (f) use of formal decision models.
2. By far the most common method of arriving at the advertising budget is to set it as a percentage of sales. The sales to which the percentage is applied are either those for the preceding budgetary period (quarter, year) or those anticipated for the coming budgetary period.
3. Theoretically, the correct way to set a profit-now advertising budget is to
   a. Measure or estimate the relevant portion of the sales response function.
   b. Translate it into a profit response function.
   c. Set the advertising budget at the point that will produce the maximum contribution to sales and fixed costs.

4. Regardless of whether the advertising sales response function is one of diminishing returns over its full range, or whether it is one of first increasing and then decreasing returns, the effective portion of the response function is the diminishing-returns portion.

5. A mathematical model for the optimum level of advertising based on a diminishing-returns response function is

$$A^* = \frac{[xb(1 - AVC)]^{1/(1-x)}}{P}$$

where A^* is the level of advertising that will maximize profits during the advertising budgetary period, x is an exponent with a value between 0 and $+1$, b is a coefficient with a positive value, AVC is the average variable cost per unit of production and of marketing other than advertising, and P is price.

6. The term $(1 - AVC)/P$ is the contribution margin for the product. It can also be written as $(P - AVC)/P$ or as mark-up on price. From the above equation, it can be seen that the optimum level of advertising is a direct function of contribution margin (or mark-up on price).

7. The four methods that are the most appropriate ones for measuring the sales-response function for advertising are on-line experiments, statistical analyses of sales data, field sales experiments, and the Delphi method.

8. Since the parameters that determine sales response to advertising (k, x, and b in the diminishing-returns model) probably change over time due to competitive activity, product change, changes in the quality of promotion, shifts in economic condition, and so forth, expensive means of measuring the parameters are difficult to justify.

9. On-line sales experiments are a relatively inexpensive and effective way of obtaining information on the sales-response function for advertising.

10. In designing on-line experiments for measuring sales-response functions for advertising, one should follow the following general guidelines:

   a. Number of experimental areas. From 2 to 30, depending on the number of areas in which the firm markets.

   b. Type of experimental areas. Sales territories or other defined geographic areas that are as nearly self-contained as possible in terms of (1) the coverage of the media that will be used, and (2) the distribution area of the middlemen used.

   c. Number of control areas. All the rest of the areas in which the "normal" advertising level is used.

   d. Levels of advertising in the experimental areas. $+50\%$, -50% of the normal level of advertising if there are only two experimental areas; $+50\%$, -50%, $+25\%$, and -25% of the normal level if there are four or more experimental areas. The basis for the calculation of the level of advertising is expenditures per capita.

   e. Method of selecting experimental areas. Random election from among all self-contained media and distribution areas available.

    f. Method of assigning level of advertising to each experimental area. Random assignment.

    g. Length of the on-line experiment. At least a year.

11. *Competitive parity* as used here means advertising at the same advertising-to-sales ratio as the average of that of one's competitors.

12. The rationale of using competitive parity as the basis for setting advertising budgets is that "on average, market factors will drive competitors to advertise at efficient levels, and that careful study of those norms can be used to guide budget setting practice."

13. If one uses the competitive-parity method of setting advertising budgets, he or she should adjust the average advertising-to-sales ratio of the competitors for any difference between their average contribution margin and that of his or her own firm.

14. The procedure for setting the advertising budget using the adjusted-competitive-parity method is:

    a. Determine the percentage of sales spent on advertising (by product, if possible) of each of the competitors.

    b. Determine the contribution margin as a percentage of sales (again, by product if possible) of each of the competitors.

    c. Plot advertising as a percentage of sales against the contribution margin as a percentage of sales.

    d. Fit a line (either statistically or visually) to the data.

    e. Pick off the percentage of sales that advertising should be from the contribution margin percentage.

    f. Forecast sales for the forthcoming period.

    g. Multiply forecast sales by the indicated percentage of sales to determine the amount of the advertising budget.

15. Using the mathematical form of the diminishing-returns response function, it can be shown that a profit-now advertising budget can be off by as much as $+25$ percent and it will reduce the contribution to profit and fixed costs by less than 1 percent.

16. Developmental research is often used to develop and evaluate alternative themes for advertising. There is little dispute between researchers and copywriters concerning the usefulness of this type of research.

17. Copy-testing research is used to evaluate the content—the copy—in ads. There is a substantial and continuing dispute between researchers and copywriters about both the accuracy and the usefulness of the copy-testing research techniques commonly used.

18. The reach (R) of an advertisement is the number (or percentage) of people (or households) that are exposed to it at least one time during a specified period (usually four weeks).

19. The frequency (F) is the number of times each person (household) is exposed to the message during a specified period.

20. The impact (I) is the effectiveness of each exposure in attaining the advertising objective(s).

21. The GRP (gross rating points) for a campaign is the product of reach times frequency, or

$$\text{GRP} = R \times F.$$

22. The WE (weighted exposures) for a campaign is the product of reach times frequency times average impact, or

$$WE = R \times F \times I$$
$$= GRP \times I.$$

23. In general, the objective of advertising campaigns is to maximize the number of weighted exposures.

24. The audience distribution is the number of copies circulated, the number of television or radio sets carrying the advertisement, or the number of billboards displaying the ad.

25. The exposed audience for each vehicle is the number of persons who actually saw or, in the case of radio, heard the ad.

26. Audience duplication among media vehicles leads to decreased reach and increased frequency for an advertisement.

27. The factors that affect the impact of an advertisement include its
   a. Acceptance and believability
   b. Audience selectivity
   c. Attention-getting ability
   d. Information-providing ability

28. The considerations that media planners should take into account in selecting media vehicles include:

   I. *MEDIA CHARACTERISTICS*
      1. Cost per thousand exposures (CPM)
      2. Relative impact
      3. Upper limit on insertions per period
   II. *MARKET CHARACTERISTICS*
      4. Population of the target segment
      5. Sales potential per person in the segment
      6. The percentage of potential realized with one, two . . . n average exposures per person
   III. *BRAND CHARACTERISTICS*
      7. Brand-purchase rate
      8. Brand-switching rate
      9. Market share
   IV. *MEDIA SEGMENT DATA*
      10. Target segment coverage
   V. *AUDIENCE DUPLICATION*
      11. Duplication in each pair of candidate media vehicles
   VI. *BUDGET*
      12. Budget for the period

29. A criterion that is sometimes used as the sole basis for choosing among media vehicles is cost per thousand exposures (CPM). As the above list of relevant considerations suggests, it is inappropriate to base vehicle choices only on CPM.

30. Linear programming is a mathematical model for finding an optimal solution for an objective function subject to a set of constraints.

31. Linear programming was applied to media planning beginning in about 1960 and is still in use today. It provides an "optimal" media

plan if one allows for the fact that the implicit assumptions in the operation of the model are that
  a. Successive purchases in a vehicle contribute equally to the effectiveness of the advertising.
  b. Repeated exposures of a single prospect contribute equally to the effectiveness of the advertising.
  c. Audience duplication is not a problem.
  d. There are no quantity discounts in media buying.
  e. Any schedule of advertisements during the period is as effective as any other schedule.

32. Sequential linear programming involves breaking the media planning period down into shorter subperiods and applying the single-stage linear programming, or another suitable model, sequentially to the subperiods. Changes in the data entered into the model for the second and subsequent subperiods can allow for most of the problems in single-stage linear programming.

33. Comprehensive analytic media-planning models exist also that overcome most of the inefficiencies of single-stage linear programming if the data required are available. However, the unavailability of empirical data for input is a major constraint on their use.

34. *Sales promotion* consists of short-term price, prize (or gift), or product incentives designed to induce purchase when offered to distributors, industrial users, or consumers.

35. Approximately twice as much money is spent on sales promotions as on advertising in the United States each year.

36. Sales promotion programs typically receive little in the way of evaluation.

37. Fraudulent redemptions are believed to account for as many as one-quarter af all coupons redeemed.

38. *Publicity* consists of the nonpersonal stimulation of demand for a product, service, or business unit by arranging to have commercially significant news about it published, broadcast, telecast, or presented on stage that is not paid for by the sponsor.

39. Aside from paying for one and not the other, the major differences in advertising and publicity lie in (a) control (advertising) versus lack of control (publicity) of the message, (b) favorable (advertising) versus favorable or unfavorable (publicity) messages, (c) generally higher credibility (publicity), and (d) the use of contrived events (publicity).

40. The budget for publicity-generating activities is normally set as a percentage of sales. The communications effects of publicity campaigns are usually evaluated on the basis of *scrap books* that contain clippings and a log of electronic media references or news items. *Tracking studies* also are sometimes used.

REVIEW QUESTIONS

15.1. What are the six major methods of setting advertising budgets? Which one of them is the most frequently used method? the least frequently used method?

15.2. Even for companies with large advertising budgets (say $100 million annually) it may not be economically feasible to conduct an expensive research project (say, $1 million) to estimate the sales response function for advertising. Why is this the case?

15.3. What are the four most appropriate methods of measuring the sales response function for advertising?

15.4. a. What does *competitive parity* mean?
       b. Why should an adjustment be made to a measurement of it before it is used for setting an advertising budget?

15.5. According to calculations based on the mathematical form of the diminishing-returns sales-response function for advertising, what is the cost of erring in setting the advertising budget as
       a. 25 percent too high?
       b. 25 percent too low?

15.6. How does one calculate the
       a. Gross rating points?
       b. Weighted exposures for a campaign?

15.7. What are the considerations that media planners should take into account in selecting media vehicles?

15.8. Why is it inappropriate to base media vehicle choices only on CPM data?

15.9. Which receives larger total annual expenditures in the United States, advertising or sales promotion?

15.10. What are the major differences in advertising and publicity programs?

DISCUSSION QUESTIONS AND PROBLEMS

15.11. Give the reasoning that leads to the proposition that it may be more profitable over the long term to advertise at a higher level than is profitable in the short term.

15.12. At one time the Armstrong Cork Company had as its advertising objectives "keeping the company's name before customers and attracting the attention of those who are not buying now by (a) providing salesmen an access to prospects, (b) making prospects easier to sell to, (c) publicizing the Armstrong name, and (d) carrying the sales message beyond the range of personal coverage."

Is this a desirable set of objectives? Why or why not?

15.13. The managing director of Ogilvy and Mather (Canada), Limited, a major Canadian advertising agency, states that:

a. "Advertising . . . is as essential, for certain products, as the raw materials, the skilled workmanship, and the machinery."

b. "No manufacturer in his senses spends a cent more on anything than he has to. And that applies to advertising."

Do you agree with these statements? Why or why not?

15.14. The following step-by-step method has been proposed as one that will provide a "perfect measurement" of the contribution of advertising to sales and profits:

First, make a list of all the working functions of the business (research and development, maintenance, accounting, sales, etc.). (But do not include advertising.)

To each one of the listed functions, allocate the exact amount of sales or profit which can properly be credited to that activity.

Add up the allocations.

Deduct the sum of these allocations from the known total of sales or profit for the business.

What remains is the contribution of advertising.*

Is this an adequate justification for the fact that precise estimates of proven validity of advertising's contribution to sales and profits are generally not available? Why or why not?

15.15. One of the central convictions concerning advertising held by Leo Burnett, long-time head of the Chicago advertising agency that bears his name, was:

The most powerful advertising ideas are nonverbal, and take the form of visual quality statements made by archetypes whose true meanings lie too deep for words: a strong man on horseback, a benevolent giant, a playful tiger. The richest source of these archetypes is to be found at the roots of our own culture—in American history, mythology and folklore.†

a. Can you identify advertising campaigns that use such cultural archetypes?

b. Do you agree or disagree that nonverbal symbols of this type are the "most powerful" means of communicating?

*From J. M. Wallace, "A Perfect Measurement of Advertising's Contribution to Marketing," *Journal of Marketing*, July 1966, 16.

†Carl Hixon, "Leo," *Advertising Age*, February 8, 1982, M8.

    c. Is it unethical to associate a cultural archetype with a product through advertising? Explain.

15.16. It has been asserted that:
    a. "Two brands, one with a 25% share of market and the other with a 65% share—even if everything else about their markets and copy performance were identical to each other—should not have their advertising dollars allocated in the same way."
    b. "A difference between two products in the length of purchase cycle has logical and demonstrable consequences in the way their advertising dollar should be spent."
    c. "Different brand switching rates call for different media strategies."
        1. Do you agree with the statement in (a)? If not, why not? If so, what are some of the differences in how the advertising budgets for the two brands should be allocated differently?
        2. Do you agree with the statement in (b)? If not, why not? If so, what are the major "logical and demonstrable consequences" in the way the advertising dollars of the two brands should be spent?
        3. Do you agree with the statement in (c)? If not, why not? If so, what different media strategies might be called for with a brand in a low versus one in a high brand switching product category?

15.17. One of the variables that appears to be positively associated with the A/S ratio is contribution margins on sales.
    a. Would you expect this to be the case intuitively? Explain.
    b. Would you predict this would be the case from the Dorfman–Steiner theorem? Explain.
    c. Would you expect this to be the case from the diminishing-returns quantitative model? Explain.

15.18. "Wild Kingdom," a television program sponsored by the insurance company Mutual of Omaha, is introduced with the following statement:

> As a result of high operations efficiency, Mutual of Omaha can sponsor the program you are about to see without increasing the cost of our policies.

Do you believe this statement is likely to be true? Why or why not?

15.19. "The problem of clutter is not so much a function of the number of commercials on television as it is a function of the array of commercials shown. Many of the commercials seen by viewers are irrelevant to their information requirements. People who own no dogs are treated to dog food commercials; people who have no children are 'entertained' with ads for diapers; and people who do not suffer from dandruff are subjected to ads for various concoctions designed to remove its causes."
    a. How could "clutter" of this kind be avoided on television?
    b. Should the method(s) indicated in your answer to (a) be adopted? Why or why not?

15.20. One reason that has been advanced to explain why the creative people in advertising agencies generally do not like evaluative copy-testing research has been expressed in the following syllogism:

a. Since creative people in agencies are highly articulate people who prefer verbal descriptions (which they understand and use) to quantitative descriptions (which they understand poorly and seldom use);

b. and the results of evaluative copy tests are usually reported in numbers rather than in words;

c. and since people usually do not like things they neither understand nor use;

d. it follows that the creative people in advertising agencies should not be expected usually to like evaluative copy testing.

Does this seem to be a reasonable and adequate explanation of the fact that the "creatives" in ad agencies typically don't like evaluative copy testing? Explain.

15.21. As indicated in the text, fraud is estimated to account for as much as a quarter of all coupons redeemed. What do you believe to be the major sources of fraudulent redemptions?

15.22. A Gallup poll was taken in the early 1980s to determine how the public ranked the professions listed below in order of their reputation for honesty, integrity, and ethical standards. In alphabetical order, the professions that were ranked are:

advertising practitioners	lawyers
auto salespersons	local office holders
bankers	ministers
building contractors	newspaper reporters
business executives	pharmacists
college professors	policemen
congressmen	real estate dealers
dentists	senators
doctors	state office holders
engineers	stockbrokers
funeral directors	TV reporters
insurance salespersons	union leaders

a. Rank these professions from high to low in terms of your perception of the members' reputation for honesty, integrity, and ethical standards.

b. What steps might an association of the members of the profession last on your list take to:
1. Improve ethical standards?
2. Communicate that improvement to the general public?

15.23. A poll taken in the United States in 1987 in which people were asked to rank their favorite athletes showed that 8 of the top 10 were black. Yet 9 of the top 10 sports-figure endorsers in 1987 were white. None of the 10 most popular sports figures were women, but 2 women were tied for tenth in endorsement fees.

Favorite Athlete	Endorser and Estimated Fee	
Walter Payton (football)	Arnold Palmer (golf)	$8M
Michael Jordan (basketball)	Jack Nicklaus (golf)	6M
Julius Erving (basketball)	Boris Becker (tennis)	6M
Earvin "Magic" Johnson (basketball)	Greg Norman (golf)	4.5M
Isaiah Thomas (basketball)	Michael Jordan (basketball)	4M
Dominique Wilkins (basketball)	Ivan Lendl (tennis)	3M
Larry Bird (basketball)	John Madden (former football coach)	3M
Anthony Webb (basketball)	Jim McMahon (football)	3M
Dan Marino (football)	Dennis Conner (yachting)	2M
Lawrence Taylor (football)	Chris Evert (tennis)	2M
	Martina Navratilova (tennis)	2M

a. Is the disparity between popularity and endorsements evidence of racism? Explain.
b. Is the absence of women in the list of favorite athletes evidence of sexism? Explain.

Endnotes

[1] B. T. Gale, "The Impact of Advertising Expenditures on Profits for Consumer Businesses," The Ogilvy Center for Research and Development, 1987.

[2] D. Berger, "How Much to Spend?" presentation to the Advertising Research Foundation Conference, March 18, 1980, 19.

[3] J. Simon, "Are There Economies in Advertising?" Journal of Advertising Research, June 1965, 15–20.

[4] J. Simon and J. Arndt, "The Shape of the Advertising Response Function," Journal of Advertising Research, August 1980, 11–28.

[5] D. S. Tull, J. H. Barnes, and D. T. Seymour, "In Defense of Setting Budgets for Advertising as a Percent of Sales," Journal of Advertising Research, December 1978, 49–50.

[6] J. Dean, "How Much to Spend on Advertising," Harvard Business Review, January 1951, 70.

[7] For a good general discussion of formal decision models for setting advertising budgets, see G. L. Lillien and P. Kotler, Marketing Decision Making: A Model Building Approach, Harper & Row, 1983, 492–501. References to specific models include the following: J. D. C. Little, "BRANDAID: A Marketing Mix Model," Operations Research, Vol. 23, 1975, 628–673; D. B. Montgomery and A. J. Silk, "Estimating Dynamic Effects of Marketing Communications Expenditures," Management Science, 1972, B485–B501: M. Nerlove and K. J. Arrow, "Optimal Advertising under Dynamic Conditions," Econometrica, May 1962, 129–142; A. G. Rao and P. B. Miller, "Advertising/Sales Response Functions," Journal of Advertising Research, 1975, 7–15; R. Schmalensee, "A Model of Advertising and Product Quality," Journal of Political Economics, Vol. 86, 1978, 485–903; and H. L. Vidale and H. B. Wolfe, "An Operations Research Study of Sales Response to Advertising," Operational Research Quarterly, Vol. 5, 1957, 370–381.

[8] This derivation is taken from D. S. Tull, V. R. Wood, D. Duhan, T. Gillpatrick, K. R. Robertson, and J. G. Helgeson, "'Lever-aged' Decision Making in Advertising: The Flat Maximum Principle and Its Implications," Journal of Marketing Research, February 1986, 27.

[9] J. D. C. Little, "A Model of Adaptive Control of Promotional Spending," Operations Research, November 1966, 1078.

[10] Berger, "How Much to Spend?" 20.

[11] Lillien and Kotler, Market Decision Making, 501.

[12] That this is true theoretically is demonstrated by the $(1 - AVC)/P$ term in the diminishing-returns model. It is shown to be true empirically by P. Farris and S. Albion, "Determinants of the Advertising-to-Sales Ratio," Journal of Advertising Research, February 1981, 19–27.

[13] Tull et al., " 'Leveraged' Decision Making," 28.

[14] "Research Helps Sears Reap Optimum Impact from Ads," Marketing News, December 26, 1980, 7.

[15] For a good summary of pretesting and posttesting procedures, see J. F. Engel, M. R. Warshaw, and T. C. Kinnear, Promotional Strategy: Managing the Marketing Communications Process, 4th ed., Richard D. Irwin, 1979, Chap. 15.

[16] S. Young, "Copy Testing without Magic Numbers," Journal of Advertising Research, February 1972, 3–12.

[17] For a general discussion of advertising agency, research agency, and client views toward advertising research, see "Market/ Advertising Research," Advertising Age, October 20, 1980, S1–S40 (Section 2).

[18] For an elaboration of this position, see L. D. Gibson, "What's Going On in Copy Research Anyway?" Twelfth Attitude Research Conference, Hot Springs, Virginia, April 1981.

[19] For an evaluation of the reliability and validity of copy testing, see K. J. Clancy and L. E. Ostlund, "Commercial Effectiveness Measures," Journal of Advertising Research, February 1976, 23–34; and L. C. Winters, "The Relationship of Advertising Pretesting and Tracking Studies of Awareness and Attitude,"

Attitude Research Conference, Scottsdale, Arizona, February 1982.

[20]J. S. Wright, D. S. Warner, W. L. Winter, Jr., and S. K. Ziegler, *Advertising*, 4th ed., McGraw-Hill, 1977, 585.

[21]"Crayola Betting on Its Market," *Advertising Age*, July 24, 1978, 4.

[22]For a description of the methods used by the two firms and the differences in results, see N. Howard, "Troubles in the Numbers Game," *Dun's Review*, June 1978, 102–108.

[23]D. B. Lucas and S. H. Britt, *Measuring Advertising Effectiveness*, McGraw-Hill, 1963, 225.

[24]C. A. Ramond, *Advertising Research: The State of the Art*, Association of National Advertisers, 1976, 58.

[25]This list and description of consideration is adapted from J. D. C. Little and L. M. Lodish, "A Media Planning Calculus," *Operations Research*, January–February 1969, 32–33.

[26]Consider the choice between *Time* and *Sports Illustrated* black-and-white full-page ads. If CPM were the only criterion advertisers were using to choose between the two, all advertisers would initially choose *Time* (CPM = $2.15) instead of *Sports Illustrated* (CPM = $2.33). The high demand for insertions in *Sports Illustrated* would drive up the CPM for it and the zero demand for *Time* insertions would force its CPM down. An equilibrium would be reached when the CPMs became equal and advertisers became indifferent to which magazine was read. The same logic applies across media vehicle options as a whole.

[27]As described in Ramond, *Advertising Research*, 70.

[28]A clearly written article that describes the application of linear programming to media planning is J. F. Engel and M. R. Warshaw, "Allocating Advertising Dollars by Linear Programming," *Journal of Advertising Research*, September 1964, 42–48.

[29]See, for example, W. T. Moran, "Practical Media Decisions and the Computer," *Journal of Marketing*, July 1963, 26–30.

[30]Little and Lodish, "A Media Planning Calculus," 1–5.

[31]S. Bernstein, "Promotion's New Thrust," *Advertising Age*, September 26, 1988.

[32]For examples of testing methods, see "Effective Promotions Require Research at Every Stage," *Marketing News*, October 3, 1980, 14; and C. E. Boudreau, "Testing Plays Vital Role in Premium Promotion," *Advertising Age*, October 1, 1979, S–6.

[33]A study that provides empirical evidence of this is J. A. Dodson, A. M. Tybout, and R. Sternthal, "Impact of Deals and Deal Retraction on Brand Switching," *Journal of Marketing Research*, February 1978, 77–81.

[34]"GF Trims Its Use of Coupons," *Advertising Age*, December 7, 1981, 22.

[35]N. Howard, "Coping with Coupon Fraud," *Dun's Review*, May 1978, 74.

[36]A. M. Merims, "Marketing's Stepchild: Product Publicity," *Harvard Business Review*, November–December 1972, 111–112.

[37]Both the sales and the advertising data are given in D. S. Tull, "A Re-Examination of the Causes in the Decline in Sales of Sapolio," *The Journal of Business of the University of Chicago*, April 1955, 132.

PERSONAL SELLING AND SALES MANAGEMENT

Personal selling and sales management have entered the computer age. With that entry has come a new "high-tech," skill-driven image once reserved for more glamorous areas of marketing. Following are some examples of the use of computers in personal selling.

Portable computers with modems are used to simplify paperwork and speed order processing. With modems, electronic order forms can transfer and process client desires instantly from the nearest telephone. Black & Decker, for one, does this.

Spreadsheets such as Lotus 1-2-3 and Microsoft Excel allow recording and accounting to proceed with a minimum of pain, giving greater access to current information about prospects and product lines. Salespeople can keep track of and report expenses easily with computers, too.

Electronic file cabinets, known as databases, permit salespeople to examine individual accounts, product lines, and schedules, thereby encouraging individual attention where necessary. Standard Insurance generates individualized policies on the spot simply by feeding critical individual information into a computer.

Word-processing programs permit "personalized" form letters for customers when a special announcement may stimulate a client to purchase something.

Electronic calendars can flag impending deadlines (e.g., Today you must call on the customer who 60 days ago said, "See me again in 60 days") and enable analysis of time usage. Milton Bradley, a toy manufacturer, uses electronic calendars to list stores a salesperson has not called on since a given date.

Computer programs (such as Sales Edge and Prospecting)[1] allow sellers to analyze potential customers psychologically. Young salespeople can use computers to tap the knowledge of experienced salespeople.[2]

Sometimes even the customer is a computer, as when computerized inventory monitors flag an impending shortage for a customer and automatically place an order.[3]

The use of computers by sales representatives is advancing rapidly both in terms of quantity of usage and in terms of the ever-more-sophisticated software available.

Sales managers today also use computers extensively.[4] Computer spreadsheets can help managers find information to assess sales potential, improve account product mix, reduce account costs, improve return on assets, and teach sales representatives. For example, sales managers can identify how efficient each salesperson is on a per-call basis in terms of expenses, time management, and sales. A sales manager can examine each phase of the salesperson's activities directly for its contribution to profit. The manager can then coach the salesperson about how to call on clients more efficiently to optimize effectiveness and profits. The CIBA-GEIGY pharmaceutical division uses computers to align territories.[5] Some companies keep a computerized sales information system with market information, company transaction data, and marketing program evaluation information.[6] All of this new power makes sales management more challenging, more complex, and more competitive.

In this chapter we consider personal selling and sales management. The first section deals with the basic phenomenon of personal selling, the second with managing that phenomenon.

PERSONAL SELLING

Personal selling is worth studying. Some estimates of the number of salespeople in the United States exceed 11.8 million, although about half of these people are retail salesclerks.[7] Most analyses of careers for people with academic degrees in marketing suggest that sales and sales management are the most likely starting places. And many career paths in selling are quite lucrative, because of the potential for commissions and bonuses, and are potential routes to upper levels in the company for talented employees, because of the high visibility of measures of sales effectiveness to top management. Management notices sales.

Personal selling probably has a more outdated and unfair stereotype than any other job category. One survey of 1,000 college students in 123 colleges revealed the following unfair stereotypes:[8]

- Salespeople must lie and be deceitful in order to succeed.
- One must be arrogant and overbearing to succeed in selling.
- The personal relationships involved in selling are repulsive.
- Selling benefits only the seller.
- Salespeople are prostitutes because they sell all of their values for money.
- Selling is no job for a person with talent and brains.

Yet transactions in personal selling, as with all marketing transactions, will lead to good long-term arrangements only if they are based on the truth, on trust, and on mutual benefit. Especially in many industrial selling settings, salespeople need the product knowledge of an engineer, the organizational understanding of a personnel manager, and the interpersonal skills of a minister. When a salesperson must call on the same client again and again, a nasty reputation will certainly hinder effective selling. Salespeople often like their clients, and vice versa. That liking is part of the selling process and will not grow through deceit and obnoxiousness.

What Salespeople Do

Many people outside of industry do not understand what salespeople do. The popular conception is articulately expressed by the main character in Eugene O'Neill's play *The Iceman Cometh*: "It was like a game, sizing up people quick, spotting what their pet pipe dreams were, and then kidding them along that line, pretending you believed what they wanted to believe about themselves. Then they liked you, they trusted you, they wanted to buy something to show their gratitude."[9]

A more objective list of what salespeople do resulted from a comprehensive study by William Moncrief III.[10] He interviewed a wide range of salespeople and conducted several focus groups to develop a list of 123 activities of sales personnel. Then he surveyed 1,393 industrial salespeople. From a factor analysis of the results, he isolated 10 basic activities of salespeople: selling, working with orders, servicing the product, information management, servicing the account, conferences and meetings, training and recruiting, entertaining, out-of-town travel, and working with distributors. Exhibit 16–1 gives more detail about what each of these activities entails.

From examining the patterns of the activities in Exhibit 16–1, Moncrief identified six categories of industrial sellers. The following list covers the basic types of salespeople currently active in settings other than retail.

- *Institutional sellers* constitute 15 percent of industrial sellers, and they rank high in selling and entertaining, and high in dealing with the ultimate customer. They tend not to deal with distribution or shelf stocking.
- *Order takers*. This group, which is the smallest with only 9 percent, ranks high, as you might expect, in dealing with orders, including writing them up and dealing with order problems. It also emphasizes account service. These people deal with inventory and shelf stocking more than travel and entertainment. Their products tend to be nontechnical. The rapid growth of industrial telemarketing may reduce this category even more because customers can place many orders over the telephone.

EXHIBIT **16-1**

Activities of Salespeople*

1. *Selling* consists of basic selling activities such as overcoming objections, and planning and making sales presentations. The salesperson prospects, selects the product to take on calls, prepares the sales presentation, identifies the person in authority, calls on the account, and then helps the client plan.
2. *Working with orders* involves activities related to the order. These activities include writing up the order, working with lost orders, handling shipment problems, expediting orders, and handling back orders.
3. *Servicing the product* is technical in nature. All of these activities indicate a relatively complex product that might require installation and maintenance. The salesperson might typically test the product, teach safety instructions, and order accessories. Computer systems and industrial machinery are product examples.
4. *Information management* involves communication. Tasks include receiving feedback from customers and then relaying information to management. This factor also contains the activities of checking in with supervisors and providing technical information.
5. *Servicing the account* consists of tasks usually performed at the customer location. These activities include inventory control and stocking shelves. This factor also includes two promotional activities, handling local advertising and setting up and working with point-of-purchase displays.
6. *Conferences and meetings* consist of attending a conference, working a conference, and setting up trade shows and exhibits, as well as attending sales meetings, attending training sessions, and filling out questionnaires.
7. *Training and recruiting* include looking for new salespeople, training new salespeople, traveling with trainees, and helping management plan sales activities.
8. *Entertaining* includes taking a client for drinks or dinner, hosting a party for the client, or taking the client golfing or to a ball game. It's tough work, but somebody has to do it.
9. *Out-of-town travel* is just what it appears to be.
10. *Working with distributors* centers on middlemen (and middlewomen). The salesperson sells to or establishes relations with distributors and collects past due accounts.

*From Moncrief, "Selling Activity and Sales Position Taxonomies for Industrial Salesforces," 268–270.

- *Missionary salespeople* include more people than any other category—29 percent, to be exact. These people typically do not take orders, service accounts, or service products. They travel a lot, and they sell to distributors and exhibitions. Their goal usually is to create new accounts.
- The *trade servicer* resembles the institutional seller. Sales and service occupy the time of this 18 percent of industrial selling people. They service the product and service the account. In contrast to institutional sellers, these people deal more with inventory, stocking, and promotion.
- *Trade sellers* account for 12 percent of industrial sellers. Distribution activities keep these people busy. They do not service accounts, as trade servicers do. Bids, pricing, and customer credit are major concerns for these people, who often emphasize first-time sales.
- The *other* category includes 16 percent of the respondents but is otherwise difficult to classify. "Others" tend to score at or near the bottom on almost all activities. They may be too diverse to define, or they may simply have low energy.

Salespeople engage in many activities, from the missionary salespeople, who hardly ever take orders, to the order takers, who do almost nothing else. And when one also considers retail salespeople, the diversity becomes even greater. For example, the salesperson at a small bicycle shop may also repair the most intricate mechanisms of bicycles, order inventory for the shop, and even handle the shop's payroll. But he or she probably never sells products unrelated to bicycles. On the other hand, the retail salesperson at K-Mart who handles bicycles may also deal with 1,000 other products and may not have expertise about the complexity of bicycles or ever personally deal with the inventory or payroll staff.

Within a company, the success of a particular salesperson probably depends primarily on three activities.[11]

1. *The number of sales calls made.* If all other things are equal, more sales calls will probably result in more sales. But if making many calls on poor prospects is emphasized over making a few careful calls on prime prospects, more calls can hurt success.
2. *The quality of sales calls made.* Three factors enhance the quality of the call: Calls that present the right information, communicate it effectively, and promote good relations with the client are most effective. Ignoring any of these factors may lower the quality, and therefore the effectiveness, of the call.
3. *Allocation of sales effort.* The salesperson must balance the need to service current clients with the desire to find new clients. The salesperson must balance how much attention larger and smaller clients receive. And the salesperson must visit hostile as well as friendly clients. Some balance among all of these factors will lead to maximum profit. Finding that

EXHIBIT **16-2**

Super Seller Shares Secrets

As a ten-year-old fifth grader at Manhattan's Chapin School, Markita Andrews sold 2,640 boxes of Girl Scout cookies during the three-week drive, topping the 2,256 boxes she had sold the year before and preserving her ranking as the number one Girl Scout cookie salesperson in New York City. Her success has landed her guest appearances on *Good Morning America*, *That's Incredible*, and *Late Night with David Letterman*, and in a motivational film about her success. Even *People* magazine could not resist commenting on this super seller.

Here is what Markita said about the secrets of her success:

Number of sales calls made. Markita knocked on 1,100 doors.

Quality of sales calls made. Only 1 of those 1,100 refused to buy.

Allocation of sales effort. Markita said, "I sell mostly in our apartment complex. There are nine buildings, and they're 30 stories high, with 400 apartments in each."

As with every successful salesperson, Markita knows her product and knows her market research: "We sell seven kinds of cookies, and I've tried a box of every kind. Chocolate mints are the best selling. This year, we have a new cookie, Chocolate Chunks, which were second best."

Her good attitude about her job and her customers probably also help contribute to her success. "I enjoy selling because I get to meet a lot of people, and I get to see the people from last year and the year before."*

*"Selling Is Child's Play," *Sales & Marketing Management*, Vol. 128, May 17, 1982, 38–39.

right balance is one of the challenges of selling. And it's a challenge the computer has simplified.

A typical finding in many selling situations, whether consumer or industrial, is that 20 percent of the clients account for 80 percent of the business. It is necessary to allocate sales effort in such a manner that these high-volume clients receive sufficient attention to obtain their business. If every client received exactly the same amount of attention, whether planning to purchase $5 or $5 million, some high-volume purchasers might be lost while saving an inconsequential account.

Steps in a Typical Sales Call

Every sales call is unique to some extent, but most calls follow a relatively common pattern. The logic of selling in part dictates that each of several steps be considered in any effective sales presentation because the typical buyer passes through several steps along the way. One popular account of this sequence from the customer's point of view is known as **AIDAS theory**,[12] after the first letter of the word for each step—**attention**, **interest**, **desire**, **action**, and **satisfaction**. It would make no sense to try to sell the product (action) if the customer did not want it (desire), for example.

Another perspective on these same six steps is the seller's. Generally the sales call is divided into six sequential steps, as depicted in Figure 16–1.

Locating and Qualifying Prospects: The first step is, of course, finding people who might want to buy the products. The difficulty of this step can vary from case to case. Sometimes potential buyers come to sellers, especially in response to ads, direct mail, and trade shows. Satisfied customers may also direct other buyers to a salesperson, either spontaneously or in response to a direct question. Directories, ranging from the *Thomas Register of American Manufacturers* to the Yellow Pages, list potential customers. "Cold calls" also can generate prospects. That is, simply knocking on doors may reveal potential buyers, although this method is quite difficult and usually quite expensive given the limited success most people have. To qualify a potential buyer once he or she has been found, it is necessary to establish that the client has both the organizational

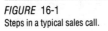
FIGURE 16-1
Steps in a typical sales call.

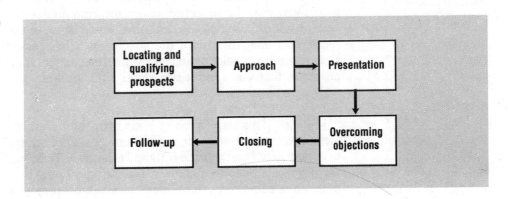

authority and the financial resources necessary for the purchase. In some industrial settings, discovering who has authority may be one of the biggest challenges of the sale.

The Approach: This requires, first of all, knowing the norms of contacting the person who might buy. Should you make an appointment? Should you write an introductory letter or phone ahead? To what extent do you have to struggle to get past "gatekeepers" (e.g., receptionists)? Second, the approach requires a good introduction to the potential customer. First impressions matter. A proper introduction and perhaps some endearing conversation about common topics such as sports or the weather often provide a good starting point, although the norms will vary considerably from situation to situation. Japanese businesspeople usually begin with a formal exchange of business cards and the reading of them. The key point is to establish sufficient rapport to transact business without wasting precious time.

The Presentation: This is the meat of the sales encounter. Here interest in what is being sold must solidify and desire must begin to form. The customer must learn why it would be beneficial to have what the salesperson is offering. Skillful demonstrations may help here. All sales presentations should be planned, but whether totally structured presentations are desirable depends on the situation. To the extent that the salesperson is learning about the potential client's desires as the conversation progresses, the salesperson ought to form the persuasive communication to those specific desires.

Overcoming Objections: When people express objections, they at least are opening the opportunity for a dialogue, and salespeople ought to view that opportunity as a positive turn of events. Sometimes objections clarify the nature of the competition or the true concerns driving the final purchase decision. Anticipated objections can be covered in the presentation, but some unanticipated or rare objections often arise. The salesperson ought to deal with objections as effectively as possible, all the time preserving rapport. Usually the first step is to clarify the objection. ("Your concern is _____? That is a very good question.") The objections may be handled by introducing new facts. ("Our product can do that. I must have forgotten to mention that product benefit in my presentation.") Other times reviewing facts is helpful. ("You think it's too expensive? Let me review all of the important benefits of this product.") In some cases the objections may appear to be insurmountable. One strategy here is to show that the objection is not insurmountable after all. Sometimes it is best to wind down the presentation, leave without attempting to close, and return at a later time with the answer in hand, perhaps after discussing the situation with a sales manager. Sometimes, if competitors can solve critical problems that you cannot solve with your product, you may simply need to walk away without a sale.

Closing: This step involves asking for the order. Sometimes a seller is reluctant to try to close for fear of failure. A skillful salesperson, however, learns to anticipate when the time is right. Perhaps the potential buyer asks a question that implies a pending purchase, such as specifying purchase conditions ("We must have delivery by next week") or option preference ("Do they come in blue?"). Sometimes a seller will use a **trial close** to gain a sense of where the buyer's thought processes are, perhaps trying to elicit specification of purchase conditions ("Would you like a blue one?" or "What form of payment will you use?" or "Would you prefer three or four?"). In this way, the seller can ease the buyer into a decision.

A great deal has been written about closing techniques, in some cases pushing it to a studied art.[13] Conventional wisdom is that a **direct close** ("How many will you buy?") should be used only when a purchase is virtually certain. Once a potential purchaser has committed to *not* buying something, it is very difficult ultimately to obtain a purchase. Gimmicks, however, are no substitute for an effective presentation and a convincing sale. Excessive reliance on gimmicks can often do more damage than good. On the other hand, an unclosed sale is no sale at all.

Several of the more common closing techniques include the following:[14] The **assumptive close** relies on activities that assume the order is a foregone conclusion. Sellers check on the correct street address for delivery as the order form is being completed. In the **summary close**, the seller reviews all of the benefits that will accrue to a purchase at this time. The **puppy dog close** hands possession over to the customer before a decision is made. The logic behind this close? Once a product is used, similar to a puppy dog who has come to your home before you have decided you want a pet, it is difficult to refuse to accept something you already have. The **negative close** implies that failure to purchase now will result in later delivery, higher prices, or some other undesirable outcome. The **concession close** offers some special additional benefit, perhaps an additional discount or an advertising allowance. The **physical close** demands some physical action of the buyer, such as accepting the pen to sign the order or receiving the car keys, that symbolizes a close has been made before the actual event has occurred.

Follow-up: This often is forgotten or underemphasized. First, the departure from the selling situation should involve as much social grace as the approach. Exchange pleasantries and offer any additional service that is available (e.g., brochures about other products). If no sale was made, immediate notes describing what happened and what should happen next ought to be formed. If a sale was made, reassurance of a good decision is appropriate. The salesperson should also check after delivery to find out if the product is satisfactory and if the customer understands all of the aspects of usage.

Selling and Other Types of Communication

The major advantage of personal selling over any other type of marketing communication, such as advertising, is that the seller immediately receives feedback on how the client responds with eye glances, facial expressions, and verbal responses (especially in telemarketing—see Exhibit 16–3) to each statement you make. Thus, you can tailor the selling effort to each client, depending on that person's concerns, needs, desires, and dreams. You can carry on a dialogue in which each statement you utter depends on the response to your previous statement. In a sense, the personal selling process segments the market

EXHIBIT **16-3**

Telemarketing

In recent years, the high cost of face-to-face personal selling has spurred companies to consider telemarketing as an alternative. Sam Summers of TechTel Communicators in Phoenix claims that each face-to-face sales call costs $220, and many calls may be necessary for even a single sale. Telephone calls, on the other hand, are far less expensive because the cost of travel and travel time is replaced by the much lower cost of telephone tolls.

Summers uses computers in conjunction with telemarketing to provide sales representatives with easy, immediate access to the most complex and detailed product information and customer information. This information can be moved off and on the computer screen quickly with the "click of a mouse" from a scripted survey or a prepared sales pitch. The computer can also automatically dial the telephone and produce "personalized" follow-up letters.

Summers tested telemarketing when selling expensive medical equipment for blood allergy screening. At first, doctor-clients displayed skepticism, but soon they learned to appreciate the quick responses and low pressure associated with telemarketing. The result was a tenfold increase in revenue over that generated by the field sales force, and 5,000 new customers. One salesperson could telephone 12 prospects in the time it takes for one face-to-face sales call.*

Telemarketing works better for some types of sales than others. Marketing directly to random consumers in their homes usually is not very effective. Many consumers believe they receive too many undesired phone calls soliciting contributions or seeking to sell unwanted products. Unwanted telephone calls bother all of us to some extent. In other media we can more easily screen and ignore unwanted or commercial messages. For example, with unsolicited mail we can postpone opening it until a later, more convenient time, or we can simply discard it without it disrupting our venture of the moment. But with the telephone, the only way to separate important or desired calls from unwanted ones is to listen to the caller long enough to gauge the purpose of the call. Screening calls usually disrupts current activities. People who work nights and sleep at home during the day know of this disruption.

For certain elderly or physically impaired people, answering the phone and screening the call require considerable effort. Getting to the phone may be difficult, and the call may come at an inappropriate time, such as in the middle of a therapy session in which timing matters or during daytime sleep associated with recovery from illness. For these people, the invasion of privacy from unwanted calls can be especially pernicious.

In many states the law requires telephone solicitors to identify themselves ("Hello. I am John Doe"), their employer ("I work for ABC Fundraising, Inc."), and the purpose of the call ("We have been hired by XYZ Charity to request donations") within 30 seconds. Otherwise, the call is classified as deceptive and illegal. Then the caller must ask whether the receiver wants to hear the presentation. ("May I explain why we want your donation?") If the consumer does not give permission, the caller must hang up.

Often for business-to-business transactions, however, telemarketing is preferred to face-to-face selling because it is simpler, faster, and less imposing. For a straight rebuy of an inexpensive, low-technology product (e.g., a paper clip), the hassle of face-to-face transactions hardly seems justified given the nature of the task. When segments are highly fragmented or geographically dispersed, telemarketing may provide the savings edge that maximizes competitiveness. Sales managers often like telemarketing because they can monitor activity level and quality much more easily for telemarketing than for face-to-face selling. The disadvantages of telemarketing are the inability to use sight, smell, taste, and touch; the inability to monitor nonverbal cues; and the inability to "size up" a potential customer in terms of responsiveness or capacity to follow through with the purchase.† Usually a long-distance carrier (e.g., AT&T, MCI) or Regional Bell Operating Company (e.g., NYNEX, US WEST, AmeriTech) will gladly discuss and teach a small company how to increase the use of the telephone in sales.

---

*"Automated Telemarketing Lowers Costs of Selling to Professionals," *Marketing News*, March 14, 1986, 44.
†Gordon J. Bolt, *Practical Sales Management*, Pitman, 1987.

down to the individual customer. With customers who purchase large volumes—imagine you are selling tires and your customer is General Motors—even the product can be modified to satisfy the customer's specifications.

Whether personal selling or advertising works more effectively depends upon communication goals and the nature of the selling task. Consider the relative emphasis on advertising versus selling by Avon and Revlon, two giants in the cosmetics industry. Avon chooses to emphasize individualized communication and personal selling, whereas Revlon prefers mass communication and advertising. Although advertising costs far less per exposure than personal selling, personal selling has a greater impact on each consumer. Both companies generally have done well in spite of their very different approaches to marketing the same types of products.[15] Although Avon has increased its presence in retailing,[16] especially in international markets, personal selling still dominates its communications efforts.

SALES MANAGEMENT

Sales managers must oversee the sales staff. They must ensure that the objectives of the company for the sales force are planned and executed as effectively as possible. They must guide the sales staff to sell the "right combination of products with the right emphasis in the right locations and in the right way."[17] And they must help the sales force achieve its potential.

Setting Objectives

The first task of the sales manager is to define objectives. These objectives provide standards for comparison to allow the manager to ask, "How well is the sales force doing?" The issue is perhaps more complex than it sounds because several goals may all be possibilities.[18] Usually several of the following criteria are goals, some more important than others. Which goals are most important will vary from company to company, from product to product, and even vary from one salesperson to another.

- *Contribution to profit* may be the primary goal a company establishes for its sales force. Sales volume and product mix usually influence profit, as well as the cost of selling activity.
- *Return on assets* may be a major goal of the sales force. This goal is similar to the profit criterion except that it also takes into account the capital investments for selling activities in such categories as offices, automobiles, and warehouses.
- *Sales cost ratio* is the scale many companies use to evaluate the success of their sales force. Sales expenses divided by dollar sales volume is the criterion here. A 4 percent expense ratio looks better than 8 percent. But if the former represents $4 million in sales and the later represents $73 million in sales, the worse ratio could nevertheless reflect more profit.
- *Market share* may sometimes be the objective of the sales force. For example, imagine a competitive industry such as personal computers, where many players are being eliminated because their volume is too

small to keep production costs competitive. Sales management may not really care about short-term profit if market share is growing and prospects for long-term survival and profit look good. Another example may be in an industry where regulation may soon change the marketplace. In the beer industry, some companies have emphasized market share more than profit, perhaps in fear of regulations restricting beer advertising. Those regulations could essentially freeze both market share and potential for long-term profit if and when they take effect. Sales managers may direct their people dealing with retailers to build market share for now and wait until later to worry about profit.

- *Achievement of company or business unit marketing goals* may imply improved perception, increased knowledge of a company, or wider acceptance of a particular point of view. Concern for long-term profits may again subordinate desire for short-term profit. The company or business unit objectives should expand corporate objectives and emanate from a clear understanding of what the competition is doing.

SALES MANAGERS' TOOLS

Once objectives have been defined, the sales manager has several tools for achieving these objectives. Managing the sales force requires the manager to decide how many salespeople to hire, how to select them, how to train them, where to assign them, how to motivate (and compensate) them, and what standard operating procedures to institutionalize. These decisions will influence how many calls salespeople make, how much effort they put forth, and how good their efforts are in terms of communication effectiveness, message content, and interpersonal effectiveness. In short, these things are what sales managers control. How well these things are controlled will influence sales and company success. Let us therefore consider each one of these tools in more detail.

How Many Salespeople to Hire?

Three theories dominate thinking on this question.[19] The first theory implies that you ought to hire *as many as you can afford*. Divide the dollars available (or in some cases the percentage of sales allocated to selling expenses) by the costs to support one salesperson, and the result is the number of salespeople to hire. The problem with this approach is that it fails to consider communication needs and potential market. For example, early in the product life cycle, it may be desirable to hire more salespeople than you can currently afford, in anticipation of future sales to anticipated customers. On the other hand, a product in a declining life cycle stage may not require as much sales staff support as the available money could support.

The second theory implies that you ought to hire *as many as you need to do the job*. In this approach you consider the number of customers, both current and potential (*n*), the ideal frequency of calls (*f*), and the typical length of calls (*l*), including travel time. These three numbers are multiplied together and divided by the selling time one salesperson has available (*st*). More specifically, the formula looks like this:

$$\text{Number of salespeople} = \frac{n \times f \times l}{st}$$

This formula can be modified to consider how size and type of customer influence sales force size, but it fails to take into account how expenditures and profits are influenced by sales force size. From this formula you know how many people to hire to cover the work, but most companies are more concerned with profit than with covering the work. This formula does not consider how to maximize profit. In addition, the typical length of calls may not be the ideal length. For example, perhaps longer calls that increase service would result in more sales, or perhaps quicker calls would allow for more calls and would therefore have a positive effect on overall sales.

The third theory of sales force size, incremental benefit, implies that you should hire *as many as possible until the probable gross profit on new business corresponds to the cost of adding a new salesperson*. The logic of this theory is that each new salesperson will probably generate new business and allow other salespeople to spend more time servicing current accounts, both of which will increase sales. But with a finite sales potential, at some point too many salespeople will be chasing too few customers, with the result that a new salesperson will cannibalize old accounts to some extent and will cut into profits more than it costs to maintain that salesperson. Computer models have been developed to help produce optimal allocations.[20] One problem with this approach, as well as with the other two, is that sales force needs will change with economic conditions. The insensitivity of the first approach to product life cycle factors is also an issue with this approach. Finally, none of these approaches considers who the salespeople are and how their effectiveness may vary in different conditions. For example, some salespeople thrive on heavy workloads, whereas others experience frustration and discouragement.

Theories about how to budget for a sales force mirror theories about sales force size. Once management determines how many people to hire and how to compensate them, the costs have been determined. Certainly with the last two theories on size—"as many as you need" and "incremental benefit," size determines budget. With the first approach—"all you can afford"—budgeting implications are tautological. The parallel theory of budgeting is that you simply budget the same as last year after correcting for inflation and changing needs. Percentage of sales sometimes is also used as a criterion.[21]

How to Select Salespeople

The selection of good people for sales jobs is vital for the success of a sales organization. The exact formula for a successful salesperson varies from situation to situation.[22] For example, skill with electrical engineering may help to sell computers but may not help at all to sell paints. No *single* factor is crucial for the success of a salesperson. Nevertheless, several attributes usually do seem to contribute to success, especially if they are used intelligently and in conjunction with situation-specific skills. For example, in one study, 100 sales managers identified what they wanted in sales personnel. In order of importance, they listed **maturity**, **personal selling and sales management skills**, **appearance**, **cooperativeness**, **communication and public speaking skills**, **disposition**, **punctuality**, and **mannerisms**.[23] In short, they wanted people with diligence, dedication, and selling and social skills.

One research study[24] found that good salespeople tend to be tall, physically impressive, and energetic. They are willing and able to work long hours. Recognition for accomplishments is important among effective salespeople. They are not highly educated but are intelligent and interested in a wide variety of topics. They are not especially sensitive or perceptive of the feelings of others. And they view selling as a professional career, with few ambitions beyond selling.

Another study[25] reviewed the scholarly literature on selling effectiveness and identified the following sources of effectiveness, in this order: personal factors, selling skill, role variables, aptitude, motivation, and organizational and environmental factors. Personal factors include categories such as age, height, marital status, and education. Apparently knowing about the objective situation of a person's life provides useful information about his or her potential in sales.

The stage of a salesperson's career may influence whether that person will respond to particular tasks with enthusiasm.[26]

- During the stage of **exploration**, people still have not defined their career goals and have only a vague concept of how their personal abilities map onto the available opportunities. People are trying to learn about their jobs and are attempting to define themselves occupationally. People at

EXHIBIT **16-4**

Anne Harleman, Sales Representative

Who are the people who work in selling? As you might guess with such a large professional category, the answers are diverse and complex. One of the 11.8 million people in selling is Anne Harleman, a 30-year-old media sales representative for *Time*. When Anne graduated from Denison University in Granville, Ohio, she wanted to find work that would be interesting and would allow her to meet people. She snatched up her first opportunity as a sales representative for the Essex County newspapers. She started this career at a time when women have enjoyed increased opportunities and acceptance in the selling field.* She later became ad director of the New England Real Estate Directory before accepting her current position at *Time*. She is also a member of the board of governors for the Boston Lantern Club for print reps.

By any measure, Anne has been quite successful. *Advertising Age* recently honored her as one of the 100 "Best and Brightest Media Sales Reps" in the entire United States.† People at *Time* believe that her success is due primarily to her knowledge and her willingness to help clients, even when a sale is not on the line. Anne likes the "chance to become an expert in so many fields," as well as the people with whom she works.

---

*J. E. Swann, D. R. Rink, G. E. Kiser, and W. S. Martin, "Industrial Buyer Image of the Saleswoman," *Journal of Marketing*, Winter 1984, 110–116.
†M. Kingman, "Advertising Age's 100 of the Best and Brightest Media Sales Reps," September 14, 1987, 38, 56.

this stage probably cost less to hire but lack many of the skills associated with more advanced stages.

- The second stage is **establishment**. People at this stage commit themselves to a career and try to establish secure roots in their profession and community. They use skills acquired in the exploration stage to seek financial and personal success. People at this stage respond well to opportunity and challenge, yet they are still learning some of the fine points that will influence their careers.

- **Maintenance** follows establishment. People reassess what they have accomplished and seek to hold their own. Frequently people at this stage reach an organizational plateau.[27] Salespeople at this stage worry about threats from innovations and ambitious younger employees. Preserving standing and status are among the concerns here. These people have high levels of skill but may be somewhat less hungry for advancement than people in the establishment stage. They are less likely to change jobs than people in the earlier stages.

- During **disengagement**, people launch the transition to retirement. People who have worked for a long time often have an identity associated with their jobs. For example, if you ask someone in the maintenance stage, "Who are you?" he or she will most likely tell you how he or she earns a living. Thus, people in this stage must rethink who they are. They must cope with the financial, health, and personal aspects of aging in a society that has less respect for senior citizens than in, say, Far Eastern societies. Although people in this career stage may have fewer years of anticipated continuation of their present job than people in earlier stages, often skills in this group are at very high levels. For example, the sales manager's desire for a mature person in a sales job will often best be satisfied by someone who is advanced in age. Some companies often try to discard older employees too soon, and competitors who will hire away these employees approaching retirement may find a wealth of skill to use.

The management of different salespeople at different career stages varies considerably. Sales managers, for example, must evaluate participation, performance, and progress within the context of career stage.[28] Many management decisions will vary depending on career stage: attitudes and behaviors, sense of opportunity, the salesperson–supervisor relationship, and tactics for motivation. Just as in baseball, coaching a Little Leaguer is quite different from coaching an old pro in the majors.

How to Train Salespeople

"Whom one recruits is important, but probably not as important as what one does with the recruits—and to them—after they have been hired."[29] Companies spend a great deal of money each year—often in the tens of thousands of dollars per person—training both new and seasoned salespeople. Training provides the opportunity to wed the wisdom of experience with the enthusiasm of the newcomer.

Every person in sales must have a thorough understanding of the company's products and customers. Customers resent uninformed salespeople. Salespeople may lose many opportunities by failing to recognize how attributes of their products fit with potential customer needs. Training provides the opportunity to learn about each product to be sold and how it is positioned relative to the competition. Different customers in different situations require different treatment, and the effective salesperson must understand how to deal with the different contexts that will be encountered.[30]

The new salesperson must learn the basic facts about a company and how it operates. What are its policies? Who are its clients? How does it approach clients? What are the corporate philosophy, ideals, and culture? A typical new salesperson may know almost nothing of the collective wisdom a company has gathered about selling during its existence. Yet that new person needs to know quite a lot before attempting even one call on a real customer, lest both the customer and the salesperson leave the encounter frustrated and unaware of opportunities that existed for mutual benefit. Other important topics for a new salesperson to master include routing, time management, listening and communications skills, sensitivity to the social skills of others, and incidental requirements (e.g., the company requires monthly self-evaluations). The trained salesperson must be capable of calling on customers effectively with the right presentation to the right person at the right time.

The seasoned veteran must learn about changes in products and policies, and continuing education refreshes the knowledge of even the most effective and successful employee. Selling skills and interpersonal skills can always improve.[31] And morale may rise simply as a result of spending time away from routine selling.

Even if little new is learned from continuing training, it provides an opportunity for salespeople to network and to share battle stories. Salespeople can develop social support networks among themselves. After a sales training session, they may feel more comfortable contacting someone from a different region about how to deal with a particularly troublesome set of circumstances. Having support from others is quite important because people in selling often experience frustration and even humiliation from potential customers who decide not to buy. To approach a fifth client in a friendly, positive manner after the first four calls have ended with rude rejections demands a lot of inner strength. That type of strength and resiliency may be one of the most important attributes for success in selling careers. And sales training can nurture that attribute.

College students should have special knowledge about methods that can be used to teach, regardless of whether the teaching is sales training or marketing management. Sales training can take the form of straight lectures, case discussions, brainstorming, role playing, reading of the text, individualized training at a computer terminal, or demonstrations. Some companies today use VCR tapes of lectures as a way to control the high cost of sales training, although this method reduces the benefits from networking. The use of videotape equipment to provide the salesperson with an opportunity for self-evaluation can be especially effective. Watching a tape of one's own performance increases consciousness of self-presentation. On-the-job training also is popular, although salespeople on straight commission may resent a "tag-along" student. The trainer should probably receive special compensation above the commission for this type of training. What type of training is most appropriate depends on the communications needs in the particular context.

Where to Assign Salespeople

In some cases territory assignment is simple and obvious, but in other cases it is quite complex. Territory definition influences allocation of sales effort and efficiency of calls. Thus it indirectly influences sales force productivity and effectiveness. The goal of territory definition is usually to create relatively equal workloads and sales potential for each member of the sales staff while maximizing coverage and minimizing travel time for everyone. Sometimes a company may want unequal territories, with small territories for trainees and large ones for proven sales force members, for example. Sometimes, such as in real estate sales, the company may not even want territories.

The process of defining territories involves several steps. First, a geographical control unit is defined, such as a zip code, a county, or a state. For each control unit, the sales manager must estimate current sales and sales potential. It is also necessary to estimate how long calls will be in each area and how much travel time is required between calls. The sales manager must also know how many salespeople will be available. Then a number of territories are defined to correspond with the number of salespeople. Usually some starting point is selected for each territory, such as a city, a regional office, or a home address for a current salesperson. Control units are aggregated based on proximity until satisfactory territories are defined.

Consider the following situation: Three salespeople, John, Bob, and Mary, are available for Springfield. Springfield has seven zip codes, 00001 to 00007. About 38 percent of the current and potential sales for the market are in zip code 00001, the downtown core, and the remaining market for sales and potential sales are spread evenly across the remaining six zip codes. The zip codes are roughly in a row, such that 00001 is closest to 00002 and farthest from 00007. Bob and Mary live in 00002 and John lives in 00007. It would be reasonable to make 00001 into Territory 1; 00002, 00003, and 00004 into Territory 2; and 00005, 00006, and 00007 into Territory 3. The stronger seller between Bob and Mary would be assigned the most important territory, and the two other territories would be assigned based on who lives nearest to them. (In other words, the better salesperson between Bob and Mary would be assigned to Territory 1, the weaker to Territory 2, and John to Territory 3.)

FIGURE 16-2
Sales territory assignment.

	Territory 1	Territory 2			Territory 3		
	x City center	x Mary's home x Bob's home					x John's home
Market %	38%	10%	10%	11%	11%	10%	10%
Zip codes	00001	00002	00003	00004	00005	00006	00007

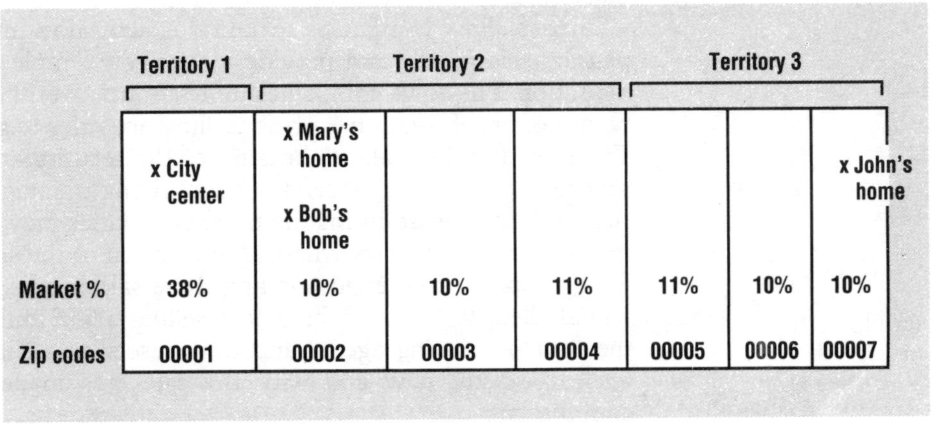

Today, many decisions about territory assignment are developed with the help of a computer. Several programs have been developed to maximize profit.[32] Although these programs have been designed to maximize profit, they do not take into account every possible variable that can contribute to profit, such as salesperson effectiveness. And even with information they do use, they are only as effective as the information is accurate. Sometimes estimates of sales potential may be quite subjective and may hamper the accuracy of the computer projections. But a careful analysis of the factors that create effectiveness will improve on wild guesses.[33]

A second problem has to do with customers that become national accounts. Sometimes several accounts are so important or so big that they require individual attention. For example, Nike, the sports shoe and clothing company, has seven national accounts that it treats separately from all other accounts due to the size and distribution channel issues. One of the seven, for example, is J. C. Penney, the large clothing retailer with its own channels of distribution. Another is Sears, and another is the military. It is more efficient for both Nike and Penney or Sears if decisions about Nike sales to Penney, Sears, or the military are made at the national level. Usually national accounts are large-volume customers with their own systems of distribution and national purchasing.[34]

Once territories are defined, routing becomes an issue. Salespeople and their managers need to develop routes that will allow for the best service of customer needs with a minimum amount of wasted travel. The more efficient the routing, the more time available for selling and the less travel expense. Telemarketing may provide an opportunity to reduce travel time and expenses.

How to Motivate and Compensate Salespeople

The most important motivating factor is the pay the salesperson earns. For some people selling can be quite lucrative, but this will depend in part on how compensation works. Some companies provide a straight salary, some use strictly commission, and many use a combination of the two. The choice of which system to use depends on how best to link management and salesperson objectives.[35]

Salaries allow companies to know exactly how much it will cost to compensate salespeople and provide a relatively simple way of computing compensation. They give companies more control over the salespeople, which may be important if a number of nonselling activities (e.g., service) are important. Trainees often like salaries because of the security and stability salaries represent in the face of an uncertain future. Long training programs usually necessitate salary, at least during the training. Salaries may apply most appropriately to team-selling contexts where identification of the source of a sale is difficult. For example, if two engineers and three salespeople have worked with a potential client for six months before selling a $4.3 million computer system to the four purchasing agents and three users at a client company, it may be unclear exactly how and why the sale was made and who deserves the commission.

The disadvantages of salaries are many. For one thing, salaries excessively compensate the weakest salespeople. Because they provide less incentive than commissions, salaries lead to situations where sales managers may have to supervise their employees more carefully. When overall sales are low, companies have large sales expenses relative to sales revenue.

Commissions involve paying a percentage of gross sales or profits to the person or people who generated the business. Often the income potential is very high with commissions. They provide very strong incentives; therefore, skilled salespeople find them attractive. Salespeople on straight commission tend to be quite independent and hard working. And a company's expenses are tied directly to sales revenue. Although commissions have declined in popularity over the years, many industries still use them, such as door-to-door sales companies (e.g., Avon), real estate, life insurance, and stock brokerage. Companies in which face-to-face selling is important or in which market conditions change rapidly usually benefit from use of commissions.[36]

Commissions also have several drawbacks. Often the lowest-paid employees resent the system. People who have better territories or better circumstances may receive rewards in excess of their efforts, although others do not. During recessions and bad times, erratic sales may disrupt many commission-based salespeople, and they may be forced to seek employment elsewhere. One way to smooth out this difficulty is to allow salespeople to draw against future commissions, in order to smooth over the deepest valleys on the sales graph. Another way to correct this situation is to provide for some minimum salary and then apply a commission or bonus on top of that when sales warrant additional reward.

The most popular compensation package is some combination of reward, commission, and perhaps bonus.[37] Although these combination plans are more difficult to explain and administer, they permit salespeople to have some basic support during bad times yet allow for incentives during good times. Companies can design compensation packages based on their specific needs, and plans can be adapted to changing conditions.

Beyond compensation, many companies try to provide other opportunities to motivate the sales staff.[38] Bonuses may be given to people who achieve some goal, such as exceeding quota or having highly rated service to clients. Contests, quota awards, recognition rewards, and praise all can help salespeople feel confident about their activities. Even the evaluation process can be rewarding if handled properly. Some people consider a pleasant work environment where people are treated fairly to be worth a lot.

Evaluating Salespeople

Every person has expectations about performance.[39] It is necessary to evaluate any business activity against those expectations for purposes of reward, promotion, and improvement.

Various companies use various means of performance evaluation.[40] Quantitative evaluations are especially popular, and with good reason. The information used is generally easy to measure, accurate, unbiased by personal prejudice, and important to company goals. The information used may rely on dollar or unit sales, or the emphasis may be on contribution to profit. New accounts, conversion rates, and expenses can also be considered. These approaches may fail to consider the dramatic swings that can take place in markets, however, sometimes far beyond the control of the salesperson. For example, a drop in oil prices hurts Texas more than Maine, and it may influence sales of business computers by the salesperson in Texas more than by the salesperson in Maine. Although some effects of conditions can be statistically removed, those statistical revisions are not necessarily entirely accurate and therefore never are entirely satisfactory. But quantitative measures do have pragmatic appeal.

For some companies, individual evaluation may dominate performance reviews. Self-evaluation can play a significant role in job performance evaluation, especially when instruction is the main goal of evaluation. Some companies use customer evaluation as an element of judgment. And the sales manager's evaluation in one form or another almost always enters into judgments about salespeople. Sales managers may sometimes play favorites and may sometimes not know enough about what salespeople actually do when alone with a potential client, thus leading the sales managers to overemphasize quantitative measures.[41] They may also attend too much to effort and not enough to task difficulty, again leading to unfair evaluations.[42]

A complete questionnaire designed to measure all aspects of sales performance has been used with some success.[43] The researchers started with a large pool of topics for evaluating sales performance, and through statistical means they reduced the dimensions necessary to judge sales performance down to five: **meeting sales objectives**, **technical knowledge**, **providing information**, **controlling expenses**, and **sales presentations**. Any evaluation of sales performance ought to include these topics if they are relevant to the specific context.

Systems and System Selling

Some organizations prefer to purchase systems rather than individual products, and this preference creates an opportunity for the marketer willing to provide a system. A **system** is:

> A package composed of a commodity product and one or more other products and related services sold as a single unit. The price is based on the system's ability to add a unique value that the commodity product alone cannot offer.[44]

This system approach to selling transforms the commodity into a product with attributes more like a branded product. It can be promoted based on special attributes. Even products that initially do not resemble commodities often are quickly copied by competitors, and the copying transforms the unique product into a commodity. Therefore, clusters of products and services add unique attributes that can again give the product noncommodity status. Of course, those attributes will have to benefit the buyer in order to be attractive. Indeed, the development of a system is aimed at solving buyer problems.

Consider a company marketing an industrial emission control device. The device per se could quickly be copied by competition and become a commodity. But if our company can promise additional benefits, such as solving the environmental problem rather than simply selling a product that will help solve the emission problem, then a system sale may be in the works. The system could promise relief from the buyer's staff diversion by providing continuing expertise on controlling emissions, relief from repetitive governmental contacts by providing an environmental "paperwork" service, relief from major capital investment by providing appropriate financial considerations, relief from unpredictability of costs by reliance on a monthly service fee, and relief from unreliability of system operation by providing ongoing operation of the system. If the buying company does not want to get involved in the emission control business, the packaged service may seem quite attractive.

Sometimes systems emerge from patterns of patents and unique skills or technology that a company possesses. If all solutions to a problem are sold rather than only one product, each interlocking part of the system can generate additional profit for the seller. Often the military will purchase one weapons system from one vendor, even though the weapons system has hundreds or even thousands of elements.

SUMMARY OF IMPORTANT POINTS

1. Personal selling and sales management have entered the computer age.
2. There are 10 basic activities of salespeople: selling, working with orders, servicing the product, information management, servicing the account, conferences and meetings, training and recruiting, entertaining, out-of-town travel, and working with distributors.
3. Types of salespeople include institutional sellers, order takers, missionary salespeople, trade servicers, trade sellers, and others.
4. Within a company, success in selling probably depends on three things:
   a. Number of sales calls made
   b. Quality of sales calls made
   c. Allocation of sales effort
5. Allocation of sales effort necessitates focusing on large-volume clients. Unpleasant calls and calls on potential customers usually are necessary.
6. One account of the selling sequence from the customer's point of view is known as AIDAS theory, after the first letter of the word for each step—*attention, interest, desire, action,* and *satisfaction.*
7. Steps in the selling process from the salesperson's perspective include locating and qualifying prospects, the approach, the presentation, overcoming objections, the closing, and follow-up.
8. Types of closing include the trial, direct, assumptive, summary, puppy dog, negative, concession, and physical.
9. Personal selling has an advantage over other types of marketing communication because the seller immediately receives feedback on how the client responds.

10. Telemarketing allows more efficient selling in some cases.
11. The first task of the sales manager is to define objectives. These may include contribution to profit, sales volume, and product mix; return on assets; sales cost ratio; market share; and achievement of company or business unit marketing goals.
12. The sales manager must decide how many people to hire, which people to hire, and how to train them. He or she must also determine routes and territory assignment, motivation strategies, compensation, and evaluation standards.
13. Any evaluation of sales performance ought to include the following topics if they are relevant to the specific context: meeting sales objectives, technical knowledge, providing information, controlling expenses, and sales presentations.
14. The selling of systems rather than of single products often increases the number of interdependent orders.

REVIEW QUESTIONS

16.1.   How are computers used in sales? in sales management?

16.2.   What are the basic types of sales activities?

16.3.   Describe the basic characteristics of each of the following types of industrial salespeople:
a. Institutional sellers
b. Order takers
c. Missionary salespeople
d. Trade servicers
e. Trade sellers

16.4.   What are the three main contributors to selling success?

16.5.   Describe the basic trade-offs in the allocation of sales effort. Why does allocation of sales effort matter to such a great extent?

16.6.   What are the steps in a typical sales call?

16.7.   Describe each of the following types of closing:
a. Trial
b. Direct
c. Assumptive
d. Summary
e. Puppy dog
f. Negative
g. Concession
h. Physical

16.8.   What are the advantages and disadvantages of telemarketing?

16.9.   Describe each of the following types of sales management objectives:
a.   Contribution to profit
b.   Return on assets
c.   Sales cost ratio
d.   Market share
e.   Achievement of company marketing goals

16.10. What are the main tools of sales managers?

16.11. Describe the major approaches to determining how many salespeople to hire.

16.12. Describe the major issues in selecting salespeople.

16.13. How should salespeople be trained?

16.14. How should sales territories be assigned?

16.15. Discuss approaches to motivating and compensating salespeople.

16.16. How should salespeople be evaluated?

16.17. Why should companies seek to use system selling?

DISCUSSION QUESTIONS AND PROBLEMS

16.18. To what extent are stereotypes of salespeople unfair? Does the fairness differ for encyclopedia versus computer salespeople?

16.19. Why do the authors disagree with Eugene O'Neill's characterization from *The Iceman Cometh*?

16.20. Salespeople must perform a variety of tasks in a typical sales presentation. What is the most difficult task for a salesperson to perform?

16.21. Sales managers must perform a variety of tasks in order to manage their staffs effectively. What is the most difficult task for a sales manager to perform?

16.22. If you just founded a new software company, how would you compensate your sales force? How would you evaluate its members?

16.23. Some sales managers "motivate" their sales force by encouraging members to borrow heavily to obtain expensive consumer goods (e.g., fancy cars). The idea is that someone deep in debt will work harder than someone experiencing little economic pressure. Is this approach ethical? Is it likely to be effective?

16.24. How might closing tactics be different for people selling:
a. Media time to advertisers
b. New cars to consumers
c. Five million dollar pieces of capital equipment

PROJECTS

16.25. Rent a copy of the film *Death of a Salesman* and view it. How is personal selling portrayed in that play? Is the portrayal fair? Is it still contemporary?

16.26. Interview three salespeople and ask them how they cope with unsuccessful calls. Why would coping with unsuccessful calls be critical for success as a salesperson?

16.27. Obtain a copy of an expert system program that helps you portray the sales client psychologically (e.g., Sales Edge or Prospecting). Pretend that your best friend is also your potential client and interact with the program on that basis. Do the results ring true? Are they truly unique, or do they simply describe what is true of everyone ("Although you sometimes feel shy, you have big dreams.")?

16.28. Choose a product or service. Do research on it and then make a formal sales presentation to your professor or class.

Endnotes

[1]"Better Than a Smile: Sales People Begin to Use Computers on the Job," *The Wall Street Journal*, September 13, 1985, 25.

[2]R. H. Collins, "Artificial Intelligence in Personal Selling," *Journal of Personal Selling and Sales Management*, May 1984, 58–66; M. Steinberg and R. E. Plank, "Expert Systems: The Integrative Sales Management Tool of the Future," *Journal of the Academy of Marketing Science*, Summer 1987, 55–62.

[3]H. L. Mathews, D. T. Wilson, and K. Backhaus, "Selling to the Computer Assisted Buyer," *Industrial Marketing Management*, 6, 1977, 307–315.

[4]G. D. Hughes, "Computerized Sales Management," *Harvard Business Review*, March–April, 1983, 102–112; R. H. Collins, "Salesforce Support Systems: Potential Applications to Increase Productivity," *Journal of the Academy of Marketing Science*, Summer 1987, 49–54.

[5]Louis A. Wallis, *Computers and the Sales Effort*, The Conference Board, 1986.

[6]C. W. Stryker, "How to Keep Your Sales Information System Up to Date," *Business Marketing*, August 1985, 1–18.

[7]*Statistical Abstracts, 1985*, Table 676, 402.

[8]D. L. Thompson, "Stereotype of the Salesman," *Harvard Business Review*, January–February 1972, 20–162; see also N. M. Ford, "Stereotype of the Salesman: The Huckster Image Thieves," *Sales Management Bulletin*, Vol. 1, Issue 4, American Marketing Association, 1–2.

[9]E. O'Neill, *The Iceman Cometh*, Random House, 1946.

[10]W. C. Moncrief III, "Selling Activity and Sales Position Taxonomies for Industrial Salesforces," *Journal of Marketing Research*, August 1986, 261–270.

[11]P. Henry, "Manage Your Sales Force as a System," *Harvard Business Review*, March–April 1975, 85–119.

[12]R. R. Still, E. W. Cundiff, and N. A. P. Govoni, *Sales Management: Decisions, Strategies, and Cases*, 4th ed., Prentice-Hall, 1981.

[13]R. Cialdini, *Influence*, Quill, 1984.

[14]Gordon J. Bolt, *Practical Sales Management*, Pitman, 1987; G. D. Hughes and C. H. Singler, *Strategic Sales Management*, Addison-Wesley, 1983.

[15]D. J. Dalrymple, *Sales Management: Concepts and Cases*, John Wiley & Sons, 1982.

[16]P. Sloan, "Avon Plans Mass-Retail Expansions," *Advertising Age*, October 26, 1987, 2.

[17]Ibid., 85.

[18]Ibid.

[19]D. J. Dalrymple, *Sales Management: Concepts and Cases*; D. S. Tull and D. I. Hawkins, *Marketing Research: Measurement and Method*, 4th ed., Macmillan, 1987.

[20]L. M. Lodish, "A User-Oriented Model for Sales Force Size, Product, and Market Allocation Decisions," *Journal of Marketing*, Summer 1980, 70–78.

[21]D. J. Dalrymple and H. B. Thorelli, "Sales Force Budgeting," *Business Horizons*, July–August 1984, 31–36.

[22]B. A. Weitz, "Sales Effectiveness through Adaptation to Situational Demands," in *Personal Selling: Theory, Research, and Practice*, J. Jacoby and C. S. Craig (eds.),Lexington Books, 1984.

[23]*Marketing News*, January 13, 1978, 13.

[24]L. M. Lamont and W. J. Lundstrom, "Identifying Successful Industrial Salesmen by Personality and Personal Characteristics," *Journal of Marketing Research*, November 1977, 517–529.

[25]G. A. Churchill, Jr., N. M. Ford, S. W. Hartley, and O. C. Walker, Jr. "The Determinants of Salesperson Performance: A Meta-Analysis," *Journal of Marketing Research*, May 1985, 103–118.

[26]W. L. Cron and J. W. Slocum, Jr., "The Influence of Career Stages on Salespeople's Job Attitudes, Work Perceptions, and Performance," *Journal of Marketing Research*, May 1986, 119–129.

[27]J. Slocum and W. Cron, "Job Attitudes and Performance during Three Career Stages," *Journal of Vocational Behavior*, April 1985, 126–145.

[28]William L. Cron, "Industrial Salesperson Development: A Career Stages Perspective," *Journal of Marketing*, Fall 1984, 41–52.

[29]Churchill et al., "Determinants of Salesperson Performance," 117.

[30]B. A. Weitz, H. Sujan, and M. Sujan, "Knowledge, Motivation, and Adaptive Behavior: A Framework for Improving Selling Effectiveness," *Journal of Marketing*, October 1986, 174–191.

[31]H. Hakansson, J. Johanson, and B. Wootz, "Influence Tactics in Buyer-Seller Processes," *Industrial Marketing Management*, Fall 1977, 319–332.

[32]L. M. Lodish, "Sales Territory Alignment to Maximize Profit," *Journal of Marketing Research*, February 1975, 30–36; A. A. Zoltners, "Integer Programming Models for Sales Territory Alignment to Maximize Profit," *Journal of Marketing Research*, November 1976, 426–430.

[33]R. W. LaForge, C. E. Young, and B. C. Hamm, "Increasing Sales Productivity through Improved Sales Call Allocation Strategies," *Journal of Personal Selling and Sales Management*, November 1983, 52–59.

[34]T. H. Stevenson and A. L. Page, "The Adoption of National Account Marketing by Industrial Firms," *Industrial and Marketing Management*, Vol. 8, 1979, 94–100.

[35]R. Y. Darmon, "Compensation Plans That Link Management and Salesman's Objectives," *Industrial Marketing Management*, Vol. 11, 1982, 151–163.

[36]"Researchers Develop Objective Approach to Paying Salespeople Salaries or Commissions," *Marketing News*, October 26, 1984, 2.

[37]Still, Cundiff, and Govoni, *Sales Management*.

[38]O. C. Walker, Jr., G.A. Churchill, Jr., and N. M. Ford, "Motivation and Performance in Industrial Selling: Present Knowledge and Needed Research," *Journal of Marketing Research*, May 1977, 156–168.

[39]R. Oliver, "Expectancy Theory Predictions of Salesmen's Performance," *Journal of Marketing Research*, August 1974, 243–253.

[40]D. N. Behrman and W. D. Perreault, Jr., "Measuring the Performance of Industrial Salespersons," *Journal of Business Research*, Vol. 10, no. 3, 1982, 355–370.

[41]A. B. Cocanougher and J. M. Ivancevich, "'BARS' Performance Rating for Sales Force Research," *Journal of Marketing*, July 1978, 87–95.

[42]J. C. Mowen, J. E. Keith, S. W. Brown, and D. W. Jackson, Jr., "Utilizing Effort and Task Difficulty Information in Evaluating Salespeople," *Journal of Marketing Research*, May 1985, 185–191.

[43]Behrman & Perreault, "Measuring the Performance of Industrial Salespersons."

[44]M. Hanan, J. Cribbin, and J. Donis, *Systems Selling Strategies*, AMACOM, 1978.

MANAGEMENT OF DISTRIBUTION

Whereas Paul Revere's distribution "system" for his silversmith shop in Colonial Boston consisted of handing the custom-made silver, copper, and brass products to his customers when they came in to pick them up, it was not feasible for most companies to distribute their products directly to buyers even then. The majority of companies manufacturing consumer products during Colonial times found it expedient to sell through retailers, and many used wholesalers as well.

As companies have grown larger and as markets have expanded, the proportion of manufacturing companies selling and delivering consumer products over the counter has undergone a continuing decline, though it by no means has disappeared. Even the distribution of illegally distilled whiskey, once sold and delivered almost exclusively from the front doors of shacks housing stills (or the back doors of shacks housing distillers), has undergone a metamorphosis in the way it is distributed to consumers. According to the Treasury Department, the modern-day moonshiner:

> Is a large-scale producer at the center of a wholesale distribution network, sending his illegally produced hootch to metropolitan areas . . . where you have the lower income people who drink it. The whiskey moves from the manufacturer to wholesalers who distribute it to retailers, usually in homes. The average retailer buys several gallons . . . and sells [it] by the drink or half-pint.[1]

Similarly, most legal consumer products are distributed through marketing channels that include one or more middlemen. These channels have to be established and, unless the manufacturer sells directly to the user, the channel maintained in the proper amounts in appropriate locations, and timely delivery made to the buyer. Members have to be recruited, trained, motivated, persuaded to buy, serviced, and compensated.

Companies also must deal with the problems associated with the physical distribution of their products. Starting with sales forecasts and production (or procurement) planning, an inventory of products must be maintained in the proper amounts in appropriate locations, orders must be processed, and timely deliveries must be made to the buyers.

In this chapter we consider these two primary problems in the distribution of products—establishing and maintaining marketing channels, and managing the physical distribution system of the firm.

MARKETING CHANNELS: THEIR NATURE, CHOICE, AND MANAGEMENT

The Nature of Marketing Channels

A *marketing channel* is

> The set of firms or individuals that participate in the production, sale, distribution, and purchase of a given good or service.

Thus, the marketing channel just described for illegally produced whiskey can be depicted as

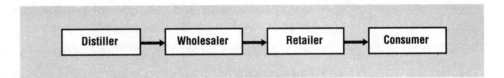

This channel contains two intermediaries (or middlemen)—wholesalers and retailers—as well as the producer (the first seller) and the consumer (the last purchaser) of the product. The channel has evolved from direct sale to the use of middlemen because it is economically more efficient to distribute that product with middlemen than without them.

Why should it often be more efficient for a producing company to sell through middlemen than to distribute its products itself? The answer to this question is not difficult to formulate. The middleman distributes the products of more than one producer (engages in multiple-line selling) to the same customer base and, by so doing, spreads the cost of selling and delivering across the producers it serves.

This principle is illustrated in Figure 17–1. If there were an industry in which four producers were each selling directly to eight customers, as shown in Figure

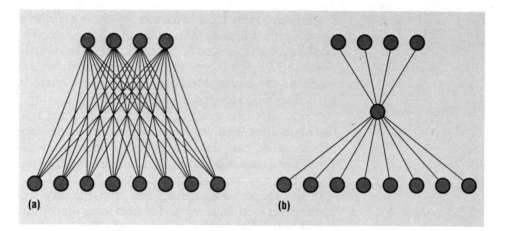

FIGURE 17-1a
Direct sale from buyer to seller.

FIGURE 17-1b
Sale through middleman.

(a)   **(b)**

17–1a, all producers would require a total of 32 sales calls to reach every customer. If a middleman were inserted in the channel, however, and the eight customers were all the same for each producer, a total of only 12 calls (or only a little more than a third of those required for direct marketing) would be required (Figure 17–1b). The potential for savings in each round of sales calls is obvious. Some additional savings also accrue from the joint delivery to the customer of an assortment of products from several producers.

Middlemen perform a number of important functions in the distribution of products. They:

- Conduct research on markets to locate and determine the requirements of potential customers.

- Promote the products they carry through catalogs, trade shows, and advertising.

- Match assortments and quantities of goods desired by customers with those available from the channel member.

- Sell the product through personal sales calls or by telephone.

- Finance the producer indirectly by reducing inventory requirements, and finance the customer directly by extending credit when required.

- Standardize and grade when required (agricultural products).

- Physically distribute the product through storing and transporting it.

- Service products and provide advice on their use as required.

- Assume risks associated with owning, storing, selling, financing, transporting, and servicing of products.

Each of these functions has to be performed by someone in the channel—if not by an intermediary, then by the producer or the user. None of the functions can be performed without cost. For this reason, and because of the economies of multiple-line selling, one should always be suspicious of claims such as:

Marketing Channels Most Frequently Used

Marketing channels necessarily start with the producer of the product or service and end with the consumer or industrial user. As shown in Figure 17–2, there are five major channels in use by producers of consumer products. A brief discussion of each of these channels follows.

Consumer
Products
Channels

Discussing only the five major channels may create the impression that the distribution of consumer products is much more standardized than it actually is. Producers may have their marketing effort organized by product line or by market, may have sales offices or branches, and may extend licenses or franchises. There are also other variations on the channels shown, especially those involving wholesalers. Some channels have as many as three specialized types of wholesalers. To keep the discussion manageable, however, we consider only the five most common consumer products channels.

FIGURE 17-2
The five major distribution channels used by producers of consumer products.

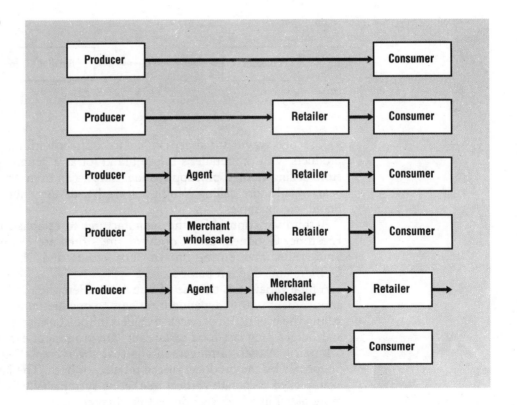

Direct to Consumer: This is the shortest, simplest, and often the most expensive channel. The producer may sell by catalog, by telephone, by direct mail, by magazine or newspaper, by television or radio, or house to house. Matchbooks, cards left on car windshields, and bill and package inserts are other media used for direct selling.

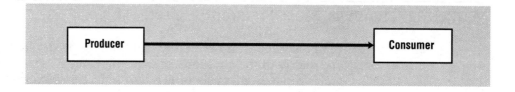

Leading direct marketers in the United States include Avon Products (cosmetics, jewelry), Time, Inc. (magazines), CBS (records, tapes), World Book Encyclopedia, Colonial Penn (insurance), and Franklin Mint (coins, engravings, figurines).

Direct to Retailer: This channel is used in a number of different ways. The most common way is for large retailers to buy products directly from the manufacturer and sell them under the manufacturer's brand. A Safeway store selling Del Monte canned pineapple or a Walgreen's drug store selling Johnson & Johnson's Tylenol are examples.

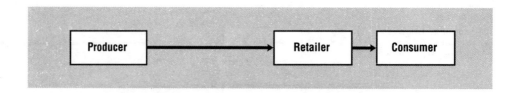

A second way is for large retailers to contract with manufacturers to supply products with the retailer's house brand (or as a generic product). A Safeway store selling canned pineapple under Safeway's own Townhouse brand, or a Sears retail store selling Whirlpool washer-dryers under the Sears Kenmore brand, are examples.

A third variation is for the manufacturer to establish its own retail stores. Firestone, Goodrich, and Goodyear tire stores are examples, as are Kinney, Stride Rite, and Buster Brown shoe stores and Sherwin-Williams, Fuller-O'Brien, and Glidden paint stores.

A final variation is the use of franchises. Here the producer has a contractual arrangement with independent owners to operate outlets under the name and selling the product or services specified in the contract. McDonald's, Wendy's, and Burger King fast-food restaurants are prominent examples.

Implicit in these arrangements is that the wholesaling functions are being performed by the producer or the retailer, or both. The last two variations are examples of corporate vertical marketing systems (VMS). We discuss VMSs in more detail in a later section of this chapter.

Producer to Agent to Retailer: A manufacturer may elect to have an agent take over all or part of the personal selling that would otherwise be performed by its own sales representatives. Agent wholesalers—variously known as manufacturers' agents, brokers, selling agents, or by other names—sell products but never take title and often do not physically take possession of them. With agents selling to the retailers instead of the manufacturer's own sales force, this channel is essentially no different from the preceding one.

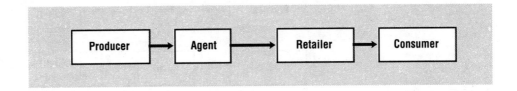

Manufacturers' agents are an example of agents used in the furniture industry, as are food brokers in the food industry.

Producer to Merchant Wholesaler to Retailer: Merchant wholesalers take title to and possession of the products they sell. This is the most common channel for marketing consumer goods. It is in especially wide use by the smaller manufacturers and retailers.

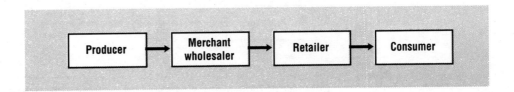

Producer to Retailer via Agent and Merchant Wholesalers: An example of the use of this channel is afforded by the food industry. Here, food brokers may be used to sell to large retailers (chains), whereas the company's own sales force is used to sell to wholesalers (who in turn sell to smaller retailers), or the brokers may be used to sell both to the chains and to the wholesalers.

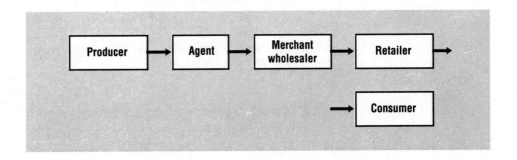

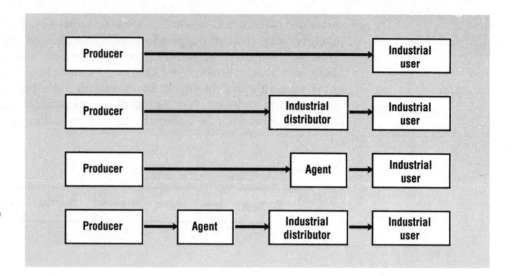

FIGURE 17-3
The four major distribution
channels used by producers of
industrial products.

Industrial Products Channels

Four channels are commonly used by producers of industrial goods. They are shown in Figure 17–3.

Producer Direct to Industrial User: This is the most important marketing channel in terms of dollar volume of industrial products sold. Commercial aircraft, machine tools, structural steel products, and industrial chemicals are examples of products sold directly to users.

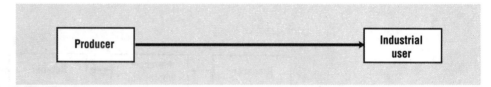

Producer to Industrial Distributor: The industrial distributor is the retailer of the industrial goods field. Hand and small power tools, pneumatic equipment, generators, and industrial finishes are examples of products sold through industrial distributors.

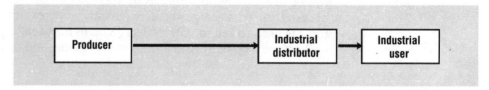

Producer to Agent to Industrial User: Agents are often used for selling directly to industrial buyers. Examples are the use of manufacturers' agents to sell

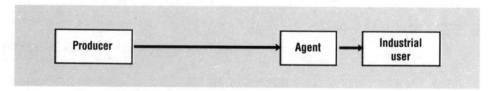

machine tools to automobile parts manufacturers, and to sell solid-state components to computer and other electronic equipment manufacturers. Heavy or bulky items are often sold by agents and then shipped directly from the factory to avoid extra shipping and handling charges.

Producer to Industrial User via Agent and Industrial Distributor: Agents are used to call on industrial distributors in product lines where unit sales are too low to permit each manufacturer to make sales calls, but the economies of multiple-line selling permits the agent to make sales calls profitably. Abrasives, lubricants, and industrial supplies are examples of products marketed through this channel.

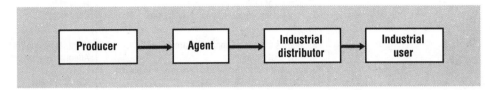

CHOOSING MARKETING CHANNELS

Choice Considerations

Choosing a marketing channel is a decision that should be made with care. There are at least two reasons for exploring the alternatives and choosing among them carefully:

1. The marketing channel chosen is usually a critically important factor in the success or failure of the product or service. A poorly chosen channel can result in ineffective presentation of the product and its features, limited purchase opportunities by customers, inappropriate pricing, poor customer service, inadequate customer financing, loss of control by the producer, and high channel maintenance costs. A good choice, on the other hand, can reverse these unwanted consequences.
2. Changing marketing channels is time-consuming, disruptive, and expensive. Unlike prices and advertising campaigns, distribution channels cannot be changed quickly and at low cost.

Choosing a marketing channel results in an economic tug-of-war between selling directly to the buyer (and the attendant greater control of sales effort, price, delivery, service, and customer relations) and selling through intermediaries at a lower cost.

The choice of a channel is affected by characteristics of the product or market, the company, and the available channel members. Although there is no formula that can be used for choosing, a careful analysis can point to the channel that will serve the needs of the company best.

A desire for efficiency and for control will lead to a producer's deciding to sell directly to the ultimate user as long as it can do so at a cost no higher than through an intermediary. If it is clear that the producer's cost will be greater

Table 17–1 Characteristics of the Product, Market, Company, and Available Channel Members That Affect Marketing Channel Choice

Characteristics	Desired Length of Channel	
	Direct or One Middleman	Two or More Middlemen
Product or market		
1. Number of customers and frequency of purchase	Few/infrequent	Many/frequent
2. Cost of the product	High	Low
3. Level of service required	High	Low
4. How technical the product is	Highly technical	Nontechnical
5. Length of shelf life	Short	Long
6. Weight or bulk	Heavy/big	Light/small
7. Geographic concentration of the market	Concentrated	Diffuse
Company		
8. Degree of channel control desired	Wants tight control	Does not need tight control
9. Financial situation	Adequately financed	Inadequately financed
10. Degree of potential internal multiple-line selling	High	Low
11. Propensity to assume risk	Above average	Below average
Channel member availability		
12. Intermediaries available	Marginal	Good

than that of one or more intermediaries, a choice has to be made. The considerations that need to be included in the choice of a channel are summarized in Table 17–1. A discussion of them follows.

1. Number of customers and frequency of purchase. Cigarettes, canned foods, magazines, and drug sundries are consumer products that have a large number of purchasers who tend buy them frequently. Each is distributed widely through retail outlets that are served by wholesalers. Industrial supplies such as small hand tools, abrasives, and paints and lubricants exhibit the same pattern.

The principle involved is that *the larger the number of purchasers or the more frequently products are purchased, other things being equal the greater the need for at least one wholesaler in the channel.* This principle exists for three reasons. First, products that are widely bought obviously have to be equally widely distributed just to make them available to their customers. Second, products that are purchased frequently tend to be purchased on the most convenient basis, and therefore need many outlets. Third, frequent purchase tends to result in high product turnover rates, and so frequent stocking is required. Using wholesalers is usually the most economical way to call on and supply a large number of retailers or industrial distributors.

2. Cost of the product. In the early 1980s, costs of producing microcomputers began to fall sharply and, almost immediately, "computer stores" began to spring up to sell them and their accessories and supplies. Computer stores had never existed until then. Prior to that time, new computers had been sold exclusively to the user by the sales representatives of the manufacturing company. Now the sales representatives began selling the computers to the computer stores.

The principle at work here is that *the gross margin per average sale is an important determinant of which, if any, intermediaries are used.* As the gross margin for each computer sale decreased (along with its cost), it became uneconomical for computer manufacturers to have representatives selling them directly to the one-at-a-time buyer. Computer stores took over that task and the representatives began to sell to them.

This is not true for large-volume buyers, however. Apple still sells computers directly to school districts and universities, for example, because the gross margin per sale is large enough to make it profitable to do so. Even a low-cost per-unit item such as a can of a soft drink can be sold directly to the retailer (but not to the consumer) if the number of units sold is large enough. Coca-Cola and Pepsi-Cola bottlers sell and make delivery directly to retailers, for example, but their lower-market-share competitors typically do not. Industrial fasteners (nuts and bolts, and so forth) are an example of a low-cost per-unit industrial item that is often sold directly to large users.

3. Level of service required. When Henry Ford began his automobile business in the early 1900s, he sold his cars directly to buyers. The same method of selling was followed in the 1920s when his company began to manufacture and sell the then-famous Ford Tri-Motor airplane. Only later did he set up a dealer network for Ford cars, and the airplanes were always sold directly to the user.

There were no doubt several common threads running through the initial decision to sell both of these products directly. One of them was the need for competent servicing for both products. When competent service is required for the continued satisfactory performance of a product (and, thus, for maintaining the good reputation of a product and the sellers of it), it should be provided either by the manufacturer or by the final seller of the product under authorization by the manufacturer.

The principal involved insofar as the length of the channel is concerned is that *the degree of control required to ensure that high-quality local servicing of the product is available usually results in either direct sale or sale through a single intermediary.*

4. How technical the product is. An integral part of the sale of many highly technical products is engineering advice on how to use them and what kind of performance could be expected in a particular application. For example, Tektronix, a manufacturer of sophisticated electronic measurement and test equipment, frequently receives requests for engineering advice of that kind.

Factory training of intermediary personnel to qualify them as competent application engineers is expensive and time-consuming, and may have to be repeated whenever there is a major design change. For this reason, the applications engineering service usually is provided by the manufacturer. Since it also is often an important determinant of whether a sale is made, the applications engineer typically doubles as a sales representative, and so such products are marketed by direct sale. (This is the case for Tektronix.)

The principle involved, then, is that *highly technical products tend to be sold directly from the manufacturer to the buyer* because (a) engineering advice is often an integral part of the sale, (b) competent advice can most economically be provided by the manufacturer, and (c) as long as engineers have to be present anyway, it is economically efficient to have them also serve as sales representatives.

5. Length of shelf life. Clothing designed by Christian Dior, fresh fish, and new Beaujoulais wine all have short marketing channels for the same reason—they have a short shelf life.

The principle here is that *the limited length of time that products with short shelf lives remain salable requires that they be distributed through a marketing channel with few delays for inventory and sale—a short marketing channel.*

6. Weight or bulk of the product. Household fans are light and not very large, and so are not very expensive to ship or to store. Air conditioners, however, are heavy and bulky and therefore are expensive and difficult to warehouse and deliver. A manufacturer of this (heavy and bulky) type of product would be well advised to consider selling direct or else using an agent, a middleman who sells but usually does not keep an inventory of the product. The product is shipped directly to the customer from the manufacturer.

The principle involved is to *keep the distribution channels for heavy or bulky products as short as possible to keep the physical handling of them to a minimum.*

7. Geographic concentration of the market. It is economically feasible for manufacturers to bypass wholesalers and sell lobster pots (traps for catching lobsters) directly to fishing cooperatives and marine supply stores along the New England coast because of the small area in which the market is concentrated. It is not economically practicable for the Eagle Co., a manufacturer of fishing rods, reels, lures, line, and other fishing accoutrements, to circumvent the wholesaler, however, as the retailers of its products are spread throughout the country.

The applicable principle is that *geographically concentrated markets permit marketing channels with fewer intermediaries than those that are geographically dispersed.*

Company
Characteristics

8. Degree of channel control desired. In marketing L'Eggs (its brand of panty hose) through supermarkets, the Hanes Corporation decided to use its own sales representatives to call on the stores rather than to use wholesalers. A major reason for that decision was to ensure that an adequate number of stores stocked the L'Eggs line, that the display racks in each store were kept neatly with a full inventory of sizes, that the racks were kept in a prominent location in the store, and that there was rapid feedback to the company on sales results. Since the product was introduced at a time (the late 1960s) when grocery wholesalers and food brokers were just beginning to get experience in carrying nonfood products, the marketing manager was afraid that using one or both of these types of middlemen might not provide the desired degree of control.

The principle involved is that, other things being equal, *the fewer the number of middlemen used, the greater the degree of control that can be exercised.*

9. Financial situation. Since for Hanes to sell directly to the supermarkets was an expensive alternative, the use of wholesalers would have been necessary if the company had not been in good financial shape. A financially strong company can establish its own sales force, provide warehousing for its products, and grant credit to buyers, whereas a financially weak company may be dependent on middlemen to provide these services.

The principal involved is that *it is preferable to select an (otherwise) less desirable channel that is affordable than a more desirable one that is not*. If the product prospers, a change can be made later when the more expensive channel can be afforded.

10. Degree of potential internal multiple-line selling. Companies that have several product lines that can be sold on the same sales call have a greater potential for circumventing the wholesaler than do those a with single product line. The Procter & Gamble Company, for example, sells its many lines of products (grocery, paper, soaps and detergents, and others) to supermarkets through its own sales force rather than using wholesalers. (In fact, it has more than one sales representative calling on the same accounts—one for soaps and detergents, another for paper products, and so on.)

The principle involved is that *the more product lines the company has that can be sold on the same sales call, the greater the potential for bypassing the wholesaler*.

11. Propensity to assume risk. Many companies when introducing a new product line do so using wholesalers (agent or merchant) rather than establishing a sales force to sell directly to retailers or industrial distributors. They do this for perhaps several reasons—the wholesalers in effect provide a ready-made sales force with lower start-up costs. Coverage and sales effectiveness being the same, using wholesalers also incurs less risk.

Other factors being the same, one reduces financial risk whenever one can convert a fixed cost into a variable cost. Since the fixed costs of using middlemen, as opposed to bypassing them, are less, the risk involved in using them is less.

The principle involved, then, is that *the greater the desire to reduce financial risk, the less desirable direct selling becomes*.

Channel Member Availability

12. Intermediaries available. The wholesalers and retailers that one might want are not always available. For example, when the management of Renault, the French automobile manufacturer, decided it wanted to expand its marketing effort in the United States, it found that obtaining distribution through independent automobile dealers of the quality it wanted was simply not possible—most of the desired dealers were unwilling to switch from the lines of automobiles they were already selling. Obtaining a dealer network was an important consideration in the subsequent decision by Renault to acquire a major interest in American Motors.

The principle here is something of a tautology: *When intermediaries of the quality desired are not available, it may be necessary for the company establishing the channel to set up its own intermediaries*.

Multiple Marketing Channels

So far, we have discussed the choice of a marketing channel as if only a single channel were going to be used. In practice, however, many companies use two or more channels to distribute the same product. Some examples:

> Apple markets its minicomputers to the consumer through computer stores, but sells to educational institutions through its own sales representatives.
>
> Mitsubishi sells its cars in the United States under Chrysler model names and through Chrysler dealers and also under its own brand and model names through its own network of independent dealers.
>
> Sears sells the same products through its retail stores, through catalogs by mail, and through catalog stores.

There are four reasons for using more than one channel:

1. To increase the profit from the existing level of sales. Apple uses its own salespeople to sell to the educational market because it is more profitable to sell directly to it than through computer outlets.

2. To increase overall sales. Mitsubishi sells through both Chrysler and its own dealers because it increases sales from what they would be from selling through only a single channel.

3. To use the channels that are appropriate to sell to each of a number of different market segments. The educational market for computers requires more technical advice and service than does the home computer market, and so selling direct is a more appropriate channel than going through a computer store.

4. To provide a hedge if one channel doesn't produce as well as expected. Both Avon and Fuller Brush, companies whose names for years were synonymous with house-to-house selling, now have begun to sell through catalogs because (a) it is difficult to recruit salespersons and (b) two-income households result in no one being home during the day.

The most common form of multiple-channel distribution occurs when a company sells a product under its own brand name but also sells the same product to retailers for resale under the retailers' brands. This is the so-called **house brand policy**. It not only increases sales but, if the manufacturer has an experience curve with any appreciable degree of slope, it reduces costs for the units produced for both channels. This is the case for Mitsubishi producing the house brand cars for Chrysler.[2]

CHANNEL MANAGEMENT

Competent management of a distribution channel requires making and implementing decisions in the areas of recruiting, training, motivating, servicing, compensating, evaluating, and replacing channel members.

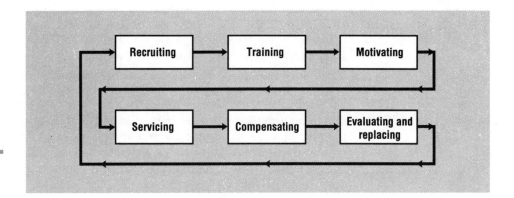

FIGURE 17-4
Decision areas for distribution
channel management.

Recruiting Channel Members

Some producers are able to attract qualified middlemen, and so **recruiting** is not a serious problem. For example:

> When the Ford Motor Company was developing the Edsel in the early 1950s, the management decided that it would not have dual dealerships. This meant that the company had to recruit a national dealership organization from scratch. This turned out not to be a problem; by the time it was ready to introduce the Edsel (1957), the company had recruited 1,200 highly qualified dealers. Many of them had been Buick and Oldsmobile dealers for General Motors, some had switched from Dodge and Chrysler dealerships for the Chrysler Corporation, and some had moved over from handling Ford products. All of the dealers had difficult years (and not a few defected) until the Edsel was taken off the market. (One of the ex-Ford dealers had had the leading Ford agency in Manhattan. It was an agonizing and highly risky decision to change to the Edsel and, as it turned out, a costly one as well.)

Other companies either face situations in which appropriate distributors do not exist, or else are unable to attract many of those they would like to take on the product. Personal computers emerged in the early 1980s with no suitable outlets to handle them. IBM therefore was forced to start its own computer stores until suitable independent outlets became available.[3] All of the Japanese car manufacturers had to accept dual dealerships when they introduced their products in the United States. It was only as sales and market share increased for the more popular makes that companies were able to develop dealerships of their own.

Whatever the situation faced by the company recruiting channel members, decisions must be made as to the minimum qualifications that a candidate member must have before it will be accepted. These qualifications include customers served, competing lines carried, financial situation, past sales and growth record, and reputation for service to its customers.

Training Middlemen Personnel

Depending on the type of product, **training** of middlemen personnel may be required in one or both of two areas: selling and servicing.

If the product is a technical one—a line of watches, an engine analyzer for automobile repair shops, home computer software—it may be desirable for middlemen personnel to be trained in the pertinent selling points for it. The training may be as limited as preparing a manual for middlemen sales representatives to as elaborate as offering special training courses for them. For example, Compaq Computer Corp. puts out a manual and a videotape for sales reps on each of its products. It also provides a computerized test on each product, which the representatives take and return to Compaq for scoring.

The training support for servicing of technical products also ranges from provision of manuals to service training courses. For example, Compaq puts out a servicing manual as well as offering regular service courses at regional locations for each of its computers.

Motivating Distributors

Appropriate **motivational strategies** depend in part on the stakes of the producers and middlemen involved. The dependence of distributors on a particular brand or line of products can range from as low as 1 or 2 percent of sales to 50 percent or more. The stake of producers that use middlemen can vary between a few percent to 100 percent of sales.

For a **high-stakes producer**, **high-stakes distributor** situation, a voluntary partnership is an appropriate strategy. Although the relationship is not a legal one, the producer looks on and treats the middlemen as if they were the distributing arm of a vertically integrated system, and encourages the distributors to view themselves as a part of the same system. The intent is to build a planned, managed system of distribution that meets the needs of both the producer and the distributors.[4] Some of the actions that are taken by the producer in implementing such a strategy are

- Establish a distributor relations planning unit within the marketing department whose responsibility is to identify distributor needs and develop programs to help meet them.
- Meet with the distributors and jointly plan the sales goals, inventory levels, merchandising and advertising programs, and sales training needs.
- Conduct marketing research studies by industry, product, and geographic area and provide the results to the distributors.

The marketing research efforts of one company, the Parker-Hannefin Corporation, a major hydraulics products manufacturer, is described in part in the box on the facing page.

The distributor agreement of Parker-Hannefin requires "each distributor to forward to Parker's market research division a photocopy of every invoice for the sale of a Parker product. The invoices are sorted and analyzed by industry, product, and customer, to enable Parker to develop distribution programs that mirror changing market conditions. One such program produces a series of market research reports tailored to each distributor. The reports analyze the distributor's sales and recommend customers that should be targeted for greater sales effort, products that should be promoted to various potential customers, and types of marketing techniques the distributor should use."*

*J. A. Narus and J. C. Anderson, "Turn Your Industrial Distributors into Partners," *Harvard Business Review*, March–April 1986, 67.

As the degree of producer or distributor dependence on each other declines, the need for a full-partnership distributor strategy decreases. Most producers in a **low-stakes producer**, **low-stakes distributor** situation use a strategy of cooperation instead. They use such motivational techniques as high margins, sales contests, and advertising and display allowances to try to gain distributor cooperation. This strategy is not as effective as a partnership strategy because it is a piecemeal approach that doesn't rest on an understanding of the distributor's needs and problems. It is a lower-cost strategy than the full-partnership approach, however, and so the benefits versus the costs of cooperation may be better in this situation than for a partnership.

Servicing

Sound *servicing* of distributors includes the prompt shipment of orders, promotional and sales support, and helping with customer problems. As one source states it:

Distributors want delivery within stated lead times, quality products that are not defective, adequate promotional and merchandising support, and rapid technical problem-solving assistance. Manufacturers must coordinate sales activities with those of the transportation and manufacturing people so that delivery promises will be kept.[5]

Compensating

Compensation for the distributor comes from the discounts allowed on the products sold. As discussed in the pricing chapter (13), the discounts that apply to distributors that are commonly used by producers include trade (a general discount for the type of distributor involved), promotional (for cooperative advertising, installing retail displays, or other specified promotional services), cash (payment within a specified time period), and quantity (a schedule relating quantities purchased and unit prices).

Other discounts are sometimes used for motivational purposes, however. They include discounts for maintaining a specified level of inventory, for meeting sales quotas, and for effective servicing of customers.

Evaluating and Replacing

Evaluation must be carried out by the producer to determine how well each middleman is performing. The criteria used for evaluation include whether the distributor is meeting sales quotas, whether the expected level of inventory is being maintained, how promptly customer deliveries are made, how cooperative the distributor is in company training programs, how well promotional allowances are used for their intended purpose(s), and the quality of the distributor's sales program.

If, after such an evaluation, a distributor is dropped, a decision has to be made about *replacement*. If the decision is to replace, recruiting must be carried out based on the criteria discussed earlier.

How and By Whom Control Is Exercised

The overall success of a marketing channel with intermediaries necessarily depends on each member's successfully performing its responsibilities. Although it often operates as a loose coalition of manufacturer, wholesalers, and retailers, each of whom negotiates aggressively with the others to serve its own ends as well as it is able, a dominant member can often serve common, as well as its own, interests better by exerting control over the actions of the other members.

The member that emerges as dominant can be the manufacturer, a wholesaler, or a retailer. It is often, although by no means always, the member whose brand appears upon the product. (The more the owner of the brand promotes it, the larger the market share; and the more financially secure the brand owner is, the more likely this is to be the case.) Thus, Procter & Gamble is the dominant member of the channels it uses for distributing its products in supermarkets, whereas Safeway is the dominant member of the channel for its Townhouse house brands. McKesson-Robbins, the drug wholesaler, tends to dominate with its own brand the channel in which it distributes drug products, and RCA dominates the channel for its TV sets (except those sold through Sears under the Kenmore brand).

The benefits dominant members attempt to achieve include price maintenance, coordinated and cooperative advertising, territorial integrity, and operating efficiencies. These benefits are all evidenced by well-run franchise operations (McDonald's fast-food restaurants, Avis Rent-A-Car, Coca-Cola bottling companies, Holiday Inns, and AAMCO Transmissions, for example), the channel with perhaps the greatest amount of control by the dominant member.

Control is exercised primarily by economic and legal means. Sanctions, either threatened or actual, are the principal economic means of exerting control. They include loss of discounts from not buying a sufficient quantity in a stated time period, rationing during times of shortage, dropping or reducing cooperative advertising, forcing purchase of complementary products (tying contracts), failure to provide an appropriate amount of personal selling effort, and shipping late or reducing inventory below a desired level. The ultimate sanction is for a channel member to drop from, or to be dropped from, the channel.

As hundreds of court cases attest, not all of these sanctions are legal. The dominant member is usually the defendant in such cases, as it is the one that typically has taken the action that brought about the suit.

Legal Aspects of Control

There are seven methods of control on which legislation and a substantial amount of legal precedent bear. The legal status of these methods is discussed briefly below.

1. *Selection of channel members.* The manufacturer has the right to select the middlemen through whom it will distribute its products, as do the middlemen to determine which products they will carry, as long as there is no intent to create a monopoly. However, manufacturers cannot drop a middleman as a punitive action for not following directives on price or for carrying competitive products.

2. *Resale price maintenance.* Manufacturers cannot require wholesalers and retailers to sell their products at a price stipulated by the manufacturer. They can suggest resale prices, but cannot penalize a channel member not charging the suggested prices by not selling to it or by taking other punitive action.

3. *Exclusive dealing.* Whether a manufacturer legally can require a middleman to carry its products exclusively depends on the circumstances. It is legal if, in the opinion of the court, it does not substantially lessen competition or tend to create a monopoly. For example, it is usually found to be illegal if the manufacturer has a sizable share of the market, as exclusive dealing would be viewed as substantially lessening competition. If, on the other hand, the manufacturer has only a small share of the market, it normally will be considered legal.

4. *Discrimination in price.* A manufacturer cannot discriminate in price between middlemen by amounts greater than the savings in cost from the way it manufactures, delivers, or sells to the one receiving the lower price. In order to be legal, differences in the price charged for purposes of control therefore would have to be limited to this cost saving.

5. *Exclusive territories.* Exclusive territories are legal as long as the court's opinion is that they do not substantially lessen competition or tend to create a monopoly. Since small companies are much less of a threat than are large companies to bring about either one of these consequences from exclusive territory assignments, small companies are much more likely to be allowed to make such agreements.

6. *Tying contracts.* Tying contracts require the purchase of complementary products (IBM computer paper with IBM minicomputers, General Motors authorized parts with General Motors cars, Gillette shaving cream with Gillette razors, and the like). Although there are some exceptions, (for example, a new company attempting to enter the market), the usual finding is that such contracts are illegal.

7. *Cooperative advertising allowances.* The giving or withholding of advertising allowances is a method sometimes used by producers to attempt to exert control over middlemen. Unless it can be shown that the middleman has not used the allowance for its intended purpose, it is illegal to discriminate in this way.

Vertical Marketing Systems as a Means of Assuming Control

A fully integrated *vertical marketing system* (VMS) is

a marketing channel in which manufacturing and the successive stages of distribution are operated as a unified system.

Four types of VMSs can be distinguished based on varying degrees of ownership:

1. *Administrative VMS.* A system in which a single dominant firm in effect administers the channel by virtue of its market power.

Table 17–2 Types and Examples of Vertical Marketing Systems

VMS Type	Owner/Dominant Member	Example
Administrative Dominant member "administers" the channel by virtue of its market power.	Manufacturer Wholesaler Retailer	General Electric McKesson-Robbins Sears, Roebuck
Contractual Firms at each stage of the channel agree to coordinate their manufacturing and marketing efforts.	Manufacturer Wholesaler Retailer	Firestone dealer stores Rexall drug stores Ben Franklin stores
Franchise Franchisees contract to provide approved products or services using the trade name, under the terms and conditions and in the area specified by the franchisor.	Manufacturer Wholesaler Retailer/service	Coca-Cola bottlers McDonald's fast foods Holiday Inn
Corporate A single company owns all the manufacturing, wholesale, and retailing operations.	Manufacturer Wholesaler Retailer	Sherwin-Williams paints W. W. Grainger electric supply* Brooks Bros. clothing

*An electrical supplies wholesaler with sales of over $500 million.

2. *Contractual VMS*. A system in which firms at each of the stages of the channel agree contractually to integrate and coordinate their manufacturing or marketing activities.
3. *Franchise VMS*. A system in which firms are licensed to use the trade name of the franchisor and to provide approved products or services in a specified location or area under contractually specified terms and conditions.
4. *Corporate VMS*. A system in which a single company owns all of the manufacturing, wholesaling, and retailing operations.

Each of these types of VMS can have as its dominant member or owner a manufacturer, wholesaler, or retailer. Examples of each of these types of VMS and the three owner/dominant firm versions of each are shown in Table 17–2.

Vertical marketing systems have become such an important factor in the distribution of consumer products and services that one observer has stated: "VMSs have become the dominant mode of distribution in consumer marketing, serving as much as 64 percent of the total market."[6] The growth to that level reflects the importance of control at all stages of the distribution of products and services.

PHYSICAL DISTRIBUTION

Physical distribution is sometimes called the "other half" of marketing, a term descriptive of both its differentiation in function and its importance. The customer analysis and demand-generating activities of marketing—marketing research, product planning and development, pricing, promotion, and personal selling—culminate in an order being placed, the first half of the marketing process. At that point the physical distribution activities—order processing, inventory maintenance and control, storage, and transportation and delivery–take over to finish the marketing task. It is only with the successful and timely completion of both sets of these marketing activities that the customers' needs can be met.

Physical distribution can be defined as:

> The set of activities that are required to carry out the delivery of products and services ordered by the customer.

As we see from Figure 17–5, the activities involved in physical distribution include order processing, inventory maintenance and control, storage, and transportation and delivery. Sound physical distribution management will mean that these activities will be planned and carried out in such a way as to ensure timely deliveries of undamaged products by economically efficient means.

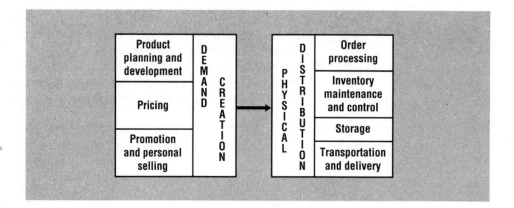

FIGURE 17-5
"The two sides of marketing"—demand creation and physical distribution.

Order Processing

Order processing has a history of being treated primarily as a part of the accounting cycle rather than as an important first step in the delivery of products to customers. The order typically came (and, in many instances, still comes) to the Accounting Department, where it was entered in a sales ledger, a credit check was made on the customer, and, two or three days later, copies were sent to the Sales Department, to the warehouse or distribution center, and to the Shipping Department. Shipping notified Accounting after shipment, and Accounting billed the customer. If there were a "stockout" condition, the warehouse sent the order back to Accounting with a notation to that effect which in turn notified both the customer—perhaps 10 days after the order had been received—and the Sales Department that a back order was being placed.

The recognition that such a system is costly has led to much more efficient processing of orders in better-managed companies. Lever Brothers, for example, has an order-processing system in which the order is entered into a central computer as soon as it is received that, in the space of a few seconds, checks the credit standing of the buyer and determines whether the items ordered are in stock. If stock is not available, it enters a back order and prints out a notice to the customer indicating the expected shipping date. If stock is available, it enters the order in a general sales ledger and in the sales account of the person making the sale (for purposes of a later calculation of commission). It also determines from which distribution center location(s) the products should be shipped, transmits the order there along with three recommended carriers for making the shipment, sends a copy of the order to the Sales Department with a notation of the distribution center(s) of origin and the probable day of shipment, updates the inventory record, orders additional units to be produced if that is appropriate, and bills the customer.

There are logical extensions to even this system—the customer placing the order through its computer on-line to the supplier's computer, the supplier billing through its computer back to the customer's computer, and the customer paying by electronic fund transfer via customer computer → customer's bank computer → supplier's bank computer → supplier's computer. Each of these extensions has been introduced, and in a few short years will be commonplace functions of fully computerized ordering–shipping–perpetual inventorying–billing–payment systems.[7]

Inefficiency in supplying the customer, either from a bad-order processing system or from too many "stockouts," comes at a substantial cost. Three types of costs associated with late shipments to customers are: (1) loss of interest earnings due to shipment delays leading to payment delays, (2) lost sales, and (3) customer reprisals (reducing the amount of shelf space assigned to the product, not participating in promotions, dropping the product, and so forth).

Loss of interest earnings as a result of shipment delays is the lowest of the three costs, but it can nonetheless add up to surprising amounts. For example, with an annual interest rate of 10 percent and a three-day delay in payment resulting from the same delay in shipment, Lever Brothers would lose in excess of $1 million per year from forgone interest earnings!

We discuss the costs of lost sales and customer reprisals in a later section.

Inventory Maintenance and Control

Maintaining an inventory obviously involves costs as well. These are out-of-pocket carrying costs consisting of five components: (1) ordering costs, (2) interest, (3) space costs, (4) inventory risk costs (obsolesence, damage, and pilferage), and (5) inventory service costs (insurance and taxes). Each of these costs appears as an item in the income statement or balance sheet.

For retailers and wholesalers, these costs are high in even the most efficiently run companies, but sound inventory management can substantially help keep them in control. The extent of the costs of carrying an inventory are reflected in part by the fact that 30 to 40 percent of the typical wholesaler's assets, and 40 to 60 percent of the average retailer's assets, are in inventory. That they are susceptible to sound control procedures is indicated by data that show that the 25 percent of wholesalers who are most efficient in handling inventory have a sales-to-inventory ratio that is more than three times as high as the 25 percent who are the least efficient. For retailers the comparable figure is lower, but still the most efficient retailers have sales-to-inventory ratios that are more than two times higher than the least efficient ones.[8] The message from these data is clear: Inventory costs are sufficiently high that controlling them should be a continuing management concern, and sound management can do much to reduce them.

The objective of sound *inventory control* is to:

Maintain inventory at a level at which the sum of the opportunity costs of stockouts and the out-of-pocket ordering and carrying costs is at a minimum.

This optimum inventory level occurs when the sum of these two types of costs associated with inventory for each product is at a minimum.

Determining Inventory Levels by Type of Stock

It is convenient to think of inventory for each product as being divided into three different types based on the purposes of the stock. As shown in Figure 17–6, these three types of stock are the

1. *Working stock.* The stock required to fill the customer orders expected before the next reorder is placed.
2. *Lead-time stock.* The stock required to fill the orders expected between the times that the reorder is placed and the new supply is received.
3. *Safety stock.* The stock required to allow for errors in estimating the proper levels of working stock.

Economic Order Quantity = Level of Working Stock + Lead-Time Stock: At any one time for a given product and for a particular company, the level of demand, quantity discounts, promotional discounts, transportation charges, interest and other carrying expenses, and order-processing costs combine to result in an order of one particular quantity costing less per unit to buy and to hold in inventory than that for any other quantity ordered. That quantity is known as the **Economic Order Quantity** (EOQ).

This quantity determines the maximum level of the working stock (WS) plus lead-time stock (LTS) that should be carried, or:

$$EOQ = \max \{WS + LTS\}.$$

By definition, this is the lowest-cost maximum level for the sum of those two inventory components.

A simple example will illustrate how the working and lead-time stocks interrelate, and when reorders should placed. Suppose that, for a particular product, the EOQ is 100 units, and a reorder in that amount has just been received. (A sample calculation yielding an EOQ of 100 units is given shortly.) Further suppose that demand averages 10 units per day, and that the lead time for a reorder to be received is three days. The lead-time stock (the stock required to fill customer orders between the time the reorder for 100 units is placed and the time it is received) is then 3 days × 10 units per day = 30 units. The working stock is the remainder, or 100 − 30 = 70 units, a seven-day supply. Seven days later, when the 70 units of working stock have been sold, a reorder point will have been reached, and so an order for another 100 units should be placed. If all is according to plan, it should arrive three days later, just as the

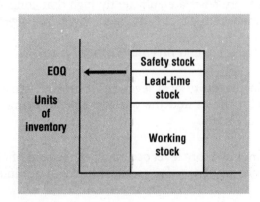

FIGURE 17-6
The economic order quantity (EOQ) and the working stock, lead-time stock, and safety stock components of inventory.

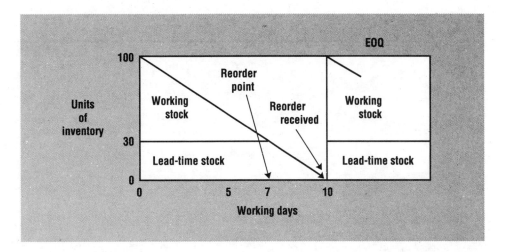

FIGURE 17-7
Inventory cycle for working and
lead-time stocks.

lead-time stock runs out. The cycle is then repeated. An inventory cycle for this example is shown in Figure 17–7.

How does one determine the EOQ? It is calculated by determining the quantity that will have the lowest average total use per unit, that is, the lowest sum of the acquisition costs plus the carrying costs. This minimum point is shown graphically at EOQ in Figure 17–8. It can be calculated by the formula given in Exhibit 17–1.

Determining the Level of Safety Stock: The costs of lost interest on payments, lost sales, and customer reprisals due to late shipments can be very high. These costs can be avoided if large enough safety stocks are kept on hand, but the costs of keeping inventories large enough to avoid stockouts completely is prohibitive. The proper level of safety stock is one that balances the cost of the potential stockouts against carrying costs in such a way as to minimize the sum of the two.

Three kinds of information are required to determine the level of safety stock for each product that will make the greatest contribution to profit:

1. Realistic cost estimates of lost sales and customer reprisals as a result of each stockout during a specified time period.

FIGURE 17-8
Determining the economic order
quantity (EOQ) graphically.

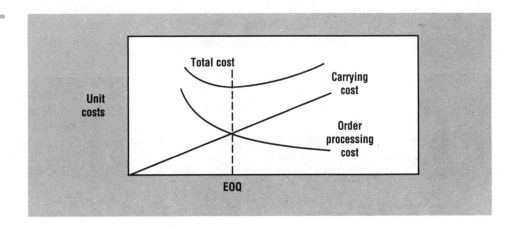

EXHIBIT **17-1**

Calculating the Economic Order Quantity (EOQ)

The formula for the Economic Order Quantity is

$$EOQ = \sqrt{\frac{2DR}{I}}$$

where

D = annual demand in units,
R = cost of placing an order, and
I = annual carrying cost per unit.

For example, assume that the annual demand for a product (D) is 2,000 units, the cost to place each order (R) is $25.00, and the annual carrying charge is $10.00. The EOQ is then found to be

$$EOQ = \sqrt{\frac{2 \times 2,000 \times 25}{10}}$$
$$= \sqrt{10,000}$$
$$= 100 \text{ units}$$

It should be noted that some simplifying assumptions are implicit in this formula. It assumes that demand is independent of inventory (other than for delivery), the annual demand can be forecast accurately, that there is a constant cost for placing each order, and that the carrying cost per unit is constant. And it does not take into account quantity discounts.

2. The levels of safety stock at which 0.1, 1, 2, . . . n stockouts can be expected to occur during that same time period; and

3. Carrying costs at the differing levels of safety stock.

By multiplying the estimated cost of each stockout (CS) times the number of stockouts expected for a given level of safety stock (N_i) and adding the ordering and carrying cost for that same level of safety stock (CC_i), one obtains an estimate of the total costs of maintaining that level of safety stock (TC_i), or:

$$TC_i = CS(N_i) + CC_i$$

By making this calculation over the appropriate range of levels of safety stock, one can determine which level will have the lowest total cost, and can maintain the safety stock at that level.

But first one has to develop realistic estimates of each of the three cost variables in the above equation.

1. Cost of stockouts. The cost from lost sales, due either to inefficient order handling or stockouts, can be substantial. For example, one study for a supplier of packaged goods showed that:

> . . . If the delivery from manufacturer to distributor was two days late, the distributor ran out of stock only 15 percent of the time. If delivery was four days late, the chance increased to 30 percent. If delivery was seven days late, the chance rose to 60 percent. If the distributor's warehouse was out of stock for two days, 10 percent of the retail stores ran out of that item. When the warehouse was out of stock as long as four days, 25 percent of the stores ran out of the item. Finally, by the time the warehouse had been out of the item as long as six days, 50 percent of the stores had none of it.[9]

For stockouts, the number of days the warehouse will be out of stock is the lead time required to order and receive a shipment of the product.

Frequent late shipments to customers can lead to customer reprisals in the form of allocation of less shelf space, carrying a smaller inventory of the product, declining to participate in product promotions (on the grounds that shipments will probably not be on time), or dropping the product completely. If the product is dropped, it will very likely become more difficult, if indeed it is possible at all, to get the customer to carry a new product introduced in the future by the same supplier.

In the study for the supplier of consumer packaged goods, it was found that:

"... Distributors' buyers became sufficiently frustrated to retaliate against this manufacturer if it were late in three out of any four consecutive deliveries."[10] The combination of the costs of lost sales and of customer reprisals for a shipment that was two days late were found to amount to 9 percent of the contribution to profit for the order, and, if it were seven days late, the loss incurred was 46 percent[!] of the contribution.[11]

It is apparent from these examples that one has to obtain information not only from customers but from the customers of customers as well to determine the costs of stockouts. The Marketing Research Department, or an outside research agency, will typically be employed for this task.

2. The expected number of stockouts at different levels of safety stock. Most well-managed companies now have their orders for inventory, the processing of customer orders, and their inventory records computerized. If computer entries in the correct amounts are made each time an order is received for inventory, each time that an order is shipped from inventory, and each time there are returned or damaged items, the **perpetual inventory** figure that results for a product should be a close approximation of the actual number of units on hand. (Mistakes in entries can be made, of course, and it will not reflect lost or stolen units.) The perpetual inventory is updated periodically by a **physical inventory**—an actual count of the items on the shelf or in the bin.

Given the computer inventory record for a product over a sufficient time period, it is possible to estimate what level of inventory (including safety stock) would have been required to fill, on the average, 95 percent, 99 percent, 99.9 percent, or any other percentage of the orders received.

If such a record is not available, one can be constructed using internal records. Starting with a physical inventory amount at the beginning of the period of interest, adding amounts received from suppliers and returned by customers, and deducting amounts shipped to customers and returned to suppliers will give a reconstructed perpetual inventory. The estimates of the level of inventory required to fill any given percentage of orders, on the average, can then be made from this reconstructed inventory.

Seasonal sales variations will obviously need to be taken into account in the amounts of inventory carried in each season.

3. Carrying costs for safety stock. Carrying costs for inventoried units are determined by standard cost accounting methods. Although it could be argued conceptually that per-unit carrying costs for safety stocks are different than they are for working and lead-time stocks (handling costs for safety stocks are less, interest and obsolescence costs are higher because each unit tends to remain in inventory longer), no distinction in the costs of carrying the three different types of stocks is usually made.

Supplying Materials and Parts on a "Just-in-time" Basis	Just-in-time delivery, or **kanban**, was originated by the Toyota Corporation in Japan to keep inventory, and thus inventory costs, to the bare minimum necessary for production. As practiced by Toyota and other companies in Japan, it largely refers to scheduling of raw materials or parts supplied by manufacturers to other, original-equipment manufacturers (OEMs), rather than to the scheduling of parts supplied by distributors to OEMs or to retailers. In Japan distances are much smaller, and, in addition, there is a tradition of suppliers' locating plants close to major customers. In the United States manufacturers typically are located much farther away from their customers, on the average, and so there is less direct selling.

As of 1985, more than 100 manufacturers in the United States were known to have tried the method.[12] Many distributors are involved as suppliers if, when the manufacturer decides to convert to just-in-time, the distributor is given a Hobson's choice of either being a part of the system or losing the business to a distributor that will.

Many distributors are turning to offering just-in-time deliveries as a marketing tool. An example is a distributor of electrical supplies, the United Electrical Company:

> United feared a French competitor might lure away a customer, the Ex-Cell-O Corp. United could not compete on price and so decided to help cut Ex-Cell-O's costs by providing better service. United offered to help Ex-Cell-O trim inventory costs by guaranteeing delivery of electrical controls a day before they were needed on the production line.... Ex-Cell-O is still a United customer.[13]

There are usually three effects on distributors such as United that become part of customer just-in-time systems: higher sales, increased inventory, and increased turnover rate.[14] The higher sales and increased turnover of course have favorable effects on gross contribution margin, whereas increased inventories have an unfavorable effect. A logical move to cut the added costs of increased inventory is for distributors to install their own just-in-time system and require their suppliers to start making deliveries on a tighter schedule.

Storage

Storage, depending on its purpose, is carried out in one of two types of facilities—a warehouse or a distribution center. A **warehouse** is designed and operated primarily for longer-term storage of raw materials or products. A **distribution center** has as its primary purposes the consolidation of shipments from different production points and the processing of orders and shipment of products to customers. The distribution center concept is the one that ties directly into marketing.

As is the case with each of the other elements of a successfully managed marketing program, the system for handling and storage of inventories through distribution centers needs to be designed with the needs of the customer in mind, but not to the exclusion of considering the costs involved. The decisions that are central insofar as marketing is concerned are those relating to the number, size, and location of distribution centers.

The immediate interests of marketing are best served with a large number of smaller distribution centers located near concentrations of customers. Such facilities are almost certain to cost more to acquire and to operate than a smaller number of centers, however. There are a number of reasons for this—per-square-foot building costs are usually higher for smaller buildings, larger facilities can be operated more efficiently in terms of labor, more facilities mean more double shipments of products, and total inventories rise as the number of locations increases.

A balance has to be struck between the demands of customer service and the added costs involved as service is improved. The dangers involved in considering only costs is illustrated by the experience of a firm that built a large, automated distribution center, only to have to abandon it a short time later:

Designed and built by a large wholesale drug firm located in a major urban area, the automated distribution center was intended to replace a number of smaller, manually operated warehouses spotted at various locations in the city. Land costs required building the center some distance from the city.

Obviously, the economics of closing down the older, inefficient warehouses and replacing them with a centralized, automated facility were good, or the firm would not have undertaken the project. Once in operation, the distribution center realized its promise and enabled the firm to pass along part of the savings to customers—a decided competitive advantage. Or so it appeared. But after only a few weeks of operation at the new center, the firm's management woke up to the chilling realization that customers didn't care that much about saving money. They wanted fast—almost immediate—service, and it was abundantly evident that deliveries from a facility some 30 miles from downtown couldn't be made that quickly, automation or no automation. The company had begun to lose customers—primarily pharmacies—at an alarming rate to competitors who were operating smaller satellite distribution facilities within the city and were capable of making fast delivery. The high costs of maintaining inventories at several locations were, in effect, being paid for willingly by customers in return for quick service.

The company moved out of its new facility and back into the city.[15]

Siting models range from the relatively simple, one location center-of-gravity model[16] to elaborate, computerized multilocation models.[17] Some dramatic results have been reported from the use of computerized models:

Hunt-Wesson Foods saved over a million dollars ("in the low seven figures") per year by using a computerized model to redesign its distribution system.[*]

The H. J. Heinz Company reduced the number of domestic distribution centers from 43 to 30, with a concomitant reduction in cost but an improvement in delivery time to customers.[†]

A computer simulation at Electrolux compared costs of operating its Atlanta distribution center with those at three other sites. The simulation showed costs would drop if the center were moved to Charlotte, N.C. The move was made and, despite the fact that carriers made general rate increases, the company cut its total distribution costs by 5 percent.[‡]

[*]Geoffrion, "Better Distribution Planning."
[†]Shycon and Maffei, "Simulation."
[‡]"Saving Money When Freight Rates Are Computerized," *Business Week*, February 25, 1980, 111–115.

Marketing managers are well advised to participate in the planning and operation of such models. The marketing representative should insist that the model used includes allowances for the effects of shipping delays on demand. He or she should also ensure that whatever computerized model that is used is validated appropriately. This can be done by comparing the model's "predictions" of costs with the actual costs for some previous year, running sensitivity analyses by making changes in the historical data (freight rates, for example) for that same year and seeing if the model's cost predictions track them well, and by running "extreme case" analyses (large changes or shifts in the geographic pattern of demand, substantial changes in freight rates, and so forth) and seeing if the solutions of the model seem to be reasonable.

Transportation and Delivery

The third largest expense of manufacturers, after labor and materials, is transportation. It typically amounts to from 10 to 30 percent of their total costs.

Most companies of any size have a traffic manager. Since the deregulation of air cargo rates in 1978 and of truck and rail rates in 1980, the traffic manager has been able to negotiate rates with carriers and thus to exercise considerably more control over both transportation costs and the services carriers provide. The decisions the traffic manager is responsible for that bear directly on marketing typically include:

- **Determining rates**—Finding the lowest quoted rate for shipping the company's products.
- **Negotiating rates and services**—Obtaining lower rates or additional services (expediting, reconsignment, diversion, and the like) by negotiation with the carrier.
- **Selecting carriers**—Choosing carriers that offer the best delivery time–reliability–services–rate combination.
- **Managing company-owned transportation equipment.**

The computer has begun to play a substantial role in the managing of the transportation function. There are agencies (such as Distribution Sciences, Inc., of Chicago) that have developed software and a computerized database that provide, for a given destination for a variety of carriers, the rates, routing, and a rating for each. When needed, shipment consolidation recommendations can be obtained from the same software package. In addition, the program can be used to conduct an audit of the freight bill after the shipment has been made.

There are also computer programs available for the routing of delivery vehicles in cities. If there are 10 deliveries to be made in the city, for example, entering data on the distance between each set of delivery points will allow the computer to determine what the shortest overall route is.[18]

The Place of Physical Distribution in the Company Organization

There are almost invariably partisan and conflicting interests in the management of physical distribution activities from the Manufacturing, Accounting, Finance, and Marketing departments. Manufacturing would like sizable production runs that permit it to get the production process running smoothly, that lower costs, and that reduce the number of changeovers each year. The result is higher inventories—and higher carrying costs. The larger inventories also tie up company capital, which makes for added problems for finance. Accounting prefers to handle order processing so that it can control the credit check and billing of customers. Slower order filling and shipment times often result when it has those responsibilities. Marketing forecasts sales and would like adequate support in providing fast and reliable service to the customer.

There has been a growing recognition of the need to manage the order-processing, inventory, storage, and transportation functions as an integrated whole. This has resulted in many companies' assigning the responsibilities for these functions to a single physical distribution executive reporting to the same level as the heads of the Marketing, Manufacturing, and Finance departments. Two examples:

> The Whirlpool Corporation reorganized its distribution activities by placing them under a vice-president of distribution. It took the unusual step of assigning the responsibility for sales forecasting to the new vice-president, along with order processing and the other physical distribution functions. The rationale for assigning sales forecasting to the Distribution Department was to match authority and responsibility more closely insofar as inventory control was concerned.*
>
> Nalley's Fine Foods made an organizational change similar to that of Whirlpool by also integrating the distribution functions under a vice-president. Reporting to the vice-president, along with a traffic manager and a distribution manager, is a production planning and inventory control manager. The production-planning function was brought over from Manufacturing to provide greater control insofar as inventories are concerned.

*T. J. Murray, "A Powerful New Voice in Management," *Dun's Review*, April 1976, 71.

An integrated organization for the physical distribution activities seems appropriate. To whom it reports is not of great importance. The central concern, to Marketing as well as to the company as a whole, is that it maintain a reasoned balance between cost and service to the customer.

1. A *marketing channel* is the set of firms or individuals that participate in the production, sale, distribution, and purchase of a given good or service.
2. *Middlemen* perform the functions of:
   a. Conducting research on markets to locate and determine the requirements of potential customers.
   b. Promoting the products they carry through catalogs, trade shows, and advertising.
   c. Matching assortments and quantities of goods desired by customers with those available from the channel member.
   d. Selling the product through personal sales calls or by telephone.
   e. Financing the producer indirectly by reducing inventory requirements, and financing the customer directly by extending credit when required.
   f. Standardizing and grading when required (agricultural products).
   g. Physically distributing the product through storing and transporting it.
   h. Servicing products and providing advice on their use as required.
   i. Assuming risks associated with owning, storing, selling, financing, transporting, and servicing of products.
3. The marketing channels most used for marketing *consumer* products (not in order of frequency of use) are:
   a. Direct to consumer
   b. Direct to retailer
   c. Producer to agent to retailer
   d. Producer to merchant wholesaler to retailer
   e. Producer to retailer via agent and merchant wholesalers
4. The marketing channels most used for marketing *industrial* products (not in order of frequency of use) are:
   a. Producer direct to industrial user
   b. Producer to industrial distributor
   c. Producer to agent to industrial user
   d. Producer to industrial user via agent and industrial distributor
5. The choice of a channel is affected by characteristics of the product or market, the company, and the available channel members.
6. The principles involved in choosing *distribution channels* include:
   a. Product or market considerations
      1. The larger the number of purchasers or the more frequently products are purchased, other things being equal, the greater the need for at least one wholesaler in the channel.
      2. The gross margin per average sale is an important determinant of which, if any, intermediaries are used.
      3. The degree of control required to ensure that high-quality local servicing of the product is available usually results in either direct sale or sale through a single intermediary.

4. Highly technical products tend to be sold directly from the manufacturer to the buyer because (a) engineering advice is often an integral part of the sale, (b) competent advice can most economically be provided by the manufacturer, and (c) as long as engineers have to be present anyway, it is economically efficient to have them also serve as sales representatives.

5. The limited length of time that products with short shelf lives remain salable requires that they be distributed through a marketing channel with few delays for inventory and sale—a short marketing channel.

6. The distribution channels for heavy or bulky products should be as short as possible to keep the physical handling of them to a minimum.

7. Geographically concentrated markets permit marketing channels with fewer intermediaries than those that are geographically dispersed.

b. Company characteristics

8. The fewer the number of middlemen used, the greater the degree of control that can be exercised.

9. It is preferable to select an (otherwise) less desirable channel that is affordable than a more desirable one that is not.

10. The more product lines the company has that can be sold on the same sales call, the greater the potential for bypassing the wholesaler.

11. The greater the desire to reduce financial risk, the less desirable direct selling becomes.

c. Channel member availability

12. When intermediaries of the quality desired are not available, it may be necessary for the company establishing the channel to set up its own intermediaries.

7. The four reasons for using more than one channel are:

a. To increase the profit from the existing level of sales

b. To increase overall sales

c. To use the channels that are appropriate to sell to each of a number of different market segments

d. To provide a hedge if one channel doesn't produce as well as expected

8. Competent management of a distribution channel requires making and implementing decisions in the areas of recruiting, training, motivating, servicing, compensating, evaluating, and replacing channel members.

9. For a high-stakes producer, high-stakes distributor situation, a voluntary partnership is an appropriate strategy.

10. The major methods used by manufacturers to establish and control distribution channels and the legal status of these methods are

a. Selection of channel members. The manufacturer has the right to select the middlemen through whom it will distribute its products, as do the middlemen to determine which products they will carry, as long as there is no intent to create a monopoly.

b. Resale price maintenance. Manufacturers cannot require whole-salers and retailers to sell their products at a price stipulated by the manufacturer.

c. Exclusive dealing. Whether a manufacturer's requirement that a middleman carry its products exclusively is legal depends on the circumstances.

d. Discrimination in price. A manufacturer cannot discriminate in price between middlemen by amounts greater than the savings in cost from the way it manufactures, delivers, or sells to the one receiving the lower price.

e. Exclusive territories. Exclusive territories are legal as long as the court's opinion is that they do not substantially lessen competition or tend to create a monopoly.

f. Tying contracts. Although there some exceptions (for example, a new company attempting to enter the market), the usual finding is that tying contracts are illegal.

g. Cooperative advertising allowances. It is illegal to discriminate between distributors in granting such allowances.

11. The major activities involved in *physical distribution* are order process-ing, inventory maintenance and control, storage, and transportation and delivery.

12. The objective of sound *inventory control* is to maintain inventory at a level at which the sum of the opportunity costs of stockouts and the out-of-pocket ordering and carrying costs is at a minimum.

13. The three types of costs associated with late shipments to customers are (a) loss of interest earnings due to shipment delays' leading to payment delays, (b) lost sales, and (c) customer reprisals (reducing the amount of shelf space assigned to the product, not participating in promotions, dropping the product, and so forth).

14. The three types of stock that make up an inventory are

a. *Working stock.* The stock required to fill the customer orders ex-pected before the next reorder is placed.

b. *Lead-time stock.* The stock required to fill the orders expected be-tween the times that the reorder is placed and the new supply is received.

c. *Safety stock.* The stock required to allow for errors in estimating the proper levels of working or basic stock.

15. The economic order quantity (EOQ) is the sum of the working stock and the lead-time stock, or: EOQ = WS + LTS.

16. The usual effects on distributors who become part of customer just-in-time systems are higher sales, increased inventory, and increased turnover rate.

17. Siting models can be validated by (a) comparing the model's "predic-tions" of costs with the actual costs for some previous year; (b) run-ning sensitivity analyses by making changes in the historical data (freight rates, for example) for that same year and seeing if the model's cost predictions track them well; (c) running "extreme case" analyses (large changes or shifts in the geographic pattern of demand, substan-tial changes in freight rates, and so forth) and seeing if the solutions of the model seem to be reasonable.

18. The decisions the traffic manager is responsible for that bear directly on marketing typically include:

a. *Determining rates.* Finding the lowest quoted rate for shipping the company's products.

b. *Negotiating rates and services.* Obtaining lower rates or additional services (expediting, reconsignment, diversion, and the like) by negotiation with the carrier.

c. *Selecting carriers.* Choosing carriers that offer the best delivery time–reliability–services–rate combination.

d. *Managing company-owned transportation equipment.*

REVIEW QUESTIONS

17.1. What is a *marketing channel*?

17.2. What is *multiple-line selling*? What effect does this practice have with respect to inducing companies to use middlemen to sell their products rather than to sell them themselves?

17.3. What functions do middlemen perform in the distribution of products?

17.4. What are the major channels in use for consumer products? for industrial products?

17.5. What is the major distinction between *merchant wholesalers* and *agents*?

17.6. What are the characteristics of the product, market, company, and available channel members that affect marketing channel choice?

17.7. a. What are the major methods of control used by manufacturers on members of their distribution channel(s)?
   b. What is the legal status of each of these methods?

17.8. a. What is a vertical marketing system (VMS)?
   b. What are the four types of VMSs based on pattern of ownership?

17.9. What are the four principal activities involved in the physical distribution of the product?

17.10. What are the three types of costs associated with late shipments to customers?

17.11. What is the objective of sound *inventory control*?

17.12. Describe the three types of stock carried in an inventory.

17.13. What is an *economic order quantity*? How is it determined?

17.14. How is the level of the *working stock* determined? of the *lead-time stock*? of the *safety stock*?

17.15. What is the difference between a *warehouse* and a *distribution center*?

17.16. How can one go about validating a *computerized site location model*?

17.17. What are the major decisions of traffic managers that bear directly on the marketing program of the firm?

DISCUSSION QUESTIONS AND PROBLEMS

17.18. Evaluate the claim "BECAUSE WE SELL DIRECTLY FROM THE FACTORY, WE SAVE YOU WHAT THE MIDDLEMAN WOULD HAVE COST!"

17.19. Describe the marketing channel(s) you believe would be appropriate for the following products and services:
   a. A fill-in-the-spaces personal will form valid in all 50 states.
   b. A super lightweight racing bicycle retailing for more than $1,000.
   c. Luxury boats 35 feet or more in length and selling for $50,000 and up.
   d. A new line of low-priced, highly advertised cosmetics.
   e. Textbooks for colleges and universities.

17.20. What marketing channels do you believe would be appropriate for:
   a. Minicomputers?
   b. Computer paper?
   c. Printers?
   d. Software?
   Explain your reasoning for each product.

17.21. Should automobiles be sold by catalog? Why or why not?

17.22. As a soon-to-be university graduate, what marketing channels should a friend who does not have a job after graduation use to get one?

17.23. Assume that an automobile dealer forecasts demand for the coming year at 2,000 new cars. Further suppose that the cost of placing an order for new cars is $25, and the annual carrying cost per car is $1,000.
   a. What is the EOQ?

      b.   What is the sum of the ordering and carrying costs per year at that EOQ?

      c.   Suppose a mistake is made in determining EOQ such that the orders placed each time are 25 percent higher than the actual EOQ. What would be the net percentage difference in the sum of the ordering and carrying costs per year when ordering this amount as opposed to the costs calculated in (b)?

      d.   Suppose a mistake is made in determining EOQ such that the orders placed each time are 25 percent lower than the actual EOQ. What would be the net difference in the sum of the ordering and carrying costs per year when ordering this amount versus the costs calculated in (b)?

      e.   Do you believe that the assumption implicit in the EOQ formula that demand is independent of inventory (other than for delivery) is realistic in the case of an automobile dealer? Why or why not?

17.24.   The problem statement is the same as in 17.23 except demand is estimated to be 4,000 cars annually. Answer parts (a), (b), (c), and (d) as given in 17.23.

17.25.   The problem statement is the same as in 17.23 except carrying costs are $2,000 per car. Answer parts (a), (b), (c), and (d) as given in 17.23.

17.26.   Suppose the manager of an independent (nonchain) shoe store estimates demand for a brand of shoes sold in the store at 4,000 pairs. Assume that the annual carrying cost per pair is $2.50 and that ordering costs are $50 per order.

      a.   What is the EOQ?

      b.   What is the sum of the ordering and carrying costs per year at that EOQ?

      c.   Suppose a mistake is made in determining EOQ such that the orders placed each time are 25 percent higher than the actual EOQ. What would be the net percentage difference in the sum of the ordering and carrying costs per year when ordering this amount as opposed to the costs calculated in (b)?

      d.   Suppose a mistake is made in determining EOQ such that the orders placed each time are 25 percent lower than the actual EOQ. What would be the net percentage difference in the sum of the ordering and carrying costs per year when ordering this amount versus the costs calculated in (b)?

      e.   Do you believe that the assumption implicit in the EOQ formula that demand is independent of inventory (other than for delivery) is realistic in the case of a shoe store? Why or why not?

17.27.   The problem statement is the same as in 17.26 except demand is estimated to be 8,000 pairs of shoes annually. Answer parts (a), (b), (c), and (d) as given in 17.26.

17.28.   The problem statement is the same as in 17.26 except carrying costs are $5 per pair. Answer parts (a), (b), (c), and (d) as given in 17.26.

17.29. Under what conditions might the use of the EOQ to determine the amount to order be inappropriate? Explain.

17.30. What research technique(s) would be appropriate for getting information from customers concerning the levels of service that might cause reprisals? Explain.

17.31. Why should the level of the safety stock fluctuate much less than the level of the working and lead-time stocks?

17.32. Where do you believe the responsibility for physical distribution activities should be located in the organization of the firm? Why?

17.33. It has been stated that "computers have been more widely used in the physical distribution of products than in any other area of marketing." Can you think of another area of marketing in which computers might be used more? Explain.

PROJECTS

17.34. Interview three local retail store managers to determine what the channels of distribution are for the products they handle.

17.35. (To be done in conjunction with question 17.20.) Interview the managers of three local minicomputer stores to determine what the channels of distribution are for the products listed in question 17.20. Ask them for explanations of any differences between the actual channels and your answers for question 17.20.

17.36. Interview the person in charge of inventories in each of three local manufacturing firms to determine how he or she determines the level of working, lead-time, and safety stocks for each product manufactured.

17.37. Interview the person in charge of inventories for dry groceries in each of three local supermarkets to determine how he or she determines the level of working, lead-time, and safety stocks for a typical product carried.

Endnotes

[1] This reference is used only to illustrate how widespread the use of marketing channels is, and not to condone their use in marketing illegal products. Washington (AP), February 18, 1972.

[2] *New York Post*, May 1, 1981, 59.

[3] IBM sold the last of its retail stores in 1986. "IBM's 84 Retail Stores Sold to Nynex," *New York Times*, April 23, 1986, D1, D2.

[4] This strategy is sometimes known as *distribution programming*. For a discussion of the partnership/distribution programming approach, see J. A. Narus and J. C. Anderson, "Turn Your Industrial Distributors into Partners," *Harvard Business Review*, March–April 1986, 66–71; and B. C. McCammon, Jr., "Perspectives for Distribution Programming," in *Vertical Marketing Systems*, L. P. Bucklin (ed.), Scott-Foresman, 1970, 32–45.

[5] Narus and Anderson, "Turn Your Industrial Distributors," 70.

[6] P. Kotler, *Principles of Marketing*, 3rd ed., Prentice-Hall, 1986, 419.

[7] M. Kacker, "Wholesaling Ignored Despite Modernization," *Marketing News*, February 15, 1986, 35.

[8] These data are for a sample of more than 1,000 wholesalers and 1,000 retailers in 10 different industries and are taken from *1986–87 Industry Norms and Key Business Ratios*, Dun & Bradstreet Credit Services, 1987.

[9] H. N. Shycon and C. R. Sprague, "Put a Price Tag on Your Customer Servicing Levels," *Harvard Business Review*, July–August 1975, 76.

[10] Ibid.

[11] Ibid.

[12] D. Hutchins, "Having a Hard Time," *Fortune*, June 9, 1986, 64.

[13] "Distributors Bow to Demands of 'Just-in-Time' Delivery," *The Wall Street Journal*, June 30, 1986, 25.

[14] Hutchins, "Having a Hard Time," 64.

[15] W. Blanding, "How Physical Distribution Helps Sales," *Sales Management*, August 19, 1974, 36.

[16] D. S. Tull and D. I. Hawkins, *Marketing Research: Method and Measurement*, 4th ed., Macmillan, 1987, 676–678.

[17] See, for example, A. A. Keuhn and M. J. Hamburger, "A Heuristic Program for Locating Warehouses," *Management Science*, Vol. 9, 1963, 643–666; H. N. Shycon and R. B. Maffei, "Simulation—Tool for Better Distribution," *Harvard Business Review*, Vol. 10, May 1967, 65–75; D. J. Bowersox, "Planning Physical Distribution Operations with Dynamic Simulation," *Journal of Marketing*, January 1972, 17–25; M. M. Connors, C. Coray, C. J. Cuccaro, W. K. Green, D. W. Low, and H. M. Markowitz, "The Distribution System Simulator," *Management Science*, 1972, B425–B453; and A. M. Geoffrion, "Better Distribution Planning with Computer Models," *Harvard Business Review*, July–August 1976, 92–99.

[18] For a description of how such a program works, see C. M. Guelzo, *Introduction to Logistics Management*, Prentice-Hall, 1986, 81–83.

CHAPTER 18

RETAILING AND WHOLESALING MANAGEMENT

The traditional image of retailing and wholesaling has been that of stodgy, slow-moving businesses that held limited promise for the future. Their reputations were for paying low salaries and offering slow advancement, often on a seniority basis. College and university graduates honored these reputations by taking care during job searches to avoid both fields.

Whatever the justification may have been for such an image, it has been an unfair characterization since the early 1970s. Since that time, both fields have evolved into much more dynamic, faster-moving businesses in which competent young managers are paid well and are able to advance rapidly. Retailing management, in particular, has come to be recognized as a "young person's" field.[1]

What caused these two fields to undergo this kind of transformation? The major reason is the electronic computer. The more-progressive firms discovered that the electronic computer could help provide information on many of the problem areas in retailing and wholesaling, and permit managers to make better and more timely decisions. Their competitors soon found that they too had to turn to the computer if they wanted to stay competitive.

An illustration of the extent to which computers are being used by progressive managers in these two fields is the computerized information system described in Exhibit 18–1. It is being used by the management of a local super-

EXHIBIT **18-1**

Computerized Management Information System of a Local Supermarket Chain

Step 1: Raw data flow from stores and warehouses to a mainframe computer at chain headquarters. Included are sales records from checkout stands, data on product delivery schedules, employee work schedules, energy use, and the amount of time products spend in chain warehouses before they are shipped to stores.

Step 2: The data are processed to help make better decisions about what products to sell, how to display them, and how to make their storage and delivery more efficient. Headquarters can determine which brands in a product class make the most money, for example, and cut back on the least profitable ones. Or it can use computer-projected cost estimates to guage how profitable a new brand of the same product might be. The computer output can also suggest whether products

should be delivered directly to stores or go a central warehouse first.

Step 3: Headquarters sends its recommendations back to the store and to warehouse managers and their assistants. These instructions include detailed schematics of every shelf, showing the store manager where to display each of the 17,000 products sold. Prices are also recommended for some of the products.

Step 4: Headquarters also sells some of the data generated in Step 1 to manufacturers for use in product planning.

Source: Adapted from "At Today's Supermarket, the Computer Is Doing It All," *Business Week*, August 11, 1986, 64–65.

market chain and has improved its decision making—and return on equity—substantially.

In this chapter we examine the nature of retailing and wholesaling, the types of institutions that serve each, and the decisions that must be made in managing each of the two types of businesses.

RETAILING

The Nature of Retailing

Retailing includes

> all the activities directly related to selling goods or services to consumers for personal, nonbusiness use.

It doesn't matter if the sale is made by a clerk in Macy's, by the ticket clerk in a booth at the ballpark, through an order placed in a Sears' catalog, by a hot dog vendor on a street corner, by an Avon lady at the customer's home, or through a vending machine in a hotel lobby; it is a retail sale as long as it is sold to a consumer for personal use rather than to a buyer for business use. The sale can be made "at wholesale" at a manufacturer's outlet at the factory, or by a grocery wholesaler selling in case lots, and as long as the purchase is made for personal rather than business use, it is a retail sale.

Retailing is the largest single industry in the United States in terms of number of employees. Almost one person of every seven employed is in retailing.[2] (The ratio for wholesaling is about 1 person in 18.) Annual sales of retailers are subtantially greater than that of any single manufacturing or service industry in the United States with the exception of wholesaling. Total annual sales at retail are slightly more than one-half those at wholesale.[3] Wholesale sales are greater than retail sales because wholesalers sell to manufacturers as well as to retailers, and wholesalers sell to other wholesalers in trade channels in which more than one wholesaler is used ([food processor] → [food broker] → [merchant wholesaler] → [grocery stores], for example).

Types of Retailers

Retailers have been remarkably creative in the types of retailing establishments they have developed. In Colonial America the prevailing type of establishment selling products to consumers was the general store, but even then there were specialty stores (saddlery, boot, and candle shops, and hardware stores, for example) and itinerant peddlers. This beginning has evolved into the extensive array of retailing outlets existing today.

Every store and each direct sales, automatic vending, and selling-in-the-home organization differs in some respects from others. A natural and useful way in which to classify retailing units is by the *strategic choices* that have been made that account for the major characteristics of the operation.

A major set of strategic choices that must be made in retailing, as in all other marketing areas, relate to the mix variables of product, price, promotion, and place (distribution). In addition, the ownership or affiliation of the retailing unit plays a considerable strategic role in determining how the unit operates.

A classification using the major strategic choices relating to product line(s), price, promotion, place, and ownership or affiliation is given in Table 18–1.

Table 18–1   Retail Outlets Classified by Major Strategic Choices

Product: Product Line(s) Carried	Price: Relative Price Charged	Promotion: Nature of Customer Contact	Place: Location	Ownership/ Location

Less than a full line
  Specialty stores
  Convenience
    stores
  Single-line stores
  Supermarkets
Two lines
  Combination
    stores
Multiple-line
  Department
    stores
  Hypermarkets
Service
  establishments
	Low price
	  Box store
	  Warehouse store
	  Discount store
	  Catalog order
	Medium-price
	Prestige-price
		In-store
		Nonstore
		  Direct marketing
		  Mail, TV,
		    telephone
		In-home
		  Salesperson
		  Electronic
		    retailing
		Automatic vending
			Downtown
			Suburban
			  shopping center
			Neighborhood
			  shopping center
			Stand-alone
				Independent
				  stores
				Corporate chain
				Voluntary chain
				Franchise
				Consumer
				  cooperative

The Product Variable: Product Line(s) Carried

An important basis for classifying retail stores is the product line(s) sold. Clothing stores, computer stores, automobile dealerships, liquor stores, and supermarkets are examples of types of single-line stores. But meaningful classifications can also be made for outlets that carry less than a full line, called specialty stores (men's or women's apparel, computer stores) and convenience stores (rapid-turnover grocery items); two lines, known as combination stores (groceries and drugs); and those that carry multiple lines, department stores and hypermarkets. Service establishments are, as the name indicates, shops that provide services to consumers (restaurants, hotels, appliance repair).

Each of these types of stores is described briefly below:

Specialty stores. Specialty stores carry less than a full line of products but offer a wide choice in terms of model, size, style, color, and other important attributes in the assortment carried. They are usually located in central business districts and shopping centers. Examples of specialty stores are those operated by Computerland, Thom McAn shoes, Ross apparel stores, and Brentano bookstores.

Convenience stores. Convenience stores carry a limited line of rapid-turnover food, beverage, and drug items. In addition, many of them have gasoline pumps. They stay open long hours, have neighborhood locations, and cater to neighborhood and drive-in customers who need fill-in merchandise or a snack. They charge higher prices and so have substantially higher margins than do supermarkets (although the margins have been reduced from their once higher levels).[4] The principal convenience store chains in the United States are 7-Eleven, Circle-K, National Convenience Stores, and Arco.

Supermarkets. A supermarket is defined by the Food Marketing Institute as a "self-service food store with grocery, meat, and produce departments, and minimum annual sales of $2 million."[5] Supermarkets typically carry an assortment of 15,000 to 17,000 food, drug sundry, and convenience items (women's hosiery, cosmetics, and so forth). There has been a trend over the years for supermarkets to increase in size. The average supermarket is now approaching 20,000 square feet—almost one-half acre—in size. Safeway and Kroger's are examples of U.S. chains of supermarkets.

Combination stores. A combination store has both a supermarket and a full-line drugstore with a common checkout area. This merging of lines results in some scale economies with respect to management, building, energy, and labor (particularly checkout labor) costs. The two lines also complement each other well since the supermarket half of the business generates substantially greater traffic for the drug store half than would a free-standing drug store, whereas drug items have substantially higher margins than do food items.[6]

Department stores. A department store is a large retail outlet that handles a variety of lines of products, has wide assortments in each, and is organized into separate departments for purposes of buying, promotion, service, and control.[7] In recent years, department stores have begun to organize their departments as specialty stores to compete more successfully with that type of store.[8] There are several large department store chains including the May Company, Dayton-Hudson, R. H. Macy, and Federated. The stores of Sears, J. C. Penney, and K-Mart also fall within the department store definition given at the beginning of this section. They are sometimes called mass-merchandising department stores to distinguish them from the more-traditional department stores.

Hypermarkets. The hypermarket combines the supermarket, department store, and specialty and service shops in one oversize, single-level store. Hypermarkets originated in France in the 1960s, spread throughout Europe, and have since been introduced (and reintroduced) in the United States. (They were originally tried in the United States in the early 1970s and had, at best, a lukewarm reception. In the mid 1980s they began to be introduced again, this time with more (apparent) success.[9] The typical hypermarket is more than 10 times the size of the average supermarket (but a quarter or more of the space in the typical hypermarket is devoted to food), has all the departments of the traditional department store, and has specialty shops along a mini-mall. A restaurant and service shops (shoe repair plus others) are also usually located on the mall. It may have 40 or more checkout lanes.[10]

Service establishments. Service establishments provide educational services (universities, vocational schools), food and lodging (restaurants, hotels), legal advice (lawyers' offices), health care (hospitals, dentists), personal care (beauty shops, dry cleaning, laundries), repairs (shoes, appliances, automobiles), financial services (banks, brokerage offices), and the like.

The economic importance of service establishments in the United States is indicated by the fact that they employ more persons and originate a higher percentage of national income than wholesaling and other retailing establishments combined. (They employ almost 21 million persons compared with about 20 million for wholesaling and other retail establishments, and they originate approximately 16 percent of national income as opposed to about 15 percent for wholesale and retail middlemen.)[11]

The Price Variable: Price Lines Carried

The types of outlets using a price appeal as the principal element of strategy include box stores, warehouse stores, full-line discount stores, and retail catalog showrooms:

Box stores. Box stores, also called limited-line or limited-item stores, were introduced into the United States from Germany in the mid 1970s. Box stores carry only fast-turnover, staple grocery products (normally no more than 600–1,000 items). They usually have only one brand and one size per item, with stockouts and changes in brands occurring often. Products are displayed in cut cartons, customers do their own bagging, there is little or no advertising, and store hours are limited. Individual items are not priced, there is no check cashing, and credit cards are not honored. Operating costs are very low, running in the range of 6 to 8 percent of sales. Reflecting these costs, prices are the lowest in the grocery field.

Warehouse stores. A warehouse store operates much like a box store, but on a larger scale. It may carry as many as 8,000 products, including vegetables, meats, dairy products, and frozen foods. They operate on gross margins of 11 to 13 percent of sales, compared with the average of 21 to 22 percent for supermarkets.

A central operating principle of both box and warehouse stores is to obtain a high rate of stock turnover. Because of the types of merchandise they carry, their low prices (which encourage consumers to buy in larger quantities), and a policy of buying for "just-in-time" delivery, both types of stores have substantially higher average rates of stock turnover than do supermarkets.

Full-line discount stores. The typical full-line discount store carries lines of products comparable to those of a department store, although they are lower in price. The discount store generally has less-expensive locations, buildings, and fixtures; has a smaller number of sales clerks for a given amount of sales; and provides fewer other services than does the average department store. National-branded merchandise, priced low and advertised heavily, is its primary patronage appeal. Perhaps the prototype of the successful full-line discount store is a K-Mart outlet.

Retail catalog showrooms. Retail catalog showrooms have a customer area with catalogs and desks for the customer to use in making out an order. Once the order is made out, it is given to a sales clerk for checking, and then to a stock clerk for filling. Repeat customers may be sent a catalog, so they can make out the order at home. Unlike ordering by mail from a catalog, however, the merchandise can be obtained only by picking it up at the showroom.

The products carried in a retail catalog showroom are typically nationally branded, high-markup items on which prices can be compared easily, and for which they can be reduced appreciably given low operating costs. Four lines of these products—jewelry (including watches), housewares, electronics, and gifts—account for about 70 percent of catalog showroom business.[12]

The Promotion Variable: Nature of Customer Contact

Thus far we have considered only types of retailers who operate stores the customer must go to in order to make a purchase. There are other types of retailers who contact the customer and make the sale at a place other than a conventional retail store. Although in the generic sense this is known as *nonstore* retailing, the popular term for it is *direct marketing*. Customer contact at locations other than a retail store can be made through any communications medium—in person, by telephone, by mail, by package inserts, or through the electronic media of radio, television, and, more recently, the home computer. Merchandise can be displayed and sold through vending machines and electronic kiosks. A *direct marketer* is an organization that uses one or more of these media to promote and to sell products.

About one of every seven dollars of retail sales in 1987 in the United States was made by direct marketers. By order of importance in terms of sales, direct marketing by telephone is first, followed by mail (catalogs and direct mail), print and electronic media, vending machines, and in-home sales.[13] Multiple-media campaigns are not unusual (see box).

> Citicorp, a New York bank, decided to market a program of second-mortgage loans on homes. As a means of generating prospect lists and obtaining applications, it tested four different direct marketing campaigns. The first consisted of a direct mail piece containing an application and a self-addressed return envelope. The second consisted of the same basic direct mail package but included a toll-free number and an invitation for the person to call to ask questions or to have the application completed over the telephone. The third campaign tested used the same direct mail package plus a business-reply coupon asking for more information. People who sent in the coupon received a telephone call. The fourth test campaign was the same as the third, with newspaper ads containing a toll-free number added.
>
> The best results were from test campaigns three and four. The bank management decided to use campaign four because, even though it cost slightly more than campaign three, it generated 15 percent more loans.

Source: Adapted from E. Roman, "Telemarketing Rings in New Business Era," *Advertising Age*, January 27, 1986, 50.

The nature of the major direct marketing methods is as follows:

Marketing by telephone (telemarketing). The first major sales campaign incorporating telephones (20 million households were called) was conducted by the Ford Motor Company in 1962. Selling by telephone has expanded greatly in both extent of use and degree of sophistication since then. It is used in both industrial and consumer marketing programs. In industrial marketing, the telephone call is used essentially as a substitute for a sales call at the customer's place of business. In consumer marketing, in-store retailing is replaced by direct contact with the customer via telephone. The consumer's number may have been obtained from a list broker furnishing a list screened by area to reflect average household income. The call may have been dialed by a computer and the sales message presented by a telephone salesperson operating from a market-tested script but trained to answer questions and objections. The order is taken and the product shipped directly to the customer.

The question of the telephone subscriber's right to privacy arises with the increasing use of telephone selling. Twenty-six states already regulate the use of automated telephone equipment in telemarketing.[14] So-called asterisk laws—laws that would make it illegal to place sales calls to telephone subscribers who have an identifying mark by their telephone book listing—also are being considered by several states.

Marketing by mail. Two major forms of retailing by mail are used, catalogs and direct mail. Each year an estimated 8 to 10 billion catalogs are sent to U.S. consumers—100 to 125 per household.[15] They are sent by catalog retailers offering products in such categories as general merchandise (Sears [although Sears may break up its general merchandise catalog into a series of specialty catalogs],[16] J. C. Penney), ready-to-wear (Avon Fashions, Brooks Brothers), and sporting goods (L. L. Bean, Eddie Bauer). And the number of catalogs distributed is small in comparison to the direct mail pieces sent out. Direct mail is used by companies offering such products and services as collectibles (Franklin Mint), encyclopedias (World Book), and insurance (Colonial Penn). Automobiles were once sold by mail,[17] and today one can order Christmas trees[18] and hamburgers[19] by mail.

Marketing through the electronic and print media. Direct-response ads, either soliciting a coupon return for further information or an order directly, have long appeared in newspapers and magazines. More recently, they have appeared with increasing frequency on television and radio. The advertisement generally includes a toll-free (800) number to call. The product advertised can be bought and paid for by giving a credit card number over the telephone. The potentially most significant development in recent media retailing, however, is a 24-hour-per-day U.S. cable network devoted exclusively to selling products. The merchandise sold ranges from costume jewelry to expensive electronics, and usually is bought at closeout prices. Prices are generally substantially lower than those for the merchandise at more conventional outlets.[20]

Vending machines. The first known vending machine dispensed holy water for a five-drachma coin in Egyptian temples about 215 B.C. And machines in the United States provided cigars and candy before the turn of this century. About $1 of each $100 of retail sales in the United States each year is made by the 4.5 million or so vending machines. In order of total sales made, the major products sold through vending machines are cold drinks (canned, bottled, and in cups), cigarettes, candy and snacks, and newspapers. About one-third of all sales are made in factories and office buildings (a panty hose marketer has begun test marketing its products through vending machines in dining rooms of law and accounting offices),[21] and in institutions such as hospitals and colleges and universities.

Vending machines are increasingly being used for dispensing services as well as products. The automatic teller machines (ATMs) in banks have been emulated by airlines and ski areas selling tickets to credit card customers through self-service computer terminals, and by car-rental companies having self-service computerized return programs. (Automatic teller machines have not been as successful in reducing human teller lines as bankers expected, however.)[22] Similar machines are used for a variety of other services, and electronic kiosks sell merchandise through video catalogs.

> **In-home marketing.** This method of retailing has not only survived from the itinerant peddler of Colonial times but, until the past few years at least, has continued to grow while doing so. One estimate is that as many as 5 million persons were engaged in direct-to-home selling in 1983.[23]

The number of direct-to-home sales representatives very likely has declined in recent years, however. The typical salesperson is a woman, often a housewife, who works part time. In a period of economic recovery, such as the early to mid 1980s, the opportunities for part-time work multiply. Many heads of household who were unemployed during a recession also go back to work as economic times improve, making a part-time income in the family less important. The result is that the ability to recruit new sales representatives by direct-to-home marketers falls off, and turnover increases. The sales forces of Avon, Mary Kay, Amway, and other large direct-to-home marketers all declined during the most recent upturn.[24]

The principal products sold in customers' homes are cosmetics (Avon, Mary Kay), encyclopedias (Encyclopedia Britannica, World Book), vacuum cleaners (Kirby, Electrolux), vitamins and health foods (Shaklee), and plastic dishes and food containers (Tupperware).

The Advantages and Disadvantages of Direct Marketing: Marketing directly through use of the telephone, mail, electronic and print media, and in-home selling has several advantages compared with in-store retailing, including:

- Direct marketing offers the ability to focus marketing efforts much more effectively in terms of selling to the target markets selected.
- It has the ability to contact prospective customers directly rather than waiting for them to appear in the store.
- It is a more convenient way for the customer to buy.
- It is frequently a lower-cost way of doing business (although not always) than through a conventional retail store.
- Conventional retailers can use direct marketing methods as a complement to in-store retailing to cultivate market segments they could not otherwise reach.
- It requires less capital to go into business.

There are, of course, disadvantages to direct marketing as well, including:

- There is a general aura of suspicion attached to direct marketers and their claims until they become well known and established that is not encountered by conventional retailers (or at least not experienced to the degree that it is by direct marketers).

- Direct marketing methods are generally intrusive on consumer privacy. Excessive intrusiveness has led to legislation regulating and restricting door-to-door selling, preventing the use of automatic devices in making telephone calls for the purpose of selling products or soliciting funds, and prohibiting the disclosure of personal financial information by creditors to the developers of telephone and mailing lists.
- Except for direct-to-home marketing, merchandise cannot be inspected prior to purchase.
- Because the purchaser cannot inspect the merchandise, liberal return policies are required.
- Some forms of direct marketing (notably direct-to-home marketing) are relatively expensive.

The Place Variable: Location of the Retail Outlet

The basic kinds of locations for retail stores are central business district, planned shopping center, neighborhood business district, string street, and stand-alone. For most types of stores (classified by type(s) of product line carried), two or more of these kinds of retail areas are viable possibilities. Table 18–2 shows typical locations by retail area for various types of stores.

Once the retail area is chosen, a specific location within it has to be selected. Many considerations enter into this decision—they include the availability of store locations, rental or building costs, location of complementary stores, location of competitive stores, parking availability, and traffic patterns.[25]

Table 18–2 Typical Locations for Stores Classified by Line(s) of Products Carried

Location	Potential for Customer Access	Typical Mix of Stores
Central business districts, large neighborhood business districts and suburban shopping centers	Easy access by public transportation and automobile, easy parking, sizable potential for walk-in customers	Stores with shopping goods (department stores, specialty stores), some service establishments (medical and dental offices, restaurants, banks)
Smaller neighborhood business districts and suburban shopping centers, string streets	Easy access by public transportation and automobile, potential for neighborhood walk-in trade	Some specialty stores (furniture, clothing, electronics and appliances, automobile dealers), supermarkets, stores with convenience items (variety stores, hardware stores, drug stores), many service establishments (cleaners, bank branch offices, medical and dental offices, insurance offices)
Stand-alone locations	Potential for large amount of space, good access by public transportation and automobile, neighborhood walk-in trade	Convenience stores, supermarkets, combination stores, some department stores, hypermarkets, some automobile dealerships and discount stores, nurseries, some service establishments (motels, restaurants)

Retail Outlets Classified by Ownership and Affiliation: There are a variety of ownership and affiliation arrangements in the retail field. The most important of these are independents, corporate chains (including franchise chains), voluntary chains, and consumer cooperatives.

Independents have no affiliation with other organizations directly involved in retailing. Independent retailers who own one outlet and are not affiliated with any other business organization involved in the retail field make up by far the largest number of retailers in the United States. They are mostly small in size and are owner-operated, and they have the advantages of more personalized relationships with customers and greater flexibility in operations than do large, multi-unit retailers. They have the disadvantages of low buying power and consequent higher costs of merchandise, plus higher operating costs as a percentage of sales than larger competitors. This generally means that the prices of independents are higher than those of multi-unit retail outlets carrying the same lines.

Corporate chains. A corporate chain is a multi-unit retailing organization under common ownership with centralized management, purchasing, and warehousing of products. Chain store units are much larger in size on the average than are independent stores. The advantages and disadvantage of corporate chains versus those of independent retailers are largely reversed. Corporate chains tend to be more impersonal in customer relations and are not as flexible in buying for local market segments as independents. However, they are able to buy at lower prices and operate with greater efficiency and, as a consequence, sell at lower prices than their independent counterparts. Price is apparently more important than personality; multi-unit retailers have increased their overall share of retail sales in the United States in recent years until they now have more sales than do independents and voluntary chains combined.[26] Examples of corporate chains include Safeway and Kroger's supermarkets, Dayton-Hudson and R. H. Macy department stores, and Sears and K-Mart mass-merchandise stores.

The large corporate chains have now become powerful enough to ask for payment for stocking new products.

In New York, Shop Rite Stores asked for $86,000 to stock $172,000 worth of Old Capital microwave popcorn, then tossed the brand out six weeks later when it didn't sell well. Curtice-Burns, Inc. has to pay $1 million up front to chains across the nation just to get shelf space for some of its $1.79-a-can pie fillings. And in New England, a supermarket chain asked Pillsbury Co. for more money to stock a new brownie than Pillsbury had budgeted for the product's introduction in the entire country.*

*Supermarkets Demand Food Firm's Payments Just to Get on the Shelf," *The Wall Street Journal*, November 1, 1988, A1.

Franchises. Franchising involves a contractual agreement in which the franchisee is granted the right to engage in offering, selling, or distributing goods or services under a marketing plan prescribed in substantial part by the franchisor and using the franchisor's identifying trademark or tradename.[27] Franchise chains in the United States started in 1851 when the Singer Sewing Machine Company set up a chain of sewing machine dealers. Franchising has expanded rapidly since then, and now generates about one-third of all retail sales in the United States.

The bulk of the capital necessary for opening an outlet is put up by the franchisee. (See Exhibit 18–2 for the cost to the franchisee to start a new franchise for some well-known companies.) In addition, once the franchise has attained a specified sales volume, the operator pays a royalty fee to the franchisor, ranging from as little as 2 to as much as 10 percent of sales, and often a fee for corporate advertising as well. (The royalty fee for Kentucky Fried Chicken franchises is 3 percent, with an added 1.5 percent for advertising, for example.) In return, the franchisor usually provides training, an operations manual, promotional assistance, a known tradename, and a defined trade territory.

Voluntary chains. As a means of competing with corporate chains, some independents have joined in organizations called voluntary chains. Some of these organizations are sponsored by wholesalers and others are organized and operated by the member retailers (sometimes called cooperative chains). In both types of chains, joint purchasing and common merchandising and advertising programs are carried out. Examples of the wholesaler-sponsored voluntary

EXHIBIT **18-2**

Buying in—The Average Amount Required by a Franchisee to Start a New Franchise*

Franchisor	Type of Business	Investment Required
AAMCO Transmissions	Car transmission service shops	$101,000
Athlete's Foot Marketing Associates	Athletic shoe and clothing shops	$107,500 to 157,500
Baskin-Robbins	Ice cream stores	$50,000
Dunkin' Donuts	Doughnut shops	$45,000 to 58,000
Entre Computer Centers	Computer stores	$125,000
Godfather's Pizza	Pizza parlors	$200,000 to 285,000
McDonald's	Hamburger restaurants	$300,000 to 360,000
Moto Photo	One-hour film-processing labs	$160,000
Pier 1 Imports	Gift and home furnishings stores	$100,000 to 130,000
Southland Corp.	7–Eleven convenience markets	$37,075

*Does not include real estate costs.
Source: *The Wall Street Journal*, May 19, 1986, 14D.

chain include the ACE hardware and IGA food stores. The retailer-sponsored chains include True Value hardware stores and Associated Grocers food stores.

Consumer cooperatives. Consumer cooperatives are retail stores (usually food stores) that are owned by their customers. They are founded when consumers are dissatisfied with the price or the quality of products offered by existing retailers. The consumers contribute the start-up capital required by buying shares in the cooperative. They usually hire professional managers to operate the stores in accordance with policies established through the vote of the owners.

Cooperatives have not been as successful in the United States as they have been in Europe. One reason for foods is that it is difficult to provide lower-priced or higher-quality products than the national chains with their volume buying and low profit margins (from 1 to 2 percent of sales).

Managing a Retailing Operation

The principal marketing decision areas in retailing are the target market, location, assortment of products and services, inventories, departmental layout and product shelf location, price, promotion, and method of control. With the exception of layout and product shelf location, decision making in each of these areas is not unique to retailing. The principles involved in making inventory, price, promotion, and control decisions in retailing are substantially the same as for types of businesses, and so do not need to be discussed again here. Because retailing has unique problems associated with selecting target markets and making decisions about location, product and service assortment, and layout and product shelf location, they are discussed in this section.

The Target Market

The first and, very likely, most important decision in setting up a retailing operation is who will make up the *target market*. What makes this probably the most important management decision is that it will be a primary deter-

FIGURE 18-1
The principal decision areas in retailing and their effects on sales, costs, and operating profits.

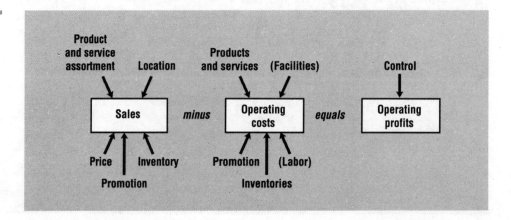

minant of the store's sales potential, as well as being central to the location, product assortment, service level, pricing, and promotion operating decisions. If a children's clothing store is to be opened, for example, and the target market is to be the parents of middle- and upper-income families with children ages three to nine, the product assortment, the quality level, the services provided (the policies on alterations, delivery, and returns, for example), the pricing, and the promotion for the store almost certainly will be different than if the target market were to be lower-income families. The location of the store is likely to be affected as well.

The choice of an appropriate target market can be aided substantially by market research. Demographic data on populations by area down to the census tract or zip code level are available from U.S. Bureau of the Census data. Many services that provide these and other data on floppie disks are available commercially.[28] And a determination of the number and quality of competitors already serving one or more candidate target markets in an area of interest can be done quickly and inexpensively through the Yellow Pages and store visits.

Location

There is a saying among retailers that three factors are critical to success: "location, location, and location."

Locating a retail store involves two sequential decisions—deciding first on the trading area and then selecting the specific site within it. Making the first of these decisions involves a **trading area analysis**. This requires, for each of the candidate areas, an evaluation of the following factors:

1. *POPULATION SIZE AND CHARACTERISTICS.* Does the area have a population of sufficient size with the desired characteristics to meet the target market requirements? (For example, Toys "R" Us requires a market area of at least 250,000 people, of which 25 to 28 percent must be children.)
2. *ECONOMIC BASE.* Is the economy diversified, relatively free from seasonal and cyclical fluctuations, and likely to grow?
3. *COMPETITION.* Do the number and quality of the competing stores currently in the area allow for one or more new stores to enter successfully? (Many chain retailers will not enter a trading area unless it can support multiple stores because of economies in distribution and advertising.)
4. *LABOR.* Is an adequate labor pool available at affordable wage rates?
5. *AVAILABILITY OF STORE LOCATIONS.* Are there acceptable store sites available for leasing or owning (whichever is required) at affordable prices?
6. *LOCAL REGULATIONS.* Are the levels of licensing costs and taxes acceptable?

Once a trading area is chosen, a specific site within it has to be selected. This involves an evaluation of the following factors for each alternative being considered:

1. *PARKING.* Are the number and location of parking spaces within an acceptable distance from the store adequate for both customers and employees?

2. *TRANSPORTATION.* Is adequate mass transportation to the site available? Is there acceptable access from major thoroughfares and freeways? Can deliveries be made easily?
3. *FOOT TRAFFIC.* Is the foot traffic of the appropriate type of people at the site large enough?
4. *VEHICULAR TRAFFIC.* Is there an adequate number of vehicles of the appropriate kind at the site? Is there traffic congestion?
5. *STORE COMPOSITION.* Is the mix of stores near the site complementary? Are competitive stores located an appropriate distance away?
6. *THE SITE ITSELF.* Is the site visible? Is the building of the proper size, configuration, and condition?
7. *OCCUPANCY TERMS.* Are the leasing or purchasing costs affordable? Are there restrictive operating regulations involved (hours, required contribution to a common advertising fund, required participation in sales, and so forth)?

Obtaining and evaluating the data required for both the trading area analysis and specific site evaluation are made much easier by reference to soundly written texts on retailing. They provide both an elaboration of each of the factors (example: a way of defining an "appropriate person" to be included in a count of foot traffic is a person carrying a shopping bag) and references to the sources of the secondary data required.[29]

Assortment of Products Carried and Services Provided

The quality of the merchandise lines carried and the level of service provided generally go hand-in-hand. Both are largely determined by the choice of target market. If high-income, upscale consumers are targeted, quality merchandise with a high level of services (liberal return policy, alterations, delivery) is required to meet their expectations. If low-income consumers are the market segment sought, lower-quality products with few services are indicated.

Deciding on the assortment of products carried within the line(s) is not this straightforward, however. Assortments can be either *wide* or *narrow*—many or few product categories carried—and *deep* or *shallow*—large or limited assortments with each category. In combination, this results in four assortment strategies: wide and deep, wide and shallow, narrow and deep, and narrow and shallow. The advantages and disadvantages of each of these strategies are given in Table 18–3.

The assortment decision may be constrained by either financial or space considerations, or both. It obviously is more costly to carry a "wide and deep" than a "narrow and shallow" assortment. And, just as obviously, the wide and deep assortment will require substantially more space. Width or depth may have to be curtailed because of these considerations.

Departmental Layout and Product Shelf Location

What kind of a traffic pattern should the store have?

Where in the pattern should high-profit and low-profit items be located?

How much space should be allocated to each product category?

Where in the traffic pattern should preplanned purchase items be placed? impulse items be located?

Table 18–3   Product Assortment Alternatives

Advantages	Disadvantages
Wide and deep (many product categories, large assortment in each)	
Broad market	High inventory investment
Full stocking of products	Unfocused image
High level of traffic	Many items have low turnover
Customer loyalty	Merchandise ages, becomes obsolete
One-stop shopping	
No disappointed customers	
Wide and shallow (many product categories, limited assortment in each)	
Broad market	Limited variety
High level of traffic	Disappointed customers
Emphasis on convenience customers	Weak image
Less costly than wide and deep	Many items have low turnover
One-stop shopping	Reduced loyalty
Narrow and deep (few product categories, large assortment in each)	
Specialist image	Limited variety
Full stock in the product category(ies)	Limited market
Customer loyalty	Limited traffic
No disappointed customers	
Less costly than wide and deep	
Narrow and shallow (few product categories, limited assortment in each)	
Aimed at convenience customers	Limited variety and traffic
Least costly	Disappointed customers
High turnover	Weak image
	Reduced loyalty

Source: Adapted from B. Berman and J. R. Evans, *Retail Management: A Strategic Approach*, 3rd ed., Macmillan, 1986, 295. Used with permission.

Which shelf space locations should be used for high-profit items? low-profit items?

These are only a few of the questions that need to be answered in designing the layout for a retail store. A poorly designed layout, both in the location of departments and in the location of products within them, can be costly in terms of lost sales. A bad layout can shunt customers past departments in which purchases would otherwise have been made, and place low-profit items in store and shelf locations that should have high-profit items.

How are the appropriate in-store and shelf locations for products to be determined? There are three sources of information that can be used for making them: conventional wisdom, customer traffic studies, and in-store location experiments.

Conventional Wisdom on Store and Shelf Location for Products: The accumulated experience of retailing professionals concerning store layout in general and the location of specific departments in particular is valuable because it reflects what retailers have found works—and doesn't work—in overall layout patterns, allocation of shelf space, store location of product categories, and shelf location of products.

▪ *LAYOUT PATTERNS.* There are two general patterns of layouts for stores, grid and free-flow. The **grid pattern** is the one used by virtually all supermarkets and drug stores. It has straight primary aisles with narrower secondary aisles intersecting at right angles. The ***free-flow pattern*** tends to be used by department and specialty stores. It has curved primary aisles (often arranged in a rough, concentric fashion) on which the major departments are located. Secondary aisles lead into and through the departments.

The two are used for different purposes. The grid pattern is designed for efficient, self-service shopping for largely preplanned purchases. The free-flow pattern is used for shopping situations in which the customer would like to browse, and receive help from a salesperson when required. The grid reduces losses from shoplifting but results in less impulse buying, compared with the free-flow layout.

▪ *ALLOCATION OF FLOOR SPACE.* There are two general methods for allocating store space by department, the model-stock and the sales-productivity ratio. The ***model-stock approach*** allocates space based on the depth of the assortment; the retail manager first decides with what depth the product category will be carried and then assigns the space necessary for that assortment level. In the ***sales-productivity ratio approach***, space is allocated proportionally to the sales or profit contribution per square foot.

The differences in the two are more of timing and style than of substance. The two approach the same objective—profit—in different ways. The model-stock method requires the retail manager, in effect, to decide on the most profitable assortment level given the square footage required. The sales-productivity ratio method specifies the space required, and thus the assortment level, given the profit per square foot.

▪ *IN-STORE LOCATION OF PRODUCT CATEGORIES.* The conventional decision rules for locating departments within the store are to (a) place the highest profit departments in the areas with the highest traffic flows, (b) group the departments by either level of purchase motivation or market segment, and (c) place necessary items or services at the back or on the top floor of the store. The reason for the matching of profitability and traffic flow levels is obvious. The logic of grouping departments by level of purchase motivation (impulse items near the front of the first floor of a department store, for example) is also apparent. Grouping all the departments carrying products appealing to teens, or to affluent women, also makes obvious good sense. Supermarkets generally have dairy products at the rear of the store, and department stores have cafeterias and credit offices on the top floor, in accordance with the "put the necessary items or services at the back or top floor of the store" rule.

▪ *SHELF LOCATION OF PRODUCTS.* The decision rule generally used with respect to shelf location is to *place the most profitable products at the most visible locations*—at eye level, at the end of the aisle, and at the checkout counter. There is a growing practice in food marketing for manufacturers to pay the store for high-visibility locations for displaying their products. In this case, the fee paid represents a part of the product's profit to the store, and so affects the shelf-location decision in accordance with the rule.

▪ *CUSTOMER TRAFFIC STUDIES.* Figures 18–2a and b show the before and after traffic studies and purchases made in a produce department in a supermarket. The *x*'s on the diagrams indicate purchases made. An inspection of Figure 18–2a indicates that traffic is concentrated on the more popular, salad-type vegetables,

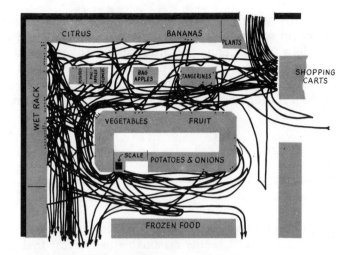

FIGURE 18-2a
Traffic pattern and purchases in a supermarket produce department before relocation of salad vegetables.

Source: Food Marketing Institute, *Store Managers' Guide 156, Customer Traffic Studies.* May 1966, 4.

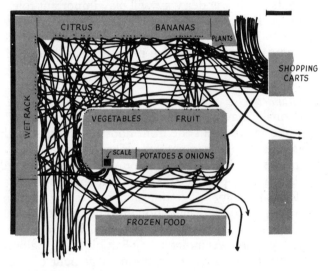

FIGURE 18-2b
Traffic pattern and purchases in a supermarket produce department after relocation of salad vegetables.

Source: Food Marketing Institute, *Store Managers' Guide 156, Customer Traffic Studies.* May 1966, 4.

and that these vegetables are grouped at one end of the rack. Interspersing the salad vegetables with others on the rack therefore might spread out the traffic and increase sales of the other vegetables and melons. Figure 18–2b shows the traffic pattern and purchases that resulted from such a change. Overall sales did increase appreciably after the relocation of the salad vegetables.

Traffic flow studies are not difficult to conduct, nor are they expensive. And as the example indicates, they may result in reducing congestion and increasing sales. (For a description of how to conduct a traffic study, see minicase IV-10, "Traffic Flow in a Supermarket," at the end of this section.)

▪ *IN-STORE LOCATION EXPERIMENTS.* You may remember from Exhibit 18–1 that the staff at the headquarters of the local supermarket "sends its recommendations back to the store and to warehouse managers and their assistants. These instructions include detailed schematics of every shelf, showing the store manager where to display each of the 17,000 products sold." These recommendations are based in part on the kinds of location decision rules described earlier, and in part on in-store experiments.

With stores that are equipped to obtain data from universal product code checkout scanning, in-store location experiments are easy to conduct. For example, a simple before and after experiment can be run by obtaining sales data for a given period for two products in their present locations, switching the locations, and then obtaining sales data for the two products for a similar period. If a significant overall sales gain results, the actual location switch can be made.

The Future of Retailing

Retailing is such a dynamic field that forecasting future developments is a very risky endeavor. It seems reasonable to forecast that extensions of two developments already under way will play important roles in retailing in the future, however. Both are based on technology that is now available, but is almost certain to improve substantially through the next decade. These are the expanded use of operating data in decision making and the growth in electronic retailing.

Expanded Use of Operating Data in Decision Making: People in the trade traditionally have viewed retailing and wholesaling as "bring it in the back door and move it out the front door" businesses without much being known about what happens in between. The major problem in managing both of these businesses has been the large number of item–brand–size–style–flavor–color combinations (up to 100,000 for both large retailers and wholesalers) and the resulting difficulty of getting and processing demand and cost information quickly and economically enough to permit sound merchandising decisions.

This has changed with the advent of UPC checkout scanning and the electronic computer. As indicated by Exhibit 18–1, major inroads already have been made by this technology in the management of supermarkets. The first scan for checkout took place in a supermarket in 1974. As of the end of 1988, more than 16,000 supermarkets were equipped for checkout scanning, and it is in the early stages of adoption by department and specialty stores.[30] This automated system for recording purchases will allow inventory management by item, automatic computer reordering, and closer tracking of the sales effects of advertising, promotions, displays, and markdowns. And, in conjunction with software that has been developed to determine direct costs on a product-by-product basis, the contribution to profits and fixed costs by item can be determined routinely. (For a description of one such costing system, see p. 593.) Decisions on product lines carried, depth of assortment per line, and location in the store will be based on more data (and more reliable data) than ever before.[31]

Growth in Electronic Retailing: For the past decade, seers of the future in retailing have been forecasting that at-home buying through electronic catalogs displayed on television, and ordering by the home computer, would be commonplace in the "next five years." Although electronic kiosks have enjoyed a modest amount of success, electronic direct marketing to the home has largely been limited to ads for a single product (specialty items such as records, and books, magazines). The potential is there, however, and it seems reasonable to expect that electronic catalogs will replace a part of the print catalogs now being distributed each year.

WHOLESALING

The Nature of Wholesaling

Wholesalers are firms that sell to retailers, industrial users, or nonprofit institutions, but not to consumers.

Except when manufacturers sell direct (and thus perform their own wholesaling function), wholesalers act as intermediaries between the producer and the non-household buyer.

Wholesale sales average about 60 percent of the total sales of goods and services in the United States during an average year. About 1 of every 18 employed persons works for a wholesaling firm.

Types of Wholesalers

A variety of wholesalers have evolved in response to competitive pressures and the needs of differing industries. They can best be classified by the nature and extent of the functions they perform, and who owns and operates them.

The four major categories of wholesale middlemen are the full-function and limited-function wholesalers, the agent middlemen, and the manufacturer's sales offices and branches. The full- and limited-function wholesalers are independently owned and operated business firms, whereas the manufacturer's sales offices and branches are owned and operated by the manufacturer. Agent middlemen are independent business concerns, but work for the manufacturer (in all instances except for brokers, who sometimes represent the buyer). The major types of wholesalers that fall into each of these categories are:

Full-Function
Wholesalers

Merchant wholesaler. Handles consumer goods and sells to retailers and service firms. Takes title, carries inventory, and offers a full range of services to customers.

Industrial distributor. Performs the same functions as the merchant wholesaler, but in the industrial goods field. Sells to manufacturers and service firms.

Limited-Function Wholesalers

Drop shipper. Sells and takes title to products that are "drop shipped"—shipped directly from the manufacturer to the customer—rather than carried in inventory. Drop shippers operate in industries in which shipping costs make up a large percentage of the delivered costs of the products, such as building materials and coal.

Wagon distributor. Sells and makes deliveries from a truck (a wagon in earlier times, hence the name) at the time of the sale. Operates almost entirely in the food field handling perishable or semiperishable products such as fruits and vegetables, ice cream, potato chips, and candies.

Rack jobber. One or more rack jobbers supply most of the products found on display racks in supermarkets—paperback books, women's hosiery, sunglasses, and the like. The rack jobber keeps the racks stocked and charges the retailer only for the merchandise sold.

Cash and carry wholesaler. Performs as a merchant wholesaler or industrial distributor except does not extend credit or make delivery. Operates chiefly in nonperishable foods in consumer goods, and in industrial supplies in the industrial goods field.

Agent Middlemen

Broker. Negotiates sales by representing the seller (usually) or the buyer (occasionally). Brokers do not take title, carry inventory, or make delivery. They operate mostly in the food field.

Commission merchant. Operates primarily in agricultural product sales in central markets. Receives the products from the manufacturer or grower and sells them on a consignment basis, remitting the proceeds after deducting commission and costs of handling.

Manufacturer's agent. Has a contractual agreement with the manufacturer to sell its products in a given territory with an agreed-on rate of commission. Operates in both consumer and industrial product lines.

Sales agent. Agrees contractually to sell the entire output of the manufacturer. May help finance the principal as well. Sales agents are found chiefly in textiles, apparel, food, and some metal products.

Auction house. Holds auctions where products are displayed and sold for a commission. Are important in the wholesaling of used cars and in such agricultural products as tobacco and livestock.

Manufacturer's Sales Offices and Branches

Sales office. Owned and operated by the manufacturer, but physically separated from the plant. Does not carry inventory.

Sales branch. Same as a sales office, except carries inventory.

Table 18–4   Major Types of Wholesalers and the Functions They Perform

Wholesaler Type	Buys/Assembles	Carries Inventory	Handles Full Line
Full-function			
Merchant wholesaler	X*	X	X
Industrial distributor	X	X	X
Limited-function			
Drop shipper	O*	O	O
Wagon distributor	X	X	O
Rack jobbers	X	X	O
Cash and carry	X	X	X or O
Agent middlemen			
Broker	O	O	O
Commission merchant	O	O	O
Manufacturer's agent	O	O	X or O
Sales agent	O	O	O
Auction house	O	O	O
Wholesaler Type	**Takes Title**	**Sells**	**Delivers**
Manufacturers			
Sales office	O	O	X or O
Sales branch	O	X	X or O

*X indicates that the function is performed, O that it is not.

The full range of functions performed by each type of wholesaler is shown in Table 18–4.

Managing a Wholesaling Operation

The principal marketing decision areas in wholesaling are location, assortment of products and services, inventories, physical distribution, price, promotion, method of control, and relations with retailers. The last of these areas, relations with retailers, is the only one unique to wholesaling. The principles involved in making inventory, price, promotion, physical distribution, and control decisions in wholesaling are substantially the same as for other types of businesses, and so do not need to be discussed again here. Retailing has unique problems associated with making location and product and service assortment decisions, however, and so they, along with wholesaler–retailer relations, are discussed in this section.

Location

Locating a wholesaling establishment has essentially the same problems as locating a retail store, with one important addition. With in-store retailing, the sales clerk is in the store, and the customer comes there to make the purchase. For most retail purchases, delivery is not required. In wholesaling, the sales representative goes to the customer, and delivery is required for most sales. This means that the cost of selling and of delivery are much more affected by the weighted average customer-to-establishment distance in wholesaling than in retailing.

It therefore becomes important to try to minimize these costs by locating near the "center" of the wholesaler customer locations, where *center* is defined as the point that will give the lowest overall travel costs + shipping costs. A widely used model that does this for shipping costs (it does not take the travel costs of sales representative directly into account) for a single warehouse location is the so-called center-of-gravity model. It requires locating customers by coordinates on a grid, and estimating the average amount shipped to each annually. Given these data, the coordinates of the least-cost location can be estimated using simple weighted averaging procedures.[32]

Product Assortment and Services Provided

As in location, product assortment decisions for wholesalers are similar to those of retailers. Nevertheless, the services provided by wholesalers vary considerably from those provided by retailers. Some of them are services that we do not associate with traditional wholesaling.

An example of a nonwholesaling service is rack jobbers' providing the display racks and keeping them stocked in retail stores. In recent years the range and extent of nonwholesaling services being supplied by wholesalers have often been computer-based, and have increased. Some wholesalers now lease electronic ordering equipment to retailers, provide price labels, and offer shelf-management plans. Foremost-McKesson, a large drug wholesaler, has even begun acting as a middleman between drug stores and insurance offices by processing medical insurance claims.[33]

Such services add value to the wholesaler's role in the distribution channel. The wholesaler should provide them as long as they contribute to overall net profits, either directly by costing less than the retailer is charged for them or indirectly by increasing retailer patronage.

Wholesaler–Retailer Relations

An area of apparent increasing conflict between wholesalers and retailing is the slowness of retailers to pay, and the taking of unauthorized discounts when they do.

Important customers of suppliers have long been known to pay slowly, and to take the 2 percent discount on a 2/10/net 30 invoice, even if the payment is made 45 days later. The high interest rates of the early 1980s, and the consequent increased emphasis on money management by retailers to keep interest costs down, has brought about even greater aging of wholesaler accounts receivable, plus a tendency for some customers to deduct unauthorized allowances. When the wholesaler complains and tries to obtain reimbursement, a customer is sometimes lost. The incident in the box below is an example.

Aside from the loss in revenue in which such unauthorized deductions result, there is a question of the legality of allowing them. If discounts are not available on a proportionally equal basis to other retailers, the supplier is technically in violation of the Robinson-Patman Act.

> Arizona Wholesale Supply Co. filed suit against Carter-Hawley-Hale Stores, Inc. and its Broadway Southwest unit in the amount of $53,000 for "illegally deducting discounts for prompt payment" and "for taking unauthorized advertising allowances and other unpaid invoices." According to Arizona Wholesale's credit terms, Broadway Southwest would have been entitled to a 2 percent discount on merchandise paid for within 20 days. The department store "failed to pay certain invoices within the credit terms" but it "deducted the 2 percent anyway," Arizona Wholesale alleged in the lawsuit.

Source: Adapted from "Wholesalers Caught in a Squeeze by Retailers," *The Wall Street Journal*, May 29, 1986, 6.

Each time a wholesaler is faced with an unauthorized discount being taken, a decision must be made whether to contest it. If it is not contested, it is an open invitation to have the same deductions taken from subsequent invoices; if it is contested, a customer may be lost.

The Future of Wholesaling

Discussions of "the future of wholesaling" in marketing texts of 20 years ago generally centered on the "circumvention" of the wholesaler—how wholesalers in general, and full-function wholesalers in particular, in the United States were being replaced by vertical marketing systems. The forecast was that manufacturers and large retailers would assume most of the wholesaling functions, with assistance as needed from limited-function and agent middlemen to fill distributional niches. Overall, independently owned and operated wholesaling businesses were expected to undergo an appreciable decline over the next decade or so.

These predictions could hardly have been more wrong. They were made at a time when the trend in overall wholesale sales, and in the sales of wholesalers who take title to the products they sell, had declined steadily as a percentage of gross national product since 1950. The forecasters were extrapolating these trends. This was the time when wholesalers had just begun to modernize their operations with the aid of computers, and the trends began to reverse themselves. Today, although total wholesale sales in the United States still do not constitute as high a percentage of GNP as they did 40 years ago, there has been a substantial resurgence in their percentage. And the sales of wholesalers who take title to the products they sell is some 5 points *higher* as a percentage of GNP than it was in 1950.

The authors lay no special claims to clairvoyance. However, with the continuation of the computer "revolution" in wholesaling management—and *revolution* is probably not too dramatic a word to use to describe what has happened in the field—there is no apparent reason why wholesaling should not at least maintain its present position in distribution.

SUMMARY OF IMPORTANT POINTS

1. *Retailing* includes all the activities directly related to selling goods or services to consumers for personal, nonbusiness use.
2. Retailing is the largest single industry in the United States in terms of number of employees, and is second only to wholesaling in terms of sales.
3. The types of retail stores classified by product line(s) carried or services provided include:
   a. *Specialty stores.* Carry less than a full line of products but offer a wide choice in terms of model, size, style, color, and other important attributes in the assortment carried.
   b. *Convenience stores.* Carry a limited line of rapid-turnover food, beverage, and drug items.
   c. *Supermarkets.* Self-service food stores with grocery, meat, and produce departments, and minimum annual sales of $2 million.
   d. *Combination stores.* Have both a supermarket and a full-line drug store with a common checkout area.
   e. *Department stores.* Large retail outlets that handle a variety of lines of products, have wide assortments in each, and are organized into separate departments for purposes of buying, promotion, service, and control.
   f. *Hypermarkets.* Combine the supermarket, department store, and specialty and service shops in one oversize, single-level store.
   g. *Service establishments.* Provide educational services, food and lodging, legal advice, health care, personal care, repairs, financial services, and the like.
4. The types of retail outlets using price appeal as the principal element of strategy include
   a. *Box stores* (also called limited-line or limited-item stores). Carry only fast-turnover, staple grocery products (normally no more than 600–1,000 items) and operate on the lowest margin of any food stores (6 to 8 percent).
   b. *Warehouse stores.* Operate much like box stores, but on a larger scale. They may carry as many as 8,000 products, including vegetables, meats, dairy products, and frozen foods. They operate on gross margins of 11 to 13 percent of sales.

    c. *Full-line discount stores.* Carry lines of products comparable to those of a department store, although they are lower in price.

    d. *Retail catalog showrooms.* Have a customer area with catalogs and desks for the customer to use in making out an order. The merchandise is obtained only by picking it up at the showroom.

5. A *direct-marketer* is a retail organization that markets by sales representative calling in the home, by telephone, by mail, by package inserts, or through the electronic media of radio, television, or the home computer. Merchandise can be displayed and sold through vending machines and electronic kiosks.

6. Retail outlets classified by ownership and control include:

    a. *Independents.* Retailers who own one outlet and are not affiliated with any other business organization involved in the retail field.

    b. *Corporate chains.* A multi-unit retailing organization under common ownership with centralized management, purchasing, and warehousing of products.

    c. *Franchises.* Retail stores whose owners have entered into a contractual agreement that gives them the right to engage in offering, selling, or distributing goods or services under a marketing plan prescribed in substantial part by the franchisor and using the franchisor's identifying trademark or tradename.

    d. *Voluntary chains.* Associations of independents either organized and operated by the member retailers (sometimes called cooperative chains) or sponsored by wholesalers for purposes of joint purchasing and carrying out common merchandising and advertising programs.

    e. *Consumer cooperatives.* Retail stores (usually food stores) that are owned by their customers.

7. The principal marketing decision areas in retailing are the target market, location, assortment of products and services, inventories, departmental layout and product shelf location, price, promotion, and method of control.

8. There are two general pattern of layouts for stores, grid (used by virtually all supermarkets and drug stores) and free-flow (used by most department and specialty stores).

9. The conventional decision rules for locating departments within the store are to (a) place the highest-profit departments in the areas with the highest traffic flows, (b) group the departments by either level of purchase motivation or market segment, and (c) place necessary items or services at the back or on the top floor of the store.

10. Wholesalers are firms that sell to retailers, industrial users, or nonprofit institutions, but not to consumers.

11. The four major categories of wholesale middlemen are the full-function and limited-function wholesalers, the agent middlemen, and the manufacturer's sales offices and branches.

12. Full-function wholesalers include:

    a. *Merchant wholesalers.* Handle consumer goods and sell to retailers and service firms. Take title, carry inventory, and offer a full range of services to customers.

b. *Industrial distributors.* Perform the same functions as the merchant wholesaler, but in the industrial goods field.

13. Limited-function wholesalers include:

   a. *Drop shippers.* Sell and take title to products that are "drop shipped"—shipped directly from the manufacturer to the customer—rather than carried in inventory.

   b. *Wagon distributors.* Sell and make deliveries from a truck (a wagon in earlier times, hence the name) at the time of the sale. Operate almost entirely in the food field handling perishable or semiperishable products such as fruits and vegetables, ice cream, potato chips, and candies.

   c. *Rack jobbers.* One or more rack jobbers supply most of the products found on display racks in supermarkets—paperback books, women's hosiery, sunglasses, and the like.

   d. *Cash and carry wholesalers.* Perform as merchant wholesalers or industrial distributors except do not extend credit or make delivery.

14. Agent middlemen include:

   a. *Brokers.* Negotiate sales by representing the seller (usually) or the buyer (occasionally). They do not take title, carry inventory, or make delivery. They operate mostly in the food field.

   b. *Commission merchants.* Receive the products from the manufacturer or grower and sell them on a consignment basis, remitting the proceeds after deducting commission and costs of handling.

   c. *Manufacturer's agents.* Have contractual agreements with manufacturers to sell their products in a given territory with an agreed-on rate of commission.

   d. *Sales agent.* Agree contractually to sell the entire output of the manufacturer. May help finance the principal as well. They are found chiefly in textiles, apparel, food, and some metal products.

   e. *Auction houses.* Hold auctions where products are displayed and sold for a commission.

15. Manufacturers' sales offices and branches include:

   a. *Sales office.* Owned and operated by the manufacturer, but physically separated from the plant. Do not carry inventory.

   b. *Sales branch.* Same as a sales office, except carries inventory.

16. The principal marketing decision areas in wholesaling are location, assortment of products and services, inventories, physical distribution, price, promotion, method of control, and relations with retailers.

REVIEW QUESTIONS

18.1.   What is the definition of *retailing?*

18.2.   What is a useful way to classify retailers?

18.3. How do retail stores vary with respect to strategic choices of the management?

18.4. Name and give examples of at least three generic types of retail stores classified by number of product line(s) carried. (Example: single-line stores = clothing stores, computer stores, and automobile dealerships.)

18.5. What is a:
a. Specialty store?
b. Convenience store?
c. Supermarket?
d. Combination store?
e. Department store?

18.6. Give five examples of *service establishments*.

18.7. Describe a:
a. Box store
b. Warehouse store
c. Full-line discount store
d. Retail catalog showroom

18.8. What are the two major types of *nonstore retailers*?

18.9. What is a *direct marketer*?

18.10. What is an *asterisk law*?

18.11. What are the advantages and disadvantages of *direct-to-home marketing*?

18.12. What is an *electronic kiosk*?

18.13. What are the basic kinds of locations for retail stores?

18.14. What is a:
a. Corporate chain?
b. Voluntary chain?
c. Franchise?
d. Consumer cooperative?

18.15. What are the *principal decision areas* in retailing?

18.16. What factors should be evaluated in a competently conducted *retail trade area analysis*?

18.17. What factors should be evaluated in selecting the *specific site* for a retail store within a trading area?

18.18. What are the three primary sources of information for determining appropriate *in-store* and *shelf locations* for products?

18.19. What is *wholesaling*?

18.20. What is a:
  a. Merchant wholesaler?
  b. Industrial distributor?
  c. Drop shipper?
  d. Wagon distributor?
  e. Rack jobber?
  f. Cash and carry wholesaler?
  g. Broker?
  h. Commission merchant?
  i. Manufacturer's agent?
  j. Sales agent?
  k. Auction house?
  l. Sales office?
  m. Sales branch?

18.21. What are the principal *marketing decision areas* in wholesaling?

DISCUSSION QUESTIONS AND PROBLEMS

18.22. According to the definitions of retailing and wholesaling given in the text (pp. 591 and 609, respectively), in which classification, if either, would you say each of the following transactions falls?
  a. A university student registering and paying tuition for classes for the coming term?
  b. Furniture that was bought from a furniture wholesaler by a furniture retailer to use in her own home?
  c. A trip to the dentist for having one's teeth cleaned?
  d. A trip to work on the subway?
  e. Using the services of an accountant to assist in making out one's personal tax return?

18.23. Given that products usually are sold by retailers at a substantial markup over the wholesale price, how do you account for the fact that total wholesale sales in the United States each year are almost twice total retail sales?

18.24. As price competition intensifies from the cloning of IBM minicomputers, what actions would you expect:
  a. IBM

b. Computer retailers

to take? Explain.

18.25. Until after World War II, the stacks of university libraries were closed to library patrons. If someone wanted to check out a book, he or she gave the call number to a library clerk who in turn gave it to a "runner" to find and bring back the book it identified. What parallels, if any, do you see between the advent of self-service in grocery stores and its use in libraries?

18.26. In Russian retail stores the customer:
   a. Selects the item he or she wants to buy,
   b. Tells the sales clerk,
   c. Who writes its price on a ticket and gives it the customer,
   d. Who takes it to a clerk at a cash register and pays for it.
   e. The clerk gives the customer the cash register receipt and the ticket.
   f. The customer takes both back to the sales clerk,
   g. who gives the customer the item.
   Sizable queues are the rule at all three stops. Why do you think such a system would be used?

18.27. Box stores tend to locate near supermarkets, but warehouse stores often have isolated locations. Why should there be a difference in the locations of the two types of stores?

18.28. Should consumers have the right to prevent telephone sales calls by having an asterisk placed by their listing in the phone book? Why or why not?

18.29. It is standard practice in any sizable telemarketing operation to have supervisors monitor some of the sales calls. California, Georgia, and Michigan have laws prohibiting the monitoring of telephone calls unless permission is obtained from both parties in advance. Should the monitoring of telephone sales calls by supervisors who have not received the sales prospect's permission be interpreted as violating these laws? Why or why not?

18.30. The Internal Revenue Service approached mailing list brokers with the intent to purchase lists of high-income households to be used to check against lists of taxpayers. Was this an appropriate use for the mailing lists? Why or why not?

18.31. Sears, Roebuck management views the catalogs it issues as being useful to the company for promotional purposes as well as for selling products. Suggest three promotional functions the catalog might serve.

18.32. Several tests have demonstrated the consumer's reluctance to buy even well-known brands of hosiery and other staple apparel items through vending machines. What do you believe are the underlying reasons for the refusal to buy these products through this kind of outlet?

18.33. One suggested form of market testing new brands of cigarettes and snack items is to place various versions of them (different formulations, packages being considered) at different prices in vending machines. Do you think this would provide a valid method of predicting the best-selling version and the most profitable price if the new product were to be introduced and sold at conventional retail outlets? Why or why not?

18.34. Since the success or failure of a direct mail campaign depends at least in part on getting the recipient to open the envelope, many direct mail envelopes are designed to give the impression that the contents are something they are not (a check from the government, a notice from the IRS, for example). Suppose that once such a "camouflaged" envelope is opened the recipient finds that the offer is an honest one and the mailing piece is done with sincerity and integrity. Is the deception to get the recipient to open the envelope ethical? Why or why not?

18.35. Give two examples of specialty retail stores (by line(s) carried, not specific stores) that you believe would likely use the *model-stock* approach to allocating floor space by department, and two that probably use the *sales-productivity ratio* approach. Explain why you chose the types of stores you did.

18.36. Suppose that you are considering buying a fast-food franchise. The estimated total of the cost of the franchise plus the site and building is $1.2 million. You plan to invest $200,000 of your own money and pay off the remainder in five annual installments of $200,000 plus interest. Suppose you estimate that the net cash flow (after principal and interest costs) will average 10 percent of sales. Further suppose that you estimate sales will increase by 12 percent each year.

If your objective is to have a net present value of $1.0 million with five years of operation at a discount rate of 25 percent, and an estimated value of $1.5 million for the fixed assets and business as a going concern at the end of the five years, how much would first-year sales have to be in order to realize that?

18.37 Although retailing is an innovative field, not all of the new developments tried succeed. Included among the innovations that have failed are:

a. A gasoline distributor offered a contract under which the car that the customer drove to work would be filled with gasoline regularly, the oil checked, and the windshield cleaned, all at the workplace parking space of the car.

b. An inventor patented a tilted, top-loading grocery shelf in which packages or cans could be placed on their side and dispensed at the push of a button at the bottom of the columns in much the same manner as a vending machine. Higher shelving could be used (since the consumer didn't have to reach to take the package or can off the shelf), and the older merchandise was automatically dispensed first.

c. A circular department store with aisles radiating from a central hub on each floor was designed and built by Macy's. A parking ramp wound up the circumference and there was parking on each level. Customers therefore could drive directly to the floor on which they intended to do a major part of their shopping. Elevators (both passenger and freight) and escalators were located in the central hub. Explain why you think each was unsuccessful.

Source: Adapted in part from S. C. Hollander, "Retail Classifications Easy to Oversimplify: Hollander," *Marketing News,* July 13, 1979, 10.

PROJECTS

18.38. With another member of your class, visit a retail store that uses a UPC checkout scanning system and interview a member of the management about how the information from it is used. Visit a second retail store carrying the same product lines that does not use a UPC checkout scanning system and interview a management member about how the information obtained through checkout scanning in the first store is obtained in this store. Prepare a report on your findings.

18.39. With another member of your class, visit a wholesaling firm in your area that has computerized its operations and interview the management about how the computer is used. Visit a second wholesaling firm that does not use computers and interview the management about how the same operations are carried out. Prepare a report on your findings.

18.40. Assume that you and another member of your class plan to open a retail store offering a product or service of your choice. With the other class member, prepare
a. A marketing plan
b. A financial plan
for the first three years of operations of the firm. Prepare a report containing both plans that is suitable for submitting to a bank to obtain a loan to finance the store.

Endnotes

[1]"Store Managers Assuming Major Roles in Retail Businesses," *Marketing News,* June 6, 1986.

[2]U.S. Bureau of the Census, *Statistical Abstract of the United States, 1985,* U.S. Government Printing Office, 390, 781.

[3]Ibid., 781, 790.

[4]"Convenience Stores Try Cutting Prices and Adding Products to Attract Women," *The Wall Street Journal,* July 3, 1987, 13.

[5]"FMI Redefines the Supermarket," *Progressive Grocer,* April 1981, 44.

[6]"The Nielsen Researcher," No. 2, 1980, 8.

[7]Adapted from the definition given in B. Berman and J. R. Evans, *Retail Management: A Strategic Approach,* 3rd ed., Macmillan, 1986, 101.

[8]"Department Stores Shape Up," *Fortune,* September 1, 1986,

50–52; and "Specialty Store Chains Do Better Than Department Stores in 1986 Net Sales," *Marketing News*, February 1, 1988, 14.

[9]"The Return of the Amazing Colossal Store," *Business Week*, August 22, 1988, 59.

[10]"French-Run Hypermarket a U.S. Hit," *Herald-Tribune*, February 11, 1985, 7; and "Hypermarkets in the U.S.A.: A Bigg's Success—Oui or Non?" *Chain Store Age Executive*, September 1985, 25–26.

[11]U.S. Bureau of the Census, *Statistical Abstract*, 780, 781.

[12]Berman and Evans, *Retail Management*, 104.

[13]Sales estimates by method of direct marketing include sales to businesses as well as to consumers. The sources for the ranking of methods in terms of importance are E. Roman, "Telemarketing Rings in New Business Era," *Advertising Age*, January 27, 1986, 50; and D. Rotbart and L. P. Cohen, "The Party at Mary Kay Isn't Quite So Lively These Days as Recruiting of Saleswomen Falls Off," *The Wall Street Journal*, October 28, 1983, 12.

[14]"Resistance, Restrictions Plague Industry," *Marketing News*, August 1, 1986, 9.

[15]K. T. Higgins, "Boom Time for Cataloguing Is Quieting Down," *Marketing News*, August 2, 1985, 11.

[16]"Last Chapter for Big Catalog? Sears Eyes Specialty Books," *Advertising Age*, July 18, 1988, 26.

[17]"Cars Once Sold by Mail," *The Oregonian*, February 18, 1976, 8.

[18]"Can't Find Right Christmas Tree? Now You Can Order One by Mail," *The Wall Street Journal*, December 14, 1982, 27.

[19]"White Castle Boosts Market via Mail-Order Shipments," *Advertising Age*, November 29, 1982, 52W.

[20]M. Kaplan, "Shoppers Tune in National Cable Network," *Advertising Age*, March 6, 1986, 35.

[21]"Marketing" column in *The Wall Street Journal*, November 8, 1988, B1.

[22]"ATMs Not the Time Savers Some Bankers Expected," *Marketing News*, March 28, 1988, 8.

[23]Rotbart and Cohen, "The Party at Mary Kay."

[24]P. Sloan, "Avon Ladies to Toughen Up Sales Pitch," *Advertising Age*, March 12, 1984, 12. See also "Avon Crawling," *Forbes*, April 21, 1986, 72–73.

[25]See Berman and Evans, *Retail Management*, 216–227, for a detailed discussion of these considerations.

[26]1982 *Census of Retail Trade*.

[27]Adapted from J. L. Fels and L. G. Rudnick, *Investigate Before Investing*, International Franchise Association, 1976, 7.

[28]One such database is "Your Marketing Consultant" published by Market Statistics, a Division of Bill Communications. A general reference to computerized databases is R. N. Cuadra, D. M. Abels, and J. Wranger (eds.), *Directory of Online Databases*, Cuadra Associates, published semiannually.

[29]An especially good source for this purpose is Berman and Evans, *Retail Management*, Chaps. 7 and 8.

[30]See, for example, "UPC Scanning Scores OK in Bullock's Test," 61–64, and "Will Department Stores Be the Next UPC Stronghold?" 64—both in *Chain Store Age Executive*, December 1985; and "Price Marking Goes On-line," *Chain Store Age Executive*, July 1983, 96–97.

[31]For an elaboration on these uses, see G. Phillips, "Marketing in the New World of Scanners," *Viewpoint*, May–June 1986, 2–5.

[32]Determining warehouse locations using this model is discussed in D. S. Tull and D. I. Hawkins, *Marketing Research: Measurement and Method*, 4th ed., Macmillan, 1987, 676–678.

[33]"Foremost-McKesson: The Computer Moves Distribution to Center Stage," *Business Week*, December 7, 1981, 115.

MINICASES

MINICASE **IV-1**

Federal Express: How Many Assembly/Sorting/Dispersal Locations?

Federal Express was started in 1973 to provide overnight delivery of goods and information between major cities in the United States. As the growth of both the company and its competitors since then attests, it was a service for which there was a definite need. Television had speeded up the fashion cycle, necessitating rapid movement and replacement of inventories. New design philosophies had emerged that were based on replacing components at the site rather than returning the unit to a depot for repair or servicing. Maintaining inventories of expensive products at multiple locations had become more and more expensive. Rapid communication of orders, contracts, authorizations, instructions, and other kinds of communications and information had become a necessity for many firms. A reliable, inexpensive overnight delivery service from one metropolitan area to another was a welcome solution for these and other delivery problems.

To get thousands of letters and packages picked up in one city and delivered the next morning in another city requires one or more centrally located facilities for assembling, sorting by destination, and dispersal (ASD facilities). A critical initial decision was how many ASD facilities the system should have. The number of facilities is critical with respect to both time and cost. The system was being designed to take only 14 hours from the time in the late afternoon that a loaded Federal Express airplane lifted off the runway at the first of five collection cities until another Federal Express airplane arrived at the last of five delivery cities the next morning. Saving only a few minutes at any stage in the system could have a ripple effect on other stages. For example, time saved could allow later pickup or earlier arrival at the destination. Earlier arrival at the destination city the next morning would permit trucks waiting at the airport to get into the city before the heavy morning traffic, and thus save even more time. The number of ASD locations would also affect the number of aircraft required and the total number of miles flown each day, both having an obvious bearing on costs.

There were proponents of one, two, and three ASD locations. A location would have to be at a city with generally good weather, and one with an airport equipped for takeoffs and landings in bad weather. If one ASD facility were to be decided on, it was to be located somewhere near the center of the weighted market potential of the sending and receiving locations for the entire country. If two facilities were to be used, one was to be located near the center of the weighted market potential for an Eastern region, and the other near the center of the weighted market potential of a Western region; the two regions would be defined geographically such that they had roughly equal market potentials. If three facilities were decided on, there would be Eastern, Midwestern, and Western regions, each having a central location selected by the same general approach as for the two-facility solution.

1. How should the management of Federal Express have gone about getting information in order to make the number-of-ASD facilities decision?
2. What decision do you believe should have been made? Why?

Tuning the Marketing Program of the Pillsbury Company— The Dorfman and Steiner Theorem

The Dorfman and Steiner Theorem,[*] derived mathematically, states that at the optimum level of each of the mix variables:

Profit is maximized when the nonprice variables are each making a marginal contribution to profit that is equal to their individual marginal costs, and price is at the point where marginal revenue equals marginal cost.

When these conditions are met, the following equation applies:

Price elasticity of demand (absolute value) = $\dfrac{\text{Dollar sales}}{\text{Advertising expenditures}}$ (advertising elasticity)

= $\dfrac{\text{Dollar sales}}{\text{Distribution expenditures}}$ (distribution elasticity)

= $\dfrac{\text{Price}}{\text{Average unit production costs}}$ (quality elasticity)

or, in symbols:

$$\mid e_p \mid \ = \ \frac{PQ\,e_A}{A} = \frac{PQ\,e_D}{D} = \frac{P\,e_R}{c}.$$

All the terms in the equation should be familiar with the possible exception of *elasticity*. Elasticity is a term from economics that is defined for each of the mix variables as follows:

Price elasticity of demand = $\dfrac{\text{Percentage change in quantity sold}}{\text{Percentage change in price}}$

Advertising elasticity = $\dfrac{\text{Percentage change in dollar sales}}{\text{Percentage change in advertising expenditures}}$

Distribution elasticity of sales = $\dfrac{\text{Percentage change in dollar sales}}{\text{Percentage change in distribution expenditures}}$

Quality elasticity = $\dfrac{\text{Percentage change in dollar sales}}{\text{Percentage change in unit costs associated with quality changes}}$

The staff of the Marketing Services Department of the Pillsbury Company has made the estimates shown below of advertising and price elasticities of five of their products:

Product	Advertising Elasticity	Price Elasticity
A	.10	−2.10
B	.15	− .85
C	.13	−1.30
D	.20	−1.30
E	.70	−2.80

a. Calculate the percentage of sales that should be spent on advertising each product according to the Dorfman and Steiner Theorem.

b. What assumptions are implicit in the calculation made in your answer to a.? Explain.

c. If Gold Medal flour and Betty Crocker cake mix were two of the products in the list above, which two would they likely be? Explain.

---

[*]R. Dorfman and P. O. Steiner, "Optimal Advertising and Optimal Quality," *American Economic Review*, Vol. 44, December 1954, 27–34. See also the discussion in E. Douglas, *Economics of Marketing*, Harper & Row 1975, 460–463.

Does the Use of Humor in Bank Commercials Make Them Laugh All the Way to the Bank?

Society National Bank of Cleveland used the commercial given below on radio as part of a campaign to promote its new bill-paying service. The commercial was written and taped by a comedy team of "Dick and Bert" (Dick Orkin and Bert Berdis):

"Doctor, I have this mental block."
"I see."
"I can't say B...b...b...b..."
"Easy!"
"They're driving me crazy."
"Describe them."
"Hateful things that come every month."
"Celebrity roasts on TV?"
"No. B...b...b...b..."
"Bills?"
"Right! Help me, doctor."
"Go to Society National Bank."
"They'll help me with b...b...b...?"
"Mr. Porter, why don't we substitute another word instead of 'bills'? Say, 'elbow.'"
"Society will take care of my . . . elbows?"
"Yes, with their bill-paying telephone service."
"How does that . . ."
"You phone the bank to pay all your bills."

"Even my electric elbow?"
"Of course. No checks or envelopes to write. Society makes it easy and convenient."
"Oh good, cuz I can do without elbows."
"Huh?"
"Doctor, I was substituting elbows for . . ."
"Oh, I remember."
"Is the elbow-paying service expensive?"
"No. And it's free for the first six months."
"Now I can call Society to pay my son Elbow's tuition."
"Your son's name is Elbow?"
"Actually, it's B...b...b..."
"I see."
"Doctor, how can I thank you?"
"My elbow will be in the mail."*

Should this commercial

1. Have been used as written? Why or why not?
2. Have been revised before being used? Explain.
3. Not have been used at all? Explain.

---

*Given in Michael Vermeulen, "*Times* Men of the Year," *TWA Ambassador*, April 1979, 34.

Avon Products: The Case of the Missing Saleswomen

Avon is in trouble. As a major in-home marketer of cosmetics, jewelry, and personal care products, company sales depend on having a large, well-trained, highly motivated force of saleswomen calling on customers. Recruiting in the United States has become increasingly difficult, however, and turnover has risen. The result is a domestic sales force that has become smaller in size and shorter in experience.

An Avon representative is an independent dealer, not an agent or employee of the company. Representatives buy products from the company and sell them by calling on customers in their homes. Almost all representatives are women who work on a part-time basis. They have an assigned territory of about 100 homes, all in the neighborhood in which they live, if possible. Representatives are assigned to group sales leaders responsible for training and supervising their charges.

There are about 1.4 million representatives worldwide, of which approximately 400,000 are in the United States. The overall number has stayed about constant at that level since 1982. However, that has been the result of a rise in the number of representatives abroad each year offsetting a decline in the number in the United States. Since reaching its all-time high of 440,000 in the United States in 1982, the number has fallen each year to its present level of slightly less than 400,000. Fewer than two-thirds of U.S. households are called on by Avon representatives.

All in-home marketers—Mary Kay, Tupperware, and others—have experienced the same problem in recruiting and retaining sales representatives. It is not difficult to find the reasons for these difficulties. The improvement in the economy has provided increased job opportunities for women, especially in part-time work. The economic recovery has also resulted in lower unemployment, reducing the number of households in which the wife needs to work to help support the family. At the same time, companies such as Avon have encountered new competition in cosmetics marketing from combination stores and other mass merchandisers that have moved aggressively into this high-margin product line. Commissions earned on sales of cosmetics by Avon and Mary Kay representatives have not been helped by this increased competition.

What actions might Avon management take to counter the recruiting and retention problems it faces?

R. L. Financial Consulting

The two sales associates of R. L. Financial Consulting, Penn Rettig and Mary Nelson, each prepared a draft of a letter to send to prospective clients. Each was then edited by Richard Lessnick, the owner of the business. The edited versions are as follows:

Small businesses encounter many problems during the business day. Analyzing financial problems requires accurate records and detailed interpretation. Professional expertise will benefit most businesses and aid in their successful operation.

Since you're in business to make money, it's important to make financial decisions from accurate records. Interpretation, budgeting and forecasting are drawn from these records. More than ten years' experience in this field gives us an expertise which will be used to help you in the financial planning of your business.

Some of the services we offer are listed below:

—Accounting systems
—Financial statements: comparative and percentaged
—Tax planning
—Loan application packages
—Year-round service

We take pride in our small office which, by design, enables us to provide you with continuous and personal service. All systems and services are tailored to meet your explicit needs. Complete financial statements are customized to meet your requirements through the use of our small-business computer. Completed statements are then reviewed by you and a member of our staff at predetermined intervals during the year.

To acquaint you with our services, we provide the initial consultation at no charge. Charges are based on each particular business due to the variety of business requirements. Anticipated costs are discussed prior to performing any services.

We would appreciate the opportunity to serve you. Call today to schedule your initial consultation.

Sincerely,

Mary Nelson
Sales Associate

Do you have financial questions about your business that no one seems to answer?

Is your accountant just an accountant and nothing more?

At R. L. Financial Consulting we offer you more personalized service, because we take an active interest in the TOTAL financial environment in which your business must compete. Not only do we offer custom-tailored accounting services, we also answer many important financial questions, such as:

—Are you utilizing your cash where it will do the most good?
—Should your company buy or lease?
—Are you charging enough for your services/products?
—Do you know how to analyze your sales to see which products are profitable for you and which are not?
—How do your expenses compare to those of similar firms?
—How fast should your company grow consistent with sound financial management?
—Are you taking full advantage of the tax regulations regarding independent businesses?

At R. L. Financial Consulting we are here to make sure that you have the accurate, up-to-date information you need to make the right financial decisions for your business, at a price you can afford. To acquaint you with our services, we provide the initial consultation at no charge. Charges are based on each particular business due to the variety of business requirements. Anticipated costs are discussed prior to performing any services.

If you feel that last year's profits were not what they should have been, or that you paid too much in taxes last year, then give us a call. We appreciate the opportunity to serve you.

Penn Rettig   Mary Nelson   Richard Lessnick
Sales Associate   Sales Associate   Financial Consultant

1. What were the appeals used in each of the two letters?
2. What other appeals might have been used?
3. If one of the two letters was to be mailed without further editing or revision, which should have been used? Why?

Using Test Market Consumer Diary Panel Data to Forecast New Product Sales: The Parfitt and Collins Model

A useful model of new product sales incorporating the purchase frequency of the product is one based on the model proposed by Parfitt and Collins.* Consumer diary panel data from one or more test market areas are used to make the forecast.

In this model, sales in any period (S_t) are the sum of sales to initial purchasers (I_t) and sales to repurchasers (R_t) or

$$S_t = I_t + R_t.$$

For estimation purposes, the terms on the right side of this equation need to be expanded. Sales to initial purchasers in the period are the product of the market potential for initial sales (MPI) times the *penetration rate* (PR_t), the proportion of buyers who buy the new product in that period for the first time, or:

$$I = (MPI)(PR_t).$$

Similarly, sales to repurchasers in the period are the product of its market potential (MPR) times the repurchase rate (RR), or:

$$R_t = (MPR_t)(RR).$$

The market potential for repurchase sales is equal to initial sales and repurchase sales made one purchase interval (i) earlier, or:

$$MPR_t = I_{t-i} + R_{t-i}.$$

Reassembling the equation for sales in a given period, we have:

$$S_t = (MPI)(PR_t) + (I_{t-i} + R_{t-i})(RR).$$

The operation of this model for various purchase intervals is illustrated in the table below. Assumed values for MPI, PR_t, and RR are given there, and sales for each year are calculated using the model. You should work through the table to be sure you understand how the sales estimates for each year for each purchase interval are derived. Note also how both the pattern and the level of sales are affected by the purchase interval.

*J. H. Parfitt and B.J.K. Collins, "The Use of Consumer Panels for Brand Share Predictions," *Journal of Marketing Research*, May 1968, 131–146.

Illustration of Operation of New Product Sales Model for Three Different Purchase Intervals

Potential market for initial purchases (MPI) = 100,000 units
Penetration rate (PR_t):

Year 1	2%	Year 3	8%
Year 2	5%	Year 4	8%	Year 5	7%

Repurchase rate (RR_t): .50

	Purchase Interval								
Years After Introduction	5 years			2 years			1 year		
	Initial Purchase Col. 1	Repurchase Col. 2	Total Unit Sales Col. 3	Initial Purchase Col. 4	Repurchase Col. 5	Total Unit Sales Col. 6	Initial Purchase Col. 7	Repurchase Col. 8	Total Unit Sales Col. 9
1	2,000	0	2,000	2,000	0	2,000	2,000	0	2,000
2	5,000	0	5,000	5,000	0	5,000	5,000	1,000	6,000
3	8,000	0	8,000	8,000	1,000	9,000	8,000	3,000	11,000
4	8,000	0	8,000	8,000	2,500	10,500	8,000	5,500	13,500
5	7,000	0	7,000	7,000	4,500	11,500	7,000	6,750	13,750

(Continued on page 630)

The model indicates that four variables are involved in new product sales forecasting: market potential for sales to initial purchases, penetration rate, purchase frequency/purchase interval, and repurchase rate.

1. Extend the table above through Year 8 given the following penetration rates:

   Year 6   6%
   Year 7   4%
   Year 8   2%

2. Recalculate columns 7, 8, and 9 of the table on page 629 to obtain pessimistic and optimistic sales forecasts using the values of penetration and repurchase rates given in the table on the right.

	Penetration Rate	
	Pessimistic Forecast	**Optimistic Forecast**
Year 1	1.5%	2.5%
Year 2	3.75	6.25
Year 3	6.0	10.0
Year 4	6.0	10.0
Year 5	5.25	8.75
Repurchase rate (all years)	0.40	0.60

What conclusions do you reach about the sensitivity of the forecasts to these rates?

Using Test Market Consumer Diary Panel Data to Forecast New Product Sales: The Fourt and Woodlock Model

The Fourt and Woodlock model* can be used to forecast new product sales from consumer purchase diary panel data in market test areas. The Fourt and Woodlock model is

$$q_t = rx\,(1-r)^{t-1}$$

where

q_t = penetration rate in period t

r = rate at which penetration takes place (value is between 0 and 1)

x = maximum penetration expressed as a percentage of all potential buying units

t = time period

1. Assume that it is estimated from the consumer panel data for a product in test market that in each period one-fourth of all potential buyers who have not previ-ously bought the product will buy it ($r = .25$), and that the maximum percentage of the potential buyers who will eventually buy the product is 40 percent ($x = 40\%$). Calculate the percentage of the total potential buyers who will make first purchases during each of its first five periods after introduction.

2. Estimate the penetration rate for a new product for each of the first five periods after introduction when:
   a. $r = .20, x = .40$
   b. $r = .20, x = .50$
   c. $r = .30, x = .40$
   d. $r = .30, x = .50$

What tentative conclusions do you reach about the sensitivity of the penetration rate to r and x?

---

*L. A. Fourt and J. W. Woodlock, "Early Prediction of Market Success for New Grocery Products," *Journal of Marketing*, October 1960, 31–38.

The *Harvard Business Review*: Circulation Down or Turning Around?

The *Harvard Business Review* (HBR) no doubt graces more corporate coffee tables than any other journal published by an academic institution. Since its founding in 1922, it has been the chronicler of the latest developments to ensure corporate growth and prosperity, and the first to reveal that they no longer work as well as they once did. Reflecting the prestige of the Harvard Business School, its articles have been cited in speeches and debates as if they were the ultimate authority on the point at issue. If corporate America were to adopt a secular bible, much of it would come from the *Harvard Business Review*.

Yet by the early 1980s, a nagging suspicion had arisen that it had become more of a symbol to be displayed than a source of advice to be read. One faculty member admitted that in recent years "it wasn't what one thought it should be" and that "most people don't read it." This suspicion was confirmed when circulation began to slide. In early 1985, circulation was 242,000. Less than two years later (late 1986) it had fallen to about 200,000. Advertising pages had also declined from 460 in 1985 to 440 in 1986.

A new editor, Theodore Leavitt, a professor of marketing at the school, was appointed after the circulation decline began.

He made a trip around the country to interview readers and then began to make the changes he thought were needed to raise both circulation and readership.

1. Look at issues of the *HBR* during the 1980–1984 period. What do you think might have caused the circulation decline beginning in 1985? Give examples from specific issues.
2. Look at issues from 1987 to the present. What steps do you think the new editor took to try to bring circulation back up? Give examples from specific issues.
3. What other steps do you think might have been taken? Explain.
4. Check the latest issue of *Standard Rate and Data Service* (Business Publications Rates and Data section, class 20, library call no. HF 5905.S723) in your university library to determine the current circulation of the *HBR*. What conclusions do you reach about how effective the steps taken by the new editor have been?

Gerber Products Company: Closet Teenage Consumers

Gerber Products Company is well known as the principal marketer of baby foods in the United States. (It has more than one-half of the U.S. market for prepared baby foods.) Recently the Sales Promotions department at Gerber's anonymously conducted a "secret snack sweepstakes" with advertisements in several teen magazines, including *Glamour* and *Seventeen*. The ads contained a self-addressed, tear-out postcard on which readers were asked to write their name and address and send it in. The address on it did not identify Gerber as the recipient. (It consisted only of a post office box number in Chicago.)

Some 30,000 readers responded and requested a sample of the unidentified snack. Each respondent was sent a free jar of Gerber's dutch apple dessert and a coupon entitling her or him to another free jar at a local supermarket. About one-half of the coupons were redeemed.

This response indicated that a sizable proportion of teens tried the product and liked it. To see if teens might be a viable market segment for Gerber desserts, they tried some brand-named ads in the same magazines. Some of the ads offered 50 cents off coupons on any Gerber dessert, and others offered to provide such coupons to anyone who wrote to the company. Very few teenagers took advantage of either offer.

1. What marketing strategy would be involved if the company attempted to market the baby food desserts to teenagers?
2. Why do you think the teenagers would respond favorably to the anonymous ads but largely ignore the named-brand ads?
3. Are there market segments other than the parents of babies in which there might be closet consumers of the desserts? of the vegetables? of the pureed meats? How would you determine if this is the case?
4. Prepare a recommended marketing campaign for the teenage market for the desserts.
5. How could such a campaign be tested before a final decision is made about running it? If it were tested, what testing program should be used? Why?

Traffic Flow in a Supermarket

The procedure for studying consumer traffic recommended by the Food Marketing Institute* is:

1. Diagram the department or section to be studied plus a portion of adjacent departments or sections. (Adjacent departments may influence the traffic flows in the area being studied.) Make a clear designation of entry and exit points for the area. Make about 100 copies of the diagram.

2. Survey a peak traffic period. (You may want to survey a slack period later.) Stand in a spot where all or part of the traffic in the area can be observed. Do not make it obvious to a customer that you are tracing his or her shopping path through the area.

3. On one of the copies of the diagram, trace that customer's path through the area as soon as he or she passes the point of entry.

4. Make a solid line recording the path of the customer. Place an *X* where the customer purchases an item. If the customer handles an item but doesn't place it in the shopping cart, place an *o* at the display. This may indicate a quality, signing, or price problem.

5. When one customer leaves the area, start charting the next customer who enters.

6. When approximately 100 customer patterns have been drawn, the analysis can begin. Place all of the diagrams in a pile in random order. Take every third diagram and copy each of these to a master diagram.

7. Factors to look for in the analysis include:
   a. Parts of the display that are heavily and lightly shopped
   b. How completely the areas are being shopped
   c. Whether there are bottlenecks and, if so, where they are located
   d. Whether the size of the display is out of proportion to sales

8. The actions to be taken include:
   a. Relocating items by placing the higher-demand items in the present lightly shopped areas
   b. Eliminating bottlenecks by moving easily removable displays

The figure below depicts the results of one such study of a produce department during a peak traffic period.

1. Why might it be desirable to survey the area during a slack period?

2. Why chart 100 customers and use only 33 of the charts in the analysis?

3. What refinements might be made of the procedure outlined above?

4. What are the principal problems, if any, suggested by the master diagram?

5. What corrective actions, if any, need to be taken?

*Source: The figure and most of the text for this minicase are taken from Food Marketing Institute, Store Managers' Guide 156, *Customer Traffic Studies*, May 1966, 4. Used with permission.

APS Inc.: What Steps Should It Have Taken as Customers in Its Biggest Market Segment Started Going Out of Business?

APS Inc. is the nation's second-largest auto parts distributor. It markets both national-brand and private-brand parts through independent parts wholesalers. The wholesalers in turn sell to service stations, professional mechanics, and auto parts retailers.

In the mid 1970s about 40 percent of the sales of APS wholesalers were to gasoline service stations doing repair work. In 1975 there were more than 147,500 service stations in the United States. (See the table below.). Then the OPEC-induced precipitous rise in oil prices and the resulting higher gasoline prices, smaller cars, and a 55-mile-per-hour national speed limit reduced gasoline consumption to the point that the oil companies started cutting back on their retailing operations. Some 16,000 service stations had gone out of business by 1978, and the forecast was for another 10,000 or so to disappear in the next two years. As stations closed, their repair business shifted to automobile dealers, tire dealers (Goodyear, Firestone, and others), mass merchandisers (Sears, J. C. Penney, and others), and muffler shops (Midas). These companies buy their parts directly from manufacturers, for the most part, and so they bought APS parts only on an emergency basis.

There were about 1,500 APS wholesalers. There was little turnover, and the number had remained at about this same level for the past several years. Although the proportion of their sales going to service stations reflected the decline in the number of stations, wholesaler sales were holding up overall. This was in part because of the increasing number of automotive parts retailers to serve a growing do-it-yourself market. Drivers were keeping cars longer, and the recent models contained intricate, costly devices to save fuel and control pollution. Rising costs were causing more and more car owners to do their own repairs.

Still, the shifts taking place in the business were of concern to the APS management. They had already moved into foreign markets (Belgium, Venezuela, and Mexico) and had acquired some of its suppliers, but there might be other steps they should take. The data in the table below were compiled to help in considering what actions they should take, if any, to counter the drop in the number of service stations or to take advantage of other trends.

Number of Outlets Handling and Using Automotive Parts, 1970, and 1975–1978

Year	New and Used Car Dealers (000s)	Auto and Home Supply Stores (000s)	Gasoline Service Stations (000s)	Wholesale Motor Vehicle and Auto Equipment Dealers (000s)
1970	31,067	na	146,616	28,715
1975	30,006	31,427	147,576	29,324
1976	29,519	33,079	142,025	36,041
1977	29,614	34,815	139,509	38,026
1978	29,801	36,021	130,697	37,236

What actions, if any, should the APS management have considered taking? Why?

General Mills: Familiarity, Quality Assessment, and Use of Brands of Products

In an early study of the competitive position of its brands vis-à-vis that of other brands in packaged-food product lines, General Mills obtained the data shown in the table below. The data on packaged pie mixes were obtained through interviews of a random sample of 850 housewives and those for ice cream from a random sample of 500 housewives, all residents of Chicago.*

Brand	Percent of Respondents Who Knew Brand	Percent of Users Who Give Brand Top Rating	Percent of Respondents Now Using Brand
Packaged Pie Mix			
A	70.8	24.3	11.3
B	55.2	26.8	6.1
C	51.0	44.2	10.9
D	46.2	20.8	4.2
E	23.3	24.2	3.3
Ice Cream			
A	33.8	67.5	21.4
B	51.8	67.6	17.8
C	26.8	50.0	8.6
D	16.8	53.6	3.6
E	37.8	26.5	3.2

*G. H. Brown, "Measuring Consumer Attitudes towards Products," *The Journal of Marketing*, April 1950, 691–706.

1. Suppose the General Mills pie mix was Brand C. Based on these data and assuming the Chicago respondents were representative of those in all areas in which General Mills products were marketed, what action(s) do you think General Mills should have taken?

2. Suppose the General Mills ice cream was Brand D. Based on these data and the same assumption concerning representativeness as stated in question 1, what action(s) do you think General Mills should have taken?

3. If you were to use this method of obtaining information on the competitive position of the brands of a company for which you were conducting a marketing audit, what other questions would you want to ask during the consumer interviews? Why?

Pricing of the Jaguar XJ12

The launch of the Jaguar XJ12 in 1972 was beset with problems. By the scheduled time for the introduction, 500 cars had been completed, but not distributed, before arguments over labor rates sent the production workers out on strike and closed the factory. British Leyland, the manufacturer of the Jaguar, did not allow the labor dispute to delay the launch date, and around £60,000 was allocated for press advertising during July 1972. All the British and European road tests, which form a vital part of any vehicle launch program, had to be conducted with just four cars that the management had managed to smuggle out of the factory through the picket lines.

The XJ12 was acknowledged as a superb product and demand was tremendous, building up to a two-year waiting list by the end of the year. Price was identified as a major factor stimulating this market response; the product offered was of very high quality for the recommended retail selling price.

The inevitable happened. In October 1972, a second-hand XJ12 was auctioned off for £1,500 (about $3,000) more than list price. Even one year after the strike had been settled and full production resumed, a significant premium above list price was still being obtained for second-hand vehicles.

The board of directors of British Leyland was criticized for this black market situation. The critics maintained that a market-based pricing method would have resulted in a higher price while still satisfying actual purchasers.

The company replied that it had costed out the vehicle as accurately as possible and was quite satisfied with the levels of profit. It was considering an attempt to eliminate the black market by legal means through the insertion of an anti-resale clause in the original contract of sale. Critics were advised to remember that the XJ12 price could not be allowed to get too far out of line with the XJ6 (the previous model), and the recommended price was perfectly equated with the planned production volumes for this vehicle.

1. What were the apparent primary pricing objectives of the management of British Leyland? Explain the basis for your inference.
2. What collateral pricing objectives might have been present in the pricing of the XJ12? Explain the basis for your inference.
3. For the objective of "maximizing stockholder wealth," what price should have been charged? Why?

Adapted from R. Harrison and F. M. Wilkes, "A Note on Jaguar's Pricing Policy," *European Journal of Marketing*, Vol. 7, no. 3, Winter 1973–1974, 242–246. Used with permission.

Sears, Roebuck: Paint Department Price Experiment

Paint has always been a product subject to frequent sales in general-merchandise department stores such as Sears, Penney's, and K-Mart because mark-ups are substantially higher than for most of the other merchandise carried.

The manager of the paint department at one Sears store came to the conclusion that frequent sales on interior house paints might not be desirable. She reasoned that individual rooms or the interiors of houses are painted only every few years and consumers probably have low brand loyalty for any one brand. They might well just "shop the sales" for a week or two before they got ready to paint and buy whatever brand of the quality they want that is available at the best price.

She decided that she would run an experiment on pricing Sears best brand of interior paint and see how prices seemed to affect sales and contribution to profits and fixed costs. If the results gave a clear indication of a most profitable price, she would keep the brand at that price most of the time with only one or two sales a year. If, on the other hand, there were a range of prices over which contribution was roughly the same, she would set a usual price near the top of the range but have more frequent sales. For the sales she would set the price at the low end of the range.

She decided that she would keep a record of not only Sears' prices and quantities sold, but the prices of the comparable brands of paint sold by Montgomery Ward's, Penney's, and K-Mart as well. She planned to change prices every two weeks and to keep doing that for five months.

The results are shown in the table below.*

The transfer price to the department was $6.40 per gallon for the August through January period. A part of the department manager's compensation was based on contribution.

1. What price policy should the department manager follow?
2. What price(s) should she set?

	Sears		Competitor Average Price/Gallon		
Period	Price/ Gallon	Gallons Sold	Montgomery Ward's	K-Mart	Penney's
August 19–September 1	$11.99	178	$11.99	$ 9.69	$12.49
September 2–September 15	9.49	675	11.20	11.99	11.10
September 16–September 29	10.99	397	9.60	11.99	12.49
September 30–October 13	8.99	833	11.40	11.99	12.49
October 14–October 27	11.49	212	11.99	9.99	12.49
October 28–November 10	11.99	302	11.99	11.75	12.49
November 11–November 24	9.99	514	11.99	11.99	10.10
November 25–December 8	8.99	462	10.45	11.99	10.70
December 9–December 22	8.49	90	10.60	11.99	12.49
December 23–January 5	9.49	321	11.99	11.99	12.49
January 6–January 19	11.99	714	11.99	11.99	12.49

*Data have been disguised, but the same price–quantity sold patterns were retained.

Pricing of Pampers

After several years of development by the Procter & Gamble Company, Pampers, the disposable diaper, was test marketed in Peoria, Illinois, in 1961. The price of 10 cents per diaper was based on the estimated costs of producing and selling 400 million diapers annually.

The Peoria test was a major disappointment. It indicated that the most Procter & Gamble could hope to sell nationally was fewer than 200 million diapers per year.

A marketing research study conducted in the Peoria area indicated that price was the major problem. Consumers liked the disposable diaper, but at 10 cents per diaper the cost of using them was too high.

The average cost of producing and marketing Pampers at an annual rate of 400 million per year was estimated to be 3.0 cents per diaper. Procter & Gamble's analysts estimated that if 1 billion diapers could be produced and sold per year (in a total estimated domestic market of 15 billion diaper changes per year), the production and marketing costs could be reduced to 2.4 cents per diaper. At a retail price of 6 cents per diaper, this would allow the same percentage mark-ups in the distribution channel and Procter & Gamble to make the same total amount of profit (although the profit per unit would be lower).

In 1964, Pampers was test marketed again, this time in Sacramento, California, and at a price of 6 cents per diaper. It was an immediate success, with respect to both trial and repeat-purchase rates. Additional test markets were conducted that confirmed the Sacramento findings. The decision to go to national distribution was made as a result of these tests.

Until mid 1970, demand for the product was greater than could be supplied. The price was kept constant, however, and supplies were allocated to supermarkets carrying the product. By the middle of 1970, almost 20 years after the idea of a disposable diaper was first considered, Pampers was available in sufficient quantity to satisfy demand throughout the United States. By 1976, almost half the babies in the country were wearing Pampers.

1. Is this an example of a profit-oriented or a share-oriented, or a combination profit- and share-oriented pricing policy? Explain.
2. From the data given, estimate the level of the experience curve for Pampers.

White Mountain Motor Company: Pricing of the Long-Life Pick-up/Delivery Vehicle

The specifications issued by Eagle Air Express for the next generation of pick-up and delivery vehicles called for, among other things, a use life of 24 years. Since Eagle planned to buy almost 3,000 of the vehicles and since the U.S. Postal Service, United Parcel Service, and the other air express companies presumably would be purchasing similar vehicles, obtaining the order was attractive.

Several companies designed vehicles that they hoped would meet the 24-year use life requirement. After a specified time to allow for research and development for these new vehicles, Eagle ran accelerated use tests on prototypes of them at a testing facility near Laredo, Texas. Among other stringent requirements in the test, each vehicle was required to run over 35,000 potholes. The vehicle designed by the White Mountain Motor Company (named the Long-Life Pick-up/Delivery Vehicle (LLPDV, usually referred to as the PDV) was the only one of the vehicles tested that passed the longevity requirement. (It would require an engine change after 12 years, however.)

The competition for the contract came down to the PDV and an updated version of the current generation of vehicles being used by Eagle, the AJ8-D. The AJ8 series was manufactured by Lake Erie General Corp. and the -D version had a use life of 12 years as estimated from the test.

White Mountain management believed the PDV had some operating advantages over the AJ8 in addition to the longer use life. The LLPDV had an aerodynamic design that reduced air resistance. This both increased gasoline mileage and made the vehicle more stable. It also was designed so that the width between the front wheels was less than that between the back wheels. This gave the PDV a shorter turning radius than the AJ8-D and made it more maneuverable in general.

White Mountain began to work out a price for the PDV. The estimated average total cost of the PDV over the 2,950 units to be purchased by Eagle came out to be just under $9,000 each. The White Mountain management recognized that the relevant cost to the purchaser of a vehicle was its *life cycle cost*—the purchase price plus the costs of operation and maintenance over its use life minus the salvage value when it was to be replaced. Further, it understood that since the operation and maintenance costs would be incurred over an extended period and the purchase price was to occur at the start of the use life, the appropriate way to treat the operation and maintenance costs, and the salvage value, was to discount them to the present.

To make a valid comparison of the costs of owning and operating the PDV with the AJ8-D, it was necessary to estimate the present value of the costs of operation and maintenance of the PDV for its 24-year estimated life, and the present value of the costs of owning and operating two AJ8s, the second one purchased at the expiration of the estimated 12-year use life of the first. The estimates of the purchase price of the AJ8 and the current (nondiscounted) operating costs, maintenance costs, and salvage values for the PDV and AJ8 are shown in the table below.

Estimates of AJ8-D Purchase Price and Operating and Maintenance Costs and Salvage Prices for the PDV and AJ8-D*

Item of Cost	PDV	AJ8-D
Price for initial AJ8-D		$8,618
Operating costs/year	$ 670	745
Maintenance costs/year	280	280
New engine cost	1,500	—
Price for second AJ8-D	—	8,618
Incremental value per year of PDV due to maneuverability	50	
Salvage value	350	500
Discount rate	7.0%	

*All costs and the salvage prices are estimated in current dollars for the year incurred or realized.

1. What is the life cycle cost of the AJ8-D?
2. What is the economic value to the customer of the PDV?
3. What price should White Mountain management set for the PDV?

The Wichita *Eagle-Beacon*: Improving Subscriber Deliveries

The circulation director for the Wichita *Eagle-Beacon*, a morning and Sunday newspaper in the Knight-Ridder chain, had been keeping track of subscriber complaints for several years. For the past two years they had been slowly edging upward, and had recently reached slightly more than 2 complaints per 1,000 deliveries. He knew this was higher than it should be and, since poor delivery service was the most frequently cited reason for stopping subscriptions, something needed to be done to make deliveries more reliable.

An objective of no more than 1 complaint per 1,000 deliveries was set, and a program was begun to try and achieve it.

What steps might have been taken to help reduce complaints? Explain.

MARKETING ORGANIZATION, CONTROLS AND AUDITS, AND INTERNATIONAL MARKETING

V

If structure in fact follows strategy, as the organizational dictum says it should, the way in which the marketing activities of the company are organized reveal much about the company's marketing strategy. Similarly, if the caliber of controls is a measure of mastery, the nature and extent of the controls used will disclose much about the competence of the marketing manager.

Not since the time of the colonies has international trade been so important to the American economy—and to the American company—as it is today. International marketing is a central task, perhaps *the* central task, involved in international trade.

This section begins with a chapter on marketing organization and is followed by one on marketing controls and audits. The section concludes with the chapter on international marketing.

CHAPTER 19

MARKETING ORGANIZATION

In 1980, Eastman Kodak had a single marketing unit that was responsible for the marketing of 30,000 products. The overall company organization was divided into both product divisions and market regions; however, the marketing organization was centralized into a "Marketing Division." The vice-president and general manager of the Marketing Division was in charge of a sales department, an advertising department, a department of distribution, and a marketing research department that served all products and geographic regions. Pricing recommendations originated at the product division level, but the Marketing Division vice-president had to approve them before they went into effect.

One executive being responsible for the prices for 30,000 products, in addition to all the other decisions involved in marketing them, led to unavoidable bureaucratic delays. It became evident to the company president that changes needed to be made to streamline the organization.

Suppose you had been the person in charge of a marketing reorganization study. With what primary questions would you have been concerned?

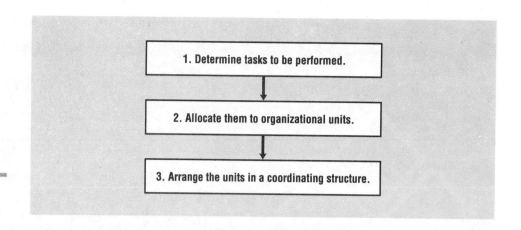

FIGURE 19-1
Steps in the design of an
organization.

Three primary considerations would have been:

1. What are the tasks that should be performed?
2. How should these tasks be allocated to organizational units?
3. How should these units be joined in a coordinating structure?

These questions translate directly into the steps for designing an organization shown in Figure 19–1. They are the steps involved in organizing any activity in which two or more persons are involved, be it as sizable and as complicated as an Eastman Kodak Company or as small and as straightforward as a two-person business.

This chapter is concerned first with a discussion of these steps as they apply to the organizing of marketing activities. The findings of a study on how companies actually organize their marketing efforts are then discussed.

STEPS IN ORGANIZING THE MARKETING FUNCTION

1. The Marketing Tasks to Be Performed

Earlier (in Chapter 1) we defined *marketing management* as

the making and implementing of the decisions necessary for the marketing of specific ideas, goods, and services.

The decisions made concern the analysis, planning, organizing, conducting, and controlling of those activities designed to develop, price, promote, and distribute products and services to target markets.

These are the general tasks that have to be performed in any marketing program. Each of these tasks can be (and should be) broken into several subtasks for organizing purposes. For example, the *distribution* of products involves such activities as the development of distribution channels, inventory management, warehousing, order processing, transportation, dealer relations, and distribution cost analysis.

Lists of marketing mix element subtasks are given in Exhibit 19–1.

EXHIBIT **19-1**

Common Marketing Organizational Units

SALES MANAGER	ADVERTISING MANAGER	MARKETING RESEARCH MANAGER	DISTRIBUTIONS MANAGER

Region
   A
   B
   . . .
Sales training
Sales rep recruiting
Sales compensation
Development of distribution
   channel(s)
Dealer relations
	Product advertising
	Corporate advertising
	Agency liaison
	Advertising budgeting
		Demand analysis
		Surveys
		Forecasting
		Industry data
		Competitor data
			Warehousing
			Transportation
			Order processing
			Development of distributions
			   channel(s)
			Dealer relations
			Distribution cost analysis
			Inventory management

MARKETING PLANNING MANAGER	PROMOTIONS MANAGER	MERCHANDISING MANAGER	CUSTOMER SERVICES MANAGER
Strategic planning Operational planning New product planning	Price promotions Coupon promotions Sampling Games . . .	Dealer aids Sales incentives Point-of-purchase advertising Cooperative advertising	Repairs Applications engineering Credit Warranties

GROUP MARKET MANAGER	GROUP PRODUCT MANAGER	INTERNATIONAL MARKET MANAGER	NEW PRODUCT MARKETING
Manager industrial products Manager consumer products . . .	Brand manager Product A Brand manager Product B . . .	European market Asian market . . .	New Product A New Product B . . . New product planning

MARKETING CONTROLLER	PRICING	PUBLIC RELATIONS	
Budgeting Expense accounts Sales analysis	Product line A Product line B . . .	Customer relations Dealer relations Governmental relations	

2. The Allocation of Tasks to Organizational Units

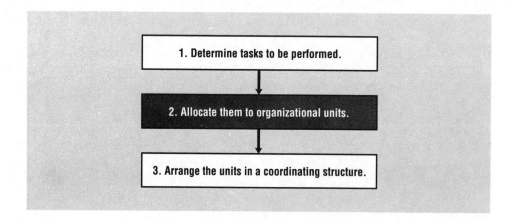

A set of marketing organizational units that commonly are found in companies (although all of them seldom are found in the *same* company) is shown in Exhibit 19–1. The tasks that are typically assigned to each unit are also shown there.

Responsibilities of the Chief Marketing Executive

Whereas, by definition, each marketing task has to be performed in a marketing *program*, it doesn't necessarily have to be performed by a marketing *department*.

The last study on the responsibilities of marketing managers on a task-by-task basis was published in 1976.[1] Although the study was completed more than a decade ago, it was carried out at a time when the organizational emphasis on marketing had been under way for at least 20 years. Its findings therefore perhaps remain reasonably representative of the organizational assignments today.

The study indicated that most marketing managers had responsibility for marketing planning (about 90 percent) and for marketing research (approximately 80 percent), and about two-thirds of them had responsibility for advertising and sales promotion. Roughly 60 percent were responsible for product planning, and about half had responsibility for pricing and field sales management. Only about one-third of them had responsibility for "dealer relations."

These findings indicate that responsibility for one or more of the four elements of the marketing mix often resides in a department other than Marketing. This implication is substantiated by the findings of a study presented later in the chapter about how companies organize their marketing efforts.

3. Deciding on the Marketing Organizational Structure

Virtually every company, even the very small ones, has a **Sales Department**, and all but the smaller companies have an **Advertising Department**. Standardization stops once we get beyond these organizational units, however. The needs of the company in terms of the product markets it serves and the organizational preferences and style of its management conspire to make for different groupings of marketing tasks.

Structure Follows Strategy

In 1980, Eastman Kodak had strategies formulated by product lines and by geographic regions (particularly in Europe and South America). It had organized its domestic manufacturing and engineering activities by product group, and had plants in each of the major countries in which it marketed internationally. Yet at the same time, Marketing was organized as a single "division" responsible for all products and all geographic regions.

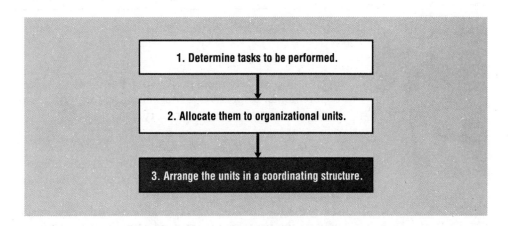

"Form follows function" is a well-known principle for designing buildings. "Structure follows strategy" is an analogous principle for designing organizations. Even a casual examination of the Kodak organization indicates that marketing was not organized in a way that reflects the company's strategies. One of the guiding precepts of the reorganization in 1980 was to correct this mismatch of organization with strategy.

Evolution of the Organization of Marketing Activities

The Six Stages of Marketing Organizational Development

Organization evolves as companies grow and markets change. Six general stages of organizational development can be discerned. These stages are depicted in Figure 19–2.

Stage 1—The "Sales Only" Department: A sales department is central to the marketing effort since "nothing happens in business until a sale is made." Until the late 1800s, the only department formally concerned with marketing in the typical company in the United States was the Sales Department. Although its chief responsibility was calling on and making sales to customers, it usually also was responsible for whatever advertising the company did.

As shown in part *a* of the figure, the product design, pricing, and physical distribution functions of marketing were typically carried out in this form of

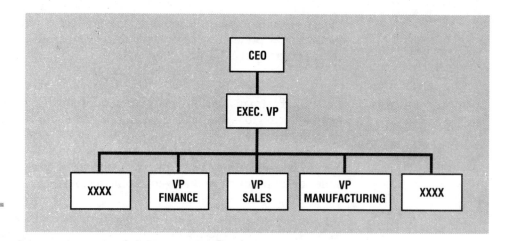

FIGURE 19-2a
Sales department only.

organizational arrangement by the Engineering, Finance, and Manufacturing departments, respectively. Marketing research on a formal basis was not begun until after the turn of the century.

Stage 2—The Sales Plus Advertising Department: By the 1880s, several of the larger companies marketing consumer goods had begun to advertise them extensively. (Products being advertised nationally included Hire's root beer, Ivory soap, Kodak cameras, and Pillsbury's flour.)[2] These companies found that the growing amount of responsibility and effort involved in conducting their advertising programs warranted establishing separate advertising departments.

Other than the very small ones, most companies today have a separate part of their organization devoted to advertising. It may or may not be a part of a marketing department, however. A separate advertising department that is on the same level as the sales department (as shown in part *b* of the figure) is not uncommon. In this form of organization the product design, pricing, and distribution functions typically remain in the Engineering, Finance, and Manufacturing departments, respectively.

FIGURE 19-2b
Sales plus advertising
departments.

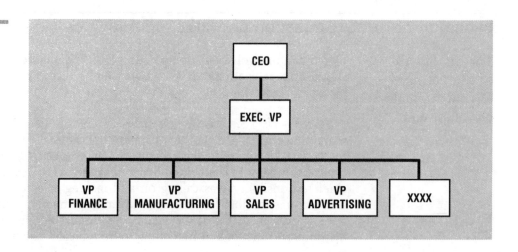

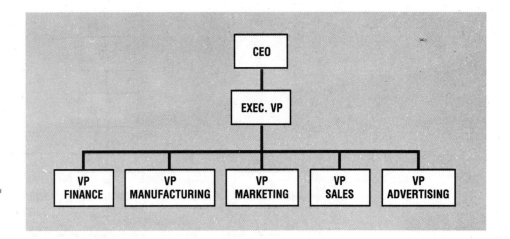

FIGURE 19-2c
Sales plus advertising plus
marketing departments.

Stage 3 — The Sales Plus Advertising Plus "Marketing" Department: As long as a company can sell all it can produce at terms that are acceptable to it, there is little incentive to "market" rather than just to "sell." For many consumer goods companies, the sellers' market that had existed in the United States since its founding came to an end in the 1920s. It is significant in this respect that the first book published with the word "marketing" in its title was in 1920.[3] (Perhaps as valid a marker as any of the end of the sellers' market era is the recognition by Henry Ford in 1926 that he could not successfully continue to "give them any color they want as long as it is black" and, by extension, any model they wanted as long as it was a Model T. It was in that year, after 18 years of producing nothing but black Model T's, that the Ford Motor Company shut down for several months to retool and to start producing Model A's — and in a variety of colors.)

It was in the 1920s that the first "marketing departments" began to appear and the terms marketing manager and marketing strategy began to gain currency.[4] Rarely did these new departments include the sales or advertising function, however. Rather, they were most often concerned with organizing and operating a marketing research section[5] and assimilating one or more of the product planning, pricing, or distribution functions that had until then been the responsibility of other departments. As the brand manager system (to be discussed shortly) gained acceptance in the 1930s, the brand managers and group brand managers involved often became a part of the Marketing Department.

The type of organization shown in part *c* of the figure is a common one today, especially among companies that use brand managers.

Stage 4 — The Functionally Integrated Marketing Department: The functionally integrated marketing department is one in which the chief marketing executive has responsibility for each of the four marketing mix elements — for promotion (for sales and advertising, as well as for any sales promotional activities that are carried out), for pricing, for product development, and for distribution. The responsibility for marketing research also falls within the functionally integrated department. There is no delegation of any of these responsibilities by product or market, however. Part *d* of the figure depicts this form of marketing organization.

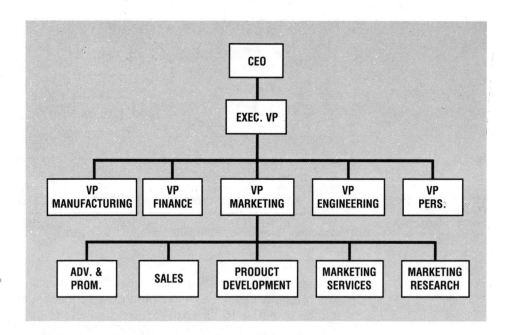

FIGURE 19-2d
The functionally integrated
marketing departments.

Stage 5—The Product-Oriented or Market-Oriented Integrated Marketing De-partment: As companies grow in size, a functionally organized department becomes too cumbersome to provide the attention needed and to act with the speed required to stay competitive in specific products and geographic regions. At some point there is usually a delegation of the marketing for groups of products, geographic areas, or both, with the chief marketing executive retain-

FIGURE 19-2e
The product market-oriented
integrated marketing department.

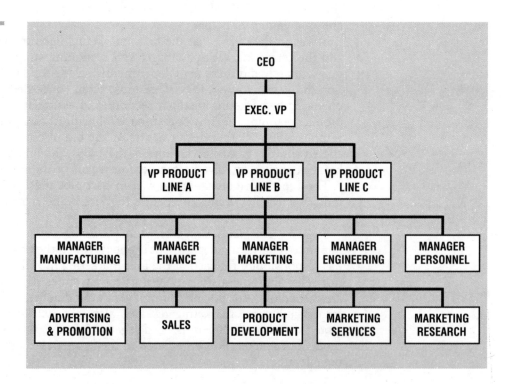

ing the final responsibility for them. A product-oriented integrated marketing organization is shown in Figure 19-2e and a market-oriented integrated marketing organization is shown in part f of the figure.

Stage 6—The Decentralized Marketing Department: A pronounced evolutionary change has taken place since 1950 in large companies in the organizational location of their marketing activities. In these companies, there has been a decided shift *downward* in the organizational level for which the responsibility for carrying out most marketing activities is located. In general, there has been a shift from the corporate to the divisional level, with some companies even shifting responsibility for the marketing of the products of a strategic business unit (SBU) down to that level.

The marketing reorganization of Eastman Kodak mentioned at the beginning of the chapter resulted in marketing's being decentralized by forming marketing departments within each of the several product divisions. There is a straightforward reason for shifts of this kind. The "large" company of 1950 was often a single-product-line firm that was not divisionalized. The large firm of today

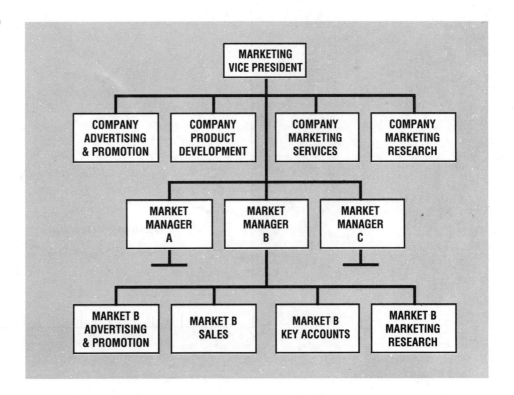

FIGURE 19-2f
The market-oriented integrated marketing organization.

almost always has divisions in a number of industries, and is often multinational in nature as well. Figure 19–3 illustrates the dramatic change from nondivisionalized to divisionalized organization of large companies from 1950 to 1970.

The responsibility for the marketing activities of the company, which necessarily had been at the corporate level before, tended to move to the division when it was established. As shown in Table 19–1, most marketing-related activities in companies that have divisions or subsidiaries are carried out predominantly at the divisional, subsidiary, or SBU level. Responsibility for only those marketing activities that are more nearly corporate-wide in nature (corporate advertising, policy decisions with respect to the advertising agency used, research on markets, research on competitors, economic research) or are not related to the businesses of any of the divisions or subsidiaries (developing new

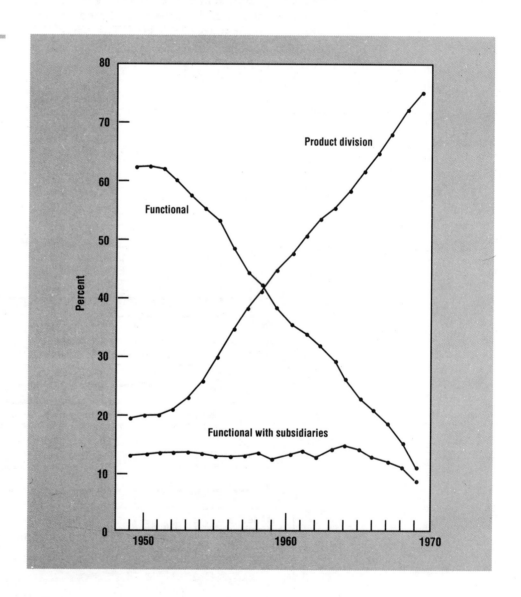

FIGURE 19-3
Shift from nondivisionalized to divisionalized organization of Fortune 500 companies, 1950 to 1970.

Table 19–1 Locations of Marketing-Related Activities

Activity	Companies in Which Some Kind of Indicated Activity Exists (%)	
	Corporate or Group* Level	Divisional or Other Operating Level*
Advertising and promotion		
Corporate advertising	84%	11%
Product advertising	48	84
Sales promotion	39	88
Advertising agency policy decisions	79	51
Sales and distribution		
Sales†	28	88
Dealer relations	28	83
Physical distribution	48	75
Business research and analysis		
Research on markets	90	76
Research on competitors	84	81
Economic research	96	38
Sales forecasting	59	89
Products (excluding R&D)		
Major new products related to existing lines	55	85
Major new products not related to existing lines	90	54
Planning		
Preparation of marketing plans	49	90
Product pricing	45	90

Source: Adapted from D. S. Hopkins and E. L. Bailey, *Organizing Corporate Marketing*, Report No. 845, The Conference Board, 1984, 20. The data are based on information provided by 294 multibusiness manufacturing companies. Percentages in the table may add across to more than 100 percent because of the possible reported location of activities in the same category at more than one organizational level in a company. The percentages are calculated by dividing the usable responses in each category by 294, and so in some instances add across to less than 100 percent due to item nonresponse.
*All of the companies have operating divisions or other operating units, such as subsidiaries or SBUs. About two-thirds of the companies are also organized into groups of divisions or subsidiary companies.
†These percentages are averages of sales to "national" accounts and other customers.

products not related to existing product lines) are conducted primarily at the corporate level.

Organizing the Integrated Marketing Department

Ways of
Organizing
Marketing

Marketing departments can be organized by marketing function, by market, by product, or by combinations of these basic organizational arrangements known as a ***matrix organization***.

Organization by Marketing Function: The most common form of marketing organization is the one in which the marketing department is divided according to ***function***. A typical fully integrated department organized in this way has a sales manager (who often is in charge of developing and maintaining channels of distribution as well as managing the sales force), an advertising and sales promotions manager, a product development manager, a marketing administration manager (whose responsibilities include pricing and marketing planning, among others), and a marketing research manager, all of whom report to a marketing vice-president. An organization chart for such a department is shown in part d of Figure 19–2.

As shown in Table 19–2, a functionally organized department works best when both the products sold and the markets for them are relatively homogeneous. In such a situation there is no need to specialize either by *market* or by *product*, the two major competing ways of organizing a fully integrated department.

Because of the requirement of (relative) homogeneity of both products and markets, the functional form of organization is typically found in smaller companies. The Eastman Kodak Company and Pepsi are exceptions—both are very large companies that have organized their marketing departments on a functional basis. In both cases, this no doubt is because the products produced and the markets served are relatively homogeneous—in the one case both products and markets are closely concerned with photography and in the other with soft drinks. Specialization, either by product or by market, is therefore not required.

Organization by Market: When a company sells its products to many markets, each with differing characteristics and requirements, efficiency sometimes requires that a marketing program be organized by individual market rather than by function only. This permits specialization by market as well as by function and thus provides more expertise in dealing with the requirements of both. IBM is an example of a company that has found this method of organizing its marketing effort desirable; it has a public-sector marketing group along with several different industry marketing groups. One of its competitors, Hewlett-Packard, has recently dropped its product-oriented marketing organization and now also uses a market orientation.

By convention, when one speaks of a department organized by *market*, market refers to a market segment other than a geographic territory. If a department is organized on a straight functional basis in all respects other than having separate sales forces in each of several geographic territories, for example, it is still referred to as having a functional organization.

An organization chart for a marketing department organized by market was given in Figure 19–2f. As shown there, the basic functional organization is

Table 19–2 Form of Organization of Fully Integrated Marketing Departments by Degree of Homogeneity of Products Sold and Markets Served

	Homogeneous Markets	Heterogeneous Markets
Homogeneous products	Organization by function	Organization by market
Heterogeneous products	Organization by product	Matrix organization

retained, but it is partially decentralized by market. Instead of a single sales force, the market managers each have a sales force for their respective markets. There may also be advertising and marketing research staffs within each of the market organizations if the market is large enough to warrant them.

A statement made earlier was that "... efficiency sometimes requires that a marketing program be organized by individual market rather than by function only." This is true, but it should not be interpreted to mean that organizing by market is a less-expensive way to organize the marketing effort. The contrary is true—it almost always costs *more* to organize by market than by function alone. The higher costs are due both to the added supervisory personnel required—a sales supervisor in each market, for example, rather than a manager for a single sales force—and to added costs of sales calls. When customers in different markets are located in the same city, sales representatives from each of the appropriate sales forces must travel to that city to call on them. When a single customer has requirements that fall into two or more different markets, multiple sales calls will be made on the same company by different sales representatives of the company. The added personnel and travel that these extra calls entail increase sales force costs compared with those of territorially based sales organizations.

Still, when markets differ substantially in how they buy or use a product, it may well be more efficient to organize by market than by function because of the higher sales that result.

Organization by Product: When there is not much difference between markets but products vary substantially, it may be desirable to organize by product. This permits specialization by product as well as by function—product development personnel, sales representatives, advertising staff persons, and others each can become very familiar with the products with which they deal as well as being competent in their own functional specialty. The advantages that organizing by product provide led to the general divisionalizing of large companies that occurred in the United States between 1950 and 1970.

An organization chart for a basic product-oriented marketing department can be developed quickly and easily from Figure 19–2e by exchanging the word *product* (or *product line*) for *market* in the middle and bottom rows of boxes. ("Market manager B" therefore becomes "Product manager B," "Market B sales" becomes "Product B sales," and so forth.)

Examples of this basic product orientation in the organization of marketing departments are not difficult to find. For example, USX (formerly U.S. Steel) has divided its marketing efforts by its coal chemical and steel product lines; Borden Chemicals by the adhesives and the industrial chemicals it manufactures and markets; and the Ford Motor Company by vehicles (cars and trucks) and replacement parts.

A closely allied variant of the basic product orientation in the organization of marketing departments is even much more common, however. It is the brand management form of organization initiated and made famous by Procter & Gamble and Johnson & Johnson and since adopted in one form or another by large numbers of packaged consumer goods companies. Some industrial goods producers use it as well.

The **brand management system** is one in which a person is assigned responsibility for coordinating the marketing efforts for one or more brands.[6] A common form of arrangement is for the brand manager to be given a budget for the marketing of each brand and to "buy" the sales support, advertising and marketing research, and other services from the company that the brand requires. This allows the brand to become a profit center and the brand manager to have profit responsibility. Approximately 60 percent of all brand managers in the United States are held accountable for the profitability of their brands.[7]

Most brand managers are responsible for several brands, some having more than 10. The median number appears to be three or four.[8] If there are very many brand managers in the organization, they typically report to a group brand manager. In an integrated marketing organization, the group brand manager in turn reports to the chief marketing executive.

The brand management system has the obvious advantage of decentralizing and focusing the sales and advertising and other marketing efforts on a brand in an otherwise centralized organization in which each brand might not get individual attention. One study indicates that 85 percent of large consumer packaged goods companies had brand managers, as did 55 percent of large industrial goods companies.[9] Among the well-known companies that have brand managers are General Foods, Miller Brewing, Max Factor, Pillsbury, Union Carbide, and Uniroyal. Even the U.S. Postal Service has a number of "brand" managers.

This system is not without problems, however. Unless a budget is provided with which to "buy" the needed sales and advertising and other marketing support, brand managers have to rely on persuasion to get the needed services for their brands. Even with budgetary support, the functional heads from whom they "buy" recognize that the brand manager is a captive customer who has little negotiating power. For brand managers who have profit responsibility and who are rewarded commensurately with the profit performance of their brands, there is an incentive not to "invest" in the brand to build market share (by, say, keeping the price down or keeping advertising budgets up) if this is detrimental to short-term profits. There has also been a relatively high level of turnover because:

> ... The job attracts high potential, well-motivated individuals who consider brand management a stepping stone to higher management. To attract and to hold good people companies in the past have advanced them from assistant to associate to brand manager to group brand manager fairly rapidly.[10]

For these and other reasons, there has been a reported trend toward making the brand manager primarily a planner and coordinator and moving the decision-making responsibility to higher levels in the organization. Some companies, such as Pepsi and Levi-Strauss, have dropped it altogether. There does not appear to be any general trend toward discontinuing this method of organization, however.

The Matrix Organization: The distinguishing characteristic of a ***matrix marketing organization*** is that it:

> Combines two or more of the functional, product, and market dimensions at the same level, with the functional specialists, product, or market managers each reporting to two or more persons.[11]

One version of a matrix for a marketing organization is shown in Figure 19–4. In this example, groups of functional specialists are assigned to a particular market manager and to the appropriate functional manager to work on their specialty in that market. This feature of having persons report to more than one superior is at once the major strength, and the primary weakness, of this method of organization. It is a strength because it gives, in this example, both the market manager and the functional manager authority commensurate with their responsibilities. The market manager has the responsibility of meeting a target sales level for each of the products sold in his or her market, for example. The sales representatives assigned to that market can then be directed to take the actions necessary, in the market manager's opinion, to realize those levels of sales. The sales manager has the responsibility for recruiting, selecting, training, assigning, evaluating, and compensating those same sales representatives. He or she also has the necessary authority to meet those responsibilities.

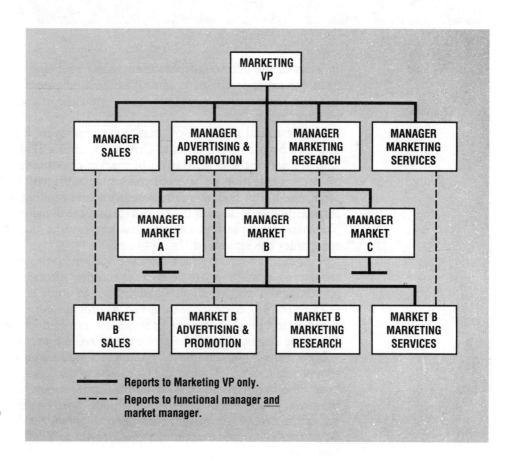

FIGURE 19-4
Example of matrix organization.

The weakness of the matrix system is obvious—it violates the traditional principle of unity of command. Reporting to two superiors simultaneously almost always leads to uncertainty and ambiguity on the part of the subordinates and often leads to conflict between superiors. As a result, matrix organizations have been described as "stressful places in which to work."

It is also the most-expensive form of organization. It requires more managers, more negotiation between managers, and more meetings with subordinates to relay decisions and to answer questions than any of the other forms of organization.

The matrix system has perhaps been used most widely by highly technical companies in their attempts to apply technical expertise to a variety of markets. It is also used by chain retailing organizations (J. C. Penney, for example), which have buyers reporting to both the executive responsible for store operation and the one responsible for merchandise buying. It is also used in the marketing organizations of Citibank and Dow-Corning. (Dow-Corning uses a three-dimensional form involving functions, products, and markets.)

AN OVERVIEW OF HOW MARKETING IS ORGANIZED IN COMPANIES

In view of the current corporate emphasis on being "market driven" and the need for an appropriate organization to implement market strategies effectively, it is surprising how little is known about marketing structure in American businesses.

The empirical literature on marketing organization is limited in both scope and number of investigations. One finds empirical studies in three areas: (1) case studies of the organization of marketing activities of (a few) companies; (2) the organization of selected marketing subfunctions (the national account force, the brand management system) across companies;[12] and (3) marketing responsibilities located at the corporate and the divisional levels of companies.[13] Nowhere does one find an overview of how the marketing functions within companies are organized.[14]

A study has been conducted by the authors to provide an indication of how companies actually organize their marketing efforts. Data were obtained for 63 companies ranging in size from about $1 million to $7+ billion in annual sales.[15] The respondents were asked to provide information on the marketing organization for the *company* if there were no product divisions or subsidiaries, or for the largest *product division* or *subsidiary* if there were such.

Even though the sample of companies was taken at random, the low response rate (63 of 329 companies, or 19 percent) prevents the use of significance tests of differences among small and large companies, or consumer versus industrial goods versus service companies. Some of the differences shown in the tables below are of sufficient size to provide a basis for reaching some judgments about organizational variations across these categories of companies, however.

Fragmented versus Integrated Organizations

A ***fragmented marketing organization*** is defined as one in which a manager of one or more of the four marketing mix elements reports to someone other than the chief marketing officer. Conversely, an ***integrated marketing organization*** is defined as one in which the manager of each of the four marketing mix elements reports to the chief marketing officer.

The findings with respect to fragmentation versus integration are as follows:

	Total		Fragmented Organization		Integrated Organization	
	No.	%	No.	%	No.	%
Small companies*	25	40	7	28	18	72
Large companies*	38	60	25	66	13	34
Total	63	100	32	51	31	49
Consumer goods	28	44	14	50	14	50
Industrial goods	19	30	10	53	9	47
Services	16	26	8	50	8	50
Total	63	100	32		31	

*Companies with sales of $100 million or less were classified as *small*; those with sales greater than $100 million, and that were divisionalized or had subsidiaries, were classified as *large*.

These data indicate that

- Small-company marketing organizations tend to be less fragmented (28 percent) than those of large companies (66 percent).
- There is no apparent difference in the percentages of consumer goods (50 percent), industrial goods (53 percent), and service companies (50 percent) that have fragmented marketing organizations.

Executives in smaller companies in general tend to have a broader range of responsibilities than those in larger companies, however, and so one might expect marketing organizations in small companies to be less fragmented for this reason.

Other things being equal, is an integrated marketing organization to be preferred to a fragmented one? The answer is: In general, "yes." The reason is that the marketing mix element decisions should be made interactively. For example, it is generally not appropriate to have a high advertising budget for a product that has a low contribution margin, nor is it appropriate to have a low advertising budget for a product with a high contribution margin. Yet if one manager reporting to one superior is setting price (and thus the contribution margin) for a product, and another manager reporting to a different superior is allocating the advertising budget to that same product, it is much less likely that the two figures will each be set with full knowledge of how the other was made.

Integrated Marketing Organizations—Functional, Product-Oriented, Market-Oriented, and Matrix Organizations

The data with respect to how marketing departments in which the responsibility for all of the four mix elements is vested are organized are as follows:

	Total		Functional Organization		Product- or Market-oriented, or Matrix	
	No.	%	No.	%	No.	%
Small companies	25	40	12	48	13	52
Large companies	38	60	4	11	34	89
Total	63	100	16	25	47	75

These data suggest that:

- A substantially higher proportion of small companies have functionally organized departments (48 percent) than do large companies (11 percent). The remainder in both cases are product- or market-oriented, or organized in a matrix.

A logical explanation of this difference is that smaller companies have yet to grow to the point where the functional form of organization becomes too cumbersome to use, and so the company has not yet had to turn to product or market managers or a matrix organization to gain efficiency.

Proportions of Companies with Product-Oriented, Market-Oriented, and Matrix Organizations

Many of the companies with fragmented marketing organizations also have product and/or market managers, or matrix organizations. The total numbers (and percentages) of companies in the survey with product-oriented, market-oriented, and matrix organizations are as follows:

	Total		Product-oriented		Market-oriented		Matrix	
	No.	%	No.	%	No.	%	No.	%
Fragmented	32	51	13	41	20	63	3	9
Integrated	31	49	7	23	12	39	2	6
	63	100	20	32	32	51	5	8

These findings suggest that:

- Market managers are more common (51 percent) than product managers (32 percent).
- Matrix organizations are relatively *uncommon* (8 percent).

Despite the greater amount of attention that has been paid in the trade press to product managers, it probably should not be surprising that market managers outnumber them. Most companies that market their products nationally have regional sales (or, more recently, sales + advertising) managers, and an even greater percentage of those who market internationally have separate marketing organizations for that purpose.

Relative Frequency of Reorganization and Change of the Person in Charge of the Marketing Department

The responses for the indicated questions on the relative frequency of reorganization and the relative frequency of change of the heads of the departments in companies were:

Based on your company's experience, rank order the following areas in terms of frequency of reorganization using the number "1" for the area most frequently reorganized and the number "5" for the area least frequently reorganized:

	Number of Responses				
	1	2	3	4	5
Marketing	25	6	11	2	5
Production	9	16	6	10	6
Finance and Accounting	3	9	13	8	17
Engineering	4	7	4	14	14
Purchasing	2	10	9	8	16

Rank order the areas where changes of the person in charge occur (indicate with a "1" the area with most frequent changes to a "5" with least frequent changes):

	Number of Responses				
	1	2	3	4	5
Marketing	24	5	5	3	5
Production	6	15	8	7	6
Finance and Accounting	3	10	6	14	9
Engineering	2	7	7	8	11
Purchasing	5	3	10	6	16

These data indicate that:

- Marketing departments are the most frequently reorganized, and changes in chief marketing executives occur more frequently than that for any of the other major departments in the company, both by a substantial margin.

No data were obtained to explain why Marketing is the clear leader in both categories. A possible explanation for the relatively higher frequency of reorganization is that a company strategy change would almost always affect Marketing, whereas it might or might not affect the other departments. Some companies undergo a substantial initial reorganization and then several successive fine-tuning reorganizations over a short period to iron out problems encountered in the first one. From 1980 through 1986, Eastman Kodak had five reorganizations of Marketing to get from a functional to a product-and-market-oriented matrix organization, for example.

It is not clear whether the higher frequency of change of marketing executives is from choice or necessity on the part of the company. Whether it is their fault or not, marketing executives are probably more vulnerable to disappointing company performances than are the other department heads. Marketing managers also have substantially more exposure outside the company than do their counterparts in the other departments, and so may well receive more (unsolicited) offers for other jobs.

How Can the Marketing Manager Tell If the Organization Being Used Is Appropriate?

Although it is difficult to measure organizational effectiveness,[16] there are suggestive symptoms that, when present, ought to raise the question of whether the organization being used is the appropriate one. They include:

1. Ambiguity about and conflicts over authority to make marketing decisions.
2. Lack of consideration of effect on linked variables when a decision on a single marketing variable is made.
3. Inability of decision makers to anticipate marketing problems.
4. Information flows within the organization fail to provide decision makers with necessary information.
5. Slow reactions to changes in the marketing environment; and
6. High levels of customer complaints.[17]

SUMMARY OF IMPORTANT POINTS

1. The central questions in organizing any activity in which two or more persons are involved are:
   a. What are the tasks that should be performed?

b. How should these tasks be allocated to organizational units?

c. How should these units be joined in a coordinating structure?

2. A guiding principle in setting up a marketing organization is that "structure follows strategy."

3. Other factors being the same, the degree of homogeneity or heterogeneity of products and of markets suggests the following kinds of organizational arrangements:

	Homogeneous Markets	Heterogeneous Markets
Homogeneous Products	Organization by function	Organization by market
Heterogeneous Products	Organization by product	Matrix organization

4. A *matrix organization* combines two or more of the functional, product, and market dimensions at the same level, with the product or market managers each reporting to two or more persons.

5. The major weakness of a matrix organization is that it requires subordinates to report to more than one superior—it violates the traditional principle of unity of command.

6. **a.** A *fragmented marketing organization* is one in which a manager of one or more of the four marketing mix elements reports to someone other than the chief marketing officer.

   b. An *integrated marketing organization* is one in which the manager of each of the four marketing mix elements reports to the chief marketing officer.

7. The available evidence suggests that small-company marketing organizations tend to be fragmented less often than those of large companies. There is little difference in the percentages of consumer goods, industrial goods, and service companies that have fragmented marketing organizations, however.

8. About one-half of small companies have functionally organized departments compared with only about one-tenth of large companies. The remainder of large and small companies with integrated departments organize them by product or market, or in a matrix.

9. About one-half of all companies have market managers, whereas only about one-third have product managers. Only about one company in ten has a matrix marketing organization.

10. Marketing departments undergo more frequent reorganizations than other major departments of the company, and marketing managers change more often than any of the other department managers.

11. The symptoms of an inappropriate organization for the marketing activities of a company include:

   a. Ambiguity about and conflicts over authority to make marketing decisions.

   b. Lack of consideration of effect on linked variables when a decision on a single marketing variable is made.

   c. Inability of decision makers to anticipate marketing problems.

   d. Information flows within the organization fail to provide decision makers with necessary information.

   e. Slow reactions to changes in the marketing environment.

   f. High levels of customer complaints.

REVIEW QUESTIONS

19.1.   What are the central questions in organizing any activity in which two or more persons are involved?

19.2.   Describe in your own words the meaning of "structure follows strategy."

19.3.   Why has responsibility for the marketing operations of companies "moved down" in U.S. companies over the past 40 years?

19.4.   Other things being equal, what kind of organization should a company have that has

   a.   Heterogeneous products and homogeneous markets?

   b.   Homogeneous products and heterogeneous markets?

   c.   Homogeneous products and homogeneous markets?

   d.   Heterogeneous products and heterogeneous markets?

19.5.   What is:

   a.   A *fragmented* marketing organization?

   b.   An *integrated* marketing organization?

19.6.   a.   What is a *matrix* organization?

   b.   What is its major strength?

   c.   What is its major weakness?

19.7.   a.   About what proportion of U.S. companies have integrated marketing departments?

   b.   Does a higher proportion of small companies or of large companies have integrated marketing departments? Why do you think this might be the case?

19.8.   Are market-oriented, product-oriented, or matrix marketing organizations the most prevalent among U.S. companies? Why do you think this might be the case?

19.9. How do marketing departments compare with the departments of manufacturing, engineering, accounting and finance, and purchasing with respect to the frequency of:
a. Reorganization?
b. Change of department head?

DISCUSSION QUESTIONS

19.10. It is not unusual for two competitors selling the same products to the same markets to have organized their marketing operations differently. Is this an indication that one of them is handicapping itself with an inferior marketing organization? Why or why not?

19.11. From the evidence given in the study of marketing organization in the chapter, only about one-half of all companies have an integrated marketing organization.
    What are the major arguments that a company:
a. should have an integrated marketing organization?
b. need not have an integrated marketing organization?
c. On balance, which do you conclude is preferable?

19.12. Some companies using the brand management form of organization establish "budgets" for the operating period that allow the brand manager to "buy" the sales, advertising, promotional, and research support they need from the appropriate departments within the company. Other companies do not set budgets for the brand managers but require them to present a case to the sales manager, advertising manager, and so forth for the support they need for the period. Which method do you believe is preferable? Explain.

19.13. Why would:
a. A product-oriented organization be more expensive to operate than a functional organization?
b. A matrix organization be more expensive to operate than a product-oriented organization?

19.14. Are there likely to be any differences in the design of new products if the product-planning function is a responsibility of the Engineering Department rather than of the Marketing Department? Explain.

19.15. Is designing the marketing organization susceptible to the methods of management science? Explain.

19.16. A few years ago, Xerox Company changed from a territorial to an industry-oriented sales organization. (Instead of having a sales manager for each of several territories, it has a sales manager for each of the industries to which it markets its products.)

a. Would the change have resulted in added marketing costs? Explain.

b. What differences would result if it changed now to industry *marketing* managers?

19.17. Suppose you are the marketing manager of a microcomputer company that markets its products to the business, education, and home segments. Sales are made directly to the business and educational users, and to computer stores for the home market.

In the past, the sales force has been organized by geographic territories with a sales manager and a sales force in each territory. The territorial sales managers report to a general sales manager. You are now considering adding managers for each of the three market segments, each to report to a group market manager.

a. Should the territorial sales force be broken into business, education, and computer store specialists? Why or why not?

b. Should the territorial sales managers also report to the market manager? Why or why not?

19.18. a. Draw a chart of the marketing organization if the answers to 19.17a and b were "yes."

b. Draw a chart of the marketing organization if the answers to 19.17a and b were "no."

PROJECTS

19.19. Interview two companies that are competitors located in the city where you live or attend college to determine what their strategies are and how they have organized their marketing activities. Analyze the organizations to determine:

a. Similarities and dissimilarities in organization

b. Appropriateness of the organizations given the companies' strategies

c. Any changes you would recommend

19.20. Consult the Standard & Poor's Register of Corporations, Directors and Executives in your university library to obtain a list of the marketing executives for the Coca-Cola Bottling Company of Los Angeles, the Coca-Cola Bottling Company of Memphis, the Pepsi-Cola Bottling Company of San Francisco, and the Pepsi-Cola Bottling Company of Spokane.

From the data you obtain, what conclusions do you draw about:

a. The degree of integration of the marketing organization of the bottlers?

b. The degree of similarity or differences of the marketing organizations of the bottlers?

Endnotes

[1]Heidrick and Struggles, *Profile of a Chief Marketing Executive*, 1976. The responding chief marketing executives were from Fortune 1,000 companies. Chief marketing executives from 360 companies responded.

[2]F. Presbrey, *The History and Development of Advertising*, Doubleday, Doran & Company, 1929, 338–339.

[3]It was *The Elements of Marketing* by P. T. Cherington, published by Macmillan in 1920.

[4]For example, the term *marketing manager* is used by L. S. Lyon in his book, *Salesmen in Marketing Strategy*, Macmillan, 1926. A year later, the book by W. D. Moriarity, *Scientific Marketing Management: Its Principles and Methods*, was published.

[5]L. C. Lockley, "Notes on the History of Marketing Research," *Journal of Marketing*, April 1950, 733–736.

[6]In some companies, the person involved in the marketing of a brand that is the company's only product in that category is called a *product manager*. We use the two terms interchangeably.

[7]As reported in R. T. Hise and J. P. Kelly, "Product Management on Trial," *Journal of Marketing*, October 1978, 30; 61 percent of 198 brand managers surveyed had profit responsibility.

[8]Ibid, 31.

[9]Association of National Advertisers, *Current Advertising Practices: Opinions as to Future Trends*, 1974.

[10]V. P. Buell, "The Changing Role of the Product Manager," *Journal of Marketing*, July 1975, 10.

[11]K. Knight, "Matrix Organization: A Review," *The Journal of Management Studies*, 1976, 125.

[12]B. P. Shapiro and R. T. Moriarty, "Organizing the National Account Force," Working Paper, Marketing Science Institute, April, 1984; Hise and Kelley, "Product Management on Trial," 28–33; and L. Skenazy, "Brand Managers Shelved?" *Advertising Age*, July 13, 1987, 81, are examples.

[13]D. S. Hopkins, and E. L. Bailey, "Organizing Corporate Marketing," The Conference Board, Report No. 845, 1984.

[14]Heidrick and Struggles, the executive search service firm, conducts a periodic survey of the tasks and responsibilities assigned to the chief marketing officers of large firms. The usefulness of this survey for the purpose at hand is diminished by three factors, however: (a) it does not distinguish between corporate and divisional level marketing executives; (b) one cannot tell from the aggregated responses what proportion of companies have integrated versus fragmented marketing departments; and (c) one cannot determine the organization of the functions within the marketing department. The latest of these surveys is entitled "Chief Marketing Executive" and was conducted in 1988.

[15]The survey was conducted by mail using a random sample of 329 companies listed in Standard & Poor's Register of Corporations. One follow-up mailing was made to nonrespondents.

[16]R. M. Steers, "Problems in the Measurement of Organizational Effectiveness," *Administrative Science Quarterly*, December, 1975, 546–558.

[17]Adapted from a similar listing in B. Weitz and E. Anderson, "Organizing the Marketing Function," in B. Enis and K. Roering, *Review of Marketing*, American Marketing Association, 140.

MARKETING AUDITS AND CONTROLS

A central objective of the management of every company is to have a marketing program that is efficient from both a design and an implementation standpoint. A **design-efficient** program is one in which the marketing strategies and plans used provide the opportunity for a high level of performance. Thus:

> If Perrier, a company in France that bottles and markets spring water, developed sound strategies and plans for the introduction of its product into the United States, it would have a *design-efficient* marketing program for that purpose.

An **implementation-efficient** marketing program is one that is carried out in such a way as to achieve a high proportion of its potential at a reasonable cost. In Perrier's case:

> If the program were carried out competently so that a high proportion of its potential were actually achieved in a cost-effective manner, it would have an *implementation-efficient* program for the U.S. introduction.[1]

The design efficiency of a marketing program is measured through a marketing audit, and its implementation efficiency is measured and maintained through a system of marketing controls.

The topics of marketing design and implementation efficiency are the central concerns of this chapter.

DESIGN EFFICIENCY OF THE MARKETING PROGRAM—MEASUREMENT THROUGH THE MARKETING AUDIT

Design efficiency can be measured through an audit of the entire marketing program or just a part of it. If the audit is a review of the overall marketing program, it is customarily called a "marketing audit." It is defined as follows:

> A *marketing audit* consists of an independent, objective, and thorough review of the marketing environment and the manner in which the overall marketing program is conducted with respect to its organization, objectives, strategies, planning, and decision support systems; functional area programs; and overall marketing productivity for the purposes of determining (1) how well it is being conducted and (2) how it can be improved.

If the audit is for only a *part* of the overall marketing effort (say, of only the promotional program), it is ordinarily known as a *functional audit*.

A marketing audit is similar to a financial audit in that each requires that answers be obtained to a set of critical questions concerning the area being audited. In the case of the financial audit, many of the questions for which the representative of an accounting firm must obtain answers before making an informed judgment on the financial condition of the company are specified by the profession through the American Institute of Certified Public Accountants. No similar agency in marketing exists for codifying the questions to be asked in conducting a marketing audit. However, even in the relatively short time since marketing audits were first conducted,[2] conventional wisdom and accumulated experience have led to a working consensus on the areas to be audited and the general nature of the questions to be asked.[3]

The results of the marketing audit of a large U.S. food retailer are described in Exhibit 20–1. During the first year after the audit was completed, the company invested more than $250 million in increasing the number of its food–drug combination stores and opening limited-assortment, limited-service discount stores. During the second year after the audit, it acquired a 51 percent interest in Sav-On Drug, a large West Coast drug chain. In both years it continued to dispose of smaller stores. Profits after the audit increased steadily each year, with a total increase for a five-year post-audit period of just over 200 percent (in real terms).

EXHIBIT **20-1**

Marketing Audit of the Jewel Companies (Jewel Tea) Retailing Operations

Dissatisfied with near-static profit levels and notwithstanding the fact that it had grown to be the sixth-largest food chain in the United States, the management of Jewel Companies ordered "a massive reassessment" of the company's retailing operations.

The supermarket industry had been plagued by maturing markets, price wars, and rising costs. Whereas Jewel sales had increased by more than 26 percent over the preceding five years, profits had increased by a total of less than 7½ percent during the same period. Management commissioned a comprehensive marketing audit to find out what should be done to make its retailing operations more profitable.

The audit resulted in the following conclusions:

- The company should increase its emphasis on limited-line, limited-service discount grocery stores.

- The proportion of private-brand and generic products carried should rise, with a concomitant reduction in nationally branded and advertised products.
- Large stores offer a greater return on investment than smaller stores. The company should therefore sell, or franchise, its smaller supermarkets and concentrate on operating large stores.
- Large combination food and drug stores offer more profit potential than large food supermarkets alone. The company should expand its number of combination stores both in present markets and in areas where it does not now have stores.
- The company should also acquire, or open, large drug–general merchandise stores.

Areas That Should Be Audited and Questions That Should Be Asked

The major audit areas are specified in the definition given above. There are seven such areas: marketing environment, organization, objectives, strategies, planning and decision support systems, functional area programs, and overall marketing productivity.

An example of the types of questions that need to be raised in a *functional audit* (in this case, the promotion program) is given in Exhibit 20–2. The full schedule of questions that need to be asked in a *marketing audit* are shown in Exhibit 20–5. (Because of its length, it is given at the end of the chapter.) Note that in each exhibit, references are given for each question to the sections of this and earlier chapters that will be of assistance in answering them.

Who Should Conduct the Marketing Audit?

As even a cursory review of the questions in Exhibit 20–5 suggests, conducting a good marketing audit requires a substantial amount of effort by knowledgeable auditors. In the usual case, an auditing team is used rather than having a single person take on the entire task. The team typically consists of a chief auditor from outside the department (to ensure independence), one or more

EXHIBIT **20-2**

Appropriate Questions for a Functional Audit of Advertising, Sales Promotion, and Public Relations

1. Is there a clearly defined set of advertising objectives? Do they follow logically from the corporate and marketing objectives? Chapter 14, pp. 468–469.
2. Is the advertising budget determined by an appropriate method? Chapter 15, pp. 492–499.
3. Are media selected by an appropriate method? Chapter 15, pp. 502–510.
4. Are there clearly stated objectives for the:
   a. Sales promotion program?
   b. Public relations program?
5. Are measurements made at the appropriate times or intervals of the effectiveness of
   a. Advertising theme and copy? Chapter 15, pp. 500–502.
   b. The overall advertising program? Chapter 20, p. 679.
   c. The sales promotional program? Chapter 15, pp. 512–514.
   d. The public relations program? Chapter 15, pp. 516–517.
6. How effectively is the advertising agency performing?

persons from the Marketing Department (to collect data from inside the department), and a person from the Accounting Department (to provide financial data). The services of outside agencies may also be used from time to time (to provide independent economic or industry forecasts, conduct a customer survey, and so forth).

The selection of the chief auditor is, of course, the most critical to the success of the venture. The usual arrangement is for a consultant from outside the company to be retained to head the auditing effort. In instances in which the department being audited is in a division of a larger corporation, the chief auditor—and perhaps functional area specialists as well—may be assigned from the corporate marketing staff. (General Electric and International Telephone & Telegraph follow this practice, for example.) In either case, the person selected should be thoroughly competent in the field of marketing, and preferably should have had prior experience in conducting audits. The chief auditor should report to the executive to whom the marketing manager reports, or to the next higher level, taking care to keep the marketing manager fully informed of all findings.

Before the appointment of the chief auditor is made final, agreements should be reached concerning the objectives of the audit and questions to be answered, the data to be made available by the company and those to be generated by the auditors (including outside agencies), who the inside members of the auditing team are to be and the time available from each, interim reporting dates, the scheduled completion date, and the budget for the audit. Having these agreements reduced to writing and signed by the persons concerned will help prevent later potential disagreements.

How Long Should the Audit Take?

Audits require from a few weeks to over a year to conduct. The length depends on the comprehensiveness of the audit and the extent to which the needed data are already available. An audit for an industrial supplier that involved relatively limited objectives and required only a survey of a sample of customers in the way of outside data was conducted by a consultant in eight weeks. At the other extreme, the audit conducted by Jewel Tea involved "a major reassessment" of its retailing operations and took nearly 18 months (Exhibit 20–1).

Although audits should be done expeditiously, undue pressure to complete them may result in corners' being cut in terms of obtaining and analyzing critical data. Sufficient time should be allowed to avoid this problem.

How Often Should an Audit Be Carried Out?

Audits often are held as a reaction to a sharp downturn in sales, unsatisfactory margin levels, or the surfacing of other marketing related problems. Had an audit been held before the crisis appeared, however, it might have been averted, or its severity at least reduced.

Audits have an obvious close association with long-range planning, and the timing of them can be tied profitably to the long-range planning cycle. Companies tend to do major revisions of their long-range plans at intervals of three, five, or ten years, depending on how dynamic the nature of their business is. A strong case can be made for conducting a marketing audit before each such revision, both for reasons of evaluating and improving the marketing program and for using the results of the audit as a major source of information to be used in preparing the plan.

MARKETING IMPLEMENTATION—MEASUREMENT AND MAINTENANCE THROUGH A SYSTEM OF MARKETING CONTROLS

The Elements of the Marketing Control System

Broadly speaking, **marketing control** includes "everything that helps ensure that the people in the organization are acting so as to implement properly the [marketing] strategy that has been agreed upon."[4] In a programmatic sense, a well-designed marketing control system consists of the following four elements:

1. Deciding on which variables are to be controlled
2. Setting a budget or a standard of performance for each

3. Measuring actual costs and performances;

4. Taking corrective action when required

The budgets and performance standards typically are stated in quantitative terms, and so the measurements of actual costs and performances necessarily are carried out numerically. Harold Geneen, the former chief executive officer of ITT, has stated that:

> The difference between well-managed companies and not so well-managed companies is the degree of attention they pay to numbers. . . . How often are the numbers reported up the chain of command? How much variation is tolerated between budget forecasts and actual results? How deep does management dig for its answers?[5]

It is clear that he was referring only to the controlling function of management when he made this statement. Sound strategic planning is not and cannot be primarily numerical in nature.

What Marketing Variables Should Be Controlled?

The first step in setting up a control system is the obvious one of deciding what variables are to be controlled. Marketing programs have both ***input and output variables*** associated with them, and variables of both types are candidates for control. As shown in Figure 20–1, the input variables are prices and the costs associated with product research and development, advertising and promotion, personal selling, distribution, marketing research, and marketing

FIGURE 20-1
Control of input and output variables in marketing.

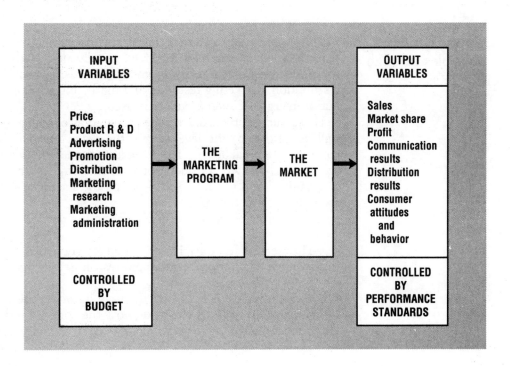

administration. These inputs are controlled by budgets. Thus, when Perrier management set up a marketing control system for its entry into the U.S. market, it had to:

1. Decide on input variables such as price, advertising expenditure, sales expenses, administrative expenses, so forth, and output variables such as sales, market share, and profit.
2. Establish the budgets (for expenditures) and performance standards (for sales, profits, and other output variables).
3. Set up a system for measuring actual costs and performance on the variables being controlled.
4. Take corrective action when needed.

It is clear how budgets can be used as a controlling device for such marketing costs as product R&D, advertising, and distribution. But how, you might ask, is *price* controlled by a budget? It is not always the case that it is, but in some companies, especially those marketing packaged consumer products, **contribution budgets** are set up. Such companies tend to do a lot of promotions (coupons, price deals) that have the effect of reducing the price to the buyer, and thus reducing the margin to the seller. As the name suggests, a contribution budget is used to control the erosion of contribution margins so that some minimum average margin is maintained.

The output variables are various measures of sales and market share, profit, communication program results, distribution channel results, and consumer attitudes and buying behavior. These outputs are controlled by performance standards.

A **performance standard** is exactly what the name implies—an expected level of performance. An example is the expected level of sales by product, territory, and market segment for the coming year.

Control of Input Variables through Budgets

An important part of the annual marketing plan is the budgets for the major marketing input variables. In it will usually be found the budgeted amounts for product research and development, advertising, promotion, personal selling, distribution, marketing research, and marketing administration, and for contribution margin (if such a budget is used).

These budgets typically will be prepared as overall amounts by function and will be neither to the level nor in the detail that is needed for purposes of control. The breakdown of the functional budgets that is needed for control will depend on two considerations: (1) the way in which the marketing effort is organized and (2) the level to which the manager(s) involved wants to exercise budgetary controls.

A basic principle involved in budgeting is that:

The person responsible for a budget should have full authority to approve or disapprove expenditures on items covered by the budget.

When this principle is followed, the way in which the Marketing Department is organized has obvious effects on how the control budgets are set up. If there are product managers, for example, a budget will very likely be desired for the product group that is assigned to each product manager. And if there are market managers, there will need to be a budget for each market.

If there are functional managers (sales manager, advertising manager), the level to which the managers are involved and to which the marketing manager wants control exercised also will obviously affect the breakdown of the functional budgets. The sales manager, for example, typically will want to control expenditures by sales territory, and the advertising manager by medium and territory. Even if the sales and advertising managers don't want to control to these levels, the marketing manager is likely to require it, both to help ensure that they meet their overall functional budgets and to exercise tighter budgetary control.

The types of input budgets that one finds in firms are:

- Contribution budgets   Overall, by product, by product line, by market
- Research and development budgets   Overall, by product, by product line
- Advertising budget   Overall, by medium, by product, by market area, by market segment
- Promotional budget   Overall, by product, by product line, by market area, by market segment
- Personal selling   Overall, by product line, by sales territory
- Marketing research   Overall, by product line, by market
- Marketing administration   Overall, by product line, by market

The usual case is that any one firm will have some, but not all, of these items budgeted. Each marketing manager or functional manager will select those controls that are needed in the situation faced by the firm and that correspond to his or her management style and preferences.

Control of Output Variables through Performance Standards

The major purposes of setting up a system of marketing controls for output variables are (1) to use the performance standards, and the measures of actual performance, as the basis for awarding or withholding incentives to improve individual performance and (2) to analyze the measures of actual performance, and the underlying causes for them, to determine ways in which the marketing program can be improved.

The incentives to individuals can be either direct or indirect in nature. An example of a control with an associated **_direct incentive_** is a sales quota for a sales representative which, when met, results in a bonus. If the bonus is large enough, the salesperson will alter his or her behavior—make more calls, try harder to make a sale on each call—to try and earn it.

More often, however, the incentive is an **_indirect incentive_**; if the performance measurements indicate the person has continued to meet or exceed the appropriate standards, he or she will be retained and given pay increases. Those whose performance is not up to standard are put on notice that there is a need to improve.

Just as the annual marketing plan contains budgets for the major marketing input variables, it also contains performance standards for the major output variables. It will almost always specify the expected levels of sales and market share by product line, and may give the planned levels of profit by product line as well. Some annual plans will also specify the expected levels of advertising effectiveness in terms of consumer awareness and consumer preference by product line, and of distribution effectiveness measured by the number of distribution points attained by product line as well.

The performance standards given in annual marketing plans typically need to be extended to individual products and sales territories, and to specific persons in the organization—brand managers, sales representatives, media buyers, and others—for reasons of control. A list of the frequently used marketing performance standards and the organizational units to whom they apply in each of the marketing functional areas is given below.

Market Share, Sales, and Sales Costs Performance Standards

The most frequently used set of performance standards are with respect to market share and sales. Those commonly set by marketing managers for sales managers, and by sales managers for territorial managers and individual sales representatives, are:

- Market share by product, and by product line (marketing manager, brand or product manager)
- Sales by product, and by product line (sales manager, brand or product manager)
- Sales force cost as a percentage of sales (sales manager, regional or territorial sales manager)
- Sales by region or sales territory (regional or territorial sales manager)
- Sales by individual sales representative (each sales representative)
- Average dollar sales per sales call (overall and by each sales representative)
- Average contribution margin per sales call
- Average number of sales calls per day (overall and by each sales representative)
- Average cost per sales call (overall and by each sales representative)
- Average entertainment cost per sales call (overall and by each sales representative)
- Average travel cost per sales call (overall and by each sales representative)
- Number of new customers per period (overall and by each sales representative)
- Number of old customers lost per period (overall and by each sales representative)

Reviewing these statistics over time and across sales territories can reveal differences that need to be explained and raise questions that need to be answered. How has the Des Moines territory consistently managed to maintain a lower ratio of sales cost to sales than any other territory? Why have entertainment costs risen over each of the past several years? What are the differences between the three best- and the three worst-performing territories in terms of average number of calls per sales representative? number of new customers gained and old customers lost per period? average revenue per sales call? average contribution margin per sales call?

Such analyses often lead to identifying problems and may suggest corrective actions that should be taken as well. After reviewing the increasing costs of providing company cars to sales representatives, a food company changed over to providing allowances for use of personal cars for business travel. A pump company found that a substantial portion of the average time spent on each call was involved in doing applications engineering, and so set up training programs in how to optimize the use of their pumps in various kinds of fluid- and gas-moving systems. Ducommun Metal, a large metal wholesaling firm, changed the basis for paying commissions from sales to the contribution.margins of sales made by their sales representatives after an analysis of commissions paid revealed that some of the higher-paid representatives were below average in terms of contribution margin brought in.

We discuss the ways in which market share and sales data are analyzed for control purposes in a subsequent section of the chapter.

Advertising and Sales Promotion Performance Standards

The advertising manager should be concerned with collecting and analyzing data concerning:

- The cost per thousand (CPM) of potential buyers reached (by campaign, by type of medium, and by medium vehicle)
- The number of inquiries generated (by campaign, by type of medium, by medium vehicle)
- The cost per inquiry (by campaign, by type of medium, by medium vehicle)

Similarly, the manager(s) concerned with sales promotion (the sales promotion manager, the brand managers) should maintain data on:

- The cost of each deal, sampling, demonstration, display, coupon campaign, or other promotional device
- The number of deals sold, coupons redeemed, inquiries generated, and so forth, for each promotion
- The reduction in contribution margin per promotional campaign

CPM data are available from secondary sources (as described in Chapter 15), and the remainder of the advertising and sales promotion data can be generated by internal record keeping. These statistics can therefore be maintained at a low cost, a cost so low in fact that the managers concerned (advertising manager, promotion manager, brand managers) cannot afford to be without them.

There are other advertising performance standards that need to be considered, but whose use comes at some cost. Chief among these are communication standards. If, after considering the cost of collecting the data required, the manager concerned decides to establish controls in this area, standards may be set and tracking studies conducted to measure performance conducted:

- Before–after consumer awareness
- Before–after consumer attitudes
- Before–after consumer predisposition to buy

(See Chapter 14, for a discussion of communication objectives.)

Distribution Performance Standards

Following the cost of production, distribution is typically the largest single cost for a product. It therefore warrants careful management. The manager(s) concerned with distribution normally will need to monitor and control:

- The average overall distribution cost per unit (by product, by distribution channel, by region)
- Average shipping costs per unit (by product, by type of carrier, by region)
- Average inventory costs per unit (by product, by region)
- The percentage of distribution outlets handling the product (by product, by region)

Observation suggests that, on the average, firms have paid considerably more attention to developing lower-cost methods of producing products than they have to reducing the costs of distributing them. Competent management of course requires a diligent search for economies in both areas.

Analysis of Sales and Market-Share Data for Control Purposes

Sales Analyses
Sales analyses are conducted for one, or both, of two purposes: (1) to determine what causes differences, either high or low, in actual sales versus sales-performance standards and (2) to determine how the marketing program can be made more efficient.

Sales Analysis for Determining Causes of Differences between Actual Sales and the Performance Standard: A **sales control chart** is:

> A chart with upper and lower sales control limits on which sales are plotted each period (usually a week, month, or quarter) to determine if an unusually high or low sales amount is or is not a random variation.

Such charts are helpful for determining when the differences between actual sales and the performance standard should be investigated. The control chart was originally developed for quality control in manufacturing. The upper and lower control limits are set using statistical techniques.

Suppose, for example, that All-American Markets, Inc., a convenience store chain in the Phoenix and Los Angeles areas, had established upper and lower control limits around the expected sales for each of its stores. Further suppose that the sales performance for Store 33 for the past 20 months has been plotted and appears as shown in Figure 20–2.

It is evident from the chart that the store's sales performance for the twentieth month is out of control, rather than just experiencing an isolated bad month. Even though they had remained within the lower control limit, sales had been falling for the four previous months, and in the last month they fell below the acceptable control limit.

Having established that this is not just a random occurrence, the management of All-American can look into the circumstances surrounding the sales decline to try to determine its causes. Has a new supermarket come into the neighborhood? Has a nearby plant shut down? Are there extensive repairs being made to the arterial on which it is located? Are there personnel problems in the store?

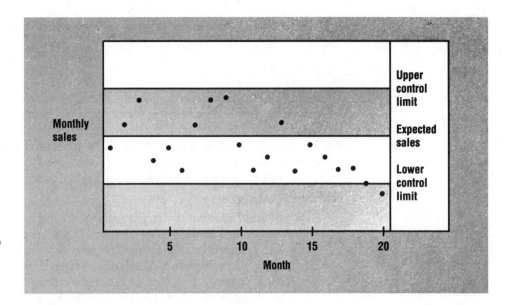

FIGURE 20-2
Control chart and data for sales of
a convenience market for the past
20 months.

Sales Analysis for Helping to Make the Marketing Program More Efficient:
Analyses of sales invoices and of sales call reports should be made periodically
for the purpose of seeing what actions might be taken to increase the overall
efficiency of the marketing program. From a joint analysis of the reports of
sales calls made and the invoices of sales sent to customers, for example, a few
of the many questions that need to be answered and the corrective actions
that, if needed, can be taken, include the following:

1. What proportion of sales (last quarter, during the last two quarters) were
made to the 25 percent of our customers with the lowest average purchases?
What proportion of sales calls were made to these same customers? Does there
appear to be a disproportionate sales effort?

Possible corrective actions: Call on these customers less often? Drop some of
them completely?

2. What proportion of shipments (during the last two quarters, last year)
was made to customers in each sales territory? Do these data suggest that (a)
our sales territories may need realigning? (b) our physical distribution system
may need revamping?

Possible corrective actions: Set up sales territories with more nearly equal potential? Add one or more warehouses? Drop one or more warehouses?

3. What proportion of sales (by product) had to be back-ordered (during the
last quarter)?

Possible corrective action: Selective increase in inventory levels?

4. What customers show a downward trend in purchases (over the last 8,
12 quarters)?

Possible corrective action: Sales manager and sales representative make joint calls
on these customers to determine causes, what can be done to correct them?

5. Are there assortments of products that tend to get ordered by some customers, by certain market segments?

Possible resulting action: Suggestion selling (when Item A is ordered suggest Items B, C)?

Market-Share Analyses

Whereas the measurement of sales by territory or product (or product line) is a straightforward accounting problem using sales invoices, the measurement of market share involves obtaining data on the size of the market(s) for which the market-share estimates are desired. As discussed earlier (Chapter 9) markets can be defined as being either potential, available, served, or penetrated markets, and they can be measured either as overall markets or by market segments.

- The *potential market* is the potential total industry sales for all market segments under conditions of optimum development.

  If Nike determines that there is a potential, under conditions of optimum market development, to sell an average of two pairs of sports shoes per person between the ages of 6 and 60 in the United States per year, the size of the potential market can be found as two times the number of people in that age range.

  Measuring market share on the basis of the potential market size is usually appropriate because, as the name indicates, it is useful to know what share of the potential market is being obtained.
- The *available market* is the potential market less those buyers who lack interest or resources.

  The available market is therefore measured by industry sales for the time period of interest. It is a common basis for market-share measurements because industry sales data are usually easily obtainable (from trade associations, syndicated services, or government agencies).

  Company sales as a proportion of industry sales are of most interest as a market-share measurement when the company has a product line that is broad and is widely distributed. It might not be a very good basis for measuring market share for Nike, however, as the company has deliberately chosen to follow quality and pricing policies that have kept its products out of a sizable portion of the retail outlets.
- The *served market* consists of the available market less those buyers the company has chosen not to serve.

  Nike has maintained a consistent policy of producing a quality product, pricing it at the high end of the range for sports shoes, and distributing it through the better sporting goods, shoe, and department stores. Market share measured by Nike sales as a percentage of the total sales through these types of retail stores would therefore be a suitable overall market-share measurement for the company.
- The *penetrated market* consists of the served market less purchases by those buyers from which the company has not been able to obtain business.

  Nike, no doubt, has been unable to obtain distribution in all of the sporting goods, shoe, and department stores in which it would have liked to place its shoes. A measurement of market share as the percentage of Nike sales to the total sales of sports shoes for the outlets for which it does have distribution would therefore show how well it was doing head-to-head against competitors at the average retail store level.

The company management may want market-share data on one or more of the above bases for selected market segments, as well as for the overall market. For example, Nike management might well want to know what the company's share is of the jogger, court sports, aerobic, walking shoe, and casual wear segments, as well as that of the overall sports shoe market.

Taking Corrective Action as a Result of Sales and Market-Share Analyses

How should the marketing manager decide what action to take when actual sales or market-share performance is below the standard? The recognition that actual performance is not meeting the standard should trigger a series of analytical steps of the following general nature:

1. Check to ensure that the level of performance was really too low, rather than the standard being too high. If the standard was too high, lower it and investigate no further. If it was not too high, proceed with the investigation.
2. Conduct a sales analysis to determine if the sales and market share were uniformly low, or whether they were low only in one or more sales territories or market segments.
3. a. If performance was uniformly low, look for general causes of the poor performance—such as prices being too high or new products introduced by competitors.
   b. If performance was low in selected territories or market segments, look for changes that occurred there that did not occur in territories or among market segments where performance was up to standard.
4. Conduct whatever additional investigations are required to draw conclusions concerning the cause(s) of the low performance.
5. Decide what action(s) can best be taken to correct or counteract the causes identified.

An example of this analytical procedure is given in Exhibit 20–3.

Analysis of the Contribution to Profit and Fixed Costs

The central determinant of a company's success, and ultimate survival, is profitability. The control of sales to ensure that they are at a satisfactory level is of course critical to profitable operations. The costs associated with developing, producing, and marketing products is the other half of the profit equation.

Marketing management is of course responsible only for marketing costs. It is concerned not only with the functional costs of the type budgeted in the annual plan—sales force, advertising and sales promotion, physical distribution,

EXHIBIT **20-3**

Analysis of Low Sales of Some All-American Convenience Markets in the Los Angeles Area

All-American Stores is a chain of convenience markets that began in Phoenix and expanded into other cities. Shortly after expanding into the Los Angeles area, All-American experienced sales problems with a number of stores. Sales in these problem stores were, on the average, almost 30 percent lower than the average of the other stores.

Investigations by the company had yielded no indications of problems in differences in location or nearness of competitors, or in the general level of competence of store personnel. At that point, a consultant was called in to see if he could pinpoint the problem.

Among other things, he compared the checkout tapes of three high-sales and three low-sales stores for a sample of days. The analysis revealed that the two sets of stores did not differ significantly in number of customers per day. It did show, however, that the average sale per customer for the better stores was substantially higher. Further investigation revealed that the higher-sales store personnel were engaging in "assortment" selling at the checkout stand—when customers were checking out with eggs, they were asked if bacon were needed; with shaving cream, if razor blades were needed; and so forth—whereas those at the lower-sales stores were not.

An immediate training program was started for assortment selling for checkout clerks in the problem stores. Sales soon rose appreciably.

---

and marketing administrative costs—but the allocated costs of each of these functions as they are assigned to products and product lines, market areas, and market segments, because the contribution to profit and fixed costs of each of the latter is of obvious concern in the effective management of the marketing program.

In financial accounting, marketing costs are collected as functional costs (selling costs, advertising costs, and so forth) and usually reported as a lump sum. For purposes of reporting to stockholders and government agencies, there is no need to allocate them by products, or market areas, or market segments. Managerial accounting is done for purposes of providing information to help make decisions, however. If one wants to analyze the profitability of a product line, or market area, or market segment, he or she needs to determine the income and costs pertaining directly to that marketing entity. Moreover, the principle that

> for decision-making purposes, only those revenues and marketing (and other) costs that are likely to be affected by the action being considered are relevant

has to be kept in mind in doing the analysis. For some decisions, some costs will change and others will not be affected by the action that is taken. If the possibility of discontinuing a product line is under consideration, for example, the advertising expenses for that line can obviously be affected, but the marketing manager's salary will likely remain unchanged.

Most marketing costs vary as a result of a decision change by discrete increments rather than continuously, and so we refer to them as *incremental costs*. (When the sales force is to be expanded, for example, one typically does so by adding a full-time sales representative, adding another car to the sales fleet, and so forth.) Those costs that will not be affected by the decision we refer to as *fixed costs*. When restated in these terms, the above principle becomes:

> For decision making purposes, only those marketing (and other) costs that are incremental are relevant.

By using only incremental costs, we determine the contribution to profit and fixed costs, rather than profit directly. Income statements in which fixed as well as incremental costs are allocated are known as *full-cost statements*; income statements in which only incremental costs are used are known as *contribution statements*.

An example will be useful to illustrate the difference that using only incremental costs can make in profitability analyses for decision-making purposes. Suppose a (hypothetical) manufacturer of microcomputers markets its products to the personal, business, and educational market segments. Further suppose that sales to businesses have been disappointing, and management is currently considering stopping selling to that market.

Full-cost income statements for the three market segments suggest that the business segment is incurring a loss. In Table 20–1, the analysis of profit for the three segments has included allocations of fixed as well as incremental costs to the three segments, and it shows that the business segment incurred a $3 million loss last year. Furthermore, it indicates that the personal and educational segments were both profitable, the one having earned a profit of $8.5 million and the other $4.5 million.

On the face of the results, this financial analysis would therefore lend support to a decision by management to discontinue the business segment. Remember, however, that these statements contain allocations of fixed costs—costs that would still be incurred even if the business segment were dropped. Suppose that we take out the fixed costs and so convert the full-cost statements for the three market segments into contribution statements. For this purpose, assume that the fixed costs charged to each of the expenditure items were as follows:

> Cost of goods sold had fixed costs amounting to 20 percent of total manufacturing costs for such items as manufacturing supervision and plant and equipment costs. The fixed-cost portion of the total cost of goods sold therefore came to .20 × $60 million = $12 million.

Table 20–1 Full-Cost Income Statement for a Microcomputer Manufacturer—and for the Personal, Business, and Educational Market Segments—for the Most Recent Year

	Overall (millions)	Personal Segment (millions)	Business Segment (millions)	Educational Segment (millions)
Net sales	$100.0	$50.0	$20.0	$30.0
Less: Cost of goods sold	60.0	27.0	15.0	18.0
Operating profit	$ 40.0	$23.0	$ 5.0	$12.0
Less: General and administrative expense	5.0	2.5	1.0	1.5
Marketing expenses	15.0	8.0	3.0	4.0
Research and development	10.0	4.0	4.0	2.0
Net profit <loss> before taxes	$ 10.0	$ 8.50	($ 3.0)	$ 4.5

General and administrative expense was all fixed, as it consisted of such costs as general management and staff salaries, financial costs, and so forth. It was a total of $5 million.

Marketing fixed costs came to 10 percent of the total marketing expenditures for supervision and staff costs. The fixed-cost portion of total marketing costs therefore amounted to .10 × $15 million = $1.5 million.

Research and development fixed costs made up 40 percent of the total R&D expenditures for basic research and for supervision costs. Fixed costs for R&D therefore totaled .40 × $10 million = $4 million.

The total of these fixed costs comes to $22.5 million.

Further suppose that the fixed costs were allocated to the segments in Table 20–1 on the basis of the proportion of total sales made to each segment. (There may be little in the way of an economic rationale to support such an allocation method, but it is not uncommon in full-cost allocations.) Since the personal, business, and educational segments had 50, 20, and 30 percent of the total sales, respectively, the incremental and fixed costs by expenditure item by segment would therefore have been as shown in Table 20–2.

We can now prepare the contribution statements for each of the segments. They are shown in Table 20–3.

A decidedly different conclusion emerges from the contribution statement than from the full-cost income statement. We see from Table 20–3 that, rather than the business segment costing the company $3 million in profits in the year for which the full-cost income statement was prepared, it actually contributed $2.1 million toward fixed costs and profits! As shown in the pro forma full-cost income statement shown in Table 20–4, if the company had discontinued sales to the business segment at the beginning of that year, profits would have been only $7.9 rather than $10 million.

Table 20–2   Schedule of Incremental and Fixed Costs for the Personal, Business, and Educational Segments, Microcomputer Manufacturing Company

	Incremental Costs (millions)	Fixed Costs (millions)	Total (millions)
Personal segment			
Cost of goods sold	$21.60	$ 5.40	$27.00
General and administrative	—	2.50	2.50
Marketing	7.25	0.75	8.00
R&D	2.00	2.00	4.00
Business segment			
Cost of goods sold	$12.00	$ 3.00	$15.00
General and administrative	—	1.00	1.00
Marketing	2.70	0.30	3.00
R&D	3.20	0.80	4.00
Educational segment			
Cost of goods sold	$14.40	$ 3.60	$18.00
General and administrative	—	1.50	1.50
Marketing	3.55	0.45	4.00
R&D	0.80	1.20	2.00
Total fixed costs		$22.50	

Table 20–3 Contribution Statement for a Microcomputer Manufacturer—and for the Personal, Business, and Educational Market Segments—for the Most Recent Year

	Overall (millions)	Personal Segment (millions)	Business Segment (millions)	Educational Segment (millions)
Net sales	$100.0	$50.0	$20.0	$30.0
Less: Incremental cost of goods sold	48.0	21.60	12.0	14.0
Operating profit	$ 52.0	$28.40	$ 8.0	$15.6
Less: Incremental general and administrative expense	—	—	—	—
Incremental marketing expense	13.5	7.25	2.7	3.55
Incremental research and development	6.0	2.0	3.2	.80
Contribution to profit and fixed costs	$ 32.5	$19.15	$ 2.1	$11.25
Less: Fixed costs	22.5			
Net profit (loss) before taxes	$ 10.0			

For decisional purposes, fixed costs are irrelevant and so there is no need to allocate them. Worse than simply being a waste of time, however, the allocation may result in distortions (such as those in Table 20–1) that lead to bad decisions being made.

Undesirable Behavior Resulting from Controls

In the chapter on marketing planning (Chapter 10), it was pointed out that one of the costs of planning is that it can result in altering in undesirable ways the behavior of the persons affected by it. This same observation applies to setting up and maintaining controls in the marketing program.

Misreporting is one effect. For example, sales representatives normally are required to report the number of sales calls made each day they are in the field. It is not uncommon for calls that were never made to be shown on call reports or, if made, to be hurried unnecessarily so that a higher number of calls could be reported. The misreporting of expenses, for some reason inevitably in error on the high side, is so well known that it needs no comment here.

Table 20–4 Full-Cost Income Statement for a Microcomputer Manufacturer for the Personal and Educational Market Segments for the Most Recent Year and Assuming the Business Segment Was Discontinued at the Beginning of the Year

	Overall (millions)	Personal Segment (millions)	Business Segment (millions)	Educational Segment (millions)
Net sales	$80.0	$50.000	$—	$30.000
Less: Cost of goods sold	48.0	29.100	—	18.900
Operating profit	$32.0	$20.900	$—	$11.100
Less: general and administrative expense	5.0	3.125	—	1.875
Marketing expenses	12.3	8.188	—	4.112
Research and development	6.8	4.500	—	2.300
Net profit <loss> before taxes	$ 7.9	$ 5.087	<$—>	$ 2.813

An associated kind of effect is to change the nature of an activity so that it
can be completed more quickly or more easily, and thus make the unit reporting
look better in terms of meeting performance standards. An example from the
Procter & Gamble Company given in Exhibit 20–4 illustrates this practice.

Implementation—Some General Observations

We have discussed implementation thus far only from the standpoint of control. To that we need to add observations about some characteristics of soundly
devised implementation programs.

Implementation is clearly an important area of marketing; strategies, however well conceived and designed, come to naught unless they are competently
implemented. Yet there has been little in the way of systematic investigation
of marketing implementation as a subdiscipline of marketing. What we know,
or think we know, about what characterizes good practice in implementation
is largely based on anecdotal evidence and rules of thumb. The generalizations
that follow (those that are not self-evident) should be viewed in that light.

Need for Coherence: There is a tendency for elements of strategy to become
distorted in translation into implementation programs. For example, design
engineers tend to become enamored with high-tech solutions and building
added features into products. Cost and complexity are added as a result. If the
strategy that occasioned the new product was one of using it to enter a low-
price segment, implementation will suffer unless the design engineers are held
strictly to a low-cost design goal.

Attention to Detail: Peters and Waterman report that one of the values of
the excellently managed companies they studied was "a belief in the importance of the details of execution, the nuts and bolts of doing the job well."[7]

An example is afforded by the distribution system of Frito-Lay, one of the companies they studied:

> Each driver/salesperson, no matter how experienced, must complete a ten-book programmed learning course which covers everything from the Frito-Lay theme to likely consumer behavior to how to pack the delivery truck for maximum efficiency.... Goods cannot be placed willy-nilly on the super-market shelves but must be stocked according to what the company calls "national pattern," a display set-up which specifies that the Doritos go to the left of the Fritos, and that Jalapeña Dip is never stocked to the right of Onion Dip. Failure to follow these recommendations is a disciplinary offense.[8]

Match Task Demands and Capabilities of People: Just as everyone is not a good strategist, everyone is not a good implementer. There is evidence that older, more-experienced people are better than younger people at implementation, whereas younger people may do just as well, or better, at formulating strategy.[9] (This suggests that the traditional pattern of early career assignments being implementation-oriented with good performance being rewarded by promotion to assignments that are strategy-oriented may be the reverse of what it should be.)

There is also evidence that the conventional "gunslinger" image of good implementers and "ivory tower" image of good strategists is not correct since "there are *no* stereotypical personality correlates that differentiate good implementers from good strategists."[10]

The association between age and implementation skills suggests that they may be experientially acquired. This in turn implies that (1) it may be difficult to select good future implementers from a group of inexperienced job candidates, (2) implementation skills are probably trainable, and (3) companies might be well advised either to prolong apprentice-type assignments involving implementation, to devise training programs focusing on implementation, or both. Frito-Lay provides an example of a company that does both of these things; in addition to the training program described above for its driver/salespersons, "salespeople are not allowed to have their own route until they have served as substitutes for vacationing 'regulars' for a year."[11]

Provide Adequate Support: There are two reasons that ample financial and other means of support for implementation tasks need to be provided. First, there is the obvious need for the implementer to have the wherewithal needed to get the job done well. Skimping on support will almost inevitably mean that a poorer job is done, and that in turn may result in a false economy. Second, and maybe even more important, inadequate support sends the message to the implementer that "we don't think your job is important enough to provide you with sufficient resources to do it properly." Motivation and morale decline as a result.

Need for Continuing Monitoring by Management: There is a kind of immutable law that "what the boss pays attention to gets attention." The reverse of this maxim also unfortunately applies.

EXHIBIT **20-5**

Schedule of Questions and Useful References for Obtaining Answers for the Marketing Audit

I. Economy/Industry

1. What changes, if any, have taken place in the economy in the past three years (such as increases or decreases in the rate of inflation, rising or falling interest rates, ranges in dollar exchange rates, booms or recessions) that are likely to have significant future effects on marketing in the industry?

   Analysis of economic changes, Chapter 3, pp. 80–84.

2. What changes, if any, are likely to take place in the economy in the next five years that will have significant effects on marketing in the industry?

   Forecasting, Chapter 10, pp. 319–322.

3. What major changes are occurring that have their origin within the industry (such as new manufacturing methods, material shortages, influx of foreign competition) that are likely to have significant effects on marketing in the industry?

   Analysis of industry changes, Chapter 3, pp. 73–77.

4. What steps have been taken to counter or take advantage of these economic and industry changes? What steps are planned?

The Firm

5. Is there an appropriate balance in the emphasis given by top management to marketing along with each of the other major functions of the firm?

   Chapter 3, pp. 71–73.

The Political–Legal Context

6. Are there laws that are being proposed (in such areas as product safety, advertising, protective tariffs, consumer credit) that will affect the firm's marketing program significantly?

   Monitoring, Chapter 8, pp. 229–230.

Technological Developments

7. What major changes, if any, are occurring in the technology of the product? in packaging? in storage and transportation? in communication?

   Technological environment, Chapter 3, pp. 77–79.

8. What generic substitutes, if any, pose threats as replacements to company products? What is the earliest that each potential replacement could occur?

Demographic and Social Changes

9. What effects will projected changes in the size, age distribution, geographic distribution, and income and educational levels of the population have on the marketing of the product?

   Secondary data sources, Chapter 8, pp. 236–241.

10. What changes in the lifestyles and attitudes of consumers will likely affect the marketing of the product? What marketing changes will be required?

    Chapter 4, pp. 103–106.

Market

11. What changes are likely to occur over the next five years in market size, growth or decline, profitability, and geographic distribution?

    Forecasting, Chapter 10, pp. 319–322.

12. a. What are the principal market segments?

    Segmenting the market, Chapter 2, pp. 41–44; organization segmentation, Chapter 5, pp. 144–145.

    b. What will be the probable rate of increase or decrease for each?

    Forecasting, Chapter 10, pp. 316–324.

    c. Which are the higher-profit segments? the lower-profit segments?

    This chapter, pp. 681–685.

(Continued on page 689)

EXHIBIT **20-5**

Schedule of Questions and Useful References for Obtaining Answers for the Marketing Audit (*continued*)

d. What changes in customer needs and desires are taking place in each segment?	Chapter 4, pp. 120–122.
e. How do the customers in each segment make buying decisions?	Chapter 4, pp. 95–122; Chapter 5, pp. 138–144.

Competitors

13. What are the objectives and strategies of each of the leading competitors?	Competitor intelligence, Chapter 3, pp. 74–77.
14. How do the customers rate the company versus each of its competitors in terms of product quality, service, price, and reputation?	Competitor intelligence, Chapter 3, pp. 74–77.
15. What are the market shares of each of the competitors? Which are growing and which are declining?	Competitor intelligence, Chapter 3, pp. 74–77.
16. What are the production costs of the competitor with the highest market share? the lowest market share?	Estimating competitor costs, Appendix A, p. 749.

II. Marketing Organization
Structure

1. a. Are all marketing functions under the direction of one executive?	_____
b. Does that executive report at the same level as do the heads of finance and the major operations departments (manufacturing, merchandising, and so forth)?	_____
2. a. Are the marketing responsibilities appropriately assigned along functional, product, customer, and territorial lines?	Chapter 19, pp. 654–658.
b. Do assigned authorities match assigned responsibilities?	

Internal Effectivenss

3. Is there an appropriately designed and smoothly functioning operating system (order entry, shipping, back ordering, expense reimbursement, and so forth)?	Chapter 17, pp. 572–578.
4. Is there an appropriately designed and smoothly functioning marketing control system?	This chapter, pp. 672–677.
5. Are there any marketing personnel that are inadequately supervised or trained?	_____

Working Relationships

6. Are there good communications and working relationships between:	
a. Marketing and Sales?	
b. Marketing and Manufacturing?	Chapter 3, pp. 71–73.
c. Marketing and R&D?	Chapter 3, pp. 71–73.
d. Marketing and Finance?	Chapter 3, pp. 71–73.

III. Marketing Performance Standards

1. Do the marketing performance standards follow clearly and logically from the corporate objectives?	Chapter 10, pp. 308–309, 311–312.
2. Are they the appropriate performance standards given the economic, industry, technological, market, and competitive environments, and the company's resources?	

(*Continued on page 690*)

EXHIBIT **20-5**

Schedule of Questions and Useful References for Obtaining Answers for the Marketing Audit (*continued*)

IV. Marketing Strategies

1. Are the key marketing strategies logically designed to achieve the marketing objectives? Chapter 2, pp. 27–54.

2. Are they the appropriate strategies given the economic, industry, technological, market, and competitive environments, and the company's resources?

V. Marketing Planning and Decision Support Systems

Planning

1. Are marketing plans prepared with the full participation of the functional managers concerned?

2. Is the overall amount of resources budgeted in the marketing plan enough to achieve the stated objectives? This chapter, p. 687.

3. Have the budgeted resources been allocated optimally by functional area within marketing?

4. a. Is a track record kept of the assumptions used in arriving at the key variables in the plan (including the sales forecast), and of actual versus planned results? Chapter 10, pp. 313–314, 325.

   b. Is a review held at the end of each planning period to determine the reasons that the plan turned out well, or was inadequate or bad? Chapter 10, pp. 313–314.

Decision Support System

5. Is the marketing information system providing the data required by management on an adequate, accurate, and timely basis? Chapter 8, pp. 229–231.

6. Has marketing management made informed decisions about using the decisional models appropriate to the marketing situation of the company? Chapter 8, pp. 251–252; Chapter 11, pp. 359–361; Chapter 12, p. 397; Chapter 13, pp. 429–434, 436–441; Chapter 14, pp. 465–480; Chapter 15, pp. 496, 498–500; Chapter 16, p. 539.

VI. Functional Area Programs

Products

1. Does the company have a formal, organized approach to developing and screening new product ideas? Chapter 11, pp. 353–361.

2. Does the company routinely do concept testing before developing, and market testing and financial analyses before launching, a new product? Chapter 11, pp. 361–365.

3. Given the corporate and marketing objectives, is the portfolio of product lines an appropriate one?

4. Is the selection of products offered in each product line the appropriate one? If not, are steps being taken to add new products or phase out old ones?

5. Are there products that should have new models, styles, shapes, colors, sizes, or features? If so, are these additions now in development?

Pricing

6. Is there a clearly defined set of pricing objectives? Do they follow logically from the corporate and marketing objectives? Chapter 13, pp. 426–429.

(*Continued on page 691*)

EXHIBIT **20-5**

Schedule of Questions and Useful References for Obtaining Answers for the Marketing Audit (*continued*)

7. Are prices set on sound demand, cost, and competitive considerations?

Advertising, Promotion, and Public Relations

8. Is there a clearly defined set of advertising objectives? Do they follow logically from the corporate and marketing objectives?	Chapter 14, pp. 468–469.
9. Is the advertising budget determined by an appropriate method?	Chapter 15, pp. 492–499.
10. Are media selected by an appropriate method?	Chapter 15, pp. 502–510.

11. Are there clearly stated objectives for the:
   a. Sales promotion program?
   b. Public relations program?

12. Are measurements made at the appropriate times or intervals of the effectiveness of:

a. Advertising theme and copy?	Chapter 15, pp. 500–502.
b. The overall advertising program?	This chapter, p. 677.
c. The sales promotional program?	Chapter 15, pp. 512–514.
d. The public relations program?	Chapter 15, pp. 516–517.

13. How effectively is the advertising agency performing?

Personal Selling

14. Are there clearly stated performance standards for the sales force?	Chapter 16, pp. 538–539.

15. For meeting its performance standards, is the sales force:

a. Of sufficient size?	Chapter 16, pp. 538–539.
b. Organized properly (by territory, market, product line)?	Chapter 16, pp. 543–544.
16. Are sales quotas set by an appropriate method?	Chapter 16, pp. 544–545.
17. Is the performance of each sales representative evaluated periodically?	Chapter 16, pp. 545–546.

Distribution

18. Are there clearly defined distribution objectives?

19. Is the mix of distributors, sales representatives, and direct selling an appropriate one?

20. Are warehouse locations and inventory policies appropriate given present transportation costs, interest rates, and demand levels?	Chapter 17, pp. 573–581.

21. Is there an adequate level of service provided by:
   a. The distributors?
   b. The company?

VII. Marketing Productivity

1. Is an internal review made of budgeted and actual costs to evaluate marketing expenditure levels?	This chapter, pp. 674–678.

2. What are the present and projected contributions to fixed costs and profits of the company's products, market segments, customer groups by quartiles based on purchase quantities, territories, and distribution channels?

3. Based on the analysis of projected contributions to fixed costs and profits, should any of the company's products be phased out, market segments, territories, or smaller customers no longer served, or distribution channels discontinued?

1. A *design-efficient* program is one in which the marketing strategies and plans used provide the opportunity for a high level of performance.
2. The *design* efficiency of a marketing program is measured through a marketing audit.
3. An *implementation-efficient* marketing program is one that is implemented in such a way as to achieve a high proportion of its potential at a reasonable cost.
4. A *marketing audit* consists of an independent, objective, and thorough review of the marketing environment and the manner in which the overall marketing program is conducted with respect to its organization, objectives, strategies, planning, and decision support systems; functional area programs; and overall marketing productivity for the purposes of determining (a) how well it is being conducted and (b) how it can be improved.
5. The marketing audit normally should be conducted by an auditing team consisting of a chief auditor from outside the department (typically from outside the firm) and such other Marketing, Accounting and Finance Department representatives as required.
6. The implementation efficiency of the marketing program is measured and maintained through a system of *marketing controls*. Such a system consists of the following four elements:
    a. Deciding on which variables are to be controlled
    b. Setting a budget and/or a standard of performance for each
    c. Measuring actual costs and performances
    d. Taking corrective action when required
7. Marketing *input variables* (product research and development, advertising and promotion, personal selling, distribution, marketing research, and marketing administration) are controlled by *budgets*.
8. Marketing *output variables* (sales, market share, contribution to profit and fixed costs, communication results, distribution results, and consumer attitudes and buying behavior) are controlled by *performance standards*.
9. A basic principle involved in budgeting is that the person responsible for a budget should have full authority to approve or disapprove expenditures on items covered by the budget.
10. A *sales control chart* is a chart with upper and lower sales control limits on which sales are plotted each period (usually a week, month, or quarter) to determine if an unusually high or low sales amount is or is not a random variation.
11. The recognition that actual performance is not meeting the standard should trigger a series of analytical steps of the following general nature:
    a. Check to ensure that the level of performance was really too low, rather than the standard being too high. If the standard was too high, lower it and investigate no further. If it was not too high, proceed with the investigation.

b. Conduct a sales analysis to determine if the sales and market share were uniformly low, or whether they were low only in one or more sales territories or market segments.

c. (1) If performance was uniformly low, look for general causes of the poor performance—such as prices being too high or new products introduced by competitors. (2) If performance was low in selected territories or market segments, look for changes that occurred there that did not occur in territories or among market segments where performance was up to standard.

d. Conduct whatever additional investigations are required to draw conclusions concerning the cause(s) of the low performance.

e. Decide what action(s) can best be taken to correct or counteract the causes identified.

12. For decision-making purposes, only those revenues and marketing (and other) costs that are likely to be affected by the action being considered are relevant.

13. A *contribution* accounting statement is normally a more useful statement for making operating decisions than is an income statement.

14. Setting up a system of controls can result in undesirable behavior (misrepresenting actual performance, changing definitions of when a project is completed or what constitutes a "sales call") on the part of those preparing reports to be used for control purposes.

15. What we know, or think we know, about what characterizes good practice in implementation is largely based on anecdotal evidence and rules of thumb.

16. There is supportive, although not conclusive, evidence concerning the following generalizations about implementation:

a. There is need for coherence between strategy and implementation.

b. Careful attention to detail is important.

c. The demands of tasks and the capabilities of people assigned to carry them out should be carefully matched.

d. Adequate support should be provided.

e. Management should monitor implementation efforts carefully and continuously.

17. The association between age and implementation skills suggests that they may be experientially acquired. This in turn implies that

a. It may be difficult to select good future implementers from a group of inexperienced job candidates.

b. Implementation skills are probably trainable.

c. Companies might be well advised either to prolong apprentice-type assignments involving implementation, to devise training programs focusing on implementation, or both.

REVIEW QUESTIONS

20.1.   a. What is a *design-efficient* marketing program?
        b. What is an *implementation-efficient* marketing program?

20.2.   How is the design efficiency of a marketing program measured?

20.3.   How is the implementation efficiency of a marketing program measured?

20.4.   What is a *marketing audit*?

20.5.   Who should conduct the marketing audit?

20.6.   What are the factors that determine how long it should take to complete a marketing audit?

20.7.   How often should a company conduct a marketing audit?

20.8.   a. What are the input variables in a marketing program?
        b. How are they controlled?

20.9.   a. What are the output variables in a marketing program?
        b. How are they controlled?

20.10. What types of marketing input budgets are commonly found in companies?

20.11. What types of marketing performance standards are commonly found in companies?

20.12. For what purposes are sales analyses conducted?

20.13. What is a *sales contol chart*?

20.14. What is:
        a. The *potential* market for a product?
        b. The *available* market?
        c. The *served* market?
        d. The *penetrated* market?

20.15. How should the marketing manager decide what action(s) to take when actual sales or market-share performance is below the standard?

20.16. a. What is an *incremental* marketing cost?
        b. What is a *fixed* marketing cost?

c. Does the statement "for decision-making purposes, only those marketing (and other) costs that are likely to be affected by the action being considered are relevant" refer to *variable*, *incremental*, or *fixed* costs? Explain.

20.17. What is a *contribution* accounting statement?

20.18. What kinds of *un*desirable behavior can result from a system of controls?

20.19. What generalizations concerning implementation can be made that seem to be supported by the available evidence?

20.20. What are the logical implications of the association between age and implementation skills?

DISCUSSION QUESTIONS AND PROBLEMS

20.21. The example of the introduction of Perrier water in the United States was used at the beginning of the chapter to illustrate the concepts of marketing design and implementation efficiency. Perrier had a highly successful introduction of its product. Does this mean that the marketing program the company used was necessarily both design- and implementation-efficient? Explain.

20.22. On page 674 the statement is made that "a basic principle involved in budgeting is that the person responsible for a budget should have full authority to approve or disapprove expenditures on items covered by the budget." Can this principle be applied in a matrix form of organization? Why or why not?

20.23. Are there any basic differences between using a control chart for quality control in manufacturing and control of, say, sales in a sales territory? Explain.

20.24. A marketing *controller* is a person in the Marketing Department who has access to the company's accounting records and who performs the same functions for marketing as the controller does for the company. Is it appropriate from an organizational standpoint to establish such a position? Explain.

20.25. Give at least three common examples of "assortment" purchasing by customers of:
a. Supermarkets

b. Drug stores.

How can checkout clerks use such purchasing behavior to increase sales?

20.26. Suppose that in the schedule of incremental and fixed costs for the microcomputer manufacturer (Table 20–2), one-third of the fixed costs had been allocated to each of the personal, business, and educational segments.

a. Revise the schedule of incremental and fixed costs (Table 20–2) and the contribution statement for the company (Table 20–3) using this basis for allocation of fixed costs.

b. What would the overall profits (before taxes) of the company have been for the year of the statement if the company had discontinued sales to the business segment at the beginning of that year? Explain, using the statements prepared in (a).

c. Revise the full-cost income statement using this method of allocating fixed costs and assuming that the business segment was discontinued at the beginning of the year for which the statement applies. Check to make sure that the level of profits (before taxes) for the company shown on the full-cost income statement you have prepared is the same as that calculated in (b).

20.27. Suppose that in the schedule of incremental and fixed costs for the microcomputer manufacturer (Table 20–2) fixed costs had been allocated to each segment on the basis of 50 percent to the personal segment, 40 percent to the educational segment, and 10 percent to the business segment.

a. Revise the schedule of incremental and fixed costs (Table 20–2) and the contribution statement for the company (Table 20–3) using this method of allocating fixed costs.

b. What would the overall profits of the company have been for the year of the statement if the company had discontinued sales to the business segment at the beginning of that year? Explain, using the statements prepared in (a).

c. Revise the full-cost income statement using this method of allocating fixed costs and assuming that the business segment was discontinued at the beginning of the year for which the statement applies. Check to make sure that the level of profits (before taxes) for the company shown on the full-cost income statement you have prepared is the same as that calculated in (b).

20.28. One economist has stated that the "only decision that ought to be made about allocating fixed costs is to fire the accountant that is doing it." Do you agree with this assertion? Explain.

20.29. Compare the first four steps suggested in the procedure for determining the reasons for low sales or market-share performance (page 679) with that of designing and analyzing the results of a sales experiment. Are there similarities? Explain.

20.30. What questions in addition to those shown in Exhibit 20–4, if any, should be raised in conducting a marketing audit of a:
   a. Multibranch bank?
   b. Machine tool manufacturer that exports more than half of its output to Western Europe?
   c. Department store chain with stores in 20 large cities in the United States and Canada?
   d. Television network?

20.31. For a multidivision company, what are:
   a. the advantages
   b. the disadvantages
   of using an outside consultant as the chief auditor in a marketing audit as opposed to using a person from the corporate marketing staff in that capacity?

PROJECTS

20.32. Do a marketing audit of the approach planned by another member of this class for finding a job on graduation.

20.33. Choose a company and a product it markets that is of interest to you and explain:
   a. The potential, available, served, and penetrated markets for the product;
   b. How measurements of the overall domestic market size for each of these market definitions might be obtained;
   c. The usefulness to the company management of market-share measurements based on each market definition.

20.34. Interview the marketing manager of a local company to determine what kind of marketing control system is used.

Endnotes

[1] The terms *design efficiency* and *implementation efficiency* are similar in concept, respectively, to what Scitovsky calls "technical efficiency" and "economic efficiency." See T. Scitovsky, *Welfare and Competition*, Richard D. Irwin, 1951, Chap. 8.

[2] Booz, Allen, Hamilton, the management consulting firm, began conducting marketing audits in 1952. Elrick and Lavidge, another consulting firm, was conducting them in the mid 1950s. "It was not until the . . . seventies, however, that it began to penetrate management awareness as a possible answer to its needs." P. Kotler, W. Gregor, and W. Williams, "The Marketing Audit Comes of Age," *Sloan Management Review*, Winter 1977, 25.

[3]For example, the degree to which the same sets of questions tend to appear on schedules prepared by different persons can be seen in comparing those in A. Shuchman, "The Marketing Audit: Its Nature, Purposes, and Problems," *American Management Association*, 1959, and in Kotler et al., "The Marketing Audit."

[4]K. A. Merchant, "Progressing toward a Theory of Marketing Control: A Comment," *Journal of Marketing*, July 1988, 40–41.

[5]H. S. Geneen, "The Case for Managing by the Numbers," *Fortune*, October 1, 1984, 78–81.

[6]A step-by-step procedure for conducting a marketing audit for an industry rather than a firm is given in W. B. Tye, "Fundamental Elements of a Marketing Audit for a More Competitive Motor Carrier Industry," *Transportation Journal*, Spring 1983, 5–22.

[7]T. J. Peters and R. H. Waterman, Jr., *In Search of Excellence: Lessons from America's Best Run Companies*, Warner Books, 1982, 285.

[8]T. Bonoma, *The Marketing Edge*, The Free Press, 1985, 93.

[9]Ibid., 172.

[10]Ibid., 176.

[11]Ibid., 92.

CHAPTER 21

INTERNATIONAL MARKETING

Once a company has become established and financially secure in its own country, the management usually raises the question of whether it should market its products or services in other countries. This possibility may have been prompted by a recognition that foreign markets provide a strategic fit with domestic product markets, as a way of reducing excess production capacity, by the receipt of unsolicited export orders, by observation of a competitor that has successfully marketed abroad, or by growing domestic competition from foreign companies.

There is good reason for raising this question. Although marketing abroad is not an easy road to either increased sales or profits, many American companies have built their foreign operations to the point where they contribute a substantial portion of the company's total sales and profits. Some American corporations even derive more revenues, or more profits, or both, from sales abroad than in the United States. Exxon, Ford Motor, Pan American World Airways, Gillette, and Colgate-Palmolive are recent examples.

Whether a particular company should start marketing abroad is a general question whose answer necessarily depends on the answers to a series of specific questions that stem from it. The first is: "If we were to start doing business internationally, to what countries would we want to market, and in what sequence should we start marketing to each of them?" This is the **geographic dimension** of marketing abroad. The next question is: "What kind of an organizational arrangement would we want to make—should we organize an export department, arrange a joint venture with one or more foreign com-

699

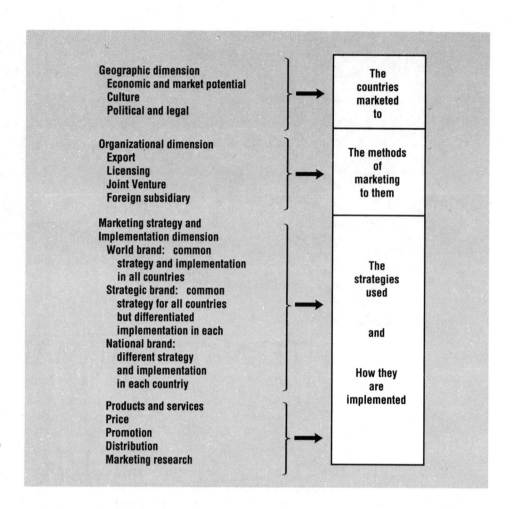

FIGURE 21-1
The dimensions of an international marketing program.

panies, or set up foreign subsidiaries?" This is the **organizational dimension** of an international marketing program. The third question is: "What kind of marketing strategy should we use in each country, and how should we put it into effect?" This is the **marketing strategy and implementation dimension** of marketing in foreign countries. These dimensions and the important considerations involved in each are shown in Figure 21–1.

The considerations and procedures involved in answering these dimensional questions are the subjects of this chapter.

THE GEOGRAPHIC DIMENSION OF MARKETING ABROAD

The choice of countries in which to market is conditioned by the elements of economics and market potential, culture, and the political and legal system. We discuss each of these elements in turn below.

Economics and Market Potential as a Screening Factor

The initial screening factor a for-profit company uses in choosing foreign markets has to be each country's economic prospects for its products. As a minimum for a country to warrant further economic consideration, it must offer sufficient **market potential** for a company's products to make entry potentially profitable. For some products it will be obvious whether the market potential of a particular country is adequate to support entry. For example, it is immediately apparent that there is a sufficient market potential in West Germany for Mobil Oil to consider marketing gasoline there, and that the potential for bourbon in Saudi Arabia would fall far short of supporting a Jack Daniels distillery. (The sale of alcoholic beverages in Arab countries is banned.) For other products the answer to the question of adequate market potential may not be at all obvious. For example, is the potential market in France for Pepperidge Farm Poultry Stuffing large enough to justify the company to begin marketing that product there?

In the nonobvious situations, making a determination of a product's market potential in a country and whether it warrants consideration for entry involves some form of marketing research. Either a tryout—or a descriptive study of some design involving demographic data, data on purchases of similar products, or a survey—will have to be conducted.

A **tryout** is a form of experimentation that is exactly what the name implies. It is a tentative, "toe-in-the-water" approach in which a small-scale marketing program is tried to see what happens. Although no statistical data are available to prove or disprove such an assertion, it is probable that this has been the most commonly used approach to determining the adequacy of market potential for entry in candidate countries. A trial introduction of Kellogg cereals in England and the franchising of 7–Eleven stores in Japan are two prominent and highly successful examples of tryouts.

Descriptive studies of market potential are discussed in the section on international marketing research later in the chapter.

Culture as an Element in the Choice of Country

The **culture** of a society can be defined as the shared set of social norms and responses that condition the population's attitudes, beliefs, and behavior. It is the basis for the common attitudes, beliefs, and modes of behavior to which members of the culture subscribe. The culture of the country is what people are referring to when they say, "I am French," or "I am Japanese," or "I am an American."

Culture has a direct influence on the choice of countries in which to market because, other things being equal, it is much easier for a company to market to another country that has a culture that is similar. Our knowledge of marketing is necessarily culture bound, and it requires less adaptation to use it successfully if the culture is similar than it does if it is different. For this reason, an American company that is considering marketing abroad will generally consider Canada and Great Britain before Japan, or even before Western European countries, as potential countries of entry. Not only is there a (substantially) common language with Canada and Great Britain, in itself an important aspect of culture, but similar consumer attitudes and buying behavior exist, as well as reasonably common methods and expectations with respect to conducting business.

Cultural considerations of course pervade the setting and implementing of marketing strategy. We consider cross-cultural analysis for the purpose of formulating marketing strategy for host countries later in the chapter.

Political and Legal Systems as a Consideration in the Choice of Country

Individual Countries

One only has to be a casual reader of the business press to quickly come to an appreciation of the importance of the host country's government to the success—or failure—of a foreign company's marketing efforts. The adverse actions of governments to which foreign companies are subject range from various forms of financial controls, limitations of the amounts of products that can be imported or sold, and regulations that restrict the company's manufacturing and marketing operations, to direct intervention in managing the company and, in extreme cases, even assuming ownership. A list of the more common forms these actions take, along with examples of their use, is given in Table 21–1.

Table 21–1   Potential Adverse Actions of Host-Country Governments toward Foreign Companies Operating There

Financial Controls
1. Imposing surcharges or special currency requirements on purchases of imports. This reduces the capability of the foreign company to compete.
   Examples: When a government becomes concerned about adverse currency flows, to discourage imports it may require that surcharges be paid. Labor governments in Great Britain have imposed such surcharges from time to time.
      When a person in Yugoslavia buys a foreign-made consumer durable (a television set, for example), he or she must pay two prices for it. One is in a "hard" Western currency that covers the foreign exchange loss the country underwent when the product was imported. The other is in Yugoslav dinars, which is to reimburse the members of the distribution channel for their costs in handling the product and provide a profit for them.
2. Requiring barter rather than payment (a form of countertrading) so that the foreign company must accept, or sell, host-country products in an amount equal to its sales in that country.
   Example: Pepsi-Cola has an arrangement with Russia by which it can sell only as much of its products in Russia as Pepsi-Cola sells of Russian Stolichnaya vodka in the United States.
3. Instituting currency controls that prohibit the company from taking specified proportions of interest, dividends, or profits from the country.
   Example: In the 1930s Joe Louis fought a heavyweight fight in Germany. The Nazi government had "blocked" the deutsche mark (prohibited it from being taken out of the country), and he had to take his earnings in the form of a shipment of ice skates.

Import Controls
4. Instituting import quotas.
   Example. The United States for many years has had an import quota on sugar.

(Continued on page 703)

Table 21–1 Potential Adverse Actions of Host-Country Governments toward Foreign Companies Operating There (*continued*)

Sales Controls

5. Restricting the purchase of foreign-made goods.
   Example: Nearly one-half of the states in the United States have "Buy America" policies for products used by the state itself.
6. Instituting boycotts.
   Example: The 20 Arabic countries in the Middle East set up a joint office in 1948 to boycott companies that were making permanent investments in Egypt. The Ford Motor Company is among the American companies whose products have been banned in Arabic countries as a result of actions of the boycott office.

Control of the Company's Operations

7. Requiring that the formulas of products be divulged.
   Example: The Indian government in 1977 decreed that Coca-Cola would have to disclose the formula for its product (and sell 60 percent of the shares of its Indian branch to Indians) or else cease operations. The Coca-Cola Company refused to disclose the formula and stopped operations in India.* But new rules were later passed which Coke decided would allow them legally to import key ingredients for the syrup, and thus preserve the secrecy of its formula. In 1988 the company applied for permission to build a plant near Delhi and to reenter the market.†
8. Imposing "invisible tariffs," that is, bureaucratic requirements for documentation, marks of origin, special labeling, and the like.
   Example: Companies trying to enter the Japanese market have complained almost universally about the difficulties they encounter in exporting goods into the country.
9. Exerting controls over the nature of the product, its price, or its promotion.
   Examples: The Indian government restricts investment by foreign companies in low-technology products, thus effectively limiting the range of products a foreign company can sell. Underwood has not been allowed to increase the price of its deviled ham in Venezuela for more than 10 years, a period during which there has been a sizable inflation.‡ Most countries have laws regulating advertising; New Zealand, for example, has 33.

Management Control or Ownership

10. Requiring "domestication" of the company, whereby local ownership in the company is increased, nationals are placed in high management positions, a higher proportion of parts have to be made locally, and so on.
    Example: The example given earlier of the Indian government's requiring Coca-Cola to sell 60 percent of its Indian branch to Indian nationals was a move toward domestication. In that connection, the minister of industry stated that the "manufacture of beverages should be 'Indianized' and the outflows of foreign exchange from the industry should be halted."**
11. Expropriation, that is, forcing the foreign corporation to sell its local business to the host government or a buyer it specifies, usually at a price set by the government.
    Example: Expropriations of North American firms has been a particular problem in South American countries over the past 20 years. During that time Peru expropriated the Standard Oil Company (New Jersey), International Tel & Tel, and Chase Manhattan holdings, and Chile expropriated the Anaconda and Kennecott subsidiaries.
12. Confiscation, that is, taking over the local business of the foreign corporation with no compensation at all.
    Example: Cuba confiscated all foreign-owned businesses when Fidel Castro came into power in 1960.

*"Cola Battle Feverish in India's Heat," *Advertising Age*, May 15, 1978, 1.
†"Coca-Cola, after an 11-Year Absence, Seeks to Re-Enter Huge Market in India," *The Wall Street Journal*, November 17, 1988, B6.
‡"Venezuela Beckons Foreign Investors, But Credibility Gap Obstructs Reentry," *The Wall Street Journal*, December 31, 1980, 10.
**New York Times*, August 9, 1977.

As the examples in the table indicate, these actions are not just idle threats. Informed estimates indicate that in the past more than 60 percent of American firms have experienced some form of detrimental action by the host government while marketing abroad for a five-year period,[1] and there is no reason to believe that that percentage has declined in recent years.

Regional Trade Organizations

There has been a post–World War II trend toward companies in the various geographic regions of the world uniting to form trading associations. The larger and more successful of these organizations are the European Economic Community (EEC),[2] the European Free Trade Association (EFTA),[3] and the Council of Mutual Economic Cooperation (COMECON).[4] Others include the Association of South East Asian Nations (ASEAN) and the Andean Pact in South America. The newest such organization is that between Canada and the United States, the Free Trade Agreement (FTA), whose provisions began to be phased in in January 1989.

The motivation for forming these organizations was generally to reduce, or to eliminate, customs and trade barriers among the participants while maintaining them to outsiders. Some, such as the EEC, have gone further. The EEC has adopted a Community-wide agricultural policy, for example, and has actively discussed adopting a common currency.

In 1992, the EEC is scheduled to have a unified, barrier-free, customs-free market of about 320 million people. It will become the largest consumer market in the world. Entry to such a market is of obvious interest to the multinational companies of all other countries.[5]

One effect of a country's belonging to one of these regional organizations is to reduce the legal risk to foreign companies doing business in it. The organization sets rules on tariffs and how its member countries can regulate foreign-company operations. To violate those rules is to risk expulsion from the organization. As long as membership by a country is viewed as being desirable, therefore, conformity to the rules has a positive value to it—and the legal risks to foreign enterprises are reduced.

World Trade Organizations

The General Agreement on Trade and Tariffs (GATT) and the United Nations Conference on Trade and Development (UNCTAD) are worldwide organizations concerned with trade and tariff regulations. GATT has as its members almost all of the important noncommunist and several of the communist countries of Eastern Europe. UNCTAD is an organization whose membership is made up primarily of third-world countries.

The broad goal of GATT has been to reduce restrictions to trade—both tariffs and nontariff barriers—on a multilateral basis. UNCTAD, on the other hand, has sought to narrow the gap between the developing and the developed economies by seeking unilateral tariff reductions and preventing "exploitation." Both organizations have had limited success in their endeavors.[6] But, as in the case of the regional trade groups, they have served somewhat to reduce the legal risks of doing business in their member countries.

Assessing Political Risk in Countries Being Considered for Entry

The extent of the financial risk in marketing abroad is, of course, partially dependent on the amount of assets that are involved. If a company is exporting through an agent in the host country, the maximum risk it can undergo is inventory and accumulated credit balances; if it has a full-fledged manufacturing and marketing subsidiary, the amount at risk is many times greater.

Despite many efforts to devise methods of assessing political risks reliably, it remains an art that depends primarily on the skills of the persons involved. Whether for this reason or some other, many (probably most) companies have no formal means of assessing political risk. The companies that do have formal, in-house risk-assessment organizations are generally the better-managed companies, and especially the better-managed companies that have large investments abroad. The Ford Motor Company is an example.[7]

Agencies are available that provide a risk-assessment service foreign marketers can buy if they are so inclined. One such service is the Business Environment Risk Index (BERI), which evaluates risk in 45 countries on a quarterly basis.[8]

There are a surprising number of publicly available sources of information that are useful for this purpose as well. Included are the Department of Commerce/International Trade Administration's *Overseas Business Reports*, the State Department's *Background Notes*, the *Public Affairs Information Service Index*, and a number of computer-based indexes. A visit to the local library will add substantially to this list.

There are divergent trends affecting political risk. The countries of the world have become economically more integrated and politically more fragmented. As a reflection of the increase in economic integration, a few countries (Singapore is a prominent example) have adopted a deliberate policy of inviting multinational companies to invest as a means to rapid industrialization. The dramatic increases in the living standard of Singapore's population during the 25 years since that policy was instituted no doubt have been highly visible to other, less-developed countries. The large debts that many of these countries have assumed also have had a positive effect in reducing punitive actions taken by them against multinational companies. They need the hard currencies these companies provide (to help make interest and principal payments on the debt). Adverse actions to multinationals are actively discouraged as well by the banks and lending agencies to which they owe the debt. At the same time, many of the third-world countries have governments that are becoming increasingly antagonistic toward what they perceive as exploitation by the West.

One political risk analyst observed that the risk for "conglomerate" investors—companies that seek to exploit in host countries profit opportunities that have no connection with what they are doing at home—are more likely targets for adverse host-government action than are "horizontal" investors—companies that produce and market the same products abroad as they do in their own countries. The reason for the perceived difference in political risk is that the conglomerates are viewed as being exploiters who contribute no added jobs or proven technology, and who will be there only as long as the venture continues to provide an acceptable return. The horizontal investor is viewed as contributing a needed product to the host-country market as well as providing additional jobs and proven technological and managerial know-how.[9]

THE ORGANIZATIONAL DIMENSION OF MARKETING ABROAD

There are four primary methods of organizing marketing efforts to foreign countries, each with a number of variations. They are the export department, using licensees, setting up joint ventures, and establishing wholly owned foreign subsidiaries.

The choice among these methods of entering foreign markets is a highly important one because it has far-reaching consequences on the marketing programs that can be used, the amount of control that can be exercised, the investment required, the degree of risk assumed, and the potential for profit.

The Export Department

Most of the successful world brands started modestly, in one market: Marlboro, Coca-Cola, Levi's, Pampers, Mars-USA, Cartier, Perrier, Bic-France, Martini, Gucci-Italy, Schweppes, and Mercedes-Benz are examples. The firms producing these products became international marketers by a process of creeping "incrementalism."[10] The smallest incremental step that a company can take insofar as organization is concerned is to market abroad through an export department. The "department" may even start with a single person, but even so, it is the place in the organization that has the necessary authorities and the associated responsibilities for exporting the company's products.

The export manager initially has to resolve the question of which countries exports should be made to (as discussed above), and then to decide how products are to be exported to the countries chosen. The three major export methods are indirect exporting, exporting through foreign distributors, and direct exporting.

Indirect Exporting

A company can sell through its own domestic sales staff to visiting foreign buyers. Buyers from foreign department stores who come to the United States to buy apparel is an example.

Another form of indirect exporting is to sell through, or to, **export management companies**, which in turn sell the product abroad. Some export management companies act as agents for companies that want to export their products. Other export management companies buy products and sell them abroad on their own account. Small companies often use an export management company because it allows them to enter the export market with little or no start-up costs in terms of either investment or acquiring expertise. The export management company typically handles all the documentation involved, as well as arranging for shipping, payment of duties, and collection of accounts.

Exporting through Foreign Distributors

The export department can set up one or more **distributors** in each country and sell to them. This requires more investment and expertise on the part of the company, but it also provides more control over the marketing of its products in the countries in which it is operating.

The export department may or may not prepare the documentation and arrange for the shipment of products to the foreign distributors. An alternative is to use a **foreign freight forwarder**. These are specialists in these areas, and if the volume sold abroad by the company is not too great, the fees they charge will be less than the cost of the company's hiring or developing its own specialists to perform these tasks.

Checklists on how to find and evaluate distributors in foreign countries are available and will prove helpful to companies with little experience in this area.[11]

Direct Exporting

Companies can solicit orders from foreign buyers through advertising, direct mail, and trade fairs, and ship directly to them. This is not unusual in industrial products (such as machinery) for which the specifications of the product can be stated in terms of internationally understood standards. Orders can be taken during exhibits at trade fairs, and from advertising and direct-mail brochures that state these specifications.

Direct exporting provides the maximum amount of control over the marketing program but, for that reason, also requires the most marketing expertise. As in exporting through distributors, foreign freight forwarders can be used for handling documentation and shipping if the company does not want to perform those tasks itself.

Licensing

Licensing is a method of obtaining both production and marketing of a company's products by a foreign company in the licensee's country. In return for an agreement by the licensee (the national company) to produce and market the products of the licensor (the international company) in a specified foreign market or markets, and to pay the licensor a stipulated amount related to the volume produced and sold, the licensor agrees to allow the use of patents, trademarks, copyrights, or manufacturing know-how within the limitations stated in the agreement.

The Culligan Company, the U.S.-based manufacturer and marketer of water softeners, is an example of a company that has used licensing successfully in more than 90 countries around the world. The Sunkist name has been licensed for use on more than 400 products in 30 countries.[12] Phillip Morris is another company that practices licensing of its brands but, in its case, it has a special reason for doing so. The governments of many countries have monopolies on the manufacture and sale of tobacco products. The only way Phillip Morris can get its products marketed in these countries is to license the government to manufacture and sell its brands.[13]

There are several advantages to using licensing as a method of entering foreign markets. They include:

1. It is a quick and easy method of entering a market.
2. It requires little capital.
3. It requires little in the way of marketing expertise.
4. It saves on tariffs and transport costs (when the licensee also produces the product).
5. It reduces the risk of financial controls being imposed, domestication, or expropriation or confiscation.

A principal concern about licensing is that after a few years, licensees may become competent enough in the production and marketing of products in the product line that they set up their own brands and "go it alone." When this happens, it amounts to the international company's having established its own competitors.

Joint Ventures

Forming a jointly owned corporation with a company in the host country has become an increasingly popular way of entering and operating in a foreign country. A study by The Conference Board some years ago (1980) indicated that half of the U.S. companies surveyed had started joint ventures in the preceding five years,[14] and there are no signs that that rate of formation has since slackened. Even in the USSR, joint ventures have flourished with the advent of the new economic restructuring; more than 60 joint ventures between Soviet and foreign companies were registered in the first half of 1988.[15]

A joint venture may be an appropriate means of entry to a foreign market for several reasons. The potential advantages include:

1. *Low investment requirements.* This is especially the case if the international company becomes the minority partner. In many countries, patents or manufacturing know-how can be capitalized (with the consent of the other party to the venture, of course), which reduces the investment required even further.

2. *Access to markets and marketing expertise.* According to one study of American firms engaging in joint ventures abroad, this was the primary reason they chose this method of entry.[16] An example of companies that have relied primarily on joint ventures are foreign automobile companies that wanted to market cars in Japan. Joint ventures proved to be the only feasible way to enter the Japanese market. For the same reason, the Nike Corporation has a joint-venture arrangement there for the marketing of its shoes and sports apparel. P&G is continuing to expand in Latin America and the Asia-Pacific regions through the use of joint ventures. The reverse of this situation for other products has also been true for some Japanese firms wanting to enter the American market; General Electric produces and distributes the Matsushita videodisc system under a joint-venture arrangement, because Matsushita did not believe it could compete successfully on its own in the highly competitive U.S. market for this product.

3. *Participation in income, growth, and equity.* Both partners can share in the earnings and growth of the new corporation—both those that are derived from the products and technology at the time the venture is formed and those resulting from the products and technology developed subsequently by the venture.

4. *Deferral of U.S. income tax.* Income realized from the venture by the U.S. partner is not subject to U.S. taxation until distributed. Depending on the host country's tax rate, the period during which income remains undistributed, and other factors, this can result in significant tax savings.

The principal drawback to the joint-venture arrangement, especially when the international company involved is the minority partner, is the lack of control. Some companies (Coca-Cola is a prominent example) refuse to enter joint ventures even when they are the majority partners for this reason. Poorly negotiated agreements can also become a millstone to either partner, sometimes for a protracted period. Within 15 years after forming a joint venture with the Rank organization in Great Britain, for example, the Xerox Corporation is reported to have paid more than $80 million to the British company simply to revise parts of the agreement that were unfavorable to Xerox.[17]

The Foreign Subsidiary

An extension of the joint-venture arrangement that moves the international company in the direction of increased ownership and control is the wholly owned subsidiary. Some companies have found it desirable to establish foreign marketing subsidiaries because they consider themselves competent to take on the marketing of their own products abroad, and because they want to maintain full control over it. They often contract out the manufacturing of their products abroad, either to manufacturers in the countries in which they are marketing or elsewhere. The Nike Germany subsidiary is an example of this approach; it does all of the marketing of the company's products in Germany, which are supplied through plants in the Far East and in various European countries that produce them under contract.

Other companies have set up foreign subsidiaries that both produce and market the products they sell. The Tektronix Company, the principal U.S. producer of oscilloscopes, has taken this organizational route in Holland. Coca-Cola also insists on 100 percent ownership of its foreign operations, including the bottling plants and marketing of its products.

The principal advantages of the foreign subsidiary compared with a joint venture are (1) the retention of control, and (2) not having to share the earnings and increase in equity with a partner, assuming, of course, that such occur. The disadvantages are that (1) it often takes longer to grow and to build earnings because of initial difficulties of obtaining distribution as a foreign company, (2) the tax savings that accrue from a joint venture will not be realized, (3) more investment is required, and (4) the risks are greater, both from the market (there is no partner with which to share them) and from host-country government policy changes (it is a completely foreign-owned corporation, rather than a partially domestic one).

Should "World Brands" Be the Norm in International Marketing?

A central issue that faces a Coca-Cola that markets in France or a Perrier that enters the market in the United States, a Gillette that exports to Great Britain or a Wilkerson that sells in the United States, or an Avia that sets up a marketing subsidiary in Germany or an Adidas that put its brand on the market in the United States is: "Should we use the same marketing program in the country that we are about to enter as we use at home?"

This issue recently received attention in the form of the "world brand" question. Leavitt[18] and others have argued that as the world has become more and more uniform—demographically, culturally, and economically—brands have not only acquired the *capability* of being marketed internationally in the same way that they are marketed in their country of origin, but that they *should be* marketed internationally in the same way.

Unquestionably there are brands that are truly world brands in terms of the way they are marketed. A world brand is not only just a product that is marketed under the same brand name in several countries. To warrant the use of that term, the brand must meet the following conditions. A ***world brand*** is

> a brand for which the product and the marketing strategy and the way it is implemented are essentially the same for each of the several countries in which it is marketed.

Coca-Cola, Procter & Gamble's Pampers (the disposable diaper), Revlon cosmetics, Gillette razors, Levi jeans, Mars candy bars, Cartier jewelry, Perrier mineral water, Bic-France ballpoint pens, Martini wines, Gucci-Italy fashion apparel, Colgate toothpaste, Schweppes soft drinks, Mercedes-Benz cars, and Marlboro cigarettes are examples of products, and TWA airline is an example of a service, that are being marketed as world brands.

In the case of TWA:

> The same product and brand name comes before the eyes of the consumers now in one country, only hours later in another. The same product and brand name is bought by Italians, the French, Germans, Americans, and just about everyone else. And certainly there are product features that every airline passenger the world over would value. For example, more room.
>
> Here's how the new wide seats in TWA's Ambassador (Business) Class were introduced in print in the U.S.A., Italy, Germany, and France. The headline the main illustration, the sub-illustration, the copy, and the TWA tag line—all are the same:
> TWA Brings In More Room
> Piu spazio con TWA
> TWA schafft Raum
> TWA installe de l'espace.[19]

The fact that there are—and should be—some brands marketed as world brands does not necessarily imply that all brands should be marketed that way,

	Differentiated strategy	Undifferentiated strategy
Differentiated implementation	1 National or regional brand	2 Strategic brand
Undifferentiated implementation	4 (necessarily an empty cell)	3 World brand

however. The options of strategy and implementation with respect to marketing abroad versus marketing in one's own country are shown in Figure 21–2. As may be seen there, three different combinations exist of differentiated versus undifferentiated strategy and differentiated versus undifferentiated implementation of strategy, one of which results in national or regional brands, another in strategic brands, and the third in world brands.

In answering the question of whether world brands should be the norm for products marketed internationally, therefore, it is necessary to examine the cells that result in national or regional and strategic brands (cells 1 and 2) in the figure to determine whether or not they should exist.

Cell 1. Differentiated Marketing Strategy and Differentiated Implementation of It—National or Regional Brands

The COMPAQ is a brand of portable personal computer that is compatible with the IBM PC. It came on the market a few years ago at the time the PC was having its rapid growth in sales. The company's strategy in the United States was to serve the same market as the PC, the brand with the highest market share, through as many reputable dealers as possible, while keeping its price noticeably lower (15 to 20 percent) than the IBM PC. The company gave larger discounts to the dealers than did IBM, and advertised just enough to make potential buyers of a personal computer aware that it was an alternative to the IBM PC. Its compatibility and portability, coupled with its lower price, combined to give it a rapid increase in sales. In the first year it was on the market, sales in the United States were more than $100 million.

When it was introduced in Great Britain, it entered a market that then had the highest per capita ownership of personal computers in the world. Most of them were British brands, however, and so the IBM PC was not in a position of market leadership. COMPAQ accordingly had to revise both its strategy and the implementation of it. The company set as its target market all prospective personal computer buyers, not just prospective IBM PC buyers. It began to advertise more heavily than it had in the United States, and to stress the functional features of its products as a

> COMPAQ, not just as an alternative to the IBM PC. Since it was no longer aiming its marketing efforts primarily at siphoning off IBM PC buyers and since the expanded advertising program was resulting in higher costs, the price was also raised to just under that of the IBM PC.

It is apparent from this example that different market conditions in different countries sometimes can dictate both different strategies and different ways of implementing them. Particularly in highly culture-bound products, such as foods and clothing, different methods of distribution, different buying habits, and different needs and attitudes may require adaptations by country or region in both the strategies used and the way they are implemented. National and **regional brands** therefore do—and should—exist.

Cell 2. Undifferentiated Strategy with Differentiated Implementation —Strategic Brands

With respect to advertising, the director of research of a major advertising agency some years ago observed the following:

> Some companies have adopted an approach ... to advertising ... that we may ... call *partial standardization*. By that I mean a common basic strategy is used worldwide. But the specific advertising executions [implementations] are determined locally.[20]

This approach, an undifferentiated strategy but with differentiated implementation, is what we have termed a **strategic brand**. This practice has continued for many products.

There are often requirements for adaptations of the other marketing mix variables as well. Full-line product strategies may have to be pared because the local market cannot support the costs of an extensive line of products. Changes in products may have to be made to adapt to local needs and preferences. Some examples of some necessary changes are:

> Nestle's Nescafe coffee has a strong international identity. Yet it is blended and flavored differently in each of the major markets to suit local tastes.*
>
> Black & Decker, the power-tool maker for both the consumer and professional markets, cannot standardize its products completely because of different safety and industrial standards, and different electrical systems. "U.S. designs are often unacceptable to Europeans, and even colors have different acceptance levels."†
>
> A Japanese toymaker who sold Barbie dolls in Japan had near-zero sales until, after many years of trying, it finally convinced Mattel, Inc. to allow a change to a less-Western look for the doll. After the toymaker "reduced her bosom, turned her blue eyes brown, and darkened her blonde hair," sales zoomed to nearly 2 million units in a two-year period.‡

*"Which Way to the Global Village," *Advertising Age*, April 29, 1985, 20.
†"Global Approach Seeks Similarities in Markets," *Marketing News*, October 11, 1985, 12.
‡"Standardization Not Standard for Global Marketers," *Marketing News*, September 27, 1985, 3.

In some cases a brand cannot be used for legal reasons. (The Ford Motor Company could not use the brand name Mustang in Germany, for example, because it was already in use by a maker of bicycles.) A company that has a policy of owning and managing its own domestic distribution centers may, for political, legal, or financial reasons, find it prudent or even necessary to use public or privately owned warehouses in some foreign countries. And pricing strategies may have to be changed to adapt to differing competitive conditions. The concept of the strategic brand is therefore a viable and valid one.

Advantages and Disadvantages of World Brands

From the foregoing examination of cells 1 and 2, it is apparent that a world brand (as we have defined it) should be used only in situations in which a careful analysis of the market and its legal setting indicates that the domestic marketing strategy and the way it is implemented are appropriate. When this is the case, there are definite advantages to the use of the world brand, including the following:

1. *An economic advantage.* Standardization of products, distribution methods, and advertising copy (with the exception of translation into local languages) for the world brand results in definite economies of scale, in terms of both production and marketing.
2. *A time advantage.* Centralization permits changes in world brand strategy and its implementation to be made more quickly. New products can be introduced in foreign markets faster.
3. *A learning advantage.* It makes the sharing of experience across countries possible; lessons learned in one country can be considered for use in another.
4. *A "quality control" advantage.* Since distribution methods and promotional programs are standardized for the world brand, there are common bases for judging how well each is being implemented in each country.
5. *A consistency of image and positioning advantage.* The image and positioning of the product across countries will be the same, and so the earlier advertising will have laid the groundwork for use of international media as they become more widely used.

There are potential disadvantages, however. They include:

1. *A "less than best fit" opportunity cost.* There are always potential opportunity losses in specific countries from a "less than best fit" of the strategy and implementation that a world brand involves.
2. *The "NIH" excuse.* Since both the strategy and its implementation were "Not Invented Here," the local manager always has this NIH factor to explain a disappointing performance when a world brand strategy is being used.
3. *Lowered local morale.* The marketing personnel in the countries where a world brand strategy is being used invariably experience a decline in morale when it is introduced. They view it (and rightly so) as reducing local marketing prerogatives and lowering their managerial status in the company.

Whether a world brand strategy should be used for a particular product must then be decided based on the net benefits or costs that accrue from these advantages and disadvantages.

Strategic Product Considerations

Whether the same product will be marketed in every country is a central element of the worldwide marketing strategy. When entering a new market, the company has three alternatives with respect to the product to be sold: (1) it can market products identical to the ones sold at home—a **standardized product strategy**, (2) it can adapt the product to meet the needs and desires of the buyers in that country—a **customized product strategy**, or (3) it can develop a totally new version of the product—an **adaptive product strategy**.

Marketing a standardized product in every country leads to faster cost and price reductions, and so leads to higher sales. Increased sales, in turn, bring still more cost reductions. This reinforcing effect in terms of cost reduction results from the workings of the experience curve. It has obvious implications for the domestic market as well as for the foreign ones.

The differences in costs between a standardized and an adaptive product strategy can be substantial. There are always at least some research and development costs for a new product, and the fact that the company will incur such costs is, of course, always recognized when an adaptive strategy is adopted. What often isn't recognized, however, is that the innovative strategy can lead to substantially *higher production costs* for both the product sold at home *and* the new product sold abroad.

An actual example (but with assumed data) will illustrate this point:

> The management of Canon, a Japanese company, had the plain paper copier that so was successful against Xerox designed for the major markets in the West. It was not designed for the Japanese market because it was too small.*
>
> Suppose that Canon is selling 25 percent of its copier output abroad (an assumed percentage that is no doubt less than Canon's actual percentage). Suppose further that the first unit cost for the product was $10,000 and that the relevant experience curve is at the 80 percent level.
>
> Consider two situations: (1) a standardized product is sold both at home and abroad and (2) the same product is still sold at home but an innovative product is sold abroad. Assume that the innovative product also has a first unit cost of $50,000. Assuming that different production processes are required, as shown in Table 21–2, those sold at home will cost almost 10 percent more (9.7%), and those sold abroad will cost about 56 percent more (56.3%) than when the products are standardized.

*S. N. Chakravarty, "The Croissant Comes to Harvard Square," Forbes, July 14, 1986, 69.

These cost differences are the maximum that would be likely to occur in the assumed situation because they assume that none of the experience producing the standard product for the domestic market can be passed on to production

Table 21–2 Unit Costs When Copiers Sold at Home (75% of Total Output) and Abroad (25% of Total Output) Are Standardized and When They Are Differentiated—80 Percent Experience Curve

Standardized Products		Differentiated Products					
Sales at Home and Abroad (100%)		Sales at Home (75%) (Standard Product)			Sales Abroad (25%) (Innovative Product)		
Number	Last Unit Cost	Number	Last Unit Cost	Percentage Over Identical Product Cost	Number	Last Unit Cost	Percentage Over Identical Product Cost
1	$10,000				1	$10,000	—
10	4,765						
100	2,271	75	2,490	9.7%	25	3,547	56.3%
1,000	1,082	750	1,186	9.7	250	1,690	56.3
10,000	515	7,500	565	9.7	2,500	805	56.3
100,000	246	75,000	269	9.7	25,000	384	56.3
1 million	117	750,000	128	9.7	250,000	183	56.3

of the innovative product for the foreign markets. Certainly for customized product production there is likely to be a transfer of experience between it and standard product production, and so unit cost differences would be less.

Still, when one considers that a cost savings of 5 percent can easily result in doubling profits, these cost differences can be very important. When recognized, they can exert considerable economic pressures to market the standardized product, or perhaps a version of it that is only changed cosmetically, in all countries. It is only when it can be demonstrated that marketing the same product will result in substantially lower sales that it becomes profitable to change it significantly for one or more foreign countries.

There are, of course, situations where that is necessary. Food products have been changed to conform to local tastes, and clothing has been adapted to meet different size requirements and fashion demands. Household appliances have been adjusted in size to match local requirements. Substantial changes in consumer durable products in order to bring the price in reach of the average consumer may be the only way to market such products successfully in third-world and developing countries.

Strategic Pricing Considerations

Pricing Objectives   As in the domestic market, the company marketing abroad must decide whether it wants to follow a "profit now" or a "share now, profit later" strategy.

In general, Japanese companies excepted, a company management is more likely to opt for a "profit now" strategy in a foreign market than it is at home. The psychology of marketing abroad tends to make foreign operations seem less stable, and thus the desire to acquire profits early more attractive. Japanese firms, however, traditionally take the route of first attempting to build market share through offering quality products at a low price. This results in low profits, or even losses, during the first few years of operation in a given market abroad. It moves the company rapidly down the experience curve, enabling costs to be reduced rapidly. When the desired share is reached, prices can be set at a level that permits higher profits.

Once the decision on pricing strategy is made and irrespective of whether it is to try to maximize profits now or to build share and obtain higher profits later, the basic pricing methods and procedures for pricing abroad should remain the same as they are for pricing domestically. Although there will be many new costs involved in marketing products abroad, such as added transportation costs, taxes and tariffs, longer distribution channels, and exchange rate fluctuations, all with the result that prices are very likely to **escalate**—to be higher abroad than at home—the principles underlying sound pricing will not have changed simply because the price is being set in a foreign country.

Price Escalation

It is a common reaction of tourists abroad to wonder why the prices of the products made in their home country "are priced so high here." An IBM PC computer that sells for $1,500 in the United States is priced at the equivalent of $2,100 in West Germany. A bottle of Bordeaux wine that is priced at a dollar in France will be several dollars in Japan (both prices in dollar equivalents). A wall clock by a well-known Danish designer that sells for the equivalent of $30 in Denmark will be nearly $50 in the United States. Exchange rates are not a factor in these price differences because the prices in both countries are given in dollars. Why are the prices for products made in other countries usually so high?

The answer is not hard to find. Although it is true that foreign products may have an allure that adds to their demand, and thus to a higher market price— for example, French wine in Japan (and in the United States) probably is priced somewhat higher because of this—the principal reason is the added costs of transporting products to and marketing them in foreign countries.

What can the international marketer do to reduce price escalation? The following are actions that may help to keep prices down in foreign markets:

1. *Simplify the product so that price can be lowered.*
2. *Assemble or produce in the foreign country.* This may eliminate a substantial proportion of the tariffs imposed (although tariffs will still have to be paid on imported parts) and will eliminate importer margins.
3. *Shorten channels of distribution.* This may not save on marketing costs— the same economies of distribution generally apply in foreign countries as at home, and shortening distribution channels at home also may not save on distribution costs—but it will save on taxes in countries that have a cumulative value-added tax. (A cumulative value-added tax is one in which the tax is based on the sales price and is assessed each time the product is sold. The more times it is sold, the greater the compounded effect of the several tax assessments become.)
4. *Reduce the profit margin.* This may be painful but necessary in order to compete.

Transfer Pricing

Transfer prices are prices charged by one part of the company when products are transferred to other parts of the company. When each organizationally separate part of the company is responsible for its income statement, the price at which products are "sold" to other organizational units within the company becomes of obvious interest to both the buying and selling units. An AC Sparkplug supplying sparkplugs to its parent General Motors or a small motors division "selling" to an appliance division of General Electric clearly will be concerned with the prices at which products are transferred as long as their managements are held responsible for profits and losses.

The price at which products or components are transferred to foreign subsidiaries takes on other dimensions than just the effects on the income statement, however. There are at least three strategic considerations involved in setting transfer prices that affect the profitability of the corporation as a whole. They are:

1. *The effect on import duties.* The lower the transfer price, the lower (in general) the cost of the duties that will have to be paid.
2. *The effect on income taxes.* The lower the transfer price, the higher the income taxes that generally will have to be paid in the host country, but the lower the income taxes paid in the home country.
3. *The effect on dividend repatriation.* The lower the transfer price, the higher the amount of dividends that will have to be taken out of the host country directly, rather than indirectly through charging more for the products supplied.

It is apparent that in some foreign countries these considerations work contrary to each other. For example, in a host country that has high import duties, high income taxes, and restrictions on repatriations of dividends, a corporation that is shipping products to a marketing subsidiary there would like to transfer them at a low price to keep duty costs low, but would prefer to set a high transfer price to keep income taxes low and reduce the problems of repatriating dividends.

As long as the parent corporation is not restricted in terms of what transfer prices it can charge, a price that optimizes even these conflicting considerations can be determined and set. However, the use of transfer prices to manipulate duty payments and tax charges and to repatriate dividends has not escaped the attention of governmental authorities. In all countries a government agency, such as the Internal Revenue Service in the United States, has the responsibility of auditing the tax returns of foreign corporations operating in that country, and for most of these agencies a routine part of the audit is an examination to determine if transfer prices are being used for tax or financial manipulation. In cases where it is found that transfer prices are being used for this purpose, they may rule that either additional import duties or taxes have to be paid.

Exchange Rate Hedging

In marketing to companies whose currency exchange rates are not tied to the U.S. dollar (only a few countries have currencies that are pegged to the dollar), as long as the price to the buyer in the host-country currency is kept the same, the "price" received by the U.S. marketer changes as the exchange rate changes.

The exposure to risk from adverse exchange rate changes occurs for each sale to be paid in the home currency of the foreign buyer (wholesaler, retailer, or industrial firm) for the period between the time the price is set and when payment is received. This exposure can be reduced or eliminated if the seller chooses to engage in a process called hedging, however. A **hedge** occurs when the marketer engages in another transaction—often in the forward market for the host country's currency—that has an exchange rate risk in the opposite direction from the same currency for the same period. What is gained or lost on the trade transaction as a result of exchange rate fluctuation is thereby offset by what is lost or gained on the hedging transaction.

There are many methods of hedging.[21] All of them have transactions costs, however, and all require that the hedger forgo the possibility of exchange rate gain on the part of the trade transaction that is hedged. Many multinational companies choose not to hedge—in effect, decide to speculate—on at least a part of their receivables in host-country currencies.

Strategic Promotional Considerations

Advertising

Ideally, every chief advertising executive in companies marketing both domestically and abroad would like to develop campaigns that can be used effectively worldwide. Campaigns that can be used in all countries are less expensive, are faster to develop, and eliminate most of the problems of controlling strategy, content, and execution. These clearly are persuasive reasons for wanting to standardize advertising across countries, and so to treat the communication of a product's attributes and its uses as if the brand were a *world brand*.

A balancing consideration, however, is that the way in which the attributes of the product are communicated to prospective buyers is culturally the most sensitive of marketing decisions. It is not just that an advertising campaign developed for use in several countries may not be as effective as customized campaigns in each would be; in some cases standardized campaigns adapted for use abroad have resulted in *reduced* sales. Horror stories abound of brand names and the slogans and colors used in advertising campaigns that turned out in one or more countries to question virility, to be offensive or obscene, or even to suggest the death of the prospective user. The fact that standardized advertising may be ineffective, not to mention the possibility of its resulting in reduced sales, is a telling argument for treating the communication aspects of the marketing of each brand as if it were a *national brand*.

How should these conflicting considerations be resolved? As indicated earlier in the chapter (p. 712), a growing number of companies are moving toward the use of standardized strategy with differentiated implementation of the advertising content, the strategic brand concept insofar as communication is concerned. Companies such as Phillips, Sony, McDonald's, Gillette,[22] Royal Dutch Shell,[23] and Levi-Strauss[24] have used this approach.

A specific example of its use is provided by Royal Dutch Shell:

Some time ago Shell, like all the oil companies, was searching for a strategy to help offset the negatives generated by the oil crisis. The agency and Shell decided not to get into the explanation business, but to build positive attitudes toward Shell through a campaign positioning Shell as helping the consumer. This was done through a series of booklets giving tips on how to deal with a variety of motoring and energy-related problems.

> Since most companies were affected in the same way by the oil crisis, this strategy was deemed transferable. However, whereas the crisis was general, the specific problems were often local, geared toward individual countries' driving habits, attitudes toward their cars, home heating or cooling problems, and so on. So the particular problems treated in the booklets, and therefore in advertising, varied considerably from country to country. There were also some differences in executional style.*

*J. Stewart, "Maybe It Will Work There—An Approach to Advertising for Multinational Clients," *Viewpoint,* Winter 1984, 28–29.

Sales Promotion

Sales promotions in countries throughout the world take essentially the same forms; cents-off promotions, coupons, samples, in-store demonstrations, product tie-ins, contests, point-of-purchase displays, retailer signs, and trade fairs are used in countries abroad as well as in the United States.

In the less-developed countries, sales promotions may take a larger share, and advertising a correspondingly lesser share, of the promotional budget than in the more-industrialized countries. This is because of limitations on media, especially in the rural portions of the country. Cateora described a promotional campaign used for this reason by both Pepsi-Cola and Coca-Cola in rural parts of Latin America as follows:

> ... A portion of the advertising–sales budget ... is spent on "carnival trucks" which make frequent trips to outlying villages to promote their products. When a carnival truck makes a stop in a village, it may show a movie or provide some other kind of entertainment, and an unopened bottle of the product purchased from a local retailer is the price of admission. The unopened bottle is to be exchanged for a cold bottle plus a coupon for another bottle.[25]

For industrial products, trade fairs are a major means of promotion in most foreign countries. There are more than 600 international trade fairs held annually in 70 different countries. Unlike the trade fairs in the United States, which are more concerned with exhibiting products than selling them, a central purpose of companies displaying their products in foreign trade fairs is to make sales during the fair.[26] (A periodic list of international trade fairs is provided in the U.S. Department of Commerce publication *Business America.*)

Personal Selling

The extent of the multinational company's direct involvement in personal selling abroad will, of course, depend upon how it has chosen to organize its marketing efforts abroad. If it is marketing solely through a domestic export management company, it will have no requirement at all for personal selling in foreign countries. This will also be the case if it is licensing its products to foreign companies. It is only when it sets up a joint venture or a subsidiary abroad that the company will become directly involved in personal selling in the other countries to which it is marketing.

When this is the case, the general tasks of recruiting, selecting, training, compensating, and directing the sales force remain the same—all must be performed for both the domestic and the international sales forces. There are almost always special culturally or politically determined criteria for each of these tasks in each foreign country, however. This may mean that they have to be administered differently abroad than they are at home. For example, an expatriate sales representative who has had no previous exposure to the country of his or her assignment is almost certain to require some training on the customs and special sales problems that are likely to be encountered. Sales personnel in countries with high personal income taxes also will want to have a higher percentage of their compensation in nontaxable fringe benefits and expense accounts than will their counterparts in countries with lower taxes.

The central strategic concern involving the personal sales force is whether host-country nationals should be used instead of home-country expatriates. There are advantages of each. The foreign national is fluent in the language, will not be affected by personal or family cultural adaptation programs, will know the special sales problems that may be encountered, and will probably cost less and remain on the job longer than the expatriate. On the other hand, the home-country expatriate will probably know the company, its policies, and its products better.

Recruiting of sales personnel for foreign countries has increasingly tended toward looking first for host-country nationals, and adding expatriates only in those cases where a sufficient number of qualified nationals cannot be found. In the case of highly technical products, however, better product knowledge may tip the balance toward a sales force composed largely of expatriates.

Strategic Distribution Considerations

Generally speaking, once a product is landed in a capitalist foreign country, the alternative channels for distributing it there are the same as those described in Chapter 17 for the United States. (When trading with socialist countries, the usual rule is that one sells to a government agency in charge of foreign trade, and the product is distributed by another government agency responsible for internal trade and distribution.) That is, the foreign marketer usually has choices of selling through **agent wholesalers** (manufacturers' representatives, brokers, factors, drop shippers), **merchant wholesalers** (distributors, jobbers, full-service importers), **retailers or industrial suppliers** (chain, independent), or **direct to consumers or industrial buyers**, or some combination of the above.

It is perhaps something of a simplification (but, if so, not much of one) to say that the choice of distribution channels abroad is governed by the same considerations, and made by the same process, as described in Chapter 17 for the domestic market. If it is a simplification, it is because of unfamiliarity with the names and exact functions performed by each of the possible channel members. Once confusion on these questions is cleared up, the choice will need to be made on the bases of consideration of functions desired for the middlemen to perform, availability of middlemen performing them, coverage, cost, efficiency, and control–the same considerations involved in choosing a domestic channel of distribution.

This is not to say that the same distribution channels will necessarily be chosen. Avon is now marketing its facial cream in the Republic of China through department stores, the first time it has distributed any of its products through retailers.[27]

International Marketing Research

Marketing researchers in the United States, and the executives who use their findings, are accustomed to dealing with a sizable market that has a common culture and speaks a common language (and they are familiar with both), has well-developed sources of secondary information, and has a populace that is mostly literate, is relatively open about giving answers to questions asked by strangers, and is largely reachable by telephone.

This felicitous combination of attributes for conducting marketing research is not found in any other part of the world. The United States, although far from being the *largest* country in the world, is the largest *market* for products with a common language and a single culture. (China, the world's largest country, has a population that is roughly five times as large but a gross national product that is only one-tenth that of the United States.) Although some Western industrialized countries have high per capita gross national products, well-developed sources of secondary data, and high literacy rates, all are substantially smaller than the United States in terms of market size. Telephone ownership is lower in most countries, and substantially lower in third-world and Socialist bloc countries. And in many other countries, including both those that are industrialized and those that are less-developed, cultural constraints prevent obtaining marketing research information on an easy, open basis.

Of particular concern is the imposition of sophisticated marketing concepts and complex research techniques that the respondents will not understand because they are not a part of the respondents' culture.[28] At best, this results in obtaining no data because of respondent lack of comprehension. At worst, bad data are obtained without the researcher and the client ever realizing that that is the case.

The effects of these differences is that, in addition to the usual problems of domestic research, the researcher abroad has extra problems with which to cope. They include:

1. *Cost versus value of research.* The smaller market, the lack of secondary data, the need to translate questionnaires into other languages and dialects, and the inability to reach many consumers by the use of mail questionnaires or telephone result not only in higher per-respondent costs, but in a higher cost of research as a percentage of prospective payoff from it as well. The ratio of the cost to the expected value of research projects in foreign countries therefore is normally higher—sometimes substantially so—than it is in the United States.

2. *Research projects may have to be conducted to provide primary data to describe what would have been disclosed by secondary data in the United States.* A central statistic of importance in the marketing of products is the total size of the market. In a country such as Bolivia, for example, whose last census of either the population or commercial and industrial activity was in the 1950s, obtaining reliable data to estimate market size requires generating it oneself.

3. *Consumer studies may largely have to be conducted by personal interview rather than by mail questionnaire or telephone in some countries.* Low literacy rates and lack of telephones may leave little in the way of an alternative to

personal interviewing. Whereas this may not be bad from a reliability and validity standpoint, it will almost always increase costs substantially.

4. *The lack of secondary data for use as sampling frames may result in having to use convenience or judgment samples rather than quota or random samples.* If recent data are not available that describe (in terms of relevant demographic groups) or provide a list of the population of interest, quota samples cannot be taken. Random samples are limited in this case to those taken with the aid of maps. Convenience and judgment samples will in many situations become the only viable choices.

This recounting of the problems of doing research abroad should not be interpreted to mean that good, cost-effective research cannot be conducted in foreign countries. Obviously this is not the case. Costs rise and problems multiply, though, and both the client and the researcher should anticipate that this will happen.

Doing Cross-Cultural Research

The fact that the research is being conducted in a different culture requires that the relevant cultural assumptions be determined. These come into play in three important areas: (1) the cultural significance of the product, (2) the nature of the purchase decision and buying process, and (3) how the product is used.

The Cultural Significance of the Product: Products may well signify different things in different cultures. Any well-conceived marketing plan has to take into account the cultural meaning of the product if it is to be successful.

In the United States, for example, fur coats have come to be regarded by a sizable portion of the population as an indication of callousness toward nature. In West Germany, on the other hand, they are regarded as an important means to display accumulated wealth. Any effort to market fur coats in the two countries would clearly need to be based in part on an understanding of the way the product is viewed in each.

The Nature of the Purchase Decision and Buying Process: Purchase decision processes and the way products are bought vary substantially across cultures. Marketing a product is made much easier if the channels used and the appeals made reflect the local cultural arrangements.

For example, Arab societies typically are male-dominated to the extent that only the small, routine purchase decisions are made by women. When Singer first started to market sewing machines in Arab countries, it was aware of this fact and was careful to market it to be purchased by the husband for his wife, rather than by the wife for herself. The appeal to the husband was that the wife could be much more productive in her home sewing, and a better-dressed household would reflect favorably upon its head.

The Way the Product Is Used: The way a product is used can have significant effects on both the way it is designed and the appeals that are made in communicating its attributes.

A prepared food product that needed only to be heated before serving was introduced in Japan by a U.S. company. The company was aware that a high percentage of Japanese households had an electrically heated pot for cooking rice, and so the advice given on the package was to use that pot for its preparation. Japanese housewives refused to do this, and rejected the product as a consequence, because of the pride they take in cooking rice well, and the importance they attach to not using the rice pot for any other purpose for fear it will adversely affect the taste of the rice.

WORKING ABROAD AND YOUR CAREER IN THE COMPANY

Your company has offered you a comparable position in the London office. Should you take it? The accumulated experience of many executives who have accepted overseas assignments suggests that it may not be a good idea insofar as your career in the company is concerned. Excerpts from an article dealing with this question indicate why:

> What can be so bad about an off-shore posting to London or Paris? First is the very real possibility of being passed over for promotions or being left out of succession plans being cooked up in the home office. . . . Then there is the worry of coming home a stranger. Returning executives sometimes find themselves without familiar faces to greet them, without appropriate jobs waiting, and without much status. Former colleagues may have risen to positions you had aspired to; mentors may have retired or moved on; policies for grooming talent might have changed.[29]

But there are pluses to such assignments as well. The experience of living and working in a foreign country provides not only an exposure to a foreign culture but a platform from which to gain a better understanding of your own. The job abroad typically results in an increase in salary in the neighborhood of 20 percent, plus hardship compensation, plus moving costs, plus assistance with housing costs. And the experience in working in an overseas office where there is much more authority and responsibility than in a comparable domestic position is a valuable one.

There are indications that some multinationals are beginning to require foreign experience of their younger executives.[30] If your company is one of these, the answers to questions 2 and 3 below are likely to be in the affirmative. You should still ask yourself questions 1 and 4, however. If your company does not require foreign experience for advancement, you will be wise to consider all of the following questions before accepting a position abroad:

1. Do I, and does my family, adapt easily to unfamiliar situations?
2. Is there an agreed-on period that I will be there?
3. Is there a reentry program in the company that guarantees that I will not be penalized for having worked abroad?
4. If things do not work out to my satisfaction on return to my own company, am I willing to change companies?

SUMMARY OF IMPORTANT POINTS

1. The major dimensions of the decision concerning marketing abroad are (a) geographic, (b) organizational, and (c) strategic.
2. The *culture* of a society can be defined as the shared set of social norms and responses that condition the population's attitudes, beliefs, and behavior.
3. The major adverse actions that host-country governments may take toward foreign companies operating there are:
   a. Imposing surcharges or special currency requirements on purchases of imports.
   b. Requiring barter rather than payment (a form of countertrading) so that the foreign company must accept, or sell, host-country products in an amount equal to its sales in that country.
   c. Instituting currency controls that prohibit the company from taking specified proportions of interest, dividends, or profits from the country.
   d. Instituting import quotas.
   e. Restricting the purchase of foreign-made goods.
   f. Instituting boycotts.
   g. Requiring that the formulas of products be divulged.
   h. Imposing "invisible tariffs," that is, bureaucratic requirements for documentation, marks of origin, special labeling, and the like.
   i. Exerting controls over the nature of the product, its price, or its promotion.
   j. Requiring "domestication" of the company, whereby local ownership in the company is increased, nationals are placed in high management positions, a higher proportion of parts have to be made locally, and so on.
   k. Expropriation, that is, forcing the foreign corporation to sell its local business to the host government or a buyer it specifies, usually at a price set by the government.
   l. Confiscation, that is, taking over the local business of the foreign corporation with no compensation at all.
4. There are four primary methods of organizing marketing efforts to foreign countries, each with a number of variations. They are (a) the export department, (b) using licensees, (c) setting up joint ventures, and (d) establishing wholly owned foreign subsidiaries.
5. There are three major exporting methods: (a) indirect exporting, (b) exporting through foreign distributors, and (c) direct exporting.
6. The advantages of using licensing as a method of entering foreign markets include:
   a. It is a quick and easy method of entering a market.
   b. It requires little capital.
   c. It requires little in the way of marketing expertise.
   d. It saves on tariffs and transport costs (when the licensee also produces the product).

e. It reduces risk of financial controls being imposed, domestication, or expropriation or confiscation.

7. The advantages of using the joint venture as a method of entering foreign markets include:
   a. Low investment requirements
   b. Access to markets and marketing expertise
   c. Participation in income, growth, and equity
   d. Deferral of U.S. income tax

8. **a.** The principal advantages of the foreign subsidiary compared with a joint venture are:
   (1) The retention of control
   (2) Not having to share the earnings and increase in equity with a partner
   b. The disadvantages are that:
   (1) It often takes longer to grow and to build earnings because of initial difficulties in obtaining distribution as a foreign company.
   (2) The tax savings that accrue from a joint venture will not be realized.
   (3) More investment is required.
   (4) The risks are greater.

9. A *world brand* is a brand for which the product and the marketing strategy and the way it is implemented are essentially the same for each of the several countries in which it is marketed.

10. A *national* or *regional brand* results from a differentiated strategy and a differentiated implementation, a *strategic brand* from an undifferentiated strategy and a differentiated implementation, and a *world brand* from an undifferentiated strategy and an undifferentiated implementation.

11. **a.** The potential advantages of a world brand are (1) production economies, (2) time savings, (3) cross-country learning, (4) added "quality" control for the marketing program, and (5) consistency of image and positioning.
   b. The potential disadvantages are (1) a "less than best fit" opportunity cost, (2) the "not invented here" excuse, and (3) lowered local morale.

12. The steps that the international marketer can take to reduce price escalation of its products in foreign markets include:
   a. Simplifying the product so that price can be lowered.
   b. Assembling or producing in the foreign country.
   c. Shortening channels of distribution.
   d. Reducing the gross margin if necessary.

13. There are at least three strategic considerations involved in setting *transfer prices* that affect the profitability of the corporation as a whole. They are:
   a. The effect on import duties
   b. The effect on income taxes
   c. The effect on dividend repatriation

14. A *hedge* occurs when the marketer engages in another transaction—often in the forward market for the host country's currency—that has

an exchange rate risk in the opposite direction from the same currency for the same period.

15. **a.** The advantages of hiring foreign nationals for the sales force are that they:

   (1) Are fluent in the language

   (2) Will not be affected by personal or family cultural adaptation programs

   (3) Will know the special sales problems that may be encountered

   (4) Will probably cost less and remain on the job longer than the expatriate

   b. The disadvantage is that the home-country expatriate will probably know the company, its policies, and its products better.

16. In addition to the usual problems of domestic research, the researcher abroad often has to cope with the problems of:

   a. Higher per-respondent costs and (probable) lower value of the research information.

   b. Research projects having to be conducted to provide primary data to describe what would have been disclosed by secondary data in the United States.

   c. Consumer studies that may largely have to be conducted by personal interview rather than by mail questionnaire or telephone in some countries.

   d. The lack of secondary data for use as sampling frames resulting in having to use convenience or judgment samples rather than quota or random samples.

REVIEW QUESTIONS

21.1. What are the major dimensions of the decision concerning marketing abroad?

21.2. What is the meaning of *culture*?

21.3. What are the major adverse actions that host-country governments may take toward foreign companies operating there?

21.4. For what do the following acronyms stand?
   a. GATT
   b. EEC
   c. ASEAN
   d. UNCTAD
   e. EFTA

21.5. What are the primary methods of organizing marketing efforts to foreign countries?

21.6. What are the major methods of exporting?

21.7. What are the advantages of licensing as a method of entering a foreign market?

21.8. What are the advantages of a joint venture as a way of entering a foreign market

21.9. What are the principal
a. advantages
b. disadvantages
of the foreign subsidiary compared with a joint venture for entering a foreign market?

21.10. What is a *world brand*?

21.11. Define:
a. A national or regional brand
b. A strategic brand
c. A world brand
in terms of strategy and implementation.

21.12. What are the potential
a. advantages
b. disadvantages
of a world brand?

21.13. What steps can the international marketer take to reduce the price of its products abroad?

21.14. What are the strategic considerations in setting transfer prices for products delivered from the home to the host country?

21.15. What is a *hedge*?

21.16. What are the
a. advantages
b. disadvantages
of hiring foreign nationals for the sales force?

21.17. In addition to the usual problems involved in domestic research, with what other problems does the researcher abroad often have to cope?

DISCUSSION QUESTIONS

21.18. There is a grocery supermarket in the basement of most major department stores in European cities, but not in the major department stores in American cities. Why do you think this difference exists?

21.19. The hypermarket (a very large store containing a supermarket, drug store, general merchandise department store, specialty shops, and service establishments such as beauty parlors and shoe repair shops) was started in France more than 20 years ago and has grown rapidly throughout Europe and the United Kingdom ever since. It was not introduced in the United States until about 10 years after its debut in France, and has grown very slowly here. Why do you think this is the case?

21.20. Every culture attaches meanings to colors. In the United States, for example, yellow is associated with cowardice, green with envy, red with anger (or passion), and so forth. White in the West is associated with purity but in the Far East it commonly signifies death and mourning.

What would you say are generally indicators of "safe" colors to use in logo and package designs in marketing a product in a foreign culture?

21.21. What indications for organizing international marketing are suggested in the statement "The world has become economically more integrated but politically more fragmented?"

21.22. "In creating a true world brand, aren't you going to be creating a product that in each country will be vulnerable to domestic competitors adding local variations that make it more appealing to that market, advertising it using local appeals, and pricing it for less because it is locally manufactured, and by so doing end up taking your market away?" Comment.

21.23. A U.S. company introduced a laundry product with stain-removing enzymes in Peru. The ads that were used, which had been successful in other countries, showed "biosolves," little cartoon enzymes with big mouths noisily "eating" dirt from clothes.

The product did badly, and some research revealed the reason. Peruvian women traditionally have boiled clothes with soap before washing them in the usual ways. The ads reinforced their belief that boiling was necessary to kill germs by showing them that there were germs (the voracious cartoon figures) in the clothes. They used the enzyme as a soap, adding it to the clothes before boiling. Boiling killed the enzymes, destroying the stain-removing properties of the product.

Seeing that the product did nothing for their clothes, the women usually didn't buy it again.

How should the company have gone about correcting this marketing error?

21.24. "The world brand supporters in effect argue that the marketer should focus on the similarities among national markets. But we have spent the last 30 years learning to profit from differences among segments in domestic markets. Why should we throw that experience away and go for world brands in international marketing?" Comment.

21.25. In general, what kinds of products lend themselves to becoming world brands?

21.26. Is the use by ESSO of the "Tiger in the Tank" campaign in the United States and abroad as:

Stop 'n Tijger in uw Tank (Holland)

Mettez un tigre dans votre moteur (France)

Metti un tigre nel motore (Italy)

Pack 'n Tiger in den Tank (West Germany)

an example of a *world brand* or a *strategic brand* approach insofar as advertising is concerned? Explain.

21.27. "The cost savings for global advertising campaign production are insignificant compared with media costs. And what savings there are hardly offset the risk that one campaign will be equally effective everywhere." Comment.

21.28. "There are those who argue that the difference in languages is a sufficient reason in itself to prevent a world brand from succeeding. But Mozart, Ming vases, and Rembrandt have always communicated universally. Nonverbal communication knows no language barrier." Comment.

21.29. If you were a marketer of fur coats in West Germany, how would the prevailing view of such coats being a means of displaying accumulated wealth affect your choice of distribution channel, the prices you set, and the advertising appeals you used?

21.30. Fill in the cells in the following table:

Unit Costs When Products Sold at Home (75% of Total Output) and Abroad (25% of Total Output) Are Standardized and When They Are Differentiated—80 Percent Experience Curve

Standardized Products		Differentiated Products					
Sales at Home and Abroad (100%)		Sales at Home (50%) (Standard Product)			Sales Abroad (50%) (Innovative Product)		
Col. 1 Number	Col. 2 Last Unit Cost	Col. 3 Number	Col. 4 Last Unit Cost	Col. 5 Percentage Over Identical Product Cost	Col. 6 Number	Col. 7 Last Unit Cost	Col. 8 Percentage Over Identical Product Cost
1	$10,000				1	$10,000	—
10	_____	5	_____	_____%	5	_____	_____%
100	_____	50	_____	_____	50	_____	_____
1,000	_____	500	_____	_____	500	_____	_____
10,000	_____	5,000	_____	_____	5,000	_____	_____
100,000	_____	50,000	_____	_____	50,000	_____	_____
1 million	_____	500,000	_____	_____	500,000	_____	_____

21.31. Compare the tabular values obtained in your answer to problem 21.30 with those in Table 21–2 in the text. What conclusions do you reach about the production savings on the Canon copiers
a. sold in Japan
b. sold abroad
if 50 percent of the sales (instead of 25 percent as in Table 21.2) were made abroad?

21.32. Fill in the table shown in problem 21.30 with the percentage sold at home being 33 percent instead of 50 percent. (Be sure to make the appropriate changes in the quantities in columns 3 and 6 before you make any calculations.)

21.33. Compare the tabular values obtained in your answer to problem 21.30 with those in Table 21–2 in the text. What conclusions do you reach about the production savings on the Canon copiers
a. sold in Japan
b. sold abroad
if 67 percent of the sales (instead of 25 percent as in Table 21–2) were made abroad?

Endnotes

[1]*The Wall Street Journal*, April 16, 1981, 1.

[2]West Germany, France, Italy, the United Kingdom, Spain, the Netherlands, Belgium, Denmark, Greece, Portugal, Ireland, and Luxembourg.

[3]Austria, Norway, Sweden, Switzerland, Iceland, and Finland.

[4]The communist bloc countries of Bulgaria, Czechoslovakia, Hungary, East Germany, Poland, Rumania, and the USSR.

[5]For a discussion of the EEC and the implications of "1992" to companies outside its borders planning to market there, see "Reshaping Europe: 1992 and Beyond," *Business Week*, December 12, 1988, 48–73.

[6]"GATT in the Doldrums," *The Economist*, November 26, 1988, 14–15; and "The General Agreement to Talk and Talk," *The Economist*, December 10, 1988, 68–69.

[7]"Integrating Political Risk: Ford Unit Uses Several Levels of Analysis," *Business International*, June 22, 1984.

[8]F. T. Haner, "Rating Investment Risks Abroad," *Business Horizons*, April 1979. 23.

[9]D. A. Schmidt, "Analyzing Political Risk," *Business Horizons*, July–August 1986, 43–50.

[10]See S. H. Robock and K. Simmonds, *International Business and Multinational Enterprises*, 3rd ed., Richard D. Irwin, 1983, 273, and "How Global Concepts Get Started," *Advertising Age*, March 11, 1985, 22–28, for elaboration of the "creeping incrementalism" approach.

[11]See, for example, "Finding a Distributor Takes Planning and Skill: A BI Checklist," March 8, 1985, 74–75, and "How to Evaluate Foreign Distributors," May 10, 1985, 145, 148—both in *Business International*.

[12]"Sunkist a Pioneer in New Products, Promotions," *Advertising Age*, November 9, 1988, 140.

[13]V. Terpstra, *International Marketing*, 3rd ed., The Dryden Press, 1983, 347.

[14]Reported in F. K. Berlew, "The Joint Venture—A Way into Foreign Markets," *Harvard Business Review*, July–August 1984, 48.

[15]"Russian Bear Bullish on Marketing," *Marketing News*, November 21, 1988, 1.

[16]L. T. Wells, "Joint Ventures," *European Business*, Summer 1973, 73–79.

[17]As reported in Terpstra, *International Marketing*, 353.

[18]T. Levitt, *The Marketing Imagination*, Free Press, 1983, Chapter 2.

[19]J. Stewart, "Maybe It *Will* Work There—An Approach to Advertising for Multinational Clients," *Viewpoint*, Winter 1984, 29–30.

[20]L. Light, "How BBDO Approaches the Problems of Multinational Advertising," Multinational Marketing Seminar, Dusseldorf, West Germany, February 2, 1976.

[21]See Robock and Simmonds, *International Business*, 536–543.

[22]L. Light, "How BBDO Approaches the Problems."

[23]R. W. Fox, "Can an International Campaign Get Much Better?" *International Advertiser*, July–August 1981, 16–18.

[24]D. Chase and E. Bacot, "Levi Zipping Up World Image," *Advertising Age*, September 14, 1981, 34.

[25]P. R. Cateora, *International Marketing*, 5th ed., Richard D. Irwin, 489.

[26]"Small U.S. Firms Use European Trade Fairs as an Inexpensive

Way to Tap New Markets," *The Wall Street Journal*, November 12, 1981, 25.

[27]"Avon Adds China to Its List of Foreign Markets," *Marketing News*, October 15, 1982, 1.

[28]"Third World Research Is Difficult, But It's Possible," *Marketing News*, August 28, 1987, 50.

[29]M. Salsman, "Pits in the Overseas Plum," *Forbes*, February 10, 1987, 132.

[30]"More U.S. Firms Insisting on Overseas Experience," *International Herald-Tribune*, July 15, 1988, 11.

MINICASES

Researching the West German Market

The following statement on the need to research the West German market, and how to do it, appears in *How To Approach the West German Market—Information for Exporters from Abroad*, published by the German Foreign Trade Information Office, Cologne, 1982, page 23:

An exporter who has selected the Federal Republic of Germany as a potential market has to realize that he will run into strong competition. For almost all imaginable products and services are being offered in this market by domestic manufacturers or exporters from abroad. That is why it is important, even before advertising and surely before making specific offers, to carry out a careful investigation of the prospective German market. Bc⁺h the strength and nature of competition and the suitability of the product intended for export have to be considered. Here are some ways of sizing up the competition:

1. Come and have a personal look. Use a visit to make contacts with manufacturers, distributors, and marketers in your field, or in related fields.
2. Consult German technical journals and trade magazines. A host of technical journals and trade magazines, containing business and production data, are published on the German market. (For publishers' addresses see "Leitfaden für Presse und Werbung," Section 4.3 [of this publication] or ask the German Foreign Trade Information Office.)
3. Peruse mail order catalogs. Such catalogs can be remarkably helpful sources of information. In their pages you will find insights about prices, fashions, forms, patterns, color, designs—plus the whole range of consumer goods now being offered on the German market.
4. Read import and production statistics. The official statistics of the German "Statisches. Bundesamt" (see Section 3.3 of this publication) contain most informative data. They give you an idea of average prices of German products compared with prices for the same products from other exporting countries. A clue—in the case of high import quotas for certain products, chances are that they are not being made in sufficient quantities at home, and therefore represent a promising item of export.

A market research effected by using the means described above will at the same time reveal whether the exporter's own product has a chance to be launched successfully on the German market, i.e., whether it can compete in quality and presentation, conforms to standards, fashions and consumer tastes, and meets the technical requirements of the German processing industry.

This first market analysis must be followed by continuous observation of the market developments so that the supplier can adapt his offer to the needs of the customer and to changing market conditions.

Will following these instructions provide a satisfactory knowledge of the prospective German market for an exporter's product? Explain.

J. Smith Company: Price Change Analysis

In the book *Practical Marketing Audits* (by John Naylor and Alan Wood and published by John Wiley and Sons, 1978), the authors give an example of an analysis of a proposed price change. The actual data for Product Line C of the J. Smith Company on average net price, unit sales, and gross margin for the past two years, and the projected data for the current year, are presented as follows:

Product Line	Unit Sales	Average Net Selling Price	Percentage Gross Margin
Year before last			
C	30,000	$4.20	52%
Last year			
C	38,000	$3.80	58%
Current year (projection)			
C	42,000	$3.40	62%

The authors make the following comments concerning these data (p. 116):

The rate of unit increase is decreasing steadily. It would appear, therefore, that the forecast unit increase is unlikely in view of the price/volume relationship. Our objective should be to maximize gross margin, but the figures indicate a potential reduced margin based on forecast units and price. Given this situation it is a simple matter to project graphically the trend in units against price and margin against units. The resultant graphs clearly show that it would be profitable to maintain price and current unit volume.

1. Prepare a graph and make the projection of units against price and margin against units. Do the "resultant graphs clearly show that it would be profitable to maintain price and current unit volume"? Explain.
2. Suppose you were the marketing manager of the J. Smith Company. Based on the data and the analysis presented, would you accept this recommendation from the auditor? Why or why not?

Technoscope, Inc.: What Transfer Price to Set?

Technoscope, a company manufacturing microscopes in both the United States and Holland, supplies components from the United States that are needed to produce the finished product in Holland. The cost of the parts, including shipping to Rotterdam but excluding import duty there, is $10 per unit.* The company historically has maintained a policy of transferring the components at cost, believing that this allows a more ready comparison of the operating results of the Dutch subsidiary with those in the United States.

Recently, however, this policy came into question. It was suggested that, although profits of the Dutch subsidiary obviously would fall, the profits of the overall corporation might be higher if the transfer price for the components were raised from $10 to $15 per unit (both including shipping costs but excluding import duty).

The person assigned to analyze this proposal assembled the following data pertaining to the question:*

1. Variable manufacturing costs other than those associated with the transfer of the parts from the United States average $30 per unit.
2. Fixed, general and administrative, and marketing costs average $35 per unit.
3. The import duty on the parts is 10 percent of declared value.

4. The forecast of sales for the next three years is for an average of 200,000 units to be sold each year at a price equivalent to $100 per unit (not including value added tax) in Dutch guilders.
5. The price will not be changed regardless of the decision on what transfer price to charge.
6. Corporate income taxes on profits in excess of the (equivalent of) $1 million are 60 percent in Holland and 48 percent in the United States.
7. Holland and the United States are signatories to a tax treaty that stipulates that profits earned in the host country will be taxed there, but not taxed again in the home country.

Assuming that there are no problems with repatriation of dividends from Holland, and that the Dutch tax authorities would not intervene if the intracompany price for the parts were raised, from the standpoint of the corporation as a whole, would a transfer price of $15 be preferable to one of $10?

---

*Dollar amounts and the import duty percentage have been rounded for ease of computation.

Phineas Pitney & Co.: Audit of Market Size and Company Sales

Phineas Pitney & Co. is a manufacturer of voting and vote-tabulation machines. Its voting machines allow the voter to insert a specially prepared ballot and register choices by punching a hole in a designated spot next to the name of each candidate for whom he or she wishes to vote. The ballots are later read and tabulated by another Phineas Pitney machine.

The company makes an "A" and a "B" model of the voting machine, and a single model of the reader/tabulator machine.

The reader/tabulator can process 4,800 average-sized ballots per hour.

A marketing audit for the company was conducted in the last quarter of a recent year. Among the data collected and analyzed by the auditor were those shown in the following table:

Suppose you had been the auditor. What marketing problem(s), if any, would the data in the table have suggested that you would want to investigate further?

Product	Last Year			Projected This Year			Planned Next Year		
	Industry Sales*	Company Sales*	Market Share	Industry Sales	Company Sales	Market Share	Industry Sales*	Company Sales*	Market Share
Model A	$ 398,700	$ 30,702	7.7%	$ 409,200	$ 35,600	8.7%	$ 410,000	$ 41,000	10.0%
Model B	494,900	151,432	30.6	483,200	149,800	31.0	489,000	159,000	32.5
Reader/ tabulator	187,100	27,319	14.6	175,300	14,900	8.5	182,000	20,000	11.0
Total	$1,080,700	$209,453		$1,067,700	$200,300		$1,081,000	$220,000	

*Sales in units.

Operating Results of Large U.S. Multinationals

The table below contains a list of all U.S. multinationals in a recent year that received either more than one-half of their revenues or more than one-half of their operating profits, or both, from their operations abroad.

What conclusion do you draw from the table concerning:

a. Foreign operating profits as a percentage of foreign sales compared with U.S. operating profits as a percentage of U.S. sales?

b. Return on foreign investment compared with return on U.S. investment?

Large U.S. Multinational Companies That Receive More Than One-Half of Their Revenues or Operating Profits from Other Countries

Company	Foreign Revenues as a Percentage of Total	Foreign Operating Profit as a Percentage of Total	Foreign Assets as a Percentage of Total
Exxon	70.1	56.7	52.3
Texaco	67.0	59.7	55.4
Chase-Manhattan	65.0	60.0	57.5
CPC International	64.4	56.3	64.9
J. P. Morgan	63.3	67.4	56.6
Citicorp	62.0	54.0	60.6
Colgate-Palmolive	58.7	63.2	46.9
Gillette	57.3	50.6	57.0
Irving Bank	57.1	63.9	51.4
Pfizer	56.8	60.8	47.3
Standard Oil of California	53.9	39.9	45.6
Philbro-Salomon	53.3	97.4	61.0
Bank-America	52.7	55.1	42.8
American International	48.9	58.3	45.1
Ford Motor	48.4	P/D*	62.5
International Tel. & Tel.	47.3	58.8	37.7
Digital Equipment	39.1	50.7	33.8
Safeway Stores	24.7	76.4	28.4
Allied Corp.	24.4	70.9	23.9
Phillips Petroleum	21.3	51.1	21.8

*Profit over deficit.

All-Purpose Plastics

All-Purpose Plastics produces and markets plastics to industrial users, both in the United States and abroad. The company manufactures three types of plastics—ABS, PVC, and CPVC. CPVC has never had a very high sales volume, and the marketing manager wondered if it should be discontinued. Early in the year he asked the chief accountant to have one of his people prepare an analysis of the profitability for the past year for each of the three product lines. At the same time, he asked the marketing research director to make an analysis of the marketing effort being expended on CPVC. If it turned out that CVPC lost money in the past year and if it appeared that the expenditures now being made on marketing it would be better spent on the two other products, he decided that he would recommend that the company stop manufacturing it.

Two weeks later he received a reply from the accountant who had been assigned to do the profitability study. It contained an income statement for the company for the previous year broken down by product line, and a memo explaining how he had made the breakdown. Excerpts from the memo are reproduced below.

Excerpts from the Accounting Report

I have made the analysis of profit by product line for last year that you requested. As you see from the enclosed statement (Table A), most of the profit came from the PVC line, ABS was marginally profitable, and CPVC showed almost a $150,000 loss.

In evaluating the CPVC loss (of $143,000), you should know how I spread the cost items. The way the amount for each cost item for each product was arrived at was as follows:

Cost of Goods Sold (in 000s)	ABS	PVC	CPVC
Labor	$1,001	$ 755	$ 464
Materials	2,633	1,876	1,113
Manufacturing overhead	216	164	101
Total	$3,850	$2,795	$1,678

Table A   Full-Cost Income Statement for the All-Purpose Plastics Company, and for the ABS, PVC, and CPVC Product Lines (in millions)

	Overall	ABS Product Line	PVC Product Line	CPVC Product Line
Net sales	$12,162	$5,527	$4,367	$2,268
Less: Cost of goods sold	8,323	3,850	2,795	1,678
Operating profit	$ 3,839	$1,677	$1,572	$ 590
Less:				
General and administrative expense	519	236	186	97
Marketing expenses	2,883	1,271	1,021	591
Engineering and R&D	210	79	86	45
Net profit ⟨Loss⟩ before taxes	$ 227	$ 91	$ 279	⟨$ 143⟩

Labor and materials were, of course, both direct costs. I spread the manufacturing overhead on the basis of labor costs for each product line.

General and Administrative
G&A was spread on the basis of product line sales.

Marketing
Marketing expenses were also spread on the basis of sales.

Engineering and R&D (in 000s)	ABS	PVC	CPVC
Process engineering	$19	$15	$ 8
R&D			
Specific to product line	6	28	15
General	34	27	14
Engineering overhead	20	16	8
Total	$79	$86	$45

(Continued on page 740)

Process engineering, general R&D, and engineering overhead were all spread to the product lines on the basis of sales.

The All-Purpose Plastics marketing department is organized such that it:

a. Has a marketing manager who directs the marketing operations of the company.

b. Has a sales force consisting of sales representatives who each sell all three plastics product lines.

c. Advertises in trade magazines and engages in sales promotion through displays at industrial shows in the United States, Western Europe, the Middle East, and Japan.

d. Has a marketing research staff that conducts research projects for all three products for the domestic and foreign markets.

e. Has a Transportation and Logistics Department that processes and ships orders.

It was the costs associated with these activities that the market research director needed to assign to the individual product lines. Excerpts from the report of the research director back to the marketing manager are given below.

Excerpts from the Research Director's Report

Table 1 is a spreadsheet that shows the item breakdown of each of the marketing subunits' expenses last year.

Some of these costs I could charge directly to the product lines, of course, but many of them were joint or indirect costs that I had to allocate to the product lines by using some measure—such as sales—that it seemed reasonable to assume was correlated with product line costs. (In the appendix I explain how I did this each time it was required.) The resulting costs—direct, allocated, and total—by product line are given in Table 2.

The marketing expenses by product line are shown in Table 3.

Appendix: Method of Spreading Joint and Indirect Costs

Sales calls. Only about 6 percent of the sales calls were made for a single product line, and the rest involved all three lines. I have charged product line concerned for the single-product-line calls, and the rest of the sales force expenses I have allocated on the basis of the sales proportion for each type of plastic—45.4 percent for ABS, 35.9 percent for PVC, and 18.7 percent for CPVC.

Advertising and sales promotion. Advertising expenditures are similar to sales calls in that some of them were for a single product line, but most of the ads were for all three lines. As was the case with the sales calls, I have charged the costs of the single-product-line ads directly to the product line, and the rest of the advertising costs were spread to the product lines on the basis of sales.

The sales promotion expenditures were all for industrial trade shows where all three product lines were exhibited. I have also allocated the expenses for these shows on the basis of product line sales.

Marketing research. Most of the marketing research costs could be charged directly to the product lines, and I did this on the basis of the person-days on projects spent for each. However, some of the time spent was on projects for all three lines, and I spread the costs of these on the basis of sales.

Transportation and logistics. I assigned the freight costs on the basis of the number of times each product line appeared on a sales invoice. The rest of the transportation and logistics (salaries, travel, supplies and telephone, and rent) were spread in proportion to product line sales.

Table 1   A Spreadsheet of Last Year's Marketing Expenses (in thousands)

	Sales Force	Advertising and Sales Promotion	Marketing Research	Transportation and Logistics	Marketing Manager's Office	Total
Salaries	$ 804	$ 40	$144	$107	$114	$1,209
Advertising	—	210	—	—	—	210
Sales promotion	—	249	—	—	—	249
Travel	402	50	52	3	51	558
Freight	—	—	—	346	—	346
Supplies and telephone	97	2	14	3	23	139
Rent	51	8	20	67	26	172
Total	$1,354	$559	$230	$526	$214	$2,883

(Continued on page 741)

Table 2 Allocation of Marketing Expenses by Product Line

Product Line/ Segments	Sales: Number of Sales Calls	Advertising and Sales Promotion: Number of Ads	Marketing Research: Person-Days Involved in Projects	Transportation and Logistics: Number of Orders	Marketing Manager's Office: Percentage of Sales
ABS	310	16	212	533	45.4
PVC	186	12	229	462	35.9
CPVC	124	34	276	251	18.7
Joint	10,212	249	349	—	—
	10,832	311	1,066	1,246	100.0
Expenses	$1,354,000	$210,0001* +349,000†	$230,000	346,000§ +180,000‖	$214,000
Cost/unit	$ 125.00	$675.25‡	$215.75	$277.70#	$ —
ABS					
Direct	$ 38,750	$ 10,805	$ 45,740	$148,010	$ —
Allocated	579,530	234,780	34,185	81,720	97,155
Total	$ 618,280	$245,585	$ 79,925	$229,730	$ 97,155
PVC					
Direct	$ 23,250	$ 8,105	$ 49,405	$128,290	$ —
Allocated	458,265	185,650	27,030	64,620	76,825
Total	$ 481,515	$193,755	$ 76,435	$192,910	$ 76,825
CVPC					
Direct	$ 15,500	$ 22,960	$ 59,545	$ 69,700	$ —
Allocated	238,705	96,705	14,080	33,660	40,020
Total	$ 254,205	$119,605	$ 73,625	$103,360	$ 40,020
Grand Total	$1,354,000	$559,000	$230,000	$526,000	$214,000

*Advertising.
†Sales promotion plus other expenses.
‡Average cost per ad.
§Freight.
‖Salaries, travel, telephone, and rent.
#Average freight cost per order.

Table 3 Direct and Allocated Marketing Expenses by Product Line

Costs	ABS	PVC	CPVC	Total
Direct	$ 243,305	$ 209,050	$167,705	$ 620,060
Allocated	1,027,370	812,390	423,170	2,262,930
Total	$1,270,675	$1,021,440	$590,875	$2,882,990

Marketing manager's office. The marketing manager's office expenses were spread on the basis of product line sales.

a. Calculate the contribution to fixed costs and profits made by the CPVC product line for the year for which the statements were prepared.

b. Prepare a pro forma full-cost income statement on the assumption that the CPVC product line was dropped at the beginning of the fiscal year for which the original statements were prepared.

c. What considerations other than its contribution to profit and fixed costs ought to be taken into account before making a decision to discontinue the CPVC line?

d. Based on what you are told in the case and your answers to the preceding questions, should the CPVC line be dropped? Explain.

Nike International: Taking on Adidas in Its Home Market

Nike, the producer and marketer of athletic shoes and sportswear, was the originator of waffle-soled shoes. The company capitalized on being the first on the market in the United States by an aggressive program of establishing dealerships, signing well-known athletes to contracts that required them to wear only Nike products in athletic meets, maintaining high-quality products, and keeping prices in the middle to upper end of the range. The company has done very little advertising of its products in the United States, relying on word-of-mouth advertising instead. It has been highly successful there.

When it began to market its products in West Germany, the company moved into an entirely different market situation. It was faced with a powerful competitor, Adidas, a West German company that had about 70 percent of the market. Adidas had reached this position by following much the same strategy in Germany as Nike had followed in the United States. In planning its strategy and how it should be implemented in Germany, Nike had to decide, among other things:

a. What its target market segments should be.
b. What its policy should be vis-à-vis Adidas.
c. What promotional strategy it should use.

What should Nike have decided with respect to each of these areas? Why should it have taken the actions you recommend?

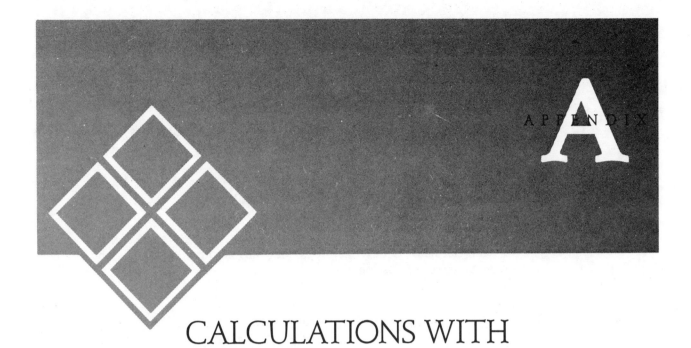

CALCULATIONS WITH EXPERIENCE CURVES*

UNIT VALUE

The formula for determining *unit cost* for a point on the experience curve is:

$$UC_i = UC_1 \times i^{-b} = \frac{UC_1}{i^b} \qquad \text{(A-1)}$$

where

UC_i = unit cost of the ith unit

UC_1 = unit cost of the first unit

i = number of cumulative units produced

b = a constant determined by the level of experience

All costs are included in the applicable cost data; marketing, engineering, production, and overhead costs are all included.

Source: Adapted from D. S. Tull and D. I. Hawkins, *Marketing Research: Measurement and Method,* 4th ed., Macmillan, 1987. Used with permission.

Example 1

Suppose a videotape recorder producer has an 80 percent curve (unit costs go down by 20 percent each time output doubles). Further suppose that the first unit cost (UC_1) was $50,000 and that we want to estimate the unit cost for the 25,000th unit.

The b value for an 80 percent curve is .322 (from Table A-1). If a calculator with y^x capability is available, the unit cost of the 25,000th unit can be estimated as:

$$UC_{25,000} = \frac{\$50,000}{25,000^{.322}} = \frac{\$50,000}{26,070} = \$1,917.91$$

If a calculator with y^x feature is not available but a log table is, the unit cost can be calculated as follows:

$$UC_{25,000} = \$50,000 \times 25,000^{-.322}$$
$$\log UC_{25,000} = \log 50,000 - .322 \log 25,000$$
$$= 4.69897 - (.322)(4.39794)$$
$$\log UC_{25,000} = 3.28283$$
$$UC_{25} = \text{antilog } 3.28283 = \$1,917.92$$

Since this is a point on an experience curve that is included in Table A-2, the unit cost for the 25,000th unit can be estimated as:

$$UC_{25,000} = \frac{UC_1 \text{ for problem} \times \text{value for 25,000 from Table A-2}}{UC_1 \text{ from Table A-2}}$$

$$= \frac{\$50,000}{\$100} \times 3.84 = \$1,920.00$$

Table A-1 Table of b Values

Experience Curve (%)	b	Experience Curve	b	Experience Curve	b
95	.074				
94	.089	84	.252	74	.434
93	.105	83	.269	73	.454
92	.120	82	.286	72	.474
91	.136	81	.304	71	.494
90	.152	80	.322	70	.514
89	.168	79	.340	68	.556
88	.184	78	.353	66	.599
87	.201	77	.377	64	.644
86	.218	76	.396	62	.690
85	.234	75	.415	60	.737

Table A-2 Experience Curve Table—Unit Values

Cumulative Output	60%	65%	70%	75%	80%	85%	90%	95%
1	$100.00	$100.00	$100.00	$100.00	$100.00	$100.00	$100.00	$100.00
10	18.32	23.91	30.58	38.46	47.65	58.28	70.47	84.44
25	9.33	13.53	19.08	26.29	35.48	47.01	61.31	78.80
50	5.60	8.79	13.36	19.72	28.38	39.96	55.18	74.86
100	3.35	5.72	9.35	14.79	22.71	33.97	49.66	71.12
250	1.70	3.23	5.84	10.11	16.91	27.40	43.20	66.46
500	1.02	2.10	4.08	7.58	13.52	23.29	38.88	63.14
1,000	.62	1.37	2.86	5.68	10.82	19.80	34.99	60.61
2,500	.31	.77	1.78	3.89	8.06	15.97	30.44	56.05
5,000	.19	.50	1.25	2.92	6.44	13.57	27.40	53.24
10,000	.11	.33	.87	2.19	5.16	11.54	24.66	50.58
25,000	.06	.18	.55	1.50	3.84	9.31	21.45	47.27
50,000	.03	.12	.38	1.12	3.07	7.91	19.31	44.90
100,000	.02	.08	.27	.84	2.47	6.72	17.38	42.66
250,000	.01	.04	.17	.57	1.83	5.42	15.12	39.86
500,000	.006	.03	.12	.43	1.46	4.61	13.61	37.87
1,000,000	.004	.02	.08	.32	1.17	3.92	12.25	35.97

AVERAGE VALUES

The formula for determining *average costs* between points on the experience curve is:

$$AUC_h^i = \frac{UC_1}{1-b} \frac{[(i+0.5)^{1-b} - (h+0.5)^{1-b}]}{i-h} \tag{A-2}$$

where

AUC_h^i = average unit costs over the range of output from h units to i units

UC_1 = unit cost for first unit

b = constant for the learning curve being used

Example 2

Suppose a new product is to be introduced, with unit costs for the first unit estimated to be $1,000. If the experience curve is estimated to be 85 percent and sales for the first year at a price of $150 are forecast to be 5,000 units, what is the estimated average cost per unit after 5,000 units have been produced?

The b value for an 85 percent curve is .234 (from Table A-1). If a calculator with y^x capability is available, the average unit cost through the 5,000th unit is calculated as

$$AUC_0^{5,000} = \frac{\dfrac{\$1,000}{1 - .234}[(5,000 + 0.5)^{1 - .234} - (0 + 0.5)^{1 - .234}]}{5,000 - 0}$$

$$= \frac{\$1,305.48[681.47 - .59]}{5,000}$$

$$= \$177.77$$

If a calculator with a y^x feature is not available but a log table is, the average cost can be calculated as follows:

$$AUC_0^{5,000} = \frac{\dfrac{\$1,000}{1 - .234}[\text{antilog } (1 - .234 \log 5,000.5) - \text{antilog } (1 - .234 \log 0.5)]}{5,000 - 0}$$

$$= \frac{\$1,305.48[681.47 - .59]}{5,000}$$

$$= \$177.77$$

Example 3

What would the estimated gross margin be for the second year if the company sold 5,000 units in the first year and forecast that 10,000 units would be sold in the second year at the same price? (Gross margin = sales − cost of goods sold.)

Estimated sales = 10,000 units @ $150.00 = $1,500,000. Estimated cost of goods sold is arrived at as follows:

$$AUC_{5,000}^{15,000} = \frac{\dfrac{\$1,000}{1 - .234}(15,000 + 0.5)^{1 - .234} - (5,000 + 0.5)^{1 - .234}}{15,000 - 5,000}$$

$$= \frac{\$1,305.48(1,580.87) - 681.47}{10,000} = \$117.42$$

$$CGS_{5,000}^{15,000} = \$117.42(15,000 - 5,000) = \$1,174,200$$

Estimated gross margin = $1,500,000 − $1,174,200 = $325,800

PLOTTING EXPERIENCE CURVES

Plotting unit costs of a product against its cumulative output using arithmetic scales (on both axes) gives a concave-upward curve of the type in Figure A-1.

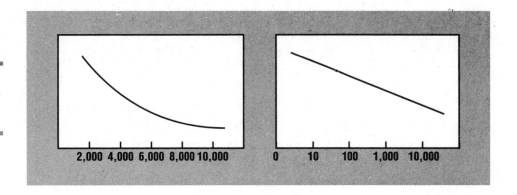

FIGURE A-1
Plot of unit costs and cumulative units produced—arithmetic scale.

FIGURE A-2
Plot of unit costs and cumulative units produced—logarithmic scale.

Plotting the same values using logarithmic scales (on both axes) gives a straight line, as shown in Figure A-2.

In plotting experience curves on log-log paper, use the following procedures:

1. Mark the units on the log-log graph paper for the unit cost and the cumulative output axes using equal powers of 10 between units (1, $1 \times 10 = 10$, $10 \times 10^1 = 100$, $100 \times 10^1 = 1,000$, and so forth, or if that does not go up far enough on the graph paper, try 1, 1, $\times 10^2 = 100$, $100 \times 10^2 = 10,000$, $10,000 \times 10^2 = 1,000,000$, and so forth.

2. *If unit cost–cumulative output data points are calculated:* Calculate the unit cost for the maximum cumulative output you think is likely to occur. Plot that cost at that cumulative output and connect it with a straight line to the first unit cost.

3. *If unit cost–cumulative output data points are obtained from actual data:* Plot the data points you have and either (a) fit a straight line to them visually or (b) fit a linear regression line to them and plot it.

4. *If first-unit cost and average cost–cumulative output data points are obtained from actual data:* Determine the applicable experience curve from two data points as described in the next section.

5. Look up the *b* value for that level of experience curve in Table A-1.

6. Use formula A-1 to calculate the unit cost for the maximum cumulative output you think is likely to occur. Plot that cost at that cumulative output and connect it with a straight line to the first unit cost.

DETERMINING THE APPLICABLE EXPERIENCE CURVE FROM ACCOUNTING DATA

Accounting data on costs usually are given as either averages or totals. The experience curve that is applicable in such cases can be determined by the following procedure:

1. Ascertain the first-unit cost from accounting data and make appropriate adjustments for inflation.

2. Determine the average unit cost for cumulative output levels h to i using accounting data.

3. By a process of trial and error, find the b value that gives an equality in formula A-2.

4. Look up the experience curve level from Table A-1.

If the historical data for the first-unit cost are not available (or judged not to be applicable), use the following procedure:

1. Determine the average unit cost for cumulative output levels h to i (AUC_h^i) and j to k (AUC_j^k)

2. Find the ratio (r) of these two averages such that:

$$r = \frac{AUC_h^i}{AUC_j^k}$$

3. Substitute the known values for $h, i, j, k,$ and r into the equality:

$$(i + 0.5)^{1-b} - (h + 0.5)^{1-b} = \frac{(i - h)r}{(k - j)} [(k + 0.5)^{1-b} - (j + 0.5)^{1-b}$$

(A-3)

4. By a process of trial and error, determine the b value that results in the equality.

5. Look up the applicable experience curve in Table A-1.

Example 4

What is the applicable experience curve where:

$$AUC_{5,000}^{7,500} = \$21.57 \text{ and } AUC_{7,500}^{10,500} = \$19.08?$$

$$r = \frac{\$21.57}{\$19.08} = 1.131$$

$$h = 5,000, i = 7,500, j = 7,500, \text{ and } k = 10,000$$

Substituting in Formula A-3:

$$(7,500 + 0.5)^{1-b} - (5,000 + 0.5)^{1-b} = \frac{2,500}{2,500} (1.131)$$

$$[(10,000 + 0.5)^{1-b} - (7,500 + 0.5)^{1-b}]$$

Let $b = .234$ (85 percent curve):

$$(7,500 + 0.5)^{1-.234} - (5,000 + 0.5)^{1-.234} = \frac{2,500}{2,500} (1.131)$$

$$[(10,000 + 0.5)^{1-.234} - (7,500 + 0.5)^{1-.234}]$$
$$929.60 - 681.47 = 1.131[1,158.82 - 929.60]$$
$$248.13 \neq 259.25, \text{ left side} < \text{right side}$$

Let $b = .322$ (80 percent curve):

$$423.95 - 322.06 = 1.131[515.23 - 423.95]$$
$$101.89 \neq 103.34, \text{ left side} < \text{right side}$$

Because the inequality is in the same direction of the two values of b but it is less for the 80 percent than for the 85 percent b value, the actual experience curve must be less than 80 percent. By continued trial and error, the b value that gives an equality is found to be (approximately) 78 percent.

COMPETITIVE COST DIFFERENTIALS THAT RESULT FROM DIFFERENT CUMULATIVE OUTPUTS

The cost advantage that the additional cumulative output resulting from a higher market share provides can be dramatic. The effects of different cumulative levels of output at different levels of the experience curve on the relative unit costs of two companies are shown in Table A-3. For example, a manufacturer with cumulative output of 1.5 times that of a competitor has a 6 percent unit cost advantage, if the experience curve applies and both are on a 90 percent curve. This enables that manufacturer to set a price that is lower than a competitor by 6 percent of the competitor's cost and still maintain the same amount of profit per unit the competitor has. This cost advantage rises to as much as 43 percent when cumulative output is 3 times as great and the applicable experience curve is 70 percent.

Table A-3 Effect of Cumulative Volume on Relative Unit Costs of Two Firms

When Cumulative Volume Produced by Manufacturer A is _____ Times That of Manufacturer B	And Both Started with the Same Initial Unit Costs and Are on the _____ % Experience Level	Unit Costs of A Are _____ % Lower Than Those of B
1.5	90	6
	80	12
	70	19
2.0	90	10
	80	20
	70	30
2.5	90	13
	80	25
	70	26
3.0	90	15
	80	30
	70	43

ESTIMATING BREAK-EVEN POINTS

Two break-even points are relevant when using share pricing for new products. The first is the number of units required to reach the point where unit costs equal price in situations where the new product is priced initially below cost. (See the figure.) This is the point where losses stop accumulating.

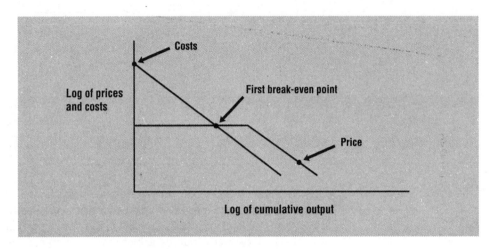

This point can be determined by setting the price equal to UC_0^i and solving for i.

Example 5

If the price of a new product is set at $5, the first-unit cost is estimated at $65, and the applicable experience curve is 80 percent, how many units must be sold before the unit cost will be equal to price?

$$UC_1 = \$65, \, b_{80\%} = .322 \text{ (from Table A-1)}$$
$$UC_i = \$5$$

Substituting into formula A-1:

$$\$5 = \frac{\$65}{i^{.322}}$$

Rearranging:

$$i^{.322} = \frac{\$65}{\$5} = 13$$

Raising both sides to the $\frac{1}{.322}$ power gives

$$(i^{.322})^{1/.322} = 13.0^{1/.322}$$
$$i = 2,883$$

Example 6

The second break-even point is the more conventional one where total revenue equals total costs. This is the equivalent of the point where price = AUC_i (since total revenue = $i \times$ price and total costs = $i \times AUC_i$). This point can therefore be determined by setting AUC_i equal to price and solving for i using formula A-2.

If the price of a new product is set at \$5, the first-unit cost is estimated at \$65, and the applicable experience curve is 80 percent, how many units must be sold before total revenues at that price will be equal to total costs?

$$AUC_i = \text{price} = \$5, \ UC_1 = \$65, \text{ and } b = .322 \text{ (from Table A-1)}$$

Substituting into formula A-2:

$$5(i) = 95.87(i + 0.5)^{.678} - 59.92$$
$$95.87(i + 0.5)^{.678} - 5i - 59.92 = 0$$

Trial-and-error solution gives $i = 9{,}593$.

COMPANY INDEX

North American Aviation Inc., 337
NYNEX, 536

Ogilvy & Mather, 180–181, 472, 523
R. E. Olds Co. (now owned by General
    Motors Corp.), 78
Omark Industries, 92
Oshkosh B'Gosh Inc., 43
Overland, Inc., 185
Overland Car Company, 78
Owens-Illinois Company, 66

Pan American World Airways, 699
Parker-Hannefin Corporation, 566–567
J C Penney Co., Inc., 37, 38, 42, 230,
    544, 594, 597, 634, 637, 658
Pepperidge Farms Inc., 701
Pepsico Inc., 336, 472–473, 561, 654, 656,
    666, 702, 719
Source Perrier, 668, 674, 695, 706, 710
Peugeot Co., 465
Pfizer Corp., 738
Philbro-Salomon, 738
Phillip Morris USA, 336, 707
Phillips N.V., 718
Phillips Petroleum, 738
Phineas Pitney & Co., 737
Pier 1 Imports, 601
Pillsbury Co., 72, 281, 494, 498, 600,
    625, 656
Pittway Corp., 425
Polaroid Corp., 380
Portland Trailblazers, 341
PPG Industries, 65
The Procter & Gamble Co., 44, 50, 60,
    73, 95, 112, 113, 118, 281, 302, 307,
    314, 368, 391, 393, 403, 408-409,
    479, 563, 568, 638, 655, 686, 708,
    710
Puma GMBH, 410

The Rand Corporation, 317
Arthur Rank Ltd., 709
Raytheon Co., 79
RCA, 33, 50, 332, 568
Red Roof Inns, 471–472
Renault Inc., 563
Revere Copper and Brass Company,
    157, 159

Revlon Inc., 536–537, 710
Rexall Drug Co., 570
Reynolds International Pen Company,
    79, 153, 448–449
RJR Nabisco, 175, 304, 308–310, 404,
    447, 510
Rockwell International Corporation, 144,
    337
Ross Corp., 593
Royal Crown Cola, 178
Royal Dutch Shell, 718

Safeway Stores Inc., 338, 556, 568, 593,
    600, 738
Sak's Fifth Avenue, 104
San Francisco Bay Area Rapid Transit,
    425
Sav-On Drug, 669
Schick (owned by Warner-Lambert Co.),
    404
Schwinn Bicycle Co., 171
Sears, Roebuck, 37, 38, 39, 43, 50, 87,
    122, 153, 168, 381, 393, 484–485,
    501, 534, 544, 556, 564, 568, 570,
    591, 594, 597, 600, 619, 637
7-Eleven Stores (owned by Southland
    Corp.), 593
Seven-Up Company, 178, 336, 420
Shaklee Corp., 598
Shell International, 44
Sherwin-Williams Co., 556, 570
Shoprite Stores, 600
Simmons Market Research Bureau, 240
Singer Sewing Machine Company, 601
J. Smith Company, 735
J. M. Smucker Co., 108
Society National Bank, 626
Sony Corp., 33, 350, 380, 718
Southland Corp., 601
Speedi-Lube Corp., 64
Sperry Corp., 315, 337, 350
Standard Oil Company (New Jersey), 703
Standard Oil of California, 738
Standard & Poor's, 666
Sterling Drug Company, 268
Stride Rite Shoes, 556
Stroh Brewery Company, 25
Studebaker Co., 78
Sunkist, 707

Sunshine Books, Ltd., 186
Sylvania Electric, 171

Technoscope, 736
TechTel Communicators, 536
Tektronix, Inc., 561, 709
Temple University Bookstore, 186
Texaco Inc., 738
Texas Instruments Inc., 29, 31, 35, 78,
    309, 410, 458
Thom McAn Shoe Co., 593
Time, Inc., 556
Toyota Motor Corporation, 5, 577
Toys "R" Us, 603
True Value Stores, 602
Tupperware Home Parties, Inc., 598, 627
TWA (Trans World Airlines, Inc.), 246,
    445, 710

U-Haul Company, 192, 198, 205–207,
    210
Union Carbide Corp., 290, 314, 656
Uniroyal Inc., 656
United Electrical Company, 578
United Parcel Service, 177, 639
U.S. Navy, 65
U.S. Postal Service, 639, 656
US WEST Communications, 536
USX, 51, 274, 655

Volkswagen of America, 5

Walgreen Drugstores, 556
Wendy's International, 280, 556
Westinghouse Electric Corporation, 339
Weyerhauser Co., 392
Whirlpool Corp., 50, 393, 556, 581
White Castle Co., 25
White Mountain Motor Company, 639
Wilkerson Blade Ltd., 710
WindandSea Sailboats, Inc., 294
Wisconsin Electric Power Company, 337
World Book Encyclopedia, 556, 597, 598
Wm. Wrigley Jr. Co., 405

Xerox Corporation, 69–70, 141,
    506–509, 666, 709, 714

Yankelovich, Skelly, and White, 8, 281

NAME INDEX

SUBJECT INDEX

Distribution center, 578
  automated, 579
Distribution channel influence, 391
Distribution channels, *see* Marketing
  channels
Distribution considerations, strategic,
  720
Distribution elasticity, 625
Distribution performance standards,
  677–678
Distribution points, 279
Distributions manager, 645
Distributors, *see also* Middlemen
  compensating, 567–568
  foreign, exporting through, 706–707
  high-stakes, 566–567
  industrial, *see* Industrial distributors
  low-stakes, 567
  motivating, 566–567
  replacing, 568
  sales promotions to, 511
  servicing of, 567
  wagon, 610
Diversification, 36–37, 40–41
  product line, 392
  in reducing risk, 51
Diverters, 445
"Dogs" quadrant, 46
Dominance Model, 210
Dorfman and Steiner Theorem, 625
Double exponential smoothing, 319
DROP error, 358
Drop shippers, 610
Dun's Market Identifiers, 144
Durable producer goods, 131
Durables, cycle/recycle for, 409
Duties, import, 717

Eagle-Beacon, Wichita, minicase, 640
Early adopters, 407
Early majority, 407
Econometric analyses, 200
Economic attractiveness, 42
Economic base, 603
Economic efficiency, 697
Economic objectives, 193
Economic order quantity (EOQ),
  574–575
Economic value to customer (EVC), 438,
  439
Economies, 69
  environment of, 80–88
  functions of, 17
  global, 101
  organization of, 17
Edsel minicase, 338
Education, consumers and, 103–104
EEC (European Economic Community),
  704
Effectiveness, organizational, 663

Efficiency
  design, 669, 697
  economic, 697
  implementation, 697
  marketing, 49, 391
  technical, 697
EFTA (European Free Trade
  Association), 704
Elasticity, 625
  advertising, for products, 500
Electronic calculators, 78
Electronic data bases, 16
Electronic media, 475
  marketing through, 597
Electronic retailing, 608–609
Emotion and information processing,
  117–118
Emotional involvement in introduction
  decision, 373-375
Empiricism, rationalism versus, 16
Employees, individual, with social
  influences, 133
Emulative new products, 39, 350
Emulators, 350-351
Encoded messages, 462
Encyclopedia of Associations, 238
Endorsement fees, 526
Engineering, 8, 71–72
Engineering-related strategies, 48,
  50–51
Enjoyment in life, 112
Entertaining, 531
Environment
  competitive, *see* Competitive
    environment(s)
  economic, 88–88
  ethical, 152–156
  industry, 73–80
  legal, 159–172
  marketing, 67
  political, 156–159
  technological, 77–80
Environmental influences, 135–137
Environmental Protection Agency, 159
Environmentalist period, 158
Epistemology, 228
Equal Credit Opportunity Act, 168
Equilibration through adaptation, 115
Equity, return on (ROE), 194
Equivalent-price strategy, 444
Escalation, price, 716
"Escalator" clauses, 445
Establishment claims, 185
Establishment stage, salespeople, 541
Ethical codes, 154
Ethical environment, 152–156
Ethical values, 152
Ethics, 152
  of acquiring competitor information,
    76–77

American Marketing Association
  Code of, 155
European Economic Community (EEC),
  704
European Free Trade Association
  (EFTA), 704
Evaluation
  of containers, 370
  of middlemen, 568
  performance, 545–546
  product, 411
  of publicity program, 516–517
  of sales promotion results, 512–514
  of salespeople, 545–546
  word-of-mouth, 6
EVC (economic value to customer), 438,
  439
Exception, management by, 195
Excess plant capacity, 50
Exchange process, 4, 6–7
  rights and duties of parties in, 155
Exchange rate hedging, 717–718
Exchanges, vendor, "just–in–time," 142
Exclusive dealing, 170, 569
Exclusive territories, 569
Executive experience, 228, 229, 231–233
Executive forecasts
  accuracy of, 318
  average or consensus of individual,
    317–318
  methods of obtaining and processing,
    317
Executive judgment, 435
Executives
  marketing, *see* Marketing executives
  overseas assignments of, 723
  personal objectives of, 428–429
Exogenous factors in product life cycle,
  405
Expected, term, 212
Expected value decision making,
  374–375
Expenditures
  consumption, 80–82
  forecasting investment and operating,
    367
  investment and operating, forecasting,
    283
  nonconsumption, 80, 82
Expenses
  general and administrative, 684
  misreporting of, 685
  transportation, 82
Experience curve, 33, 435–436
  accounting data and, A–5 to A–7
  calculations with, A–1 to A–9
  forecasting costs with, 437
  formula for, 457–458
  plotting, A–4 to A–5
  pricing using, 436–437

Goods
  "inferior," 400
  producer, durable and nondurable, 131
Government
  consumers and, 100
  as customers, 156
  as marketer and competitor, 157
  secondary data from, 238
Government agencies, sales data from,
    268–269
Government purchasers, 134–135
Grid pattern, 605–606
Gross margin per average sale, 561
Gross rating points (GRP), 502–503, 505
Group market manager, 645
Group product manager, 645
Growth, market, 46–47
Growth curve, 491
GRP (gross rating points), 502–503, 505
Guidelines for public use of market and
    opinion research minicase, 343–343

Habit, 110
Harvard Business Review minicase, 631
Heaviness of products, 562
Hedging, exchange rate, 717–718
Heuristic learning, 232
High-involvement information, 115, 118
High relative value, 7
History, marketing and, 100
Honda Motor Company fender repair
    minicase, 184
Honesty, 155
"Horizontal" investors, 705
House brand policy, 564
House-to-house selling, 564
Human life cycle, 396
Humor
  in bank commercials minicase, 626
  use of, in advertising, 471–472
Hurdle rate, 285
Hypermarkets, 85, 594

I, *see* Impact
Identifiability, market, 42
Imitation, innovation versus, 16
Impact (I), 502, 503, 505–506
  estimating, 506
  relative, 507
Implementation, 14–15, 686–687
Implementation efficiency, 697
Implementation–efficient marketing
    program, 668
Import controls, foreign, 702
Import duties, 717
Importance weights and ratings,
    209–210
Improvisation, planning versus, 15, 16
Imputation method, 245
In-home marketing, 598

In-store location experiments, 607–608
In-store location of products, 606
Incentives, 675
Income
  consumers and, 104
  personal, *see* Personal income
Income taxes, foreign effect on, 717
Incremental costs, 682
Independents, 600
Indirect exporting, 706
Indirect incentive, 675
Individual employees with social
    influences, 133
Individual-marketing-decision-related
    ethics, 153–155
Individual product branding, 393, 394
Industrial demand, 129
Industrial distributors, 609
  marketing channel producer to, 558
  marketing channel producer to
    industrial user via agent and, 559
Industrial fan and blower manufacturer
    minicase, 66
Industrial markets, syndicated data on,
    240–241
Industrial products, 389
Industrial products channels, 558–559
Industrial purchasers, 134
Industrial supplies, 560
Industrial users
  marketing channel producer direct to,
    558
  marketing channel producer to, via
    agent and industrial distributor, 559
  marketing channel producer to agent
    to, 558–559
  sales promotions to, 511
Industry, 69, 265
  information from, 233
  of users, 144
Industry environment, 73–80
Industry sales, company sales as
    proportion of, 680
"Inferior" goods, 400
Inflation, 83, 451
  consumers and, 84
  marketing management and, 84–85
Influencers, 138
Informal Judgment Model, 208–209
Informal management judgment, 200
Informal screening methods, 361
Information, 114
  disclosure of, 157
  high-involvement, 115, 118
  from industry sources, 233
  from internal reports, 234
  low-involvement, 118
  monitored, 230
  new, schemas and, 115–117
  product, spreading, 403

recurrent, 230
requested, 230
sources of, 228–229
Information management, 531
Information processing
  emotion and, 117–118
  involvement and, 118
  Piaget's cognitive theory of, 113–114
  postpurchase, 118–119
Information-providing ability, 506
Information system, computerized,
    590–591
Informational content of messages,
    470–473
Informational influences on consumers,
    97, 113–119
Informing objectives, 468
Infrastructure, 136–137
  marketing, 135–136
Innovation, imitation versus, 16
Innovative new products, 38, 350
Innovators, 350, 406–407
Input variables, 673–674
  control of, through budgets, 674–675
Installations, 389
Institutional sellers, 530
Insurance costs, product liability and,
    163
Integrated marketing department,
    organizing, 653–658
Integrated marketing organization, 659
Intelligence, competitor, 74–75
Intention-to-purchase survey, 278
Interest rates, level of, 87–88
Internal development versus acquisition
    of new products, 351
Internal information search, 114
Internal multiple-line selling, potential,
    563
Internal rate of return (IRR), 284
Internal reports, 228, 229, 233–235
  information from, 234
Internal secondary data, 237
International market manager, 645
International marketing, 699–723
  geographic dimension of, 699,
    700–705
  organizational dimension of, 699–700,
    705–709
  strategic dimension of, 700, 710–723
  "world brands" in, 710–714
International marketing research,
    721–722
International research, inherent
    problems in, 721
International trade fairs, 719
Interviews, depth, 242
Introduction
  area of, 375
  timing of, 375

Marketing tasks to be performed, 644
Marketing universities minicase, 183
Marketing variables, controlled, 672–678
Masculine image, 5
Mass-merchandising department stores, 594
Materials, 389
  supplying, 577–578
Mathematical models for setting advertising budgets, 494–495
Matrix marketing organization, 657–658
Matrix organization, 653, 660
Mature market, 397, 407–408
MBO (Management by Objectives), 195
MC (marginal cost), 431–432
McGuire Act, 166
Media, 475
  electronic, see Electronic media
  print, see Print media
  selecting, 502–510
Media characteristics, 507
Media distribution, 478
Media segment data, 507
Media vehicles, specific, 503–510
MEDIAC (comprehensive analytic media-planning model), 509
Medium see Media
Meetings, 531
Memory scanning, 114
Merchandising manager, 645
Merchant wholesalers, 557, 609
Messages, 470–473
  audience for, 478
  decoded, 462
  encoded, 462
  favorable, 515
  feedback on, 463, 478
  frequency of, 476–478
  informational content of, 470–473
  medium transmitted by, 475–476
  one-sided, 472
  response to, 462
  selecting, 500–502
  transmittal of, 476–478
  two-sided, 472
  unfavorable, 515
Middlemen, 553–555; see also Distributors
  agent, 610
  evaluating, 568
  training of, 566
Miller-Tydings Act, 158, 165, 166
Minicases
  All-Purpose Plastics, 739–741
  APS Inc., 634
  Avon Products, 627
  bank commercials, 626
  Callison Company, 340
  claims in advertising, 185
  cola drinks, 185

corporate cultures of advertising agency, 180–181
Eagle-Beacon, Wichita, 640
Edsel, 338
  fast foods versus supermarkets, 63
Federal Express, 624
R. L. Financial Consulting, 628
Fourt and Woodlock Model, 630
General Mills, 635
Gerber Products Company, 632
guidelines for the public use of market and opinion research, 342–343
Harvard Business Review, 631
Honda Motor Company fender repair, 184
industrial fan and blower manufacturer, 66
Jaguar XJ12 pricing, 636
Kansas City Royals Baseball Club, 336
Kellogg Company, 182
Kitch'n Cook'd Maui Potato Chips Company, 64
market size and company sales, 737
marketing environments, 183
marketing universities, 183
multinational operating results, 738
Naturally Thin wafers, 187
Nike International, 742
North American Aviation, 337
Owen-Illinois Company social objectives, 66
Pampers pricing, 638
Parfitt and Collins Model, 629–630
Pillsbury Company, 625
PPG Industries, 65
prescription drugs by mail, 184
price change analysis, 735
Safeway Stores, Inc., 338
Sears, Roebuck, 637
Seven-Up advertising theme, 336
Speedi-Lube, 64
supermarket traffic flow, 633
telecommuting, 180
telemarketing from cell blocks, 186
Temple University Bookstore, 186
test market area selection, 339
Trailblazers and broadcasting, 341
transfer price, 736
TV woman, 187
United States Navy pilot shortage, 65
West German market, 734
White Mountain Motor Company, 639
Wisconsin Electric Power Company, 337
MIS (marketing information system), 229–231
Misreporting, 685
Missionary salespeople, 531

Mixed cash flow statements, 285–286
"Mixed" economies, 17, 18
Mock-ups, 363
Model-stock approach, 606
Modification of attributes, 356
Modified rebuy buy class, 139–140
Monitored information, 230
Monitoring by management, 687
Morphemes, 395–396
"Most likely" cash flow statements, 284–285
Motivational stategies, 566
MPR (market potential), 629
MR (marginal revenue), 431–432
Multi-attribute decisions, 207–208
Multi-attribute view of attitudes and behaviors, 109
Multidimensional scaling, 44
Multinational operating results minicase, 738
Multiple-factor indexes, 273
Multiple-line selling, 553
  potential internal, 563
Multi-product-line companies, 52

Names, brand, see Brand names of products
NARD (National Association of Retail Druggists), 184
Narrowing principle, 196–197
National Association of Retail Druggists (NARD), 184
National brands, 711-172
National Environmental Policy Act, 159
National Industrial Recovery Act, 158, 165, 166
National Purchase Diary Panel, Inc. (NPD), 239, 240
National Traffic and Safety Act, 160
National Wholesale Druggists Association, 165
Naturally Thin wafers minicase, 187
Negative close, 535
Negotiated price, 130, 442-443
Net present value (NPV), 284
New Product Idea Screening Committee, 359
New product marketing, 645
New task purchase buy class, 139–140
Newspapers, 476
NIH ("Not Invented Here") factor, 713
Nike International minicase, 742
Nonconsumption expenditures, 80, 82
Nondurable producer goods, 131
Nondurables, stable maturity for, 409
Nonestablishment claims, 185
Nonresponse error, 244-245
Nonstore retailing, 595
Nonusers versus users, 38

expected, decision making, 374–375
high relative, 7
List of (LOV), 111, 112
net present (NPV), 284
providing, 53
study of, 110–111
unit, A–1 to A–3
Value analysis, 200, 435
Value-based pricing, 438–441
Value segments, 112
Variable costs, average (AVC), 186
Vehicular traffic, 604
Vending machines, 597–598
Vendor exchanges, "just-in-time," 142
Vertical marketing system (VMS), 556, 570–571
Videotex, 80
VMS (vertical marketing system), 556, 570–571
Volume industries, 30–31
Voluntary chains, 601–602

Wagon distributors, 610
Warehouse, 578
Warehouse stores, 595
Warm relationships with others, 112

Warranties of products and services, 164
WE (weighted exposures), 502, 503
Weak products, 412
Weight of products, 562
Weighted exposures (WE), 502, 503
Well-respected, feeling of being, 112
West German market minicase, 734
"What-if" cash flow statements, 285–287
Wheeler-Lea Act, 168
White Mountain Motor Company minicase, 639
Wholesale sales, 592, 609
Wholesalers, 134, 553; see also Wholesaling
    agent, 557
    cash and carry, 610
    defined, 609
    full-function, 609
    limited-function, 610
    merchant, 557, 609
    retailers and, 612–613
    types of, 609–611
Wholesaling, 590, 609–614; see also Wholesalers

future of, 613–614
location, 611–612
managing, 611
nature of, 609
product assortment, 612
services provided, 612
Windows in quantity discounts, 448
Wisconsin Electric Power Company minicase, 337
Women, role of, 106
Word-of-mouth evaluation, 6
Word processing, 70
Word-processing programs, 528
Working stock, 573
World brand, 710
    advantages and disadvantages of, 713–714
World trade organizations, 704

Xerography, 70

Yuppies, 105

"Zero-sum" transactions, 7
Zip code penetration rates, 236